Ford Mustang II Automotive Repair Manual

by J H Haynes
Member of the Guild of Motoring Writers
and M S Daniels

Models covered
All Mustang II models

ISBN 0 85696 629 0

Printed in the USA

ABCDE
FGH
2

(4D6 - 36049)
(231)

Haynes Publishing Group
Sparkford Nr Yeovil
Somerset BA22 7JJ England

Haynes North America, Inc
861 Lawrence Drive
Newbury Park
California 91320 USA

Acknowledgements

Thanks are due to the Ford Motor Company for technical information and for use of certain illustrations.

We are especially indebted to Mike Hazelip of the British Consulate, Los Angeles, for the loan of his Mustang II which was used as the project vehicle.

About this manual

Its aim

The aim of this manual is to help you get the best value from your car. It can do so in several ways. It can help you decide what work must be done (even should you choose to get it done by a garage), provide information on routine maintenance and servicing, and give a logical course of action and diagnosis when random faults occur. However, it is hoped that you will use the manual by tackling the work yourself. On simpler jobs it may even be quicker than booking the car into a garage and going there twice to leave and collect it. Perhaps most important, a lot of money can be saved by avoiding the costs the garage must charge to cover its labour and overheads.

The manual has drawings and descriptions to show the function of the various components so that their layout can be understood. Then the tasks are described and photographed in a step-by-step sequence so that even a novice can do the work.

Its arrangement

The manual is divided into thirteen Chapters, each covering a logical sub-division of the vehicle. The Chapters are each divided into Sections, numbered with single figures, eg 5; and the Sections into paragraphs (or sub-sections), with decimal numbers following on from the Section they are in, eg 5.1, 5.2, 5.3 etc.

It is freely illustrated, especially in those parts where there is a detailed sequence of operations to be carried out. There are two forms of illustration: figures and photographs. The figures are numbered in sequence with decimal numbers, according to their position in the Chapter – eg Fig. 6.4 is the fourth drawing/illustration in Chapter 6. Photographs carry the same number (either individually or in related groups) as the Section or sub-section to which they relate.

There is an alphabetical index at the back of the manual as well as a contents list at the front. Each Chapter is also preceded by its own individual contents list.

References to the 'left' or 'right' of the vehicle are in the sense of a person in the driver's seat facing forwards.

Unless otherwise stated, nuts and bolts are removed by turning anti-clockwise, and tightened by turning clockwise.

Vehicle manufacturers continually make changes to specifications and recommendations, and these when notified are incorporated into our manuals at the earliest opportunity.

Whilst every care is taken to ensure that the information in this manual is correct, no liability can be accepted by the authors or publishers for loss, damage or injury caused by any errors in, or omissions from, the information given.

Introduction to the Mustang II

The Mustang II range of cars comprises four different models. The basic four seater hardtop design is fitted with a 2.3 liter OHC engine and four speed manual transmission. Standard features include cut pile carpeting, comprehensive instrumentation, including a tachometer, solid state ignition and front wheel disc brakes. Optional extras include automatic transmission, power steering and a 2.8 litre V6 engine. From 1975 a 5 litre V8 engine has also been available.

A three-door fastback version of the Mustang II is also available, the rear door and folding rear seats providing the advantages of a small station wagon.

The basic Mach I model is similar in shape to the 2 + 2 but is fitted, as standard, with the 2.8 liter V6 engine and power assisted disc brakes.

Top of the range is the Ghia, which must be one of the most luxuriously appointed small cars. Extensive use of sound-deadening material has been made and suspension-to-chassis insulation, ensures a level of quietness comparable with much larger cars, while the 2.3 liter engine provides small car economy.

The mechanical layout of the Mustang II is conventional with a front mounted engine transmitting drive to the rear axle through a manual or automatic gearbox and then via a driveshaft. The one-piece rear axle is located by quarter-elliptical leaf springs, while the front suspension is by independent coil springs. A 'traction-lok' differential is an optional extra.

All models in the Mustang II range are fitted with disc brakes for the front wheels and self-adjusting drum brakes for the rear wheels.

Contents

Ford Mustang II Hardtop

Ford Mustang II Ghia

General dimensions, weights and capacities

Dimensions and weights	
Overall length	175 in (4.45 m)
Overall width	70.2 in (1.78 m)
Overall height	50.3 in (1.28 m)
Wheelbase	96.2 in (2.44 m)
Curb weight (approx)	2710 lb (1230 kg)
Capacities	
Engine oil with filter change:	
2.3 l	5 US qts (4.7 liters)
2.8 l V6	5 US qts (4.7 liters)
5.0 l V8	5 US qts (4.7 liters)
Cooling system:	
2.3 l without A/C	8.7 US qts (8.20 liters)
2.3 l with A/C	10 US qts (9.46 liters)
2.8 l (manual)	9.2 US qts (8.71 liters)
2.8 l (automatic)	9.4 US qts (8.90 liters)
5.0 l without A/C	14.0 US qts (13.25 liters)
5.0 l with A/C	14.6 US qts (13.82 liters)
Transmission:	
Manual	3.5 US pts (1.6 liters)
Automatic:	
C3	8 US qts (7.6 liters)
C4	6.75 US qts (6.4 liters)
Rear axle	3.0 US pts (1.4 liters)
Fuel:	
Main tank	13 US gals (49.2 liters)
Auxiliary tank (optional extra)	3.5 US galls (13.3 liters)

Buying spare parts and vehicle identification numbers

Buying spare parts

Replacement parts are available from many sources, which generally fall into one of two categories – authorized dealer parts departments and independent retail auto parts stores. Our advice concerning these parts is as follows:

Retail auto parts stores: Good auto parts stores will stock frequently needed components which wear out relatively fast, such as clutch components, exhaust systems, brake parts, tune-up parts, etc. These stores often supply new or reconditioned parts on an exchange basis, which can save a considerable amount of money. Discount auto parts stores are often very good places to buy materials and parts needed for general vehicle maintenance such as oil, grease, filters, spark plugs, belts, touch-up paint, bulbs, etc. They also usually sell tools and general accessories, have convenient hours, charge lower prices and can often be found not far from home.

Authorized dealer parts department: This is the best source for parts which are unique to the vehicle and not generally available elsewhere (such as major engine parts, transmission parts, trim pieces, etc.).

Warranty information: If the vehicle is still covered under warranty, be sure that any replacement parts purchased – regardless of the source – do not invalidate the warranty!

To be sure of obtaining the correct parts, have engine and chassis numbers available and, if possible, take the old parts along for positive identification.

Vehicle identification numbers

The *Vehicle Identification Number* will be found on a metal tag fastened to the top of the instrument panel. It is on the driver's side and visible from outside the car.

If it becomes necessary to obtain new parts for your car, make a note of the identification number and take it along to your Ford dealer.

A *Vehicle Certification Label* is attached to the left door pillar. The label is made of special material to guard against alteration. If an attempt is made to deface or remove it, the word "void" will appear. Vehicle loading limits and tire pressures are shown on a label attached to the rear face of the right-hand door.

An *Emission Control Information decal* is located inside the engine compartment. In addition to displaying engine adjustment information it also gives the *maintenance schedule code letter* for your car (see example). This code letter is repeated on a decal stuck to the inside of the glove compartment door.

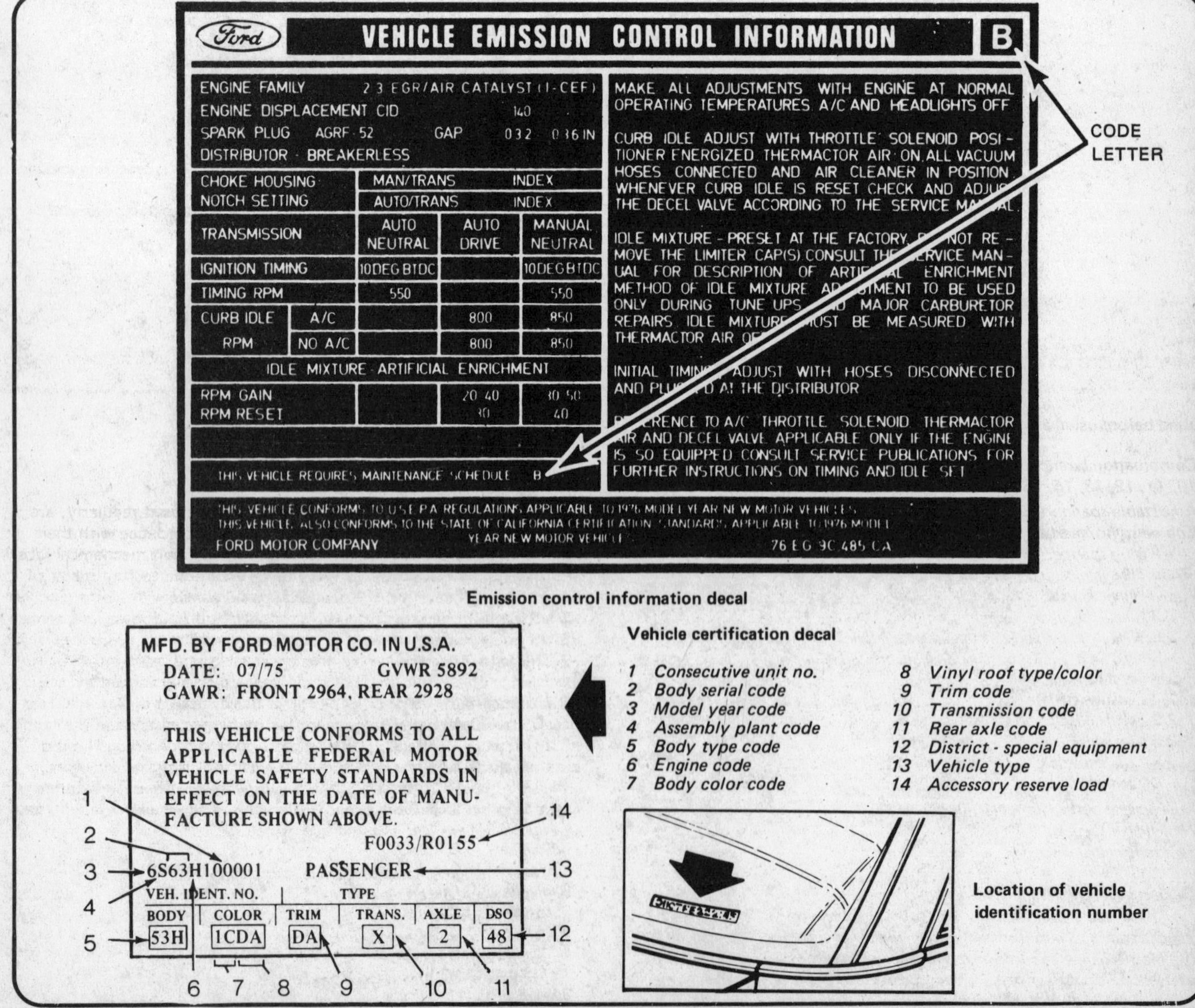

Emission control information decal

Vehicle certification decal

1 Consecutive unit no.
2 Body serial code
3 Model year code
4 Assembly plant code
5 Body type code
6 Engine code
7 Body color code
8 Vinyl roof type/color
9 Trim code
10 Transmission code
11 Rear axle code
12 District - special equipment
13 Vehicle type
14 Accessory reserve load

Location of vehicle identification number

Tools and working facilities

Introduction

A selection of good tools is a fundamental requirement for anyone contemplating the maintenance and repair of a motor vehicle. For the owner who does not possess any, their purchase will prove a considerable expense, offsetting some of the savings made by doing-it-yourself. However, provided that the tools purchased are of good quality, they will last for many years and prove an extremely worthwhile investment.

To help the average owner to decide which tools are needed to carry out the various tasks detailed in this manual, we have compiled three lists of tools under the following headings: *Maintenance and minor repair, Repair and overhaul,* and *Special*. The newcomer to practical mechanics should start off with the *Maintenance and minor repair* tool kit and confine himself to the simpler jobs around the vehicle. Then, as his confidence and experience grows, he can undertake more difficult tasks, buying extra tools as, and when, they are needed. In this way, a *Maintenance and minor repair* tool kit can be built-up into a *Repair and overhaul* tool kit over a considerable period of time without any major cash outlays. The experienced do-it-yourselfer will have a tool kit good enough for most repair and overhaul procedures and will add tools from the *Special* category when he feels the expense is justified by the amount of use to which these tools will be put.

It is obviously not possible to cover the subject of tools fully here. For those who wish to learn more about tools and their use there is a book entitled *How to Choose and Use Car Tools* available from the publishers of this manual.

Maintenance and minor repair tool kit

The tools given in this list should be considered as a minimum requirement if routine maintenance, servicing and minor repair operations are to be undertaken. We recommend the purchase of combination spanners (ring one end, open-ended the other); although more expensive than open-ended ones, they do give the advantages of both types of spanner.

Most engine fixings are to metric sizes, but both metric and AF sizes may be encountered on other parts of the car. Make sure that the threads are compatible, if possible by screwing on nuts and bolts by hand before using a wrench.

Combination wrenches - 3/8, 7/16, 1/2, 9/16 and 5/8 in AF, and 10, 11, 12, 13, 15, 16 and 17 mm
Adjustable spanner - 9 inch
Engine sump/gearbox/rear axle drain plug key
Spark plug spanner (with rubber insert)
Spark plug gap adjustment tool
Set of feeler gauges
Brake bleed nipple spanner
Screwdriver - 4 in long x ¼ in dia (flat blade)
Screwdriver - 4 in long x ¼ in dia (cross blade)
Combination pliers - 6 inch
Hacksaw (junior)
Tyre pump
Tyre pressure gauge
Grease gun
Oil can
Fine emery cloth (1 sheet)
Wire brush (small)
Funnel (medium size)

Repair and overhaul tool kit

These tools are virtually essential for anyone undertaking any major repairs to a motor vehicle, and are additional to those given in the *Maintenance and minor repair* list. Included in this list is a comprehensive set of sockets. Although these are expensive they will be found invaluable as they are so versatile - particularly if various drives are included in the set. We recommend the ½ in square-drive type, as this can be used with most proprietary torque spanners. If you cannot afford a socket set, even bought piecemeal, then inexpensive tubular box wrenches are a useful alternative.

The tools in this list will occasionally need to be supplemented by tools from the *Special* list.

Sockets (or box spanners) to cover range in previous list, and ¾ in square drive 32 mm (1¼ in AF) and 44 mm
Reversible ratchet drive (for use with sockets)
Extension piece, 10 inch (for use with sockets)
Universal joint (for use with sockets)
Torque wrench (for use with sockets)
Mole wrench - 8 inch
Ball pein hammer
Soft-faced hammer, plastic or rubber
Screwdriver - 6 in long x 5/16 in dia (flat blade)
Screwdriver - 2 in long x 5/16 in square (flat blade)
Screwdriver - 1½ in long x ¼ in dia (cross blade)
Screwdriver - 3 in long x 1/8 in dia (electricians)
Pliers - electricians side cutters
Pliers - needle nosed
Pliers - circlip (internal and external)
Cold chisel - ½ inch
Scriber (this can be made by grinding the end of a broken hacksaw blade)
Scraper (this can be made by flattening and sharpening one end of a piece of copper pipe)
Centre punch
Pin punch
Hacksaw
Valve grinding tool
Steel rule/straight edge
Allen keys
Selection of files
Wire brush (large)
Axle-stands
Jack (strong scissor or hydraulic type)

Special tools

The tools in this list are those which are not used regularly, are expensive to buy, or which need to be used in accordance with their manufacturers' instructions. Unless relatively difficult mechanical jobs are undertaken frequently, it will not be economic to buy many of these tools. Where this is the case, you could consider clubbing together with friends (or a motorists' club) to make a joint purchase, or borrowing the tools against a deposit from a local garage or tool hire specialist.

The following list contains only those tools and instruments freely available to the public, and not those special tools produced by the vehicle manufacturer specifically for its dealer network. You will find occasional references to these manufacturers' special tools in the text of this manual. Generally, an alternative method of doing the job without the vehicle manufacturers' special tool is given. However, sometimes, there is no alternative to using them. Where this is the case and the relevant tool cannot be bought or borrowed you will have to entrust the work to a franchised garage.

Valve spring compressor (where applicable)
Piston ring compressor
Balljoint separator
Universal hub/bearing puller
Impact screwdriver
Micrometer and/or vernier gauge

Dial gauge
Stroboscopic timing light
Dwell angle meter/tachometer
Universal electrical multi-meter
Cylinder compression gauge
Lifting tackle (photo)
Trolley jack
Light with extension lead

Buying tools

For practically all tools, a tool factor is the best source since he will have a very comprehensive range compared with the average garage or accessory shop. Having said that, accessory shops often offer excellent quality tools at discount prices, so it pays to shop around.

There are plenty of good tools around at reasonable prices, but always aim to purchase items which meet the relevant national safety standards. If in doubt, ask the proprietor or manager of the shop for advice before making a purchase.

Care and maintenance of tools

Having purchased a reasonable tool kit, it is necessary to keep the tools in a clean serviceable condition. After use, always wipe off any dirt, grease and metal particles using a clean, dry cloth, before putting the tools away. Never leave them lying around after they have been used. A simple tool rack on the garage or workshop wall, for items such as screwdrivers and pliers is a good idea. Store all normal spanners and sockets in a metal box. Any measuring instruments, gauges, meters, etc, must be carefully stored where they cannot be damaged or become rusty.

Take a little care when tools are used. Hammer heads inevitably become marked and screwdrivers lose the keen edge on their blades from time to time. A little timely attention with emery cloth or a file will soon restore items like this to a good serviceable finish.

Working facilities

Not to be forgotten when discussing tools, is the workshop itself. If anything more than routine maintenance is to be carried out, some form of suitable working area becomes essential.

It is appreciated that many an owner mechanic is forced by circumstances to remove an engine or similar item, without the benefit of a garage or workshop. Having done this, any repairs should always be done under the cover of a roof.

Wherever possible, any dismantling should be done on a clean flat workbench or table at a suitable working height.

Any workbench needs a vice: one with a jaw opening of 4 in (100 mm) is suitable for most jobs. As mentioned previously, some clean dry storage space is also required for tools, as well as the lubricants, cleaning fluids, touch-up paints and so on which become necessary.

Another item which may be required, and which has a much more general usage, is an electric drill with a chuck capacity of at least 5/16 in (8 mm). This, together with a good range of twist drills, is virtually essential for fitting accessories such as wing mirrors and reversing lights.

Last, but not least, always keep a supply of old newspapers and clean, lint-free rags available, and try to keep any working area as clean as possible.

Jaw gap (in)	Spanner size
0.250	¼ in AF
0.276	7 mm
0.313	5/16 in AF
0.315	8 mm
0.344	11/32 in AF; 1/8 in Whitworth
0.354	9 mm
0.375	3/8 in AF
0.394	10 mm
0.433	11 mm
0.438	7/16 in AF
0.445	3/16 in Whitworth; ¼ in BSF
0.472	12 mm
0.500	½ in AF
0.512	13 mm
0.525	¼ in Whitworth; 5/16 in BSF
0.551	14 mm
0.562	9/16 in AF
0.591	15 mm
0.600	5/16 in Whitworth; 3/8 in BSF
0.625	5/8 in AF
0.630	16 mm
0.669	17 mm
0.686	11/16 in AF
0.709	18 mm
0.710	3/8 in Whitworth; 7/16 in BSF
0.748	19 mm
0.750	¾ in AF
0.813	13/16 in AF
0.820	7/16 in Whitworth; ½ in BSF
0.866	22 mm
0.875	7/8 in AF
0.920	½ in Whitworth; 9/16 in BSF
0.937	15/16 in AF
0.945	24 mm
1.000	1 in AF
1.010	9/16 in Whitworth; 5/8 in BSF
1.024	26 mm
1.063	1.1/16 in AF; 27 mm
1.100	5/8 in Whitworth; 11/16 in BSF
1.125	1.1/8 in AF
1.181	30 mm
1.200	11/16 in Whitworth; ¾ in BSF
1.250	1¼ in AF
1.260	32 mm
1.300	¾ in Whitworth; 7/8 in BSF
1.313	1.5/16 in AF
1.390	13/16 in Whitworth; 15/16 in BSF
1.417	36 mm
1.438	1.7/16 in AF
1.480	7/8 in Whitworth; 1 in BSF
1.500	1½ in AF
1.575	40 mm; 15/16 in Whitworth
1.614	41 mm
1.625	1.5/8 in AF
1.670	1 in Whitworth; 1.1/8 in BSF
1.688	1.11/16 in AF
1.811	46 mm
1.813	13/16 in AF
1.860	1.1/8 in Whitworth; 1¼ in BSF
1.875	1.7/8 in AF
1.969	50 mm
2.000	2 in AF
2.050	1¼ in Whitworth; 1.3/8 in BSF
2.165	55 mm
2.362	60 mm

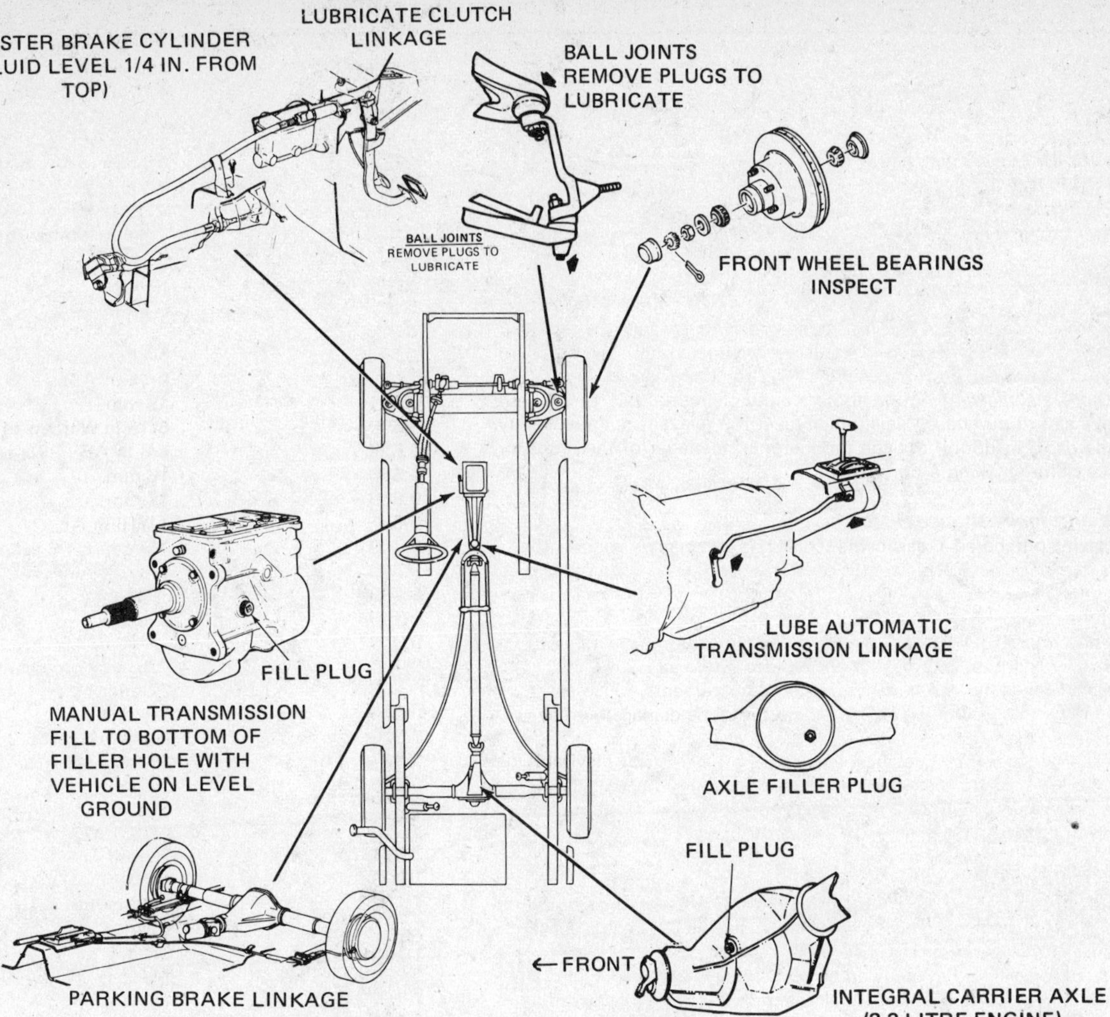

MASTER BRAKE CYLINDER (FLUID LEVEL 1/4 IN. FROM TOP)
LUBRICATE CLUTCH LINKAGE
BALL JOINTS REMOVE PLUGS TO LUBRICATE
BALL JOINTS REMOVE PLUGS TO LUBRICATE
FRONT WHEEL BEARINGS INSPECT
FILL PLUG
MANUAL TRANSMISSION FILL TO BOTTOM OF FILLER HOLE WITH VEHICLE ON LEVEL GROUND
LUBE AUTOMATIC TRANSMISSION LINKAGE
AXLE FILLER PLUG
FILL PLUG
← FRONT
PARKING BRAKE LINKAGE
INTEGRAL CARRIER AXLE (2.3 LITRE ENGINE)

Chassis lubrication and maintenance - all models

Recommended lubricants and fluids

Component	Description	Ford Specification	Component	Description	Ford Specification
Hinges, hinge check and pivots	Polyethylene Grease	ESB-M1C106-B	Automatic Transmission	Ford Automatic Transmission Fluid	ESW-M2C33-F Type F
Brake Master Cylinder	Heavy Duty Brake Fluid	ESA-M6C25-A	Manual Transmission	Ford Manual Transmission Oil	ESW-M2C83-B or ESP-M2C83-C
Front Suspension Ball Joints, Front Wheel Bearings & Clutch Linkage	Ball Joint and Multi-purpose Grease	ESA-M1C75-B	Engine	Engine Oil*	ESE-M2C101-C
Hood Latch & Auxiliary Catch	Polyethylene Grease	ESB-M1C106-B	Engine Coolant	Ford Cooling System Fluid	ESE-M97B18-C
Lock Cylinders	Lock Lubricant	ESB-M2C20-A	Steering Gear Housing (Manual & Power)	Hypoid Gear Oil	ESW-M2C105-A
Rear Axle:			Door Weatherstrip	Silicone Lubricant	ESR-M1314-A
Conventional	Hypoid Gear Oil	ESW-M2C105-A			
Traction-Lok	Hypoid Gear Oil	ESW-M2C119-A			
Power Steering (Pump Reservoir)	Power Steering Fluid	ESW-M2C128-B			

** Note engine oil of a viscosity suitable for the ambient temperature must be used. Consult the operators handbook supplied with your car.*

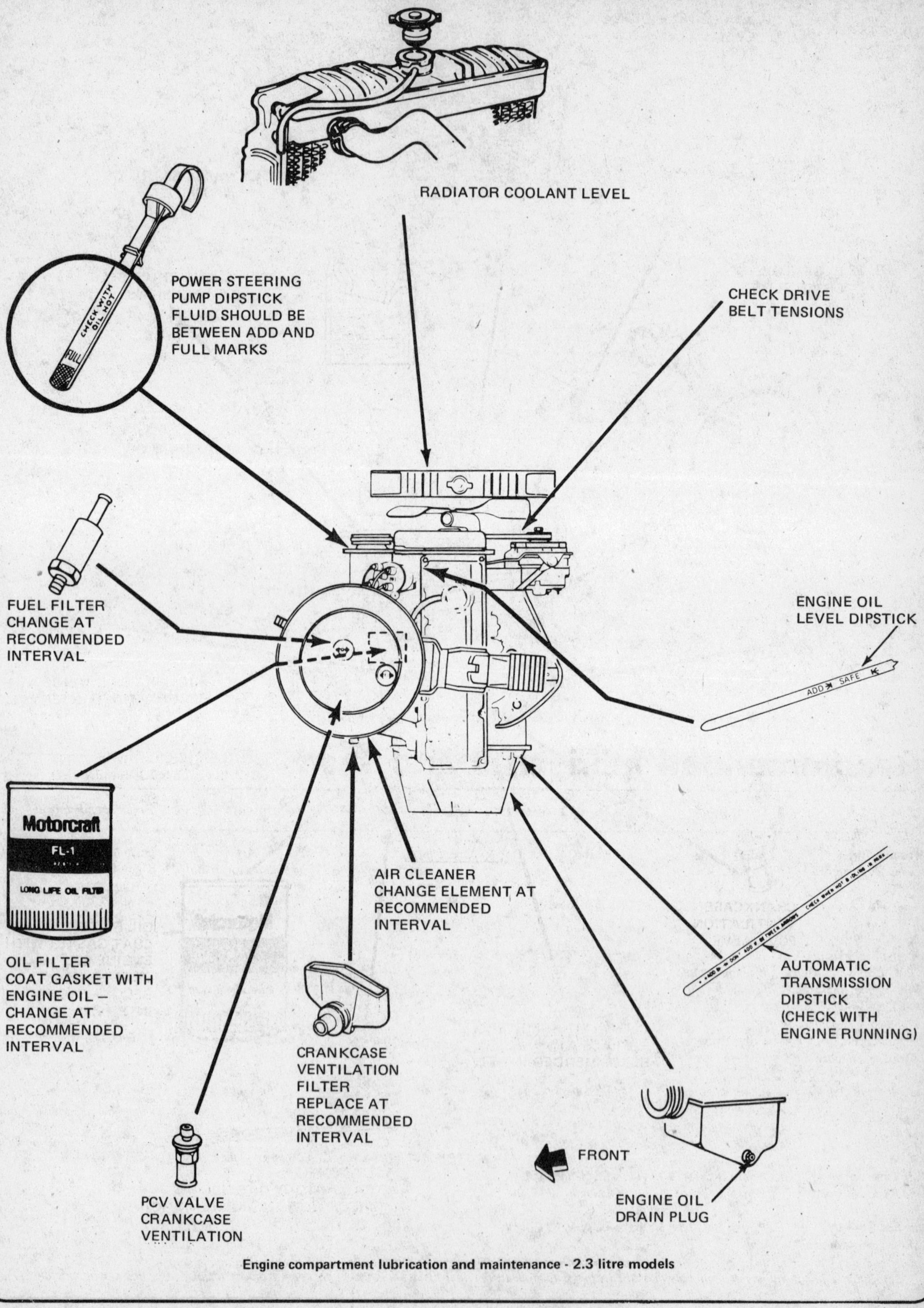
RADIATOR COOLANT LEVEL
CHECK WITH OIL HOT
FULL
POWER STEERING PUMP DIPSTICK FLUID SHOULD BE BETWEEN ADD AND FULL MARKS
CHECK DRIVE BELT TENSIONS
FUEL FILTER CHANGE AT RECOMMENDED INTERVAL
ENGINE OIL LEVEL DIPSTICK
ADD
SAFE
Motorcraft
FL-1
LONG LIFE OIL FILTER
AIR CLEANER CHANGE ELEMENT AT RECOMMENDED INTERVAL
OIL FILTER COAT GASKET WITH ENGINE OIL – CHANGE AT RECOMMENDED INTERVAL
AUTOMATIC TRANSMISSION DIPSTICK (CHECK WITH ENGINE RUNNING)
CRANKCASE VENTILATION FILTER REPLACE AT RECOMMENDED INTERVAL
FRONT
ENGINE OIL DRAIN PLUG
PCV VALVE CRANKCASE VENTILATION

Engine compartment lubrication and maintenance - 2.3 litre models

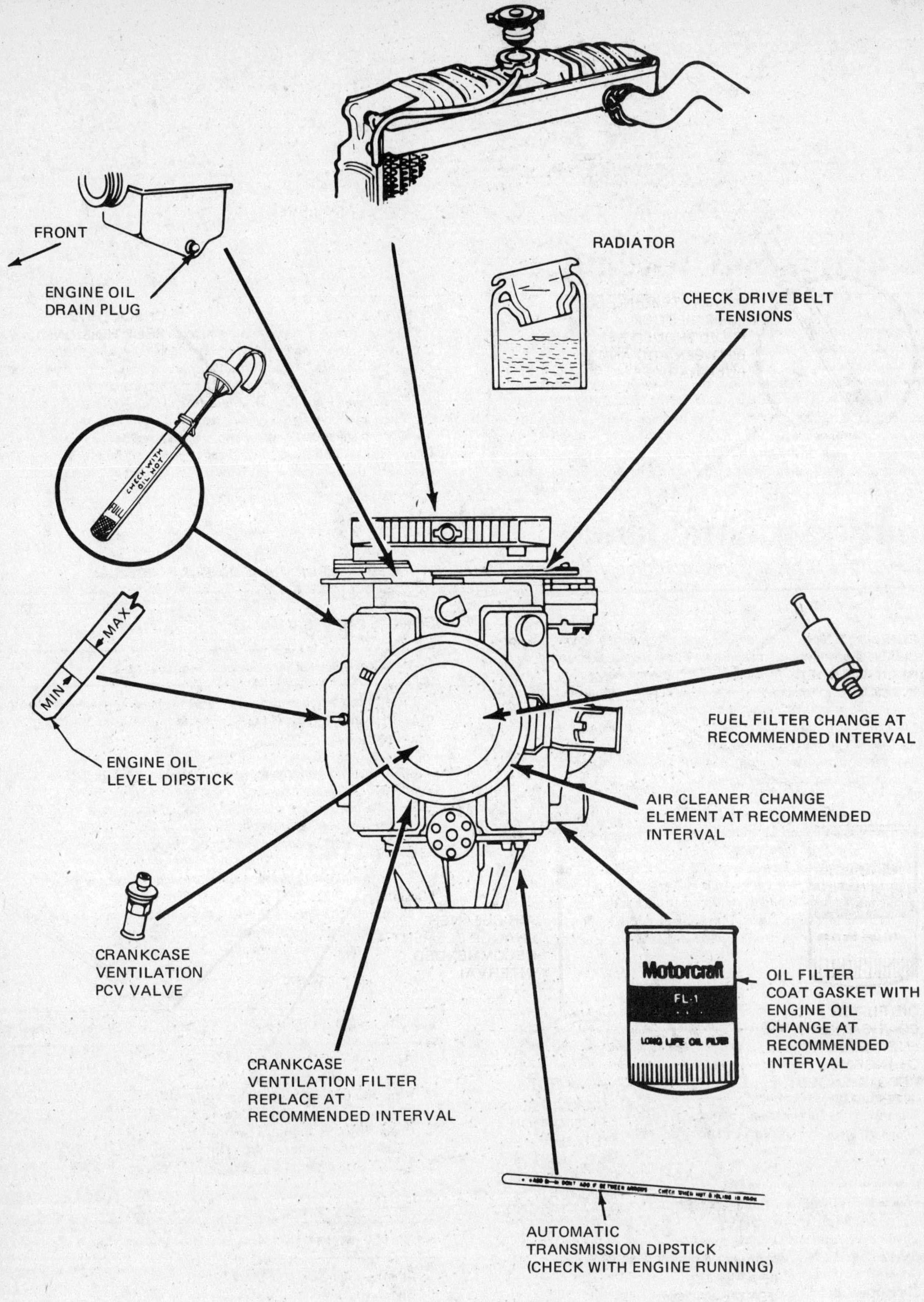
RADIATOR
FRONT
ENGINE OIL
DRAIN PLUG
CHECK DRIVE BELT
TENSIONS
CHECK WITH
OIL HOT
MAX
MIN
FUEL FILTER CHANGE AT
RECOMMENDED INTERVAL
ENGINE OIL
LEVEL DIPSTICK
AIR CLEANER CHANGE
ELEMENT AT RECOMMENDED
INTERVAL
CRANKCASE
VENTILATION
PCV VALVE
Motorcraft
FL-1
LONG LIFE OIL FILTER
OIL FILTER
COAT GASKET WITH
ENGINE OIL
CHANGE AT
RECOMMENDED
INTERVAL
CRANKCASE
VENTILATION FILTER
REPLACE AT
RECOMMENDED INTERVAL
AUTOMATIC
TRANSMISSION DIPSTICK
(CHECK WITH ENGINE RUNNING)

Engine compartment lubrication and maintenance - 2.8 litre models

Jacking and Towing

Jacking

The jack supplied with the car (photo) should only be used to raise the car for changing a roadwheel. Use a hydraulic or screw jack, preferably of the trolley type, to raise the car for repair or overhaul operations and always supplement the jack with safety stands.

To raise the front of the car, position the jack under the second crossmember. To raise the side, locate the jack under the jacking points provided for the jack which is supplied with the car. To raise the rear end, place the jack under the differential.

Never raise the front or rear of the car by means of the bumpers.

Towing

This is best carried out using special towing slings which will be provided by the rescue truck. In an emergency, attach the tow line to the outboard ends of the suspension lower arm at the front of the car or to the ends of the rear axle tubes at the rear of the car.

Remember to unlock the steering column when being towed.

When a vehicle fitted with automatic transmission is being towed, restrict the speed to 30 mph and the distance to 15 miles, otherwise the driveshaft will have to be disconnected at the rear flange. This should be done in any case if transmission damage is suspected.

Routine maintenance

For modifications, and information applicable to later models, see Supplement at end of manual

Introduction

The Routine Maintenance instructions are basically those recommended by the vehicle manufacturer. They are supplemented by additional maintenance tasks proven to be necessary.

It must be emphasised that if any parts of the engine or its ancillary equipment involved with emission control is disturbed, cleaned or adjusted the car must be taken to the local Ford dealer for checking to ensure that it still meets legal requirements.

Tasks in the maintenance instructions marked with an asterisk (*) must be entrusted to a Ford dealer.

The reader should also familiarise himself with the conditions of the vehicle warranty if the car is less than 5 years old. If the conditions of the warranty are broken or an accurate record of servicing not kept, the warranty can become invalidated.

Three maintenance schedules, A, B or C are given, these cover the variations in servicing for cars sold in different States and the type of engine fitted. To check which maintenance schedule applies to your car refer to the emission control data decal in the engine compartment (see example on page 6) or the decal inside the glove compartment door.

All models

Every 250 miles (400 km), weekly or before a long journey

Steering

Check tire pressures (when cold)
Examine tires for wear and damage
Check steering for smooth and accurate operation

Brakes

Check reservoir fluid level. If this has fallen noticeably, check for fluid leakage (photo)
Check for satisfactory brake operation

Lights, wipers, horns, instruments

Check operation of all lights
Check operation of windshield wipers and washers
Check that the horn operates
Check that all instruments and gauges are operating

Engine compartment

Check the engine oil level; top-up if necessary (photos)
Check radiator coolant level
Check battery electrolyte level

Schedules A, B and C

Every 3000 miles (5000 Km) or 3 months

The following maintenance items must be carried out at this mileage/time interval if the car is being operated in severe conditions. These are considered to be:

a) Outside temperature remains below 10°F (−12.2°C) for 60 days or more and most trips are less than 10 miles.
b) If a trailer having a total weight of more than 2000 lb. is towed over long distances.
c) Extended periods of idling or low speed operation.

For normal car operation these service items may be carried out at 6000 miles (10000 Km) or 6 month intervals.

Complete the checks in the weekly inspection plus the following:
Change the engine oil (photo)
Fit a new oil filter (photo)

Schedules A and B

Every 5000 miles (8000 Km) or 5 months, whichever occurs first

Renew the engine oil and filter
Check the ignition timing
Adjust engine idle speeds and mixture
* Check and adjust fuel deceleration valve
* Check throttle solenoid operation
Check brake master cylinder fluid level
Adjust clutch pedal free-play, if necessary

Schedule C

Every 6000 miles (10000 Km) or 6 months, whichever occurs first

Change engine oil and filter
Check transmission fluid levels (photo)
Check brake fluid level
Adjust clutch pedal free-play, if necessary
* Check fuel deceleration valve if fitted
* Adjust engine idle speed and mixture

Location of jack beneath the spare wheel

Air cleaner top cover wing nut

Removing the air cleaner element

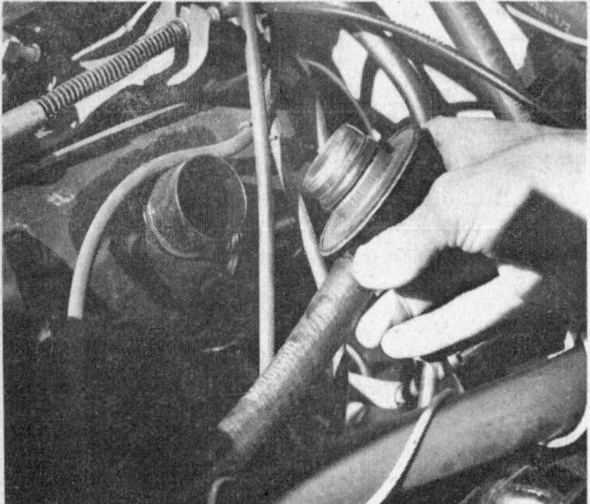
Engine oil filler cap (V6)

Automatic transmission fluid dipstick

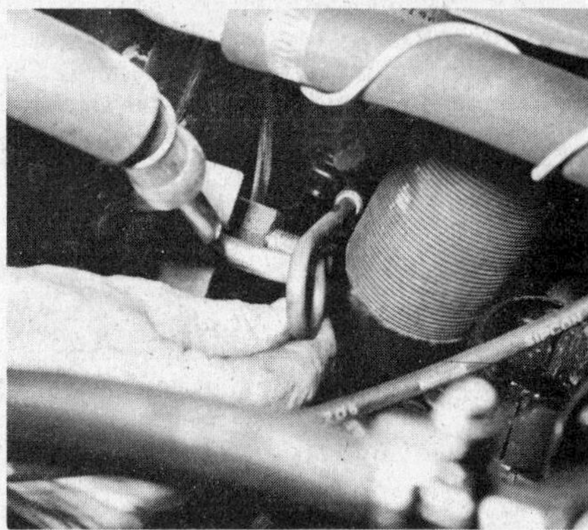
Engine oil level dipstick

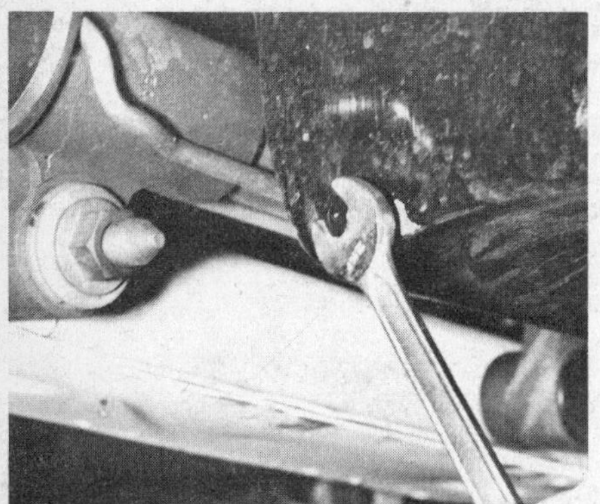
Engine oil pan drain plug

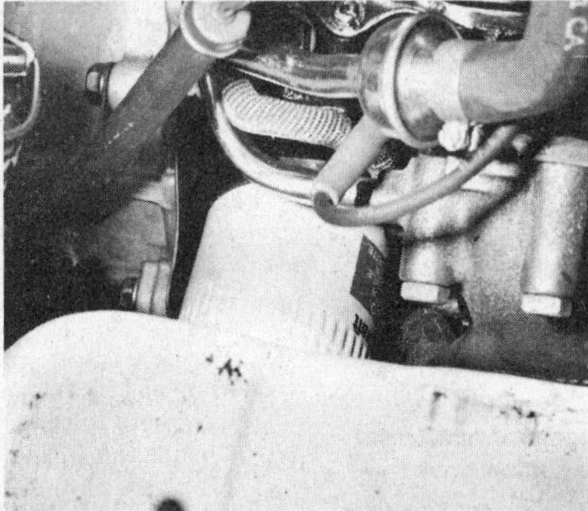
Location of oil filter

Windshield washer reservoir filler cap

Checking the brake master cylinder fluid level

General view of engine (radiator filler cap in the forefront)

Check the torque of intake manifold bolts
Lubricate exhaust control valve if fitted
Check operation of throttle and choke linkage
Renew fuel filter
Check all drivebelt tensions

Schedule C

Every 12000 miles (20000 Km) or 12 months, whichever occurs first

Adjust engine valve clearances (V6 only)
Check carburetor air cleaner element
Renew all spark plugs
Inspect spark plug wires
* Check spark control systems and delay valve
* Check EGR system and delay valve
Check condition of coolant
Inspect all drivebelts for wear and replace if necessary
* Inspect evaporative emission canister (2.3 liter engine only)
Check the torque of all engine driven accessory mounting bolts
Check front suspension and steering linkage for abnormal slackness or damaged seals
* Adjust automatic transmission bands
Inspect exhaust system and heat shields for corrosion or damage

Schedules A and B

Every 15000 miles (24000 Km) or 15 months, whichever occurs first

Note: Some of the checks below do not apply to Schedule C vehicles
Check the torque of inlet manifold bolts
Lubricate and check exhaust control valve
Check condition of coolant
Check drivebelt tensions
Check PCV system hoses
* Check thermactor system
Renew spark plugs
Inspect spark plug HT cables
Check ignition timing
Inspect distributor cap and rotor
* Check spark control system and delay valve
* Check carburetor idle speed and mixture
Check throttle and choke linkage
Check air cleaner element
* Check air cleaner temperature control and delay valve
Replace fuel system filter
Check and adjust valve clearances (V6 only)
Check the torque of engine driven accessory mounting bolts
Inspect the exhaust system and heat shields for corrosion or damage
Check transmission fluid levels
Check clutch pedal free-play and adjust if necessary

Inspect front suspension and steering for looseness or damaged seals
Have your local Ford dealer adjust the automatic transmission bands
Check brake pads and linings for wear

Schedule C

Every 18000 miles (30000 Km) or 18 months, whichever occurs first

Inspect distributor cap and rotor
Check tightness of rear spring mountings

Schedule A

Every 20000 miles (32000 Km) or 20 months, whichever occurs first

Carry out the maintenance tasks listed for schedule A and B vehicles at 15000 miles, plus the following:

Replace the PCV valve
Clean PCV system hoses
Replace crankcase filter in air cleaner
* Inspect evaporative emission canister
Inspect fuel tank filler cap, and vapor lines for leakage or deterioration.
Replace air cleaner element (photos)

Schedule C

Every 24000 miles (40000 Km) or 2 years, whichever occurs first

Dismantle, lubricate and adjust front wheel bearings
Replace crankcase filter in air cleaner
Replace air cleaner element
Inspect filler cap and fuel line for deterioration or leakage
* Check thermactor system if fitted
Check cooling system hoses for leakage
Inspect disc pads and rear brake lining for wear
Inspect all brake hoses and lines

Schedules A, B and C

Every 30000 miles (50000 Km) or 30 months, whichever occurs first

Lubricate front suspension and steering linkage
Drain and refill automatic transmission fluid
Replace coolant
Examine all brake hoses and pipes and renew if necessary
Check wheel cylinders and master cylinder for leaks and renew seals where necessary
Renew brake fluid

Chapter 1 Part A: 2300cc four cylinder engine

For modifications, and information applicable to later models, see Supplement at end of manual

Contents

Specifications

Engine (general)

Engine type	Four in-line, single overhead camshaft
Firing order	1, 3, 4, 2
Bore	3.78 in (96 mm)
Stroke	3.126 in (79.4 mm)
Cubic capacity	2294 cc (140 cu in)
Compression pressure	Lowest reading within 75% of highest reading
Oil pressure, hot	40 to 60 lb f/in^2 (2.8 to 4.2 kg f/cm^2)
Engine idle speed	See engine compartment emission control decal

Cylinder head

Valve guide bore diameter	0.3433 to 0.3443 in (8.720 to 8.745 mm)
Valve seat width:	
Intake	0.060 to 0.090 in (1.524 to 2.286 mm)
Exhaust	0.070 to 0.090 in (1.778 to 2.286 mm)
Valve seat angle	45°
Valve seat runout, max.	0.0016 in (0.041 mm)
Valve arrangement, front to rear	EI, EI, EI, EI
Gasket surface flatness	0.003 in (0.076 mm) in any 6 in (152.4 mm): 0.006 in (0.152 mm) overall
Head gasket surface finish	60 to 150 rms

Cylinder location and distributor rotation

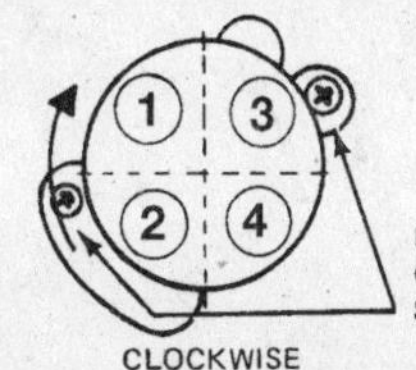

Valve springs

Spring load	71 to 79 lb at 1.56 in (32.23 to 35.87 kg at 39.6 mm) 180 to 198 lb at 1.16 in (81.72 to 89.82 kg at 29.46 mm)
Spring free-length (approx.)	1.824 in (46.33 mm)
Valve spring assembled height pad to retainer	1 17/32 in (38.89 mm)
Valve spring out of square (max)	0,078 in (1.98 mm)

Valves

Stem to guide clearance:	
Intake	0.0010 to 0.0027 in (0.0254 to 0.069 mm)
Exhaust	0.0015 to 0.0032 in (0.0381 to 0.081 mm)
Wear limit	0.0055 in (0.1397 mm)
Valve head diameter:	
Intake	1.728 to 1.744in (43.89 to 44.298 mm)
Exhaust	1.492 to 1.508 in (37.897 to 38.30 mm)
Valve face angle	44°
Valve face runout, max.	0.002 in (0.051 mm)
Stem diameter, standard:	
Intake	0.3416 to 0.3423 in (8.676 to 8.694 mm)
Exhaust	0.3411 to 0.3418 in (8.664 to 8.682 mm)
Oversize 0.008 in:	
Intake	0.3446 to 0.3453 in (8.751 to 8.771 mm)
Exhaust	0.3441 to 0.3448 in (8.740 to 8.756 mm)
Oversize 0.016 in:	
Intake	0.3566 to 0.3573 in (9.058 to 9.075 mm)
Exhaust	0.3561 to 0.3568 in (9.045 to 9.063 mm)
Oversize 0.032 in:	
Intake	0.3716 to 0.3723 in (9.439 to 9.456 mm)
Exhaust	0.3711 to 0.3718 in (9.426 to 9.444 mm)

Cylinder block

Bore diameter, standard	3.7795 to 3.7831 in (96 to 96.09 mm)
Maximum out of round	0.001 in (0.0254 mm)
Wear limit	0.005 in (0.127 mm)
Bore surface finish	18.88 rms
Taper wear limit	0.01 in (0.254 mm)
Bore diameter 0.003 in oversize	3.7825 to 3,7861 in (96.08 to 96.17 mm)
Main bearing bore diameter	2.5902 to 2.5910 in (65.79 to 65.81 mm)
Head gasket surface flatness	0.003 in (0.076 mm) in any 6 in (152.4 mm) 0.006 in (0.152 mm) overall
Head gasket surface finish	60 to 150 rms

Camshaft

Lobe lift	0.2437 in (6.19 mm)
Max. permissible lobe lift loss	0.005 in (0.127 mm)
Endplay	0.001 to 0.007 in (0.0254 to 0.178 mm)
Wear limit	0.009 in (0.229 mm)
Camshaft journal to bearings clearance	0.001 to 0.003 in (0.0254 to 0.076 mm)
Wear limit	0.006 in (0.152 mm)
Camshaft journal diameter	1.7713 to 1.772 in (44.99 to 45.01 mm)
Camshaft bearings inside diameter	1.773 to 1.7742 in (45.03 to 45.06 mm)

Camshaft drive mechanism

Face run-out max. assembled:	
Camshaft gear	0.007 in (0.178 mm)
Crankshaft gear	0.005 in (0.127 mm)

Hydraulic lash adjuster

Standard diameter	0.8422 to 0.8427 in (21.39 to 21.40 mm)
Clearance to bore	0.0007 to 0.0027 in (0.018 to 0.069 mm)
Leak-down rate for 1/8 in(3.175 mm) of travel	2 to 8 seconds
Collapsed adjuster gap at cam (allowable)	0.035 to 0.055 in (0.89 to 1.34 mm)
Collasped adjuster gap at cam (desired)	0.040 to 0.050 in (1.0 to 1.27 mm)

Auxiliary shaft

Endplay	0.001 to 0.007 in (0.025 to 0.178 mm)
Bearing clearance	0.001 to 0.0028 in(0.025 to 0.071 mm)

Crankshaft and flywheel

Main bearing journal diameter	2.3892 to 2.399 in (60.686 to 60.935 mm)
Main bearing journal run-out, max.	0.002 in (0.051 mm)
Wear limit	0.005 in (0.127 mm)
Main bearing journal thrust face run-out, max.	0.001 in (0.0254 mm)
Connecting rod journal diameter	2.0464 to 2.0472 in (51.979 to 51.999 mm)
Crankshaft free-endplay	0.004 to 0.008 in (0.102 to 0.203 mm)
Wear limit	0.012 in (0.305 mm)
Flywheel clutch face run-out	0.008 in (0.203 mm)

Crankshaft bearings

Connecting rod bearing-to-crankshaft clearance	0.0008 to 0.0026 in (0.02 to 0.066 mm)
Wall thickness, standard	0.0619 to 0.0624 in (1.572 to 1.585 mm)
Wall thickness, 0.002 in undersize	0.0629 to 0.0634 in (1.598 to 1.61 mm)
Main bearing-to-crankshaft clearance	0.0008 to 0.0015 in (0.02 to 0.038 mm)
Wall thickness, standard	0.0951 to 0.0956 in (2.416 to 2.428 mm)
Wall thickness, 0.002 in undersize	0.0961 to 0.0966 in (2.441 to 2.454 mm)

Connecting rod

Piston pin bore	0.9104 to 0.9112 in (23.12 to 23.14 mm)
Connecting rod bearing bore diameter	2.172 to 2.1728 in (55.169 to 55.189 mm)
Connecting rod side clearance (assembled to crankshaft)	0.0035 to 0.0105 in (0.089 to 0.267 mm)
Wear limit	0.014 in (0.356 mm)

Piston

Diameter:	
Standard	3.7780 to 3.7786 in (95.96 to 95.976 mm)
Coded blue	3.7792 to 3.7798 in (95.99 to 96.007 mm)
0.003 in oversize	3.7804 to 3.7810 in (96.02 to 96.037 mm)
Piston to bore clearance	0.0014 to 0.0022 in (0.035 to 0.056 mm)
Piston pin bore diameter	0.9123 to 0.9126 in (23.17 to 23.18 mm)
Ring groove width:	
Compression rings	0.080 to 0.081 in (2.03 to 2.056 mm)
Oil control ring	0.188 to 0.189 in (4.78 to 4.80 mm)

Piston pin

Length	3.01 to 3.04 in (76.45 to 77.22 mm)
Diameter, standard:	0.912 to 0.9123 in (23.16 to 23.17 mm)
0.001 in oversize	0.913 to 0.9133 in (23.19 to 23.198 mm)
0.002 in oversize	0.914 to 0.9143 in (23.21 to 23.22 mm)
Pin to piston clearance	0.0002 to 0.0004 in (0.005 to 0.01 mm)
Pin to connecting rod bushing clearance	Interference fit

Piston rings

Compression ring width	0.077 to 0.08 in (1.956 to 2.03 mm)
Compression ring side clearance	0.002 to 0.004 in (0.05 to 0.10 mm)
Wear limit	0.006 in (0.152 mm)
Oil control ring	Snug fit
Compression ring gap width	0.01 to 0.02 in (0.254 to 0.51 mm)
Oil control ring gap width	0.015 to 0.055 in (0.38 to 1.397 mm)

Oil pump

Relief valve spring tension	7.54 to 8.33 lb (3.4 to 3.78 kg) at 1.54 in (39.12 mm)
Driveshaft to housing clearance	0.0015 to 0.0029 in (0.038 to 0.074 mm)
Relief valve clearance	0.0015 to 0.0029 in (0.038 to 0.074 mm)
Rotor assembly end-clearance	0.001 to 0.004 in (0.025 to 0.102 mm)
Outer race-to-housing radial clearance	0.001 to 0.007 in (0.025 to 0.178 mm)
Oil pan capacity (approx.)	10 US pints (8¼ Imp. pints 4.7 liter)
Oil type:	**Multi-viscosity**
Below + 32°F (0°C)	5W-30/10W-30
−10°F to + 90°F (−23°C to + 32°C)	10W-30
−10°F to above 90°F (−23°C to above + 32°C)	10W-40
Above 90°F (32°C)	20W-40

Torque wrench settings

	lb f ft	kg fm
Auxiliary shaft gear bolt	28 to 40	3.9 to 5.5
Auxiliary shaft thrust plate bolt	6 to 9	0.83 to 1.2
Belt tensioner bolt:		
Pivot	28 to 40	3.9 to 5.5
Adjuster	14 to 21	1.9 to 2.9
Camshaft gear bolt	50 to 71	6.9 to 9.8
Camshaft thrust plate bolt	6 to 9	0.83 to 1.2
Carburetor to carburetor spacer stud	7.5 to 15	1.0 to 2.1
Carburetor to spacer nut	10 to 14	1.4 to 1.9
Carburetor spacer to manifold bolt	14 to 21	1.9 to 2.9
Connecting rod nut	30 to 36	4.1 to 4.9
Crankshaft damper/pulley bolt	80 to 114	11 to 15.7
Cylinder head bolt	80 to 90	11 to 12.4
Distributor clamp bolt	20 to 28	2.8 to 3.9
Distributor vacuum tube to inlet manifold - adapter	5 to 8	0.7 to 1.1
Exhaust manifold to cylinder head nut or bolt	16 to 23	2.2 to 3.2
Flywheel to crankshaft bolt	54 to 64	7.4 to 8.8
Fuel pump to cylinder block bolt	14 to 21	1.9 to 2.9

Torque wrench settings	lb f ft	kg fm
Intake manifold to cylinder head nut or bolt	14 to 21	1.9 to 2.9
Main bearing cap bolt	80 to 90	11 to 12.4
Oil pressure sending unit to cylinder block	8 to 18	1.1 to 2.5
Oil pump pick-up tube to oil pump	14 to 21	1.9 to 2.9
Oil pump pick-up tube to cylinder block	14 to 21	1.9 to 2.9
Oil pan drain plug	15 to 25	2.1 to 3.4
Oil pan to cylinder block bolts:		
M6 bolts	7 to 9	1.0 to 1.2
M8 bolts	11 to 13	1.5 to 1.8
Oil filter insert to block	20 to 25	2.8 to 3.4
Rocker cover bolts	4 to 7	0.5 to 1.0
Spark plug to cylinder head	10 to 15	1.4 to 2.1
Temperature sending unit to cylinder head	8 to 18	1.1 to 2.5
Water jacket drain plug	23 to 28	3.2 to 3.9
Water pump to cylinder block bolt	14 to 21	1.9 to 2.9
Exhaust manifold to EGR pipe - connector	25 to 35	3.4 to 4.8
EGR valve to spacer bolt	14 to 21	1.9 to 2.9
EGR tube to exhaust manifold - connector	8 to 12	1.1 to 1.6
EGR tube nut	8 to 12	1.1 to 1.6
Auxiliary shaft cover bolts	6 to 9	0.8 to 1.2
Cylinder front cover bolts	6 to 9	0.8 to 1.2
Water outlet connection bolts	14 to 21	1.9 to 2.9
Inner timing belt cover stud	14 to 21	1.9 to 2.9
Outer timing belt cover bolts	6 to 9	0.8 to 1.2
Rocker cover shield bolts	28 to 40	3.9 to 5.5
Thermactor check valve to manifold	25 to 35	3.4 to 4.8

Fig. 1.1 General view of 2.3 liter engine

1 General description

The 2300cc engine described in this Chapter is a four-cylinder single overhead camshaft unit constructed from lightweight cast-iron.

The crankshaft runs in five main bearings, and the camshaft runs in four. The main, connecting rod, camshaft and auxiliary shaft bearings are all replaceable.

The camshaft is driven from the crankshaft by a toothed belt, which also operates the auxiliary shaft. The auxiliary shaft drives the oil pump and distributor, and operates the fuel pump through an eccentric. Tension on the drivebelt is maintained by a preloaded idler pulley which runs on the outside of the belt.

A separate V-belt is used to drive the water pump, fan and alternator. V-belts are also used to drive the engine-driven accessories.

Hydraulic valve lash adjusters are used, these operating on the fulcrum point of the cam followers (rocker arms). The cylinder head is drilled to provide oil feed and return pipes for their operation.

A positive, closed-type crankcase ventilation system is used to recycle crankcase blow-by vapors back to the intake manifold.

2 Major operations possible with engine in car

The following major operations can be carried out to the engine with it in place:

1 *Removal and refitting of cylinder head*
2 *Removal and refitting of camshaft drivebelt*
3 *Removal and refitting of engine front mountings*

The camshaft can be removed after removal of the cylinder head.

3 Major operations requiring engine removal

The following major operations can be carried out with the engine out of the body frame on the bench:

1 *Removal and refitting of the main bearings*
2 *Removal and refitting of the crankshaft*
3 *Removal and refitting of the flywheel*
4 *Removal and refitting of the crankshaft rear oil seal*
5 *Removal and refitting of the oil pan*
6 *Removal and refitting of the pistons, connecting rods and big-end bearings*
7 *Removal and refitting of auxiliary shaft*

4 Methods of engine removal

The engine may be lifted out either on its own or in unit with the transmission. On models fitted with automatic transmission, it is recommended that the engine be lifted out on its own, unless a substantial crane or overhead hoist is available, because of the weight factor. If the engine and transmission are removed as a unit they have to be lifted out at a very steep angle, so make sure that there is sufficient lifting height available.

5 Engine - removal (without transmission)

Providing a good set of tools and lifting tackle is available the home mechanic should be able to remove the engine without encountering any major problems. Make sure that a set of metric sockets and wrenches is available in addition to an hydraulic trolley jack and a pair of axle stands. An assistant will make the task easier.

1 First raise the car hood and disconnect the battery leads.

2 Mark the position of the hood hinges with a pencil. Undo the retaining bolts and remove the hood.

3 Remove the air cleaner and exhaust manifold shroud.

4 If air conditioning is fitted remove the compressor unit from the engine mounting bracket but **do not** disconnect the refrigerant hoses. Position the pump out of the way without straining the hoses. **Note: If it is necessary to remove the pump from the car the hoses should be disconnected by a refrigerant specialist.**

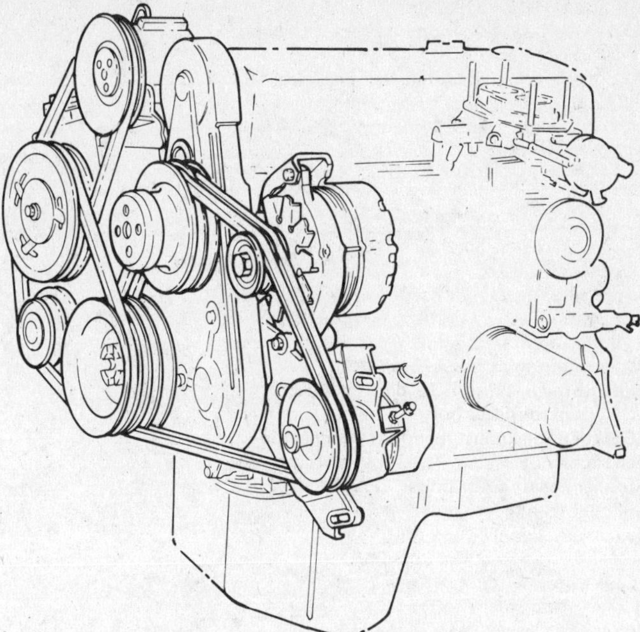

Fig. 1.2. Layout of engine accessories and drivebelts

1A

5 Remove the plug and drain the crankcase oil into a suitable container.

6 Remove the bottom radiator hose and drain the coolant.

7 Remove the top hose and transmission oil cooler hoses (if fitted) from the radiator, undo and remove the mounting bolts and remove the radiator.

8 Undo the four bolts and remove the fan.

9 If available, position the car over an inspection pit to gain access underneath, otherwise jack-up the front of the car and support it on axle stands.

10 Where applicable, remove the engine shield.

11 Remove the starter motor. Further details will be found in Chapter 10, if required.

12 *On automatic transmission models:* remove the torque converter bolt access plug. Remove the three flywheel-to-converter bolts. Remove the converter housing cover and disconnect the converter from the flywheel.

13 *On manual transmission models:* remove the flywheel cover.

14 Remove the flywheel or converter housing cover, as applicable.

15 Detach the exhaust pipe from the exhaust manifold. Remove the packing washer.

16 Remove the nuts from the engine mountings, and remove the nuts and through bolts retaining the near engine support crossmember.

17 Detach the fuel lines from the fuel pump, plugging the lines to prevent fuel spillage.

18 Where applicable, remove the power steering pump drivebelt and draw off the pulley. The drivebelt arrangement is shown in Chapter 2; refer to Chapter 11 for further information on the pump.

19 Remove the lower bolt securing the power steering pump to the bracket.

20 Lower the car to the ground.

21 Disconnect the heater and vacuum hoses from the engine. It is recommended that a sketch is made showing the various connections to avoid confusion when refitting.

22 Disconnect the power brake hose.

23 Remove the oil pressure union from the connection on the rear left-hand side of the cylinder head.

24 Detach the carburetor cable(s).

25 Disconnect the wire to the throttle solenoid and choke heater.

26 Detach the wire from the water temperature sender on the rear left-hand side of the cylinder block.

27 Disconnect the lines from the vacuum amplifier.

28 From the distributor, disconnect the coil wire and vacuum line.

29 Pull off the multi-plug from the alternator, followed by the ground wire.

30 Remove the bolt from the alternator adjusting arm.

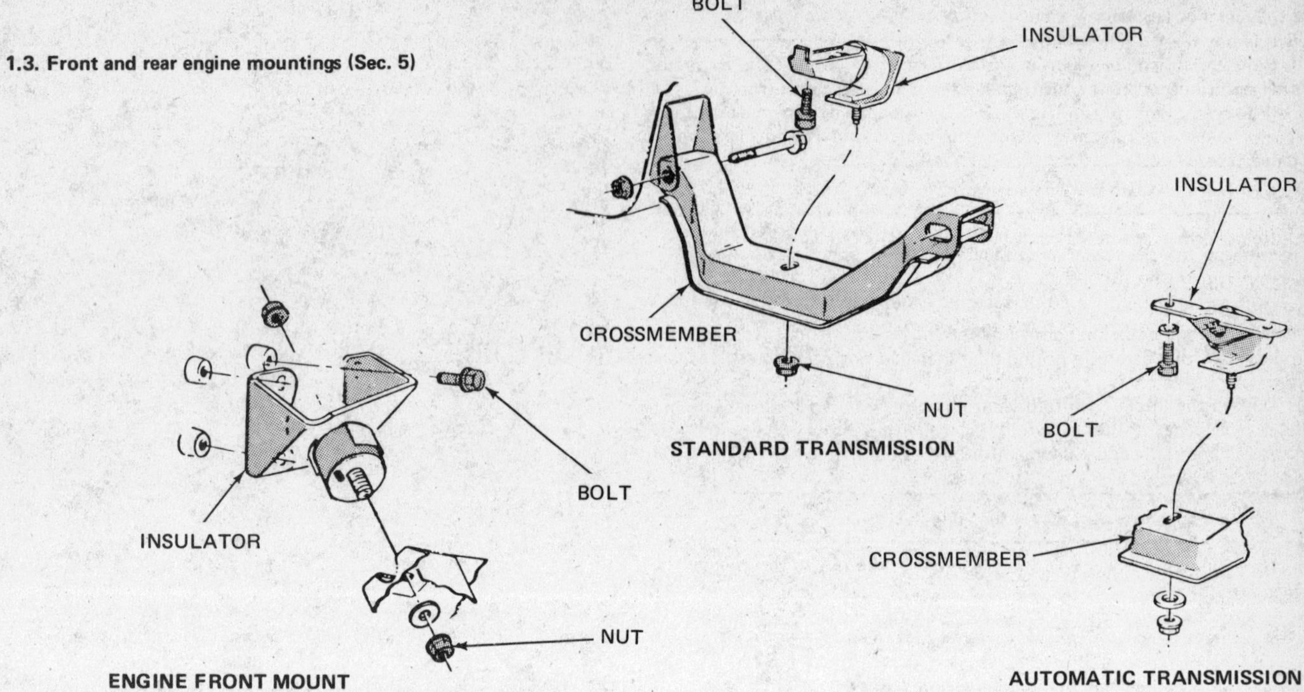

Fig. 1.3. Front and rear engine mountings (Sec. 5)

31 Remove the remaining power steering pump-to-bracket bolts, and remove the pump, (if fitted).
32 Support the weight of the transmission on a suitable jack, with a wood block interposed between the jack head and the transmission.
33 Attach the hoist hooks to the engine lifting brackets and lift the engine a little.
34 Draw the engine forward to disengage the transmission, ensuring that the transmission is still satisfactorily supported.
35 Lift the engine out, ensuring that no damage occurs to the hoses etc, in the engine compartment or to the engine mounting equipment. Transfer the engine to a suitable working area and detach the accessories. These will vary according to the engine, but would typically be:

Alternator
Thermactor pump
Air-conditioning compressor
Clutch

36 Clean the outside of the engine using a water soluble solvent, then transfer it to where it is to be dismantled. On the assumption that engine overhaul is to be carried out, remove the fuel pump, oil filter (unscrew), spark plugs, distributor (index mark the distributor body and block to assist with installation), fan, water pump, thermostat, oil pressure and water temperature senders, emission control ancillaries, etc. Refer to the appropriate Sections in this and other Chapters for further information.

6 Engine - removal (with manual transmission)

1 The procedure for removing the engine and transmission together is basically similar to that described in the previous Section. However, the following differences should be noted:

a) Disconnect the gearshift linkage from the transmission, referring to Chapter 6, as necessary.
b) Detach the propellor shaft following the procedure given in Chapter 7.
c) Disconnect the clutch operating cable from the release arm.
d) Do not remove the clutch housing bolts. These items are removed after the assembly has been removed from the car. Further information on this will be found in Chapter 6.
e) Remove the speedometer drive cable, and the transmission electrical connections. If there is any possibility of their being mixed up, suitably label them or make a sketch showing their installed positions.
f) Support the weight of the transmission in a similar manner to that described in the previous Section, paragraph 32, while the rear mounting is being detached.
g) It is a good idea to do the preliminary cleaning of the engine with the transmission still attached.

7 Engine - dismantling (general)

1 It is best to mount the engine on a dismantling stand, but if this is not available, stand the engine on a strong bench at a comfortable working height. Failing this, it can be stripped down on the floor.
2 During the dismantling process, the greatest care should be taken to keep the exposed parts free from dirt. As an aid to achieving this thoroughly clean down the outside of the engine, first removing all traces of oil and congealed dirt.
3 A good grease solvent will make the job much easier, for, after the solvent has been applied and allowed to stand for a time, a vigorous jet of water will wash off the solvent and grease with it. If the dirt is thick and deeply embedded, work the solvent into it with a strong stiff brush.
4 Finally wipe down the exterior of the engine with a rag and only then, when it is quite clean, should the dismantling process begin. As the engine is stripped, clean each part in a bath of kerosene or gasoline.
5 Never immerse parts with oilways in kerosene (eg; crankshaft and camshaft). To clean these parts, wipe down carefully with a gasoline dampened rag. Oilways can be cleaned out with wire. If an air line is available, all parts can be blown dry and the oilways blown through as an added precaution.
6 Re-use of old gaskets is false economy. To avoid the possibility of trouble after the engine has been reassembled **always** use new gaskets throughout.
7 Do not throw away the old gaskets, for sometimes it happens that an immediate replacement cannot be found and the old gasket is then very useful as a template. Hang up the gaskets as they are removed.
8 To strip the engine, it is best to work from the top down. When the stage is reached where the crankshaft must be removed, the engine can be turned on its side and all other work carried out with it in this position.
9 Wherever possible, refit nuts, bolts and washers finger-tight from

wherever they were removed. This helps to avoid loss and muddle. If they cannot be refitted then arrange them in a fashion to make it clear from whence they came.

10 Before dismantling begins it is important that a special tool is obtained for compressing the lash adjusters. This has the Ford number T74P-6565-B.

8 Cylinder head removal - engine out of the car

1 Remove the carburetor from the intake manifold using a suitable cranked wrench. For further information see Chapter 3.

2 Take off the gasket. Remove the EGR spacer, followed by the second gasket.

3 Remove any emission control system hoses and fittings from the intake manifold, carefully noting their installed positions to assist in reassembly later.

4 Loosen the intake manifold securing bolts by about ½ turn each, in the reverse order to that shown in Fig. 1.6. Then remove the bolts completely and lift away the manifold. Note the lifting eye on the No. 7 bolt.

5 Remove the timing belt outer cover (4 bolts). Note the spacers used with two of the bolts adjacent to the auxiliary shaft sprocket.

6 If major engine dismantling is going to be carried out, remove the nut and washer retaining the crankshaft pulley. If this is found difficult because the engine tends to turn over, either wedge a screwdriver in the flywheel teeth or lock the pulley using a suitable bar in the slots.

7 Draw off the pulley using a suitable puller (or carefully pry it off using a large screwdriver), then remove the belt guide.

8 Loosen the timing belt tensioner adjustment bolt to relieve the belt tension.

9 Remove the timing belt by drawing it off the sprockets.

10 Remove the timing belt tensioner from the front end of the cylinder head (2 bolts).

11 Remove the single stud and washer from the upper attachment point of the inner timing belt cover.

12 Loosen the eight screws from around the rocker cover and the two screws at the front end. Remove the screws, lift off the cover and remove the gasket. (Fig. 1.8.)

13 Loosen each cylinder head bolt slightly in the reverse order to that shown in Fig. 1.9. Then remove all the bolts with the exception of Nos. 7 and 8 which should be unscrewed so that only about two threads are engaged.

14 Using the exhaust manifold for leverage, lift it up to break the cylinder head/gasket seal.

15 Loosen the exhaust manifold retaining bolts in the reverse order

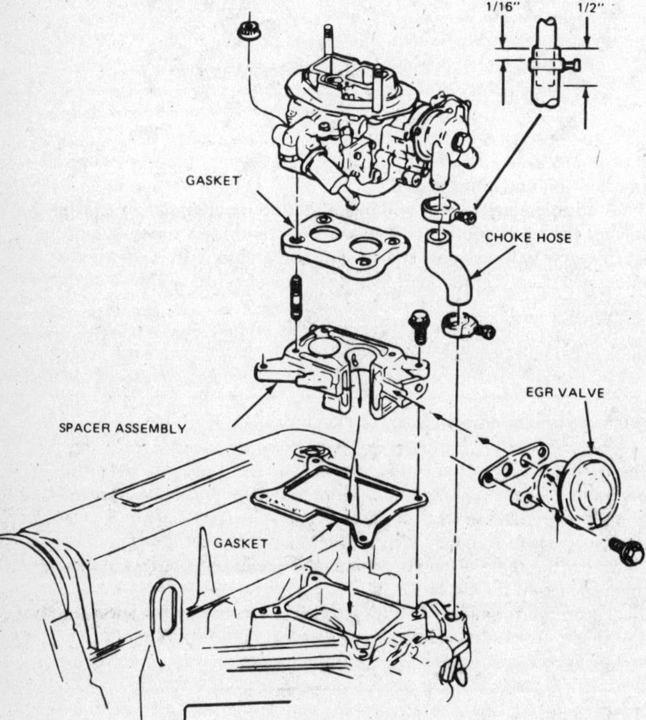

Fig. 1.4. Carburetor, EGR spacer and associated components (Secs. 8 and 63)

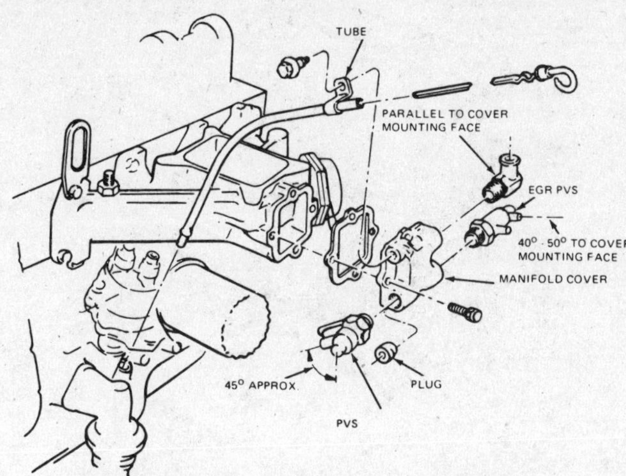

Fig. 1.5. Intake manifold ancillaries (Secs. 8 and 63)

1A

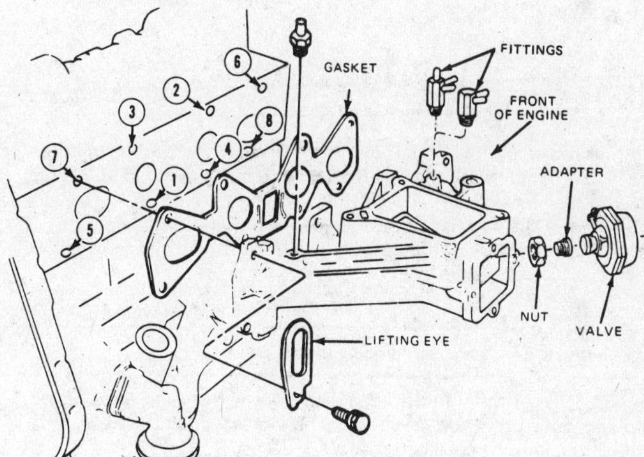

Fig. 1.6. Intake manifold and gaskets (Secs. 8 and 63)

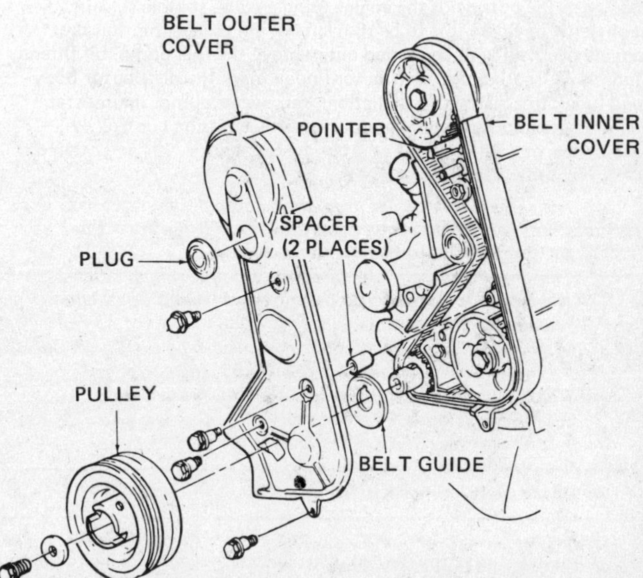

Fig. 1.7. Camshaft drivebelt outer cover assembly (Sec. 8)

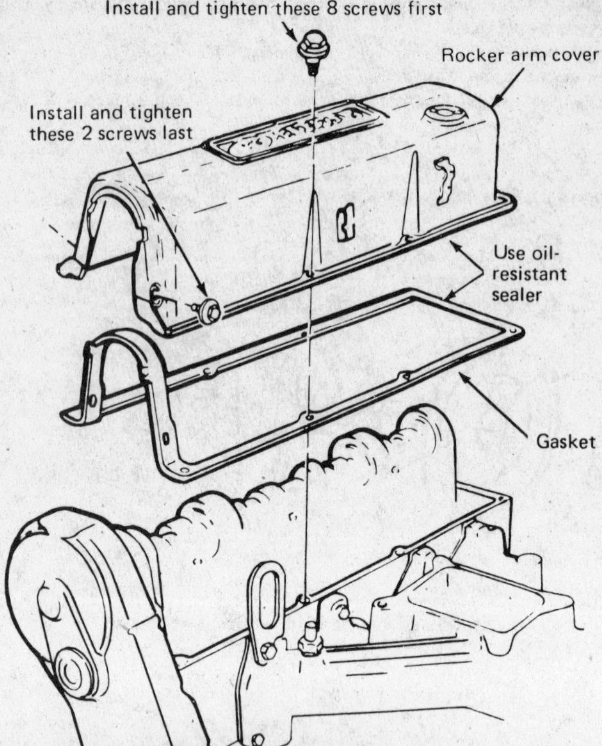

Fig. 1.8. Rocker cover and gasket (Sec. 8)

to that shown in Fig. 1.10. Remove the bolts whilst supporting the manifold then remove the manifold from the engine. Note the lifting eye on the rear bolt.

16 Remove the two remaining cylinder head bolts and lift off the head. Transfer it to a suitable workbench for further dismantling. Remove the old gasket from the block.

9 Cylinder head removal - engine in the car

1 Removal of the cylinder head with the engine in the car is very similar to the procedure given in the previous Section. However, the following points should be noted:

a) First remove the engine compartment hood for improved access.
b) Disconnect the battery ground lead.
c) Drain the engine coolant and remove the hoses connected to the cylinder head. Refer to Chapter 2, if necessary.
d) Remove the air cleaner, carburetor and emission control system items attached to the carburetor and manifolds. Refer to Chapter 3 if necessary. It is recommended that a sketch is made showing the various pipe connections to avoid confusion when refitting.
e) The camshaft drivebelt need not be completely removed unless it is to be renewed. This means that the crankshaft pulley and belt guide need not be removed.
f) Remove the appropriate drivebelts from the engine driven accessories as necessary to permit the drivebelt outer cover to be removed.
g) If air-conditioning refrigerant lines need to be disconnected, this must be carried out by a qualified refrigeration specialist.
h) Detach the spark plug leads and the oil pressure gauge connection.

10 Auxiliary shaft - removal

1 Using a metal bar to lock the auxiliary shaft sprocket, remove the sprocket retaining bolt and washer.

2 Pull off the sprocket using a universal puller, and remove the sprocket locking pin from the shaft.

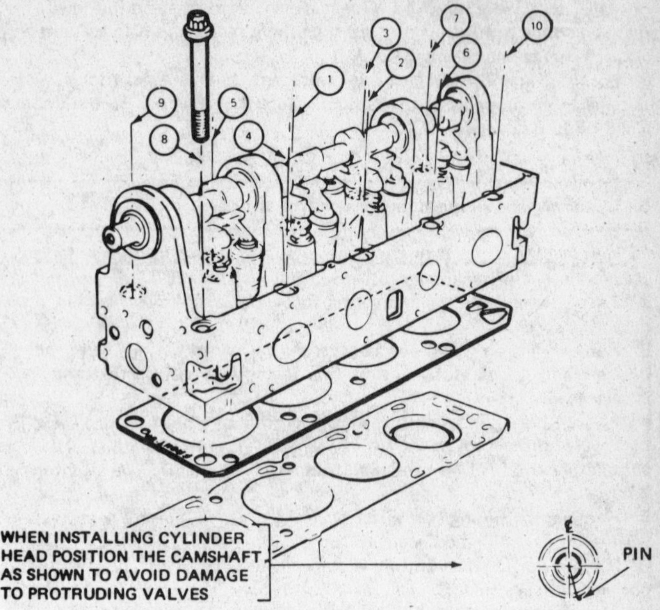

Fig. 1.9. Cylinder head bolt tightening sequence (Sec. 8)

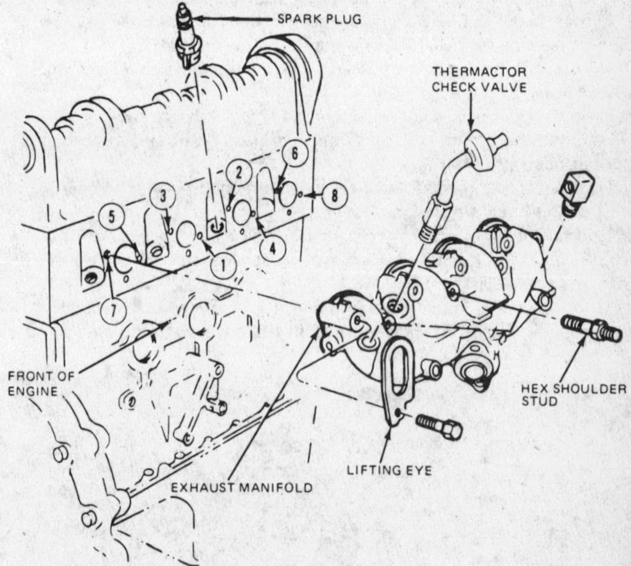

Fig. 1.10. Exhaust manifold installation (Secs. 8 and 63)

3 Remove the auxiliary shaft cover (3 screws).

4 Remove the auxiliary shaft retaining plate (2 screws).

5 Withdraw the auxiliary shaft. If this is tight, refit the bolt and washer, then use a pry bar and a spacer block to pry out the shaft.

11 Flywheel and backplate - removal

1 With the clutch removed, as described in Chapter 5, lock the flywheel using a screwdriver in mesh with the starter ring gear and undo the six bolts that secure the flywheel to the crankshaft in a diagonal and progressive manner. Lift away the bolts.

2 Mark the relative position of the flywheel and crankshaft and then lift away the flywheel.

3 Undo the remaining engine backplate securing bolts and ease the backplate from the two dowels. Lift away the backplate.

12 Oil pan, oil pump and strainer - removal

1 Undo and remove the bolts that secure the oil pan to the underside of the crankcase.

2 Lift away the oil pan and its gasket.
3 Undo and remove the screw and spring washer that secures the oil pump pick up pipe support bracket to the crankcase.
4 Using special tool 21 - 020 undo the two special bolts that secure the oil pump to the underside of the crankcase. Unfortunately there is no other tool suitable to slot into the screw head so do not attempt to improvise which will only cause damage to the screw. Later models have conventional bolts.
5 Lift away the oil pump and strainer assembly.
6 Carefully lift away the oil pump drive making a special note of which way round it is fitted.

13 Crankshaft sprocket, drivebelt inner cover and cylinder front cover - removal

1 Having already removed the crankshaft pulley (Section 8), very carefully pry off the crankshaft sprocket using a large screwdriver.
2 Remove the remaining bolt and take off the belt inner cover.

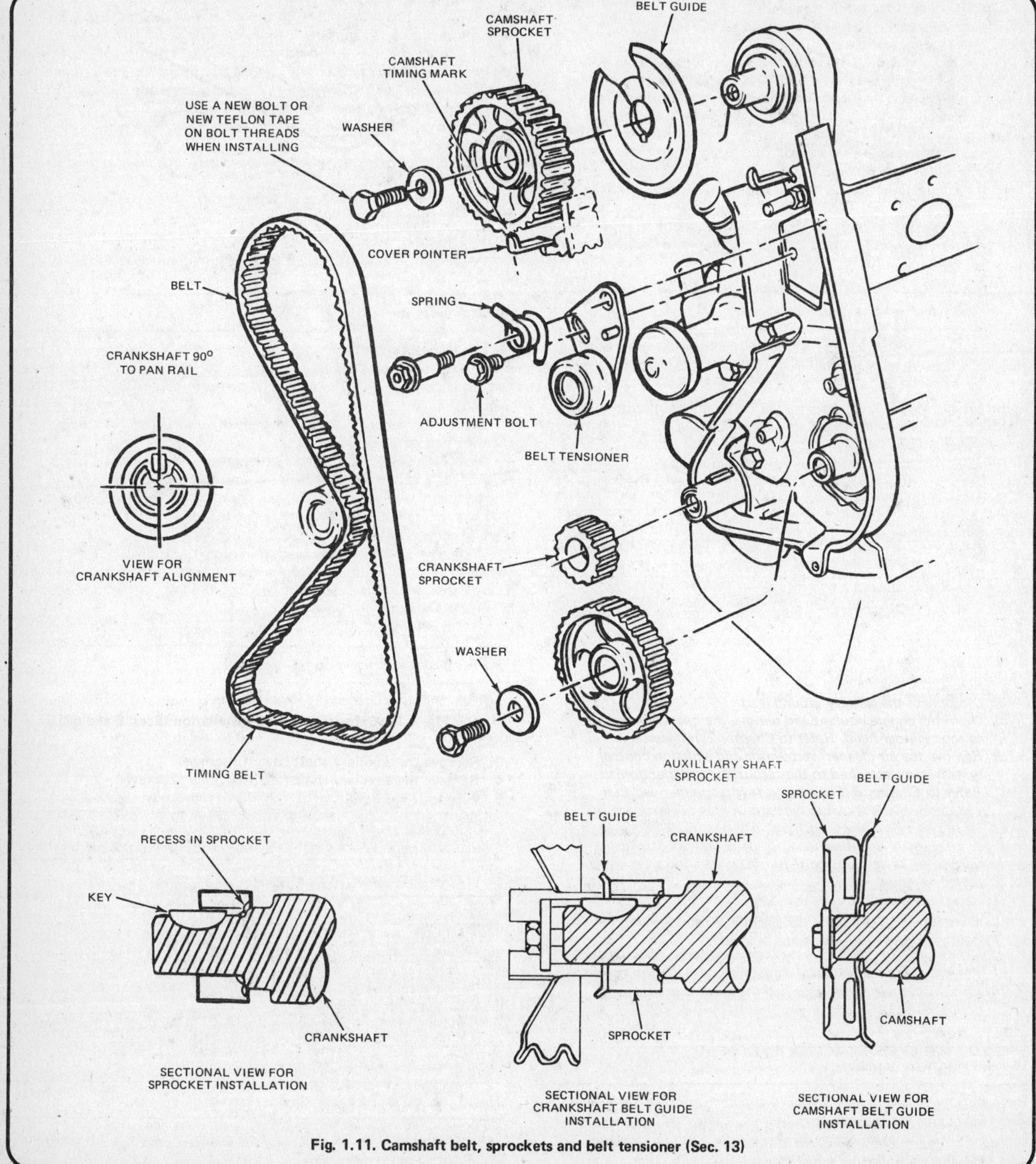

Fig. 1.11. Camshaft belt, sprockets and belt tensioner (Sec. 13)

3 Remove the two bolts and take off the cylinder front cover.
4 Remove the gasket.
5 If the crankshaft key is not a tight fit in the keyway, remove it at this stage to prevent it from being lost.

14 Pistons, connecting rods and connecting rod bearings - removal

1 Note that the pistons have a notch marked on the crown showing the forward facing side. Inspect the connecting rod bearing caps and connecting rods to make sure identification marks are visible. This is to ensure that the correct caps are fitted to the correct connecting rods and the connecting rods placed in their respective bores.
2 Undo the connecting rod nuts and place to one side in the order in which they were removed.
3 Remove the connecting rod caps, taking care to keep them in the right order and the correct way round. Also ensure that the shell bearings are kept with their correct connecting rods unless the rods are to be renewed.
4 If the connecting rod caps are difficult to remove, they may be gently tapped free with a soft-headed hammer.
5 To remove the shell bearings, press the bearing opposite the groove in both the connecting rod and its cap, and the bearing will slide out easily.
6 Withdraw the pistons and connecting rods upwards and ensure they are kept in the correct order for replacement in the same bore as they were originally fitted.

15 Crankshaft and main bearings - removal

1 Make sure that identification marks are visible on the main bearing caps, so that they may be refitted in their original positions and also the correct way round.
2 If the bearing caps are not already marked, mark them as they are removed to ensure correct installation.
3 Undo by one turn at a time the bolts which hold the five bearing caps.
4 Lift away each main bearing cap and the bottom half of each bearing shell, taking care to keep the bearing shells in the right caps.
5 When removing the rear main bearing cap note that this also retains the crankshaft rear oil seal.
6 When removing the center main bearing cap, note the bottom semi-circular halves of the thrust washers, one half lying on each side of the cap. Lay them with the main bearing cap on the correct side. On later models the shells incorporate thrust flanges, no separate thrust washers being fitted.
7 As the centre and rear bearing caps are accurately located by dowels it may be necessary to gently tap the caps to release them.
8 Slightly rotate the crankshaft to free the upper halves of the bearing shells and thrust washers which can be extracted and placed over the correct bearing caps.
9 Remove the two halves of the rear crankcase oil seal.
10 Remove the crankshaft by lifting it away from the crankcase.

16 Camshaft drivebelt - removal (engine in the car)

It is possible to remove the camshaft drivebelt with the engine in situ but experience shows that this type of belt is very reliable and unlikely to break or stretch considerably. However, during a major engine overhaul it is recommended that a new belt is fitted. To renew the belt, engine in the car:
1 Refer to Chapter 2, and drain the cooling system. Slacken the top hose securing clips and remove the top hose.
2 Slacken the alternator mounting bolts and push the unit towards the engine. Remove the drivebelt(s). **Note:** On cars equipped with a thermactor pump and air conditioning compressor these drive belts will have to be removed first (see Chapter 2).
3 Undo and remove the bolts that secure the drivebelt outer cover to the front of the engine. Lift away the cover.
4 Slacken the belt tensioner mounting plate securing bolt and release the tension on the belt.
5 Place the car in gear (manual gearbox only), and apply the brakes firmly. Undo and remove the bolt and plain washer that secures the crankshaft pulley to the nose of the crankshaft. On vehicles fitted with automatic transmission, the starter must be removed and the ring gear jammed to prevent the crankshaft from rotating.
6 Using a suitable extractor (or even a large screwdriver) carefully ease off the pulley.
7 Recover the large diameter belt guide washer.
8 The drivebelt may now be lifted away.

17 Valves and lash adjusters - removal

1 Remove the spring clip from the hydraulic valve lash adjuster end of the cam followers (where applicable). No clip is used on later models.
2 Using special tool T74P-6565-B inserted beneath the camshaft, fully compress the lash adjuster of the valve(s) to be removed, ensuring that the cam peak is facing away from the follower. This will permit the cam followers to be removed. Keep the cam followers in order so that they can be refitted in their original positions. **Note:** on some valves it may be found necessary to compress the valve spring slightly as well, in order to remove the cam followers.
3 Using a valve spring compressor, compress the valve springs and lift out the keys.
4 Remove the spring retainer and valve spring, then pry off the valve seal from the valve stem.
5 Push out the valve and keep it with its cam follower. Repeat this for the other valves.
6 Lift out the hydraulic lash adjusters, keeping each one with its respective cam follower and valve.

18 Camshaft - removal

It is not necessary to remove the engine from the car to remove the camshaft. However, it will be necessary to remove the cylinder head as described earlier in this Chapter and the cam followers as described in Section 17.
1 Using a metal bar, lock the camshaft drive sprocket. Remove the securing bolt and washer.
2 Draw off the sprocket using a suitable puller (or carefully pry it off using a large screwdriver), then remove the belt guide.
3 Remove the sprocket locating pin from the end of the camshaft.
4 From the rear bearing pedestal, remove the camshaft retaining plate (2 screws).
5 Using a hammer and a brass or aluminium drift, drive out the camshaft towards the front of the engine, taking the front seal with it. Take great care that the camshaft bearings and journals are not damaged as it is pushed out.

19 Thermostat and water pump - removal

If the cylinder head and block are being completely dismantled, the thermostat and housing, and water pump should be removed. Further information on these procedures will be found in Chapter 2.

20 Piston pin - removal

An interference fit type piston pin is used and it is important that no damage is caused during removal and refitting. Because of this, should it be necessary to fit new pistons, take the parts along to the local Ford garage who will have the special equipment to do this job.

21 Piston rings - removal

1 To remove the piston rings, slide them carefully over the top of the piston, taking care not to scratch the aluminium alloy; never slide them off the bottom of the piston skirt. It is very easy to break the cast iron piston rings if they are pulled off roughly, so this operation should be done with extreme care. It is helpful to make use of an old 0.020 inch (0.5 mm) feeler gauge.
2 Lift one end of the piston ring to be removed out of its groove and insert under it the end of the feeler gauge.
3 Turn the feeler gauge slowly round the piston and, as the ring comes out of its groove, apply slight upward pressure so that it rests on the land above. It can then be eased off the piston with the feeler gauge

stopping it from slipping into an empty groove if it is any but the top piston ring that is being removed.

22 Lubrication and crankcase ventilation systems - description

1 The pressed steel oil pan is attached to the underside of the crankcase and acts as a reservoir for the engine oil. The oil pump draws oil through a strainer located under the oil surface, passes it along a short passage and into the full-flow oil filter. The freshly filtered oil flows from the center of the filter element and enters the main gallery. Five small drillings connect the main gallery to the five main bearings. The connecting rod bearings are supplied with oil by the front and rear main bearings via skew oil bores. When the crankshaft is rotating, oil is thrown from the hole in each connecting rod bearing and splashes the thrust side of the piston.

2 The auxiliary shaft is lubricated directly from the main oil gallery. The distributor shaft is supplied with oil passing along a drilling inside the auxiliary shaft.

3 A further three drillings connect the main oil gallery to the overhead camshaft to provide lubrication for the camshaft bearings and cam followers. Oil then passes back to the oil pan via large drillings in the cylinder head and cylinder block.

4 A semi-enclosed engine ventilation system is used to control crankcase vapor. It is controlled by the amount of air drawn in by the engine when running and the throughput of the regulator valve.

5 The system is known as the PCV (Positive Crankcase Ventilation) system. The advantage of this system is that should the 'blow-by' exceed the capacity of the PCV valve, excess fumes are fed into the engine through the air cleaner. This is effected by the rise in crankcase pressure which creates a reverse flow in the air intake pipe.

6 Periodically pull the valve and hose from the rubber grommet of the oil separator and inspect the valve for free-movement. If it is sticky in action or is clogged with sludge, dismantle it and clean the component parts.

7 Occasionally check the security and condition of the system connecting hoses.

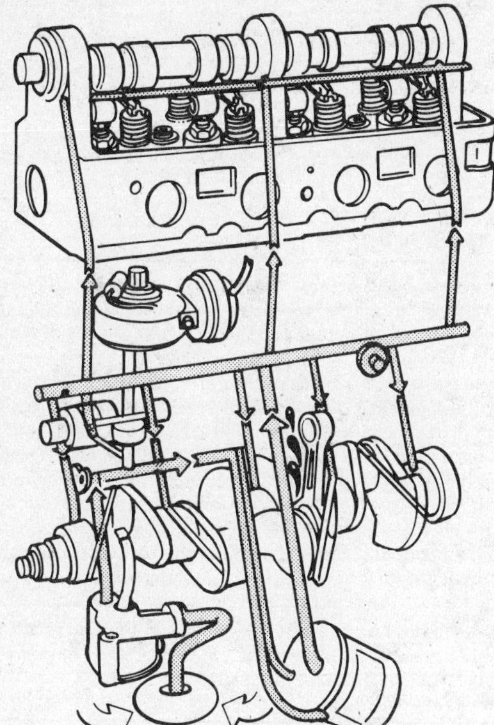

Fig. 1.12. Engine lubrication diagram (Sec. 22)

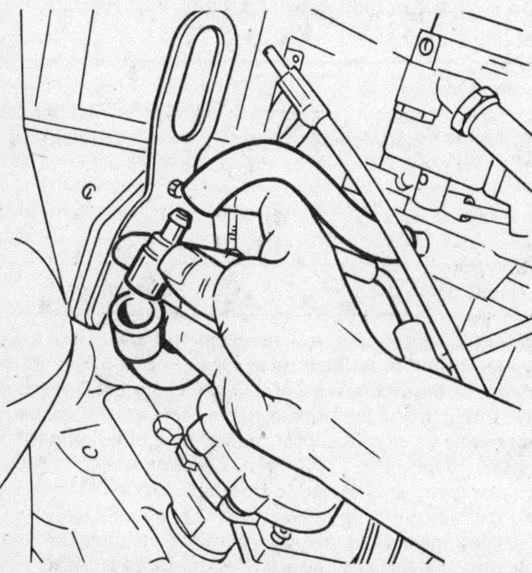

Fig. 1.14. Location of PCV valve (Sec. 22)

23 Oil pump - inspection

1 The oil pump cannot be dismantled or repaired in any way. If there is any obvious damage, or in the case of major engine overhaul, a

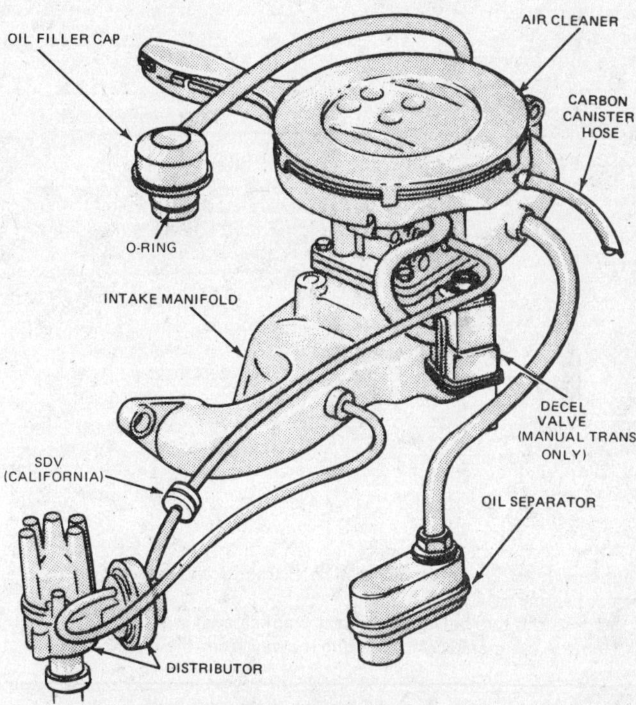

Fig. 1.13. Positive crankcase ventilation (PCV) system (Sec. 22)

Fig. 1.15. Oil pump (Sec. 23)

1A

replacement item must be fitted.
2 Detach the oil intake pipe and screen (2 screws and spring washers), and clean the parts thoroughly in gasoline.
3 Refit the intake pipe and screen, using a new gasket.

24 Oil filter - removal and refitting

The oil filter is a complete throw away cartridge screwed into the left-hand side of the cylinder block. Simply unscrew the old unit, clean the seating on the block and lubricate with engine oil. Screw the new one into position taking care not to cross the thread. Continue until the sealing ring just touches the block face then tighten one half turn by hand only. Always run the engine and check for signs of leaks after installation.

25 Engine components - examination for wear

When the engine has been stripped down and all parts properly cleaned decisions have to be made as to what needs renewal and the following Sections tell the examiner what to look for. In any border-line case it is always best to decide in favour of a new part. Even if a part may still be serviceable its life will have been reduced by wear and the degree of trouble needed to replace it in the future must be taken into consideration. However, these things are relative and it depends on whether a quick 'survival' job is being done or whether the car as a whole is being regarded as having many thousands of miles of useful and economical life remaining.

26 Crankshaft - examination and renovation

1 Look at the main bearing journals and the crankpins, and if there are any scratches or score marks then the shaft will need regrinding. Such conditions will nearly always be accompanied by similar deterioration in the matching bearing shells.
2 Each bearing journal should also be round and can be checked with a micrometer or caliper gauge around the periphery at several points. If there is more than 0.001 in of ovality regrinding is necessary.
3 A main Ford agent or motor engineering specialist will be able to decide to what extent regrinding is necessary and also supply the special undersize shell bearing to match whatever may need grinding off.
4 Before taking the crankshaft for regrinding check also the cylinder bores and pistons as it may be advantageous to have the whole engine done at the same time.
5 During any major engine repair, prise out the roller pilot bearing from the rear end of the crankshaft; this may require the use of a hook-ended tool to get behind the bearing. Fit the replacement bearing with the seal outwards (where applicable) so that it is just below the surface of the crankshaft flange.

27 Crankshaft, main and connecting rod bearings - examination and renovation

1 With careful servicing and regular oil and filter changes, bearings will last for a very long time but they can still fail for unforeseen reasons. With connecting rod bearings the indication is a regular rythmic loud knocking from the crankcase. The frequency depends on engine speed and is particularly noticeable when the engine is under load. This symptom is accompanied by a fall in oil pressure although this is not normally noticeable unless an oil pressure gauge is fitted. Main bearing failure is usually indicated by serious vibration, particularly at higher engine revolutions, accompanied by a more significant drop in oil pressure and a 'rumbling' noise.
2 Bearing shells in good condition have bearing surfaces with a smooth, even matt silver/grey color all over. Worn bearings will show patches of a different color when the bearing metal has worn away and exposed the underlay. Damaged bearings will be pitted or scored. It is always well worthwhile fitting new shells as their cost is relatively low. If the crankshaft is in good condition it is merely a question of obtaining another set of standard size. A reground crankshaft will need new bearing shells as a matter of course.

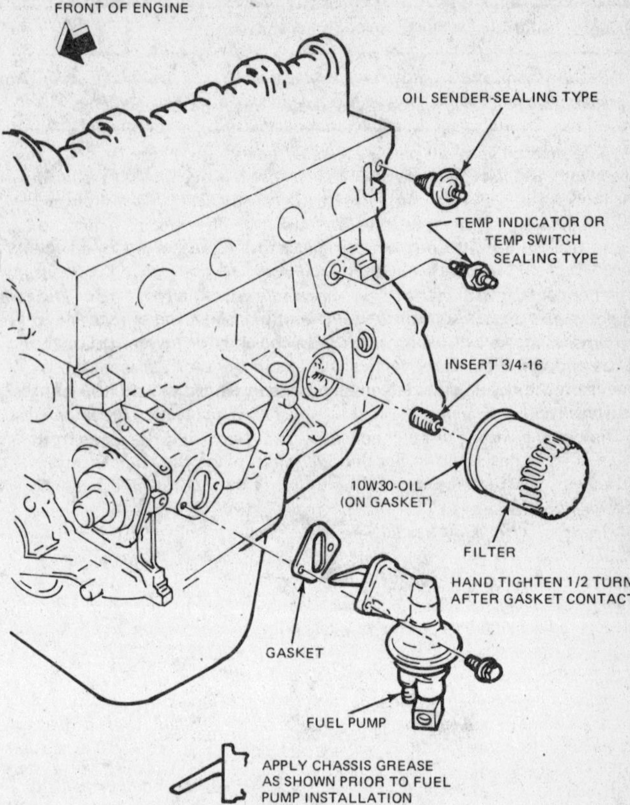

Fig. 1.16. Location of oil filter, sender units and fuel pump (Sec. 24)

28 Cylinder bores - examination and renovation

1 A new cylinder bore is perfectly round and the walls parallel throughout its length. The action of the piston tends to wear the walls at right angles to the gudgeon pin due to side thrust. This wear takes place principally on that section of the cylinder swept by the piston rings.
2 It is possible to get an indication of bore wear by removing the cylinder heads with the engine still in the car. With the piston down in the bore first signs of wear can be seen and felt just below the top of the bore where the top piston ring reaches and there will be a noticeable lip. If there is no lip it is fairly reasonable to expect that bore wear is not severe and any lack of compression or excessive oil consumption is due to worn or broken piston rings or pistons (see Section 29).
3 If it is possible to obtain a bore measuring micrometer measure the bore in the thrust plane below the lip and again at the bottom of the cylinder in the same plane. If the difference is more than 0.003 inch (0.08 mm) then a rebore is necessary. Similarly, a difference of 0.003 inch (0.08 mm) or more across the bore diameter is a sign of ovality calling for rebore.
4 Any bore which is significantly scratched or scored will need reboring. This symptom usually indicates that the piston or rings are damaged also. In the event of only one cylinder being in need of reboring, it may still be necessary for all four to be bored and fitted with new oversize pistons and rings. Your Ford agent or local motor engineering specialist will be able to rebore and obtain the necessary matched pistons. If the crankshaft is undergoing regrinding also, it is a good idea to let the same firm renovate and reassemble the crankshaft and pistons to the block. A reputable firm normally gives a guarantee for such work. In cases where engines have been rebored already to their maximum, new cylinder liners are available which may be fitted. In such cases the same reboring processes have to be followed and the services of a specialist engineering firm are required.

29 Pistons and piston rings - inspection and testing

1 Worn pistons and rings can usually be diagnosed when the symptoms of excessive oil consumption and lower compression occur and are sometimes, though not always, associated with worn cylinder bores. Compression testers that fit into the spark plug hole are available and these can indicate where low compression is occuring. Wear usually accelerates the more it is left so when the symptoms occur early action can possibly save the expense of a rebore.
2 Another symptom of piston wear is piston slap - a knocking noise from the crankcase not to be confused with the connecting rod bearing failure. It can be heard clearly at low engine speed when there is no load (idling for example) and is much less audible when the engine speed increases. Piston wear usually occurs in the skirt or lower end of the piston and is indicated by vertical streaks in the worn area which is always on the thrust side. It can also be seen where the skirt thickness is different.
3 Piston ring wear can be checked by first removing the rings from the pistons as described in Section 21. Then place the rings in the cylinder bores from the top, pushing them down about 1½ inches (38 mm) with the head of a piston (from which the rings have been removed), so that they rest square in the cylinder bore. Then measure the gap at the ends of the ring with a feeler gauge. If it exceeds that given in the Specifications, they need renewal.
4 The grooves in which the rings locate in the piston can also become enlarged in use. The clearance between ring and piston, in the groove, should not exceed that given in the Specifications.
5 However, it is rare that a piston is only worn in the ring grooves and the need to replace them for this fault alone is hardly ever encountered. Wherever pistons are renewed the weight of the four piston/connecting rod assemblies should be kept within the limit variations of 8 gms to maintain engine balance.

30 Connecting rods and piston pins - examination and renovation

1 Piston pins are a shrink fit into the connecting rods. Neither of these would normally need replacement unless the pistons were being changed, in which case the new pistons would automatically be supplied with new piston pins.
2 Connecting rods are not subject to wear but in extreme circumstances such as engine seizure they could be distorted. Such conditions may be visually apparent but where doubt exists they should be changed. The bearing caps should also be examined for indications of filing down which may have been attempted in the mistaken idea that bearing slackness could be remedied in this way. If there are such signs then the connecting rods should be renewed.

31 Camshaft and camshaft bearings - examination and renovation

1 The camshaft bearing bushings should be examined for signs of scoring and pitting. If they need renewal they will have to be dealt with professionally as, although it may be relatively easy to remove the old bushings, the correct fitting of new ones requires special tools. If they are not fitted evenly and square from the very start they can be distorted, thus causing localised wear in a very short time. See your Ford dealer or local engineering specialist for this work.
2 The camshaft itself may show signs of wear on the bearing journals or cam lobes. The main decision to take is what degree of wear justifies replacement, which is costly. Any signs of scoring or damage to the bearing journals cannot be removed by grinding. Renewal of the whole camshaft is the only solution. **Note:** Where excessive cam lobe wear is evident, refer to the note in the following Section.
3 The cam lobes themselves may show signs of ridging or pitting on the high points. If ridging is light then it may be possible to smooth it out with fine emery. The cam lobes however, are surface hardened and once this is penetrated, wear will be very rapid thereafter.
4 Ensure that the camshaft oilways are unobstructed.
5 To check the thrust plate for wear, position the camshaft into its location in the cylinder head and fit the thrust plate at the rear. Using a dial gauge, check the total shaft endfloat by tapping the camshaft carefully back-and-forth along its length. If the endplay is outside the specified limit, renew the thrust plate.

32 Cam followers - examination

1 The faces of the cam followers which bear on the camshaft should show no signs of pitting, scoring or other forms of wear. They should not be a loose sloppy fit on the ballheaded bolt.
2 Inspect the face which bears onto the valve stem and if pitted, the cam follower must be renewed.
3 If excessive cam follower wear is evident (and possibly excessive cam lobe wear), this may be due to a malfunction of the valve drive lubrication tube. If this has occurred, renew the tube and the cam follower. If more than one cam follower is excessively worn, renew the camshaft, all the cam followers and the lubrication tube. This also applies where excessive cam lobe wear is found.
4 During any operation which requires removal of the valve rocker cover ensure that oil is being discharged from the lubrication tube nozzles by cranking the engine on the starter motor. During routine maintenance operations, this can be done after checking the valve clearances.

33 Auxiliary shaft and bearings - examination and renovation

1 The procedure for the auxiliary shaft and bearings is similar to that described in Section 31 for the camshaft.
2 Examine the skew gear for wear and damaged teeth. If either is evident, a replacement shaft must be obtained.

1A

34 Valves and valve seats - examination and renovation

1 With the valves removed from the cylinder head examine the head for signs of cracking, burning away and pitting of the edge where it sits in the port. The valve seats in the cylinder head should also be examined for the same signs. Usually it is the valve that deteriorates first but if a bad valve is not rectified the seat will suffer and this is more difficult to repair.
2 Provided there are no obvious signs of serious pitting the valve should be ground with its seat. This may be done by placing a smear of carborundum paste on the edge of the valve and, using a suction type valve holder, grinding the valve in situ. This is done with a semi-rotary action, rotating the handle of the valve holder between the hands and lifting it occasionally to re-distribute the traces of paste. Use a coarse paste to start with. As soon as a matt grey unbroken line appears on both the valve and seat the valve is 'ground in'. All traces of carbon should also be cleaned from the head and neck of the valve stem. A wire brush mounted in a power drill is a quick and effective way of doing this.
3 If the valve requires renewal it should be ground into the seat in the same way as the old valve.
4 Another form of valve wear can occur on the stem where it runs in the guide in the cylinder head. This can be detected by trying to rock the valve from side to side. If there is any movement at all it is an indication that the valve stem or guide is worn. Check the stem first with a micrometer at points along and around its length and if they are not within the specified size new valves will probably solve the problem. If the guides are worn, however, they will need reboring for oversize valves or for fitting guide inserts. The valve seats will also need recutting to ensure they are concentric with the stems. This work should be entrusted to your Ford dealer or local auto-engineering

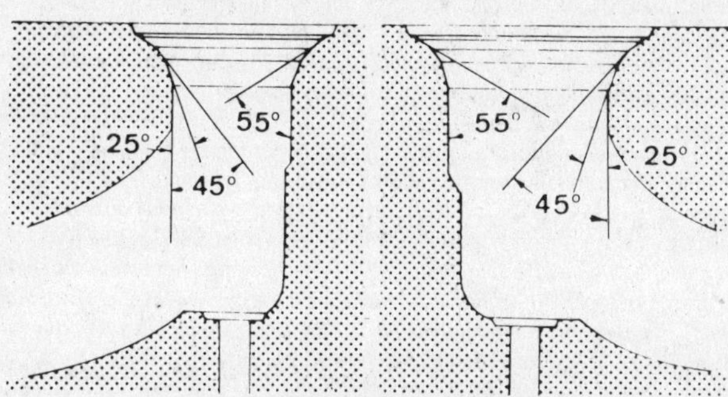

Fig. 1.17. Valve seat angles (Sec. 34)

works.

5 When valve seats are badly burnt or pitted, requiring renewal, inserts may be fitted - or replaced if already fitted once before - again this is a specialist task to be carried out by a suitable engineering firm.

6 When all valve grinding is complete it is essential that every trace of grinding paste is removed from the valves and ports in the cylinder head. This should be done by thorough washing in gasoline or kerosene and blowing out with a jet of air. If particles of carborundum should work their way into the engine they would cause havoc with bearings or cylinder walls.

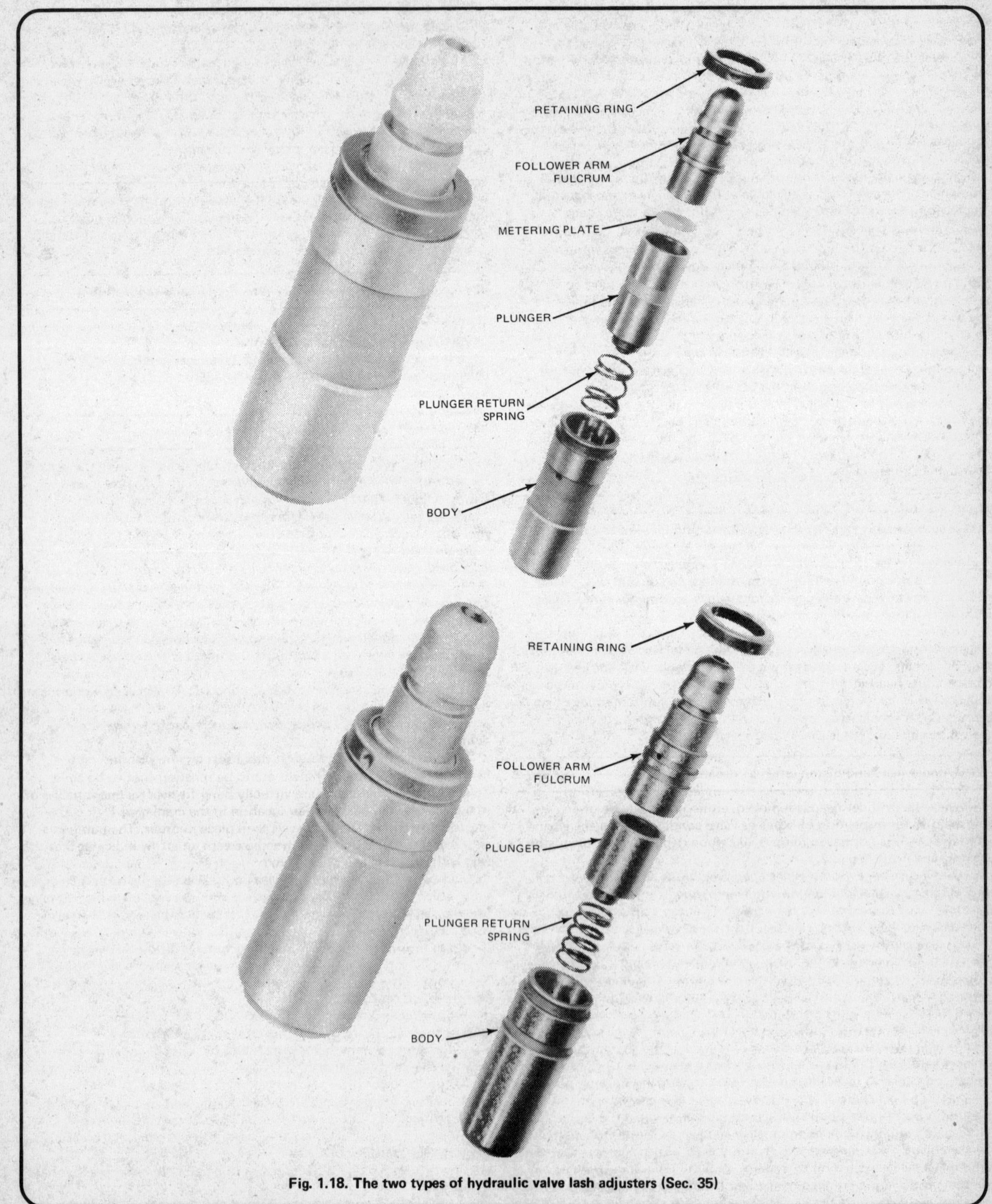

Fig. 1.18. The two types of hydraulic valve lash adjusters (Sec. 35)

35 Hydraulic lash adjusters - examination and renovation

1 Examine the outside of each lash adjuster for wear and scoring. If lightly scored, very fine emery cloth can be used to polish out the marks. However, if wear is evident, it is recommended that the complete adjuster is renewed.
2 Carefully pry off the retaining ring, take out the follower arm fulcrum and dismantle the complete adjuster. The component parts of the two different types in common use are shown in Fig. 1.18.
3 Examine all the parts of each adjuster for damage, wear, corrosion and gum deposits; obtain replacement parts for any which are unserviceable. Do not mix up the parts from the different adjusters.
4 Reassemble the adjusters, lightly lubricating the parts with engine oil. Do not attempt to fill them with oil.
5 Testing of the lifters is not practicable without the use of special equipment. However, this is available at Ford dealers or most auto-engineering workshops and can be very useful where there is any doubt about serviceability.

36 Timing gears and belt - examination

1 Any wear which takes place in the timing mechanism will be on the teeth of the drive belt or due to stretch of the fabric. Whenever the engine is to be stripped for major overhaul a new belt should be fitted.
2 It is very unusual for the timing gears (sprockets) to wear at the teeth. If the securing bolt/nuts have been loose it is possible for the keyway or hub bore to wear. Check these two points and if damage or wear is evident a new gear must be obtained.

37 Flywheel - examination and renovation

1 If the ring gear is badly worn or has missing teeth it should be renewed. The old ring can be removed from the flywheel by cutting a notch between two teeth with a hacksaw and then splitting it with a cold chisel.
2 To fit a new ring gear requires heating the ring to 400°F (204°C). This can be done by polishing four equally spaced sections of the gear, laying it on a suitable heat resistant surface (such as fire bricks) and heating it evenly with a blow lamp or torch until the polished areas turn a light yellow tinge. Do not overheat or the hard wearing properties will be lost. The gear has a chamfered inner edge which should go against the shoulder when put on the flywheel. When hot enough place the gear in position quickly, tapping it home if necessary and let it cool naturally without quenching it.

38 Cylinder head and piston crowns - decarbonisation

1 When the cylinder head is removed, either in the course of an overhaul or for inspection of bores or valve condition when the engine is in the car, it is normal to remove all carbon deposits from the piston crowns and head.
2 This is best done with a cup shaped wire brush and an electric drill and is fairly straightforward when the engine is dismantled and the pistons removed. Sometimes hard spots of carbon are not easily removed except by a scraper. When cleaning the pistons with a scraper, take care not to damage the surface of the piston in any way.
3 When the engine is in the car, certain precautions must be taken when decarbonising the pistons crowns in order to prevent dislodged pieces of carbon falling into the interior of the engine which could cause damage to cylinder bores, piston and rings - or if allowed into the water passages - damage to the water pump. Turn the engine so that the piston being worked on is at the top of its stroke and then mask off the adjacent cylinder bores and all surrounding water jacket orifices with paper and adhesive tape. Press grease into the gap all round the piston to keep carbon particles out and then scrape all carbon away by hand carefully. Do not use a power drill and wire brush when the engine is in the car as it will virtually be impossible to keep all the carbon dust clear of the engine. When completed, carefully clear out the grease around the rim of the piston with a matchstick or something similar - bringing any carbon particles with it. Repeat the process on the other piston crowns. It is not recommended that a ring of carbon is left round the edge of the piston on the theory that it will aid oil consumption. This was valid in the earlier days of long stroke low revving engines but modern engines, fuels and lubricants cause less carbon deposits anyway and any left behind tend merely to cause hot spots.

39 Valve guides - inspection

Examine the valve guides internally for wear. If the valves are a very loose fit in the guides and there is the slightest suspicion of lateral rocking using a new valve, then the guides will have to be reamed and oversize valves fitted. This is a job best left to the local Ford dealer.

40 Oil pan - inspection

Wash out the oil pan in gasoline and wipe dry. Inspect the exterior for signs of damage or excessive rust. If evident, a new oil pan must be obtained. To ensure an oil tight joint scrape away all traces of the old gasket from the cylinder block mating face.

41 Engine reassembly - general

All components of the engine must be cleaned of oil, sludge and old gasket and the working area should also be cleared and clean. In addition to the normal range of good quality socket wrenches and general tools which are essential, the following must be available before reassembling begins:

1 *Complete set of new gaskets*
2 *Supply of clean lint-free cloths*
3 *Clean oil can full of clean engine oil*
4 *Torque wrench*
5 *All new spare parts as necessary*

1A

42 Crankshaft - refitting

Ensure that the crankcase is thoroughly clean and that all oilways are clear. A thin twist drill or a piece of wire is useful for cleaning them out. If possible blow them out with compressed air.

Treat the crankshaft in the same fashion, and then inject engine oil in the crankshaft oilways.

Commence work of rebuilding the engine by refitting the crankshaft and main bearings:

1 Wipe the bearing shell locations in the crankcase with a lint-free cloth.
2 Wipe the crankshaft journals with a soft lint-free cloth.
3 If the old main bearing shells are to be renewed (not to do so is false economy unless they are virtually new) fit the five upper halves of the main bearing shells to their location in the crankcase.
4 Identify each main bearing cap and place in order. The number is cast into the cap and with intermediate caps an arrow indicates that the cap is fitted the correct way round.
5 Lubricate the new crankshaft rear oil seals in engine oil and fit one in the rear crankcase groove and the other in the rear main bearing cap groove making sure the oil seal tabs face toward the rear of the engine (Fig. 1.19).
6 Wipe the cap bearing shell location with a soft non-fluffy rag.
7 Fit the main bearing lower shells onto each main bearing cap.
8 Apply a little grease to each side of the centre bearing so as to retain the thrust washers.
9 Fit the upper halves of the thrust washers into their grooves either side of the main bearing The slots must face outwards.
10 Lubricate the crankshaft journals and the upper and lower main bearing shells with engine oil.
11 Carefully lower the crankshaft into the crankcase.
12 Lubricate the crankshaft main bearing journals again and then fit No 1 bearing cap. Fit the two securing bolts but do not tighten yet.
13 Apply a little non-setting gasket sealant to the crankshaft rear main bearing cap location.
14 Next fit No 5 cap. Fit the two securing bolts but as before do not tighten yet.
15 Apply a little grease to either side of the center main bearing cap so

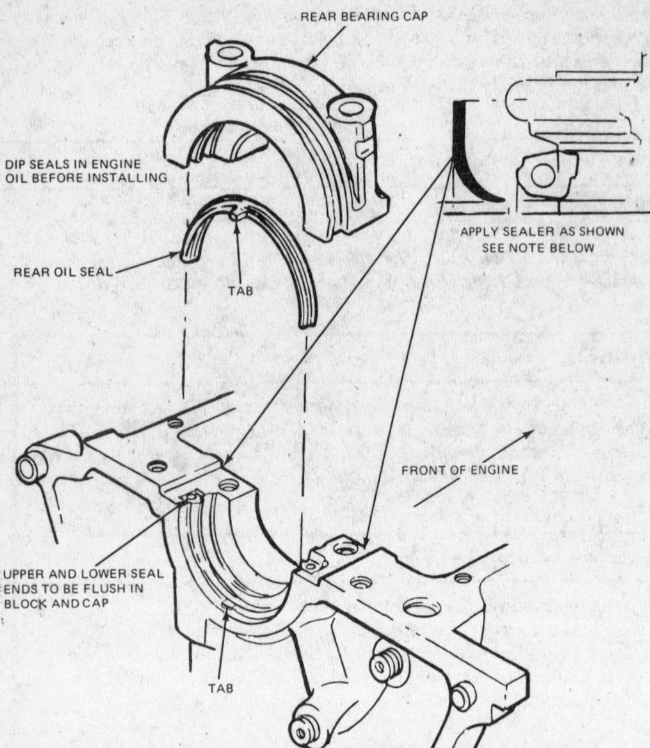

Fig. 1.19. Installation of rear main bearing oil seal (Sec. 42)

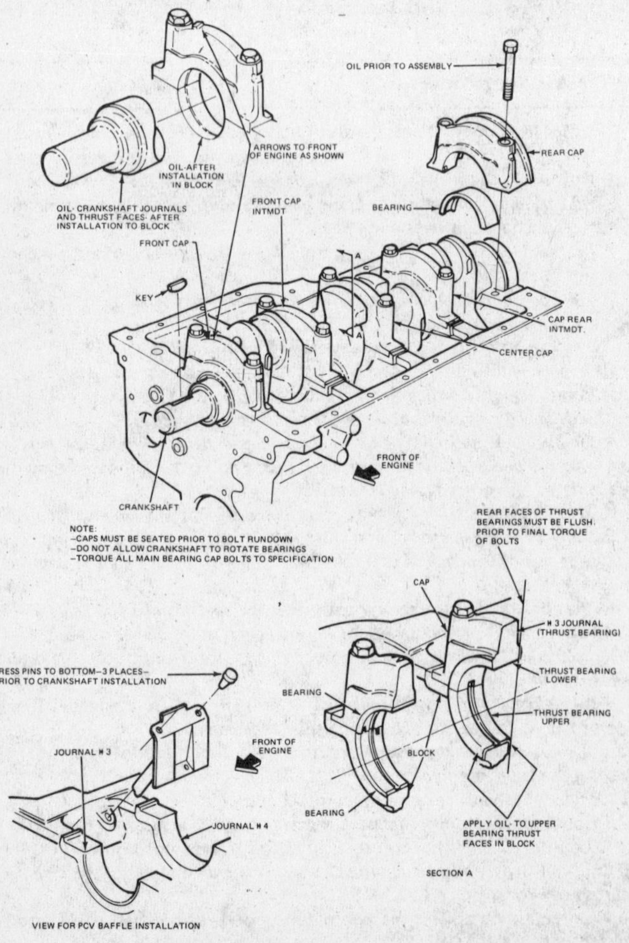

Fig. 1.20. Installation of main bearings and caps (Sec. 42)

as to retain the thrust washers (early models only with separate thrust washers). Fit the thrust washers with the tag located in the groove and the slots facing outwards.

16 Fit the center main bearing cap and the two securing bolts. Then refit the intermediate main bearing caps. Make sure that the arrows always point towards the front of the engine.

17 Lightly tighten all main bearing cap securing bolts and then fully tighten in a progressive manner to the final torque wrench setting as specified.

18 Using a screwdriver, ease the crankshaft fully forwards and with feeler gauges check the clearance between the crankshaft journal side and the thrust washers. The clearance must not exceed that given in the Specifications. Oversize thrust washers are available.

19 Test the crankshaft for freedom of rotation. Should it be stiff to turn or possess high spots, a most careful inspection must be made with a micrometer, preferably by a qualified mechanic, to get to the root of the trouble. It is very seldom that any trouble of this nature will be experienced when fitting the crankshaft.

43 Pistons and connecting rods - reassembly

As an interference fit type piston pin is used (see Section 20) this operation must be carried out by the local Ford dealer. Do not forget that the notch in the piston crown must face toward the front of the engine.

44 Piston rings - refitting

1 Check that the piston ring grooves and oilways are thoroughly clean and unblocked. Piston rings must always be fitted over the head of the piston and never from the bottom.

2 The easiest method to use when fitting rings is to wrap a 0.20 in (0.5 mm) feeler gauge round the top of the piston and place the rings one at a time, starting with the bottom oil control ring, over the feeler gauge.

3 The feeler gauge, complete with ring, can then be slid down the piston over the other piston ring grooves until the correct groove is reached. The piston ring is then slid gently off the feeler gauge into the groove.

4 An alternative method is to fit the rings by holding them slightly open with the thumbs and both of the index fingers. This method requires a steady hand and great care, as it is easy to open the ring too much and break it.

45 Pistons - refitting

The pistons, complete with connecting rods, can be fitted to the cylinder bores in the following sequence:

1 With a wad of clean rag wipe the cylinder bores clean.

2 The pistons, complete with connecting rods, are fitted to their bores from the top of the block.

3 Locate the piston ring gaps as shown in Fig. 1.21.

The oil control ring segment gaps are to be approximately 80° away from the expander gap and not in the area of the skirt. The piston should be installed in the block so that the expander gap is towards the front and the segment gap is towards the rear.

4 Well lubricate the piston and rings with engine oil.

5 Fit a universal piston ring compressor and prepare to install the first piston into the bore. Make sure it is the correct piston-connecting rod assembly for that particular bore, that the connecting rod is the correct way round and that the front of the piston is towards the front of the bore, ie, towards the front of the engine.

6 Again lubricate the piston skirt and insert into the bore up to the bottom of the piston ring compressor.

7 Gently but firmly tap the piston through the piston ring compressor and into the cylinder bore with the wooden shaft of a hammer.

46 Connecting rods to crankshaft - refitting

1 Wipe clean the connecting rod upper shell bearing location and the

underside of the shell bearing, and fit the shell bearing in position with its locating tongue engaged with the corresponding cut out in the rod.

2 If the old shell bearings are nearly new and are being refitted then ensure they are refitted in their correct locations on the correct rods.

3 Generously lubricate the crankpin journals with engine oil and turn the crankshaft so that the crankpin is in the most advantageous position for the connecting rods to be drawn onto it.

4 Wipe clean the connecting rod cap and back of the shell bearing, and fit the shell bearing in position ensuring that the locating tongue at the back of the bearing engages with the locating groove in the connecting rod cap.

5 Generously lubricate the shell bearing and offer up the connecting rod cap to the connecting rod.

6 Refit the connecting rod nuts and pinch them tight.

7 Tighten the nuts with a torque wrench to the specified torque.

8 When all the connecting rods have been fitted, rotate the crankshaft to check that everything is free, and that there are no high spots causing binding. The bottom half of the engine is now near completion.

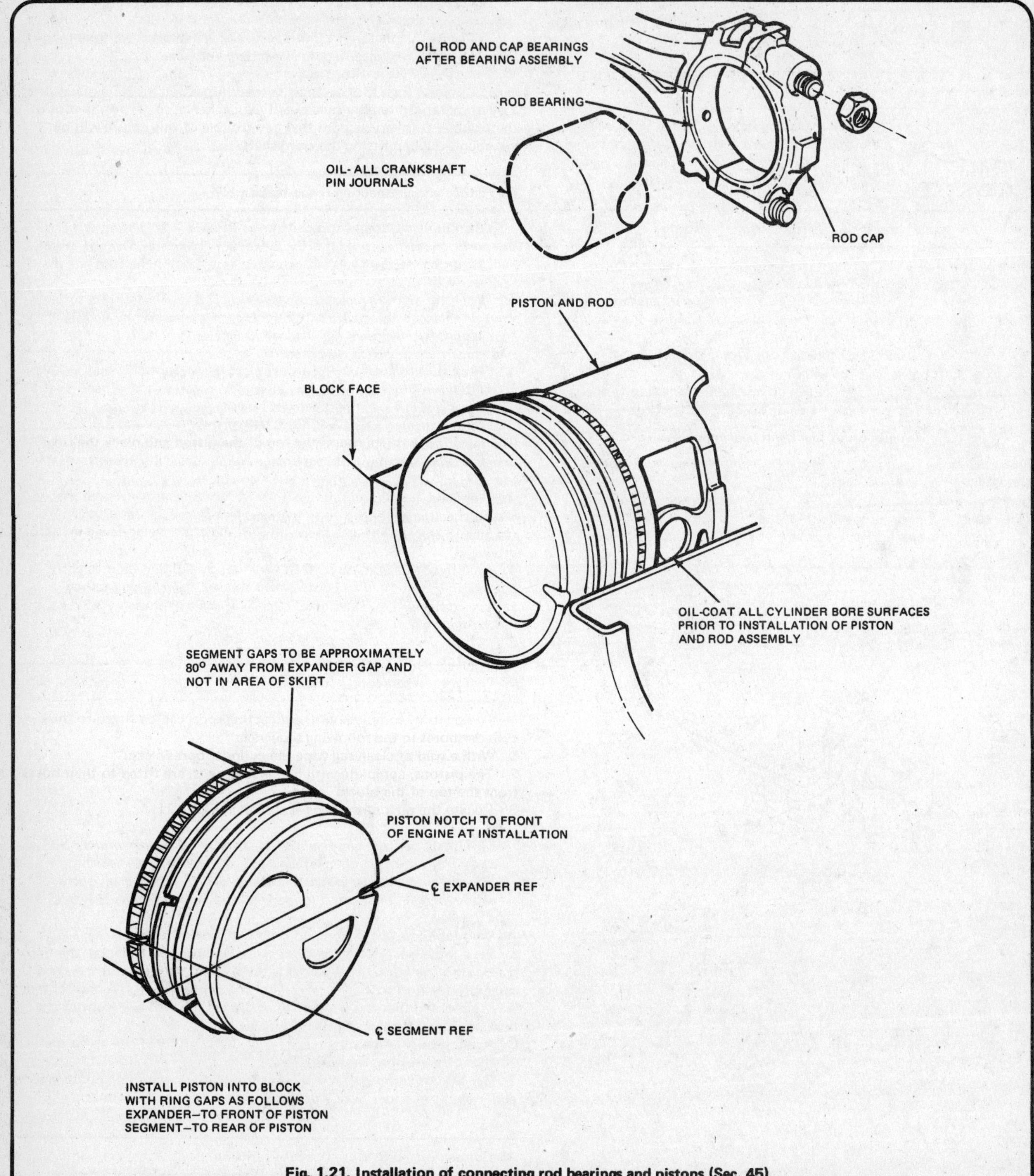

Fig. 1.21. Installation of connecting rod bearings and pistons (Sec. 45)

47 Oil pump and strainer - refitting

1 Wipe the mating faces of the oil pump and underside of the cylinder block.
2 Insert the hexagonal driveshaft (longer washer-to-tip section) into the end of the oil pump.
3 Offer up the oil pump and refit the two special bolts. Using special tool '21-020' and a torque wrench tighten the two bolts to the specified torque.
4 Refit the one bolt and spring washer that secures the oil pump pick-up pipe support bracket to the crankcase.

48 Auxiliary shaft - refitting

1 Lubricate the auxiliary shaft bearing surfaces with engine oil then insert the shaft into the block. Tap it gently with a soft-faced hammer to ensure that it is fully home.
2 Fit the retaining plate and secure it with the two screws.

49 Auxiliary shaft and cylinder front covers - refitting

Note: If only one of the covers has been removed, the existing gasket may be cut away and a new gasket suitably cut.
1 Lubricate a new auxiliary shaft seal with engine oil and fit it into the auxiliary shaft cover so that the seal lips are towards the cylinder block face.
2 Position a new gasket on the cylinder block endface; position the auxiliary shaft cover over the spigot of the shaft.
3 Fit the cover retaining bolts but do not tighten them until the cylinder front cover has been fitted or the gasket may distort.
4 Fit the cylinder front cover in a similar manner to that described for the auxiliary shaft cover.
5 Position the front cover over the crankshaft spigot and loosely fit the retaining bolts.
6 Using the crankshaft sprocket as a centralizing tool, tighten the front cover bolts to the specified torque.
7 Tighten the auxiliary shaft cover bolts to the specified torque.

50 Oil pan - refitting

1 Wipe the mating faces of the underside of the crankcase and the oil pan.
2 Smear some non-setting gasket sealant on the underside of the crankcase.
3 Fit the oil pan gasket and end seals making sure that the bolt holes line up.
4 Offer the oil pan to the gaskets taking care not to dislodge, and secure in position with the bolts.
5 Tighten the oil pan bolts in a progressive manner, to a final torque wrench setting as specified, in the order shown in Fig. 1.25.

51 Water pump - refitting

Refit the water pump to the cylinder block (if removed), referring to Chapter 2 as necessary.

52 Backplate, flywheel and clutch - refitting

1 Wipe the mating faces of the backplate and cylinder block and carefully fit the backplate to the two dowels.
2 Wipe the mating faces of the flywheel and crankshaft and offer up the flywheel to the crankshaft, aligning the previously made marks unless new parts have been fitted. A reinforcing plate is fitted to the adapter plate on automatic models.
3 Fit the six crankshaft securing bolts and lightly tighten.
4 Lock the flywheel using a screwdriver engaged in the starter ring gear and tighten the securing bolts in a diagonal and progressive manner to a final torque wrench setting as specified.
5 Refit the clutch disc and pressure plate assembly to the flywheel making sure the disc is the right way round (refer to Chapter 5).
6 Secure the pressure plate assembly with the six retaining bolts and spring washers.
7 Centralise the clutch disc using an old input shaft or piece of wooden dowel, and fully tighten the retaining bolts.

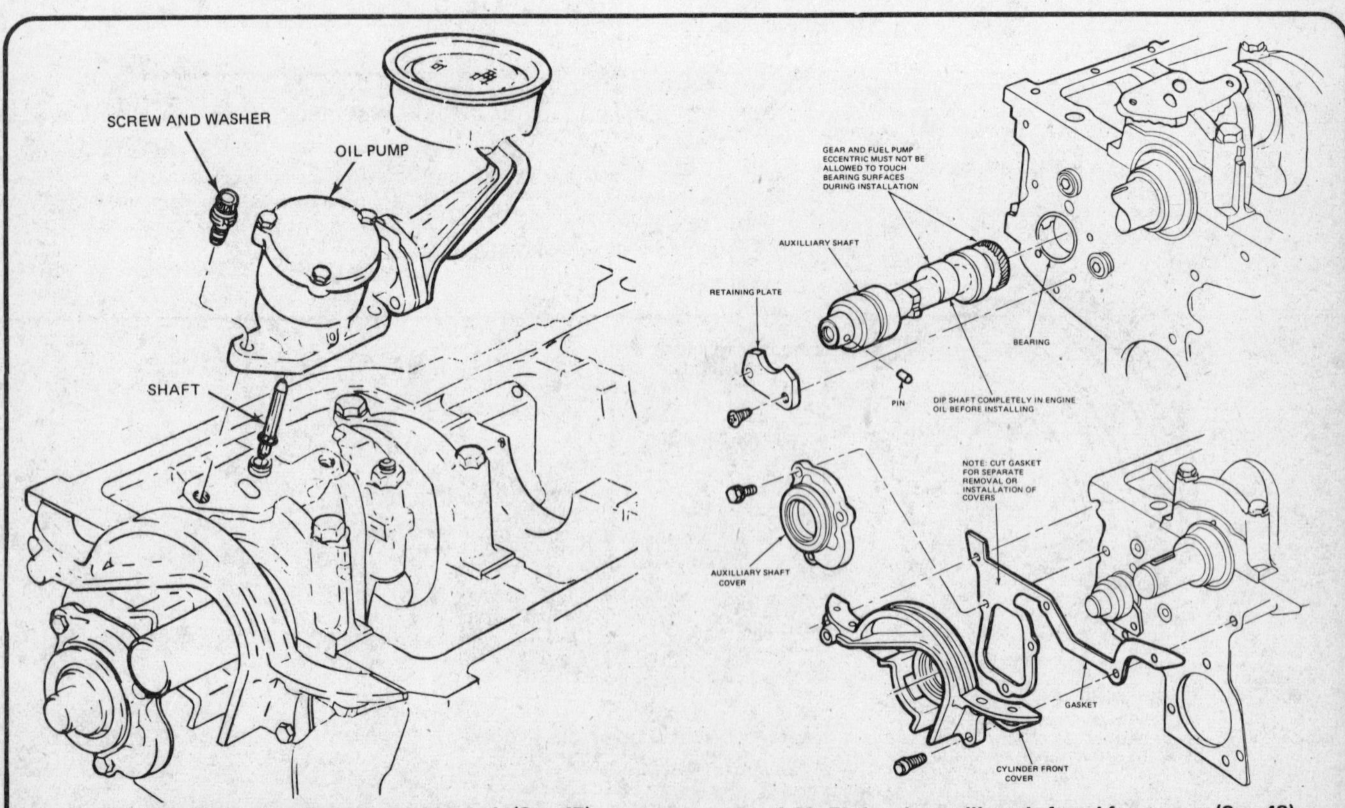

Fig. 1.22. Fitting the oil pump and driveshaft (Sec. 47)

Fig. 1.23. Fitting the auxiliary shaft and front cover (Sec. 48)

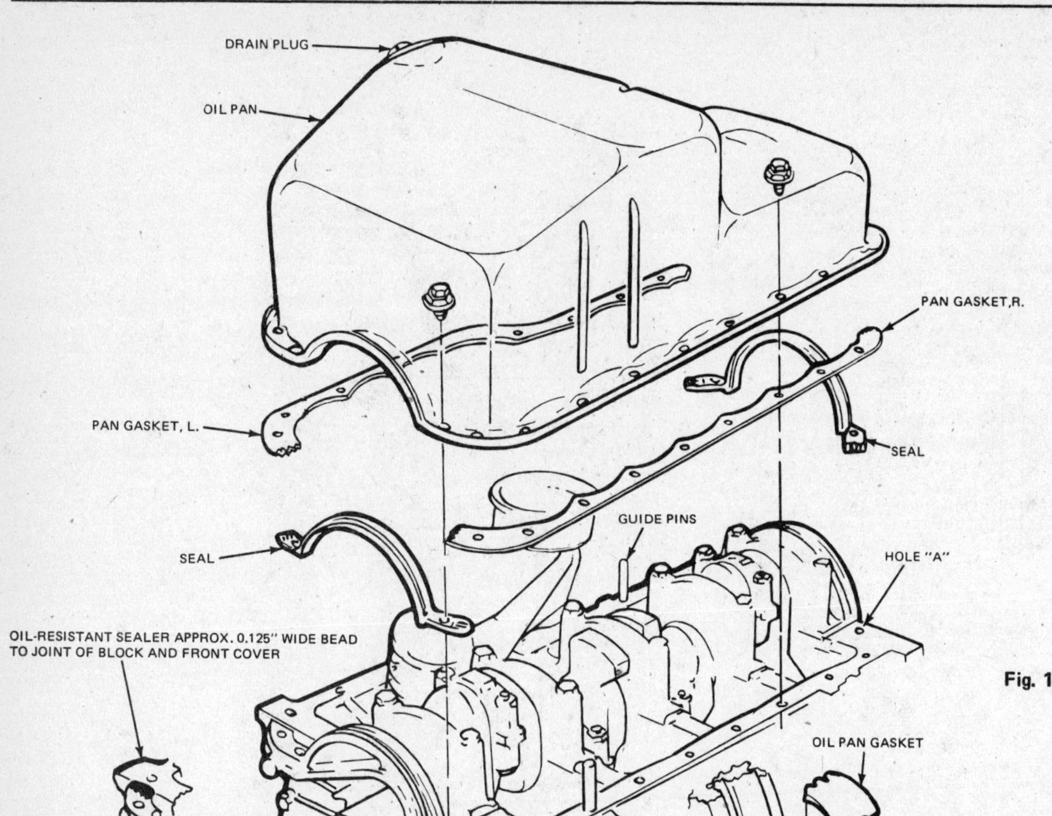

Fig. 1.24. Oil pan and gaskets (Sec. 50)

1A

Fig. 1.25. Oil pan bolts - tightening order (Sec. 50)

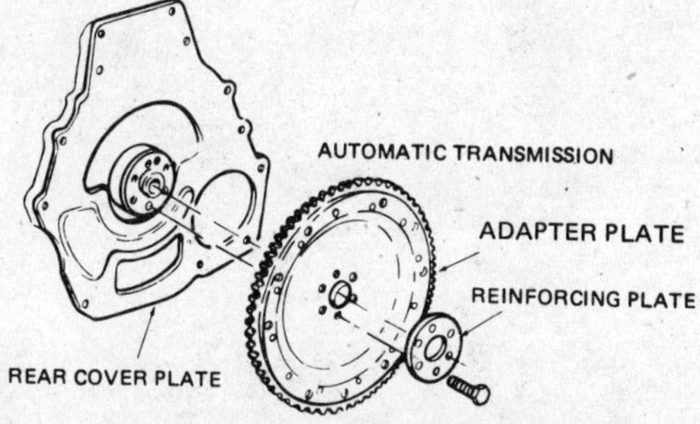

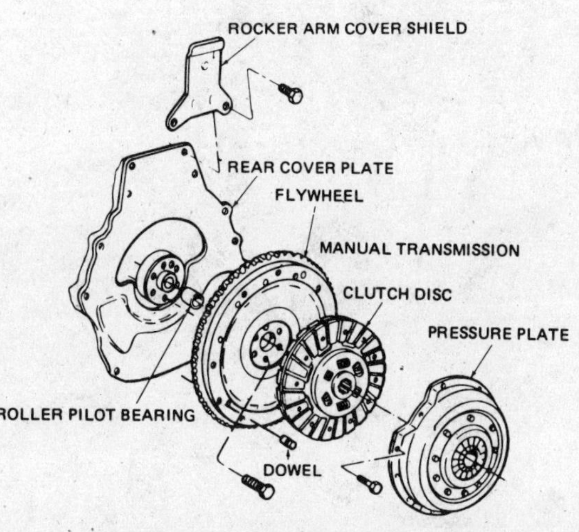

Fig. 1.26. Rear cover plate and flywheel (Sec. 52)

53 Valves - refitting

1 With the valves suitably ground in (see Section 34) and kept in their correct order, start with No 1 cylinder and insert the valve into its guide (Figs. 1.27 and 1.28).

2 Lubricate the valve stem with engine oil and slide on a new oil seal. The spring must be uppermost.

3 Fit the valve spring and retainer.

4 Using a universal valve spring compressor, compress the valve spring, until the keys can be slid into position. Note these keys have serrations which engage in slots in the valve stem. Release the valve spring compressor.

5 Repeat this procedure until all eight valves and valve springs are fitted.

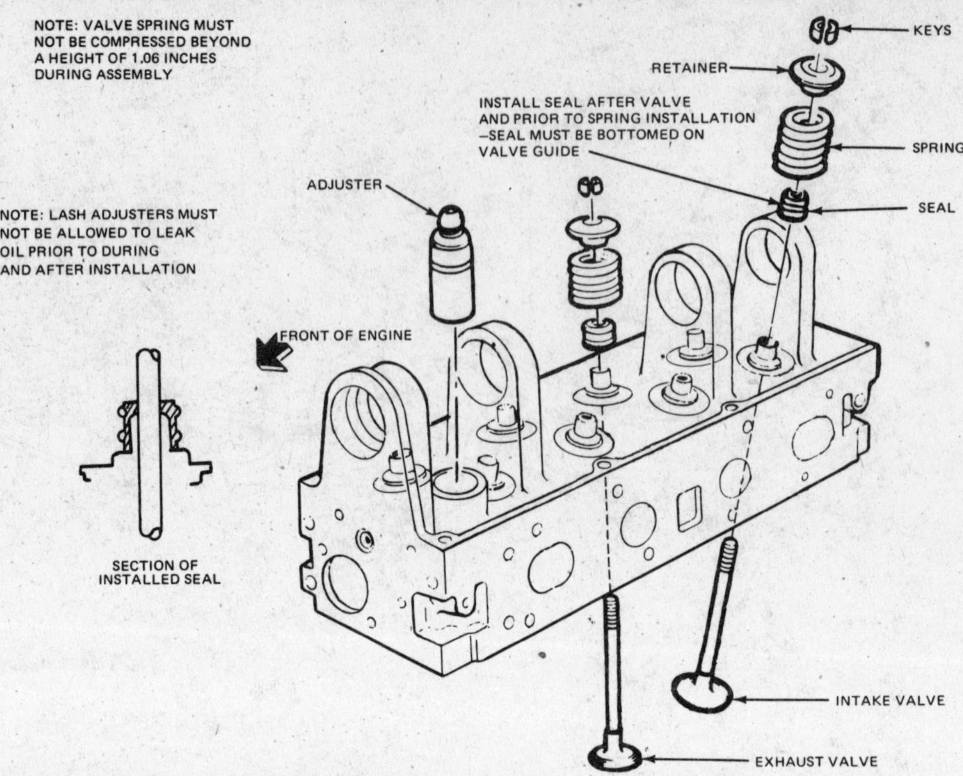
NOTE: VALVE SPRING MUST NOT BE COMPRESSED BEYOND A HEIGHT OF 1.06 INCHES DURING ASSEMBLY
KEYS
RETAINER
INSTALL SEAL AFTER VALVE AND PRIOR TO SPRING INSTALLATION –SEAL MUST BE BOTTOMED ON VALVE GUIDE
SPRING
ADJUSTER
SEAL
NOTE: LASH ADJUSTERS MUST NOT BE ALLOWED TO LEAK OIL PRIOR TO DURING AND AFTER INSTALLATION
FRONT OF ENGINE
SECTION OF INSTALLED SEAL
INTAKE VALVE
EXHAUST VALVE

Fig. 1.27. Valves and component parts (Sec. 53)

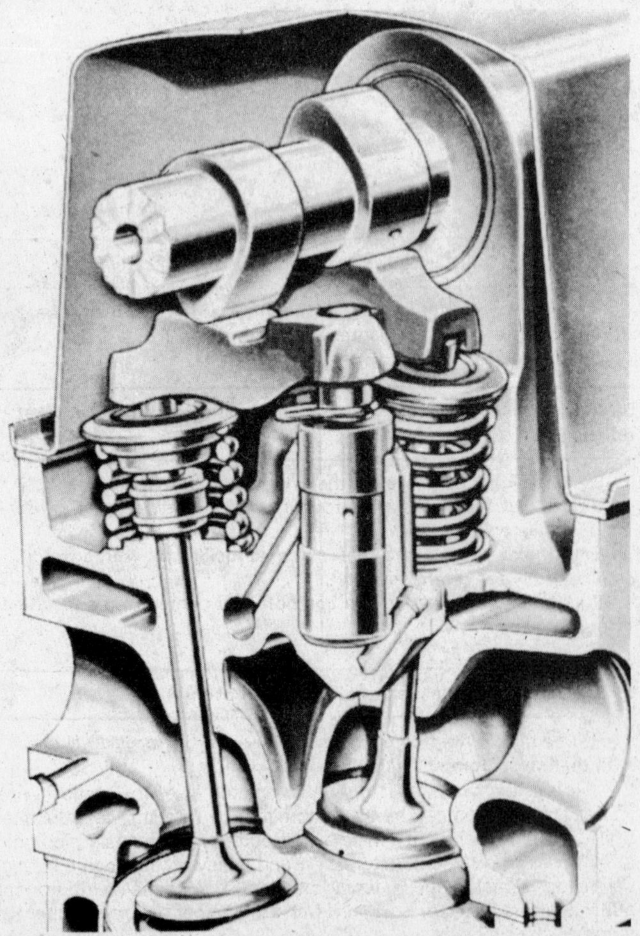

Fig. 1.28 Cutaway view of valves and lash adjusters (Sec. 53)

54 Camshaft - refitting

1 Lubricate liberally the camshaft journals and bearings with engine oil, then carefully install the shaft in the cylinder head.
2 Fit the retainer plate and screws at the rear end.
3 Lubricate a new camshaft seal with engine oil and carefully tap it into position at the front of the cylinder head.
4 Fit the belt guide and pin to the front end of the camshaft, and carefully tap on the sprocket.
5 Fit a new sprocket bolt and tighten it to the specified torque.

55 Hydraulic lash adjusters and cam followers - refitting

1 Smear the hydraulic lash adjusters with engine oil and then install each one into its respective position.
2 Smear the rubbing surface of the camshaft lobes and cam followers with engine oil.
3 Using special tool T74P-6565-B to compress each lash adjuster, position each cam follower on its respective valve end and adjuster, ensuring that the camshaft is rotated as necessary. Fit the retaining spring clips (where applicable). **Note:** On some valves it may be found necessary to compress the valve spring slightly when fitting the cam followers.

56 Cylinder head - refitting

1 Wipe the mating surfaces of the cylinder head and cylinder block.
2 Carefully place a new gasket on the cylinder block, ensuring that it is the correct way up (each gasket is marked 'FRONT UP').
3 Rotate the camshaft so that the sprocket retaining pin is in the position shown in Fig. 1.30, then position the head on the block. If the crankshaft needs to be rotated for any reason, ensure that the pistons are approximately halfway down the bores or they may contact the valves.
4 Fit and tighten the cylinder head bolts progressively to the specified torque, in the order shown in Fig. 1.9.

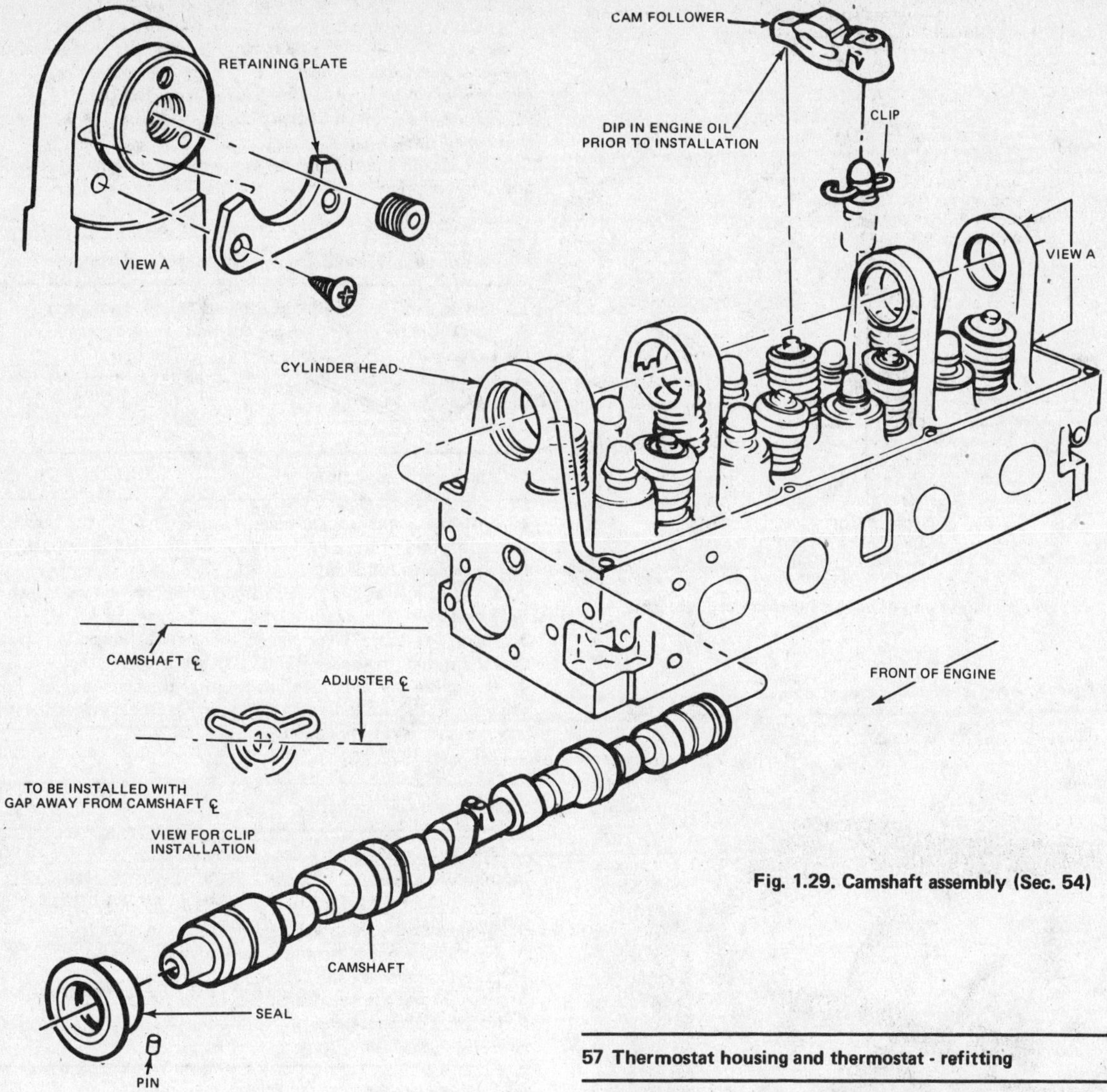

Fig. 1.29. Camshaft assembly (Sec. 54)

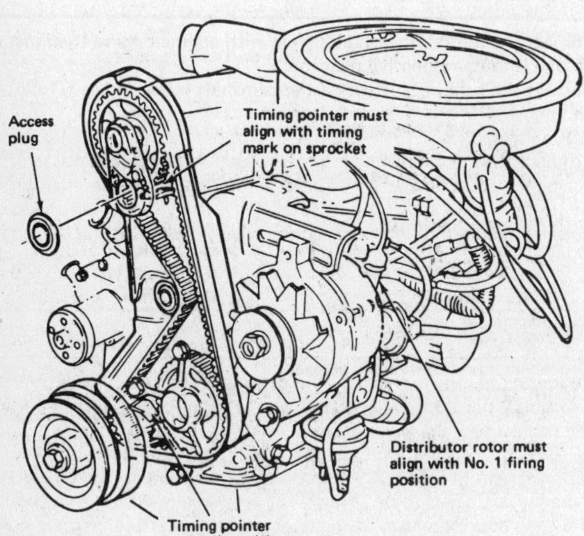

Fig. 1.30. Engine timing marks (Sec. 56)

57 Thermostat housing and thermostat - refitting

Refit the thermostat housing and thermostat to the cylinder head (if removed), referring to Chapter 2, if necessary.

58 Inner belt cover, auxiliary shaft sprocket and crankshaft sprocket - refitting

1 Refit the inner belt cover to the cylinder block (two bolts).
2 Ensure that the crankshaft sprocket key is in position, then carefully tap on the sprocket.
3 Ensure that the auxiliary shaft sprocket locking pin is in position, then carefully tap on the sprocket.
4 Fit the auxiliary shaft washer and bolt, and tighten to the specified torque.

59 Timing belt tensioner and timing belt - refitting

1 Rotate the camshaft until the index mark on the sprocket aligns with the timing pointer on the belt inner cover.
2 Rotate the crankshaft until No 1 piston is at top-dead-center (TDC). This position can be checked either by rotating the crankshaft while carefully inserting a thin screwdriver through the spark plug hole, or by positioning the belt outer cover and pulley on the engine to align the pulley 'O' mark with the timing pointer. Remove the distributor cap and make sure the rotor is aligned with the number one spark plug wire terminal.
3 Without disturbing the crankshaft and camshaft positions, refit the

1A

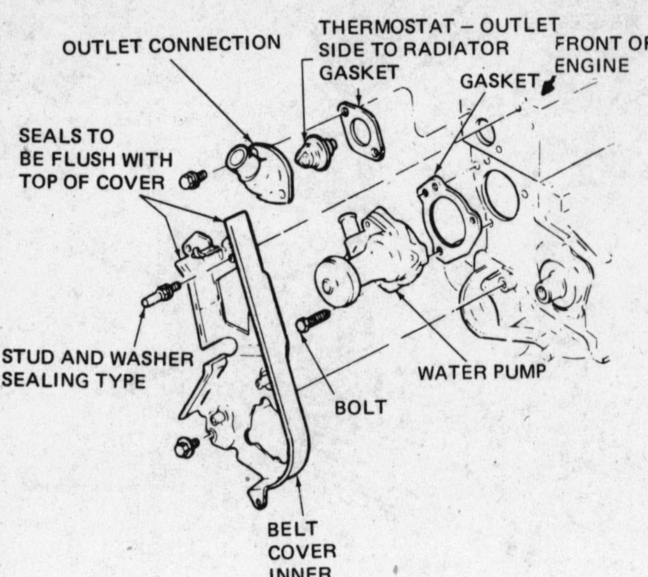

Fig. 1.31. Water pump and drivebelt inner cover (Sec. 58)

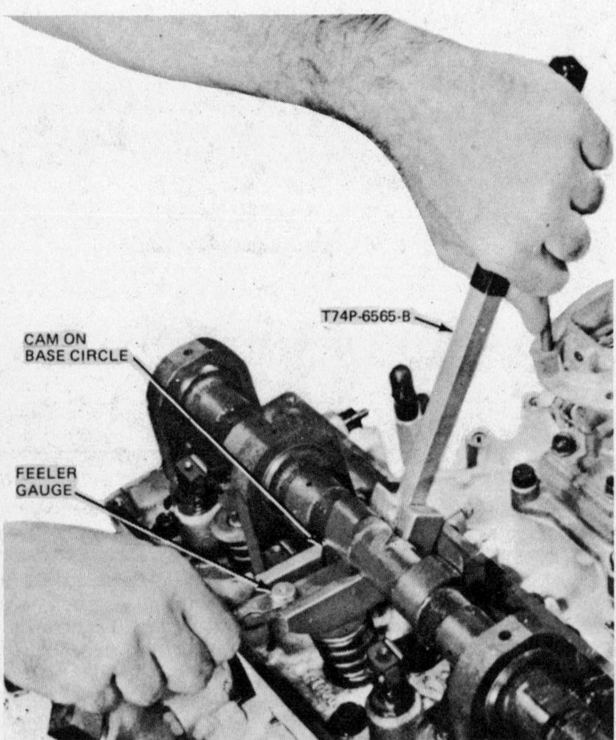

Fig. 1.32. Checking valve lash clearances (Sec. 61)

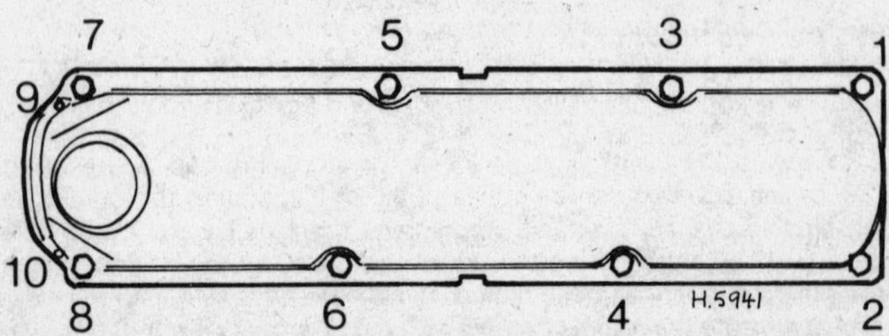

Fig. 1.33. Tightening sequence for rocker cover securing bolts (Sec. 62)

belt tensioner but do not tighten the bolts yet.

4 Install the timing belt over the crankshaft sprocket, then counter-clockwise over the auxiliary shaft and camshaft sprockets, then behind the tensioner jockey wheel. If difficulty is experienced, use a lever to pull the tensioner jockey wheel away from the belt.

5 Rotate the crankshaft two full turns in a clockwise direction to remove all slack from the belt.

6 Ensure that the timing marks are correctly aligned, then tighten the adjuster/bolts to the specified torque.

60 Belt outer cover and crankshaft pulley - refitting

1 Position the belt guide on the end of the crankshaft.

2 Install the belt outer cover, noting that spacers are used on two of the bolts.

3 Fit the crankshaft pulley, washer and retaining bolt. Tighten the bolt to the specified torque.

61 Valve lash - adjustment

1 With the engine rocker cover removed, rotate the crankshaft so that the base circle of the camshaft lobe of the first valve to be checked, is facing the cam follower.

2 Using special tool T74P-6565-B, compress the valve lash adjuster fully and hold it in this position.

3 Using a suitable feeler gauge, check that the gap is as given in the Specifications for the hydraulic lash adjuster.

4 If outside the allowable limit, either the cam follower is worn, the valve spring assembled height is incorrect, the camshaft is worn, or the lash adjuster is unserviceable.

62 Rocker cover - refitting

1 Clean the mating surfaces of the rocker cover and cylinder head, then lightly smear on a little non-setting gasket sealant.

2 Position a new gasket in the rocker cover, ensuring that the locating tabs are correctly positioned in the slots.

3 Fit the rocker cover. Fit and tighten the eight screws around the base to the specified torque.

4 Fit and tighten the two screws at the front end of the cover to the specified torque.

63 Engine - preparation for refitting

1 Having completed the engine rebuilding, it is now necessary to refit the items which were taken off prior to the commencement of major dismantling. These will differ according to the extent of the work done and the original equipment fitted, but will typically be:

a) *Oil pressure sender:* Coat threads with a non-setting gasket sealant and screw into the cylinder head.
b) *Water temperature sender:* Coat threads with a non-setting gasket sealant and screw into cylinder block.
c) *Fan:* Refer to Chapter 2, if necessary.
d) *Exhaust manifold:* Ensure that the mating surfaces are clean then apply a light even film of graphite grease. Install the manifold and tighten the bolts in two steps to the specified torque in the order shown in Fig. 1.10. Do not forget the lifting eye at No. 7 bolt.
e) *Spark plugs:* Fit new spark plugs of the type stated on the engine emission control decal.
f) *Intake manifold:* Ensure that the mating surfaces of the manifold and cylinder head are clean then install the manifold using a new gasket. Tighten the bolts in two steps to the specified torque in the order shown in Fig. 1.6. Do not forget the lifting eye at No. 7 bolt.
g) *Manifold ancillaries:* Refit the manifold ancillaries. These will vary according to the particular vehicle, but will typically be as shown in Fig. 1.5. and 1.6.
h) *Carburetor:* Install the carburetor, EGR valve and spacer assembly using new gaskets. The layout of the components is

the air cleaner at this stage. shown in Fig. 1.4. Do not forget the choke hose; do not fit the air cleaner at this stage.

j) *Fan:* Refer to Chapter 2, if necessary.
k) *Distributor:* Align the index marks and refer to Chapter 4. to ensure that the ignition timing is correct.
l) *Oil filter:* If not already fitted, refer to Section 24.
m) *Fuel pump:* Refer to Chapter 3, if necessary.
n) *Alternator:* Refit loosely; do not fit the drivebelt.
p) *Thermactor pump, compressor, PCV system, oil level dipstick, miscellaneous emission control items and associated interconnecting hoses etc.*

64 Engine - refitting (without transmission)

1 Raise the engine on the hoist and position it over the car engine compartment so that the rear end is sloping downward.
2 Lower the engine so that the exhaust manifold lines up approximately with the exhaust muffler inlet pipe.
3 *Automatic transmission:* Start the converter pilot into the crankshaft.
4 *Manual transmission:* Start the transmission main drive gear (input shaft) into the clutch hub. If necessary rotate the engine slightly *clockwise* to align the splines.
5 Ensure that the engine is settled on its mounts, then detach the hoist chains.
6 From beneath the car install the flywheel housing or converter upper attaching bolts.
7 *Automatic transmission:* Attach the converter to the flywheel and tighten the nuts to the specified torque. Refer to Chapter 7 for further information, if necessary. Install the converter bolt access plug.
8 Fit the front engine mount nuts.
9 Connect the exhaust pipe to the manifold, using a new gasket (if applicable).
10 Refit the starter motor and electrical cables.
11 Remove the plugs from the fuel lines and reconnect them to the fuel pump. If not already done, reconnect the fuel line to the carburetor.
12 Position the power steering pump on its brackets and install the upper bolts (where applicable).
13 Fit the engine shield.
14 From inside the engine compartment fit the power steering pump pulley (where applicable).
15 Reconnect the engine ground lead.
16 Fit the alternator adjusting arm bolt and the electrical connector(s).
17 Connect the wire to the electrically assisted choke.
18 Connect the coil wire and vacuum hose to the distributor.
19 Connect the vacuum amplifier.
20 Connect the wire to the water temperature sender in the cylinder block.
21 Connect the idle solenoid wires.
22 Position the accelerator cable on the ball stud and install the ball stud on the clip. Snap the bracket clip into position on the bracket. Where applicable, install the kick-down cable.
23 Refit the line to the oil pressure sender.
24 Refit the brake vacuum unit hose.
25 Reconnect the engine heater and vacuum hoses.
26 Refit the drivebelts to the engine driven accessories. Refer to Chapter 2 for the correct tension.
27 Refit the radiator. Refer to Chapter 2 if necessary.
28 Refit the oil cooler lines (where applicable).
29 Refit the radiator hoses.
30 Where applicable, refit the fan shroud.
31 Refill the cooling system with the correct amount of water/antifreeze (or inhibitor) mixture. Refer to Chapter 2 as necessary.
32 Fill the crankcase with the specified amount and type of oil.
33 Refit the air cleaner and the vacuum hoses. Refer to Chapter 3 if necessary.
34 Connect the battery leads.
35 Have a last look round the engine compartment to ensure that no hoses or electrical connections have been left off.
36 Refill the power steering system (where applicable).

65 Engine - refitting (with manual transmission)

1 The procedure for refitting the engine and manual transmission is

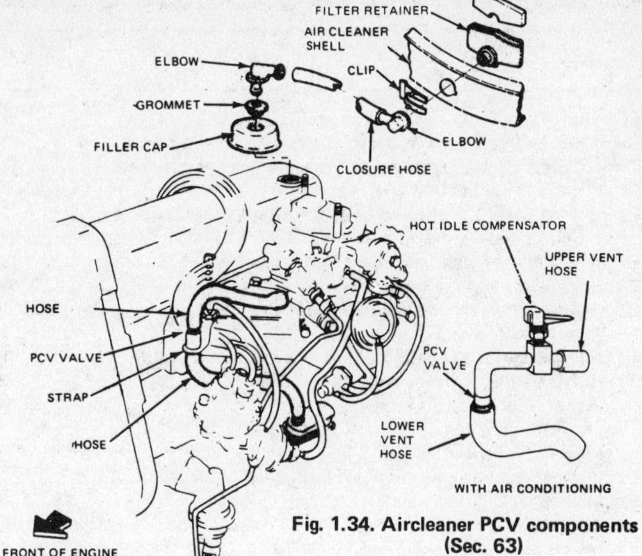

Fig. 1.34. Aircleaner PCV components (Sec. 63)

basically as described in the previous Section. However, the following differences should be noted:

a) *Support the weight of the transmission with a trolley jack prior to fitting the rear mounting.*
b) *Do not forget to reconnect the speedometer cable and transmission electrical connections. Refer to Chapter 6 for further information, if necessary.*
c) *Check the clutch adjustment after the cable has been reconnected. Refer to Chapter 5 for further information.*
d) *When reconnecting the propeller shaft, ensure that the index marks are correctly aligned. Refer to Chapter 7 for further information if necessary.*

1A

66 Engine - initial start-up after overhaul or major repair

1 Make sure that the battery is fully charged and that all lubricants, coolant and fuel are replenished.
2 If the fuel system has been dismantled it will require several revolutions of the engine on the starter motor to pump the petrol up to the carburetor.
3 As soon as the engine fires and runs, keep it going at a fast idle only (no faster) and bring it up to normal working temperature. When the thermostat opens the coolant level will fall and must therefore be topped-up again as necessary.
4 As the engine warms up there will be odd smells and some smoke from parts getting hot and burning off oil deposits. The signs to look for are leaks of water or oil, which will be obvious, if serious. Check also the exhaust pipe and manifold connections as these do not always find their exact gastight position until the warmth and vibration have acted on them and it is almost certain that they will need tightening further. This should be done, of course, with the engine stopped.
5 When normal running temperature has been reached, adjust the engine idle speed, as described in Chapter 3.
6 Stop the engine and wait a few minutes to see if any lubricant or coolant is dripping out when the engine is stationary.
7 After the engine has run for 20 minutes remove the engine rocker cover and recheck the tightness of the cylinder head bolts. Also check the tightness of the oil pan bolts. In both cases use a torque wrench.
8 Refit the hood to the previously drawn alignment marks and check that the hood fits correctly when shut.
9 Road test the car to check that the timing is correct and that the engine is giving the necessary smoothness and power. Do not race the engine; if new bearings and/or pistons have been fitted it should be treated as a new engine and run in at a reduced speed for the first 1000 miles (1600 km).
10 Bleed the power steering system (where applicable).

67 Fault diagnosis - engine

Refer to Chapter 1, Part B, Section 53, for engine fault diagnosis.

Chapter 1 Part B: 2800cc V6 engine

Contents

Specifications

Engine (general)

Engine type	6 cylinder 60° 'V' pushrod operated OHV	
Compression ratio	8.2 : 1	
Bore	3.66 in (92.96 mm)	
Stroke	2.70 in (68.58 mm)	
Capacity	170.8 cu in (2792 cc)	
Oil pressure (hot)	40-55 lb/in^2 (2.82-3.87 kg/cm^2)	
Firing order	1 - 4 - 2 - 5 - 3 - 6	
Oil capacity (including filter change)	5 US qt (4.2 Imp qt, 4.7 litres)	

Cylinder block

Bore diameter* (standard):		
Class 1	3.6616 in	(93.0046 mm)
Class 2	3.6620 in	(93.0148 mm)
Class 3	3.6624 in	(93.0250 mm)
Class 4	3.6630 in	(93.0402 mm)
**All dimensions ± 0.0002 in (0.005 mm)*		
Bore diameter* (oversize):		
0.020 service	3.6821 in	(93.5253 mm)
0.040 service	3.7018 in	(94.0257 mm)
**All dimensions ± 0.0002 (0.005 mm)*		
Main bearing bore diameter:		
Red	2.386 in	(60.6044 mm)
Blue	2.387 in	(60.6298 mm)
Thrust bearing width	0.890 - 0.892 in	(22.606 - 22.6568 mm)
Vertical inside diameter of fitted main bearing shells standard:		
Red	2.2454 - 2.2548 in	(56.990 - 57.000 mm)
Blue	2.2450 - 2.2454 in	(56.980 - 56.990 mm)

Cylinder location and distributor rotation

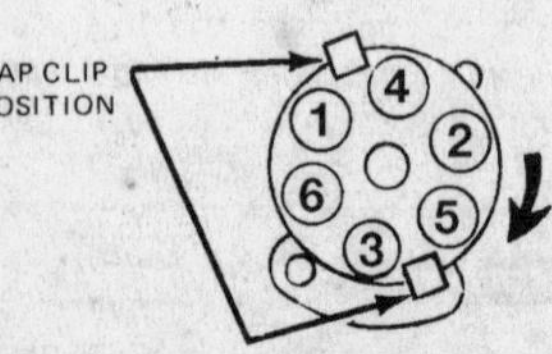

Undersize:		
0.010 ...	2.235 in	(56.769 mm)
0.020 ...	2.225 in	(56.515 mm)
0.030 ...	2.215 in	(56.261 mm)
0.040 ...	2.205 in	(56.007 mm)
Bores in cylinder block for camshaft bearings:		
Front ...	1.773 in	(45.720 mm)
No. 2 ...	1.758 in	(44.6532 mm)
No. 3 ...	1.743 in	(44.2722 mm)
Rear ...	1.728 in	(43.8912 mm)

Crankshaft

Number of main bearings	Four	
Main bearing journal diameter: Standard		
Red ...	2.244 in	(56.9976 mm)
Blue ...	2.243 in	(56.9722 mm)
Undersize:		
0.010 ...	2.234 in	(56.7436 mm)
0.020 ...	2.224 in	(56.4896 mm)
0.030 ...	2.214 in	(56.2356 mm)
0.040 ...	2.204 in	(55.9816 mm)
Main journal to bearing shell clearance:		
Standard	0.0005 - 0.002 in	(0.0127 - 0.0508 mm)
Undersize	0.0005 - 0.002 in	(0.0127 - 0.0508 mm)
Thrust bearing width:		
Bearing journal	1.039 in	(26.3906 mm)
Bearing insert	1.034 in	(26.2636 mm)
Crankshaft end play	0.004 - 0.008 in	(0.1016 - 0.2032 mm)
Connecting rod bearing journal diameter standard:		
Red ...	2.126 in	(54.0004 mm)
Blue ...	2.125 in	(53.975 mm)
Undersize:		
0.010 ...	2.116 in	(53.7464 mm)
0.020 ...	2.106 in	(53.4924 mm)
0.030 ...	2.096 in	(53.2384 mm)
0.040 ...	2.086 in	(52.9844 mm)

1B

Connecting rods

Connecting rod bearing shell vertical diameter standard:		
Red ...	2.127 in	(54.0258 mm)
Blue ...	2.126 in	(53.7718 mm)
Undersize:		
0.010 ...	2.117 in	(53.7718 mm)
0.020 ...	2.107 in	(53.5178 mm)
0.030 ...	2.097 in	(53.2638 mm)
0.040 ...	2.087 in	(53.0098 mm)
Journal bearing insert clearance:		
Standard	0.0005 - 0.002 in	(0.0127 - 0.0508 mm)
Undersize	0.0005 - 0.0025 in	(0.0127 - 0.0635 mm)

Pistons

Piston clearance ...	0.001 - 0.0025 in	(0.025 - 0.0635 mm)
Piston diameter:		
Standard	3.6605 - 3.6614 in	(92.9767 - 93.00 mm)
Oversize (0.020 in) ...	3.6802 - 3.6812 in	(93.477 - 93.5025 mm)
Oversize (0.040 in) ...	3.6999 - 3.7009 in	(93.9775 - 94.003 mm)

Piston rings

Ring gap (fitted):		
Upper compression ...	0.015 - 0.023 in	(0.381 - 0.5842 mm)
Lower compression ...	0.015 - 0.023 in	(0.381 - 0.5842 mm)
Oil control ...	0.015 - 0.055 in	(0.381 - 1.397 mm)

Camshaft

Number of bearings	4	
Bearing diameter:		
Front ...	1.650 in	(42.291 mm)
No. 2 ...	1.635 in	(41.783 mm)
No. 3 ...	1.620 in	(41.275 mm)
Rear ...	1.605 in	(40.767 mm)
Bushing inside diameter:		
Front ...	1.652 in	(41.9608 mm)
No. 2 ...	1.637 in	(41.5798 mm)
No. 3 ...	1.622 in	(41.1988 mm)
Rear ...	1.607 in	(40.8178 mm)
End play ...	0.001 - 0.004 in	(0.0254 - 0.1016 mm)

Thrust plate thickness standard:		
Red ...	0.156 in	(3.9624 mm)
Blue ...	0.157 in	(3.9874 mm)
Oversize:		
Red ...	0.161 in	(4.0894 mm)
Blue ...	0.162 in	(4.1148 mm)
Cam lift ...	0.255 in	(6.477 mm)
Cam heel to toe dimension ...	1.338 - 1.346 in	(33.9852 - 34.1884 mm)
Camshaft bearings:		
Distance from front face of cylinder block to rear side of assembled bearing		
Tolerance ...	± 0.010 in	(0.254 mm)
Front ...	0.831 in	(21.1074 mm)
No. 2 ...	6.559 in	(166.5986 mm)
No. 3 ...	11.319 in	(287.5026 mm)
Rear ...	17.091 in	(434.1114 mm)

Cylinder head

Valve seat angle ...	45°	
Valve stem diameter (inlet):		
Standard ...	0.316 in	(8.0264 mm)
Oversize:		
0.008 ...	0.325 in	(8.2296 mm)
0.016 ...	0.332 in	(8.4328 mm)
0.024 ...	0.340 in	(8.636 mm)
0.032 ...	0.348 in	(8.8392 mm)
Valve stem diameter (exhaust):		
Standard ...	0.315 in	(8.001 mm)
Oversize:		
0.008 ...	0.323 in	(8.2042 mm)
0.016 ...	0.331 in	(8.4074 mm)
0.024 ...	0.339 in	(8.6106 mm)
0.032 ...	0.347 in	(8.8138 mm)
Valve stem bore diameter:		
Standard ...	0.318 in	(8.0772 mm)
Oversize:		
0.008 ...	0.326 in	(8.2804 mm)
0.016 ...	0.334 in	(8.4836 mm)
Valve lift ...	0.373 in	(8.4742 mm)
Valve clearance (cold):		
Inlet ...	0.014 in	(0.36 mm)
Exhaust ...	0.016 in	(0.4 mm)
(hot):		
Inlet ...	0.008 in	(0.2032 mm)
Exhaust ...	0.016 in	(0.4064 mm)
Inlet valve timing:		
Opens ...	20° BTDC	
Closes ...	56° ABDC	
Exhaust valve timing:		
Opens ...	62° BBDC	
Closes ...	74° ATDC	
Valve tappet diameter ...	0.874 in	(22.1996 mm)

Torque wrench settings

	lb f ft	**kg f m**
Support bracket to engine ...	40 to 45	(5.5 to 6.2)
Support bracket to insulator ...	17 to 27	(2.35 to 3.73)
Insulator to frame ...	17 to 27	(2.35 to 3.73)
Crossmember to frame bracket ...	10 to 13	(1.38 to 1.8)
Insulator to crossmember ...	12 to 15	(1.66 to 2.07)
Insulator to transmission bracket ...	13 to 16	(1.8 to 2.21)
Transmission bracket securing bolt ...	37 to 42	(5.1 to 5.8)
Main bearing caps ...	65 to 75	(8.95 to 10.2)
Connecting rod bearing caps ...	22 to 26	(3.04 to 3.5)
Crankshaft gear ...	32 to 36	(4.4 to 4.8)
Camshaft gear ...	32 to 36	(4.4 to 4.8)
Crankshaft pulley ...	92 to 104	(12.7 to 14.4)
Flywheel ...	47 to 52	(6.45 to 7.12)
Front cover ...	12 to 15	(1.66 to 2.1)
Water pump ...	6 to 9	(0.83 to 1.24)
Oil pump ...	10 to 12	(1.38 to 1.6)
Rocker shaft supports ...	43 to 49	(5.9 to 6.76)
Oil sump (final) ...	5 to 8	(0.7 to 1.11)
Rocker arm covers (final) ...	2 to 5	(0.28 to 0.69)
Inlet manifold (final) ...	15 to 18	(2.07 to 2.49)
Cylinder head (final) ...	65 to 80	(8.95 to 11.06)
Temperature sender unit ...	8 to 12	(1.11 to 1.6)
Spark plugs ...	15 to 22	(2.1 to 3)

1 General description

The engine described in this part of the Chapter is a 6-cylinder ohv gasoline type with the cylinders arranged in a 60° 'V' formation.

The cylinder bores are machined directly into the cast iron cylinder block. The cylinder block is cast integral with the crankcase and incorporates full length water jackets. There are four large diameter main bearings each having removable caps.

A cast-iron crankshaft runs in the main bearings which are fitted with detachable steel-backed copper-lead bearing shells. The endfloat of the crankshaft is controlled by the thrust flanges on No 3 main shell bearing.

Pressed in oil seals are incorporated in the front cover and rear carrier so as to prevent oil leaks from either the front or the rear of the crankshaft. The rear oil seal in the carrier runs directly onto the crankshaft flange.

A gear on the end of the camshaft is in direct mesh with a gear on the end of the crankshaft and is driven by the crankshaft at half-engine speed. The camshaft runs in steel-backed white-metal bushings. Incorporated on the camshaft in front of the rearmost bearing journal is a skew gear and this drives the oil pump and distributor. The camshaft also drives, through an eccentric and a pushrod, the fuel pump, which is bolted to the lower left-hand side of the block.

The valves are mounted overhead and are operated by a system of rockers, pushrods and tappets from the camshaft that is placed in the valley between the two banks of cylinders. The inlet valves are of a larger diameter than those of the exhaust, to improve engine breathing. The rocker arms are mounted on a rocker shaft located on the top of each cylinder head. The valve springs are of an unusual form with close coils at one end, with the close coils fitted adjacent to the cylinder head.

The connecting rods are H-section forgings and the connecting rod caps are located by bolts and secured with two nuts. Similar to the crankshaft main bearing the connecting rod bearings are steel-backed and copper-lead lined.

The little end, sometime called the small end, is not bearing lined but is shrunk onto the piston to secure the latter in position.

Mounted onto the rear end of the crankshaft is a cast-iron flywheel (manual transmission) or adaptor plate (automatic transmission).

A steel starter ring gear is shrunk onto the outer periphery of the flywheel and engages with the starter motor driver during engine starting conditions. If an automatic transmission is fitted, the ring gear is shrunk onto the adapter plate which is attached to the torque converter. The torque converter is driven via the adapter plate to the rear crankshaft flange instead of the normal flywheel.

The engine oil pan is a steel pressing having a rear well. The drain plug is on the right-hand side of the pressing.

The hexagonal driveshaft from the distributor drives a bi-rotor type oil pump. Incorporated into the design of the pump is an oil pressure relief valve. Oil under pressure is directed via a full flow oil filter to the main, connecting rod, and camshaft bearings and to the valve lifters. As the valve lifters are hollow they control the amount of oil through the hollow pushrods to the rocker arms and valves.

There is a drilling in the cylinder block front face which supplies oil to the timing gears.

The oil from the rocker arms drains from the cylinder head and into the valve lifter chamber so lubricating the cams and distributor drive gear as it returns to the oil pan at the base of the engine.

The cylinder bores are lubricated by one squirt of oil every crankshaft revolution emitting from a small drilling in each connecting rod web. The piston pins are continuously lubricated by oil mist created by internal engine activity and also on the downward strokes by oil scraped by the oil control rings from the cylinder bores.

Located on the left-hand rocker cover top is the oil filler cap and this incorporates a filter gauze for the positive crankcase ventilation system. Any crankcase fumes are discharged into the inlet manifold under the control of an emission valve located in the left-hand rocker cover.

2 Major operations with engine in place

The following major operations may be carried out without taking the engine from the car:

1. *Removal and replacement of the cylinder heads.*
2. *Removal and replacement of the timing gear.*
3. *Removal and replacement of the front engine mountings.*
4. *Removal and replacement of the engine - gearbox rear mounting.*
5. *Removal and replacement of the camshaft.*

1B

3 Major operations with engine removed

Although it would be possible to carry out some of the following operations with the engine in the car if the gearbox and clutch were removed, it is deemed inadvisable.

1. *Removal and replacement of the flywheel.*
2. *Removal and replacement of the rear main bearing oil seal.*
3. *Removal and replacement of the oil pan.*
4. *Removal and replacement of the connecting rod bearings.*
5. *Removal and replacement of the pistons and connecting rods.*
6. *Removal and replacement of the oil pump.*
7. *Removal and replacement of the crankshaft and crankshaft main bearings.*
8. *Removal and replacement of the camshaft and bushings*

1 General view of engine compartment

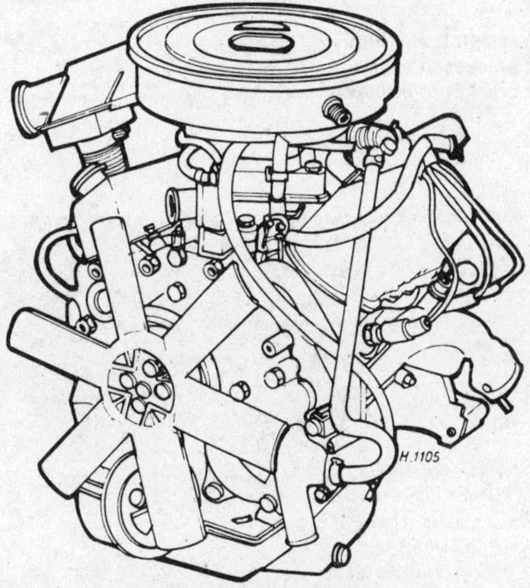

Fig. 1.35. Front, LH view of V6 engine

4 Methods of engine removal

1 On earlier models (thru 1976), the engine may be lifted out together with the gearbox or separated from the gearbox and lifted out by itself. If the gearbox is left attached the disadvantage is that the engine has to be tilted to a very steep angle to get it out, particularly when automatic transmission is fitted. Unless both the engine and gearbox are being repaired or overhauled together there is no other reason for removing them as a unit.
2 On later models, 1977 on, the engine can only be removed without the gearbox due to the design of the crossmember.

5 Engine removal without gearbox

1 This task takes about three hours. It is essential to have a good hoist. If an inspection pit is not available, two axle stands will also be required. In the later stages, when the engine is being separated from the gearbox and lifted, the assistance of another person is most useful.

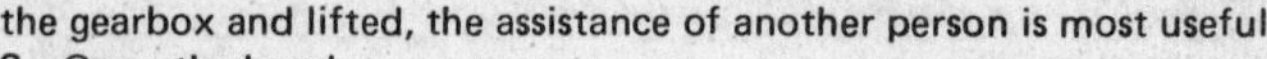

2 Open the hood.
3 Place a container of suitable size under the radiator and one under the engine and drain the cooling system, as described in Chapter 2. Do not drain the water in the garage or the place where the engine is to be removed if receptacles are not at hand to catch the water.
4 Place a container of 12 US pints (6 liters) capacity under the oil pan and remove the drain plug. Let the oil drain for 10 minutes and then refit the plug.
5 Place old blankets over the fenders and across the cowl to prevent damage to the paintwork.
6 It is easier if two assistants are available so that the hood can be supported whilst the hinges are being released.
7 Using a pencil, mark the outline of the hinges on the hood.
8 Undo and remove the four nuts and washers and bolt plates that secure the hinges to the hood (photo).
9 Release the hood stay and carefully lift the hood up and over the front of the engine compartment.
10 Disconnect the battery, release the battery clamp and lift away from its tray. Remove the battery heat shield (photos).

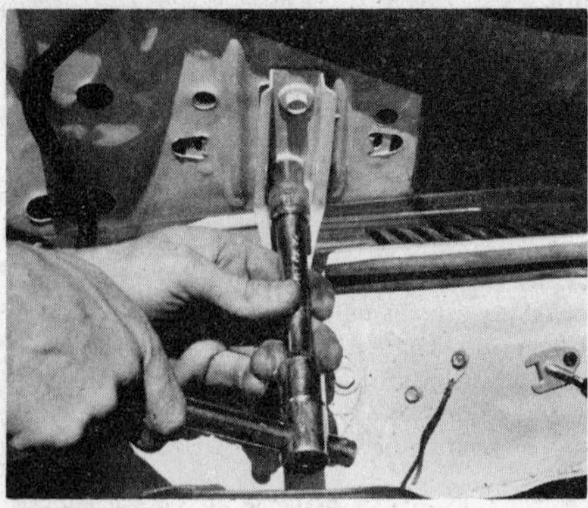
5.8 Removing the hood hinge bolts

5.10A Removing the battery inner clamp nut ...

5.10B .....and lifting out the heat shield (if fitted)

5.10C Removing the battery clamp retaining plate

5.11 Removing the air cleaner and duct assembly

5.12A Unscrewing the top hose clamp

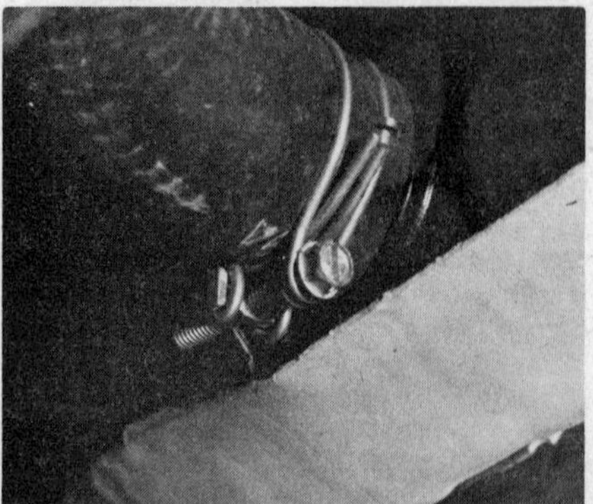
5.12B Location of bottom hose clamp

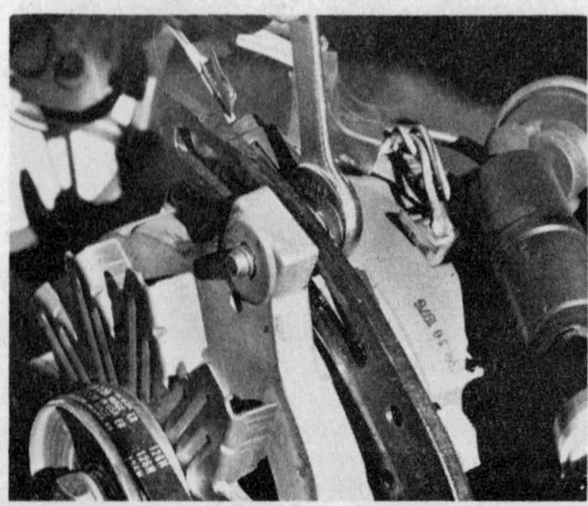
5.14 Slackening the alternator adjusting bolt

11 Refer to Chapter 8 and remove the air cleaner and intake duct assembly (photo).
12 Slacken the clips that secure the upper and lower radiator hoses and carefully remove the hoses (photos).
13 Refer to Chapter 2 and remove the radiator and its shroud.
14 Detach the terminal connector at the rear of the alternator. Slacken the mounting bolts and push the alternator towards the engine (photo). Lift away the fanbelt. Remove the alternator mounting bolts and lift away the alternator.
Note: On cars fitted with a power steering and thermactor pump and/or an air-conditioning compressor, the drivebelts for these units will have to be removed first, (refer to Chapter 2).
15 Remove the alternator bracket securing bolts and spring washers and lift away the bracket and earth cable from the side of the cylinder block.
16 Slacken the heater hose clips at the cylinder block and water pump unions and detach the hoses.
17 Remove the engine ground cable securing bolt from the engine and move the ground cable to one side.
18 Disconnect the main fuel line from the inlet side of the fuel pump and plug the end of the line to prevent syphoning of gasoline.
19 Detach the accelerator cable or linkage at the carburetor installation and inlet manifold. Further information will be found in Chapter 3.
20 When an automatic transmission is fitted, disconnect the downshift linkage.
21 Make a note of the cable connections to the ignition coil, water temperature sender unit and detach from the terminals. Also release the oil pressure gauge pressure pipe.
22 Detach the vacuum hose to the brake servo unit from the inlet manifold.
23 Disconnect the emission control pipes and electrical connections from the carburetor and inlet manifold.
24 Remove the two hoses and electrical connector from the choke thermostat housing.
25 Undo and remove the nuts that secure each exhaust downpipe to the exhaust manifolds, release the clamp plates and move the downpipes to the side of the engine compartment.
26 Chock the rear wheels, jack-up the front of the car and support on firmly based axle stands. To give better access, remove the front wheels.
27 Make a note of the cable connections to the starter motor. Detach the cables from the starter motor terminals.
28 Undo and remove the bolts and spring washers that secure the starter motor to the engine. Lift away the starter motor.
29 Undo and remove the engine front mounting through bolts at the cylinder block, and remove the rear engine mounting crossmember.

Automatic transmission

30 Undo and remove the bolts and spring washers that secure the converter inspection cover to the housing. Lift away the inspection cover.
31 Undo and remove the bolts that secure the torque converter to the adaptor plate. It will be necessary to rotate the crankshaft using a large spanner on the crankshaft pulley securing bolt.
32 Undo and remove the converter housing to engine block securing bolts and spring washers.
33 Detach the downshift rod from its bracket.

Manual transmission

34 Pull back the clutch release arm rubber boot, if fitted. Slacken the locknut and adjustment nut. Detach the inner cable from the release arm and withdraw the cable assembly.
35 Undo and remove the bolts and spring washers securing the bellhousing to the engine.

All models

36 Refit the wheels and lower the front of the car.
37 Wrap rope slings around the exhaust manifolds or if chains are to be used, mount brackets on the exhaust manifold and then attach the chain hooks to the brackets. Take up the slack.
38 Place a jack under the transmission unit to support its weight.
39 Check that all cables and controls have been detached and safely tucked out of the way.
40 Raise the engine slightly and then draw it forwards. When automatic transmission is fitted make sure that the torque converter remains attached to the transmission unit, by prying it to the rear.
41 Continue lifting the engine taking care that the backplate does not foul the bodywork.
42 With the engine away from the engine compartment lower to the ground or bench and suitably support so that it does not roll over.

6 Engine removal with manual gearbox attached (early models only)

1 Proceed exactly as described in Section 5 up to and including paragraph 19, then 21 to 29 inclusive and finally paragraph 34.
2 Unscrew the gearbox drain plug and allow the oil to drain away for five minutes. Replace the drain plug.
3 From inside the car remove the gearshift stick, (see Chapter 6).
4 Support the weight of the gearbox using a small jack located adjacent to the drain plug.
5 Undo and remove the center bolt which locates the gearbox extension housing into the support member. Then making sure the gearbox support jack is firmly in position, undo and remove the four bolts and washers that secure the crossmember to the underside of the body. Lift away the crossmember.
6 With the crossmember removed it is now an easy task to disconnect the speedometer cable from the gearbox by removing the circlip and withdrawing the cable.
7 Detach the back-up lamp cable connector at its snap-connector.
8 Wrap rope slings around the exhaust manifolds or if chains are to be used, mount brackets on the exhaust manifold and then attach the chain hooks to the brackets. Take up the slack.
9 Check that all cables and controls have been detached and safely tucked out of the way.
10 With the jack under the gearbox still in position start lifting and at the same time, once the front mountings have been cleared, move the engine forward until the propeller shaft is withdrawn from the end of the gearbox. Support the shaft on a wooden block.
11 Due to the fact that the gearbox is attached, the engine will have to be lifted out at a much steeper angle than for removing the engine on its own. As the weight is more towards the rear, it will be fairly easy to achieve the necessary angle.
12 Continue to raise the engine and move it forwards at the necessary angle. At this stage the forward edge of the bellhousing is likely to catch against the front crossmember and the tail of the gearbox will need raising until the whole unit is forward and clear of it.
13 Finally the whole unit will rise clear and if the maximum height of the lifting tackle has been reached, it will be necessary to swing the unit so that the tail can be lifted clear whilst the hoist is moved away or the car lowered from its axle stands and pushed from under the unit.
14 The whole unit should be lowered to the ground (or bench) as soon as possible and the gearbox may then be separated from the engine.

7 Engine removal with automatic transmission attached

It is recommended that the engine should not be removed whilst still attached to the automatic transmission, because of the weight involved. If it is necessary to remove both units refer to Chapter 6 and remove the transmission unit first. Then remove the engine as described in Section 5 but disregarding information on detachment from the transmission unit.

8 Engine dismantling - general

1 Ideally, the engine is mounted on a proper stand for overhaul but it is anticipated that most owners will have a strong bench on which to place it. If a sufficiently large strong bench is not available then the work can be done at ground level. It is essential, however, that some form of substantial wooden surface is available. Timber should be at least ¾ inch thick, otherwise the weight of the engine will cause projections to punch holes straight through it.
2 It will save a great deal of time later if the exterior of the engine is thoroughly cleaned down before any dismantling begins. This can be done by using kerosene and a stiff brush or more easily, by the use of a proprietary solvent which can be brushed on and then the dirt swilled off with a water jet. This will dispose of all the heavy muck and grit once and for all so that later cleaning of individual components will be a relatively clean process and the kerosene bath will not become contaminated with abrasive material.
3 As the engine is stripped down, clean each part as it comes off. Try

to avoid immersing parts with oilways in kerosene as pockets of liquid could remain and cause oil dilution in the critical first few revolutions after reassembly. Clean oilways with wire, or, preferably, an air jet. air jet.

4 Where possible avoid damaging gaskets on removal, especially if new ones have not been obtained. They can be used as patterns if new ones have to be specially cut.

5 It is helpful to obtain a few blocks of wood to support the engine whilst it is in the process of being dismantled. Start dismantling at the top of the engine and then turn the block over and deal with the oil pan and crankshaft etc., afterwards.

6 Nuts and bolts should be replaced in their locations where possible to avoid confusion later. As an alternative keep each group of nuts and bolts (all the timing gear cover bolts for example) together in a jar or tin.

7 Many items dismantled must be replaced in the same position, if they are not being renewed. These include valves, rocker arms, valve lifters, pistons, pushrods, bearings and connecting rods. Some of these are marked on assembly to avoid any possibility of mixing them up during overhaul. Others are not, and it is a great help if adequate preparation is made in advance to classify these parts. Suitably labelled cardboard boxes or trays should be used. The time spent in this preparation will be amply repaid later.

9 Engine ancillaries - removal

1 Before beginning a complete overhaul, or if the engine is being exchanged for a works reconditioned unit, the following items should be removed :

Fuel system components:
- *Carburetor*

Inlet and exhaust manifolds
- *Fuel pump*
- *Fuel lines*

Ignition system components:
- *Spark plugs*
- *Distributor*
- *Coil*

Electrical system components (if not removed already):
- *Alternator and mounting brackets*
- *Starter motor*

Cooling system components:
- *Fan and fan pulley*
- *Water pump thermostat housing and thermostat*
- *Water temperature sender unit*

Engine:
- *Crankcase ventilation tube*
- *Oil filter element*
- *Oil pressure sender unit (if fitted)*
- *Oil level dipstick*
- *Oil filler cap*
- *Engine mounting brackets*

Clutch:
- *Clutch pressure plate and total assembly*
- *Clutch friction plate and total assembly*

Optional equipment:
- *Air-conditioning compressor*
- *Power steering pump*
- *Thermactor pump*

10 Cylinder heads - removal with engine in car

1 For safety reasons disconnect the battery.

2 Remove the air cleaner from the carburetor installation, as described in Chapter 3.

3 Disconnect the accelerator linkage from the carburetor.

4 Refer to Chapter 2 and drain the cooling system.

5 Detach the HT leads from the spark plugs, release the distributor cap securing clips and remove the distributor cap.

6 Slacken the clips and disconnect the hose from the water pump to the water outlet.

7 Detach the vacuum pipe from the distributor body and carburetor installation.

8 Refer to Chapter 3, and remove the carburetor and inlet manifold assembly. This will necessitate removal of the distributor.

9 Remove the two rocker covers by undoing and removing the securing screws and lifting away together with their respective gaskets.

10 Undo and remove the three bolts and washers that secure each rocker shaft assembly to the top of each cylinder head. This must be done in a progressive manner. When the bolts are free lift away the rocker shaft assembly and oil baffles. Note to which cylinder head each rocker shaft assembly was fitted.

11 With the rocker shaft assemblies away, remove the pushrods. Keep them in order and the right way up by pushing them through a piece of stiff paper or cardboard with the valve numbers marked.

12 Detach the exhaust downpipes from the exhaust manifold and move the downpipes to the sides of the engine compartment. Leave the manifolds in place as they will act as a lever to assist removal of the heads.

13 Taking each cylinder head in turn, slacken the eight holding down bolts in the order shown in Fig. 1.39. When all are free of tension remove all the bolts.

14 On occasions the heads may have stuck to the head gasket and cylinder block, in which case if pulling up on the exhaust manifolds does not free them they should be struck smartly with a soft faced hammer in order to break the joints. **Do not** try to pry them off with a blade of any description or damage will be caused to the faces of the head or block, or both.

15 Lift the heads off carefully. Note which side each head comes from as they are not identical, and it is essential to replace them on the same bank of cylinders. Place them where they cannot be damaged. Undo the bolts holding the exhaust manifold to each head if not previously removed.

16 Remove the cylinder head gaskets. New ones will be required for reassembly.

11 Cylinder heads - removal with engine out

Follow the sequence given in Section 10, paragraphs 5 to 16 inclusive, disregarding information on parts mentioned that have been previously removed.

12 Cylinder heads - dismantling of valves and springs

1 Lay the cylinder head on its side and using a proper valve spring compressor place the 'U' shaped end over the spring retainer and screw on the valve head so as to compress the spring.

2 Sometimes the retainer will stick, in which case the end of the compressor over the spring should be tapped with a hammer to release the retainer from the locks (collets).

3 As the spring is compressed two tapered locks will be exposed and should be taken from the recess in the retainer.

4 When the compressor is released the spring may be removed from the valve. Lift off the retainer, spring and oil seal. Withdraw the valve from the cylinder head. Note that the springs are fitted with the close coils towards the cylinder head.

5 It is essential that the valves, springs, retainers, locks and seals are all kept in order so that they may be refitted in their original positions.

13 Valve rocker shaft assembly - dismantling

1 With the rocker shaft assembly on the bench tap out the pin at each end of the rocker shaft using a suitable diameter parallel pin punch.

2 Withdraw the spring washer, rocker arm, support, rocker arm spring and subsequent parts in order. Keep all parts in that order so that they may be refitted in their original positions.

14 Valve lifters - removal

1 The valve lifters may now be removed from the cylinder block by pushing them up from the camshaft (which can be revolved if necessary

to raise the valve lifters) and lifting them out. **Note:** with the engine in the car a magnet may be required to withdraw them, (see Fig. 1.42).
2 If necessary the pushrod bearing caps in each valve lifter can be taken out by first extracting the retaining circlip.
3 Make sure that all the valve lifters are kept in order so that they may be replaced in the location they came from.

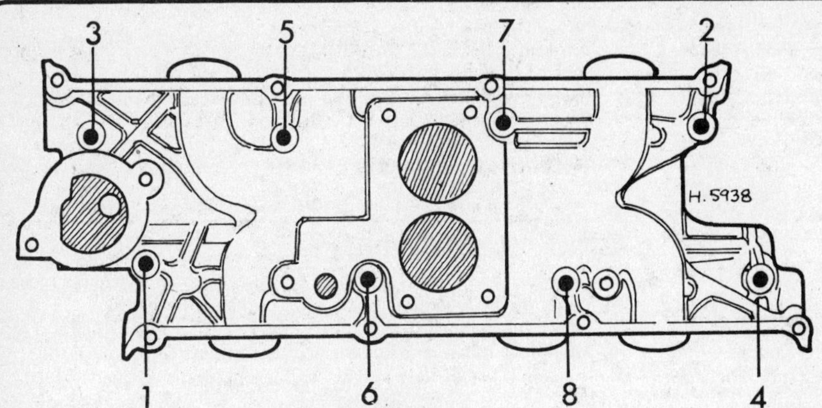

Fig. 1.36. Correct slackening and tightening sequence of inlet manifold bolts (Secs. 10 and 47)

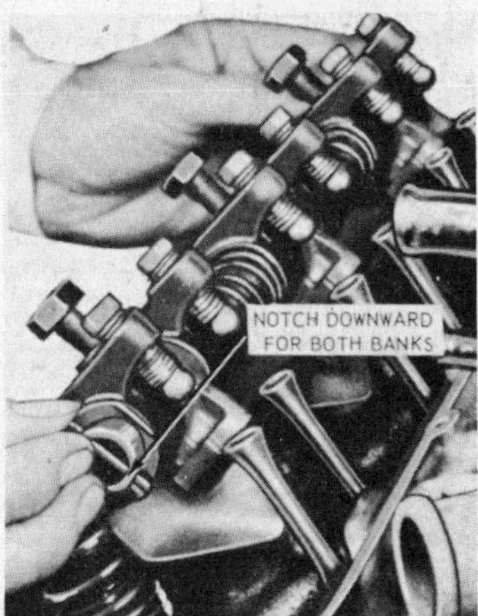

Fig. 1.37. Removing the rocker gear (Sec. 10)

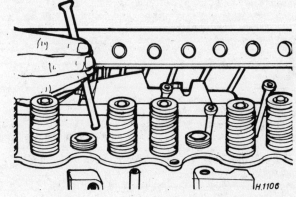

Fig. 1.38. Removing the pushrods (Sec. 10)

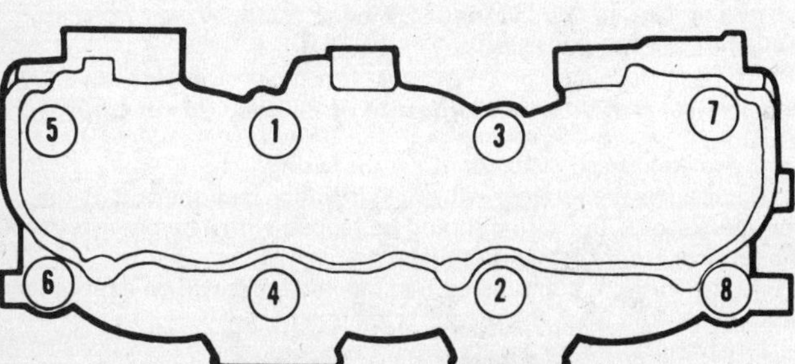

Fig. 1.39. Correct sequence for slackening or tightening the cylinder head bolts (Secs. 10 and 47)

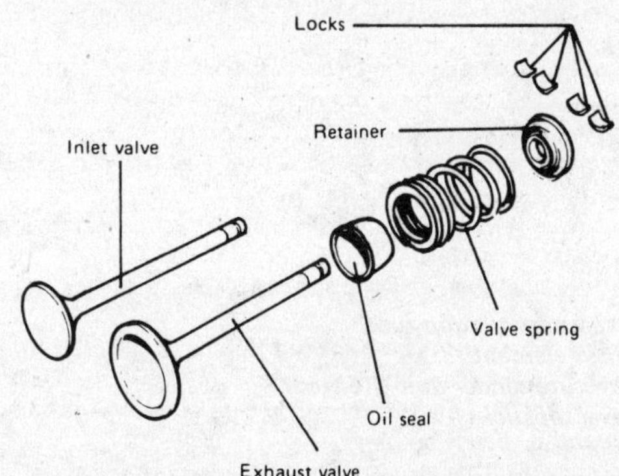

Fig. 1.40. Inlet and exhaust valve components (Sec. 12)

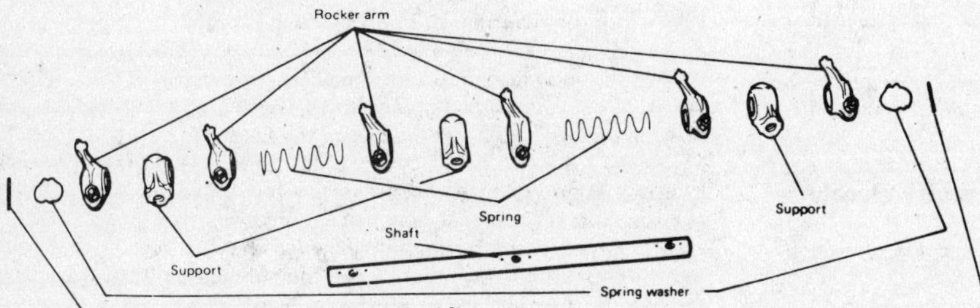

Fig. 1.41. Rocker shaft and components (Secs. 13 and 47)

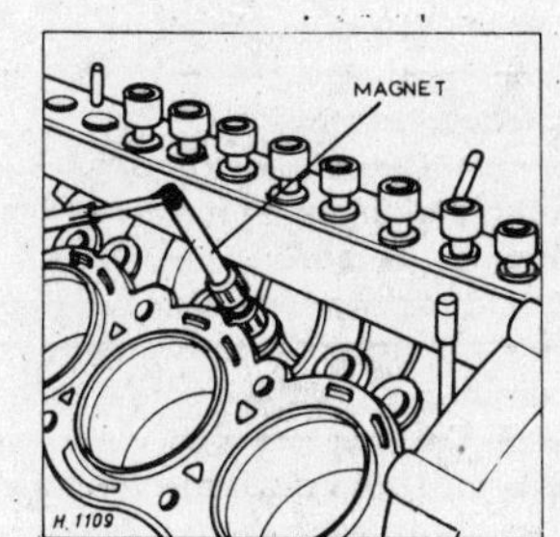

Fig. 1.42 Removing the valve lifters using a magnet (Sec. 14)

1B

15 Crankshaft pulley wheel - removal

1 Remove the bolt and washer locating the pulley to the front of the crankshaft. The pulley is keyed to the crankshaft and must be drawn off with a proper sprocket puller. Attempts to lever it off with long bladed articles such as screwdrivers or tire levers are not suitable in this case because the timing cover behind the pulley is a light and relatively fragile casting. Any pressure against it could certainly crack it and possibly break a hole in it.
2 The pulley may be removed with the engine in the car but it will be necessary to remove the radiator, and drivebelts.
3 Recover the Woodruff key from the crankshaft nose.

16 Flywheel - removal

1 Remove the clutch assembly, as described in Chapter 5.
2 The flywheel is held in position to the crankshaft by six bolts. One of these bolts is spaced unevenly so that the flywheel will only fit one position.
3 Remove the six bolts, taking care to support the weight of the flywheel as they are slackened off in case it slips off the flange. Secure it carefully, taking care not to damage the mating surfaces on the crankshaft and flywheel.

17 Oil pan - removal

1 With the engine out of the car, first invert the engine and then remove the bolts which hold the pan in place.
2 The pan may be stuck quite firmly to the engine if sealing compound has been used on the gasket. It is in order to lever it off in this case. The gasket should be removed and discarded in any case.
3 It is possible to remove the pan with the engine in the car. First withdraw the oil level dipstick.
4 Remove the bolts that secure the fan shroud to the radiator. Place the shroud over the fan.
5 Detach the battery ground cable.
6 Slacken the alternator mounting bolts and remove the fan belt.
7 Chock the rear wheels, jack-up the front of the car and support on firmly based stands.
8 Drain the oil pan after placing a container of at least 12 US pints (5.7 liters) under the drain plug and removing the plug. Allow to drain for five minutes and refit the plug.
9 Note the electrical cable connections to the starter motor and detach from their terminals.
10 Undo and remove the starter motor securing bolts and spring washers. Lift away the starter motor.
11 Undo and remove the bolts and spring washers that secure the splash shield.
12 Support the engine using an overhead hoist or crane and then undo and remove the engine front support nuts.
13 Raise the engine and place some wood blocks between the engine front supports and chassis brackets.
14 Undo and remove the bolts and spring washers that secure the clutch or converter housing cover. Lift away the cover.
15 Undo and remove the oil pan retaining bolts and lift away the oil pan. If stuck, refer to paragraph 2. Remove the pan gasket.

18 Front cover - removal

1 With the engine out of the car, remove the oil pan and crankshaft pulley wheel.
2 Undo and remove the water pump retaining bolts and lift the water pump from the front cover. It may be necessary to tap it with a soft-faced hammer if a jointing compound has been used.
3 Undo and remove the front cover securing bolts and lift away. If stuck, carry out the instructions in paragraph 2. Remove the front cover gasket.
4 If the engine is still in the car it will be necessary to remove the front oil pan bolts which run through the timing cover. It will also be necessary to remove the fanbelt, crankshaft pulley wheel and fuel pump.

19 Timing gears - removal

1 Undo and remove the bolt and washer that secures the timing gear to the camshaft.
2 To remove the gear lightly tap it at the rear, so releasing it from the camshaft. Lift away the gear and then the Woodruff key.
3 To remove the crankshaft gear use a universal puller and draw it from the end of the crankshaft. This is only necessary when the gear is to be renewed.
4 Recover the Woodruff key.

20 Camshaft - removal

1 The camshaft can be removed with the engine in the car. (Should camshaft renewal be necessary it will probably be necessary to overhaul other parts of the engine too. If this is the case engine removal should be considered).
2 Refer to Chapter 2 and remove the radiator.
3 Detach the spark plug leads from the spark plugs, release the cap securing clips and place the cap to one side.
4 Detach the distributor vacuum line and then remove the distributor as described in Chapter 4.
5 Remove the alternator as described in Chapter 10.
6 Undo and remove the screws that secure each rocker cover to the cylinder heads. Lift away the rocker covers and gaskets.
7 Refer to Chapter 3 and remove the inlet manifold and carburetor installation.
8 Undo and remove the three bolts and washers that secure each rocker shaft assembly to the cylinder heads. This should be done in a progressive manner to avoid straining the shaft. Lift away each rocker shaft assembly noting from which head each was fitted.
9 Remove the pushrods and note the location from where they came and also which way up. Keep them in order and the right way up by pushing them through a piece of stiff paper with valve numbers marked.
10 Refer to Section 17 and remove the oil pan.
11 Refer to Section 18 and remove the front cover.
12 Refer to Section 19 and remove the camshaft timing gear.
13 Undo and remove the two screws which secure the camshaft thrust plate to the cylinder block face. Lift away the plate and spacer.
14 Using a magnet recover the valve lifters from the 'Vee' in the cylinder block. Keep in order as they must be refitted in their original positions.
15 If any valve lifters cannot be removed, retain in their maximum height positions with clips.
16 The camshaft may now be drawn forwards through the cylinder block. Take care that the sharp edges of the cams do not damage the bearings.

21 Oil pump - removal

1 Refer to Section 17 and remove the oil pan.
2 Undo and remove the two bolts that secure the pump to the crankcase. Lift away the pump and recover the gasket.
3 The long hexagonal section driveshaft will come out with the pump. This is driven by the distributor shaft.

22 Pistons, connecting rods and bearings - removal

1 Pistons and connecting rods may be removed with the engine in the car, provided the oil pan and cylinder heads are first removed. The bearing shells may be removed with the heads on.
2 Slacken the two nuts holding each bearing cap to the connecting-rod. Use a good quality socket wrench for this work. A ring wrench may be used for removal only - not replacement which calls for a special torque wrench. Having slackened the nuts two or three turns tap the caps to dislodge them from the connecting rods. Completely remove the nuts and lift away the end caps.
3 Each bearing cap normally has the cylinder number etched on one end as does the connecting rod. However, this must be verified and if in doubt the cap should be marked with a dab of paint or punch mark to ensure that its relationship with the connecting rod and its numerical

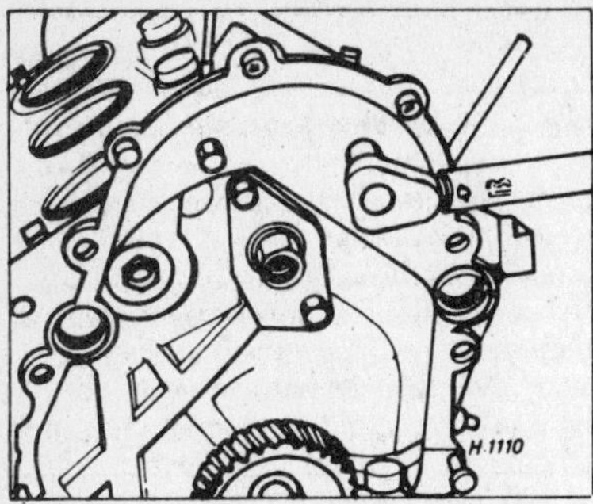

Fig. 1.43. Removing front cover securing bolts (Sec. 18)

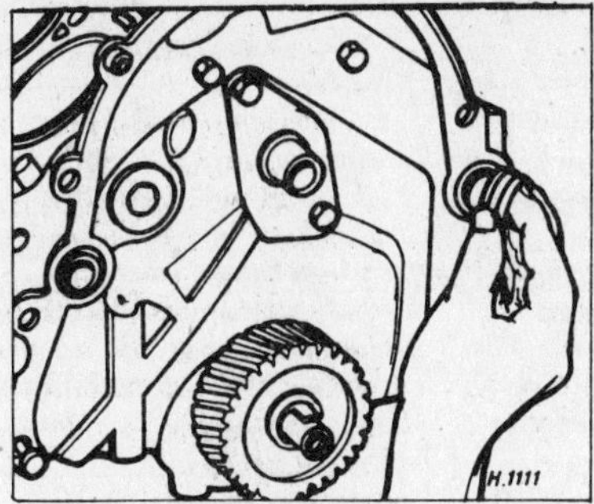

Fig. 1.44. Removing front cover plate sleeves (Sec. 18)

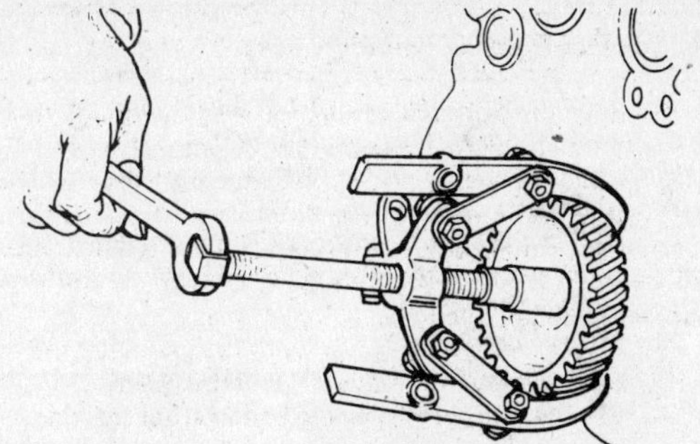

Fig. 1.45. Removing the crankshaft timing gear (Sec. 19)

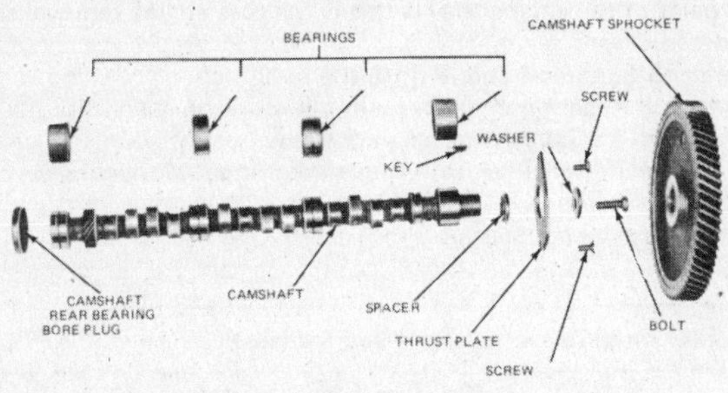

Fig. 1.46. Camshaft components and drive sprocket (Sec. 20)

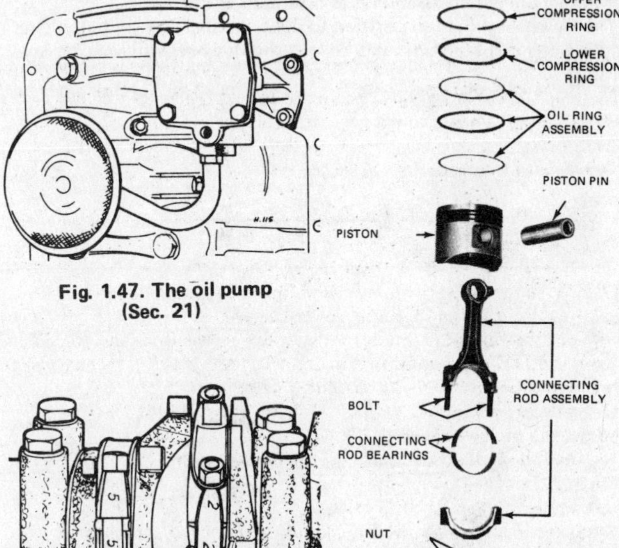

Fig. 1.47. The oil pump (Sec. 21)

Fig. 1.48. Connecting rod bearing identification marks (Sec. 22)

Fig. 1.49. Piston and connecting rod assembly (Sec. 22)

position in the cylinder block is not altered.

4 The piston and connecting rod may then be pushed out of the top of each cylinder.

5 The connecting rod bearing shells can be removed from the connecting rod and cap by sliding them round in the direction of the notch at the end of the shell and lifting them out. If they are not being renewed it is vital they are not interchanged - either between pistons or between cap and connecting rod.

23 Piston rings - removal

1 Remove the pistons from the engine.

2 The rings come off over the top of the piston. Starting with the top one, lift one end of the ring out of the groove and gradually ease it out all the way round. With the second and third rings an old feeler blade is useful for sliding them over the other grooves. However, as rings are only normally removed if they are going to be renewed it should not matter if breakages occur.

24 Piston pin - removal

The piston pins need removing if the pistons are being renewed. New pistons are supplied with new pins for fitting to the existing connecting rods. The piston pin is semi-floating - that is, it is a tight shrink fit with the connecting rod and a moving fit in the piston. To press it out requires considerable force and under usual circumstances a proper press and special tools are essential. Otherwise piston damage will occur. If damage to the pistons does not matter, then the pins may be pressed out using suitable diameter pieces of rod and tube between the jaws of a vise. However, this is not recommended as the connecting rod might be damaged also. It is recommended that piston pins and pistons are removed from, and refitted to, connecting rods, by Ford dealers with the necessary facilities.

25 Crankshaft rear oil seal - removal

It is possible to remove the crankshaft rear oil seal with the engine in or out of the car. Where the engine is being completely removed, refer to Section 26 and remove the crankshaft. The seal can then be drawn from the end of the crankshaft. With the engine in the car proceed as follows:

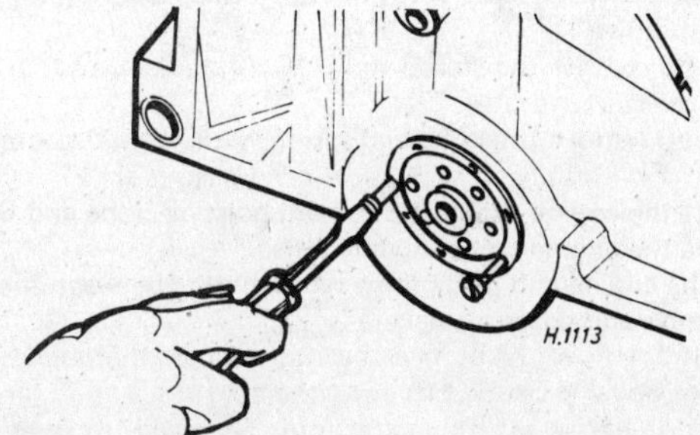

Fig. 1.50. Removing crankshaft rear oil seal (Sec. 25)

1 Refer to Chapter 6 and remove the transmission.

2 Manual gearbox: Refer to Chapter 5 and remove the clutch assembly.

3 Refer to Section 16 and remove the flywheel.

4 Undo and remove the bolts and spring washers that secure the flywheel housing and rear plate where fitted.

5 Using an awl make two holes in the crankshaft rear oil seal. Punch holes on opposite sides of the crankshaft and just above the rear bearing cap to cylinder block split line.

6 Screw two long self-tapping screws into the two holes and with pliers pull or lever out the oil seal. If tight it may be necessary to place small blocks of wood against the cylinder block to provide a fulcrum for the pliers when levering out.

7 Take extreme caution not to scratch the crankshaft oil seal surface.

26 Main bearings and crankshaft - removal

1 The engine should be taken from the car and the oil pan, cylinder heads, timing gears and pistons removed.
2 With a good quality socket wrench undo the eight bolts holding the four main bearing caps.
3 When all the bolts are removed lift out the caps. If they should be tight, tap the sides gently with a piece of wood or soft mallet to dislodge them.
4 Lift out the crankshaft.
5 Slide out the bearing shells from the caps and from the crankcase seats. Note the thrust flanges on No 3 bearing shell

27 Lubrication and crankcases ventilation system - description

1 A general description of the oil circulation system is given in Section 1 of this Chapter.
2 The oil pump is of the eccentric bi-rotor type.
3 The oil is drawn through a gauze screen and tube which is below the oil level in the well of the oil pan. It is then pumped via the full flow oil filter to the system of oil galleries in the block as previously described. The oil filter cartridge is mounted externally on the left-hand side of the block.
4 The crankcase is positively ventilated. Air enters through the oil filler cap in the left-hand rocker cover which is fitted with a washable gauze filter. Air enters directly under the rim of the cap or as in the closed system, the cap is connected to the carburetor air filter by a pipe so that filtration of the air is by existing air filter.
5 Air passes through the pushrod and oil drain channels in the tappet chamber and up the right-hand bank of the block to the right-hand rocker cover. The right hand rocker cover is fitted with an outlet connected by a pipe to the engine intake manifold. A tapered valve in the rocker cover outlet controls the outlet of fumes so that when manifold depression is high the valve closes partially, thus reducing the flow proportionally.

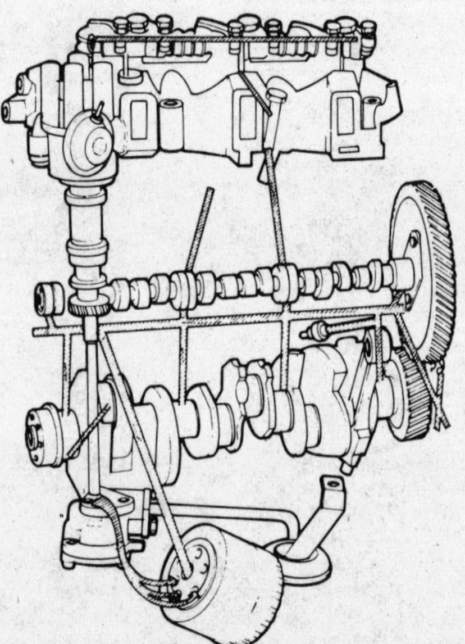
Fig. 1.51. Engine lubrication system (Sec. 27)

28 Oil filter - removal and replacement

The oil filter is a complete throwaway cartridge screwed into the left-hand side of the engine block. Simply unscrew the old unit, clean the seating on the block and screw the new one in, taking care not to cross the thread. Continue until the sealing ring just touches the block face. Then tighten one half turn. Always run the engine and check for signs of leaks after installation.

29 Engine components - examination for wear

When the engine has been stripped down and all parts properly cleaned decisions have to be made as to what needs renewal and the following sections tell the examiner what to look for. In any border line case it is always best to decide in favour of a new part. Even if a part may still be serviceable its life will have been reduced by wear and the degree of trouble needed to replace it in the future must be taken into consideration. However, these things are relative and it depends on whether a quick 'survival' job is being done or whether the car as a whole is being regarded as having many thousands of miles of useful and economical life remaining.

30 Crankshaft - examination and renovation

1 Look at the four main bearing journals and the six crankpins and if there are any scratches or score marks then the shaft will need grinding. Such conditions will nearly always be accompanied by similar deterioration in the matching bearing shells.
2 Each bearing journal should also be round and can be checked with a micrometer or caliper gauge around the periphery at several points. If there is more than 0.001 in (0.0254 mm) of ovality regrinding is necessary.

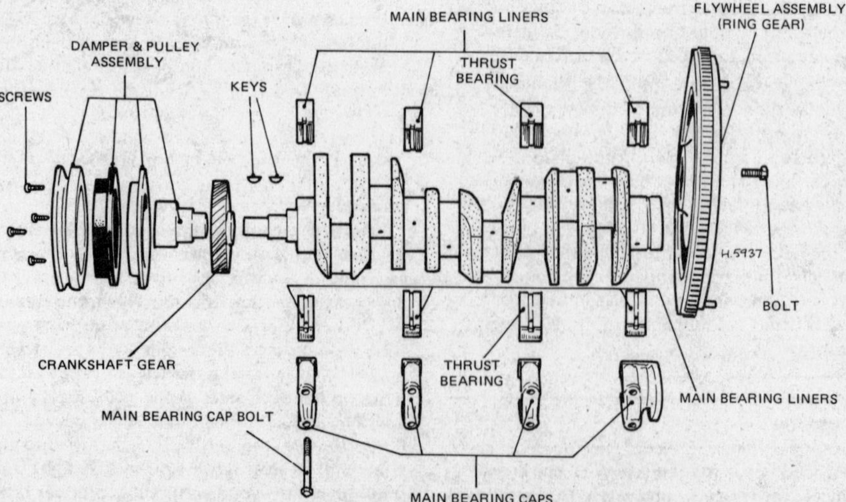

Fig. 1.52. Crankshaft and flywheel assembly (Sec. 30)

3 A main Ford agent or motor engineering specialist will be able to decide to what extent regrinding is necessary and also supply the special under-size shell bearings to match whatever may need grinding off the journals.
4 Before taking the crankshaft for regrinding, check also the cylinder bores and pistons as it may be more convenient to have the engineering operations performed at the same time by the same engineer.

31 Crankshaft (main) bearings and connecting rod bearings - examination and renovation

1 With careful servicing and regular oil and filter changes bearings will last for a very long time but they can still fail for unforeseen reasons. With connecting rod bearings the indications are regular rhythmic loud knocking from the crankcase, the frequency depending on engine speed. It is particularly noticeable when the engine is under load. This symptom is accompanied by a fall in oil pressure although this is not normally noticeable unless an oil pressure gauge is fitted. Main bearing failure is usually indicated by serious vibration, particularly at higher engine revolutions, accompanied by a more significant drop in oil pressure and a 'rumbling' noise.
2 Bearing shells in good condition have bearing surfaces with a smooth, even, matt silver/grey color all over. Worn bearings will show patches of a different color where the bearing metal has worn away and exposed the underlay. Damaged bearings will be pitted or scored. It is nearly always well worthwhile fitting new shells as their cost is relatively low. If the crankshaft is in good condition it is merely a question of obtaining another set of standard size. A reground crankshaft will need new bearing shells as a matter of course.

32 Cylinder bores - examination and renovation

1 A new cylinder is perfectly round and the walls parallel throughout its length. The action of the pistons tends to wear the walls at right angles to the piston pin due to side thrust. This wear takes place principally on that section of the cylinder swept by the piston rings.
2 It is possible to get an indication of bore wear by removing the cylinder heads with the engine still in the car. With the piston down in the bore first signs of wear can be seen and felt just below the top of the bore where the top piston ring reaches and there will be a noticeable lip. If there is no lip it is fairly reasonable to expect that bore wear is low and any lack of compression or excessive oil consumption is due to worn or broken piston rings or pistons (see next Section).
3 If it is possible to obtain a bore measuring micrometer, measure the bore in the thrust plane below the lip and again at the bottom of the cylinder in the same plane. If the difference is more than 0.003 inch (0.0762 mm) then a rebore is necessary. Similarly, a difference of 0.003 inch (0.0762 mm) or more across the bore diameter is a sign of ovality calling for a rebore.
4 Any bore which is significantly scratched or scored will need reboring. This symptom usually indicates that the piston or rings are damaged in that cylinder. In the event of only one cylinder being in need of reboring it will still be necessary for all six to be bored and fitted with new oversize pistons and rings. Your Ford dealer or local engineering specialist will be able to rebore and obtain the necessary matched pistons. If the crankshaft is undergoing regrinding it is a good idea to let the same firm renovate and reassemble the crankshaft and pistons to the block. A reputable firm normally gives a guarantee for such work. In cases where engines have been rebored already to their maximum, new cylinder liners are available which may be fitted. In such cases the same reboring processes have to be followed and the services of a specialist engineering firm are required.

33 Pistons and piston rings - examination and renovation

1 Worn pistons and rings can usually be diagnosed when the symptoms of excessive oil consumption and low compression occur and are sometimes, though not always, associated with worn cylinder bores. Compression testers that fit into the spark plug holes are available and these can indicate where low compression is occuring. Wear usually accelerates the more it is left so when the symptoms occur early action can possible save the expense of a rebore.
2 Another symptom of piston wear is piston slap - a knocking noise from the crankcase not to be confused with connecting rod bearing failure. It can be heard clearly at low engine speed when there is no load (idling for example) and the engine is cold, and is much less audible when the engine speed increases. Piston wear usually occurs in the skirt or lower end of the piston and is indicated by vertical streaks in the worn area which is always on the thrust side. It can also be seen where the skirt thickness is different.
3 Piston ring wear can be checked by first removing the rings from the pistons, as described in Section 23. Then place the rings in the cylinder bores from the top, pushing them down about 1.5 inches (38.1 mm) with the head of a piston (from which the rings have been removed) so that they rest square in the cylinder. Then measure the gap at the ends of the ring with a feeler gauge. If it exceeds 0.023 in (0.584 mm) for the two top compression rings, or 0.055 in (1.397 mm) for the oil control ring then they need renewal.
4 The groove in which the rings locate in the piston can also become enlarged in use. The clearance between ring and piston, in the groove, should not exceed 0.004 inch (0.1016 mm) for the top two compression rings and 0.003 inch (0.0762 mm) for the lower oil control ring.
5 However, it is rare that a piston is only worn in the ring grooves and the need to replace them for this fault alone is hardly ever encountered. Wherever pistons are renewed the weight of the six piston/connecting rod assemblies should be kept within the limit variation of 8 gms. to maintain engine balance.

34 Connecting rods and piston pins - examination and renovation

1 Piston pins are a shrink fit into the connecting rods. Neither of these components would normally need replacement unless the pistons were being changed, in which case the new pistons would automatically be supplied with new pins.
2 Connecting rods are not subject to wear but in extreme circumstances, such as engine seizure, they could be distorted. Such conditions may be visually apparent but where doubt exists they should be changed. The bearing caps should also be examined for indications of filing down which may have been attempted in the mistaken idea that bearing slackness could be remedied in this way. If there are such signs then the connecting rods should be renewed.

35 Camshaft and camshaft bearings - examination and renovation

1 The camshaft bearing bushings should be examined for signs of scoring and pitting. If they need renewal they will have to be dealt with professionally as, although it may be relatively easy to remove the old bushings, the correct fitting of new ones requires special tools. If they are not fitted evenly and square from the very start they can be distorted, thus causing localised wear in a very short time. See your Ford dealer or local engineering specialist for this work.
2 The camshaft itself may show signs of wear on the bearing journals, cam lobes or the skew gear. The main decision to take is what degree of wear justifies replacement, which is costly. Any signs of scoring or damage to the bearing journals must be rectified and as under-size bearing bushings are supplied the journals can be reground. Excessive wear on the skew gear which can be seen where the distributor driveshaft teeth mesh, will mean renewal of the whole camshaft.
3 The cam lobes themselves may show signs of ridging or pitting on the high points. If the ridging is light then it may be possible to smooth it out with fine emery. The cam lobes, however, are surface hardened and once this is penetrated wear will be very rapid thereafter. The cams are also offset and tapered to cause the valve lifters to rotate - thus ensuring that wear is even - so do not mistake this condition for wear.

36 Valve lifters - examination and renovation

1 The faces of the valve lifters which bear on the camshaft should show no signs of pitting, scoring or other forms of wear. They should also not be a loose fit in their housing. Wear is only normally encountered at very high mileages or in cases of neglected engine lubrication. Renew if necessary.

37 Valves and valve seats - examination and renovation

1 With the valves removed from the cylinder heads examine the heads for signs of cracking, burning away and pitting of the edge where it seats in the port. The seats of the valves in the cylinder head should also be examined for the same signs. Usually it is the valve that deteriorates first but if a bad valve is not rectified the seat will suffer and this is more difficult to repair.
2 Some inlet valve heads are coated with diffused aluminium to increase their resistance to oxidisation and to give a hard wear resistant surface on the valve seat area. These valves should in no circumstances be ground as this will remove the aluminium coating. If the valves are worn or pitted they should be replaced with a new set. These valve seats can however, be lapped with an old or dummy valve in the way described below.
3 As far as the exhaust valves and non-coated inlet valves are concerned, provided there are no obvious signs of serious pitting the valve should be ground with its seat. This may be done by placing a smear of carborundum paste on the edge of the valve and, using a suction type valve holder, grinding the valve in-situ. This is done with a semi-rotary action, twisting the handle of the valve holder between the hands and lifting it occasionally to redistribute the paste. Use a coarse paste to start with and finish with a fine paste. As soon as a matt grey unbroken line appears on both the valve and the seat the valve is 'ground-in'. All traces of carbon should also be cleaned from the head and the neck of the valve stem. A wire brush mounted in a power drill is a quick and effective way of doing this.
4 If an exhaust valve requires renewal it should be ground into the seat in the same way as an old valve.
5 Another form of valve wear can occur on the stem where it runs in the guide in the cylinder head. This can be detected by trying to rock the valve from side to side. If there is any movement at all it is an indication that the valve stem or guide is worn. Check the stem first with a micrometer at points all along and around its length and if they are not within the specified size new valves will probably solve the problem. If the guides are worn, however, they will need reboring for oversize valves or for fitting guide inserts. The valve seats will also need recutting to ensure they are concentric with the stems. This work should be given to your Ford dealer or local engineering works.
6 When all valve grinding is completed it is essential that every trace of grinding paste is removed from the valves and ports in the cylinder head. This should be done with thorough washing in gasoline or kerosene and blowing out with a jet of air. If particles of carborundum should work their way into the engine they would cause havoc with bearings or cylinder walls.

38 Timing gears - examination and renovation

Carefully inspect the gear teeth for signs of excessive wear which will cause noisy operation. When assembled to the engine the backlash must not exceed 0.004 in (0.1016 mm).

39 Flywheel ring gear - examination and renovation

1 If the ring gear is badly worn or has missing teeth it should be renewed. The old ring can be removed from the flywheel by cutting a notch between two teeth with a hacksaw and then splitting it with a cold chisel.
2 To fit a new ring gear requires heating the ring to 400° F (204° C). This can be done by polishing four equally spaced sections of the gear, laying it on a suitable heat resistant surface (such as fire bricks) and heating it evenly with a blow lamp or torch until the polished areas turn a light yellow tint. Do not overheat or the hard wearing properties will be lost. The gear has a chamfered inner edge which should go against the shoulder when put on the flywheel. When hot enough place the gear in position quickly, tapping it home if necessary and let it cool naturally without quenching in any way.

40 Oil pump - overhaul

1 The oil pump maintains a pressure of around 45 lb sq in. An oil pressure gauge is fitted to give earlier warning of falling oil pressures due either to overheating, pump or bearing wear.
2 At a major engine overhaul it is as well to check the pump and exchange it for a reconditioned unit if necessary. The efficient operation of the oil pump depends on the finely machined tolerances between the moving parts of the rotor and the body and reconditioning of these is generally not within the competence of the non-specialist owner.
3 To dismantle the pump, first remove it from the engine, as described in Section 21.
4 Remove the two bolts holding the end cover to the body and remove the cover and relief valve parts which will be released.
5 The necessary clearances may now be checked using a machined straight edge (a good steel rule) and a feeler gauge.
6 On bi-rotor type pumps the critical clearances are between the lobes of the center rotor and convex faces of the outer rotor, between the outer rotor and the pump body, and between both rotors and the end cover plate.
7 The rotor lobe clearances may be checked as shown in Fig. 1.54. The clearances should not exceed 0.006 in (0.152 mm). The clearance between the outer rotor and pump body should not exceed 0.010 in (0.254 mm).
8 The endfloat clearance can be measured by placing a steel straight edge across the end of the pump and measuring the gap between the rotors and the straight edge. The gap on either rotor should not exceed 0.005 in (0.127 mm). See Fig 1.55.
9 If the only excessive clearances are endfloat it is possible to reduce them by removing the rotors from the pump body and lapping away the face of the body on a flat bed until the necessary clearances are obtained. It must be emphasised, however, that the face of the body must remain perfectly flat and square to the axis of the rotor spindle otherwise the clearances will not be equal and the end cover will not be a pressure tight fit to the body. It is worth trying, of course, if the pump is in need of renewal any way, but unless done properly it could seriously jeopardise the rest of an overhaul. Any variations in the other clearances should be overcome with an exchange unit.
10 When reassembling the pump and refitting the end cover make sure that the interior is scrupulously clean and that the pressure relief valve parts are assembled in the correct positons.

41 Cylinder heads and piston crowns - decarbonisation

1 When cylinder heads are removed either in the course of an overhaul or for inspection of bores or valve condition when the engine is in the car, it is normal to remove all carbon deposits from the piston crowns and heads.
2 This is best done with a cup shaped wire brush and an electric drill and is fairly straightforward when the engine is dismantled and the pistons removed. Sometimes hard spots of carbon are not easily removed except by a scraper. When cleaning the pistons with a scraper take care not to damage the surface of the piston in any way.
3 When the engine is in the car certain precautions must be taken when decarbonising the piston crowns, in order to prevent dislodged pieces of carbon falling into the interior of the engine which could cause damage to cylinder bores, pistons and rings - or if allowed into the water passages - damage to the water pump. Turn the engine, therefore, so that the piston being worked on is at the top of its stroke and then mask off the adjacent cylinder bore and all surrounding water jacket orifices with paper and adhesive tape. Press grease into the gap all round the piston to keep carbon particles out and then scrape all carbon away by hand carefully. Do not use a power drill and wire brush when the engine is in the car as it will be virtually impossible to keep all the carbon dust clear of the engine. When completed carefully clear out the grease round the rim of the piston with a matchstick or something similar - bringing any carbon particles with it. Repeat the process on the other five piston crowns. It is not recommended that a ring of carbon is left round the edge of the piston on the theory that it will reduce oil consumption. This was valid in the earlier days of long stroke low revving engines but modern engines, fuels and lubricants cause less carbon deposits anyway and any left behind tends merely to cause hot-spots.

42 Rocker gear - examination and renovation

1 Check the shaft for straightness by rolling it on a flat surface. It is most unlikely that it will deviate from normal, but if it does, then a

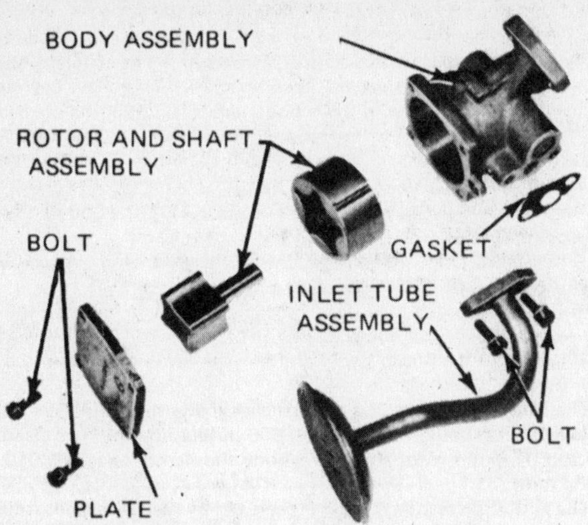

Fig. 1.53. Oil pump components (Sec. 40)

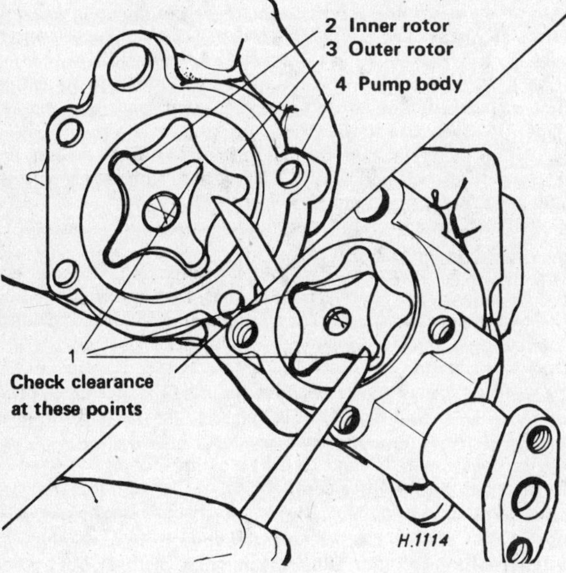

Fig. 1.54. Checking oil pump rotor clearances (Sec. 40)

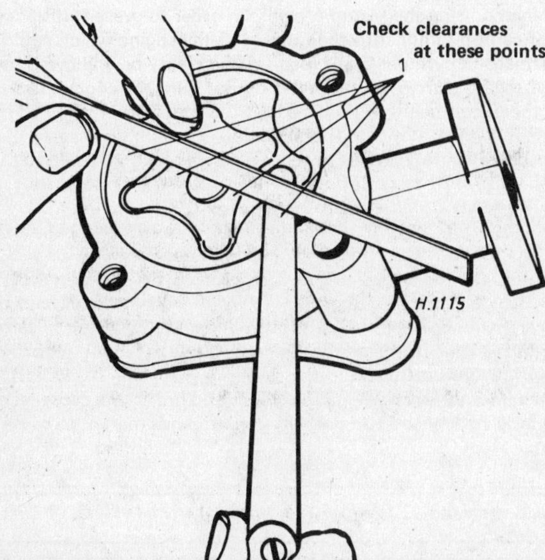

Fig. 1.55. Checking oil pump endfloat clearances (Sec. 40)

judicious attempt may be made to straighten it. If this is not successful purchase a new shaft. The surface of the shaft should be free from any worn ridges caused by the rocker arms. If any wear is evident renew the rocker shaft. Wear is likely to have occurred only if the rocker shaft oil holes have become blocked.

2 Check the rocker arms for wear of the rocker bushes, for wear at the rocker arm face which bears on the valve stem, and for wear of the adjusting ball ended screws. Wear in the rocker arm bush can be checked by gripping the rocker arm tip and holding the rocker arm in place on the shaft, noting if there is any lateral rocker arm shake. If any shake is present, and the arm is loose on the shaft, remedial action must be taken. It is recommended that any worn rocker arm be taken to the local Ford dealer or automobile engineering works to have the old bush drawn out and a new bush fitted.

3 Check the tip of the rocker arm where it bears on the valve head, for cracking or serious wear on the case hardening. If none is present the rocker arm may be refitted. Check the pushrods for straightness by rolling them on a flat surface.

43 Engine reassembly - general

1 All components of the engine must be cleaned of oil sludge and old gaskets and the working area should also be clear and clean. In addition to the normal range of good quality socket spanners and general tools which are essential, the following must be available before reassembly begins:

a) Complete set of new gaskets
b) Supply of clean rags
c) Clean oil can full of clean engine oil
d) Torque spanner
e) All new spare parts as necessary

44 Engine reassembly - camshaft, crankshaft and oil pump

1 Insert the camshaft carefully into the block, taking care not to let any of the cam lobes damage the bearing bushings.

2 Refit the camshaft thrust plate and secure it with the two screws. These screws must be tightened firmly.

3 Select the halves of the four main bearing shells which have the oil hole and grooves and place them in position in the crankcase. The notches on the ends of the shells should locate in the cut-outs in the housings. It is essential that the two surfaces coming together are scrupulously clean. Note the thrust flanges on No 3 shell.

4 Lubricate the bearings generously with clean engine oil.

5 Make sure that the crankshaft is scrupulously clean and lower it carefully into place on the bearings with the gearwheel towards the front of the engine.

6 Fit the plain bearing shells into the main bearing caps, again noting the thrust flanges on No 3 shell.

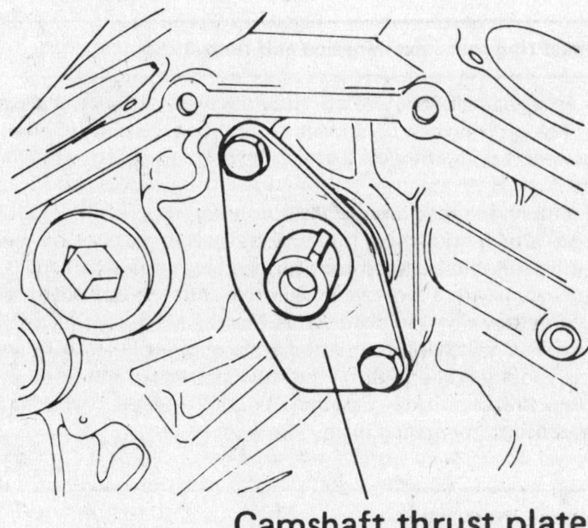

Fig. 1.56. Camshaft thrust plate (Sec. 44)

7 When the crankshaft and center bearing cap is in position the endfloat may be checked by pushing the crankshaft as far as it will go in either direction and checking the gap between the shell flange and the crankshaft web with a feeler gauge. The gap should be between 0.003 and 0.011 in (0.08 to 0.28 mm).
8 The front and rear main bearing caps do not automatically line up for bolting down and it may be necessary to tap them with a hammer handle or other soft weight to enable the bolts to pick up the threads.
9 Make sure that the bolts are clean and tighten them all down evenly to the specified torque setting.
10 Place the new crankshaft rear oil seal squarely in position with the open lip facing away from the shoulder in the bore. The seal can be tapped home squarely with a soft metal drift.
11 It is important to make sure that the seal is driven in squarely from the very start, otherwise it will buckle; if one side tends to go in too far to start with, pull it out and start afresh until it is squarely and firmly 'started' all round.
12 Lubricate the crankshaft flange well so that the seal will not run on a dry surface to start with and heat up.
13 Make sure the hexagonal driveshaft is located in the oil pump (longer section into pump) and replace the pump; tighten the two mounting bolts evenly to the specified torque setting.

45 Engine reassembly - pistons, piston rings, connecting rods, bearings, endplates, timing gear and front cover

1 The subsequent paragraphs on assembly assume that all the checks described in Sections 33 and 34 have been carried out. Also the engine has been partially assembled as described in Section 44.
2 The assembly of new pistons to connecting rods should have been carried out as detailed in Section 24. The new pistons should be supplied with rings already fitted.
3 If new rings are being fitted to existing pistons the following procedure should be followed. Having removed the old rings make sure that each ring groove in the piston is completely cleaned of carbon deposits. This is done most easily by breaking one of the old rings and using the sharp end as a scraper. Be careful not to remove any metal from the groove by mistake! Be careful not to cut your fingers either.
4 The end-gap of the new piston rings - three for each piston - must be checked in the cylinder bores as described in Section 33. It is assumed that the gap at the ends could meet with normal operating temperatures are reached and the rings would then break.
5 The minimum gap for all three rings is 0.015 in (0.38 mm). If the gap is too small, one end of the ring must be filed to increase the gap. To do this the ring should be gripped in a vise between two thin pieces of soft metal in such a way that only the end to be filed is gripped and so that it only protrudes above the jaws of the vise a very small distance. This will eliminate the possibility of bending and breaking the ring while filing the end. Use a thin, fine file and proceed in easy stages checking the gap by replacing the ring in the bore until the necessary minimum gap is obtained. This must be done with every ring, checking each one in the bore to which it will eventually be fitted. To avoid mistakes it is best to complete one set of rings at a time and replace the piston in the cylinder bore before proceeding to the next.
6 To replace the rings on to the pistons calls for patience and care if breakages are to be avoided. The three rings for each piston must all be fitted over the crown, so obviously the first one to go on is the slotted oil control ring. Hold the ring over the top of the piston and spread the ends just enough to get it around the circumference. Then, with the fingers, ease it down, keeping it parallel to the ring grooves by 'walking' the ring ends alternately down the piston. Being wider than the compression rings no difficulty should be encountered in getting it over the first two grooves in the piston.
7 The lower compression ring, which goes on next, must only be fitted one way up. It is marked 'TOP' to indicate its upper face.
8 Start fitting this ring by spreading the ends to get it located over the top of the piston.
9 The lower compression ring has to be guided over the top ring groove and this can be done by using a suitably cut piece of tin which can be placed so as to cover the top groove under the ends of the ring.
10 Alternatively, a feeler blade may be slid around under the ring to guide it into its groove.
11 The top ring may be fitted either way up as it is barrel faced.
12 With the rings fitted, the piston/connecting rod assembly is ready for replacement in the cylinder
13 Each connecting rod and bearing cap should have been marked on removal but in any case the cylinder number is etched lightly on the end of the cap and connecting rod alongside. The piston and connecting rod are also marked to show which side faces the front of the engine.
14 Start with No 1 cylinder and remove the existing oil 'glaze' from the bore by rubbing it down with very fine emery. This will break down the hardened skin and permit the new piston rings to bed down more quickly. Clean away any abrasive dust.
15 Fit a new shell bearing half into the connecting rod of No 1 piston so that the notch in the bearing shell locates in the groove in the connecting rod.
16 Push the piston into the cylinder bore (the correct way round) until the oil control ring abuts the face of the block. Then, using a piston ring compressor contract the rings and tap the piston into the cylinder. Take great care to be sure that a ring is not trapped on the top edge of the cylinder bore and when tapping the piston in do not use any force. If this is not done the rings could easily be broken.
17 When the piston has been fully located in the bore push it down so that the end of the connecting rod seats on the journal on the crankshaft. Make sure the journal is well lubricated with engine oil.
18 Maintaining absolute cleanliness all the time fit the other shell bearing half into the cap, once again with the notches in the bearing and cap lined up. Lubricate it with engine oil and fit it onto the connecting rod so that the holes in the cap fit to the dowels in the connecting rod.
19 Replace all pistons and connecting rods in a similar manner and do not make any mistakes locating the correct number piston in the correct bore. Numbers 1, 2 and 3 cylinders are on the right-hand bank and numbers 4, 5 and 6 on the left-hand bank starting from the front of the engine. However, due to the 'Vee' formation of the engine the big-end journals on the crankshaft starting at the front run 1, 4, 2, 5, 3, and 6. This is different again from the firing order so make sure you have it all clear in your mind to start with!
20 When all caps are correctly fitted tighten down the bolts to the correct torque (see Specifications).
21 The timing gears are easily fitted but care must be taken to ensure that the marks line up properly. The camshaft and crankshaft gears are keyed to their respective shafts. The timing marks are in the form of a single dimple on one tooth of each gearwheel (see Fig. 1.63).
22 Before replacing the camshaft timing gear, the front engine plate must be replaced. Select the new gasket and coat the clean face of the block with suitable sealing compound and stick the gasket to it in position. Then offer up the cover plate.
23 Bolt the cover plate up tight to the block, not forgetting to fit the support plate behind the three center bolts.
24 Fit the camshaft and crankshaft gears so that the timing marks line up. Replace the camshaft gear locking bolt and washer. Tighten the bolt to the specified torque setting.
25 If the crankshaft pulley wheel oil seal is being replaced in the front cover it will be necessary to take care in driving out the old one as the cover is a light alloy casting which will not stand rough treatment. As the old seal must be driven out from the front it is essential to find two pieces of wood thicker than the depth of the cover so that the immediate area near the seal ring may be supported.
26 With the cover firmly supported inside, it can be laid on the bench and the old seal driven out with a punch.
27 Turn the cover over and carefully tap in the new seal evenly with the inner lip facing away from the shoulder in the bore.
28 Tap the seal home finally with a block of wood.
29 Select the front cover gasket and using a suitable sealing compound position it on the engine front plate and offer up the cover.
30 Place the front cover bolts in position and screw them up loosely. Then fit the crankshaft pulley wheel onto the keyway of the crankshaft. See that the boss of the pulley is lubricated where the oil seal runs.
31 The replacement of the crankshaft pulley, before tightening the cover bolts, centralises the seal to the pulley. The bolts holding the cover may then be tightened to the specified torque setting.

46 Engine reassembly - rear plate, crankshaft pulley wheel, oil pan and flywheel

1 If the engine rear plate has been removed it should now be replaced.

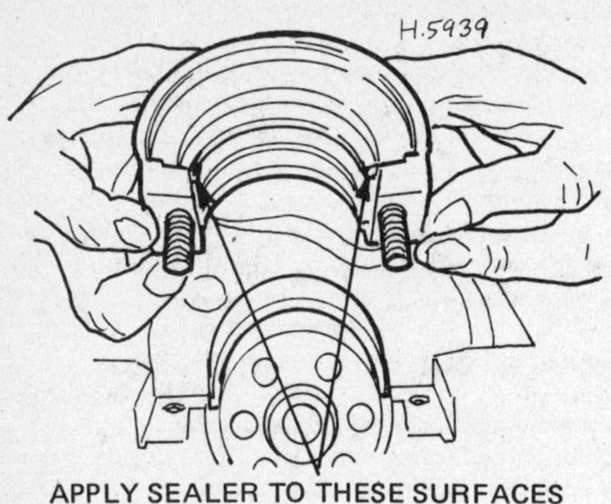

Fig. 1.58. Inserting rear bearing wedge seals (Sec. 44)

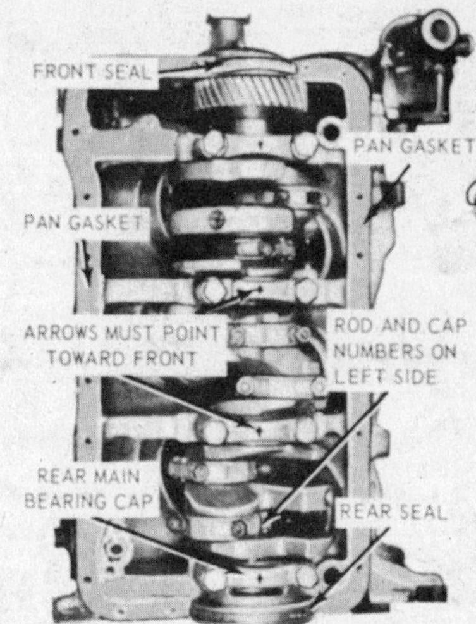

Fig. 1.59. Underside view of engine

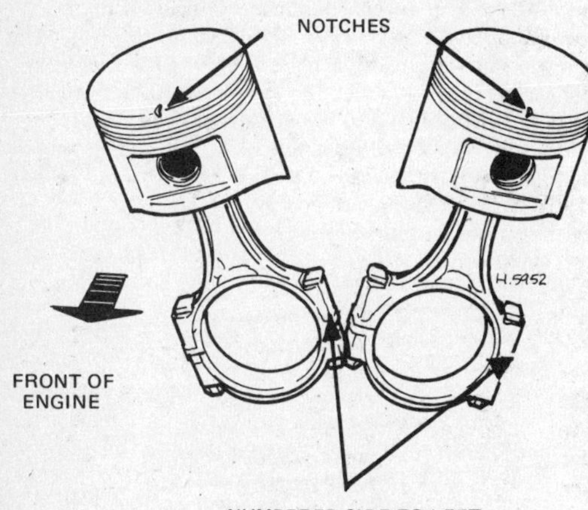

Fig. 1.60. Correct location of pistons and connecting rods (Sec. 45)

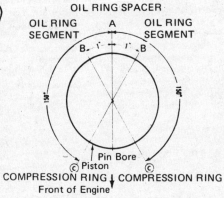

Fig. 1.61. Spacing the piston ring gaps (Sec. 45)

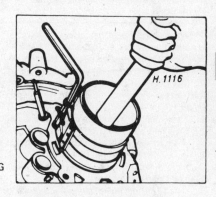

Fig. 1.62. Refitting a piston (Sec. 45)

Fig. 1.63. Alignment of timing gear marks (Sec. 45)

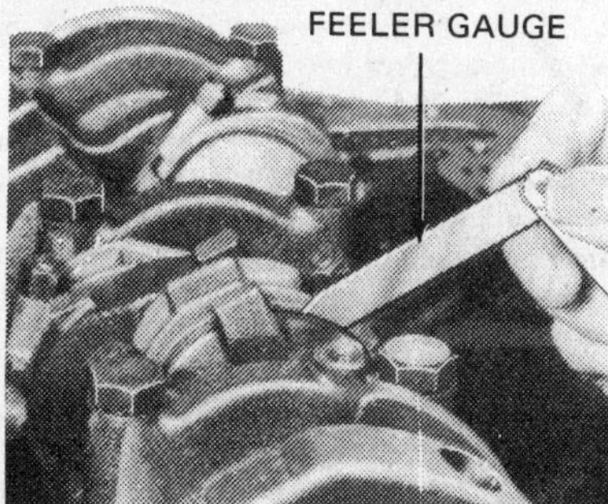

Fig. 1.64. Checking connecting rod side clearances (Sec. 45)

Make sure that both metal faces are quite clean before refitting. No gasket is used.

2 Replace the bolt and washer which locate the crankshaft pulley wheel, block the crankshaft with a piece of wood against the side of the crankcase and tighten the bolt to the specified torque setting.

3 Trim the projecting pieces of the front cover and backplate gaskets at the oil pan face of the block and front cover.

4 Trim the projecting edge of the rear oil seal carrier on the oil pan face at the rear of the crankcase.

5 Clean all traces of old gasket which may remain from the oil pan joint faces and cover the faces of both the crankcase and pan with sealing compound. The oil pan gasket is in four sections which dovetail together and these should be carefully positioned and the joints interlocked.

6 The engine is then ready for the oil pan to be replaced.

7 Clean the interior of the pan thoroughly, apply sealer to the joint edge and place it in position.

8 Replace all the oil pan bolts and tighten them evenly to the specified torque setting (Fig. 1.65).

9 The flywheel (or adapter plate) may now be replaced. Make sure that the mating flanges are clean and free from burrs and line up the bolt holes correctly. They are so positioned that they will only line up

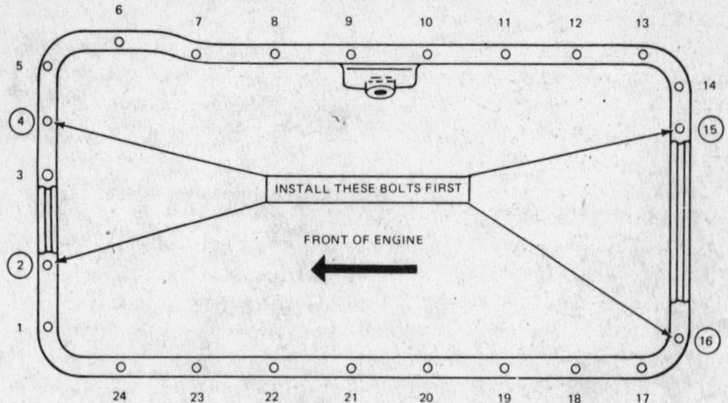

Fig. 1.65. Correct tightening sequence for oil pan bolts (Sec. 46)

in one position. Do not hammer the flywheel into position if it should be difficult to get it fully onto the flange. Support it squarely and refit the bolts, tightening them evenly so as to draw the flywheel squarely onto its seat. There are no washers and the bolts should be tightened evenly and progressively to the specified torque setting.

47 Engine reassembly - valve gear, cylinder heads, inlet and exhaust manifolds

1 When the cylinder heads have been decarbonised and the valves ground in as described in Sections 37 and 41, the cylinder heads may be reassembled. If the valves have been removed as described in Section 12 there will be no confusion as to which valve belongs in which position.
2 Make sure all traces of carbon and grinding paste have been removed, lubricate the valve stem with engine oil and place it in the appropriate guide.
3 It will then protrude through the top of the cylinder head.
4 Fit a new seal cup over the valve stem.
5 Place the valve spring over the valve stem with the close coils of the spring nearest the cylinder head.
6 Fit the circular retainer over the spring with the protruding centre boss retainer downwards.
7 Using a proper valve spring compressor tool, compress the spring down the valve stem sufficiently far to enable the two halves of the locks (collets) to be fitted into the groove in the valve stem. If necessary the locks should be smeared with grease to keep them in position. The spring compressor may then be released. Watch to ensure that the locks stay together in position as the retainer comes past them. If the retainer is a little off centre it may force one lock out of its groove in which case the spring must be recompressed and the lock repositioned. When the compressor is finally released, tap the head of the valve stem with a soft mallet to make sure the valve assembly is securely held in position.
8 Stand the engine the right way up on the bench and replace the valve lifters if they have been removed from the block. If these have been kept in order on removal, as suggested, it will be a simple matter to replace them.
9 The cylinder head gaskets are not interchangeable but are marked 'TOP' and 'FRONT' to indicate the upper surface and which end is next to the timing gear.
10 Position the cylinder heads on a clean surface, identified as to which bank (left or right) they are to be refitted.
11 Locate the gasket over the protruding spigots in the block and then place the cylinder head in position.
12 Make sure the cylinder head bolts are clean and lightly oiled and replace them. Nip them all down lightly and then tighten them in the sequence shown in Fig. 1.39. The bolts should be tightened down in three stages to the specified torque.
13 Now fit the pushrods into position, making sure that they are replaced the same way up as they came out and according to the original valve position. This will not be difficult if they have been kept in order.
Reassemble the rocker shaft assemblies in the order shown in Fig. 1.41.
14 Refit the rocker shaft assemblies to the cylinder heads and secure to the cylinder heads with the three bolts and washers.
15 The inlet manifolds may now be refitted to the cylinder heads. In view of the large area to be sealed for both air and water it is a safety measure - if not essential - to use a jointing compound. In addition to the gasket on the mating surfaces.
16 Place the inlet manifold gasket in position in the Vee so that the single square hole is on the left-hand cylinder head. The gasket is obviously incorrect if put on any other way but this is a positive guide.
17 Apply jointing compound to the mating faces of the inlet manifold. Note the square port which matches the gasket hole and port in the left-hand cylinder head.
18 Place the manifold in position taking care not to disturb the gasket.
19 Replace the manifold securing bolts, ensuring that the gasket is lined up to permit them to pick up the threads in the cylinder heads, and screw them up lightly.
20 With a torque wrench tighten the bolts down evenly to the specified torque. This tightening should also be done in stages. Any uneven or excessive tightening may crack the manifold casting so take care (Fig. 1.36).

48 Valve lash - adjustment

1 The valve stem to rocker clearance, which is in effect the mechanical free play between the camshaft and the end of the valve stem, is important to the correct operation and performance of the engine. If the clearance is too great the valve opening is reduced with consequent reduction in gas flow - and is also very noisy. If the clearance is too little the valve could open too much with the danger of hitting the crown of the piston. The clearance is checked when the tappet is on the heel of the cam (opposite the highest point) and the valve therefore closed. This position coincides with certain other valves being fully open with their tappets on the high point of the cam. This can be seen easily when the valve spring is fully compressed.
2 The table below shows the relationship between the fully open valves and the closed valves which are to be checked.

Valves open	Adjust valves
No 5 cylinder	*No 1 cylinder*
No 3 cylinder	*No 4 cylinder*
No 6 cylinder	*No 2 cylinder*
No 1 cylinder	*No 5 cylinder*
No 4 cylinder	*No 3 cylinder*
No 2 cylinder	*No 6 cylinder*

3 For valve stem to rocker clearance dimensions, refer to the Specifications Section at the beginning of this Chapter.
4 The actual adjustment procedure is straightforward. With the appropriate valve ready for checking, place a feeler gauge of the required thickness (for exhaust or inlet valve) between the top of the valve stem and the rocker arm. If it will not go in or it is too loose, screw the lash adjuster in or out until the correct setting is obtained.

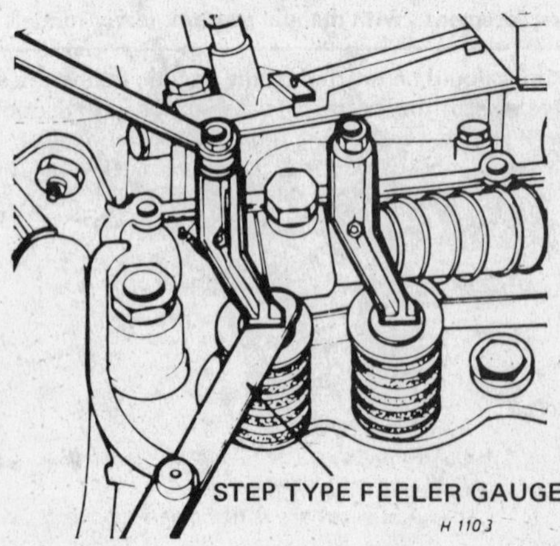

Fig. 1.66. Adjusting the valve clearances (Sec. 48)

49 Engine reassembly - fitting ancillary components

1 The exhaust manifolds are best replaced before putting the engine back into the car as they provide very useful holds if the engine has to be manhandled at all. Note that no gaskets are used on the exhaust manifolds.
2 Replace each manifold and tighten the bolts evenly.
3 The ancillary engine components must be replaced and the method of doing this is detailed in the appropriate Chapters. Section 9 of this Chapter gives a full list of the items involved. When this has been done the engine is ready to be put back in the car.

50 Engine replacement - without gearbox

1 The engine must be positioned suitably so that the sling used to remove it can be easily refitted and the lifting tackle hooked on. Position the engine the right way round in front of the car and then raise it so that it may be brought into position over the car, or the car rolled into position underneath it.
2 The gearbox should be jacked up to its approximately normal position.
3 Lower the engine steadily into the engine compartment, keeping all ancillary wires, pipes and cables well clear of the sides. It is best to have a second person guiding the engine while it is being lowered.
4 The tricky part is finally mating the engine to the gearbox, which involves locating the gearbox input shaft into the clutch housing and flywheel. Provided that the clutch friction plate has been centered correctly as described in Chapter 5, there should be little difficulty. Grease the splines of the gearbox input shaft first. It may be necessary to rock the engine from side to side in order to get the engine fully home. Under no circumstances let any strain be imparted onto the gearbox input shaft. This could occur if the shaft was not fully located and the engine was raised or lowered more than the amount required for very slight adjustment of position.
5 As soon as the engine is fully up to the gearbox bellhousing replace the bolts holding the two together.
6 Now finally lower the engine onto its mounting brackets at the front and replace and tighten down the nuts, and washers.
7 Replace all electrical connections, the fuel lines and carburetor linkages, cooling system hoses and radiator in the reverse order to that described in Section 5.
8 Reconnect the clutch cable as described in Chapter 5, replace the exhaust pipes and reconnect them to the manifold extensions, replace the plate covering the lower half of the bellhousing and remove the supporting jack.
9 Fill the engine with fresh oil and replace the coolant.

51 Engine replacement - with manual gearbox (early models only)

1 The gearbox should be refitted to the engine, taking the same precautions as regards the input shaft as mentioned in Section 50.
2 The general principles of lifting the engine/gearbox assembly are the same as for the engine above but the gearbox will tilt everything to a much steeper angle. Replacement will certainly require the assistance of a second person.
3 Lift the gearbox end of the unit into the engine compartment (unless you are fortunate enough to have a hoist with a very high lift) and then lower and guide the unit down. One of the first things to be done is to reconnect the propeller shaft into the gearbox rear extension casing so someone should be ready to lift and guide the propeller shaft into position as soon as the gearbox is near enough. This cannot be done after the unit has been lowered beyond a certain position.
4 If a trolley jack is available this is the time to place it under the gearbox so that as the engine is lowered further the rear end can be supported and raised as necessary - at the same time being able to roll back as required. Without such a jack, support the rear in such a way that it can slide if possible. In any case the gearbox will have to be jacked and held up in position when the unit nears its final position.
5 Locate the front mounting brackets on the locating bolts as described in Section 50.
6 Refit the speedometer drive cable with the gearbox drive socket and refit the circlip and bolt. This **must** be done before the gearbox supporting crossmember is in place.
7 Jack up the rear of the gearbox and position the crossmember to the bodyframe. Then replace and tighten down the four retaining bolts and the centre bolt to the gearbox extension.
8 Replace the gearbox remote control shift lever and housing as described in Chapter 6.
9 Reconnect the clutch cable and adjust as described in Chapter 5 and reconnect the back-up light wire. The final connections should then be made as described in Section 50 and in addition to the engine lubricant and coolant, the gearbox should also be refilled with fresh oil.

52 Engine - initial start-up after overhaul or major repair

1 Make sure that the battery is fully charged and that all lubricants, coolants and fuel are replenished.
2 If the fuel system has been dismantled it will require several revolutions of the engine on the starter motor to get the gas up to the carburetor.
3 As soon as the engine fires and runs keep it going at a fast tickover only (no faster) and bring it up to normal working temperature.
4 As the engine warms up there will be odd smells and some smoke from parts getting hot and burning off oil deposits. The signs to look for are leaks of oil or water which will be obvious if serious. Check also the clamp connections of the exhaust pipes to the manifolds as these do not always 'find' their exact gas tight position until warmth and vibration have acted on them and it is almost certain that they need tightening further. This should be done, of course, with the engine stopped.
5 When running temperature has been reached adjust the idling speed as described in Chapter 3.
6 Stop the engine and wait a few minutes to see if any lubricants or coolant is dripping out when the engine is stationary.
7 Road test the car to check that the timing is correct and giving the necessary smoothness and power. Do not race the engine - if new bearings and/or pistons and rings have been fitted it should be treated as a new engine and run in at reduced revolutions for 500 miles (800 km).
8 Bleed the power steering (if fitted) as described in Chapter 11.

For 'Fault diagnosis - engine' see next page

53 Fault diagnosis - engine (4 and 6 cylinder)

Symptom	Reason/s	Remedy
Engine will not turn over when starter switch is operated	Flat battery Bad battery connections Bad connections at solenoid switch and/or starter motor	Check that battery is fully charged and that all connections are clean and tight.
	Defective solenoid	Bridge the main terminals of the solenoid switch with a piece of heavy duty cable in order to operate the starter.
	Starter motor defective	Remove and overhaul starter motor.
Engine turns over normally but fails to fire and run	No spark at plugs	Check ignition system according to procedures given in Chapter 4.
	No fuel reaching engine	Check fuel system according to procedures given in Chapter 3.
	Too much fuel reaching the engine (flooding)	Check the fuel system as above.
Engine starts but runs unevenly and misfires	Ignition and/or fuel system faults	Check the ignition and fuel systems as though the engine had failed to start.
	Incorrect valve clearances	Check and reset clearances (V6 only).
	Burnt out valves Blown cylinder head gasket	Remove cylinder heads and examine and overhaul as necessary.
	Worn out piston rings Worn cylinder bores	Remove cylinder heads and examine pistons and cylinder bores. Overhaul as necessary.
Lack of power	Ignition and/or fuel system faults	Check the ignition and fuel systems for correct ignition timing and carburetor settings.
	Incorrect valve clearances	Check and reset the clearances (V6 only).
	Burnt out valves Blown cylinder head gasket	Remove cylinder heads and examine and overhaul as necessary.
	Worn out piston rings Worn cylinder bores	Remove cylinder heads and examine pistons and cylinder bores. Overhaul as necessary.
Excessive oil consumption	Oil leaks from crankshaft rear oil seal, timing cover gasket and oil seal, rocker cover gasket, oil filter gasket, sump gasket, sump plug washer.	Identify source of leak and renew seal as appropriate.
	Worn piston rings or cylinder bores resulting in oil being burnt by engine - smoky exhaust is an indication	Fit new rings or rebore cylinders and fit new pistons, depending on degree of wear.
	Worn valve guides and/or defective valve stem seals - smoke blowing out from the rocker cover vents is an indication	Remove cylinder heads and recondition valve stem bores and valves and seals as necessary.
Excessive mechanical noise from engine	Wrong valve to rocker clearances	Adjust valve clearances (V6 only)*
	Worn crankshaft bearings Worn cylinders (piston slap) Worn timing gears	Inspect and overhaul where necessary.

Note 1: When investigating starting and uneven running faults do not be tempted into snap-diagnosis. Start from the beginning of the check procedure and follow it through. It will take less time in the long run. Poor performance from an engine in terms of power and economy is not normally diagnosed quickly. In any event the ignition and fuel systems must be checked first before assuming any further investigation needs to be made.

**Note 2: The 2.3 liter engine is fitted with hydraulic valve lash adjusters which may produce a mechanical tapping noise on initial start-up. However as the engine lubricating oil circulates, and the lifters 'jump-up', the noise should disappear. If it does not, the lash adjusters should be inspected for correct operation.*

Chapter 2 Cooling system

For modifications, and information applicable to later models, see Supplement at end of manual

Contents

Specifications

System type	Pressurised, assisted by pump and fan
Thermostat	
Type	Wax filled
Location:	
2300cc (4 cylinder)	Front of cylinder head
2800cc (V6)	Bottom of cylinder block front cover
Opening temperature	188° - 195°F (86 - 91°C)
Fully open	212° - 215°F (100 - 101°C)
Radiator	
Type	Corrugated fin
Pressure cap setting	13 psi (0.91 kgf/cm^2)
Water pump	Centrifugal impeller type
Drivebelt tension	Approximately 0.5 in (13 mm) of movement at midpoint of the longest span of belt
Cooling system capacities	
2300cc without air-conditioning	8.7 US quarts (9.2 liters)
2300cc with air-conditioning	10 US quarts (9.46 liters)
2800cc without air-conditioning (manual)	9.2 US quarts (8.71 liters)
2800cc without air-conditioning (automatic)	9.4 US quarts (8.90 liters)
2800cc with air conditioning (manual or automatic)	9.4 US quarts (8.90 liters)

Torque wrench settings	**lb f ft**	**kg f m**
Fan to pulley hub	12 to 18	1.6 to 3.5
Water pump bolts	6 to 12	1.0 to 1.6
Alternator pivot bolts:		
2300cc engine	15 to 18	2.0 to 3.5
2800cc engine	40 to 50	6.0 to 7.0
Thermostat housing bolts	12 to 15	1.66 to 2.07

1 General description

The cooling system on both the 2300cc (4 cylinder) and 2800cc (V6) engines comprises a radiator connected to the engine by top and bottom water hoses, a belt-driven fan and water pump and a thermostat. Small bore hoses transfer water to the heater and automatic choke control unit.

The unit manifold is water heated and on some models the fan incorporates a temperature controlled fluid coupling which reduces power absorption and fan noise.

The cooling system is pressurised to enable a higher operating temperature to be maintained without boiling. If the water pressure within the system rises above the preset limit of the radiator cap, (see Specifications) the spring-loaded valve within the cap opens and allows the excess water to pass along an overflow pipe, thus relieving the pressure. It is therefore important to ensure that the cap has the correct pressure setting stamped on the top and that the spring and sealing washer are in good condition.

The system functions in the following fashion. Cold water in the bottom of the radiator circulates up the lower radiator hose to the water pump where it is pushed round the water passages in the cylinder block, helping to keep the cylinder bores and pistons cool.

The water then travels up into the cylinder head and circulates round the combustion spaces and valve seats absorbing more heat.

On the 2300cc engine the thermostat is located on the front of the cylinder head and when the engine reaches working temperature it opens, allowing hot water to pass along the top hose into the radiator to be cooled.

The thermostat on the V6 engine is located at the bottom of the front engine cover and when open it enables the pump to draw water from the radiator into the engine via the bottom hose.

On both engines the function of the thermostat is to restrict water flow between the radiator and engine providing fast warm-up until normal operating temperature is reached.

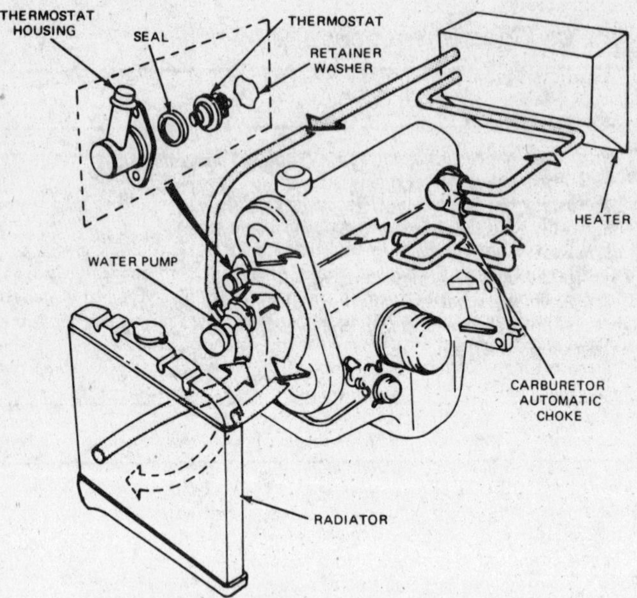

Fig. 2.1. Cooling system (2300cc engine)

2 Cooling system - draining

1 If the engine is cold, remove the filler cap from the radiator by turning the cap anticlockwise. If the engine is hot, then turn the filler cap very slightly until pressure in the system has had time to be released. Use a rag over the cap to protect your hand from escaping steam. If, with the engine very hot, the cap is released suddenly, the drop in pressure can result in the water boiling. With the pressure released the cap can be removed.
2 If antifreeze is used in the cooling system, drain it into a bowl having a capacity of at least that of the cooling system, for re-use.
3 Open the drain plug located at the base of the radiator, or remove the bottom radiator hose. Also remove the engine drain plug which is located at the rear left-hand side of the cylinder block on 2300cc engines and one on each side of the block on V6 engines. If the heater has a water control valve, open this also to drain the heat exchanger.
4 When the water has finished running, probe the drain plug orifices with a short piece of wire to dislodge any particles of rust or sediment which may be causing a blockage.
5 It is important to note that the heater on most models cannot be drained completely during the cold weather so an antifreeze solution must be used. Always use an antifreeze with an ethylene-glycol or glycerine base.

3 Cooling system - flushing

1 In time the cooling system will gradually lose its efficiency as the radiator becomes choked with rust, scale deposits from the water, and other sediment. To clean the system out, remove the radiator filler cap and drain plug and leave a hose running in the filler cap neck for ten to

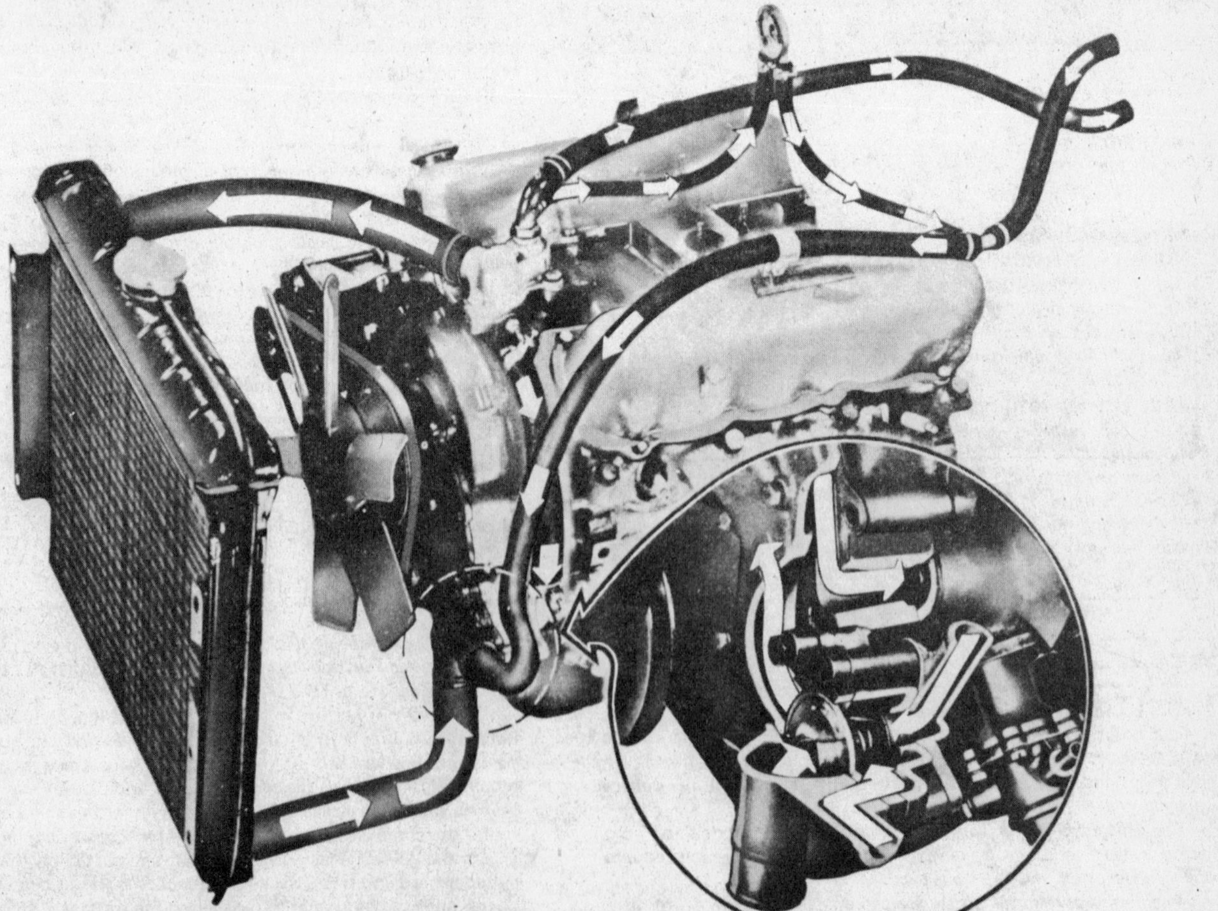

Fig. 2.2. Cooling system (V6 engine)

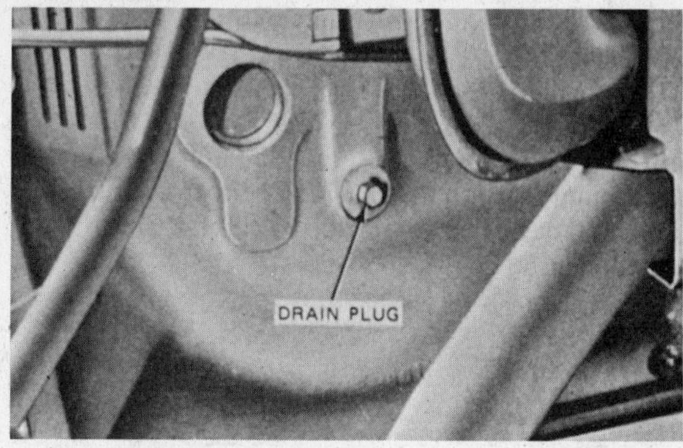

Fig. 2.3. Cylinder block drain plug (2300cc engine) (Sec. 2)

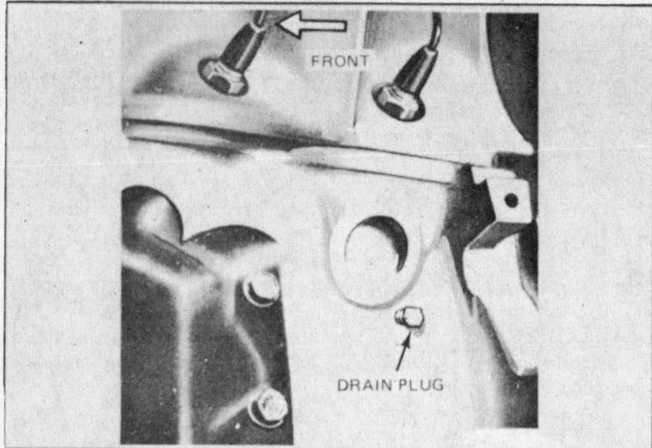

Fig. 2.4. Cylinder block drain plug (V6 engine, one each side) (Sec. 2)

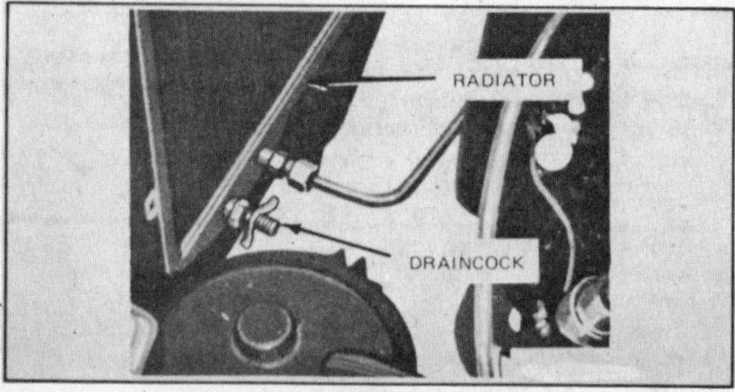

Fig. 2.5. Radiator drain tap (Sec. 2)

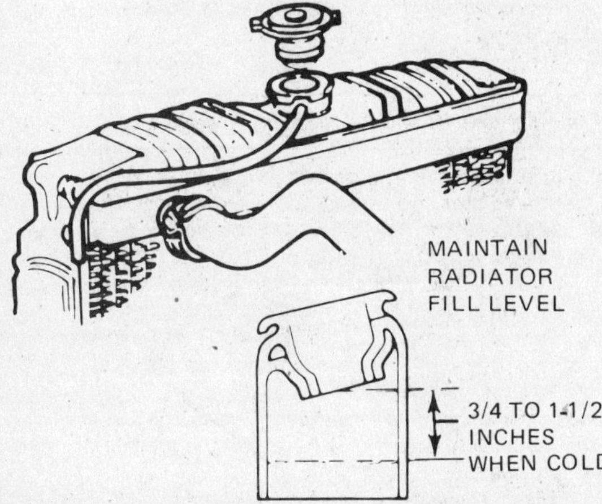

Fig. 2.6. Radiator filler cap and water level (Sec. 4)

fifteen minutes.

2 In very bad cases the radiator should be reverse flushed. This can be done with the radiator in position. The cylinder block plug is removed and a hose with a suitable tapered adaptor placed in the drain plug hole. Water under pressure is then forced through the radiator and out of the header tank filler cap neck.

3 It is recommended that some polythene sheeting is placed over the engine to stop water finding its way into the electrical system.

4 The hose should now be removed and placed in the radiator cap filler neck, and the radiator washed out in the usual manner.

4 Cooling system - filling

1 Refit the cylinder block and radiator drain plugs.

2 Fill the system slowly to ensure that no air lock develops. If the heater has a water control valve, check that it is open (control at hot), otherwise an air lock may form in the heater. The best type of water to use in the cooling system is rain water; mixed in the correct proportion with the recommended antifreeze/rust inhibitor solution.

3 Do not fill the system higher than within ¾ to 1½ inch (19 to 38 mm) of the filler neck. Overfilling will merely result in wastage, which is especially to be avoided when antifreeze is in use.

4 It is usually found that air locks develop in the heater radiator so the system should be vented during refilling by detaching the heater supply hose from the elbow connection on the water outlet housing.

5 Pour coolant into the radiator filler neck whilst the end of the heater supply hose is held at the elbow connection height. When a constant stream of water flows from the supply hose quickly refit the hose. If venting is not carried out it is possible for the engine to overheat. Should the engine overheat for no apparent reason then the system should be vented before seeking other causes. On some models a bleed nipple is incorporated in the coolant hose which runs at the rear of the engine.

6 After filling the system run the engine with the filler cap off until normal operating temperature is reached. Check the coolant level and refill if necessary.

7 Refit the radiator cap and turn it clockwise to lock it in position.

5 Radiator - removal inspection, cleaning and replacement

1 Drain the cooling system as described in Section 2 of this Chapter.

2 Slacken the two clips which hold the top and bottom radiator hoses on the radiator and carefully pull off the two hoses (photo).

3 As applicable, remove radiator upper splash shield and disconnect the hoses from the automatic transmission oil cooler. Plug the ends of the hoses to prevent fluid loss and ingress of dirt.

4 Undo and remove the four bolts that secure the radiator shroud to the radiator side panels and move the shroud over the fan blades. This

5.2 Removing top hose clamp

is only applicable when a shroud is fitted.
5 Undo and remove the four bolts that secure the radiator to the front panel. The radiator may now be lifted upwards and away from the engine compartment. The fragile matrix must not be touched by the fan blades as it is easily punctured.
6 Lift the radiator shroud from over the fan blades and remove from the engine compartment.
7 With the radiator away from the car any leaks can be soldered or repaired with a suitable proprietary substance. Clean out the inside of the radiator by flushing as described earlier in this Chapter. When the radiator is out of the car it is advantageous to turn it upside down and reverse flush. Clean the exterior of the radiator by carefully using a compressed air jet or a strong jet of water to clear away any road dirt, flies etc.
8 Inspect the radiator hoses for cracks, internal or external perishing and damage by overtightening of the securing clips. Also inspect the overflow pipe. Renew the hoses if suspect. Examine the radiator hose clips and renew them if they are rusted or distorted.
9 The drain plug and washer should be renewed if it is leaking.
10 Refitting the radiator is the reverse sequence to removal. After refilling the system run the engine and check for leaks.
11 If a transmission oil cooler is fitted, check the hoses for leaks and top-up the fluid level, if necessary.

6 Thermostat - removal and refitting (2300cc engine)

1 Partially drain the cooling system, as described in Section 2.
2 Slacken the top radiator hose to the thermostat housing and remove the hose.
3 Undo and remove the two bolts and spring washers that secure the thermostat housing to the cylinder head.
4 Carefully lift the thermostat housing away from the cylinder head. Recover the joint washer adhering to either the housing or cylinder head.
5 Withdraw the thermostat, making a note of which way round it is fitted.
6 Refit the thermostat using the reverse procedure to dismantling.
7 Always ensure that the thermostat housing and cylinder head mating faces are clean and flat. If the thermostat housing is badly corroded fit a new housing. Always use a new gasket. Tighten the two securing bolts to the specified torque.

7 Thermostat - removal and refitting (V6 engine)

1 To remove the thermostat first drain the cooling system as described in Section 2.
2 Slacken the clips that secure the radiator bottom hose and heater return hose to the thermostat housing. Carefully detach the hoses from the thermostat housing.
3 Undo and remove the three bolts and spring washers that secure the thermostat housing cover to the front cover.
4 Draw the housing from the front cover. Tap the side very gently if it has stuck to the gasket and front cover. Recover the gasket.
5 Remove the inner circular gasket and withdraw the thermostat noting which way round it is fitted (see Fig. 2.8).
6 Replacing the thermostat is the reverse sequence to removal. It is recommended that new gaskets are fitted.
7 Clean the faces of the housing and the front cover to ensure a water tight joint. If the housing has corroded badly a new one should be fitted.
8 Refill the cooling system, as described in Section 4, and finally check for water leaks.

8 Thermostat - testing

1 Remove the thermostat, as described in the previous Sections.
2 Test the thermostat for correct functioning by suspending it on a string in a saucepan of cold water together with a thermometer. Heat the water and note the temperature at which the thermostat begins to open. This should be as given in the Specifications. Continue heating the water until the thermostat is fully open. Then let it cool down naturally.
3 If the thermostat does not fully open in boiling water, or does not close down as the water cools, then it must be discarded and a new one fitted. Should the thermostat be stuck open when cold this will usually be apparent when removing it from the housing.

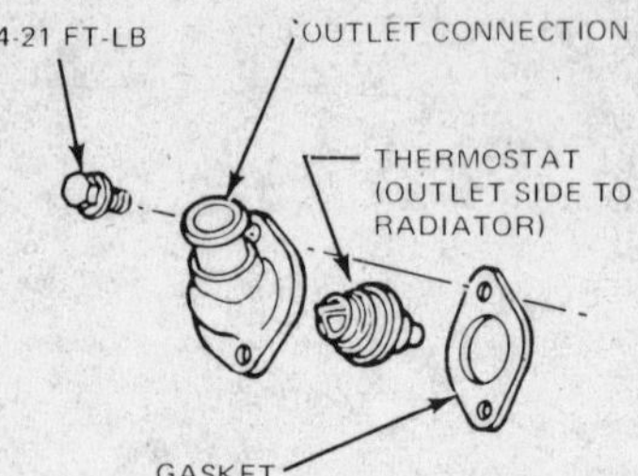

Fig. 2.7. Thermostat assembly (2300cc engine) (Sec. 6)

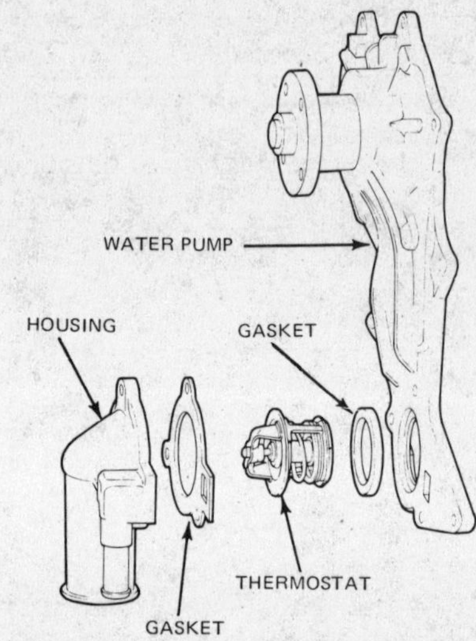

Fig. 2.8. Thermostat assembly (V6 engine) (Sec. 7)

9 Water pump - removal and refitting (2300cc engine)

1 Drain the cooling system, as described in Section 2.
2 Refer to Section 5 and remove the radiator and shroud (if fitted).
3 Slacken the alternator adjusting bolts and remove the fanbelt.
4 Undo and remove the four bolts securing the fan assembly to the water pump flange. If a viscous-drive fan is fitted refer to Section 12.
5 Remove the camshaft drive cover bolts and lift away the outer cover.
6 Undo and remove the four bolts and spring washers that secure the water pump to the cylinder block. Lift away the water pump and recover the gasket.
7 Refitting the water pump is the reverse sequence to removal. The following additional points should, however, be noted:

a) Make sure the mating faces of the cylinder block and water pump are clean. Always use a new gasket.
b) Tighten the water pump and fan bolts to the specified torque.

10 Water pump - removal and refitting (V6 engine)

1 Drain the cooling system, as described in Section 2.
2 Remove the radiator and shroud, as described in Section 5.
3 Loosen the alternator adjusting bolts and remove the drivebelt. If an air-conditioning pump is fitted the alternator and mounting bracket will have to be removed completely.
4 Remove the fan and pulley from the pump.
5 Unscrew and remove the bolts and washers that secure the water pump assembly. Note the location of the bolts as they are of different lengths.
6 Lift away the water pump assembly. Recover the gasket if not stuck to the casting. If necessary also remove the thermostat housing from the water pump.
7 Before refitting the water pump assembly remove all traces of the old gasket and sealing compound from the front cover and water pump

assembly.
8 Carefully apply a sealer to both sides of a new gasket and accurately position on the water pump.
9 Hold the water pump in position and screw in two bolts and washers, so retaining it to the front cover.
10 Remove all gasket material from the thermostat housing mating faces. Apply a sealer to both sides of the new gasket and position on the water pump. Secure in position with the two bolts and washers.
11 Refit all remaining securing bolts and washers ensuring they are located in their original positions. Tighten in a diagonal and progressive manner to the correct torque wrench settings - see Specifications.
12 Refit the fan, drivebelt(s) and radiator; then refill the cooling system.

11 Water pump - overhaul

Water pump failure will be indicated by coolant leakage, noisy operation and/or excess movement of the drive spindle. If any of these faults are present a replacement pump must be obtained from a Ford dealer as it is not practical or even economical to attempt repairing a worn out unit.

12 Viscous cooling fan - removal and refitting

1 Remove the radiator, as described in Section 5.
2 Remove the center bolt attaching the fan assembly to the extension shaft and remove the fan.
3 Remove the four nuts and bolts securing the viscous-clutch to the fan, and separate the parts.
4 Refitting is the reverse of the removal procedure.

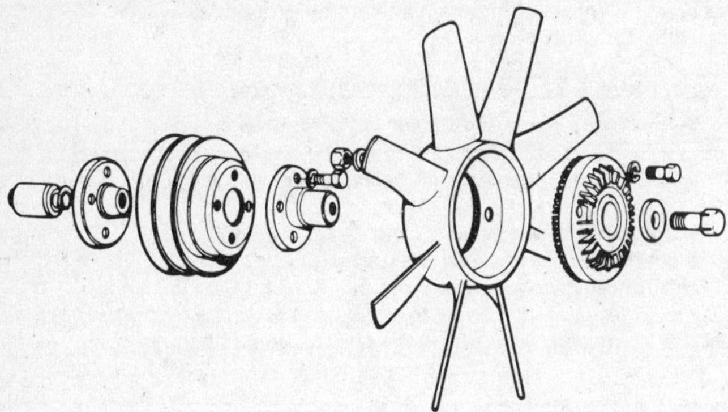

Fig. 2.9. Viscous type cooling fan (Sec. 12)

13.3 Alternator drivebelt slide adjuster

13 Drivebelts - inspection and adjusting

1 The number of drivebelts on the car will depend on which extras are fitted, ie, air-conditioning compressor, power steering pump and thermactor pump.
2 Periodically the belts should be checked for correct tension and wear. Use a flashlight and examine the inside surface of the belts for cracks and if in evidence replace the belt(s).
3 The alternator belt tension is adjusted by slackening the two lower pivot bolts and top slide bolt and moving the alternator in the required direction (photo).
4 The power steering and thermactor pump drivebelts, if fitted, are adjusted by slackening the slot bolts and screwing the adjusting bolts in or out to achieve the required belt tension. The slot bolts are then tightened.
5 When an air-conditioning pump is fitted the drivebelt tension is

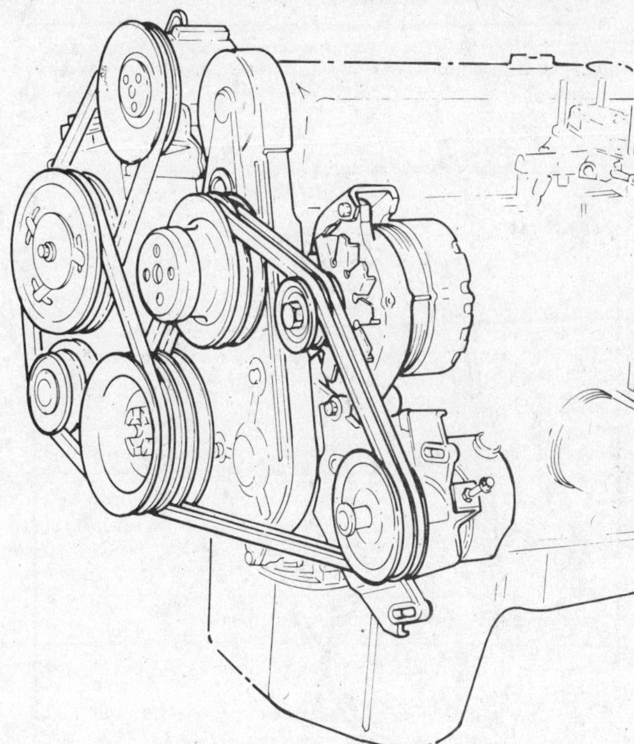

Fig. 2.10. Layout of drivebelts with all optional accessories fitted (note double fanbelt) (Sec. 13)

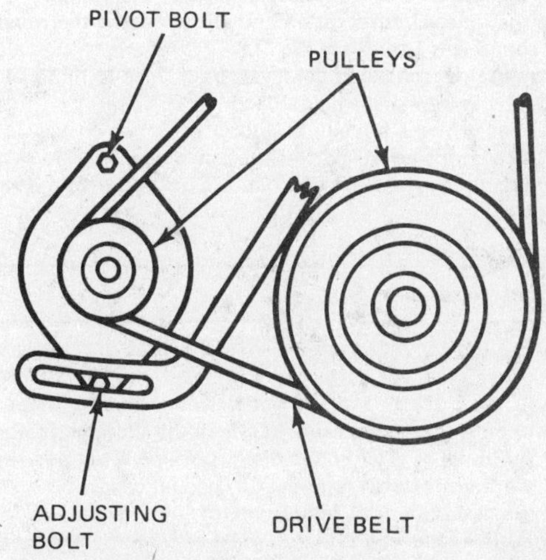

Fig. 2.11. Pivot bolt and slide adjustment - typical (Sec. 13)

2

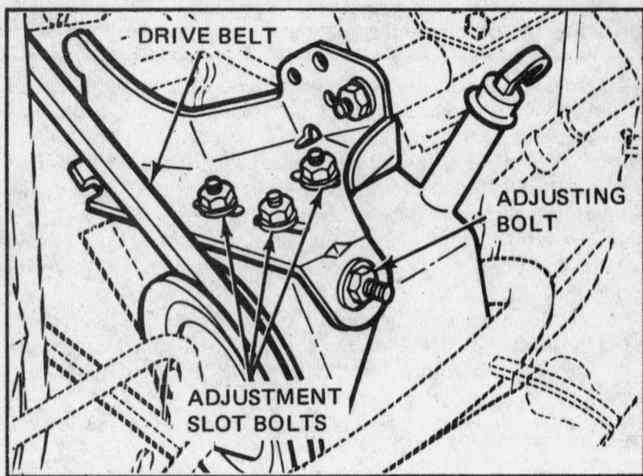

Fig. 2.12. Slotted bolt adjustment - power steering pump, typical (Sec. 13)

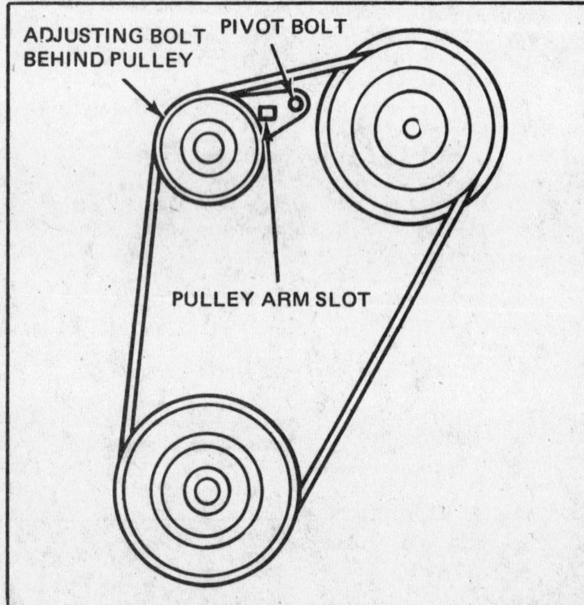

Fig. 2.13. Idler pulley adjustment - air-conditioning compressor, typical (Sec. 13)

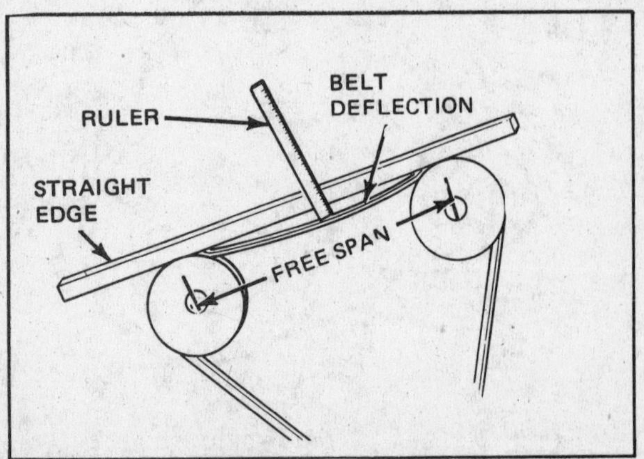

Fig. 2.14. Method of checking fanbelt tension (Sec. 13)

controlled by an idler pulley, this has a single pivot bolt and an adjusting bolt located behind the pulley.

6 To get the belts adjusted correctly the car should be taken to a Ford dealer who will have a special belt tensioning tool. However the home mechanic can obtain approximately the correct tension by adjusting the belt(s) until there is about ½ inch (13 mm) of movement midway between the pulleys.

14 Drivebelts removal and refitting

1 To remove a drivebelt, slacken the relevant accessory pivot and adjusting bolts and move it in towards the engine as far as possible. Remove the belt by lifting it over the pulley, rotating the pulley at the same time.

Note: If air conditioning and/or power steering pumps are fitted to the engine these drivebelts will have to be removed prior to the removal of the alternator/fanbelt.

2 Install the drivebelt(s) using the reverse sequence to removal. If a new belt is fitted the engine should be run for 10 minutes then switched off and the belt tension re-checked.

3 On some engines the fan is driven by twin belts and these should always be renewed as a pair.

15 Temperature gauge - fault diagnosis

1 If the temperature gauge fails to work, either the gauge, the sender unit, the wiring or the connections are at fault.

2 It is not possible to repair the gauge or the sender unit and they must be replaced by new units if at fault.

3 First check that the wiring connections are sound. Check the wiring for breaks using an ohmmeter. The sender unit and gauge should be tested by substitution.

16 Temperature gauge and sender unit - removal and refitting

1 Information on the removal of the gauge will be found in Chapter 10.

2 To remove the sender unit, disconnect the wire leading into the unit at its connector and unscrew the unit with a spanner. The unit is locked in the cylinder head just below the manifold on the left-hand side on V6 models, and on the cylinder block just below the oil pressure switch on 2300cc models. Refitting is the reverse sequence to removal.

17 Antifreeze and corrosion inhibitors

1 In circumstances where it is likely that the temperature will drop below freezing it is essential that some of the water is drained and an adequate amount of ethylene glycol antifreeze is added to the cooling system. If antifreeze is not used, it is essential to use a corrosion inhibitor in the cooling system in the proportion recommended by the inhibitor manufacturer.

2 Any antifreeze of good quality can be used. Never use an antifreeze with an alcohol base as evaporation is too high.

3 Most antifreeze with an anti-corrosion additive can be left in the cooling system for up to two years, but after six months it is advisable to have the specific gravity of the coolant checked at your local repair station and thereafter once every three months.

4 The table below gives the proportion of antifreeze and degree of protection:

Antifreeze	Commences to freeze		Frozen solid	
%	°C	°F	°C	°F
25	-13	9	-26	-15
33 1/3	-19	-2	-36	-33
50	-36	-33	-48	-53

Note: Never use antifreeze in the windshield washer reservoir as it will cause damage to the paintwork.

18 Fault diagnosis - cooling system

Symptom	Reason/s	Remedy
Overheating	Insufficient water in cooling system	Top-up radiator.
	Fan belt slipping (accompanied by a shrieking noise on rapid engine acceleration)	Tighten fan belt to recommended tension or replace if worn.
	Radiator core blocked or radiator grille restricted	Reverse flush radiator, remove obstructions.
	Bottom washer hose collapsed, impeding flow	Remove and fit new hose.
	Thermostat not opening properly	Remove and fit new thermostat.
	Ignition advance and retard incorrectly set (accompanied by loss of power, and perhaps, misfiring)	Check and reset ignition timing.
	Carburetor incorrectly adjusted (mixture too weak)	Tune carburetor.
	Exhaust system partially blocked	Check exhaust pipe for constrictive dents and blockages.
	Oil level in sump too low	Top-up oil pan to full mark on dipstick.
	Blown cylinder head gasket (water/steam being forced down the radiator overflow pipe under pressure)	Remove cylinder head, fit new gasket.
	Engine not yet run-in	Run-in slowly and carefully.
	Brakes binding	Check and adjust brakes if necessary.
Underheating	Thermostat jammed open	Remove and renew thermostat.
	Incorrect thermostat fitted allowing premature opening of valve	Remove and replace with new thermostat which opens at a higher temperature.
	Thermostat missing	Check and fit correct thermostat.
Loss of cooling water	Loose clips on water hoses	Check and tighten clips if necessary.
	Top, bottom, or by-pass water hoses perished and leaking	Check and replace any faulty hoses.
	Radiator core leaking	Remove radiator and repair.
	Thermostat gasket leaking	Inspect and renew gasket.
	Radiator pressure cap spring worn or seal ineffective	Renew radiator pressure cap
	Blown cylinder head gasket/s (pressure in system forcing water/steam down overflow pipe)	Remove cylinder head and fit new gasket.
	Cylinder wall or head cracked	Dismantle engine, despatch to engineering works for repair.

Chapter 3 Carburetion; fuel, exhaust and emission control systems

For modifications, and information applicable to later models, see Supplement at end of manual

Contents

Specifications

Fuel pump

2300cc engine:	
Type	Mechanical, driven from auxiliary shaft
Delivery pressure	4.0 to 5.5 lb/in^2 (0.28 to 0.39 kg/cm^2)
V6 engine:	
Type	Mechanical, driven from eccentric on camshaft via a pushrod

Carburetor

Type (2300 cc engine)	Motorcraft 5200 dual barrel with automatic choke
Carburetor settings:	
Fast idle speed	1800 rpm
TSP-off idle speed	500 rpm
Curb idle speed	See engine compartment decal
Electric choke heater resistance	1.3 to 3.5 ohms
Automatic choke setting	1NL
Choke plate pulldown	0.20 in (0.5 mm)
Dry float setting	0.46 in (11.7 mm)
Accelerator pump setting	No 2
Fast idle cam setting	0.1 in (2.5 mm)

Fuel tank

Normal capacity	13 US gallons (49.2 liters)
Optional auxiliary tank	3½ US gallons (13.3 liters)
Fuel filter	Disposable in-line type
Air cleaner	Replaceable paper element type
Fuel evaporative emission system	Charcoal canister type

Torque wrench settings

	lb f ft	kg f m
2300cc engine:		
Air cleaner wing nuts	1.5	0.2
Exhaust manifold flange bolts	15 to 20	2.1 to 2.8
U-bolts and clamps	28 to 33	3.9 to 4.5
Strap-type clamps	9 to 12	1.2 to 1.6
V6 engine:		
Exhaust manifold bolts	16 to 23	2.2 to 3.1
Exhaust silencer clamps	25 to 35	3.4 to 4.8
Inlet pipe flange nuts	17 to 25	2.35 to 3.4
'O' ring insulator brackets to floor panel	9	1.2

1 General description

The fuel system on the Mustang II cars comprises an underflow gas tank at the rear of the car with interconnecting fuel pipes to the mechanical fuel pump and twin choke carburetor. To increase the range of the car an optional overload fuel tank of 3½ US gallons (13.3 liters) capacity can be fitted.

Because a catalytic converter is fitted in the exhaust system as an aid to emission control, only unleaded fuel must be used with an octane rating of 91.

To conform to the regulations imposed in the USA for controlling engine emission, the fuel system has been modified and further information will be found in the relevant sections of this Chapter. Before starting any work on the fuel system refer to Section 2.

2 US Federal regulations - emission control

The fuel system has been modified so that the car will comply with the USA Federal Regulations covering emission of hydrocarbons and carbon monoxide. To achieve this the ignition system must be accurately set using special equipment (see Chapter 4) before any attempt is made to adjust the carburetor or its controls. Thereafter the fuel system may be reset but once again special equipment must be used. The information contained in this Chapter is given to assist the reader to clean and/or overhaul the various components but when completed the car must be taken to the local Ford dealer for final adjustments to be made. Failure to do this will probably mean that the car does not comply with the regulations unless you possess suitable exhaust gas analysing equipment.

3 Thermostatic air cleaner and duct system - general description

1 The air cleaner on both the 4-cylinder and V6 engines is retained on studs projecting from the carburetor air inlet by four wing-nuts. (On some later models a single wing-nut is used.)

2 An additional feature is the control system for intake air to ensure that fuel atomisation within the carburetor takes place using air at the correct temperature. This is effected by a duct system which draws in fresh air, or pre-heated air from a heat shroud around the engine exhaust manifold. The component parts of a typical system are shown in Fig. 3.1.

3 Operation of the system can be summarized as follows:

When the engine is cold, heated air is directed from the exhaust manifold into the air cleaner, but as the engine warms up cold air is progressively mixed with this warm air to maintain a carburetor air temperature of 105 to 130°F (40.5 to 76.8°C). At high ambient temperatures the hot air intake is closed off completely.

The mixing of air is regulated by a vacuum operated motor on the air cleaner inlet duct, which is controlled by a bi-metal temperature sensor and cold weather modulator valve. Operation of the system is best understood by referring to Fig. 3.3 which shows the routing of the intake air under different temperature conditions.

An additional feature on cars with catalytic converters or Cold Temperature Actuated Vacuum (CTAV) systems is an ambient temperature sensor mounted within the air cleaner. This switch is operated by ambient temperature changes and under certain conditions will override the cold weather modulator system. For further information see Section 30.

4 Thermostatic air cleaner - testing

Vacuum motor and valve assembly

1 Check that the valve is open when the engine is switched off. Start the engine, and check that the valve closes when idling (except where the engine is hot). If this fails to happen, check for disconnected or leaking vacuum lines, and for correct operation of the bi-metal sensor (see below).

2 If the valve closes, open and close the throttle rapidly. The valve should open at temperatures above 55°F (12.7°C) during the throttle operation. If this does not happen, check the valve for binding.

Bi-metal switch

3 The bi-metal switch can be checked by subjecting it to heated air, either from the engine or from an external source (eg, a hair dryer). **Do not immerse it in water or damage may occur.**

Cold weather modulator valve

4 Without the use of a supply of refrigerant R-12 and a vacuum source, testing is impractical. If the modulator valve is suspected of being faulty it should be tested by your Ford dealer.

5 Air cleaner and element - removal and refitting

1 Disconnect the vacuum hoses from the vacuum motor and intake manifold (or T-connection).

2 Detach the air intake ducts.

3 Remove the wing nut(s) attaching the air cleaner body to the carburetor air horn studs.

4 Where applicable, detach the catalyst switch connectors and any remaining vacuum hoses, noting where they were fitted, and remove the air cleaner (photo).

5 Remove the air cleaner top cover, and take out the element (photo).

6 Refitting is the reverse of the removal procedures, using new gaskets a as applicable.

6 Fuel pump - description (2300cc engine)

The fuel pump is located on the lower left-hand side of the engine and is driven from the auxiliary driveshaft by an actuating lever. The pump is a sealed unit and cannot be dismantled. If it develops a fault it must be discarded and a new one fitted.

3

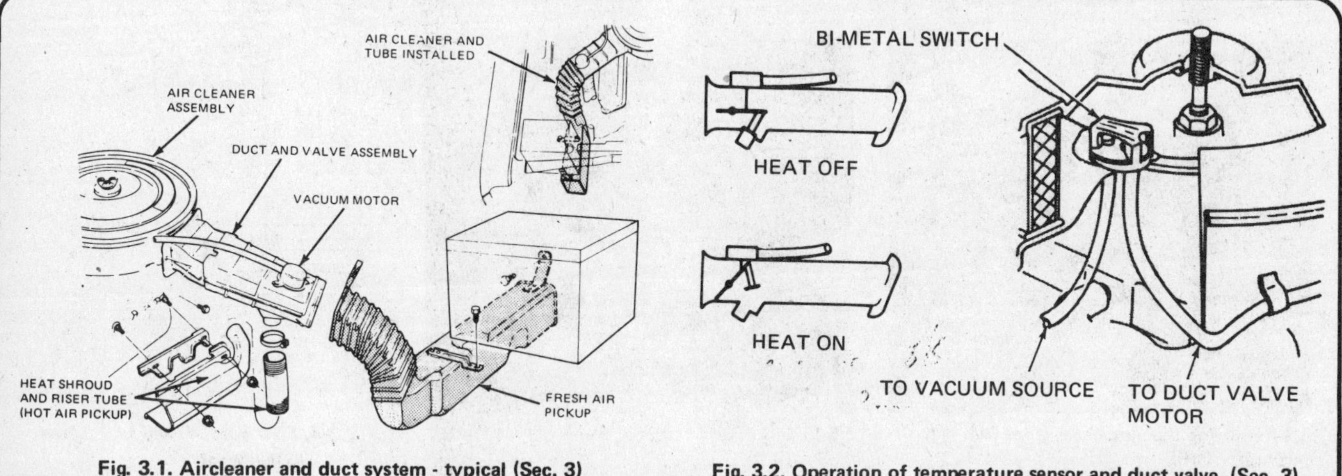

Fig. 3.1. Aircleaner and duct system - typical (Sec. 3)

Fig. 3.2. Operation of temperature sensor and duct valve (Sec. 3)

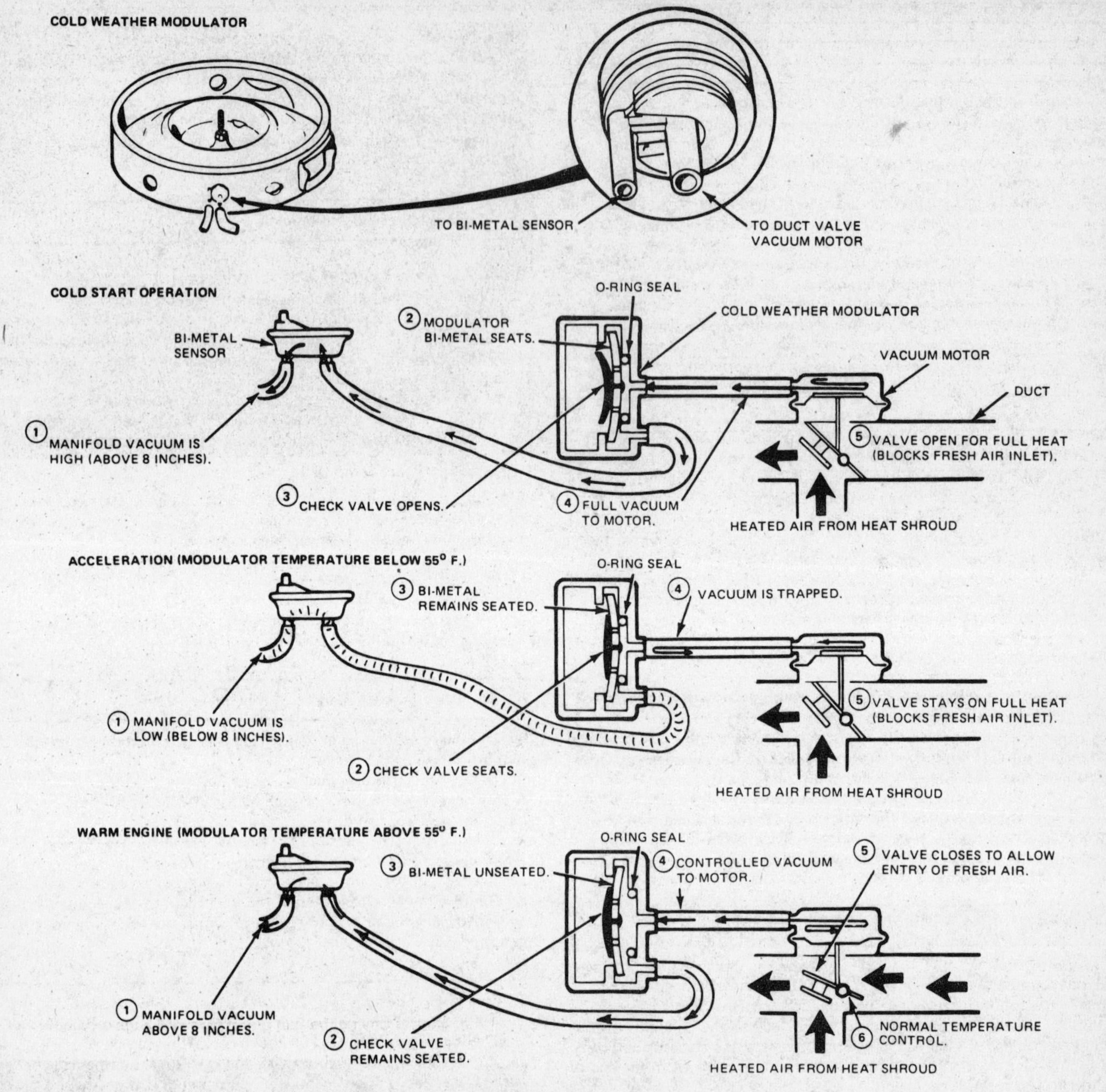

COLD WEATHER MODULATOR

TO BI-METAL SENSOR

TO DUCT VALVE VACUUM MOTOR

COLD START OPERATION

BI-METAL SENSOR

(1) MANIFOLD VACUUM IS HIGH (ABOVE 8 INCHES).

(2) MODULATOR BI-METAL SEATS.

(3) CHECK VALVE OPENS.

O-RING SEAL

COLD WEATHER MODULATOR

(4) FULL VACUUM TO MOTOR.

VACUUM MOTOR

DUCT

(5) VALVE OPEN FOR FULL HEAT (BLOCKS FRESH AIR INLET).

HEATED AIR FROM HEAT SHROUD

ACCELERATION (MODULATOR TEMPERATURE BELOW 55° F.)

(1) MANIFOLD VACUUM IS LOW (BELOW 8 INCHES).

(2) CHECK VALVE SEATS.

(3) BI-METAL REMAINS SEATED.

O-RING SEAL

(4) VACUUM IS TRAPPED.

(5) VALVE STAYS ON FULL HEAT (BLOCKS FRESH AIR INLET).

HEATED AIR FROM HEAT SHROUD

WARM ENGINE (MODULATOR TEMPERATURE ABOVE 55° F.)

(1) MANIFOLD VACUUM ABOVE 8 INCHES.

(2) CHECK VALVE REMAINS SEATED.

(3) BI-METAL UNSEATED.

O-RING SEAL

(4) CONTROLLED VACUUM TO MOTOR.

(5) VALVE CLOSES TO ALLOW ENTRY OF FRESH AIR.

(6) NORMAL TEMPERATURE CONTROL.

HEATED AIR FROM HEAT SHROUD

Fig. 3.3. Operation of cold weather modulator system on aircleaner (Sec. 3)

5.4 Removing the air cleaner from the carburetor (V6)

5.5 Location of air cleaner element

Fig. 3.4. Fuel pump fitted to 2.3 liter engine (Sec. 7)

7 Fuel pump - removal and replacement (2300cc engine)

1 Remove the inlet and outlet pipes at the pump and plug the ends to stop gas loss or dirt finding its way into the fuel system.
2 Undo and remove two bolts and spring washers that secure the pump to the cylinder block.
3 Lift away the fuel pump and gasket.
4 Refitting the fuel pump is the reverse sequence to removal but there are several additional points that should be noted:

a) Tighten the pump securing bolts to the specified torque.
b) Before reconnecting the pipe from the fuel tank to the pump inlet, move the end to a position lower than the fuel tank so that fuel can syphon out. Quickly connect the pipe to the pump inlet.
c) Disconnect the pipe at the carburetor and turn the engine over until gasoline issues from the open end. Quickly connect the pipe to the carburetor union. This last operation will help to prime the pump.

8.1 Location of fuel pump (V6)

8 Fuel pump - description (V6 engine)

1 The fuel pump on the V6 engine is located on the left-hand side of the cylinder block (photo). The pump diaphragm is operated by a rod driven by an eccentric on the camshaft. As in the case of the 2300cc engine, the pump is a sealed unit and cannot be dismantled.

9 Fuel pump - removal and replacement (V6 engine)

1 Slacken the clips and detach the inlet and outlet pipes from the pump.
2 Undo and remove the two securing bolts and washers. Lift away the pump and its gasket. The latter should be discarded and a new one obtained ready for refitting.
3 To refit the fuel pump first make sure that all traces of the old gasket have been removed from the mounting pad and pump.
4 Smear some oil resistant cement onto both sides of a new gasket and place on the flange. Check that the rod is correctly located and replace the pump. Secure with the two bolts and washers.
5 Reconnect the two pipes and check for fuel leaks.

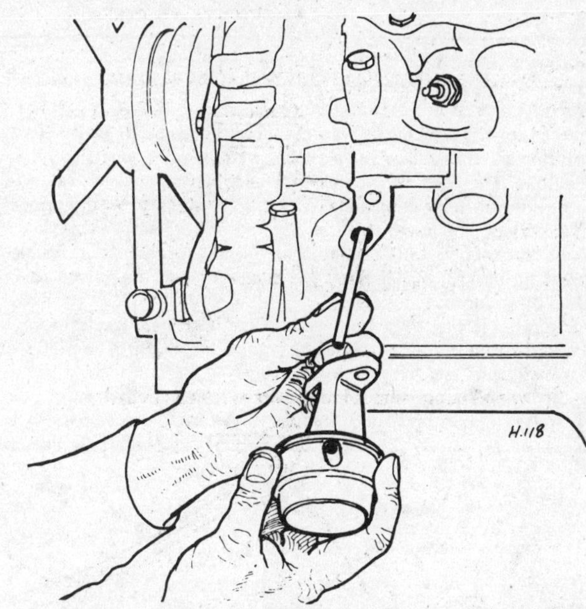

Fig. 3.5. Removing the fuel pump from V6 engine (Sec. 9)

10 Fuel pump - testing (all models)

Assuming that the fuel lines and unions are in good condition and that there are no leaks anywhere, check the performance of the fuel pump in the following manner. Disconnect the fuel pipe at the carburetor inlet union, and the high tension lead to the coil and, with a suitable container or large rag in position to catch the ejected fuel, turn the engine over. A good spurt of gasoline should emerge from the end of the pipe every second revolution.

11 Fuel filter - renewal

1 Initially remove the carburetor air cleaner.
2 Loosen the fuel line clips at the filter, pull off the fuel lines and discard the clips. On later models, unscrew the filter from the carburetor (photo).
3 Fit the replacement filter using new clips, start the engine and check for fuel leaks. **Note:** If the replacement filter shows the direction of fuel flow, take care that it is fitted the correct way round.
4 Refit the air cleaner.

11.2 Carburetor fuel filter (screw in type)

12 Carburetion - warning

1 Before making any adjustment or alteration to the carburetor or emission control systems (see Section 30), the owner is advised to make himself aware of any Federal, State or Provincial laws which may be contravened by making any such adjustment or alteration.
2 Setting dimensions and specifications are given in this Chapter where relevant to adjustment procedures. Where these differ from those

3

given on the engine tune-up decal, the decal information should be assumed to be correct.

3 Where the use of special test equipment is called-up (eg, exhaust gas CO analyzer, etc), and this equipment is not available, any setting or calibration should be regarded as a temporary measure only and should be rechecked by a suitably equipped Ford dealer or carburetion/emission control specialist at the earliest opportunity.

4 Before attempting any carburetor adjustments, first ascertain that the following items are serviceable or correctly set:

a) All vacuum hoses and connections.
b) Ignition system.
c) Spark plugs.
d) Ignition initial advance.

5 If satisfactory adjustment cannot be obtained check the following points:

a) Carburetor fuel level.
b) Crankcase ventilation system.
c) Valve clearance.
d) Engine compression.
e) Idle mixture.

13 Carburetor (Motorcraft 5200) - general description

The main parts of this carburetor are shown in Fig. 3.6. It will be seen that it is of the dual barrel, vertical downdraught design, incorporating an automatic strangler-type water heated, electrically assisted choke. The float chamber is internally vented.

The carburetor body comprises two castings which form the upper and lower bodies. The upper incorporates the float chamber cover, float pivot brackets, fuel inlet union, gauze filter, spring loaded needle valve, twin air intakes, choke plates and the section of the power valve controlled by vacuum.

Incorporated in the lower body is the float chamber, accelerator pump, two throttle barrels and integral main venturis, throttle plates, spindles, levers, jets and the enrichment valve.

The throttle plate opening is in a preset sequence so that the primary starts to open first and is then followed by the secondary in such a manner that both plates reach full throttle position at the same time. The primary barrel, throttle plate and venturi size is identical in both the primary and secondary barrels.

All the carburetion systems are located in the lower body and the main progression systems operate in both barrels, whilst the idling and the power valve systems operate in the primary barrel only, and the full load enrichment system in the secondary barrel.

The accelerator pump discharges fuel into the primary barrel.

A connection for the vacuum required to control the distributor advance/retard vacuum unit is located in the lower body.

A solenoid throttle positioner (TSP) assembly is incorporated on certain versions to prevent dieseling (running-on) after the ignition has been switched off, by allowing the throttle plates to close beyond the point required for idling.

14 Carburetor curb idle, TSP-off and fast idle speed adjustments

Note: Read Section 2 before commencing.

1 Remove the air cleaner and plug all vacuum lines at the vacuum source end.

2 Apply the parking brake and block the roadwheels.

3 Check, and adjust if necessary, the choke and throttle linkage for freedom of movement.

4 Start the engine and run it up to normal operating temperature.

5 Disconnect the EGR vacuum line at the valve, and plug the line.

6 Where applicable, set the Air-Conditioning to OFF.

7 Where applicable, remove the spark delay valve and route the primary advance vacuum signal directly to the distributor vacuum diaphragm unit (advance side).

8 Set the automatic transmission to Park, or manual transmission to Neutral, then run the engine at normal operating temperature. Check that the choke plates are closed, then set the throttle so that the fast idle adjustment screw contacts the kick-down step of the choke cam; adjust the fast idle adjusting screw to obtain the specified rpm.

9 Set the throttle to the high step of the choke cam and allow the engine to run for 5 seconds (approximately).

10 Rotate the choke cam until the fast idle adjustment screw contacts the choke cam kick-down step. Allow the engine speed to stabilize, then recheck the fast idle rpm, as described in paragraphs 8 and 9; readjust if necessary, then repeat the procedure given in the first sentence of this

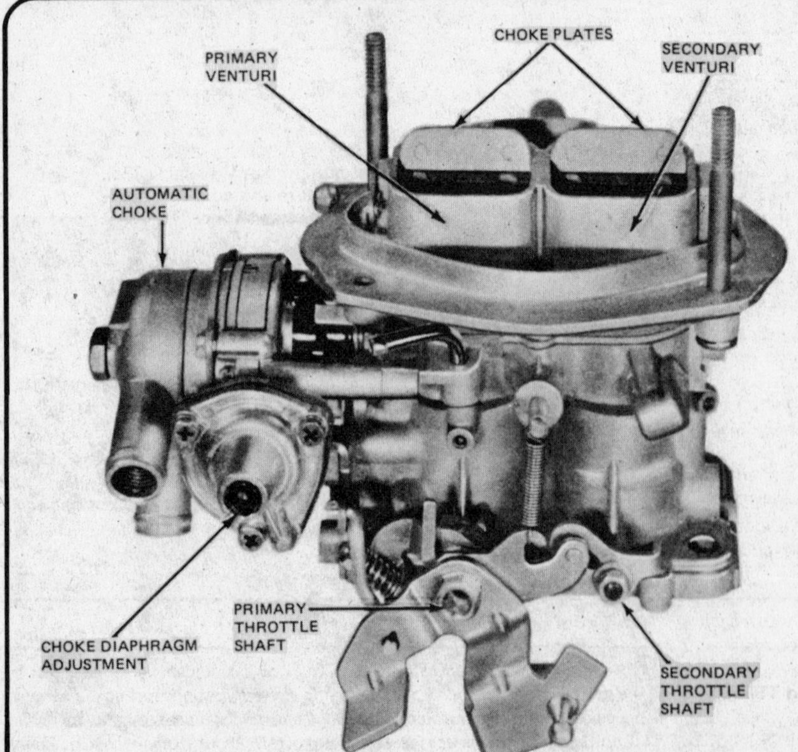

Fig. 3.6. General view of Motorcraft 5200 carburetor (Sec. 13)

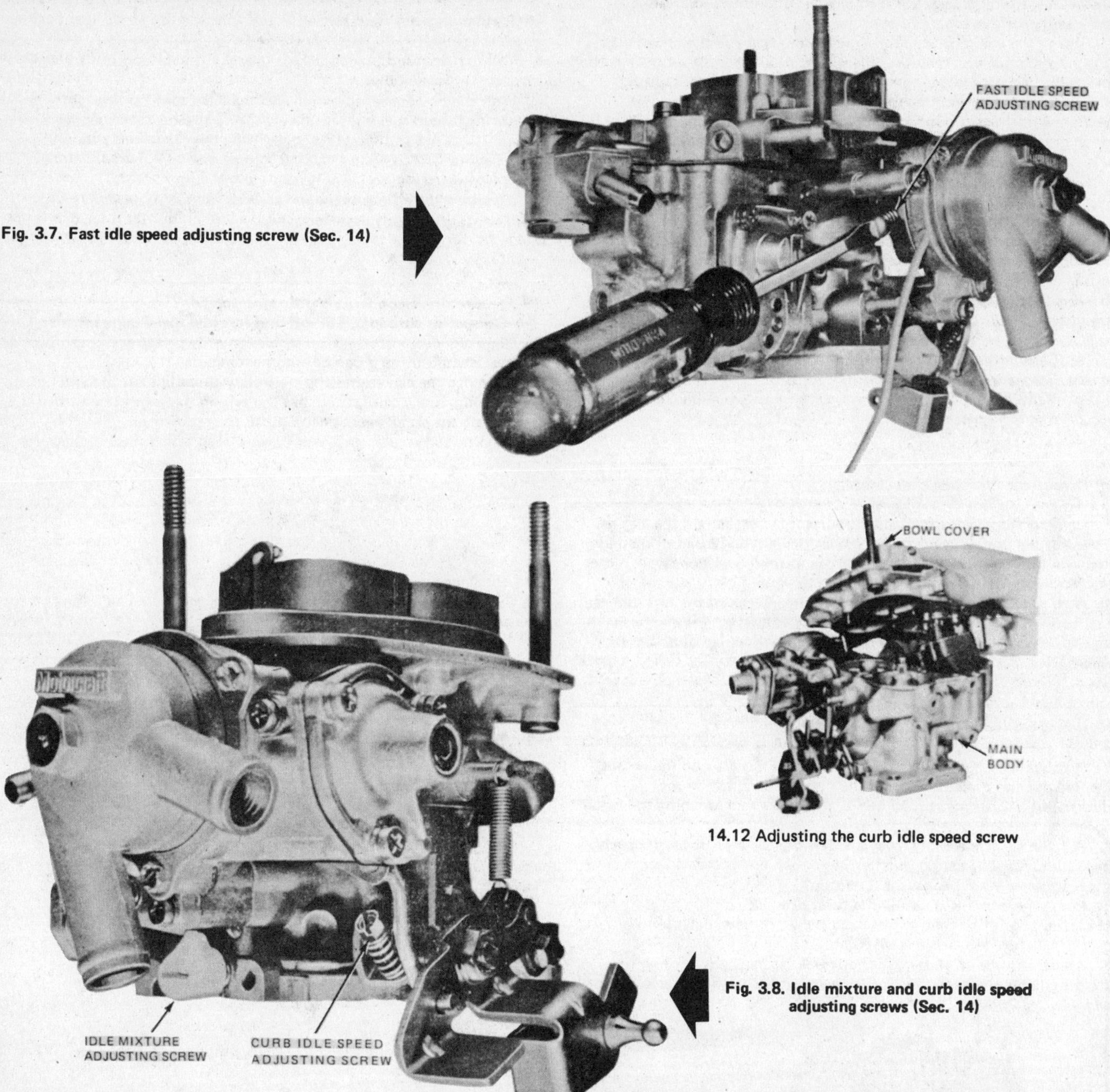

Fig. 3.7. Fast idle speed adjusting screw (Sec. 14)

14.12 Adjusting the curb idle speed screw

Fig. 3.8. Idle mixture and curb idle speed adjusting screws (Sec. 14)

3

paragraph to ensure repeatability.

11 Allow the engine to return to the normal idle, then for automatic transmission models select Drive.

12 Where no TSP assembly is fitted, adjust the curb idle screw in or out to obtain the specified curb idle speed (photo), then proceed to paragraph 15.

13 Where a TSP assembly is fitted, adjust the curb idle screw which contacts the solenoid plunger to obtain the specified curb idle speed (the solenoid is energized and the plunger extended when the ignition is ON).

14 Now collapse the solenoid plunger by forcing the throttle linkage against the plunger, grasping the throttle lever and solenoid housing between the thumb and index finger to alleviate movement of the solenoid assembly position.

15 Adjust the TSP-off adjusting screw to obtain the specified TSP-off idle speed.

16 Open the throttle slightly to allow the solenoid plunger to extend.

17 Provided that all adjustments are now satisfactory, stop the engine, then install the air cleaner and its associated vacuum lines. If the adjustments are not satisfactory, refer to paragraph 4 in Section 12.

18 Restart the engine and if necessary run it up to normal operating temperature. With the engine running at 2000 rpm (approximately) select Park (automatic transmission) or Neutral (manual transmission). Allow 5 seconds (approximately) for the speed to stabilize, then let the engine return to idle; set automatic transmission models to Drive. Recheck the curb idle speed, and if necessary readjust as described in paragraph 12 onwards.

19 Refit all vacuum lines.

15 Carburetor - idle mixture adjustment

Note: Idle mixture adjustment can only be satisfactorily carried out by the artificial enrichment method using special test equipment. The procedure given in this Section allows approximate settings to be obtained should this be necessary (eg, after carburetor overhaul). Read Section 12 before commencing.

1 Obtain the best possible idle speed using the method given in

Section 14. If the idle speed is unsteady, it should be increased sufficiently for the engine to continue running.

2 Rotate the idle mixture screws within the range of the limiting caps to obtain the most satisfactory idle speed. Where the idle mixture is too rich, indicated by a 'sooty' exhaust smoke and the engine 'hunting' (slowing down and running 'lumpily'), rotate the screws clockwise. Where the idle mixture is too lean, indicated by the engine speed tending to increase and then decrease, and possible a 'hollow' exhaust note, rotate the screws counter-clockwise.

3 Reset the idle speed as soon as the mixture is satisfactorily set, following the procedure given in Section 14.

4 If the idle mixture cannot be set satisfactorily within the range of the limiting caps, pull off the caps and adjust the mixture screws but refit the caps afterwards. In case it is not possible to obtain a satisfactory setting, rotate each screw in turn, counting the exact number of turns to just seal it, then back off the same number of turns. This will give a datum point from which adjustment can commence. Both screws can be expected to be the same number of turns from the seat when correctly set, after which the limiting cap must be refitted.

5 On completion of *any* idle mixture adjustment, ensure that the setting is checked by a Ford dealer or carburetor/emission control specialist at the earliest opportunity.

16 Carburetor - fast idle cam clearance

1 Remove the air cleaner if the carburetor is installed on the engine.

2 Insert the unmarked shank of a twist drill 0.1 in (2.5 mm) diameter between the lower edge of the choke plate and the air horn wall. **Note:** No 38 drill is 0.1015 in; No 39 drill is 0.0995 in.

3 With the fast idle screw held on the bottom step of the fast idle cam, against the top step, the choke lever tang and the fast idle cam arm should *just* be in contact. Bend the choke lever tang up or down as necessary.

17 Carburetor - choke plate vacuum pull-down

1 Remove the air cleaner if the carburetor is installed on the engine.

2 Remove the three screws and the ring retaining the choke thermostatic spring cover. Do not remove the screw retaining the water cover.

3 Pull the cover assembly away and remove the electric assist assembly.

4 Set the fast idle cam on the top step, then use a screwdriver to push the diaphragm stem back against its stop.

5 Insert the unmarked shank of a twist drill 0.20 in (5 mm) between the lower edge of the choke plate and the air horn wall. **Note:** No 7 drill is 0.201 in; No 8 drill is 0.199 in.

6 Adjust the choke plate-to-air horn wall clearance by turning the vacuum diaphragm adjusting screw, as necessary, with a hexagonal wrench.

18 Carburetor - dry float setting

1 The dry float setting can only be checked at the appropriate stage of carburetor disassembly.

2 With the bowl cover inverted, and the float tang resting lightly on the spring loaded fuel inlet needle, measure the clearance between the edge of the float and the bowl cover using the unmarked shank of a twist drill of 0.44/0.48 in (11.2/12.2 mm) diameter. **Note:** 7/16 in (11.112 mm) drill plus feeler gauges can be used.

3 To adjust the clearance, bend the float tang as necessary so that both floats are equally adjusted. Do not scratch or otherwise damage the float tang.

19 Carburetor - secondary throttle stop screw

1 The secondary throttle stop screw can only be set at the appropriate stage of carburetor disassembly.

2 Back off the screw until the secondary throttle plate seats in its bore.

3 Turn the screw until it touches the tab on the secondary throttle lever, then turn it an additional ¼ turn.

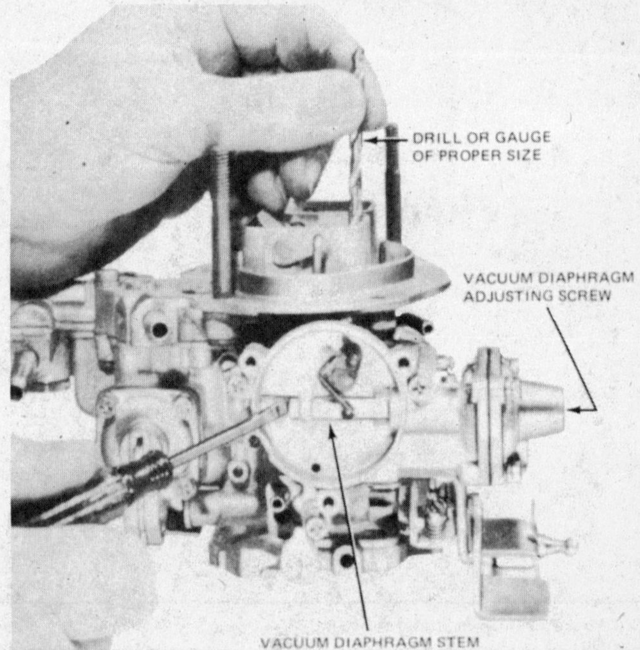

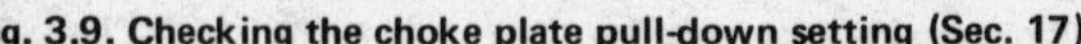

Fig. 3.9. Checking the choke plate pull-down setting (Sec. 17)

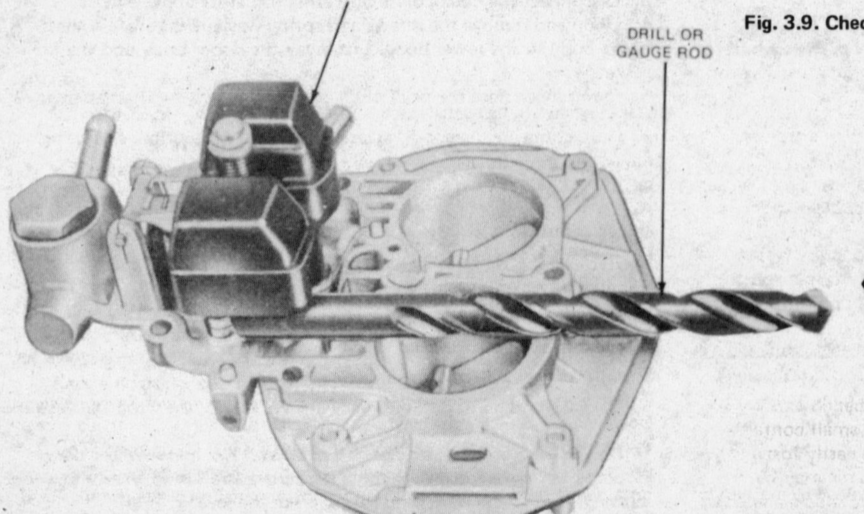

Fig. 3.10. Dry float setting (Sec. 18)

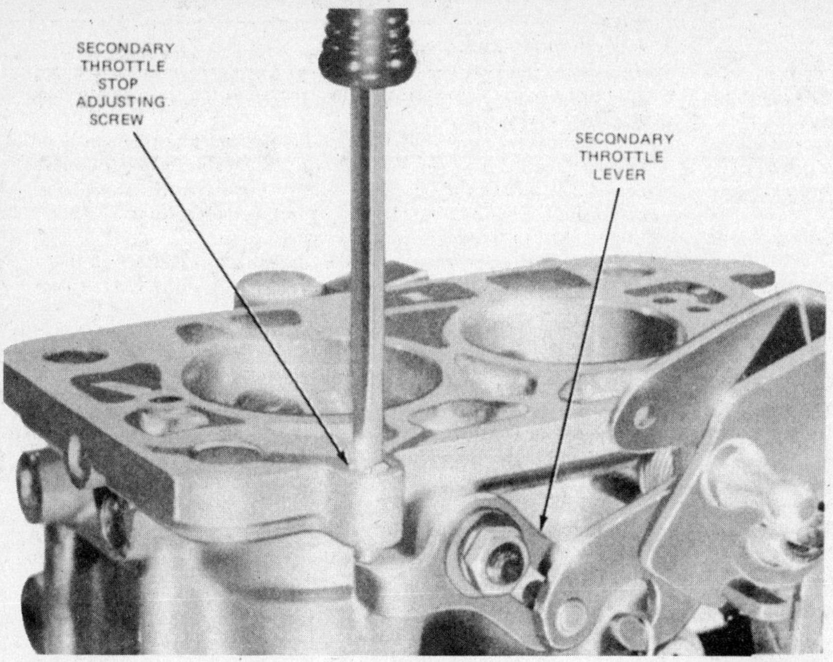

Fig. 3.11. Adjusting the secondary throttle stop screw (Sec. 19)

Fig. 3.12. Removing the bowl cover (air horn) (Sec. 21)

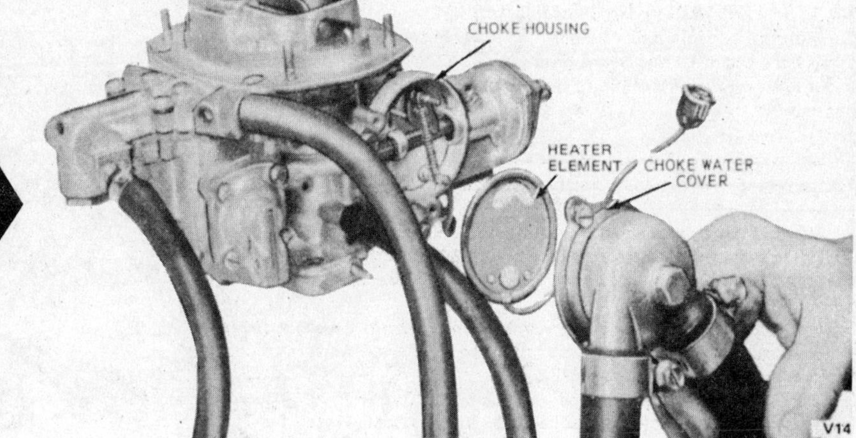

Fig. 3.13. Removing the automatic choke assembly (Sec. 21)

20 Carburetor - removal and refitting

1 Remove the air cleaner as described in Section 5.
2 Disconnect the fuel feed line from the carburetor.
3 Disconnect the electrical leads and vacuum lines from the carburetor.
4 Disconnect the throttle cable/kick-down cable from the carburetor. For further information see Section 26.
5 Partially drain the cooling system and disconnect the water hoses from the choke housing (refer to Chapter 2, if necessary).
6 Using suitably cranked ring/socket wrenches, remove the carburetor mounting nuts. Lift off the carburetor and gasket.
7 Refitting the carburetor is basically the reverse of the removal procedure, but ensure that a new flange gasket is used.

21 Carburetor - dismantling and reassembly

1 Before dismantling wash the exterior of the carburetor and wipe dry using a non-fluffy rag. Select a clean area of the workbench and lay several layers of newspaper on the top. Obtain several small containers for putting some of the small parts in, which could be easily lost. Whenever a part is to be removed look at it first so that it may be refitted in its original position. As each part is removed place it in order along one edge of the newspaper so that by using this method reassembly is made easier.

Carburetor bowl cover

2 Unscrew and remove the fuel filter retainer from the upper body. Recover the filter.
3 Disconnect the choke plate operating rod at its upper end.
4 Undo and remove the screws and spring washers that retain the upper body to the lower body. Lift away the upper body and the gasket.
5 Carefully extract the float pivot pin and lift out the float assembly followed by the needle valve.
6 Unscrew the needle valve seat and remove the gasket.
7 Remove the three enrichment valve vacuum diaphragm screws. Remove the washers and diaphragm.

Automatic choke

8 Remove the single screw and washer from the choke housing. Remove the cover and gasket.
9 Remove the thermostatic spring housing retaining ring screws. Remove the retaining ring, housing and electric choke heater.
10 Remove the choke housing assembly screws; note the long screw on the long leg of the assembly. Move the housing away from the main body, disengaging the fast idle rod. Remove the O-ring from the vacuum port.
11 Remove the choke shaft nut, lockwasher, lever and fast idle cam.
12 Remove the fast idle lever retaining screw, the fast idle lever and the spacer. Take off the screw and spring from the lever.
13 Remove the choke diaphragm cover screws. Remove the cover, spring and diaphragm/shaft.

Accelerator pump

14 Remove the four pump cover screws and the pump cover. Remove the pump diaphragm and spring.

15 Remove the pump discharge screw assembly, the discharge nozzle and the two gaskets. Remove the two discharge check balls.

Main body

16 Remove the primary high speed bleed plug and the main well tube.

17 Remove the secondary high speed bleed plug and the main well tube. Note the size of the primary and secondary plugs and tubes to ensure correct assembly.

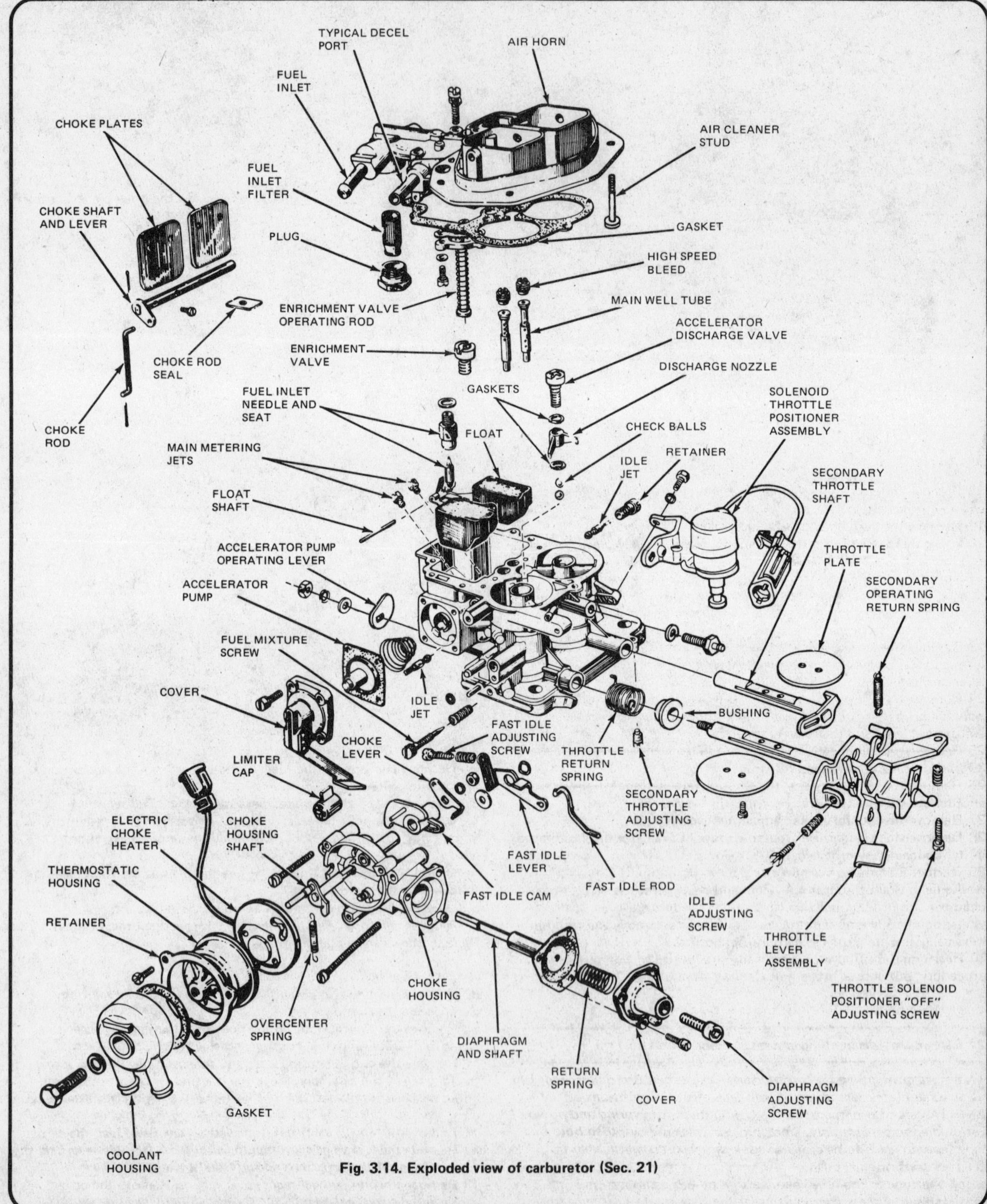

Fig. 3.14. Exploded view of carburetor (Sec. 21)

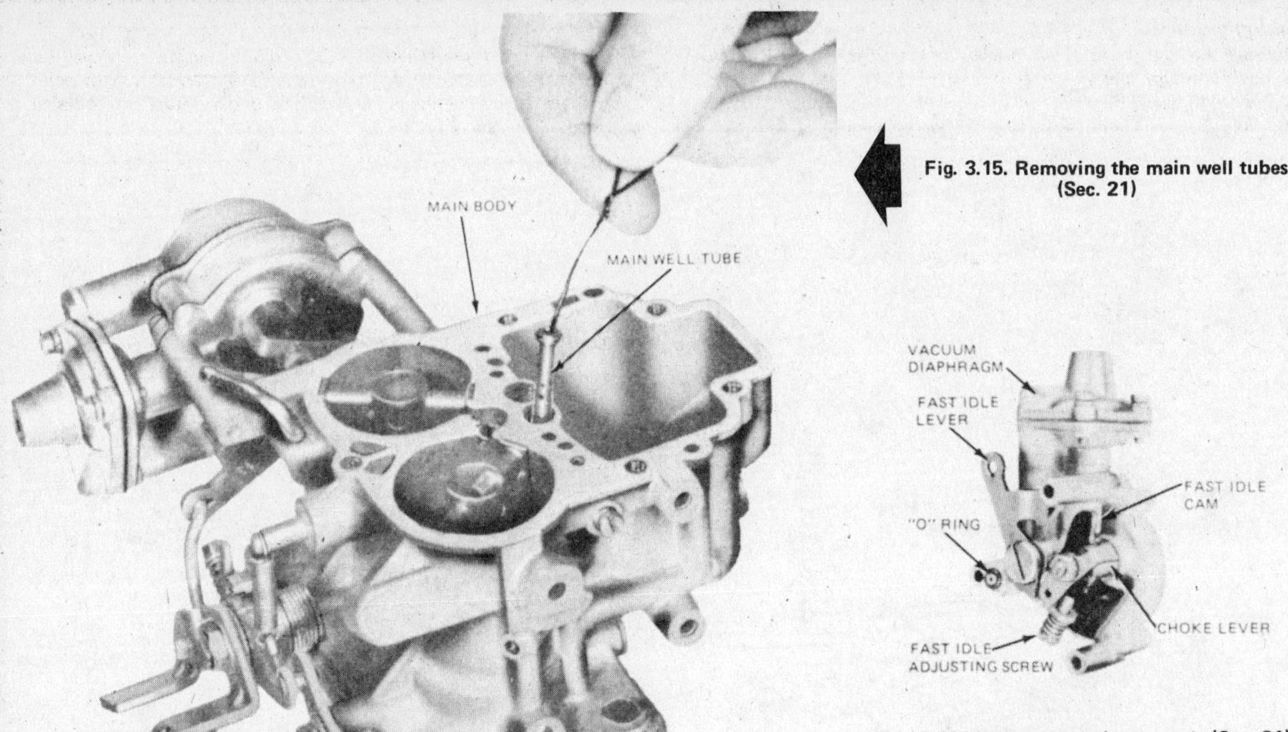

Fig. 3.15. Removing the main well tubes (Sec. 21)

Fig. 3.16. Automatic choke controls (Sec. 21)

18 Remove the primary and secondary main jets, noting their sizes to ensure correct assembly.
19 Remove the enrichment valve and gasket.
20 From the side of the carburetor body, remove the idle jet retainers and idle jets.
21 Turn the idle limiter cap counter-clockwise to the rich stop. Remove the cap, then count the exact number of turns to *just* seat the idle mixture needle. Remove the needle and spring.
22 Detach the secondary operating lever return spring.
23 Remove the primary throttle lever nut and locking tab. Remove the lever and flat washer followed by the secondary lever assembly and lever bushing.
24 Remove the idle adjustment lever spring and shaft washer. Note how the primary throttle return spring is hooked over the idle adjustment lever and the carburetor body.
25 Remove the idle speed screw and spring from the idle adjustment lever.
26 Remove the secondary throttle lever nut, lockwasher, flat washer and the lever itself.
27 Remove the secondary idle adjustment screw.
28 Remove the solenoid throttle positioner (TSP) from the carburetor body if considered necessary.
29 Dismantling is now complete and all parts should be thoroughly washed and cleaned in gasoline. Remove any sediment in the float chamber and drillings but take care not to scratch the fine drillings whilst doing so. Remove all traces of old gaskets using a sharp knife. When all parts are clean reassembly can begin.
30 Reassembly of the carburetor is essentially the reverse of the removal procedure, but careful attention should be paid to the following points:

a) Main body: Ensure that the idle mixture screws are refitted in exactly the same position as determined at paragraph 21, then install a new limiter cap with the stop tab against the rich side of the stop on the carburetor body. Now ensure that the main jets, primary and secondary main well tubes, and high speed bleeds are correctly fitted in their respective positions.
b) Accelerator pump: When refitting the return spring and pump diaphragm assembly, start the four cover screws, then hold the pump lever partly open to align the gasket; then tighten the screws.
c) Automatic choke: When installing the diaphragm adjusting screw, initially adjust it so that the threads are flush with the inside of the cover. Fit the fast idle rod with the end which has one tab in the fast idle adjustment lever, and the end which has two tabs in the primary throttle lever. Adjust the choke plate pull down as described in Section 17. Before installing the electric choke heater ensure that the choke plate is either fully open or fully closed.

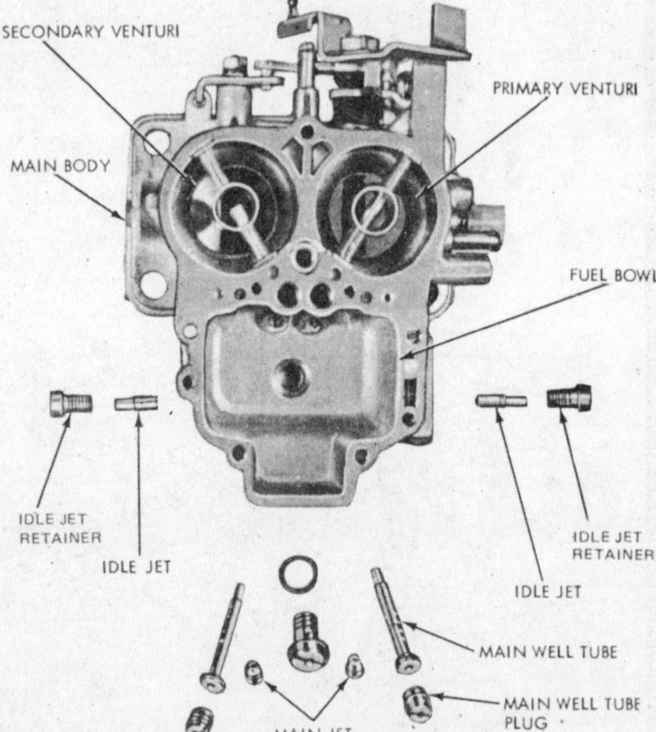

Fig. 3.17. Main metering jets and idle jets removed (Sec. 21)

d) Bowl cover: When refitting the enrichment valve vacuum

diaphragm, depress the spring and fit the screws and washers finger-tight. Hold the stem so that the diaphragm is horizontal, then tighten the screws evenly. Adjust the dry float setting as described in Section 18.

22 Fuel tank - general description

The fuel tank on all Mustang II models is the flat slab type and is

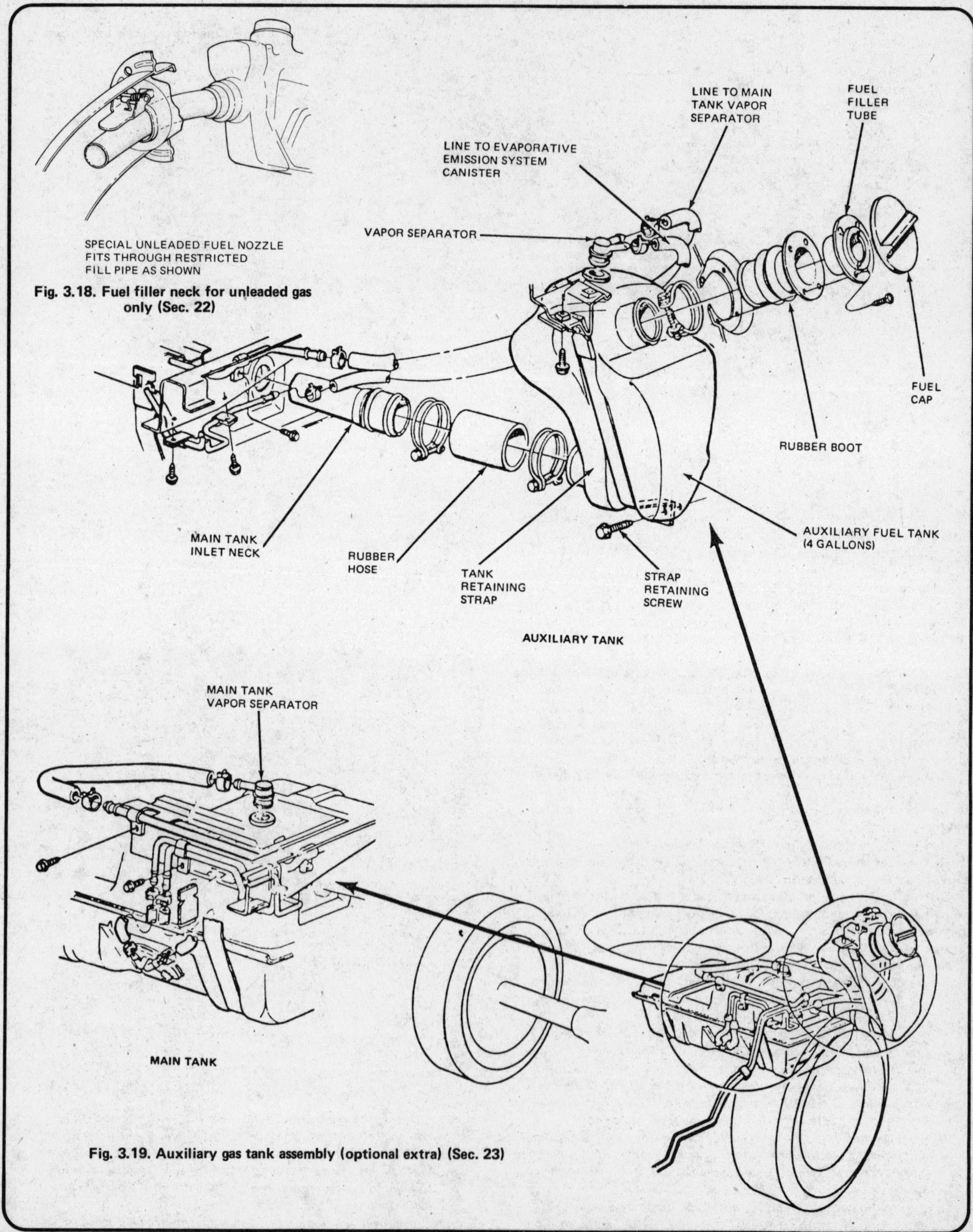

Fig. 3.18. Fuel filler neck for unleaded gas only (Sec. 22)

Fig. 3.19. Auxiliary gas tank assembly (optional extra) (Sec. 23)

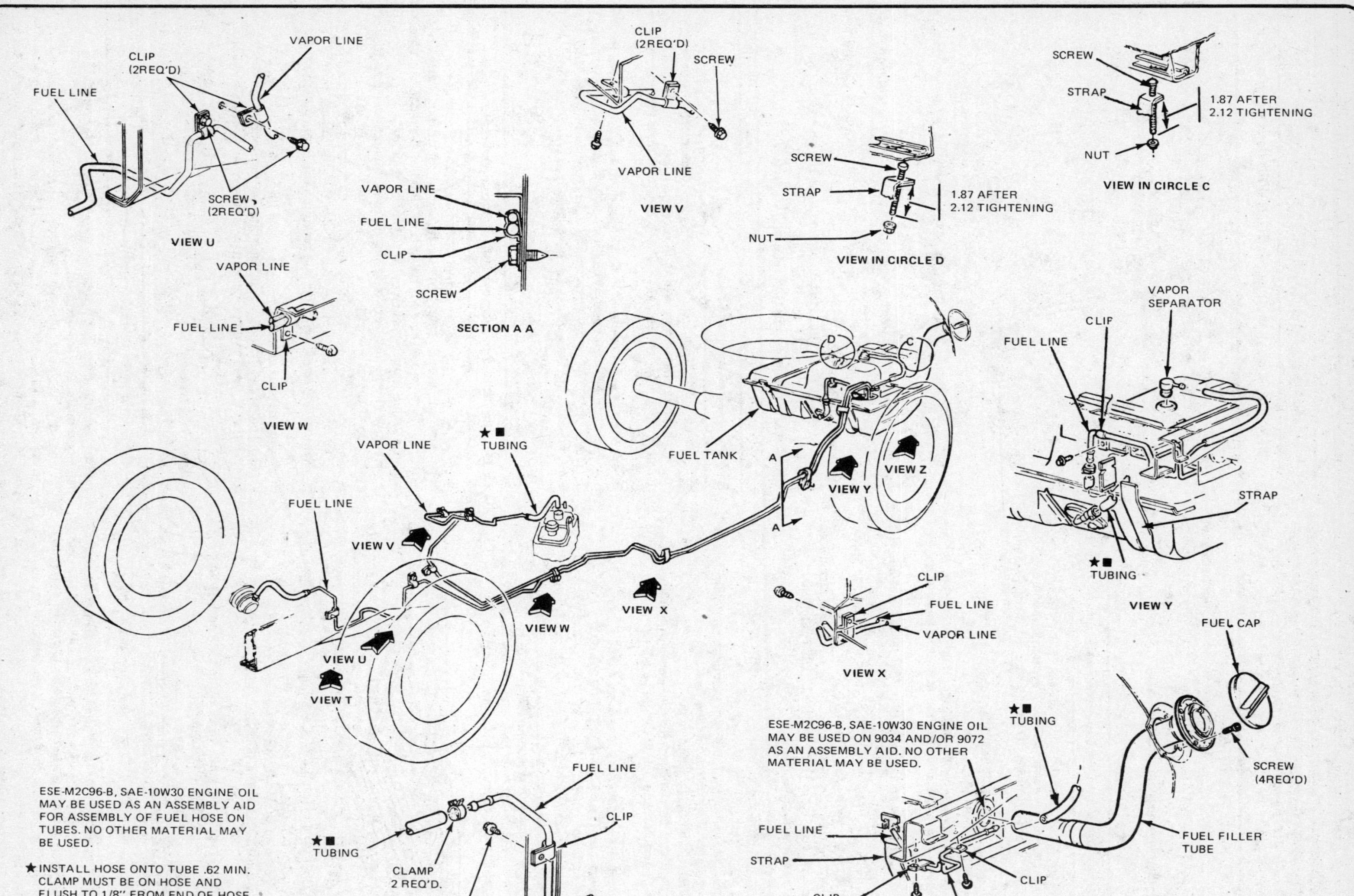

Fig. 3.20. Layout of fuel tank and fuel vapor pipelines (Sec. 24)

located beneath the floor of the rear compartment. The filler tube leads up to a gas cap on the right-hand rear side of the car. From 1975 on, the fuel filler orifice is fitted with a special restrictor to ensure that only the smaller, non-leaded refuelling nozzle can be fitted into the filler neck. Gas pumps supplying leaded fuels are fitted with a refuelling nozzle that is too large to fit in the filler neck.

To increase the fuel capacity, an auxiliary tank can be supplied as an optional extra on all Mustang II models. This tank, which has a capacity of approximately 4 gallons, is fitted between the main gas tank and the filler tube and is filled via the main tank gas cap.

23 Auxiliary tank (if fitted) - removal and replacement

1 For safety reasons disconnect the main battery terminals.
2 If the fuel gauge shows more than half full, syphon out enough fuel, using a suitable length of tubing, to ensure that the auxiliary tank is empty.
3 Remove the four screws holding the filler tube to the bodywork aperture and remove the filler tube.
4 From inside the left-side rear wheel housing, remove the four bolts that retain the inner splash panel covering the tank, and remove the panel.
5 Disconnect the hose between the main tank fuel sender unit and the fuel supply line.
6 Loosen the two clamps on the main filler tube connecting the auxil auxiliary tank to the main tank.
7 Place a container beneath the auxiliary tank to catch any residual fuel and then slide the connecting tube off the auxiliary tank neck.
8 Remove the screw holding the auxiliary tank retaining strap and remove the strap.
9 Lower the tank until the clamp holding the rubber boot to the tank filler neck can be slackened and the boot removed.
10 Lower the tank still further until the two hoses can be disconnected from the vapor separator union on top of the tank.
11 The auxiliary tank can now be lifted away.
12 Refitting the auxiliary tank is basically the reverse procedure to removal. However, the following points should be noted:

a) Do not forget to reconnect the two hoses to the vapor separator union on top of the tank before lifting the tank up into the installed position.
b) When fitting the rubber boot to the filler pipe, note that there is a notch in the boot which must be aligned with the raised rib on the auxiliary tank filler neck.
c) After the tank is installed have the system filled up and make a careful check to ensure there are no leaks.

24 Main fuel tank - removal and replacement

1 Disconnect the battery terminals.
2 Using a suitable length of pipe syphon out as much gas from the tank as possible.
3 If an auxiliary tank is fitted, remove it as described in the previous Section.
4 If the main tank only is fitted, remove the four screws securing the filler pipe to the bodywork aperture and carefully ease the bottom end of the pipe out of the sealing ring in the side of the tank.
5 Jack-up the rear of the car and suitably support it for access beneath.
6 Disconnect the fuel feed and vapor pipes at the tank and detach them from the clips along the tank front edge.
7 Disconnect the electrical leads from the sender unit.
8 Undo and remove the two support strap retaining nuts at the rear of the tank while supporting the weight of the tank.
9 Push the straps downwards and lift the tank out toward the rear of the car.
10 If it is necessary to remove the sender unit, this can be unscrewed from the tank using the appropriate Ford tool. Alternatively a suitable C-spanner or drift can probably be used, but great care should be taken that the flange is not damaged and that there is no danger from sparks if a hammer has to be resorted to.
11 Taking care not to damage the sealing washer, prise out the tank-to-filler pipe seal.

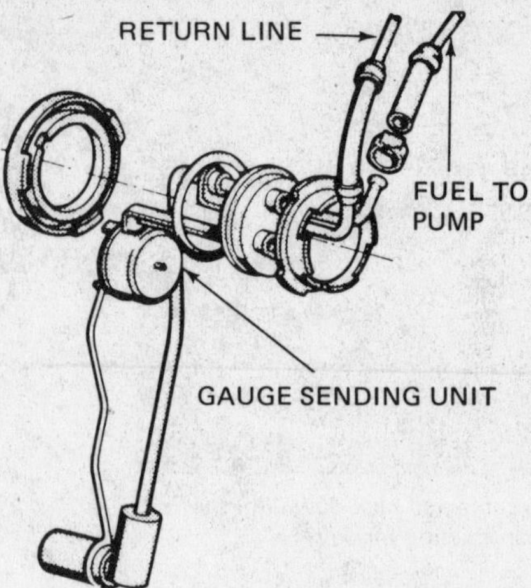

Fig. 3.21. Gas tank sender unit (Sec. 24)

12 When refitting, ensure that the rubber pads are stuck in position.
13 Refit a new filler pipe seal.
14 Refit the sender unit using a new seal, as the original one will almost certainly be damaged.
15 The remainder of the refitting procedure is the reverse of removal. A smear of engine oil on the tank filler pipe exterior will aid its fitment.
16 Do not overtighten the tank retaining strap nuts.

25 Fuel tank - cleaning and repair

1 With time it is likely that sediment will collect in the bottom of the fuel tank. Condensation, resulting in rust and other impurities, will usually be found in the fuel tank of any car more than three or four years old.
2 When the tank is removed it should be vigorously flushed out with hot water and detergent and, if facilities are available, steam cleaned.
3 Never weld, solder or bring a naked light close to an empty fuel tank, unless it has been cleaned as described in the previous paragraph, for at least two hours.

26 Throttle cable and kick-down rod - removal and replacement

1 Prise the throttle cable retainer bush from the top end of the accelerator pedal and remove the inner cable from the pedal assembly. **Note:** On later model cars the cable is retained by a Tinnerman type fastener which must be pryed off the end of the cable.
2 Remove the circular retaining clip holding the inner cable to the underside of the dash panel.
3 Remove the two screws retaining the outer cable to the dash panel.
4 Disconnect the control rod from the carburetor linkage (photo).
5 Remove the screw or spring clip retaining the outer cable to the engine bracket.
6 The complete cable assembly can now be removed.
7 To remove the kick-down rod (automatic transmission only), remove the 'C' type spring clips and pins at each end of the rod and remove the rod (See Fig. 3.22).
8 Refit the throttle cable and kick-down rod using the reverse procedure to removal.

27 Accelerator pedal - removal and refitting

1 Remove the inner throttle cable from the pedal assembly as described in the previous Section.
2 Undo the two nuts retaining the pedal to the floor bracket and remove the pedal assembly (see Fig. 3.22). **Note:** If a pedal extension pad is fitted this will have to be uncrimped from the pedal prior to pedal removal.
3 Refit the accelerator pedal using the reverse procedure to removal.

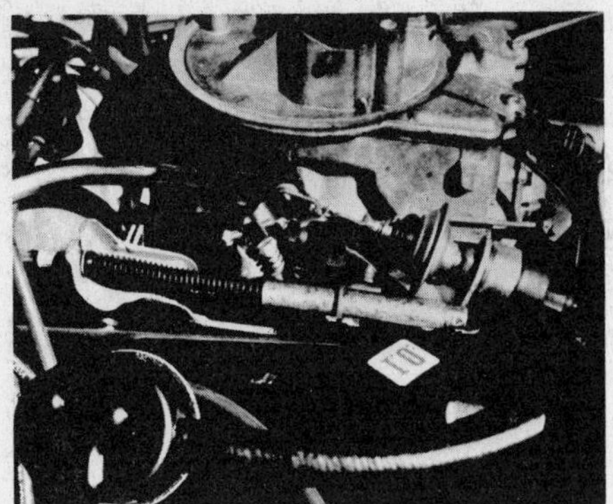

26.4 Throttle cable and kick-down linkage (automatic transmission models)

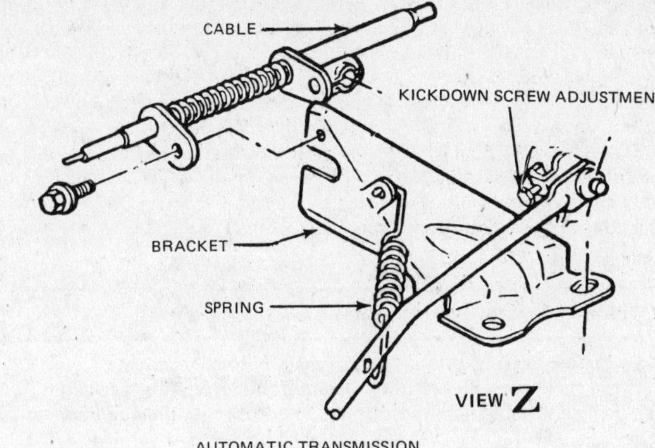

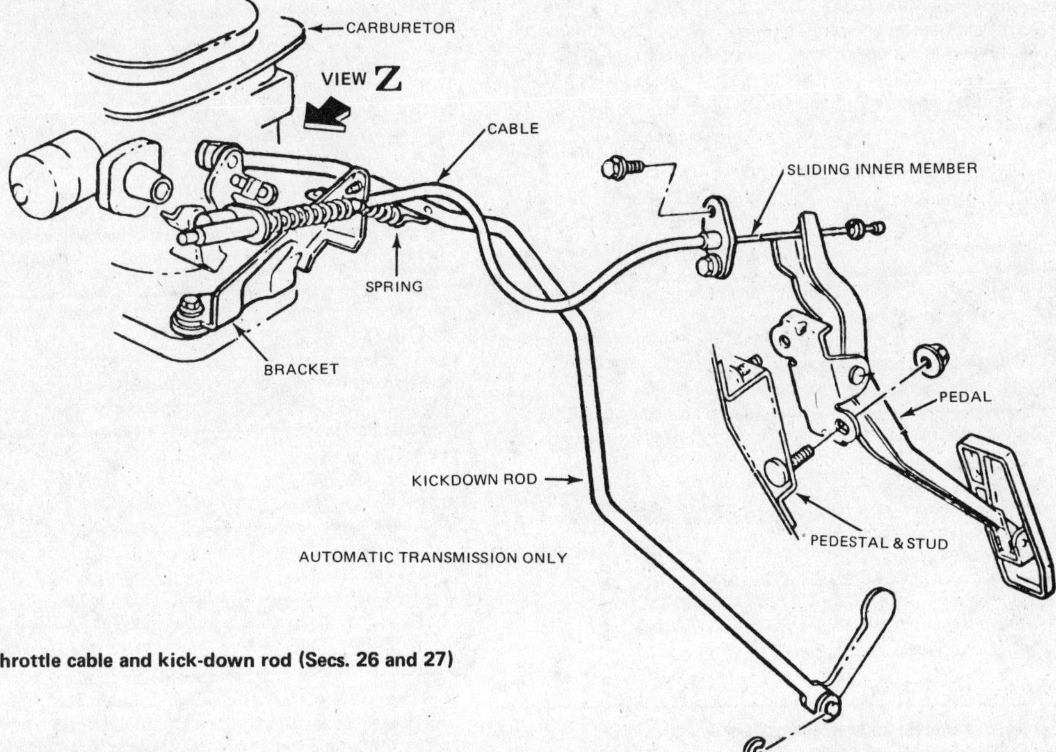

Fig. 3.22. Throttle cable and kick-down rod (Secs. 26 and 27)

28 Exhaust system - general description

V6 engines

1 The exhaust system on the V6 engined Mustang comprises single or dual pipes and resonator boxes.

2 On cars built from 1975 on a catalytic converter is fitted between the manifold and resonator box for emission control purposes.

4-cylinder engines

3 The 2.3 liter exhaust system is similar to the V6 in layout but consists of only a single pipe, resonator and muffler assembly located beneath the right-hand side of the car. At present, cars sold in the State of California only are fitted with a catalytic converter (Fig. 3.24).

4 On all models a periodic check should be made on the exhaust system for excessive corrosion and leaks. Any faults should be rectified at once to avoid contravening the Emission Control laws, or enabling carbon monoxide fumes entering the car.

29 Exhaust system - replacement

1 The exhaust systems on all models are made up of separate sections and attached together with either 'U' bolt clamps or a flange and gasket. Each system is attached to the underside of the car by brackets bolted to to insulated hangers.

2 The 2.3 liter exhaust system is in two sections comprising the front pipe connected to the exhaust manifold and then the resonator, connecting pipe and rear muffler which are welded together as one unit.

3 When a catalytic converter is fitted, it is located at the rear of the front pipe and can be removed by undoing the flange bolts.

4 The V6 layout is similar. The front pipes are attached by crossbraces and must be replaced together.

5 The right-hand side resonator and muffler are welded together but the left-hand resonator and connecting pipe can be removed as a separate unit.

6 Both catalytic converters, when fitted, can be removed separately.

7 When removing the resonator box(es) and muffler(s) it will be necessary to jack up the car body only to allow the rear axle to hang down fully. This will provide sufficient clearance for the resonator to

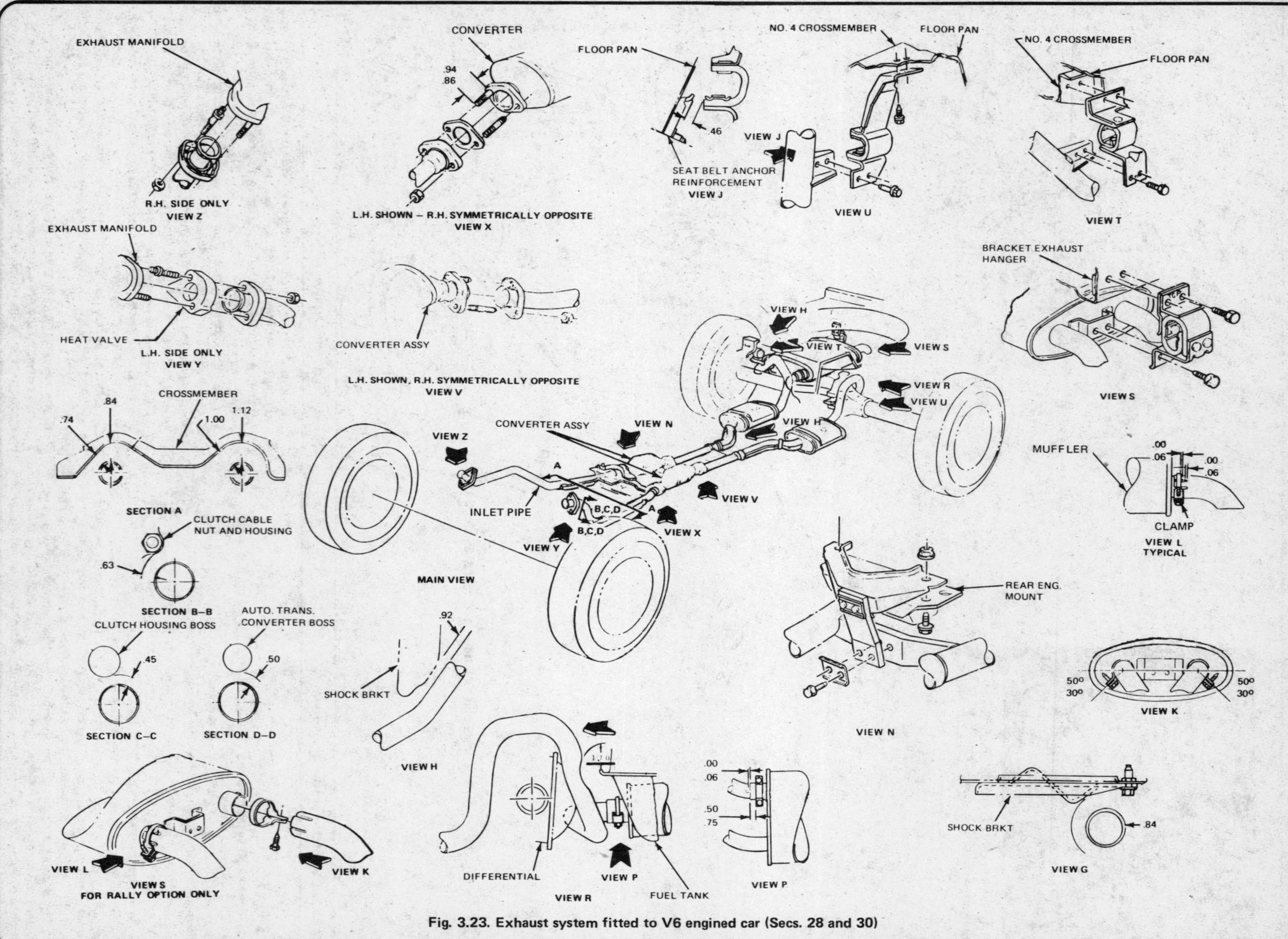

Fig. 3.23. Exhaust system fitted to V6 engined car (Secs. 28 and 30)

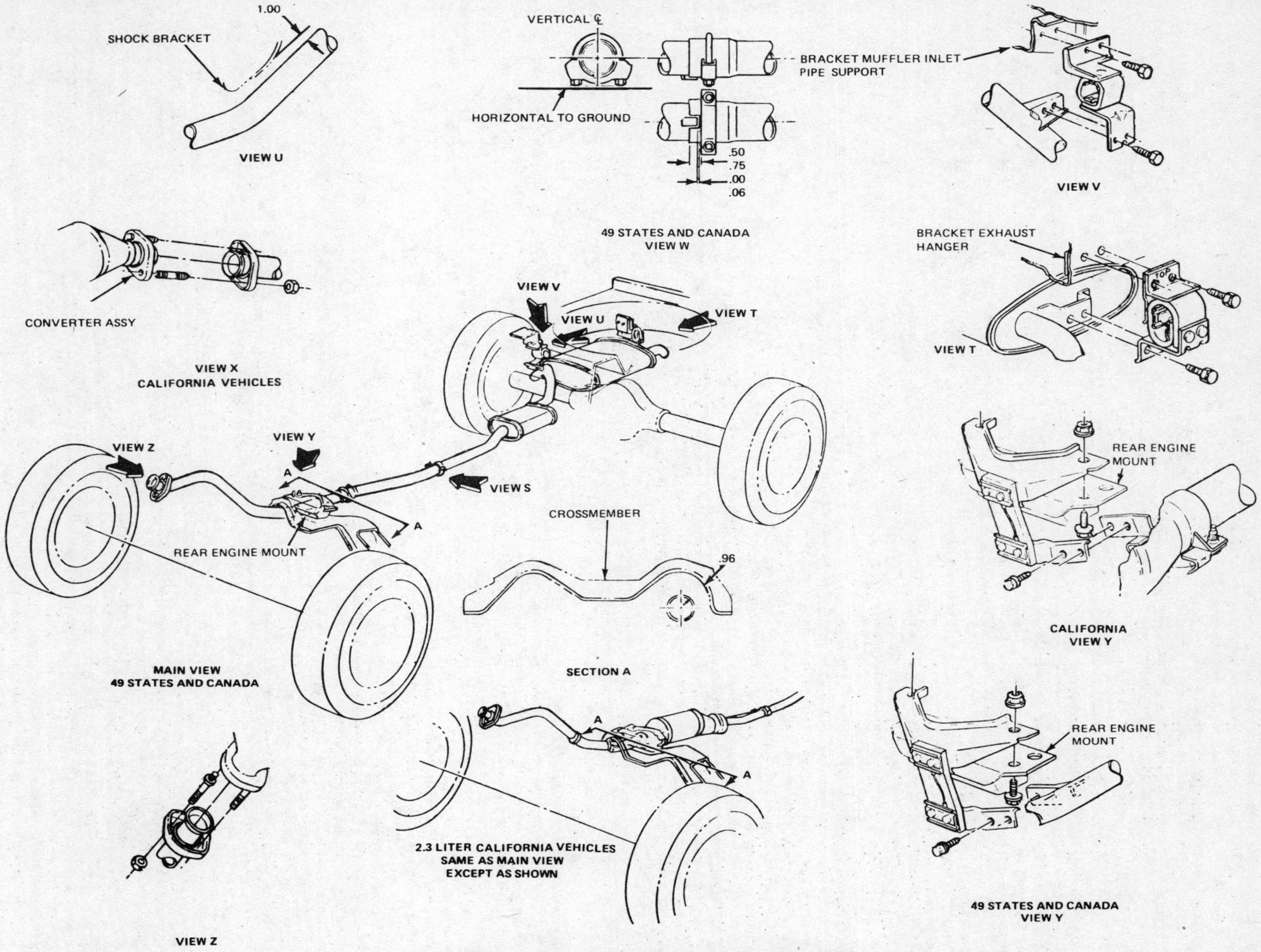

SHOCK BRACKET
1.00
VIEW U
VERTICAL ℄
HORIZONTAL TO GROUND
.50
.75
.00
.06
BRACKET MUFFLER INLET PIPE SUPPORT
VIEW V
CONVERTER ASSY
VIEW X
CALIFORNIA VEHICLES
49 STATES AND CANADA
VIEW W
VIEW V
VIEW U
VIEW T
BRACKET EXHAUST HANGER
VIEW T
VIEW Z
VIEW Y
A
VIEWS S
A
REAR ENGINE MOUNT
CROSSMEMBER
.96
REAR ENGINE MOUNT
CALIFORNIA
VIEW Y
MAIN VIEW
49 STATES AND CANADA
SECTION A
A
A
2.3 LITER CALIFORNIA VEHICLES
SAME AS MAIN VIEW
EXCEPT AS SHOWN
REAR ENGINE MOUNT
49 STATES AND CANADA
VIEW Y
VIEW Z

Fig. 3.24. Exhaust system layout 2.3 liter car (Secs. 28 and 30)

be withdrawn over the axle.
8 Although the different exhaust system sections can be renewed separately it will usually be found that if one section is badly corroded the rest of the system will be approaching the same condition. Therefore the most sensible and safest policy is to renew the complete system.
9 When refitting a flange type joint always use a new gasket.
10 Models fitted with catalytic converter(s) are fitted with a heat shield which will have to be unbolted and removed prior to replacing the exhaust system.

30 Emission control systems - general description

To conform to the USA anti-pollution laws the Mustang range of cars are fitted with several emission control devices. The specific controls fitted to each car will depend on what State the car is sold in, and emission control information for individual cars is shown on a data plate inside the engine compartment.

To cover all models, this Section describes all the emission controls that may be fitted.

Warning: Before commencing any maintenance or testing of emission control systems the owner is advised to read Section 2 of this Chapter to avoid contravening the emission control regulations.

Improved combustion (IMCO) system

1 The main features of this system are covered by the design of the engine and carburetor, and therefore require no special information. However, an electrically assisted choke heater is used as an aid to fast choke release for better emission characteristics during engine warm-up.
2 The heater is a constant temperature, positive temperature coefficient (PTC) unit, energised from the alternator field (IND) terminal, and is energised when the engine is running.
3 Incorporated with the unit is a fast idle cam latch, which holds the cam on the high position until the choke heats up and the bi-metal latch backs off to allow the latch pin and fast idle cam to rotate to the normal run position.
4 An overcenter spring assists in closing the choke plate for initial starting of a cold engine in high ambient temperatures. This spring has no effect after initial choke pull-down occurs.

Positive crankcase ventilation (PCV) system

5 The PCV system operates by drawing in air and mixing it with the vapors which have escaped past the piston rings (blow-by vapors). This mixture is then drawn into the combustion chamber through an oil separator and PCV valve.

Evaporative emission control

6 This system is designed to limit the emission of fuel vapors to the atmosphere. It comprises the fuel tank, pressure and vacuum sensitive fuel filler cap, a restrictor bleed orifice, a charcoal canister and the associated connecting lines.
7 When the fuel tank is filled, vapors are discharged to the atmosphere through the filler tube, and a space between the inner filler tube and the outer neck. When fuel covers the filler control tube, vapors can no longer escape and a vapor lock is created by the orifice; therefore there can be no flow to the vapor charcoal canister.
8 When thermal expansion occurs in the fuel tank, vapor is forced through the orifice to the canister, where it is stored when the engine is not running and is drawn into the carburetor intake system as soon as the engine is started.

Exhaust gas recirculation (EGR) system

9 This system is designed to reintroduce small amounts of exhaust gas into the combustion cycle to reduce the generation of oxides of nitrogen (NOx). The amount of gas reintroduced is governed by engine vacuum and temperature.
10 The EGR valve is mounted on a spacer block between the carburetor and manifold. A venturi vacuum amplifier (VVA) is used to change the relatively weak vacuum signal in the carburetor throat to a strong signal for operation of the EGR valve.
11 A relief valve is also used to modify the output EGR signal whenever venturi vacuum is equal to, or greater than, manifold vacuum. This allows the EGR valve to close at or near, wide open throttle, when maximum engine power is required.
12 The EGR/CSC (cold start cycle) regulates the distributor spark advance and EGR valve operation according to the engine coolant

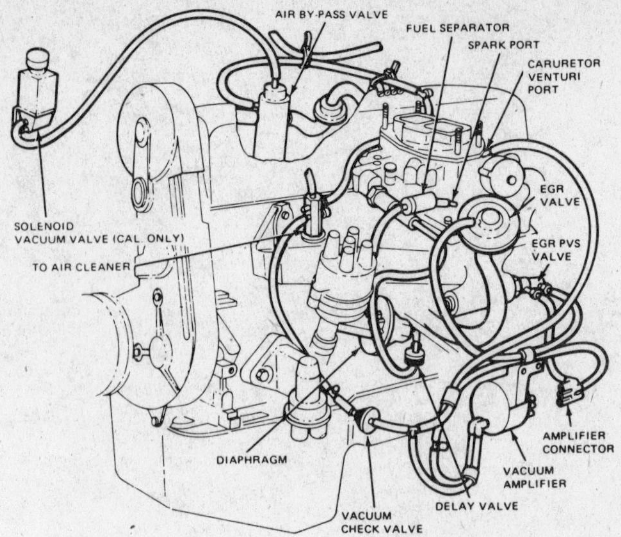

Fig. 3.25. Layout of emission control systems - typical (Sec. 30)

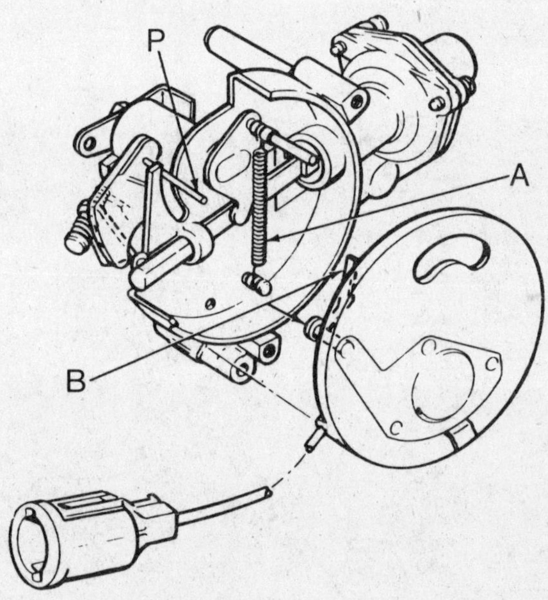

Fig. 3.26. Electrically assisted choke (Sec. 30)

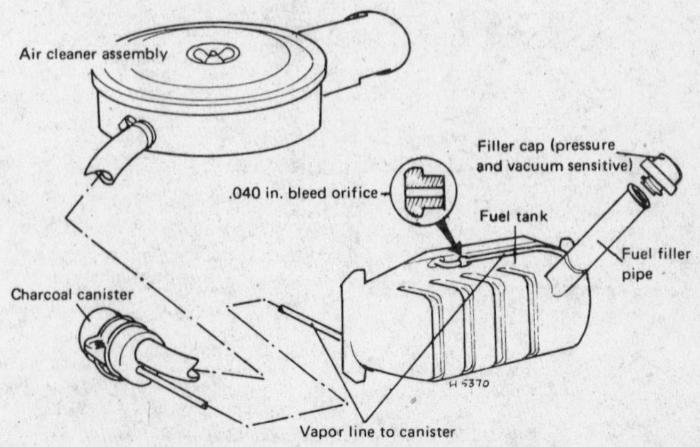

Fig. 3.27. Fuel evaporation system - typical (Sec. 30)

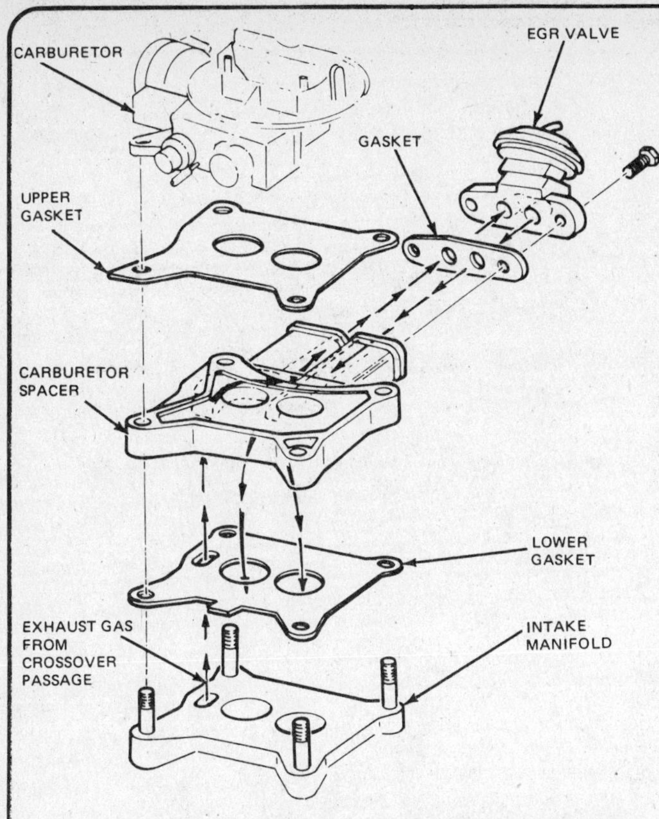

Fig. 3.28. EGR inlet manifold spacer and components (Sec. 30)

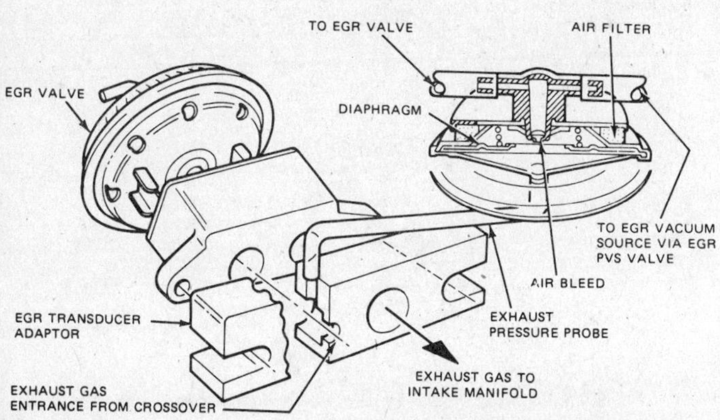

Fig. 3.29. EGR exhaust back pressure transducer (Sec. 30)

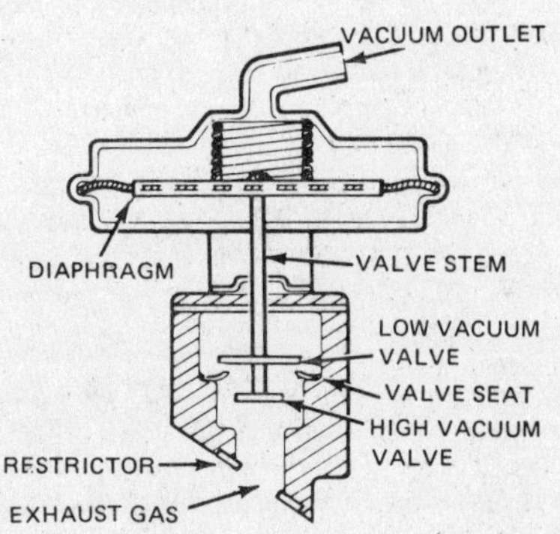

Fig. 3.30. EGR valve - typical (Sec. 30)

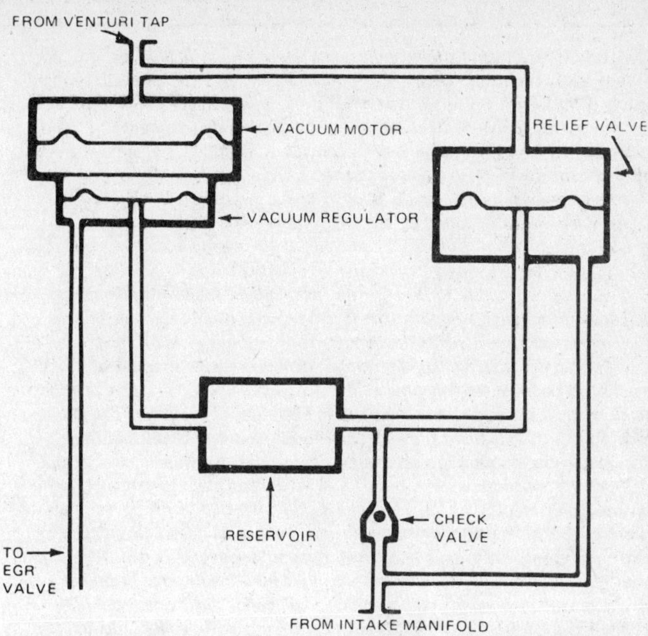

Fig. 3.31. Schematic diagram of venturi vacuum amplifier (Sec. 30)

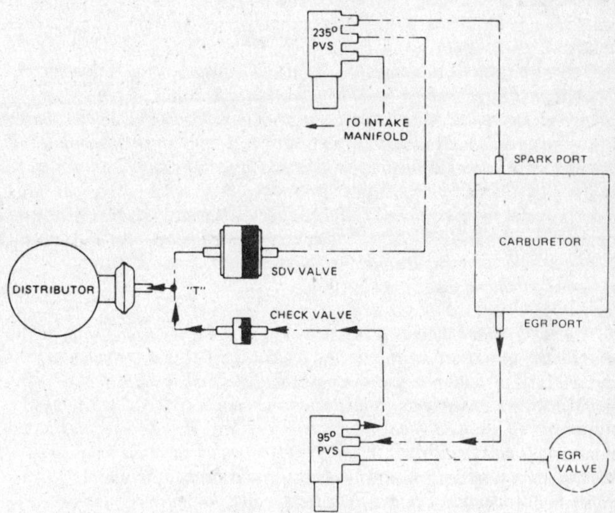

Fig. 3.32. Operation of EGR/CSC system below 82°F (Sec. 30)

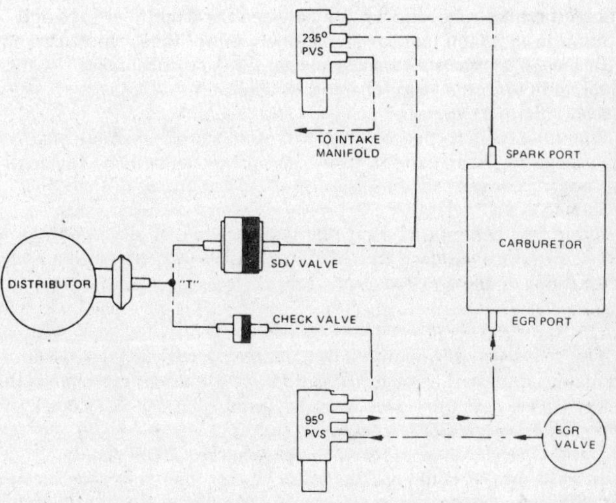

Fig. 3.33. Operation of EGR/CSC system above 95°F (Sec. 30)

3

temperature, by sequentially switching the vacuum signals. When the coolant temperature is below 82°F (27.8°C), the EGR posted vacuum switch (PVS) admits carburetor EGR port vacuum (which occurs at approximately 2500 rpm) directly to the distributor advance diaphragm through the one-way check valve. At the same time the PVS shuts off the carburetor vacuum to the EGR valve (Fig. 3.32).
13 When the engine coolant is 95°F (35°C) or above, the EGR-PVS directs carburetor vacuum to the EGR valve (Fig. 3.33).
14 At temperatures between 82 and 95°F (27.8 and 35°C), the EGR-PVS may be closed, open or in the mid-position.
15 A spark delay valve (SDV) is incorporated in the system to delay the carburetor spark vacuum to the distributor diaphragm unit for a predetermined time. During acceleration, little or no vacuum is admitted to the distributor diaphragm unit until acceleration is completed because of the time delay of the SDV and the re-routing of the EGR port vacuum at temperatures above 95°F (32°C). The check valve blocks the vacuum signal from the SDV to the EGR-PVS, so that carburetor spark vacuum will not be dissipated at temperatures above 95°F.
16 The 235°F (113°C) PVS is not strictly part of the EGR system, but is connected to the distributor vacuum advance unit to prevent over-heating while idling with a hot engine. At idle speeds, no vacuum is generated at either of the carburetor ports and the engine timing is fully retarded. However, when the coolant temperature reaches 235°F (113°C) the PVS is actuated to admit intake manifold vacuum to the distributor advance diaphragm. The engine timing is thus advanced, idling speed is correspondingly increased and the engine temperature is lowered due to increased fan speed and coolant flow.

Catalytic converter
17 On some models a catalytic converter is incorporated upstream of the exhaust front muffler (See Fig. 3.23 and 3.24). The converter comprises a ceramic honeycomb-like core housed in a stainless steel pipe. The core is coated with a platinum and palladium catalyst which converts unburned carbon monoxide and hydrocarbons into carbon dioxide and water by a chemical reaction.
18 No special maintenance of the converter is required, but it can be damaged by the use of leaded fuels, engine misfiring, excessive richness of the carburetor mixture, incorrect operation of the Thermactor system or running out of gasoline.

Inlet air temperature regulation
19 Inlet air temperature regulation is accomplished by the use of a thermostatic air cleaner and duct system (see Section 3).
20 An additional feature, incorporated on some models, is the cold temperature actuated vacuum (CTAV) system. This is designed to select either carburetor spark port vacuum or carburetor EGR port vacuum, as a function of ambient air temperature. The selected vacuum source is used to control the distributor diaphragm unit.
21 The system comprises an ambient temperature switch, a three-way solenoid valve, an external vacuum bleed and a latching relay.
22 The temperature switch activates the solenoid, which is open at temperatures below 49°F (9.5°C) and is closed above 65°F (18.3°C). Within this temperature range the solenoid valve may be open or closed.
23 Below 49°F (9.5°C) the system is inoperative and the distributor diaphragm receives carburetor spark port vacuum while the EGR valve receives EGR port vacuum.
24 When the temperature switch closes (above 65°F/18.3°C) the three way solenoid valve is energized from the ignition switch and the carburetor EGR port vacuum is delivered to the distributor advance diaphragm as well as to the EGR valve. The latching relay is also energized by the temperature switch closing, and will remain energized until the ignition switch is turned off, regardless of the temperature switch being open or closed.

Thermactor exhaust control system
25 This system is designed to reduce the hydrocarbon and carbon monoxide content of the exhaust gases by continuing the oxidation of unburnt gases after they leave the combustion chamber. This is achieved by using an engine driven air pump to inject fresh air into the hot exhaust stream after it leaves the combustion chamber. This air mixes with the hot exhaust gases and promotes further oxidation, thus reducing their concentration and converting some of them into carbon dioxide and water.
26 The air pump draws in air through an impeller type, centrifugal fan and exhausts it from the exhaust manifold through a vacuum controlled air bypass valve and check valve. Under normal conditions thermactor air passes straight through the bypass valve, but during deceleration, when there is a high level of intake manifold vacuum, the diaphragm check valve operates to shut off the thermactor air to the air supply check valve and exhausts it to atmosphere. The air supply check valve is a non-return valve which will allow thermactor air to pass to the exhaust manifold but will not allow exhaust gases to flow in the reverse direction (Figs. 3.41 and 3.42).
27 A slightly modified system may be used on some later vehicles which have catalytic converters in the exhaust system; this may incorporate a vacuum differential valve (VDV) (Fig. 3.40). A typical system is shown in Fig. 3.37 and 3.43.

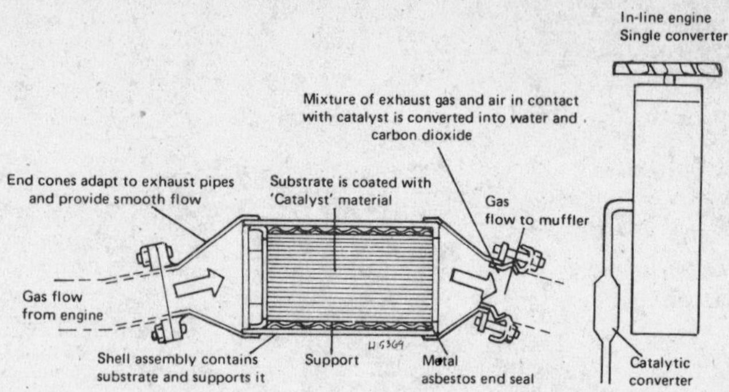

Fig. 3.34. Sectional view of catalytic converter (Sec. 30)

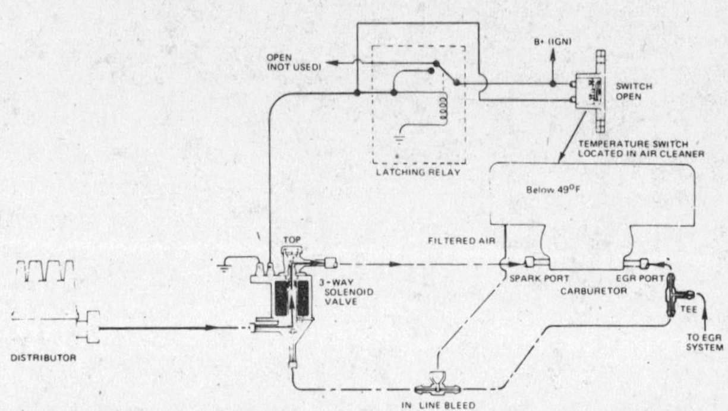

Fig. 3.35. Typical CTAV system operation below 49°F (Sec. 30)

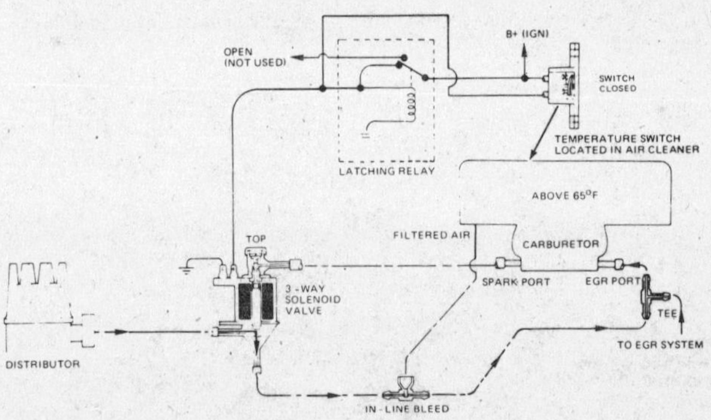

Fig. 3.36. Typical CTAV system operation above 65°F (Sec. 30)

Deceleration valve
28 A deceleration valve is used to provide an enriched mixture when the engine is on overrun with the throttle closed. The valve screws into the intake manifold and has two vacuum outlet ports. When the engine decelerates a vacuum is applied to the control port and the valve opens and allows a fuel/air mixture to by-pass the carburetor and pass directly into the intake manifold (Fig. 3.44).
29 On Mustang models with the V6 engine the system is controlled by a gearbox operated switch and solenoid valve which prevents the deceleration valve operating at speeds below 11 mph (see Fig. 3.45).

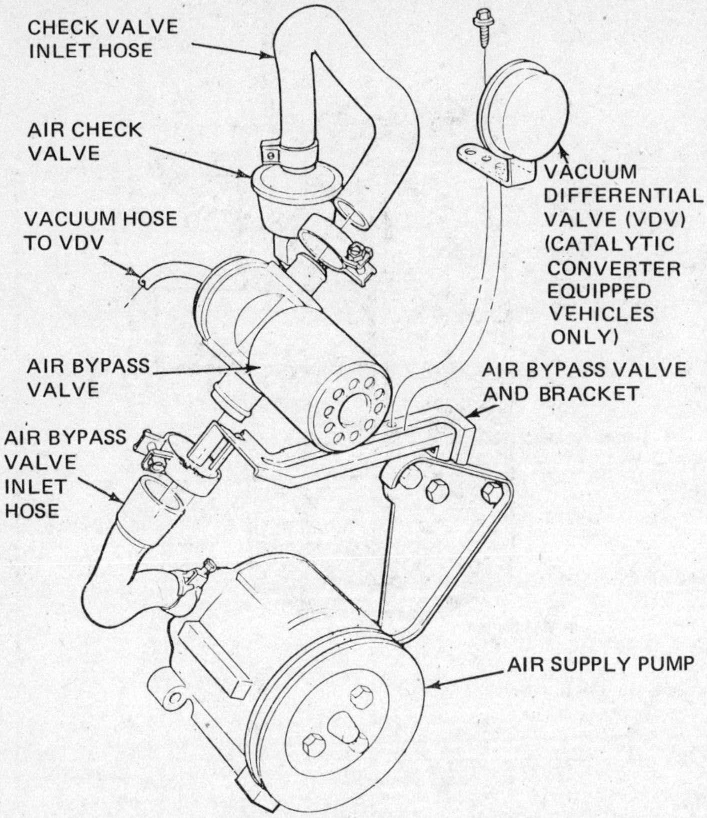

CHECK VALVE INLET HOSE
AIR CHECK VALVE
VACUUM HOSE TO VDV
AIR BYPASS VALVE
AIR BYPASS VALVE INLET HOSE
VACUUM DIFFERENTIAL VALVE (VDV) (CATALYTIC CONVERTER EQUIPPED VEHICLES ONLY)
AIR BYPASS VALVE AND BRACKET
AIR SUPPLY PUMP

Fig. 3.37. Layout of basic thermactor components (Sec. 30)

31 Emission control system - maintenance and testing

1 In view of the special test equipment and procedures there is little that can be done in the way of maintenance and testing for the emission control system. In the event of a suspected malfunction of the system, check the security and condition of all pneumatic and electrical connections then, where applicable, refer to the following paragraphs for further information.

Electrically assisted choke heater

2 The only test that can be carried out on this assembly, without special test equipment, is a continuity check of the heater coil. If an ohmmeter is available, check for the specified resistance. If no ohmmeter is available, disconnect the stator lead from the choke cap terminal and connect it to one terminal of a 12V low wattage bulb (eg, instrument panel bulb). Ground (earth) the other terminal of the bulb and check that it illuminates when the engine is running. If it fails to illuminate, check the alternator output and the choke lead for continuity. If the bulb illuminates, disconnect the bulb ground terminal and reconnect it to the choke lead. If the bulb does not illuminate when the engine is warm, a faulty choke unit is indicated.

PCV system

3 Remove all the hoses and components of the system and clean them in kerosene or gasoline. Ensure that all hoses are free from any obstruction and are in a serviceable condition. Where applicable, similarly clean the crankcase breather cap and shake it dry. Replace parts as necessary, then refit them to the car.

Charcoal canister

4 The charcoal canister is located on the right-hand side of the engine compartment. To remove it, disconnect the two hoses, then remove the three nuts securing the canister bracket to the dash panel. Remove the canister and bracket. Refitting is the reverse of the removal procedure.

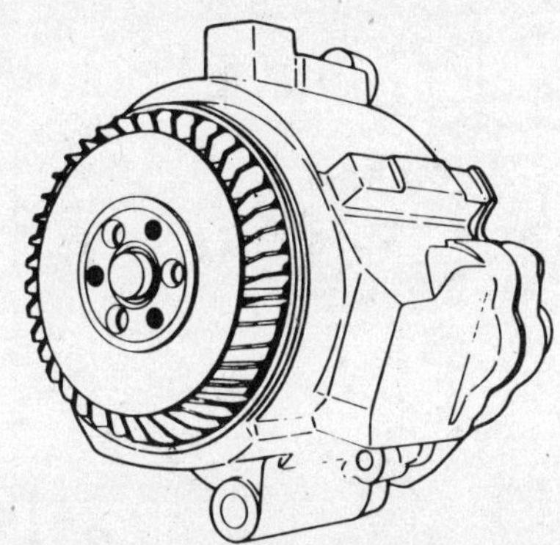

Fig. 3.38. Thermactor engine driven pump (Sec. 30)

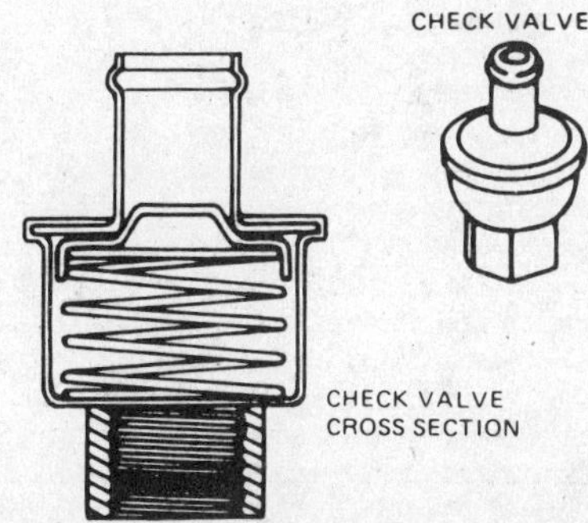

Fig. 3.39. Exhaust check valve (Thermactor system) (Sec. 30)

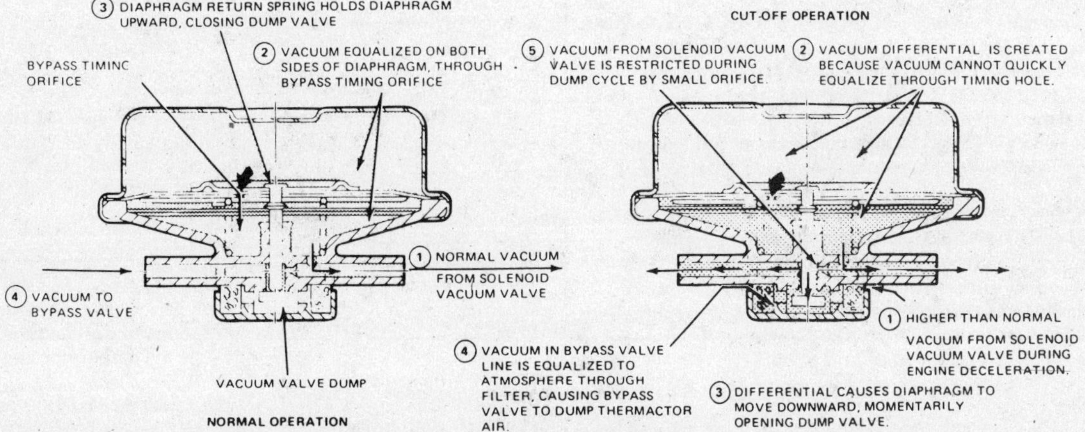

Fig. 3.40. Vacuum differential valve (systems with catalytic converter) (Sec. 30)

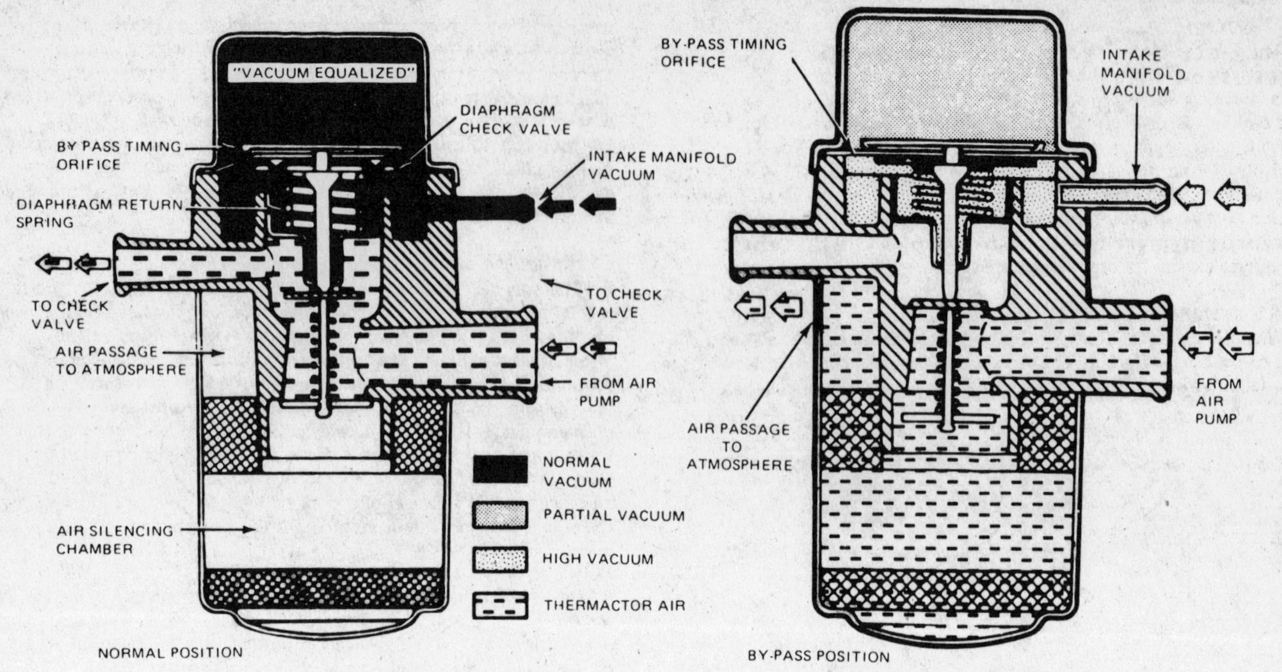

Fig. 3.41. Early type thermactor system bypass valve (Sec. 30)

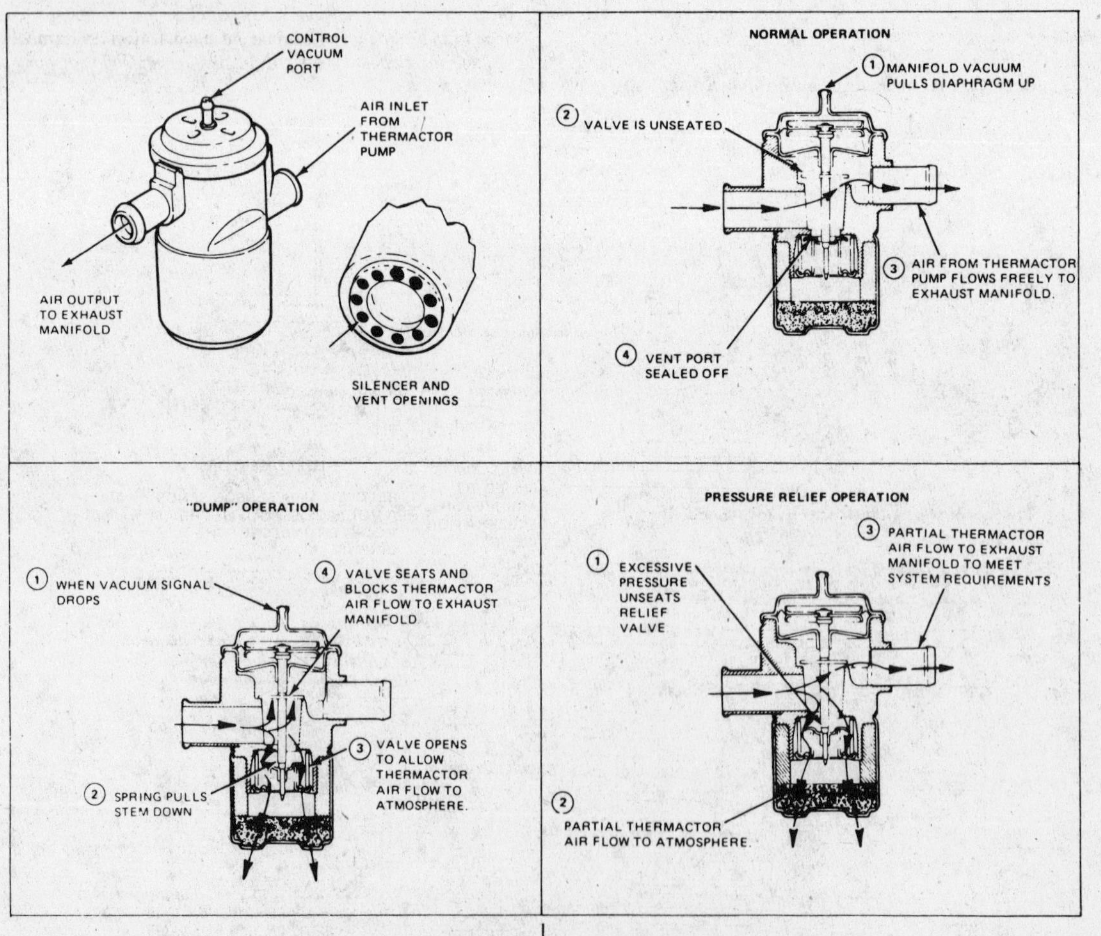

Fig. 3.42. Later type Thermactor system bypass valve (Sec. 30)

EGR system

5 The EGR valve can be removed for cleaning, but where it is damaged, corroded or extremely dirty it is preferable to fit a replacement. If the valve is to be cleaned, check that the orifice in the body is clear but take care not to enlarge it. If the valve can be dismantled, internal deposits can be removed with a small power driven rotary wire brush. Deposits around the valve stem and disc can be removed by using a steel blade or shim approximately 0.028 in (0.7 mm) thick in a sawing motion around the stem shoulder at both sides of the disc. Clean the cavity and passages in the main body; ensure that the poppet wobbles and moves axially before reassembly.

CTAV system

6 Without special equipment it is only possible to carry out electrical tests of the system circuitry. Connect one terminal of a 12V low wattage bulb (eg, instrument panel bulb) to the car ground. Connect the other terminal to point 'B' (Fig. 3.46) and remove the connector at point 'D'. Turn on the ignition; if the light illuminates, replace the latching relay. If there is no light, reconnect at point 'D'; there should now be a light. If there is none, check the temperature switch and the wiring back to the ignition switch. Provided that there is a light, disconnect at point 'D' again. There should now be a light; if there is

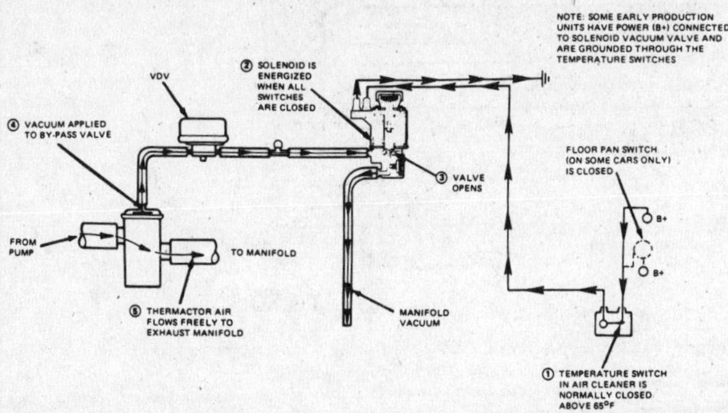

Fig. 3.43. Schematic diagram of thermactor system - typical (Sec. 30)

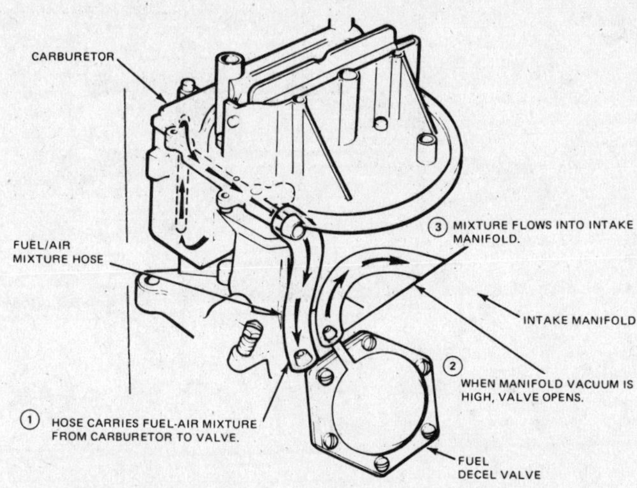

Fig. 3.44. Conventional fuel deceleration system (Sec. 30)

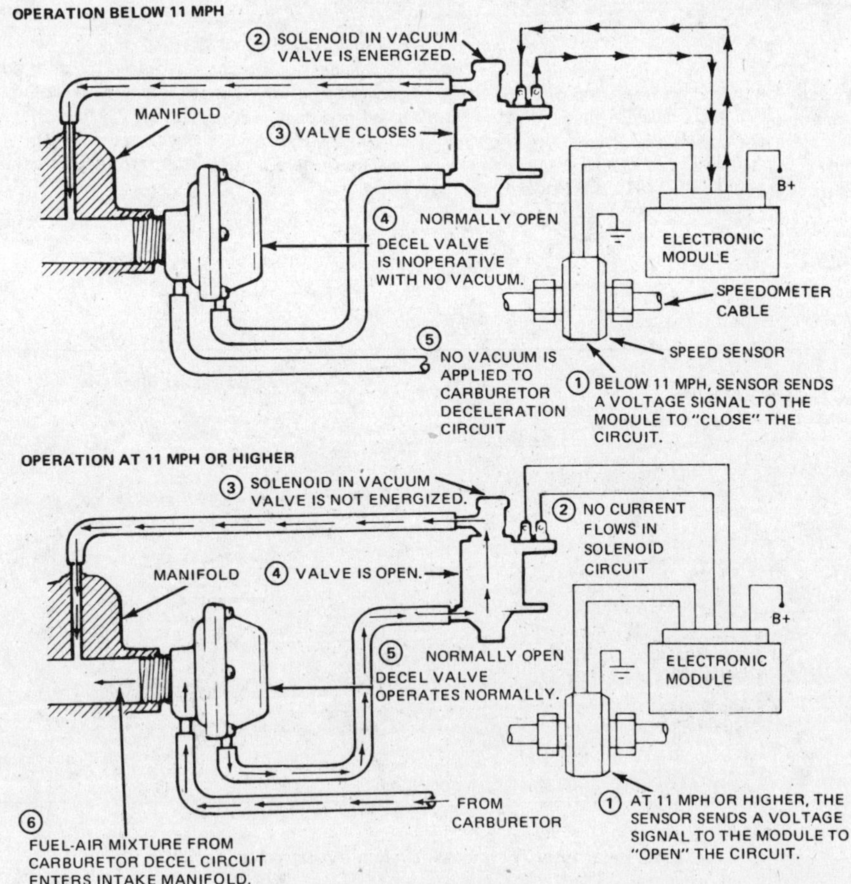

Fig. 3.45. Speed-controlled deceleration system (Sec. 30)

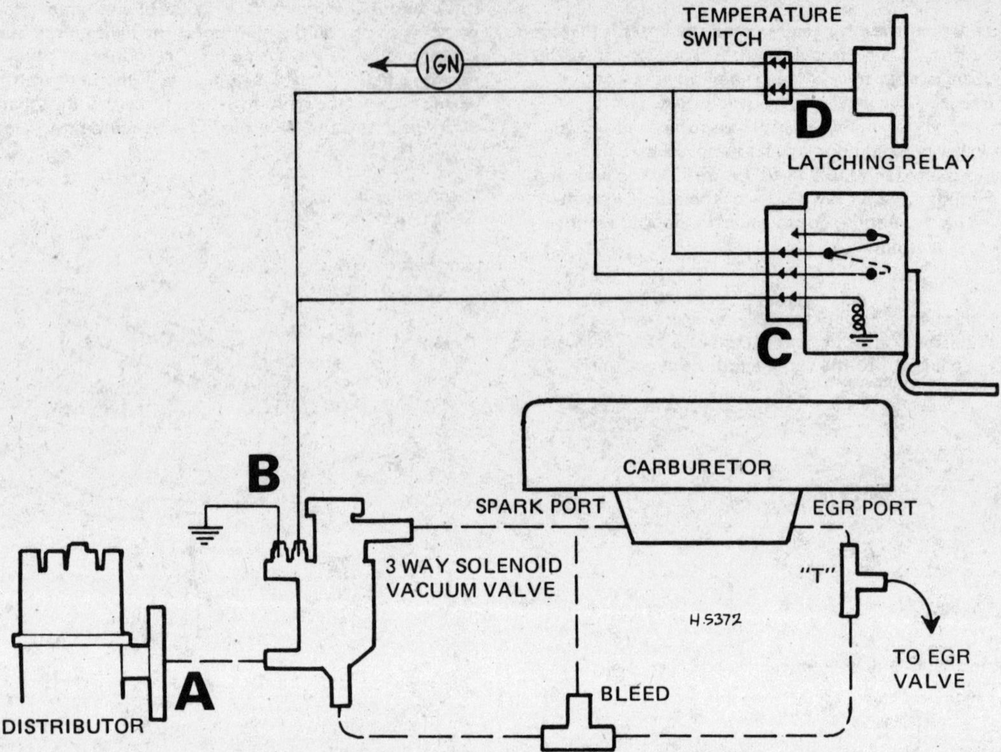

Fig. 3.46. Test connection points for the CTAV system (Sec. 31)

none, replace the latching relay. If it is possible to cool the temperature switch below 49°F (9.5°C), check that the contacts are open at or below this temperature.

Thermactor system

7 Apart from checking the condition of the drivebelt and pipe connections, and checking the pump drivebelt tension, there is little that can be done without the use of special test equipment. Drivebelt tension should be checked by a Ford dealer with a special tensioning tool. However, this is approximately equal to ½ in (13 mm) of belt movement between the longest pulley run under moderate hand pressure.

Deceleration valve system

8 Special equipment is required to carry out a complete test on the deceleration valve function and it is recommended that the car is taken to a Ford dealer. However, on 2.8 liter engines the speed control solenoid circuit can be checked by switching on the ignition and checking there is current at terminal B+ on the solenoid using a test lamp.

32 Fault diagnosis - fuel system

Symptom	Reason/s
Excessive fuel consumption *	Air cleaner choked or inlet duct system inoperative. General leaks from fuel system. Float chamber fuel level too high. Rich mixture. Incorrect valve clearances. Dragging brakes. Tires under-inflated. Faulty choke operation.

** May also be due to faulty condenser or advance/retard system in distributor OR an emission control system fault.*

Symptom	Reason/s
Insufficient fuel delivery or weak mixture	Clogged fuel line or carburetor filter. Fuel inlet needle valve stuck. Faulty fuel pump. Leaking pipe connections. Leaking inlet manifold gasket. Leaking carburetor mounting flange gasket. Weak carburetor mixture setting.

33 Fault diagnosis - emission control system

The following list is for guidance only, since a combination of faults may produce symptoms which are difficult to diagnose. It is therefore essential that a Ford dealer or emission control specialist is consulted in the event of problems occurring.

Symptom	Reason/s
Electrically assisted choke heater	
Long engine warm-up time	Faulty choke heater.
PCV system	
Fumes escaping from engine	Clogged PCV valve. Split or collapsed hoses.
Evaporative control system	
Fuel odour or rough engine running	Choked carbon canister. Stuck filler cap valve. Split or collapsed hoses.
Lean mixture, stalling	Faulty solenoid vent valve or carburetor bowl vent valve.
Thermactor system	
Fume emission from exhaust	Air pump drivebelt incorrectly tensioned. Damaged air supply pipes. Split or collapsed sensing hoses. Defective air pump. Faulty pressure relief valve.
EGR system	
Rough idling	Faulty or dirty EGR valve. Split or collapsed hoses. Leaking valve gasket.
Catalytic converter	
Fume emission from exhaust	Damaged or clogged catalyst.

Chapter 4 Ignition system

For modifications, and information applicable to later models, see Supplement at end of manual

Contents

Specifications

Spark plugs

Type:	
2.3 liter engine	Motorcraft AGRF - 52
V6 engine	Motorcraft AGR - 42
Electrode gap	Normally 0.032 in (0.8 mm), but refer to Emission Control decal inside the engine compartment
Thread size	18 mm

Coil

Type	Motorcraft 8 volt, oil filled
Ballast resistor	1.5 ohms

Distributor

Type:	
Pre - 1975 models	Moving contact breaker
1975 models on	Solid state, breakerless
Automatic advance	Vacuum and centrifugal
Direction of rotation	Clockwise
Contact breaker gap (where applicable):	
2.3 liter engine	0.027 in (0.68 mm)
V6 engine	0.024 in (0.6 mm)
Rotor air gap (solid state ignition)	7.5 k.v. (voltage drop)
Static advance (initial)	Refer to Emission control decal
Dwell angle (models with mechanical breaker)	35 - 41°
Firing order:	
2.3 liter engine	1 - 3 - 4 - 2
V6 engine	1 - 4 - 2 - 5 - 3 - 6

Note: All adjustment figures given in these specifications should be double-checked against the car's individual Emission Control decal.

Torque wrench settings	**lb f ft**	**kg f m**
Spark plugs:		
2.3 liter engine	10 to 15	1.3 to 2
V6 engine	14 to 22	1.9 to 3

1 General description (contact breaker ignition system)

In order that the engine can run correctly it is necessary for an electrical spark to ignite the fuel/air mixture in the combustion chamber at exactly the right moment in relation to engine speed and load. The ignition system is based on feeding low tension voltage from the battery to the coil where it is converted to high tension voltage. The high tension voltage is powerful enough to jump the spark plug gap in the cylinders many times a second under high compression pressures, providing that the system is in good condition and that all adjustments are correct.

The ignition system is divided into two circuits, low tension and high tension.

The low tension circuit (sometimes known as the primary) consists of the battery lead to the ignition switch, ballast resistor lead from the ignition switch to the low tension or primary coil winding (terminal 15 or +), and the lead from the low tension coil winding (terminal 1 or –) to the contact breaker points and condenser in the distributor.

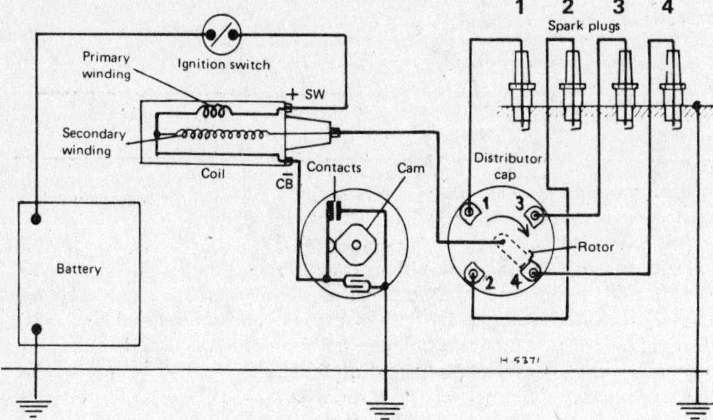

Fig. 4.1. Diagram of ignition system (4-cyl)

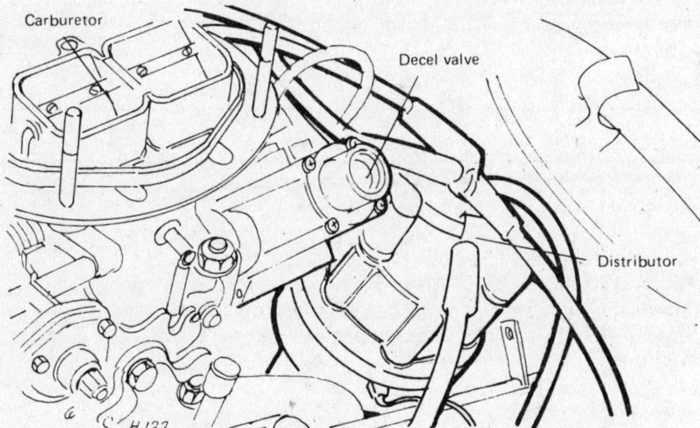

Fig. 4.2. Location of distributor on V6 engine

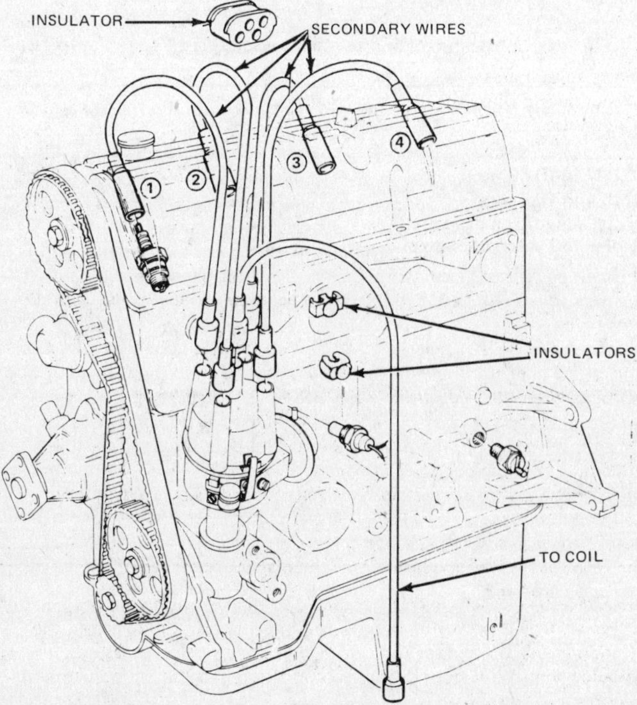

Fig. 4.3. 2.3 liter engine distributor and HT leads

The high tension circuit consists of the high tension or secondary coil winding, the heavy ignition lead from the centre of the coil to the centre of the distributor cap, the rotor arm, the spark plug leads and spark plugs.

The system functions in the following manner. Low tension voltage is changed in the coil into high tension voltage by the opening of the contact breaker points in the low tension circuit. High tension voltage is then fed via the carbon brush in the center of the distributor cap to the rotor arm of the distributor, and each time it comes in line with one of the metal segments in the cap, which are connected to the spark plug leads, the opening of the contact breaker points causes the high tension voltage to build up, jump the gap from the rotor arm to the appropriate metal segment and so via the spark plug lead to the spark plug, where it finally jumps the spark plug gap before going to ground.

The ignition is advanced and retarded automatically, to ensure the spark occurs at just the right instant for the particular load at the prevailing engine speed.

The ignition advance is controlled both mechanically and by a vacuum operated system. The mechanical governor comprises two weights, which move out from the distributor shaft as the engine speed rises due to centrifugal force. As they move outwards they rotate the cam relative to the distributor shaft, and so advance the spark. The weights are held in position by two light springs and it is the tension of the springs which is largely responsible for correct spark advancement.

The vacuum control consists of a diaphragm, one side of which is connected via a small bore tube to the carburetor, and the other side to the contact breaker plate. Depression in the inlet manifold and carburetor, which varies with the engine speed and throttle opening, causes the diaphragm to move, so moving the contact breaker plate, and advancing the spark. A spring within the vacuum unit returns the breaker plate to the normal position when the amount of manifold depression is reduced.

Some distributors are fitted with a dual diaphragm vacuum control unit.

The outer (primary) diaphragm senses carburetor vacuum just upstream of the throttle butterflies to advance ignition timing; the inner (secondary) diaphragm senses manifold vacuum. Therefore, when the manifold vacuum is high (eg, during deceleration or idling) the secondary diaphragm retards the spark. As soon as the throttle is opened, the primary diaphragm takes control and causes the spark to advance. The purpose of this system is to decrease the emission of unburnt hydrocarbons at low throttle openings.

The wiring harness includes a high resistance wire in the ignition coil feed circuit and it is very important that only a 'ballast resistor' type ignition coil is used. The starter solenoid has an extra terminal so that a wire from the solenoid to the coil supplies voltage direct to the coil when the starter motor is operated. The ballast resistor wire is therefore bypassed and battery voltage is fed to the ignition system, so giving easier starting.

On some models where an F.M. radio is fitted a 'screening can' is fitted around the distributor to suppress interference and is easily removable.

2 Ignition system servicing and Federal Regulations (all models)

In order to conform with the Federal Regulations which govern the emission of hydrocarbons and carbon monoxide from car exhaust systems, the engine, carburetion and ignition system have been suitably modified.

It is critically important that the ignition system is kept in good operational order and to achieve this accurate analytical equipment is needed to check and reset the distributor function. This will be found at your local dealer.

Information contained in this Chapter is supplied to enable the home mechanic to set the ignition system roughly so enabling starting the engine. Thereafter the car must be taken to the local Ford dealer for final tuning unless you possess the necessary equipment. Failure to do this can result in heavy penalties.

3 Contact breaker points - adjustment (contact breaker ignition system)

1 To adjust the contact breaker points to the correct gap, first release

the two clips or screws, securing the distributor cap to the distributor body, and lift away the cap. Clean the cap inside and out with a dry cloth. It is unlikely that the segments will be badly burned or scored, but if they are the cap will have to be renewed.
2 Inspect the carbon brush contact located in the top of the cap to ensure that it is not broken and stands proud of the plastic surface.
3 Lift away the rotor arm and check the contact spring on the top of the rotor arm. It must be clean and have adequate tension to ensure good contact.
4 Gently pry the contact breaker points open to examine the condition of their faces. If they are rough, pitted or dirty it will be necessary to remove them for resurfacing, or for replacement points to be fitted.
5 Presuming the points are satisfactory, or that they have been cleaned or replaced, measure the gap between the points with feeler gauges by turning the crankshaft until the heel of the breaker arm is on the highest point of the cam. The gap should be as given in the Specifications.
6 If the gap varies from the specified amount slacken the contact plate securing screw/s, V6 distributor 1 screw, 2.3 liter distributor 2 screws.
7 Adjust the contact gap by inserting a screwdriver in the notched hole in the contact breaker plate. Turn clockwise to increase, and anticlockwise to decrease the gap. When the gap is correct, tighten the securing screw/s and check the gap again (Fig. 4.4).
8 Replace the rotor arm and distributor cap. Retain in position with the two clips, V6, or two screws 2.3 liter.
9 On modern engines, setting the contact breaker gap using feeler gauges must be regarded as a basic adjustment only. For optimum engine performance, the dwell angle must be checked. The dwell angle is the number of degrees through which the distributor cam turns during the period between the instants of closure and opening of the contact breaker points. Checking the dwell angle not only gives a more accurate setting of the contact breaker gap but this method also evens out any variations in the gap which could be caused by wear in the distributor shaft or its bushings or a difference in height of any of the cam peaks.
10 The angle should be checked with a dwell meter connected in accordance with the makers' instructions. Refer to Specifications for the correct dwell angle. If the dwell angle is found to be too large, increase the points gap, if too small, reduce the gap. Always adjust the dwell angle before checking the ignition timing.

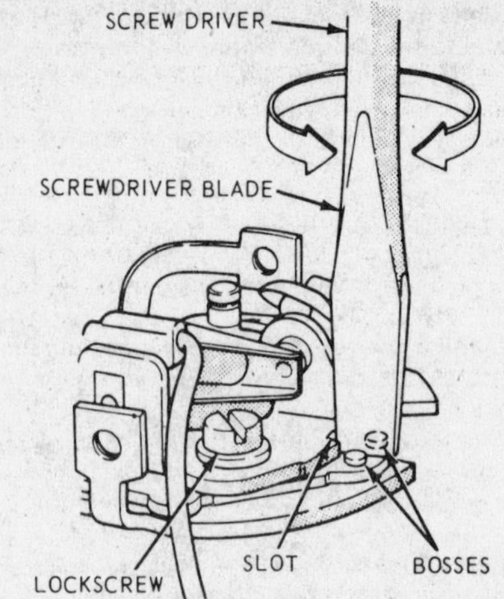

Fig. 4.4. Adjusting contact breaker gap - typical (Sec. 3)

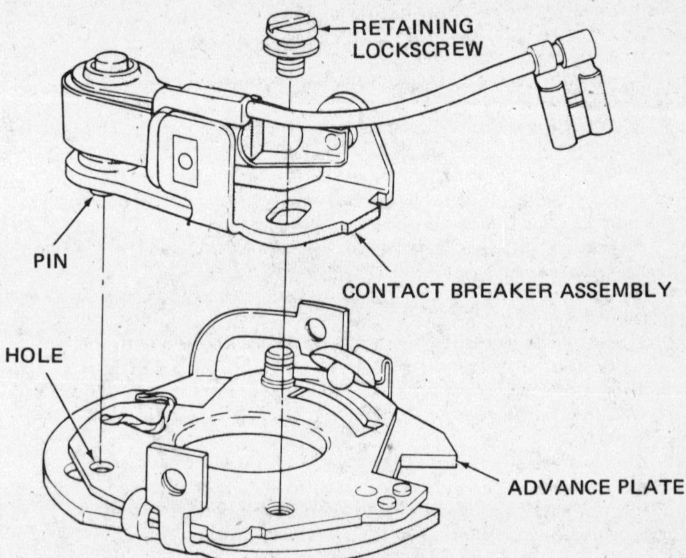

Fig. 4.5. Contact breaker and plate assembly (V6 engine) (Sec. 4)

4 Contact breaker points - removal and refitting (contact breaker ignition system)

1 If the contact breaker points are burned, pitted or badly worn they must be removed and renewed.
2 Lift off the rotor arm by pulling it straight up from the spindle.

V6 engines

a) Detach the low tension lead terminal from the internal terminal post and then undo and remove the screw that retains the contact breaker assembly to the base plate. Lift away the two contact breaker points.
b) To refit the points, first locate the fixed point and lightly tighten the retaining screws. Smear a trace of grease onto the cam to lubricate the moving point heel and then fit the moving point pivot and reset the gap as described in Section 3.

2.3 liter engines

a) Slacken the self-tapping screw that secures the condenser and low tension lead to the contact breaker point assembly. Slide out the forked ends of the lead terminals.
b) Undo and remove the two screws that secure the contact breaker points base plate to the distributor base plate. Lift away the points assembly.
c) To refit the points is the reverse sequence to removal. Smear a trace of grease onto the cam to lubricate the moving point heel, and then reset the gap, as described in Section 3.
3 Should the contact breaker points be badly worn, a new set must be fitted. As an emergency measure clean the faces with fine emery paper folded over a thin steel rule. It is not necessary to rub the pitted point right down to the stage where all the pitting has disappeared. When the surfaces are flat a feeler gauge can be used to reset the gap.
4 Finally replace the rotor arm and distributor cap. Retain in position with two clips, or screws.

5 Condenser - removal, testing and refitting (contact breaker ignition system

1 The purpose of the condenser (sometimes known as a capacitor) is to ensure that when the contact breaker points open there is no sparking across them which would waste voltage and cause wear.
2 The condenser is fitted in parallel with the contact breaker points. If it develops a short circuit, it will cause ignition failure as the contact breaker points will be prevented from correctly interrupting the low tension circuit.
3 If the engine becomes very difficult to start or begins to miss after several miles of running and the breaker points show signs of excessive burning, then the condition of the condenser must be suspect. One further test can be made by separating the points by hand with the ignition switched on. If this is accompanied by a bright flash, it is indicative that the condenser has failed.
4 Without special test equipment the only safe way to diagnose condenser trouble is to replace a suspected unit with a new one and note if there is any improvement.
5 To remove the condenser from the distributor take off the distributor cap and rotor arm.
6 *V6*: Release the condenser cable grommet from the side of the distributor body and then undo and remove the screw that secures the condenser to the distributor body. Lift away the condenser.
7 *2.3 liter:* Slacken the nut holding the condenser lead and low tension lead to the contact breaker points. Slide out the forked terminal on the end of the condenser low tension lead. Undo and

remove the condenser retaining screw and remove the condenser from the breaker plate.

8 To refit the condenser, simply reverse the order of removal.

6 Distributor - lubrication (contact breaker ignition system)

1 It is important that the distributor cam is lubricated with petroleum jelly or grease at 6000 miles (10000 km) or 6 monthly intervals. Also the automatic timing control weights and cam spindle are lubricated with engine oil.

2 Great care should be taken not to use too much lubricant as any excess that finds its way onto the contact breaker points could cause burning and misfiring.

3 To gain access to the cam spindle, lift away the distributor cap and rotor arm. Apply no more than two drops of engine oil onto the felt pad. This will run down the spindle when the engine is hot and lubricate the bearings.

4 To lubricate the automatic timing control allow a few drops of oil to pass through the holes in the contact breaker base plate through which the four sided cam emerges. Apply not more than one drop of oil to the pivot post of the moving contact breaker point. Wipe away excess oil and refit the rotor arm and distributor cap.

7.3. Removing the distributor cap retaining screws

7 Distributor - removal (contact breaker ignition system)

1 First remove the air cleaner assembly on V6 engines only (refer to Chapter 3).

2 On 2.3 liter engines fitted with a thermactor pump it will be necessary to remove the drivebelt and one mounting bolt and swing the pump to one side to allow access to the distributor.

3 Release the clips and remove the distributor cap. (On later models the distributor cap is retained by screws - see photo).

4 Disconnect the low tension wire and vacuum hose/s from the distributor body.

5 Rotate the engine until the timing pointer is lined up with the correct mark on the crankshaft pulley (see Fig. 4.7 and 4.8), check that the distributor rotor is lined up with the index mark on the top edge of the distributor body, ie, number one spark plug segment in the distributor cap.

6 Remove the distributor clamp bolt and lift out the distributor (Fig. 4.6). **Note:** The oil pump driveshaft may stick in the end of the distributor shaft and be withdrawn from the pump. If so, it must be replaced before the distributor is refitted (see Section 13).

Fig. 4.6. Distributor retaining clamp - typical (Sec. 7)

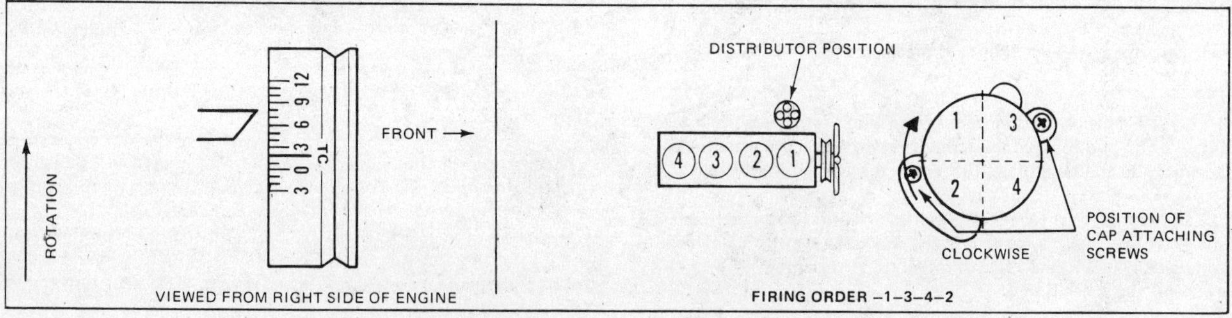

Fig. 4.7. Ignition timing marks and firing order for the 2.3 liter engine (Secs. 7, 15 and 18)

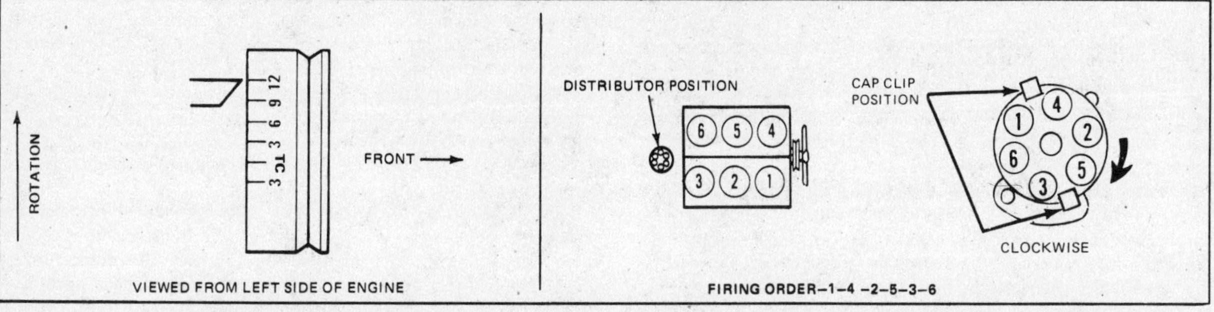

Fig. 4.8. Ignition timing marks and firing order for the V6 engine (Secs. 7, 15 and 18)

8 Distributor - dismantling (2.3 liter engine - contact breaker ignition system)

1 With the distributor on the bench, remove the cap and rotor (Fig. 4.9).
2 Remove the condenser and contact breaker assembly, as described in the previous Sections.
3 Using a small screwdriver, remove the 'C' clip retaining the vacuum advance arm to the breaker plate.
4 Undo and remove the two screws retaining the vacuum advance mechanism to the distributor body, detach the advance arm from the breaker plate and remove the vacuum unit.
5 Remove the two retaining screws and lift out the breaker plate assembly.
6 The mechanical advance is next removed but first make a careful note of the assembly, particularly which spring fits which post and the position of the advance springs. Then remove the advance springs.
7 Pry off the circlips from the governor weights pivot and take out the weights.
8 To remove the cam, take out the felt pad in the top of the cam and ease out the spring clip. Withdraw the cam assembly from the driveshaft.

9 Distributor - dismantling (V6 engine - contact breaker ignition system)

1 Initially release the two spring clips which retain the distributor cap, then pull off the cap followed by the rotor.
2 Remove the lead from the terminal and grommet in the side of the distributor body.
3 Take out the condenser retaining screw and ease the grommet out

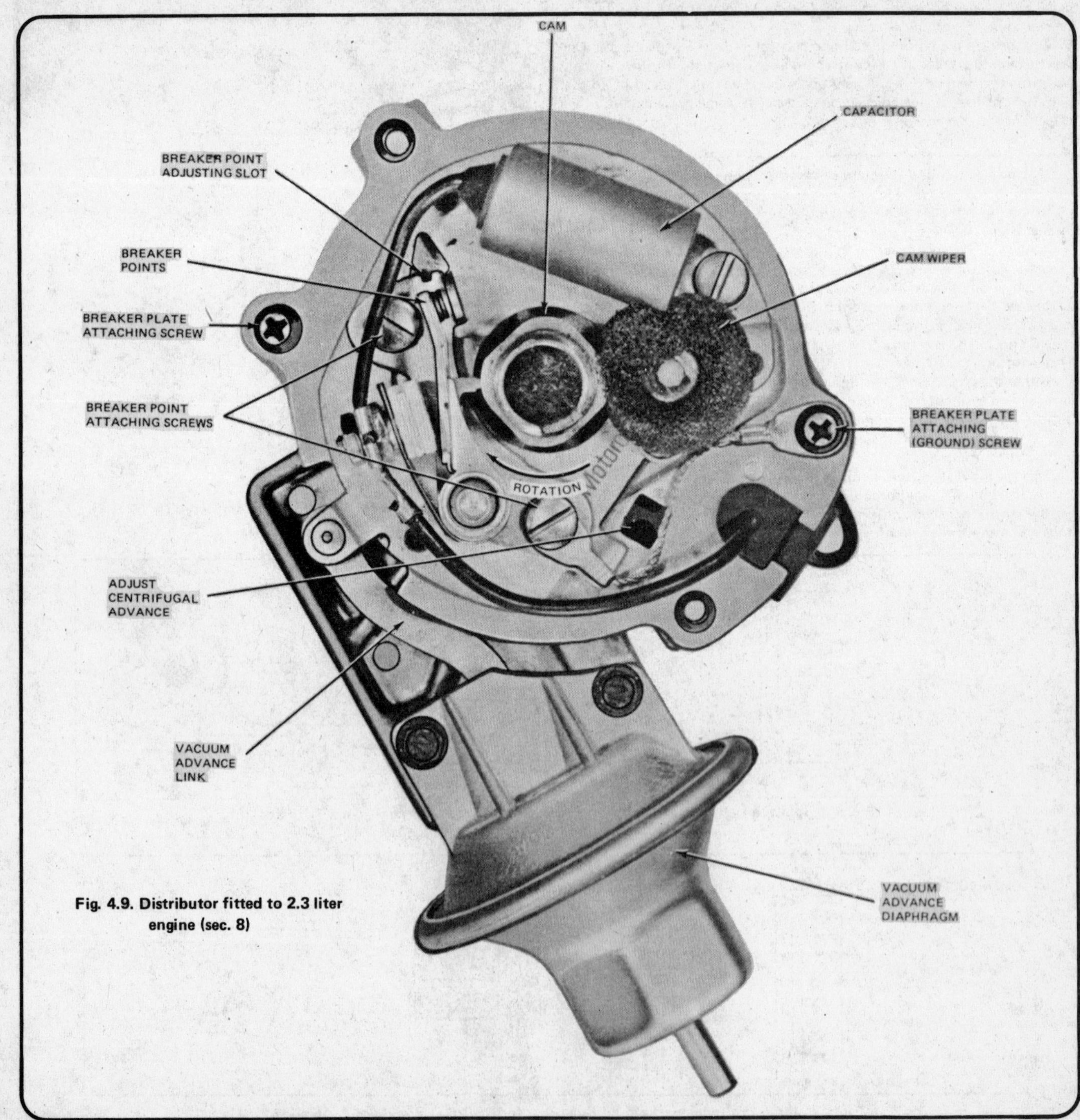

Fig. 4.9. Distributor fitted to 2.3 liter engine (sec. 8)

of the distributor body. Now remove the condenser and lead.

4 Remove the vacuum unit retaining screws and the cam wiper (which is retained by one of these screws).

5 Carefully pry off the 'C' clip retaining the vacuum advance link to the breaker plate. Disengage the link from the plate and remove the vacuum unit.

6 Remove the screws securing the cap retaining spring clips on the distributor body. These screws also retain the breaker plate which can now be pryed out of the body. Note that this step may be difficult since the body is intentionally distorted during original assembly to hold the plate in position.

7 Use a screwdriver to disassemble the points from the breaker plate.

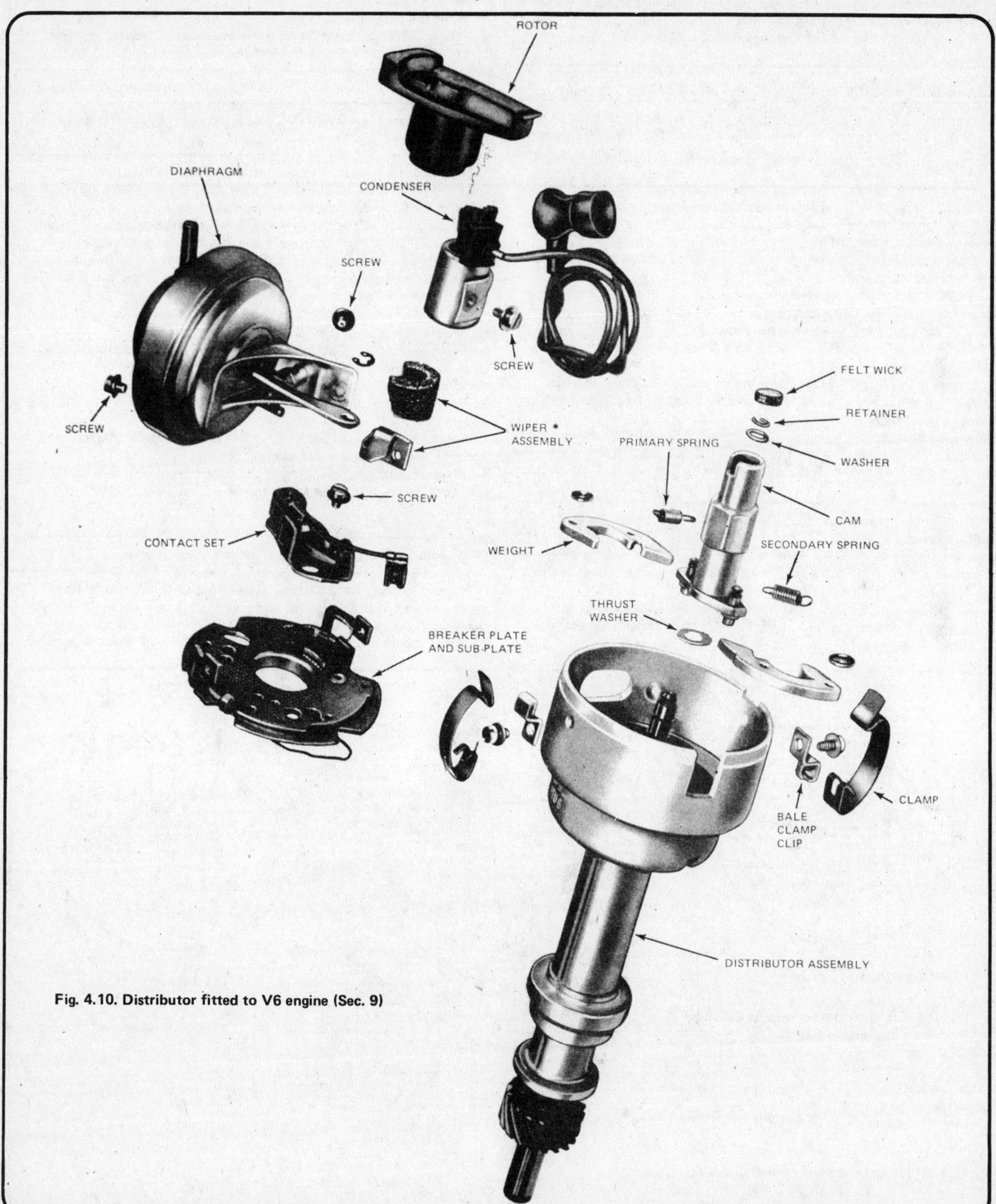

Fig. 4.10. Distributor fitted to V6 engine (Sec. 9)

4

8 Carefully disengage and remove the primary and secondary centrifugal advance springs then remove the 'C' clips from the weights. Lift off the weights.
9 Carefully pry on the lower edge of the cam using a screwdriver, to disengage the cam retaining ring. Lift off the cam, and lift off the felt wick and loose cam retaining ring.
10 If it is necessary to withdraw the driveshaft, tap out the gear lock pin with a punch and remove the gear using a suitable puller.
11 Finally remove the shaft from the distributor body.

10 Distributor - inspection and repair (contact breaker ignition system)

1 Check the contact breaker points for wear, as described in Section 3. Check the distributor cap for signs of tracking indicated by a thin black line between the segments. Replace the cap if any signs of tracking are found.
2 If the metal portion of the rotor arm is badly burned or loose, renew the arm. If only slightly burned, clean the end with a fine file. Check that the contact spring has adequate pressure and the bearing surface is clean and in good condition.
3 Check that the carbon brush in the distributor cap is unbroken and stands proud of its holder.
4 Examine the centrifugal weights and pivots for wear and the advance springs for slackness. They can best be checked by comparing with new parts. If they are slack they must be renewed.
5 Check the points assembly for fit on the breaker plate, and the cam follower for wear.
6 Examine the fit of the spindle in the distributor body. If there is excessive side movement it will be necessary to either fit a new bush or obtain a new body.
Note: It is not possible to obtain a replacement driveshaft, cam or bushes for the distributor fitted to the 2.3 liter engine and if these items are worn a new distributor assembly must be fitted.

11 Distributor - reassembly (2.3 liter engine - contact breaker ignition system)

1 Lubricate the distributor shaft with oil and refit the cam assembly.
2 Refit the cam retaining ring and felt wick.
3 Fit the advance weights in the correct position and hook on the primary and secondary springs. Lightly oil the pivots and refit the 'C' clips.
4 Fit the breaker plate into the distributor body ensuring that the retaining screw holes line up. Refit the retaining screws.
5 Position the vacuum advance unit on the side of the distributor body and fit the operating arm onto the breaker plate with the 'C' clip. Install the vacuum advance unit retaining screws.
6 Replace the contact breaker points but do not tighten the retaining screws.
7 Refit the condenser and low tension wire and grommet; ensure the two connectors are correctly fitted to the contact breaker terminal.
8 Finally reset the contact breaker points as described in Section 3 and refit the rotor arm.

12 Distributor - reassembly (V6 engine - contact breaker ignition system)

1 To reassemble, first lubricate the top of the distributor shaft with engine oil and install the cam assembly. Fit the retaining ring in the top of the cam and install the felt wick.
2 Sparingly, coat the pivot pins with oil and fit the vacuum weight and new 'C' clips. Fit the primary and secondary springs (see Fig. 4.12).
3 Position the breaker plate in the distributor body so that the mounting holes are correctly aligned, then carefully tap the plate down into its seating.
4 Fit the vacuum advance unit with the advance link over the post on the breaker plate and fit a new 'C' clip.
5 Position the cam wiper and fit the vacuum unit attaching screw through the distributor body into the cam wiper post. Now fit the remaining vacuum unit securing screw.
6 Install the contact breaker points and lightly secure them with the screw, then set the gap as detailed in Section 3.
7 Fit the terminal and grommet in the side of the distributor body and position the condenser inside the distributor.
8 Fit the securing screw through the distributor body to retain the condenser. Attach the point lead to the terminal and fit the rotor.

13 Distributor - refitting (contact breaker ignition system)

1 If the oil pump driveshaft was withdrawn with the distributor, smear one end of it with grease and insert it into the end of the distributor driveshaft.
2 Insert the distributor into the cylinder block hole ensuring the

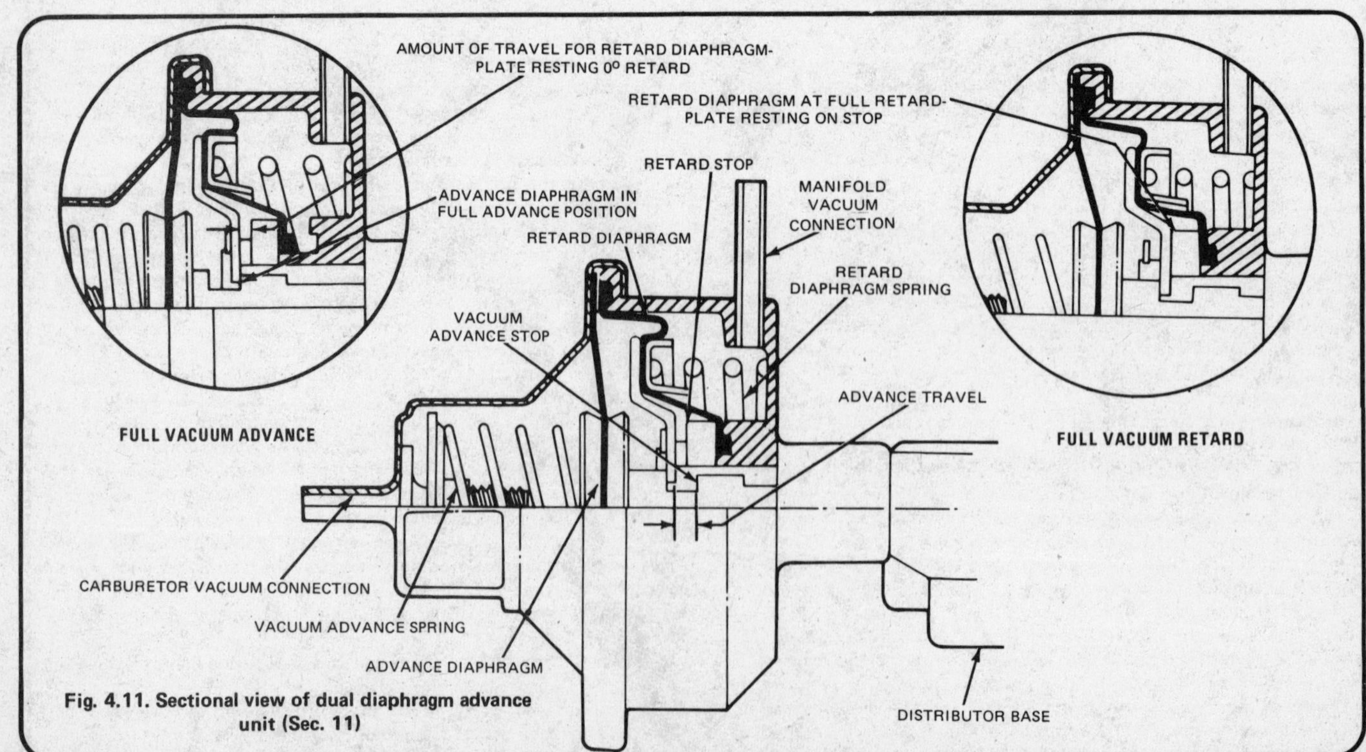

Fig. 4.11. Sectional view of dual diaphragm advance unit (Sec. 11)

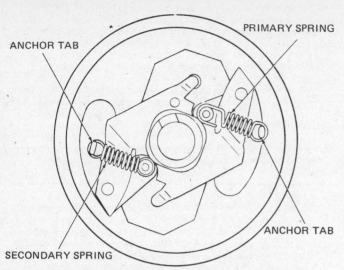

Fig. 4.12. Centrifugal advance weights and springs (Sec. 12)

pump driveshaft is correctly seated in the pump.

3 Notice that the rotor arm rotates as the gears mesh. The rotor arm must settle in exactly the same direction that it was in before the distributor was removed. To do this lift out the assembly far enough to rotate the shaft one tooth at a time lowering it home to check the direction of the rotor arm. When it points in the desired direction with the assembly fully home fit the distributor clamp plate, bolt and plain washer.

4 With the distributor assembly fitted reconnect the low tension lead. Reconnect the HT lead to the center of the distributor cap and refit the rubber union of the vacuum pipe which runs from the inlet manifold to the side of the vacuum advance unit.

5 If the engine was rotated while the distributor was removed, it will be necessary to re-time it as described in Section 15.

14 Spark plugs and HT leads (all models)

1 The correct functioning of the spark plugs is vital for the correct running and efficiency of the engine.

2 At intervals of 6,000 miles the plugs should be removed, examined, cleaned, and if worn excessively, renewed. The condition of the spark plugs will also tell much about the overall condition of the engine.

3 If the insulator nose of the spark plug is clean and white, with no deposits, this is indicative of a weak mixture, or too hot a plug. (A hot plug transfers heat away from the electrode slowly - a cold plug transfers it away quickly.)

4 The plugs fitted as standard are as listed in 'Specifications' at the beginning of this Chapter. If the tip and insulator nose is covered with hard black looking deposits, then this is indicative that the mixture is too rich. Should the plug be black and oily, then it is likely that the engine is fairly worn, as well as the mixture being too rich.

5 If the insulator nose is covered with light tan to greyish brown deposits, then the mixture is correct and it is likely that the engine is in good condition.

6 If there are any traces of long brown tapering on the outside of the white portion of the plug, then the plug will have to be renewed, as this shows that there is a faulty joint between the plug body and the insulator, and compression is being allowed to leak away.

7 Plugs should be cleaned by a sand blasting machine, which will free them from carbon more thoroughly than cleaning by hand. The machine will also test the condition of the plugs under compression. Any plug that fails to spark at the recommended pressure should be renewed.

8 The spark plug gap is of considerable importance, as, if it is too large or too small, the size of the spark and its efficiency will be seriously impaired. The spark plug gap should be set to the figure given in Specifications at the beginning of this Chapter.

9 To set it, measure the gap with a feeler gauge, and then bend open, or close, the outer plug electrode until the correct gap is achieved. The center electrode should never be bent as this may crack the insulation

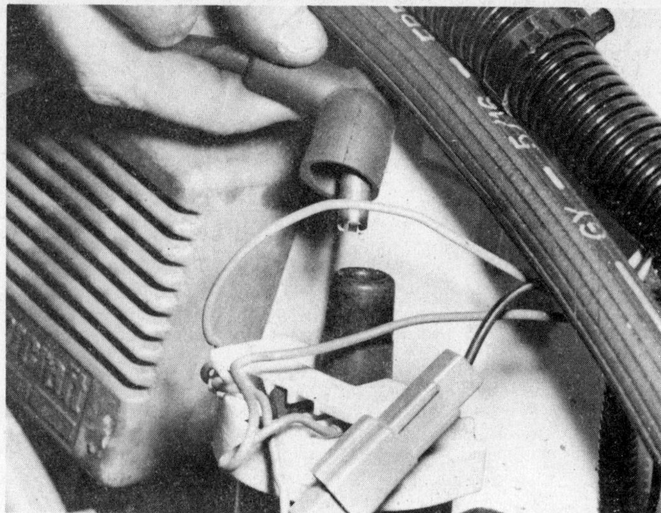

14.11 Disconnecting the HT lead from coil (electronic system)

and cause plug failure if nothing worse.

10 When replacing the plugs, remember to use new plug washers, and replace the leads from the distributor in the correct firing order.

11 The plug leads require no routine attention other than being kept clean and wiped over regularly.

At intervals of 6,000 miles, however, pull the leads off the plugs, coil and distributor one at a time and make sure no water has found its way onto the connections. Remove any corrosion from the brass ends, wipe the collars on top of the distributor, and refit the leads (photo).

15 Static ignition timing - (initial advance - contact breaker ignition system)

1 When a new gear or shaft has been fitted, or the engine has been rotated, or if a new assembly is being fitted, it will be necessary to re-time the ignition. Carry it out this way:

2 Refer to the emission control decal in the engine compartment which will give the initial advance (static) timing figure in degrees.

3 Turn the engine until No. 1 piston is coming up to TDC on the compression stroke. This can be checked by removing No. 1. spark plug and feeling the pressure being developed in the cylinder. If this check is not made it is all too easy to set the timing 180° out. The engine can most easily be turned by engaging top gear and edging the car along (except automatic).

4 Continue turning the engine until the appropriate timing mark on the crankshaft pulley is in line with the pointer (Figs. 4.7 and 4.8).

5 Now, with the vacuum advance unit pointing to the rear of the engine and the rotor arm in the same position as was noted before removal, insert the distributor into its location. Notice that the rotor arm rotates as the gears mesh. Lift out the distributor far enough to rotate the shaft one tooth at a time, lowering it home to check the direction of the rotor arm. When it points in the desired direction with the assembly fully home, fit the distributor clamp plate, bolt and plain washer. Do not fully tighten yet.

6 Gently turn the distributor body until the contact breaker points are just opening when the rotor is pointing to the contact in the distributor cap which is connected to No. 1 spark plug. A convenient way is to put a mark on the outside of the distributor body in line with the segment in the cover, so that it shows when the cover is removed.

7 If this position cannot be reached, check that the drive gear has meshed on the correct tooth by lifting out the distributor once more. If necessary, rotate the driveshaft gear one tooth and try again.

8 Tighten the distributor body clamp enough to hold the distributor, but do not overtighten.

9 The timing should then be checked with a strobe light, (see Section 17).

10 As a final check, take the car to a Ford dealer or ignition specialist who will have the proper equipment to correctly set the timing in relation to the fuel and emission control systems fitted to the car.

16 General description (electronic ignition system)

1 Later Mustang II models are fitted with an electronic (breakerless) type distributor (photo).

2 Mechanically the system is similar to the contact breaker type fitted to earlier models with the exception that the distributor cam and contact breaker are replaced by an armature and magnetic pick-up unit, (see Fig. 4.14). The coil primary circuit is controlled by an amplifier module (photo).

3 When the ignition is switched on, the ignition primary circuit is energized. When the distributor armature 'teeth' or 'spokes' approach the magnetic coil assembly, a voltage is induced which signals the amplifier to turn off the coil primary current. A timing circuit in the amplifier module turns on the coil current after the coil field has collapsed.

4 When on, current flows from the battery through the ignition switch, through the coil primary winding, through the amplifier module and then to ground. When the current is off, the magnetic field in the ignition coil collapses, inducing a high voltage in the coil secondary winding. This is conducted to the distributor where the rotor directs it to the appropriate spark plug. This process is repeated for each power stroke of the car engine.

5 The distributor is fitted with devices to control the actual point of ignition according to the engine speed and load. As the engine speed increases two centrifugal weights move outwards and alter the position of the armature in relation to the distributor shaft to advance the spark slightly. As engine load increases (for example when climbing hills or accelerating), a reduction in intake manifold depression causes the base plate assembly to move slightly in the opposite direction (clockwise) under the action of the spring in the vacuum unit, thus retarding the spark slightly and tending to counteract the centrifugal advance. Under light loading conditions (for example at moderate steady speeds) the comparatively high intake manifold depression on the vacuum advance diaphragm causes the baseplate assembly to move in a counter-clockwise direction to give a larger amount of spark advance.

6 For most practical do-it-yourself purposes ignition timing is carried out as for conventional ignition systems. However, a monolithic timing system is incorporated, and this has a timing receptacle mounted in the left rear of the cylinder block for use with an electronic probe. This latter system can only be used with special electronic equipment, and checks using it are beyond the scope of this manual.

7 Fault finding on the breakerless ignition system, which cannot be rectified by substitution of parts or cleaning/tightening connections, etc. should be entrusted to a suitably equipped Ford dealer since special test procedures and equipment are required.

17 Ignition timing (strobe lamp - electronic ignition system)

1 Refer to the vehicle engine decal to obtain the ignition timing initial advance. Locate the appropriate timing mark on the engine vibration damper on the crankshaft pulley and highlight it with a paint mark. Place a dab of paint on the timing pointer.

2 Disconnect the vacuum line from the distributor, and temporarily plug the line.

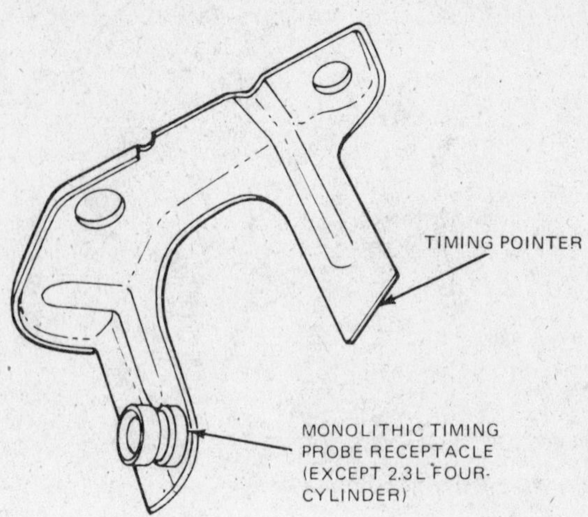

Fig. 4.13 Typical timing pointer and probe receptacle (Sec. 16)

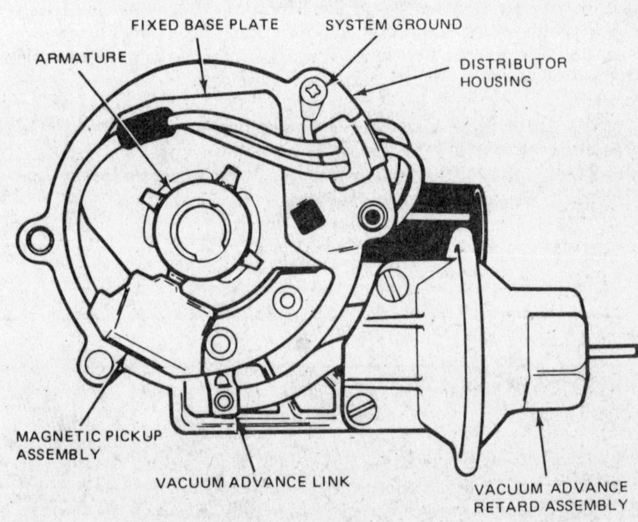

Fig. 4.14. Breakerless ignition distributor (4 cyl).

16.1 Breakerless distributor rotor and armature (V6)

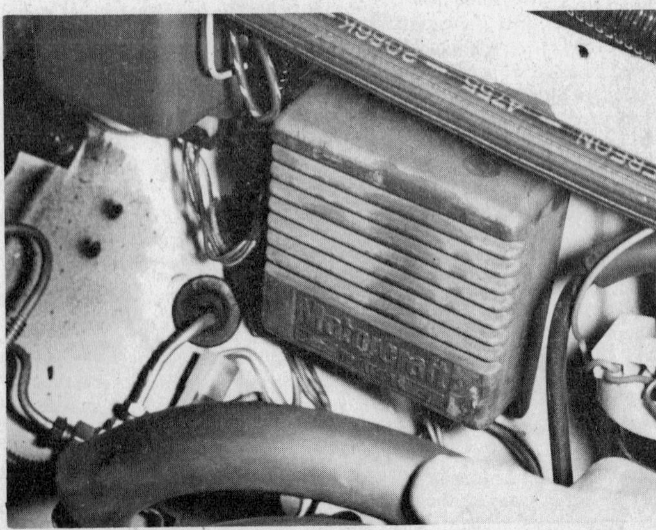

16.2 Electronic ignition amplifier module

Common spark plug conditions

NORMAL

Symptoms: Brown to grayish-tan color and slight electrode wear. Correct heat range for engine and operating conditions.
Recommendation: When new spark plugs are installed, replace with plugs of the same heat range.

WORN

Symptoms: Rounded electrodes with a small amount of deposits on the firing end. Normal color. Causes hard starting in damp or cold weather and poor fuel economy.
Recommendation: Plugs have been left in the engine too long. Replace with new plugs of the same heat range. Follow the recommended maintenance schedule.

CARBON DEPOSITS

Symptoms: Dry sooty deposits indicate a rich mixture or weak ignition. Causes misfiring, hard starting and hesitation.
Recommendation: Make sure the plug has the correct heat range. Check for a clogged air filter or problem in the fuel system or engine management system. Also check for ignition system problems.

ASH DEPOSITS

Symptoms: Light brown deposits encrusted on the side or center electrodes or both. Derived from oil and/or fuel additives. Excessive amounts may mask the spark, causing misfiring and hesitation during acceleration.
Recommendation: If excessive deposits accumulate over a short time or low mileage, install new valve guide seals to prevent seepage of oil into the combustion chambers. Also try changing gasoline brands.

OIL DEPOSITS

Symptoms: Oily coating caused by poor oil control. Oil is leaking past worn valve guides or piston rings into the combustion chamber. Causes hard starting, misfiring and hesitation.
Recommendation: Correct the mechanical condition with necessary repairs and install new plugs.

GAP BRIDGING

Symptoms: Combustion deposits lodge between the electrodes. Heavy deposits accumulate and bridge the electrode gap. The plug ceases to fire, resulting in a dead cylinder.
Recommendation: Locate the faulty plug and remove the deposits from between the electrodes.

TOO HOT

Symptoms: Blistered, white insulator, eroded electrode and absence of deposits. Results in shortened plug life.
Recommendation: Check for the correct plug heat range, over-advanced ignition timing, lean fuel mixture, intake manifold vacuum leaks, sticking valves and insufficient engine cooling.

PREIGNITION

Symptoms: Melted electrodes. Insulators are white, but may be dirty due to misfiring or flying debris in the combustion chamber. Can lead to engine damage.
Recommendation: Check for the correct plug heat range, over-advanced ignition timing, lean fuel mixture, insufficient engine cooling and lack of lubrication.

HIGH SPEED GLAZING

Symptoms: Insulator has yellowish, glazed appearance. Indicates that combustion chamber temperatures have risen suddenly during hard acceleration. Normal deposits melt to form a conductive coating. Causes misfiring at high speeds.
Recommendation: Install new plugs. Consider using a colder plug if driving habits warrant.

DETONATION

Symptoms: Insulators may be cracked or chipped. Improper gap setting techniques can also result in a fractured insulator tip. Can lead to piston damage.
Recommendation: Make sure the fuel anti-knock values meet engine requirements. Use care when setting the gaps on new plugs. Avoid lugging the engine.

MECHANICAL DAMAGE

Symptoms: May be caused by a foreign object in the combustion chamber or the piston striking an incorrect reach (too long) plug. Causes a dead cylinder and could result in piston damage.
Recommendation: Repair the mechanical damage. Remove the foreign object from the engine and/or install the correct reach plug.

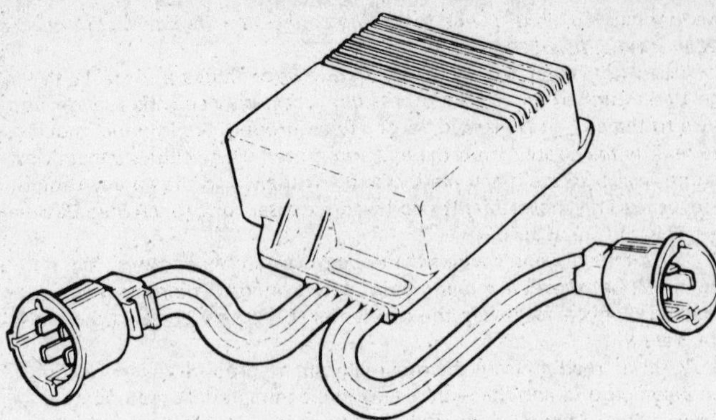

Fig. 4.15. Electronic ignition amplifier module

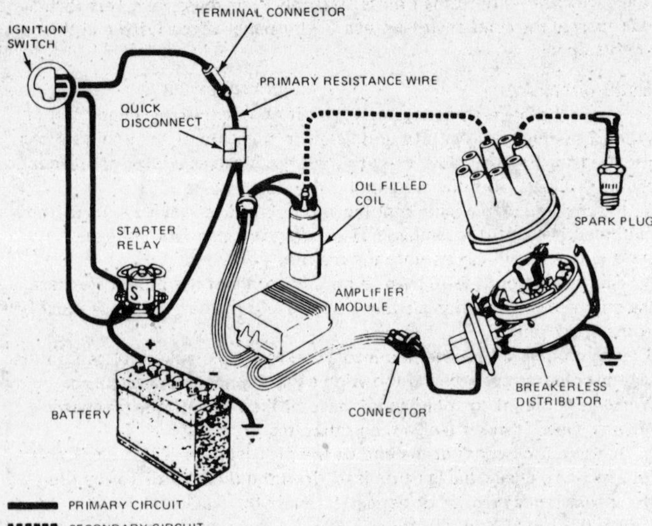

Fig. 4.16. Electronic ignition circuit diagram

3 Connect a proprietary ignition timing light in accordance with its manufacturer's instructions to No. 1 spark plug wire, then run the engine until warm. Allow the engine to idle at 600 rpm, shine the timing light onto the vibration damper and note the position of the white line with respect to the timing pointer. If the line and pointer do not coincide, stop the engine, slacken the distributor clamp bolt, run the engine again and position the distributor until the timing marks do coincide. **Note:** If the timing marks cannot be made to coincide, or if the engine will not start and the ignition timing is suspected as being incorrect, refer to Section 18 to ensure that the distributor is correctly positioned.

4 Having set the timing, stop the engine and tighten the distributor clamp bolt, then run the engine up to 2500 rpm (approx) and check that the timing advances (indicating that the centrifugal advance is operating).

5 Stop the engine, unplug and reconnect the distributor vacuum line, then again run the engine up to 2500 rpm (approx) and check that a greater amount of advance is obtained than at paragraph 4 (indicating that the vacuum advance is operating).

6 If a satisfactory result is not obtained in the tests at paragraph 4 and 5, further investigation of the distributor should be carried out by a suitably equipped Ford dealer or ignition diagnosis specialist. Overhaul kits are not available for this type of distributor and, in the event of failure, a replacement must be fitted.

7 On completion of any testing, ensure that all test connections are removed.

18 Distributor - removal and refitting (electronic ignition system)

1 Remove the air cleaner (refer to Chapter 3, if necessary).

2 Disconnect the distributor harness connector and vacuum advance line.

18.8 Crankshaft timing marks and pointer (V6)

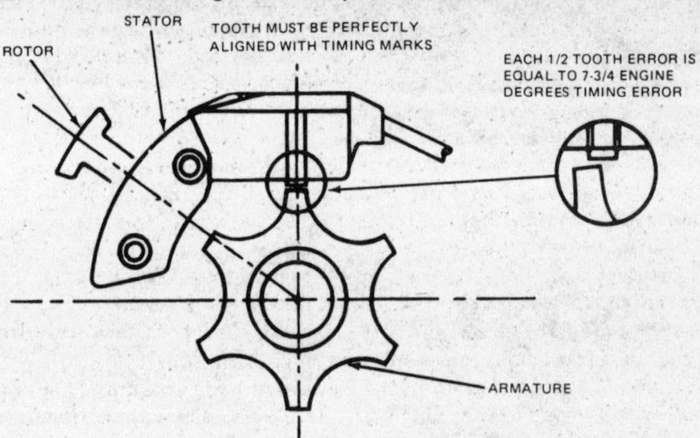

Fig. 4.17. Correct armature position for static timing, (V6 shown, but same method applies to 2.3 liter engines)

3 Remove the distributor cap and move it to one side.

4 Scribe a mark on the distributor body and engine block to indicate the installed position, then remove the distributor hold-down bolt and clamp. Lift out the distributor. **Note:** To simplify the refitting procedure, do not rotate the engine after removing the distributor unless absolutely necessary.

5 Provided that the engine has not been rotated, refitting the distributor is a straightforward reversal of the removal procedure, but it is recommended that the ignition timing is checked as described in the previous Section.

6 If the engine was rotated while the distributor was removed it will be necessary to position the engine with the No. 1 piston at tdc (top-dead-center).

7 First remove the No. 1 cylinder spark plug, (refer to Fig. 4.7 or 4.8 for the location). With a thumb placed over the spark plug hole rotate the engine until pressure is felt, indicating the No. 1 piston is rising on the compression stroke.

8 Shinea flashlight on the crankshaft pulley and continue to rotate the the engine until the timing pointer is aligned with the initial timing (static) mark on the pulley, (photo) (refer to emission control decal for the correct figure).

9 Position the distributor in the block with one of the armature 'spokes' aligned as shown in Fig. 4.17, and the rotor in the No. 1 firing position (ie, as if aligned with the No. 1 spark plug lead terminal in the distributor cap).

10 If the distributor will not fully engage, it may be necessary to crank the engine with the starter after the distributor drive gear is partially engaged, in order to engage the oil pump intermediate shaft. Loosely install the retaining clamp and bolt, then rotate the distributor to advance the timing to a point where the armature spoke is aligned properly. Tighten the clamp bolt, then refit the distributor cap, electrical leads and vacuum connection. Check the timing, as described in the previous Section.

19 Ignition system - fault diagnosis (all models)

By far the majority of breakdown and running troubles are caused by faults in the ignition system either in the low tension or high tension circuits.

There are two main symptoms indicating faults. Either the engine will not start or fire, or the engine is difficult to start and misfires. If it is a regular misfire, (ie, the engine is not running on all cylinders), the fault is almost sure to be in the secondary or high tension circuit. If the misfiring is intermittent the fault could be in either the high or low tension circuits. If the car stops suddenly, or will not start at all, it is likely that the fault is in the low tension circuit. Loss of power and overheating, apart from faulty carburetion settings, are normally due to faults in the distributor or to incorrect ignition timing.

Engine fails to start

1 If the engine fails to start and the car was running normally when it was last used, first check there is fuel in the fuel tank. If the engine turns over normally on the starter motor and the battery is evidently well charged, then the fault may be in either the high or low tension circuits. First check the HT circuit. **Note:** If the battery is known to be fully charged, the ignition light comes on, and the starter motor fails to turn the engine **check the tightness of the leads on the battery terminals** and also the security of the ground lead at its **connection to the body.** It is quite common for the leads to have worked loose, even if they look and feel secure. If one of the battery terminal posts gets very hot when trying to work the starter motor this is a sure indication of a faulty connection to that terminal.

2 One of the most common reasons for bad starting is wet or damp spark plug leads and distributor. Remove the distributor cap. If condensation is visible internally dry the cap with a rag and also wipe over the leads. Refit the cap.

3 If the engine still fails to start, check that voltage is reaching the plugs by disconnecting each plug lead in turn at the spark plug end, and holding the end of the cable about 3/16 inch (5 mm) away from the cylinder block. Spin the engine on the starter motor.

4 Sparking between the end of the cable and the block should be fairly strong with a strong regular blue spark. (Hold the lead with rubber to avoid electric shocks). If voltage is reaching the plugs, then remove them and clean and regap them. The engine should now start.

5 If there is no spark at the plug leads, take off the HT leads from the center of the distributor cap and hold it to the block as before. Spin the engine on the starter once more. A rapid succession of blue sparks between the end of the lead and the block indicate that the coil is in order and that the distributor cap is cracked, the rotor arm is faulty, or the carbon brush in the top of the distributor cap is not making good contact with the spring on the rotor arm. Possibly, the points are in bad condition, (earlier models only). Clean and reset them as described in this Chapter, Sections 2 or 3.

6 If there are no sparks from the end of the lead from the coil, check the connections at the coil end of the lead. If it is in order start checking the low tension circuit. (*The following applies to cars fitted with contact breaker type distributors only*).

7 Use a 12v voltmeter or a 12v bulb and two lengths of wire. With the ignition switched on and the points open, test between the low tension wire to the coil (it is marked 15 or +) and ground. No reading indicates a break in the supply from the ignition switch. Check the connections at the switch to see if any are loose. Refit them and the engine should run. A reading shows a faulty coil or condenser, or broken lead between the coil and the distributor.

8 Take the condenser wire off the points assembly and with the points open test between the moving point and ground. If there now is a reading then the fault is in the condenser. Fit a new one and the fault is cleared.

9 With no reading from the moving point to ground, take a reading between ground and the – or 1 terminal of the coil. A reading here shows a broken wire which will need to be replaced between the coil and distributor. No reading confirms that the coil has failed and must be replaced, after which the engine will run once more. Remember to refit the condenser wire to the points assembly. For these tests it is sufficient to separate the points with a piece of dry paper while testing with the points open.

Engine misfires

1 If the engine misfires regularly, run it at a fast idling speed. Pull off each of the plug caps in turn and listen to the note of the engine. Hold the plug cap in a dry cloth or with a rubber glove as additional protection against a shock from the HT supply.

2 No difference in engine running will be noticed when the lead from the defective circuit is removed. Removing the lead from one of the good cylinders will accentuate the misfire.

3 Remove it about 3/16 inch (5 mm) away from the block. Re-start the engine. If the sparking is fairly strong and regular, the fault must lie in the spark plug.

4 The plug may be loose, the insulation may be cracked, or the points may have burnt away giving too wide a gap for the spark to jump. Worse still, one of the points may have broken off. Either renew the plug, or clean it, reset the gap, and then test it.

5 If there is no spark at the end of the plug lead, or if it is weak and intermittent, check the ignition lead from the distributor to the plug. If the insulation is cracked or perished, renew the lead. Check the connections at the distributor cap.

6 If there is still no spark, examine the distributor cap carefully for tracking. This can be recognised by a very thin black line running between two or more electrodes, or between an electrode and some other part of the distributor. These lines are paths which now conduct electricity across the cap thus letting it run to ground. The only answer is a new distributor cap.

7 If the ignition timing is too far retarded, it should be noted that the engine will tend to overheat, and there will be a quite noticeable drop in power. If the engine is overheating and the power is down, and the ignition timing is correct, then the carburetor should be checked, as it is likely that this is where the fault lies.

Chapter 5 Clutch

For modifications, and information applicable to later models, see Supplement at end of manual

Contents

Specifications

Clutch type ...	Single dry plate, diaphragm spring	
Actuation ...	Cable	
Friction plate diameter		
2.3 liter engine ...	8.5 in (216 mm)	
V6 engine ...	9.5 in (240 mm)	
Number of springs ...	6	
Friction plate color identification (paint daub)		
2.3 liter engine ...	Yellow	
V6 engine ...	Blue	
Clutch pedal free travel ...	1 3/8 to 1 5/8 in (33 to 39 mm)	
Torque wrench settings	**lb f ft**	**kg f m**
Pressure plate to flywheel ...	12 to 24	1.64 to 3.28
Clutch housing to engine ...	28 to 38	3.9 to 5.4

1 General description

The clutch unit is of the single dry plate diaphragm spring type which comprises a steel cover dowelled and bolted to the rear face of the flywheel. It contains the pressure plate, diaphragm spring and fulcrum rings.

The clutch disc is free to slide along the splined first motion shaft and is held in position between the flywheel and the pressure plate by the pressure of the pressure plate spring. Friction lining material is riveted to the clutch disc and it has a spring cushioned hub to absorb transmission shocks and to help ensure a smooth take-off.

The circular diaphragm spring is mounted on shoulder pins and held in place in the cover by two fulcrum rings. The spring is also held to the pressure plate by three spring steel clips which are riveted in position.

The clutch is actuated by a cable controlled by the clutch pedal. The clutch release mechanism consists of a release fork and bearing. Wear of the friction material in the clutch is adjusted out by means of a cable adjuster at the lower end of the cable where it passes through the bellhousing.

Depressing the clutch pedal actuates the clutch release arm by means of the cable.

The release arm pushes the release bearing forwards to bear against the release fingers, so moving the center of the diaphragm spring inwards. The spring is sandwiched between two annular rings which act as fulcrum points. As the center of the spring is pushed in, the outside of the spring is pushed out, so moving the pressure plate backwards and disengaging the pressure plate from the clutch disc.

When the clutch pedal is released, the diaphragm spring forces the pressure plate into contact with the high friction linings on the clutch disc and at the same time pushes the clutch disc a fraction of an inch forwards on its splines, so engaging the clutch disc with the flywheel. The clutch disc is now firmly sandwiched between the pressure plate and the flywheel and the drive is taken up.

2 Clutch - adjustment

1 At the specified service intervals the clutch operating cable should be adjusted to compensate for gradual wearing of the friction disc linings.

2 To adjust the clutch, open the hood and remove the bracket that retains the cable to the left-hand fender apron.

3 Locate the clutch cable where it emerges through the dash panel at the rear left-hand side of the engine compartment and remove the retaining clip (5.3).

4 Pull the cable toward the front of the car until the adjustment nut slots are clear of the sleeve and rotate the nut away from the sleeve approximately ¼ inch (6mm).

5 Release the cable to neutralize the linkage, then pull the cable out gently until all free movement is taken up.

6 Rotate the adjusting nut toward the rear of the car until it just touches the sleeve protruding from the dash panel, then allow it to drop into the nearest notch.

7 Refit the clutch cable retaining clip and replace the cable bracket on the fender apron.

8 Check that the clutch pedal free-play travel is within the limits given in the Specifications, then take the car for a test run and check the operation of the clutch.

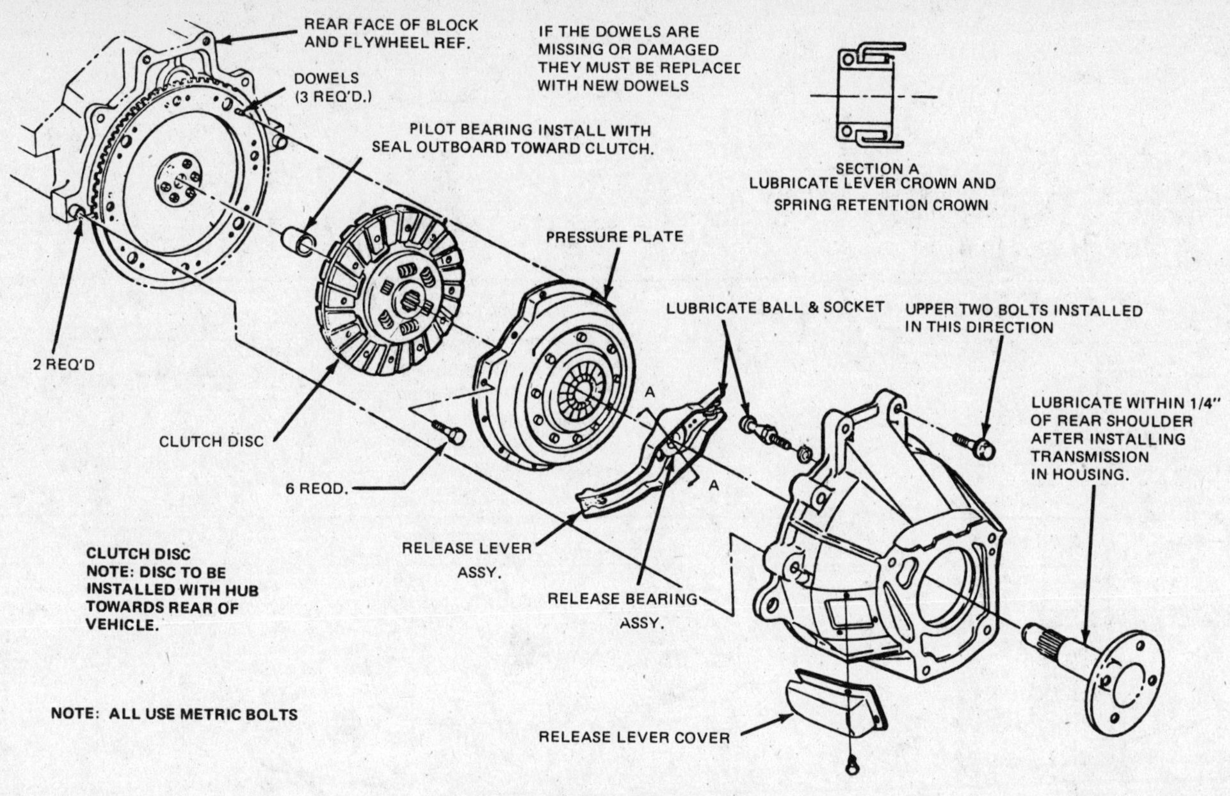

Fig. 5.1. 2.3 liter clutch assembly

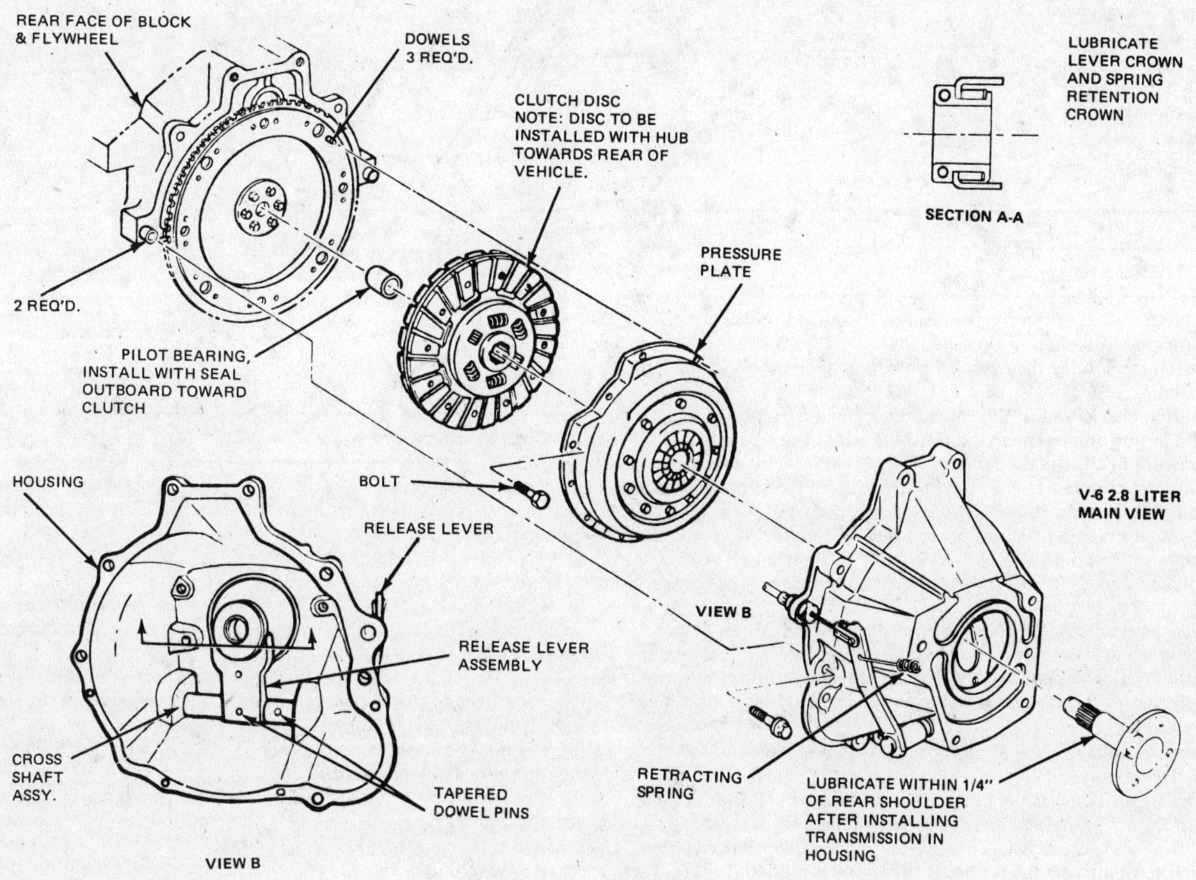

Fig. 5.2. V6 clutch assembly

5

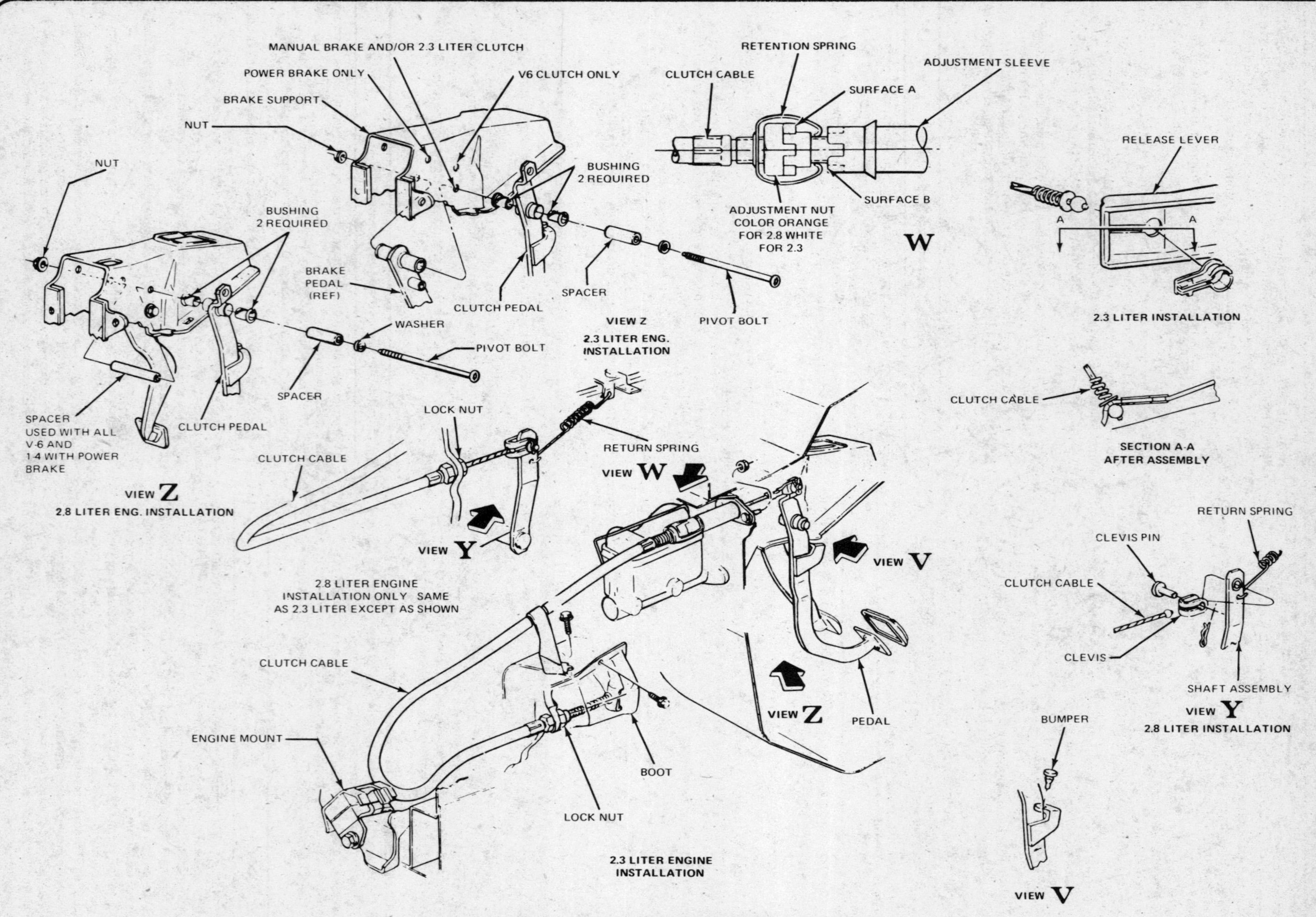

Fig. 5.3. 2.3 liter and V6 clutch cable and components

3 Clutch - removal

1 Remove the transmission as described in Chapter 6.
2 Disconnect the clutch cable from the release lever and clutch housing as described in Section 8.
3 Remove the starter motor from the front of the clutch housing (see Chapter 10).
4 Remove the bolts securing the engine rear lower plate to the front of the clutch housing.
5 Remove the bolts retaining the clutch housing to the rear of the engine block.
6 Pull the clutch housing toward the rear of the car until it clears the clutch cover assembly and lower it to the ground.
7 Scribe a mating line from the clutch cover to the flywheel to ensure identical positioning on replacement and then remove the clutch assembly by unscrewing the six bolts holding the cover to the rear face of the flywheel. Unscrew the bolts diagonally, half a turn at a time, to prevent distortion to the cover flange and to relieve the diaphragm spring tension.
8 With all the bolts and spring washers removed lift the clutch assembly off the locating dowels. The driven plate or clutch disc may fall out at this stage as it is not attached to either the clutch cover assembly or the flywheel.

4 Clutch - overhaul

1 It is not practical to dismantle the pressure plate assembly and the term 'clutch dismantling and replacement' is a term usually used for simply fitting a new clutch friction plate.
2 If a new clutch is being fitted it is false economy not to renew the release bearing at the same time. This will preclude having to replace it at a later date when wear on the clutch linings is still minimal.
3 If the pressure plate assembly requires renewal (see Section 5) an exchange unit must be purchased. This will have been accurately set up and balanced to very fine limits.

5 Clutch - inspection

1 Examine the clutch driven plate friction lining for wear and loose rivets and the plate for rim distortion, cracks, broken hub springs, and worn splines. The surface of the friction linings may be highly glazed, but as long as the clutch material pattern can be clearly seen this is satisfactory. Compare the amount of lining wear with a new clutch driven plate at the stores in your local garage, and if the linings are more than three quarters worn renew the driven plate.
2 Check the machined faces of the flywheel and the pressure plate. If either is grooved it should be machined until smooth or renewed.
3 If the pressure plate is cracked or split it is essential that an exchange unit is fitted, also if the pressure of the diaphragm spring is suspect.
4 Check the release bearing for smoothness of operation. There should be no harshness and no slackness in it. It should spin reasonably freely bearing in mind it has been pre-packed with grease.
5 Check also that the clutch pilot bearing in the center of the flywheel is serviceable. Further information on this will be found in Chapter 1 and Chapter 13.

6 Clutch - refitting

1 It is important that no oil or grease gets on the clutch driven plate friction linings, or the pressure plate and flywheel faces. It is advisable to replace the clutch with clean hands and to wipe down the pressure plate and flywheel faces with a clean dry rag before reassembly begins.
2 Place the clutch driven plate against the flywheel, ensuring that it is the correct way round. The flywheel side of the clutch driven plate is marked on the center. If the driven plate is fitted the wrong way round, it will be quite impossible to operate the clutch.
3 Refit the clutch cover assembly loosely on the dowels. Refit the bolts and spring washers, and tighten them finger tight so that the clutch driven plate is gripped but can still be moved.
4 The clutch driven plate must now be centralised so that when the engine and gearbox are mated, the gearbox input shaft splines will pass through the splines in the center of the driven plate hub.
5 Centralisation can be carried out quite easily by inserting a round bar or long screwdriver through the hole in the center of the clutch, so that the end of the bar rests in the small hole in the end of the crankshaft containing the input shaft pilot bushing. Ideally an input shaft should be used.
6 Using the input shaft pilot bushing as a fulcrum, moving the bar sideways or up and down will move the clutch driven plate in whichever direction is necessary to achieve centralisation.
7 Centralisation is easily judged by removing the bar and moving the driven plate hub in relation to the hole in the center of the clutch cover diaphragm spring. When the hub appears exactly in the center of the hole all is correct. Alternatively the input shaft will fit the bushing and centre of the clutch hub exactly, obviating the need for visual alignment.
8 Tighten the clutch bolts firmly in a diagonal sequence to ensure that the cover plate is pulled down evenly and without distortion of the flange. Finally tighten the bolts down to the specified torque.
9 Refit the clutch housing, using the reverse procedure to removal as described in Section 3.

7 Clutch release bearing - removal and replacement

1 With the gearbox and engine separated to provide access to the clutch, attention can be given to the release bearing located in the bellhousing, over the input shaft.
2 The release bearing is a relatively inexpensive but important component and unless it is nearly new it is a mistake not to renew it during an overhaul of the clutch.

2.3 liter engines

3 To remove the release bearing, first undo the retaining screws and remove the metal cover from the side of the clutch housing.
4 Slide the release lever sideways toward the opening in the side of the clutch housing until the spring clip on the lever disengages from the ball pivot.
5 To free the bearing from the release arm simply unhook it, and then with the aid of two blocks of wood and a vise, press off the release bearing from its hub.
6 Replacement is a straightforward reversal of these instructions.

V6 engines

7 The clutch release lever on the V6 engine is operated by a cross-shaft located in the bottom section of the clutch housing (see Fig. 5.2).
8 To remove the shaft, drive out the two tapered pins using a punch of a suitable diameter.
9 Withdraw the shaft from the side of the clutch housing.
10 Release the spring clips and remove the release bearing from the lever.
11 Replace the release bearing and cross-shaft using the reverse procedure to removal.

8 Clutch cable - removal and replacement

1 From the dash panel at the rear of the engine compartment, remove the cable retaining clip.
2 Pull the cable away from the dash panel sleeve and rotate the adjusting nut toward the front of the car for approximately 1 inch (25mm).
3 Remove the cable retaining bracket from the left-hand front fender apron.
4 Remove the cable end fitting from the top of the clutch pedal and push it through the dash panel.
5 Jack up the front of the car and support it on axle stands or suitable blocks.
6 On 2.3 liter cars remove the screws securing the metal release lever cover (if fitted) and remove the cover.
7 Remove the plastic cable retaining clip and remove the cable from the clutch release lever.
8 If working on a V6 engined car, remove the spring clip and clevis pin that secures the cable to the clutch release lever.
9 Remove the rear lock-nut holding the outer cable to the side of the clutch housing and withdraw the cable toward the front of the car.
10 The complete cable assembly can now be removed from the car.

11 Installation of the cable is the reverse procedure to removal. After refitting, the cable should be adjusted as described in Section 2.

9 Clutch pedal - removal and refitting

1 For safety reasons disconnect the battery negative terminal.
2 Remove the clutch cable retaining clip at the dash panel and back-off the adjusting nut approximately 1 inch (25mm) as described in the previous Section.
3 Remove the cable from the top of the clutch pedal lever.
4 Remove the clutch and brake pedal pivot nut located on the right-hand side of the mounting bracket (see Fig. 5.3).
5 Pull the pivot bolt out from the left-hand side of the mounting bracket and remove the pedal bushes and spacers.
6 The brake pedal will probably drop down when the pivot bolt is removed and a careful note should be made on the correct location of all bushings and spacers.
7 If any of the bushings are badly worn they should be renewed.
8 Refitting is the reverse procedure to removal. Use a little grease on the pedal bushings and adjust the clutch cable as described in Section 2.

10 Fault diagnosis - clutch

There are four main faults to which the clutch and release mechanism are prone. They may occur by themselves, or in conjunction with any of the other faults. They are clutch squeal, slip, spin and judder.

Clutch squeal - diagnosis and remedy

1 If, on taking up the drive or when changing gear, the clutch squeals, this is indicative of a badly worn clutch release bearing.
2 As well as regular wear due to normal use, wear of the clutch release bearing is much accentuated if the clutch is ridden or held down for long periods in gear, with the engine running. To minimise wear of this component the car should always be taken out of gear at traffic lights and for similar hold-ups.
3 The clutch release bearing is not an expensive item, but is difficult to get at.

Clutch slip - diagnosis and remedy

4 Clutch slip is a self-evident condition which occurs when the clutch driven plate is badly worn, oil or grease have got onto the flywheel or pressure plate faces, or the pressure plate itself is faulty.
5 The reason for clutch slip is that due to one of the faults above, there is either insufficient pressure from the pressure plate, or insufficient friction from the driven plate to ensure solid drive.
6 If small amounts of oil get onto the clutch, they will be burnt off under the heat of the clutch engagement, and in the process, gradually darken the linings. Excessive oil on the clutch will burn off leaving a carbon deposit which can cause quite bad slip, or fierceness, spin and judder.
7 If clutch slip is suspected, and confirmation of this condition is required, there are several tests which can be made.
8 With the engine in second or third gear and pulling lightly, sudden depression of the accelerator pedal may cause the engine to increase its speed without any increase in road speed. Easing off on the accelerator will then give a definite drop in engine speed without the car slowing.
9 In extreme cases of clutch slip the engine will race under normal acceleration conditions.
10 If slip is due to oil or grease on the linings the permanent cure is, of course, to renew the clutch driven plate and trace and rectify the oil leak.

Clutch spin - diagnosis and remedy

11 Clutch spin is a condition which occurs when there is an obstruction in the clutch, either in the gearbox input shaft or in the operating lever itself, or oil may have partially burnt off the clutch lining and have left a resinous deposit which is causing the clutch disc to stick to the pressure plate or flywheel.
12 The reason for clutch spin is that due to any, or a combination of, the faults just listed, the clutch pressure plate is not completely freeing from the driven plate even with the clutch pedal fully depressed.
13 If clutch spin is suspected, the condition can be confirmed by extreme difficulty in engaging first gear from rest, difficulty in changing gear, and sudden take up of the clutch drive at the fully depressed end of the clutch pedal travel as the clutch is released.
14 Check the clutch cable adjustment (Section 2).
15 If these points are checked and found to be in order then the fault lies internally in the clutch, and it will be necessary to remove the clutch for examination.

Clutch judder - diagnosis and cure

16 Clutch judder is a self-evident condition which occurs when the gearbox or engine mountings are loose or too flexible, when there is oil on the face of the clutch friction plate, or when the clutch pressure plate has been incorrectly adjusted.
17 The reason for clutch judder is that due to one of the faults just listed, the clutch pressure plate is not freeing smoothly from the driven plate and is snatching.
18 Clutch judder normally occurs when the clutch pedal is released in first or reverse gears, and the whole car shudders as it moves backward or forward.

Chapter 6 Gearbox and automatic transmission

For modifications, and information applicable to later models, see Supplement at end of manual

Contents

Specifications

Manual gearbox

Number of gears	4 forward, 1 reverse	
Type of gears	Helical, constant mesh	
Synchromesh	All forward gears	
Gearbox type designation	RAD	
Gear ratios	**Pre-1976**	**1976***
First	3.50 : 1	4.07 : 1
Second	2.21 : 1	2.57 : 1
Third	1.43 : 1	1.66 : 1
Fourth	1 : 1	1 : 1
Reverse	3.38 : 1	3.95 : 1
Counter gear endfloat	0.004 - 0.018 in (0.10 0.45 mm)	
Lubricant type	Ford manual transmission lube	
Lubricant capacity	3.5 US pints (2.6 Imp)	

**Refer to Chapter 13 Specifications for later models*

Automatic transmission

Type	C3 or C4
Fluid capacity	16 US pints (13 Imp)
C4 transmission gear ratios:	
First	2.46 : 1
Second	1.46 : 1
Third	1 : 1
Reverse	2.20 : 1
C3 transmission gear ratios:	
First	2.47 : 1
Second	1.47 : 1
Third	1 : 1
Reverse	2.11 : 1
Shift lever positions (both types)	P, R, N, D, 2, 1

Torque wrench settings

Manual gearbox	**lb f ft**	**kg f m**
Drain and filler plugs	25 to 30	3.4 to 4.2
Cover to gearbox case	12 to 14	1.7 to 1.9
Clutch housing to gearbox case	40 to 47	5.5 to 6.5
Clutch housing to engine	22 to 27	3.0 to 3.7
Extension housing to gearbox case	30 to 35	4.2 to 4.8

Torque wrench settings (cont)

Automatic transmission

C4	**lb f ft**	**kg f m**
Converter to flywheel	23 to 28	3.2 to 3.9
Converter housing to transmission case	28 to 40	3.9 to 5.5
Oil sump to transmission case	12 to 16	1.7 to 2.2
Converter cover to converter housing	12 to 16	1.7 to 2.2
Engine to transmission	23 to 33	3.2 to 4.6
Converter drain plug (if fitted)	20 to 30	2.8 to 4.2
Downshift lever to shaft	12 to 16	1.7 to 2.2
Filler tube to engine	20 to 25	2.8 to 3.4
Filler tube to oil pan...	32 to 42	4.4 to 5.8
Neutral switch to case	55 to 75	7.6 to 10.2
Oil cooler line connections	80 to 120	11.6 to 16.6
C3		
Torque converter housing to transmission	27 to 39	3.6 to 5.3
Disc to converter	27 to 30	3.6 to 4.1
Oil pan bolts	12 to 17	1.6 to 2.4
Downshift cable bracket	12 to 17	1.6 to 2.4
Downshift lever nut:		
Outer	7 to 11	1.0 to 1.5
Inner	30 to 40	4.1 to 5.4
Inhibitor switch	12 to 15	1.6 to 2.0
Brake band adjusting screw locknut	35 to 45	4.7 to 6.1
Fluid line to connector	7 to 10	09. to 1.4
Connector to transmission housing	10 to 15	1.4 to 2.0
Torque converter housing to engine	22 to 27	3.0 to 3.7
Torque converter drain plug	20 to 29	2.7 to 4.0
Oil cooler line to connector	12 to 15	1.6 to 2.0

Part A: Manual transmission

1 Manual transmission - general description

The manual gearboxes used on the models covered by this manual are equipped with four forward and one reverse gear.

All forward gears are engaged through synchro-hubs and rings to obtain smooth, silent gearchanges. All forward gears on the mainshaft and input shaft are in constant mesh with their corresponding gears on the countershaft gear cluster and are helically cut to achieve quiet running.

The countershaft reverse gear has straight-cut spur teeth and drives the toothed 1st/2nd gear synchro-hub on the mainshaft through an interposed sliding idler gear.

Gears are engaged by a single selector rail and forks. Control of the gears is from a floor mounted shift lever which connects with the single selector rail.

Where close tolerances and limits are required during assembly of the gearbox, selective thrust washers and snap-rings are used to eliminate excessive endfloat or backlash. This eliminates the need for using matched assemblies.

2 Transmission - removal and refitting

1 If the gearbox alone is to be removed from the car, it can be taken out from below leaving the engine in position. It will mean that a considerable amount of working room is required beneath the car, and ideally ramps or an inspection pit should be used. However, provided that suitable jacks and supports are available, the task can be accomplished without the need for sophisticated equipment.
2 Disconnect the battery ground lead.
3 From inside the car remove the two front screws from each scuff plate and the side trim panel and pull the carpet back over the gear shift lever (Fig. 6.1).
4 Remove the four bolts holding the shift lever boot retaining plate and lift the plate and boot off the lever. Remove the shift lever knob if necessary.
5 Undo and remove the three shift lever retaining bolts and remove the lever assembly.
6 Remove the propeller shaft as described in Chapter 7.
7 Remove the front exhaust pipe section from the manifold flange and the front of the resonator box or converter, if fitted (two pipes on V6 cars).
8 Disconnect the clutch cable from the clutch release lever and the side of the clutch housing (see Chapter 5).
9 Remove the starter motor retaining bolts and move the motor towards the front of the car.
10 Disconnect the back-up lamp switch wires and the seat belt sensing switch wires if fitted.
11 Remove the speedometer cable retaining screw and pull the cable out of the extension housing.
12 Support the rear of the engine with a block of wood placed on top of a jack and remove the rear engine mounting crossmember.
13 Remove the two bolts that retain the gearbox extension crossmember and remove the crossmember.
14 Gradually lower the engine by means of the jack until there is sufficient clearance to remove the four bolts retaining the transmission assembly to the clutch housing.
15 Support the weight of the transmission and undo and remove the four bolts.
16 Carefully withdraw the transmission away from the clutch housing and lower it to the ground.
17 When refitting the transmission, ensure that the clutch release lever and bearing are correctly located in the clutch housing.
18 Apply a smear of light grease on the transmission input shaft splines and then install the transmission using the reverse procedure to removal. **Note:** It may be necessary to rotate the engine to align the clutch disc and input shaft splines.
19 Refill the transmission with oil.

3 Transmission - dismantling

1 Place the complete unit on a firm bench or table and ensure that you have the following tools available, in addition to the normal range of wrenches etc.

a) Good quality snap-ring pliers, 2 pairs - 1 expanding and 1 contracting.
b) Copper-headed hammer, at least 2 lb.
c) Selection of steel and brass drifts.
d) Small containers.
e) Engineer's vise mounted on firm bench.
f) Selection of steel tubing.

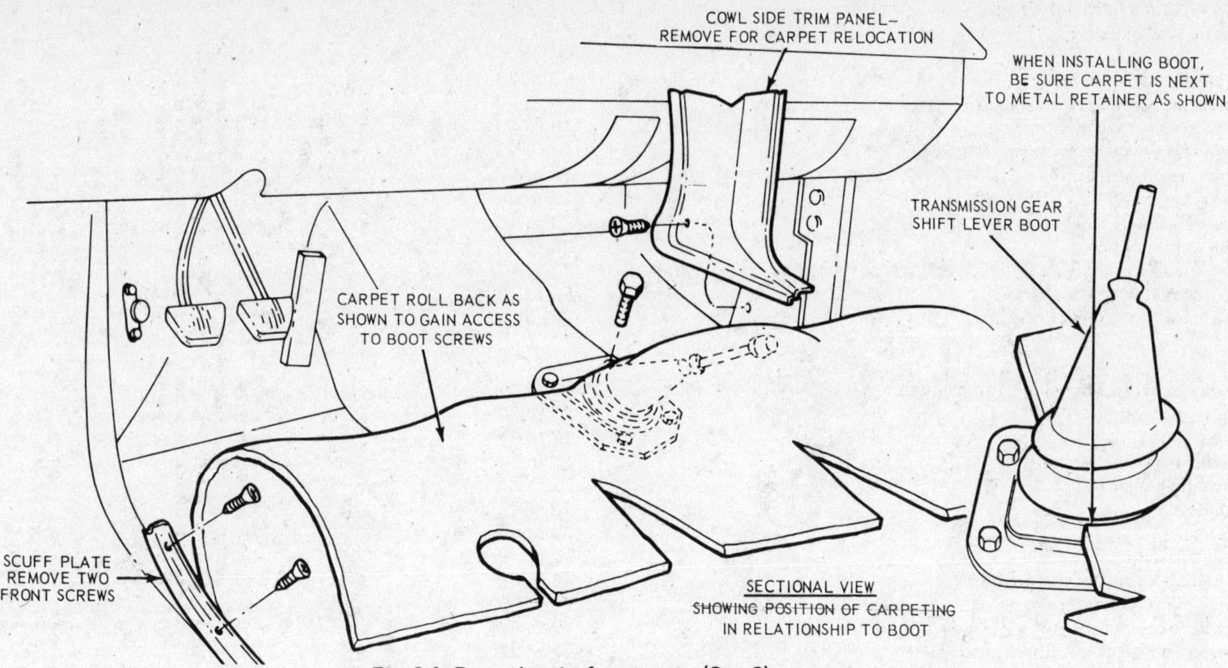

Fig. 6.1. Removing the front carpet (Sec. 2)

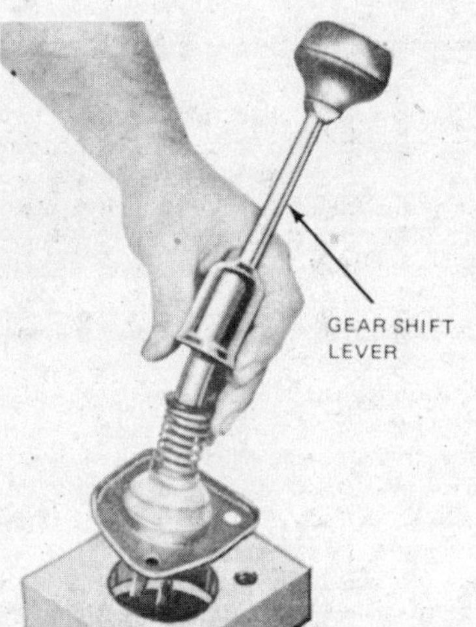

Fig. 6.2. Removing the shift lever (Sec. 2)

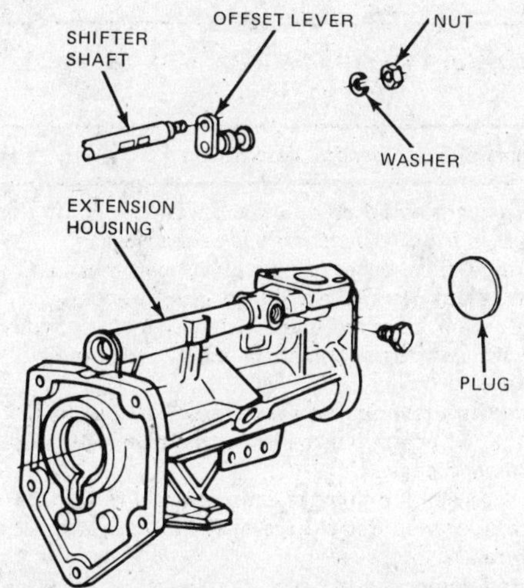

Fig. 6.3. Extension housing components (Sec. 3)

2 Any attempt to dismantle the gearbox without the foregoing is not impossible, but will certainly be very difficult and inconvenient.
3 Read the whole of this Section before starting work.
4 Using a brass drift, drive out the access plug at the rear of the extension housing by inserting the drift through the shift lever locating hole.
5 Working through the access hole, remove the offset lever retaining nut and washer and remove the lever (see Fig. 6.3).
6 Remove the bolts holding the extension housing to the transmission case and withdraw the extension housing taking care not to bend the selector rod.
7 Remove the screws retaining the top transmission cover plate and lift off the cover complete with selector shaft and forks. Remove the gasket. Turn the gearcase upside down to drain the oil, a drain plug is not fitted.
8 Undo and remove the bolts securing the input shaft retainer at the front of the transmission casing and take off the retainer and gasket.
9 Using a small screwdriver, remove the spring-clip retaining the reverse gear selector lever. Remove the lever and unscrew the pivot bolt from the side of the casing.
10 Remove the inner and outer snap-rings that retain the output shaft bearing and lever out the bearing using two screwdrivers placed in the outer snap-ring groove. Take care not to damage the transmission casing or output shaft (Fig. 6.5).
11 Take off the snap-ring securing the speedometer drivegear to the input shaft and slide the gear off. Do not lose the lock ball. On later transmissions, the speedometer gear is an interference fit on the shaft, no locking ball or circlips being used. Mark the position of the gear on the shaft before removal. The gear is very tight and a puller or press will be needed to withdraw it.
12 Remove the large outer snap-ring that retains the input shaft bearing and lever out the bearing using the method described previously.
13 Withdraw the input shaft and bearing, 4th gear and synchro-ring from the front of the transmission casing.
14 Carefully remove the output shaft and gear train by lifting it forward and up through the top of the casing.
15 Drive out the roll pin from the reverse idler gear shaft and slide the shaft out through the rear of the casing.
16 Using a drift of a suitable diameter, carefully drive out the countershaft from the front of the casing and then lift out the countershaft gear cluster, roller bearings, plain and thrust washers up through the top of the casing (Fig. 6.6).
17 Turning to the top cover assembly (Fig. 6.7), first remove the

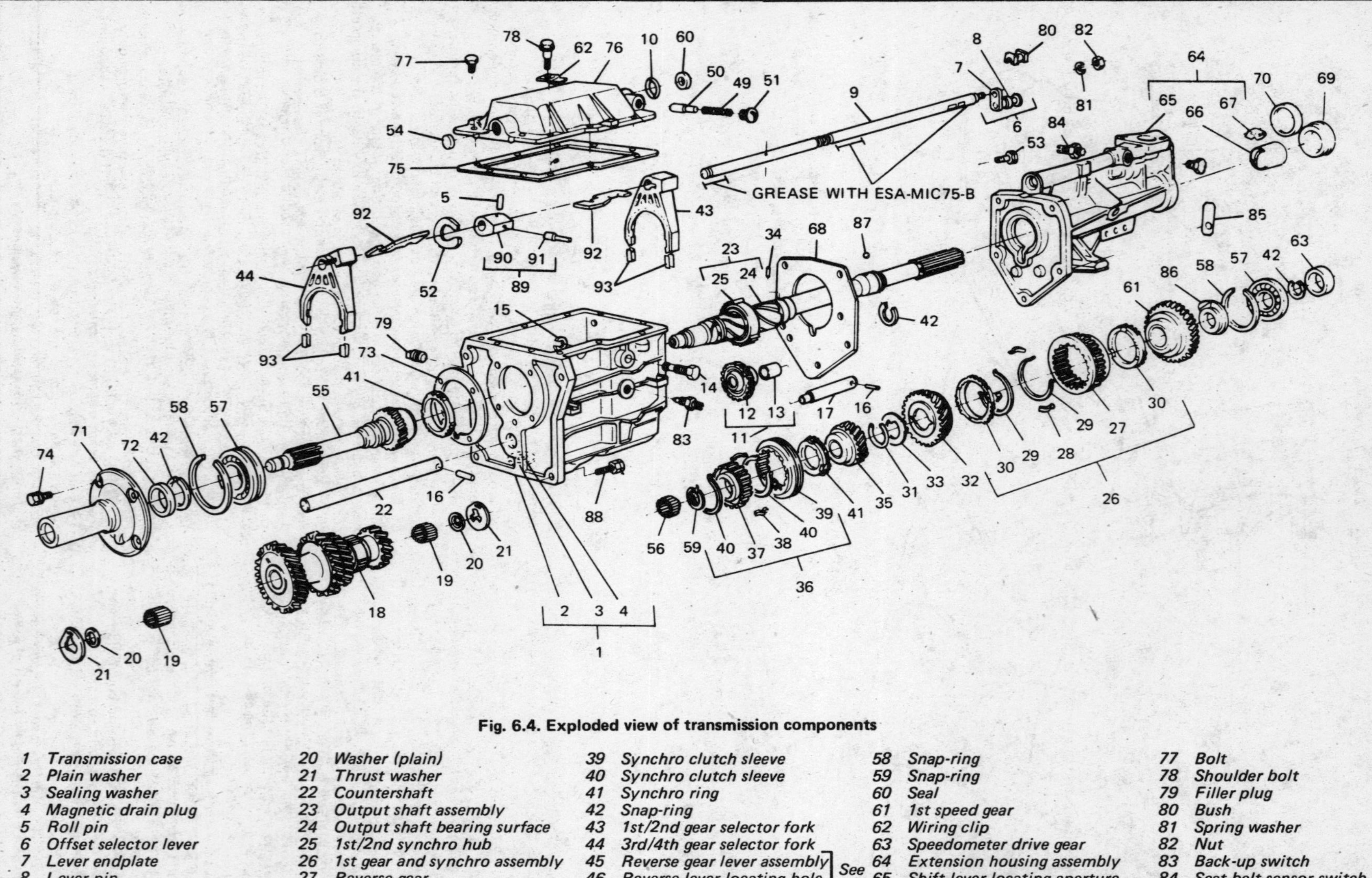

Fig. 6.4. Exploded view of transmission components

1 Transmission case
2 Plain washer
3 Sealing washer
4 Magnetic drain plug
5 Roll pin
6 Offset selector lever
7 Lever endplate
8 Lever pin
9 Gear selector shaft
10 'O' ring seal
11 Reverse idler assembly
12 Reverse gear
13 Spacer
14 Pivot bolt
15 Retaining clip
16 Roll pin
17 Reverse idler shaft
18 Countershaft gear cluster
19 Roller bearings
20 Washer (plain)
21 Thrust washer
22 Countershaft
23 Output shaft assembly
24 Output shaft bearing surface
25 1st/2nd synchro hub
26 1st gear and synchro assembly
27 Reverse gear
28 Synchro hub insert
29 Synchro hub spring
30 Synchro ring
31 Snap-ring
32 2nd speed gear
33 Thrust washer
34 Roll pin
35 3rd speed gear
36 3rd/4th synchro assembly
37 3rd/4th synchro hub
38 Synchro hub insert
39 Synchro clutch sleeve
40 Synchro clutch sleeve
41 Synchro ring
42 Snap-ring
43 1st/2nd gear selector fork
44 3rd/4th gear selector fork
45 Reverse gear lever assembly } See Fig. 6.7.
46 Reverse lever locating hole } See Fig. 6.7.
47 Reverse lever pivot hole } See Fig. 6.7.
48 Reverse gear selector fork } See Fig. 6.7.
49 Interlock spring
50 Interlock plunger
51 Interlock retaining screw
52 Interlock plate
53 Retain bolt
54 Welsh plug
55 Input shaft
56 Roller bearings
57 Input shaft bearing
58 Snap-ring
59 Snap-ring
60 Seal
61 1st speed gear
62 Wiring clip
63 Speedometer drive gear
64 Extension housing assembly
65 Shift lever locating aperture
66 Extension housing bush
67 Reverse gear stop plate
68 Gasket
69 Oil seal
70 Plug
71 Input shaft retainer
72 Seal
73 Gasket
74 Bolt
75 Gasket
76 Transmission cover
77 Bolt
78 Shoulder bolt
79 Filler plug
80 Bush
81 Spring washer
82 Nut
83 Back-up switch
84 Seat belt sensor switch
85 Ident tag
86 Thrust washer
87 Lock ball
88 Retaining bolt
89 Selector assembly
90 Selector arm
91 Roll pin
92 Selector arm plate
93 Fork inserts

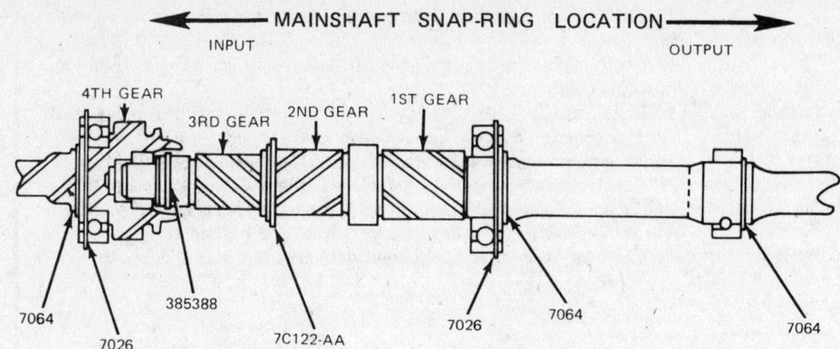

Fig. 6.5. Snap-ring locations and part numbers (Secs. 3, 5, 6 and 7)

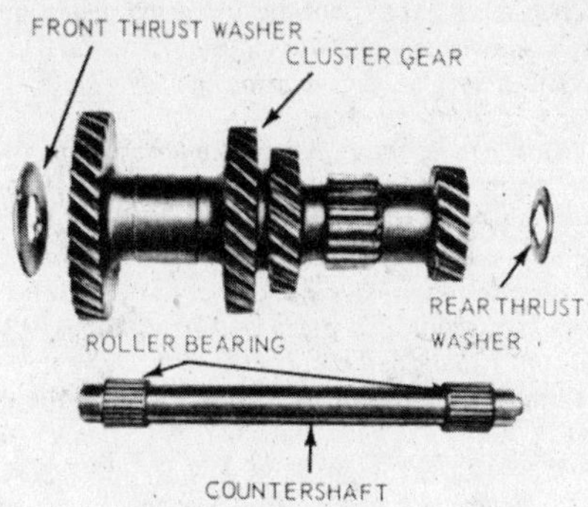

Fig. 6.6. Countershaft gear assembly (Secs. 3, 4 and 7)

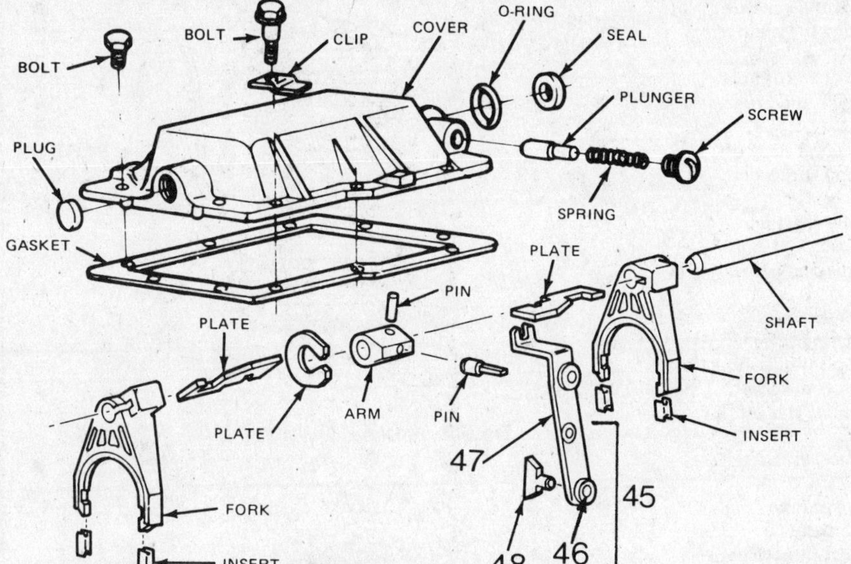

Fig. 6.7. Top transmission cover and components (Sec. 3). (For numbered items see the caption to Fig. 6.4)

detent retaining screw and lift out the spring and plunger.
18 Pull the selector shaft toward the rear of the cover and turn counter-clockwise.
19 Using the correct size punch, drive out the roll pin that secures the selector arm and interlock to the shaft.
20 Slide the selector shaft out from the rear of the cover taking care not to damage the 'O' ring and seal.
21 Remove the selector arm and interlock plate.
22 Remove the 1st/2nd speed selector fork and the 3rd/4th speed selector fork taking care not to lose the two nylon inserts on each fork.
23 The gearbox is now stripped right out and must be thoroughly cleaned. If there is any quantity of metal chips and fragments in the bottom of the gearbox casing it is obvious that several items will be found to be badly worn. The component parts of the gearbox and countershaft should be examined for wear. The input and output shafts assemblies should be broken down further as described in the following Sections.

4 Transmission - examination and renovation

1 Carefully clean and then examine all the component parts for general wear, distortion, slackness of fit, and damage to machined faces and threads.
2 Examine the gearwheels for excessive wear and chipping of the teeth. Renew them as necessary.
3 Examine the countershaft for signs of wear, where the countershaft gear cluster roller bearings bear. If a small ridge can be felt at either end of the shaft it will be necessary to renew it.
4 The four synchro-rings are bound to be badly worn and it is false economy not to renew them. New rings will improve the smoothness and speed of the gearchange considerably.
5 The needle roller bearings located between the nose of the output shaft and the annulus in the rear of the input shaft are also liable to wear, and should be renewed as a matter of course.
6 Examine the condition of the two ball bearing assemblies, one on the input shaft and one on the output. Check them for noisy operation, looseness between the inner and outer races, and for general wear. Normally they should be renewed on a gearbox that is being rebuilt.
7 If either of the synchro-hubs are worn it will be necessary to buy a complete assembly as the parts are not sold individually.
8 The nylon inserts on the selector forks should be renewed even though they may appear to be in good condition. If any of the inserts have broken up, allowing wear on the fork assembly itself, the complete fork should be renewed unless the wear is minimal.
9 If the bushing bearing in the extension is badly worn it is best to take the extension to your local Ford garage to have the bearing pulled out and a new one fitted.
10 The oil seals in the extension housing, input shaft bearing retainer and top cover should be renewed as a matter of course. Drive out the old seals with the aid of a drift or broad screwdriver. It will be found that the seals come out quite easily.
11 With a piece of wood to spread the load evenly, carefully tap new seals into place ensuring that they enter their housings squarely.
12 The only point on the output shaft that is likely to be worn is the nose where it enters the input shaft. However, examine it thoroughly for any signs of scoring, picking up, or flats, and if damage is apparent, renew it.

5 Input shaft - dismantling and reassembly

1 The only reason for dismantling the input shaft is to fit a new ball bearing assembly, or, if the input shaft is being renewed and the old bearing is in excellent condition, the fitting of a new shaft to an old bearing.

2 With a pair of expanding snap-ring pliers remove the small snap-ring which secures the bearing to the input shaft.
3 With a soft-headed hammer gently tap the bearing forward and then remove it from the shaft.
4 When fitting the new bearing ensure that the groove cut in the outer periphery faces away from the gear. If the bearing is fitted the wrong way round it will not be possible to fit the large snap-ring which retains the bearing in the housing.
5 Using the jaws of a vise as a support behind the bearing tap the bearing squarely into place by hitting the rear of the input shaft with a plastic or hide faced hammer.
6 Finally refit the snap-ring which holds the bearing to the input shaft.

6 Output shaft - dismantling and reassembly

1 The output shaft has to be dismantled before some of the synchro-rings can be inspected. For dismantling it is best to mount the plain section of the shaft in a vise fitted with jaw protectors.
2 As each component is removed from the shaft make a careful note of its position and then place it on a clean sheet of paper in the order of removal.
3 First remove the snap-ring from the front of the shaft and slide off the 3rd and 4th speed synchro-hub assembly, synchro-ring and 3rd speed gear.
4 Remove the next snap-ring and thrust washer from the shaft and slide off the 2nd speed gear and synchro-ring.
5 The 1st/2nd gear synchro-hub is fixed to the shaft and cannot be removed.
6 Turning to the rear of the shaft, remove the thrust washer and using a punch of the right diameter, drive out the roll (spring) pin from the shaft. Note that this pin locates and drives the oil slinger type thrust washer in addition to retaining the 1st speed gear on the shaft.
7 Slide the 1st speed gear and synchro-ring from the shaft. The output shaft is now completely dismantled.
8 If it is necessary to dismantle the synchro-hubs and sleeves, first etch alignment marks on each component.
9 Push the sleeves off the hubs and remove the inserts and insert springs, making a careful note which way round they are fitted.
10 Do not mix the 1st/2nd synchro-hub components with those from the 3rd/4th synchro-hub assembly.
11 To assemble a synchro-hub, first position the sleeve on the hub making sure the etched marks line up.
12 Fit the three inserts and retain in position with the springs. Make sure the bent tab on each spring is located in one of the inserts and that the springs face in opposite directions (see Fig. 6.8).
13 To reassemble the gears and synchro-hubs onto the shaft, first fit a synchro-ring on the 1st speed gear cone and slide the gear and synchro-ring onto the rear end of the shaft, making sure that the inserts in the synchro-hub are engaged in the notches in the synchro-ring.
14 Tap the roll pin into the shaft to retain the 1st speed gear assembly.
15 Install a synchro-ring onto the cone of the 2nd speed gear and slide the two components onto the front end of the shaft; again make sure that the synchro-ring notches engage with the synchro-hub inserts.
16 Fit a new thrust washer on the shaft and retain it with a new snap-ring.
17 Fit the synchro-ring onto the 3rd speed gear cone and slide them onto the shaft.
18 Install the 3rd/4th speed synchro-hub onto the shaft making sure the synchro-ring notches engage with the inserts on the synchro-hub.
19 Fit a new snap-ring to retain the 3rd/4th speed gear synchro-hub.
20 Turning to the rear end of the shaft fit a new thrust washer behind the 1st speed gear and make sure the washer engages with the roll pin and the groove in the washer faces toward the first gear.
21 The output shaft is now completely reassembled.

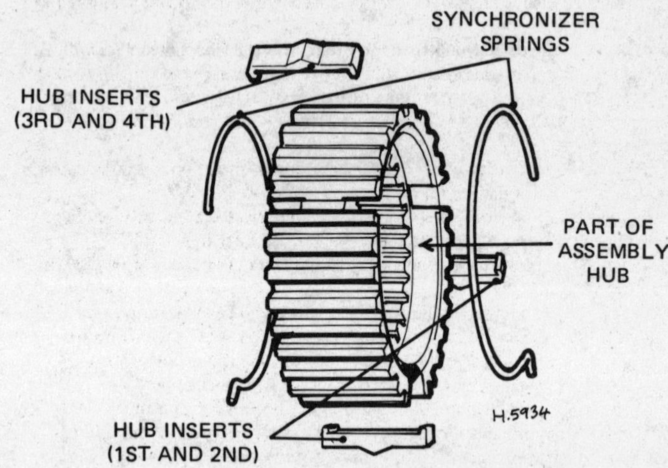

Fig. 6.8. Synchro-hub assembly (Sec. 6)

Fig. 6.9. Removing the front output shaft snap-ring (Sec. 6)

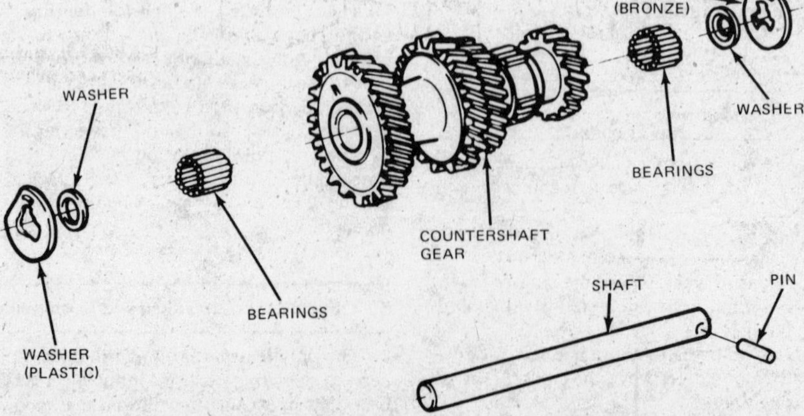

Fig. 6.10. Countershaft components (Secs. 3, 4 and 7)

7 Transmission - reassembly

1 Firstly, insert the reverse gear idler shaft into the rear of the transmission case. Hold the spacer and reverse gear in position (gear teeth facing the front of the casing) and slide the shaft fully home.
2 Smear some grease into each end of the countershaft gear cluster and carefully insert the roller bearings. Ideally a dummy shaft of the same outside dimensions as the countershaft but shorter, should be placed inside the countershaft gear cluster to hold the bearings in place.
3 Stick the nylon washer and thrust washer onto each end of the countershaft gear cluster with grease (see Fig. 6.10).
4 Carefully lower the gear cluster and washers into the casing until the bore of the gear cluster lines up with the countershaft holes in the front and rear sections of the casing. Check that the thrust washers are also lined up.
5 Insert the countershaft from the rear of the transmission casing and gently tap it through the gear cluster driving out the dummy shaft.
6 If a dummy countershaft was not used insert the countershaft the same way, but take great care not to dislodge any roller bearings or thrust washers.
7 When the countershaft is fully home check that the roll pin on the rear end of the shaft is seated in the casing groove.
8 Check that the countershaft gear cluster rotates smoothly with no harshness that might indicate dislodged roller bearings.
9 Install the output shaft and gear cluster into the casing through the top access hole.
10 Fit a new snap-ring in the groove around the rear bearing assembly and carefully drive the bearing along the output shaft until it enters the aperture in the rear of the casing. Note that the groove in the bearing must be positioned toward the rear of the casing.
11 Install a new bearing retainer snap-ring on the output shaft.
12 Check that the roller bearings are correctly located in the end of the input shaft with grease and retained with a new snap-ring.
13 Insert the input shaft, 4th gear and synchro-ring assembly through the front of the casing, making sure the end of the output shaft is correctly located in the roller bearing recess of the input shaft.
14 Fit a new snap-ring in the front bearing groove and tap the bearing along the input shaft until it enters the aperture in the casing. Carefully tap the bearing fully home.
15 Fit a new front bearing retainer snap-ring onto the input shaft.
16 Install the input shaft retainer using a new gasket.
17 Apply gasket sealer to the bearing retainer bolts and torque them up to the figure given in the Specifications.
18 Install the reverse idler gear shift lever making sure the fork is correctly positioned in the idler gear groove.
19 Screw the reverse lever pivot bolt into the side of the casing and align the reverse lever onto the pivot; retain it in place with the spring clip.
20 To reassemble the top cover, first make sure the new nylon inserts are correctly fitted on the forks and then insert the selector arm plates into the shift forks (Fig. 6.11).
21 Place the two selector forks in the correct position inside the top cover.
22 Install the selector arm through the interlock plate and position both components in the cover with the wider leg of the interlock plate facing down toward the inside of the transmission casing.
23 Fit a new 'O' ring and oil seal into the rear selector shaft hole in the top cover.
24 Smear some light grease onto the selector shaft and slide it into the rear of the cover and through the selector forks and selector arm assembly.
25 Align the hole in the selector arm and shaft and drive in the roll pin until it is flush with the arm.
26 Install the detent plunger and spring, apply some gasket sealant on the retaining plug threads and screw in.
27 Check the movement of the selector forks in each gear position by operating the selector shaft.
28 Place a new gasket on the top of the casing. Position the gears and selector forks into the 1st or 3rd gear position and fit the top cover.
29 Screw in the two shoulder bolts first and then install the rest of the cover bolts and tighten to the specified torque. Note that some of the bolts are used to retain cable clips.
30 Fit the speedometer drive gear locking ball into the hole in the output shaft, hold the ball in position and slide the drivegear over it. Secure with a snap-ring.
31 Place a new gasket over the rear end of the transmission casing and install the rear extension housing.
32 Apply sealer to the extension housing retaining bolts and tighten to the specified torque.
33 Fit the offset lever onto the end of the selector shaft and secure with the nut and washer. Take care not to overtighten the nut. Torque to 8 - 12 lb f ft (1.1 - 1.5 kg fm).
34 Insert the gearshift lever into place and check the operation of all four gear positions.
35 Smear some gasket sealer around the edge of the access plug and install it in the rear of the selector shaft housing using a plastic faced mallet.
36 The transmission is now ready to be re-installed into the car (see Section 2).

6

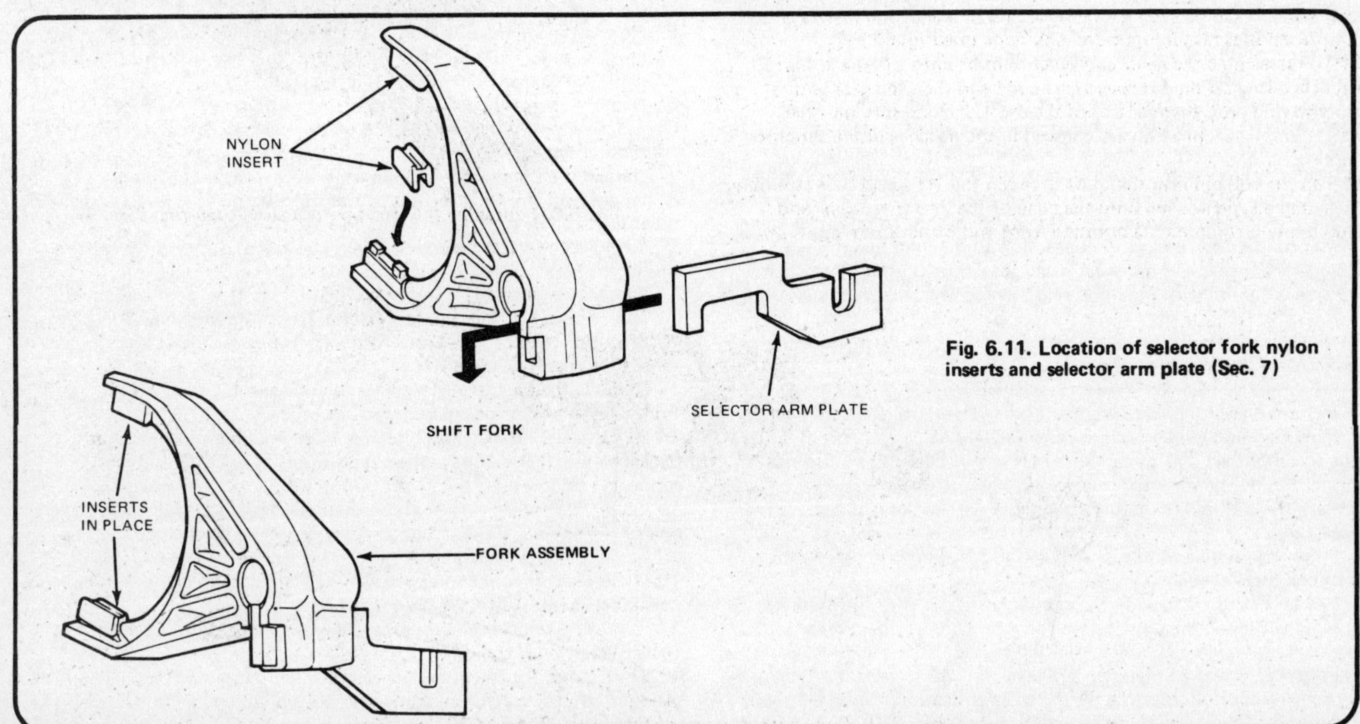

Fig. 6.11. Location of selector fork nylon inserts and selector arm plate (Sec. 7)

8 Fault diagnosis - manual gearboxes

Symptom	Reason/s	Remedy
Weak or ineffective synchromesh	Synchronising cones worn, split or damaged	Dismantle and overhaul gearbox. Fit new gear wheels and synchronising cones.
	Synchro-ring worn, or damaged	Dismantle and overhaul gearbox. Fit new synchro-rings.
Jumps out of gear	Broken gearchange fork rod detent spring	Dismantle and replace spring.
	Gearbox coupling dogs badly worn	Dismantle gearbox. Fit new coupling dogs.
	Selector fork rod groove badly worn	Fit new selector fork rod.
Excessive noise	Incorrect grade of oil in gearbox or oil level too low	Top-up gearbox with correct grade of oil. grade of oil.
	Bush or needle roller bearings worn or damaged	Dismantle and overhaul gearbox. Renew bearings.
	Gear teeth excessively worn or damaged	Dismantle, overhaul gearbox. Renew gear wheels.
	Countershaft thrust washers worn allowing excessive end play	Dismantle and overhaul gearbox. Renew thrust washers.
Excessive difficulty in engaging gear	Clutch cable adjustment incorrect	Adjust clutch cable correctly.

Part B: Automatic transmission

9 Automatic transmission - general description

1 The automatic transmission takes the place of the conventional clutch and gearbox, and comprises the following two main assemblies:

a) A three element hydrokinetic torque converter coupling, capable of torque multiplication at an infinitely variable ratio.
b) A torque/speed responsive and hydraulically operated epicyclic gearbox comprising a planetary gearset providing three forward ratios and one reverse ratio.

2 Due to the complexity of the automatic transmission unit, if performance is not up to standard, or overhaul is necessary, it is imperative that this be left to the local main agents who will have the special equipment for fault diagnosis and rectification. The content of the following Sections is therefore confined to supplying general information and any service information and instruction that can be used by the owner.
3 The automatic transmission fitted to the Mustang II models is manufactured by Ford and is either the C3 or C4 type depending on the year of manufacture and engine size. Both types of transmission are very similar, but where there are major differences these are described under a separate Section heading. A transmission oil cooler is fitted as standard and ensures cooler operation of the transmission under trailer towing conditions. A vacuum connection to the inlet manifold provides smoother and more consistent downshifts under load than is the case with units not incorporating this facility.

10 Transmission - fluid level checking

1 Before attempting to check the fluid level, the fluid must be at its normal operating temperature (approximately 65°C /150°F). This is best accomplished by driving the car for about 5 miles (8 km) under normal running conditions.
2 Park the car on level ground, apply the handbrake and depress the brake pedal.
3 Allow the engine to idle, then move the selector through all the positions three times.
4 Select 'P' and wait for 1 to 2 minutes with the engine still idling.
5 Now withdraw the dipstick (engine still idling), wipe it clean with a lint-free cloth, replace it and withdraw it again. Note the oil level and, if necessary, top-up to maintain between the 'MAX' and 'MIN' dipstick markings. Only fluid meeting the stated specification should be used; this is applied through the dipstick tube (photo).

11 Transmission - removal and refitting (C3)

1 If possible, raise the car on a hoist or place it over an inspection pit. Alternatively, it will be necessary to jack-up the car to obtain the maximum possible amount of working room underneath.
2 Place a large drain pan beneath the transmission sump (oil pan) then, working from the rear, loosen the attaching bolts and allow the fluid to drain. Remove all the bolts except the two front ones to drain as much fluid as possible, then temporarily refit two bolts at the rear to hold it in place.
3 Remove the torque converter drain plug access cover and adapter plate bolts from the lower end of the converter housing.
4 Remove the three adapter plate-to-converter attaching bolts, cranking the engine as necessary to gain access by means of a spanner on the crankshaft pulley attaching bolt. **Caution: Do not rotate the engine backwards.**
5 Rotate the engine until the converter drain plug is accessible, then remove the plug, catching the fluid in the drain pan. Fit and tighten the drain plug afterwards.
6 Remove the propeller shaft, referring to Chapter 7, as necessary. Place a polythene bag over the end of the transmission to prevent dirt from entering.
7 Detach the speedometer cable from the extension housing.
8 Disconnect the shift rod at the transmission manual lever, and the downshift rod at the transmission downshift lever.
9 Remove the starter motor retaining bolts and position the motor out of the way.
10 Disconnect the starter inhibitor (neutral start) switch leads.
11 Disconnect the vacuum lines from the vacuum unit.
12 Position a trolley jack beneath the transmission and raise it to *just* take the transmission weight.
13 Remove the engine rear support to crossmember nut and the transmission extension housing crossmember.
14 Remove the inlet steady pipe rest from the inlet pipe and rear engine support. Disconnect the exhaust pipe at the manifold and support it to one side (two pipes on the V6).
15 Lower the trolley jack slightly, then place another jack to the front end of the engine. Raise the engine to gain access to the upper converter housing-to-engine attaching bolts.
16 Disconnect the oil cooler lines at the transmission and plug them to prevent dirt from entering (Fig. 6.15).
17 Remove the lower converter housing-to-engine bolts, and the transmission filler tube.
18 Ensure that the transmission is securely mounted on the trolley jack, then remove the two upper converter housing-to-engine bolts.
19 Carefully move the transmission rearwards and downwards, and

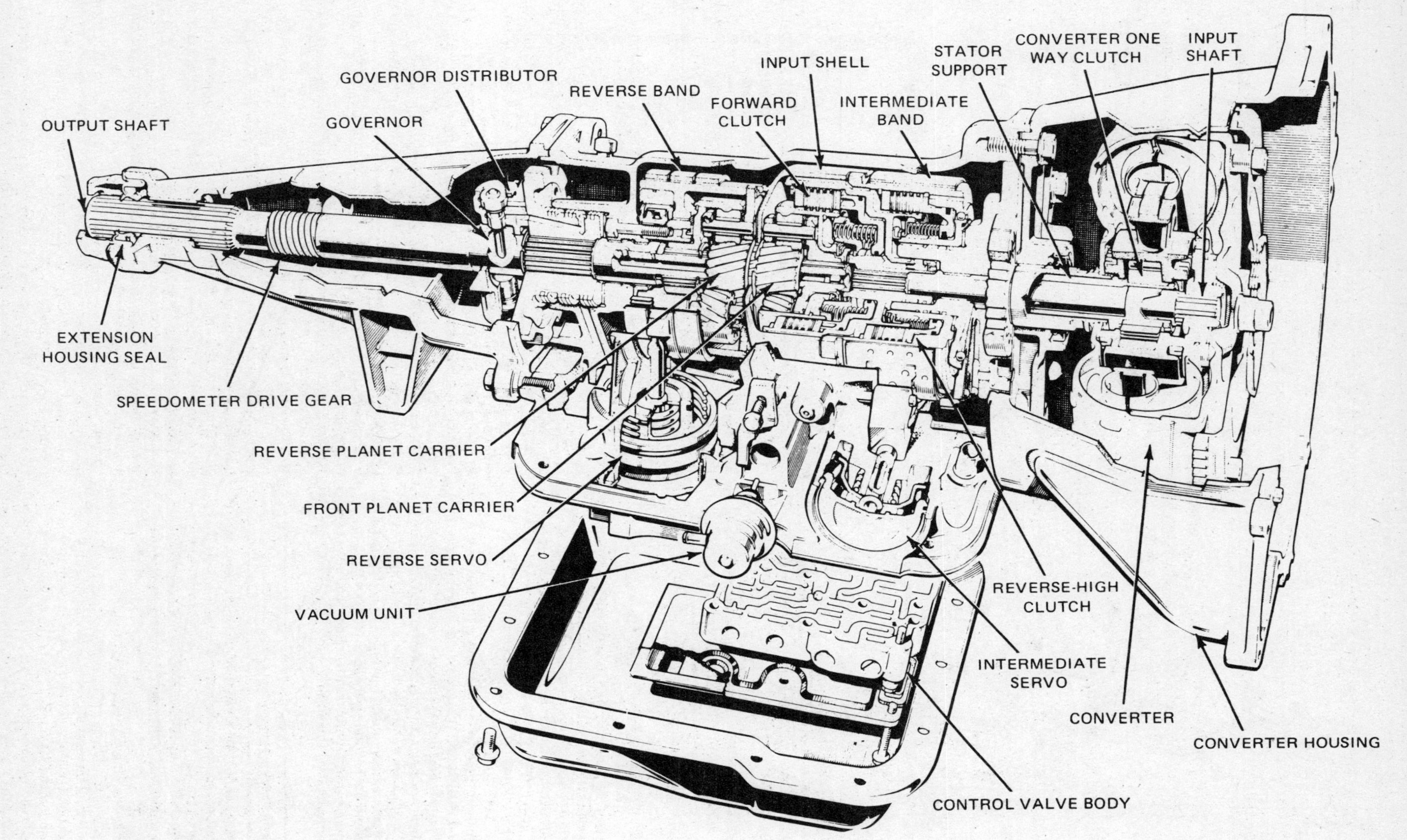

Fig. 6.12. Sectional view of C3 automatic transmission

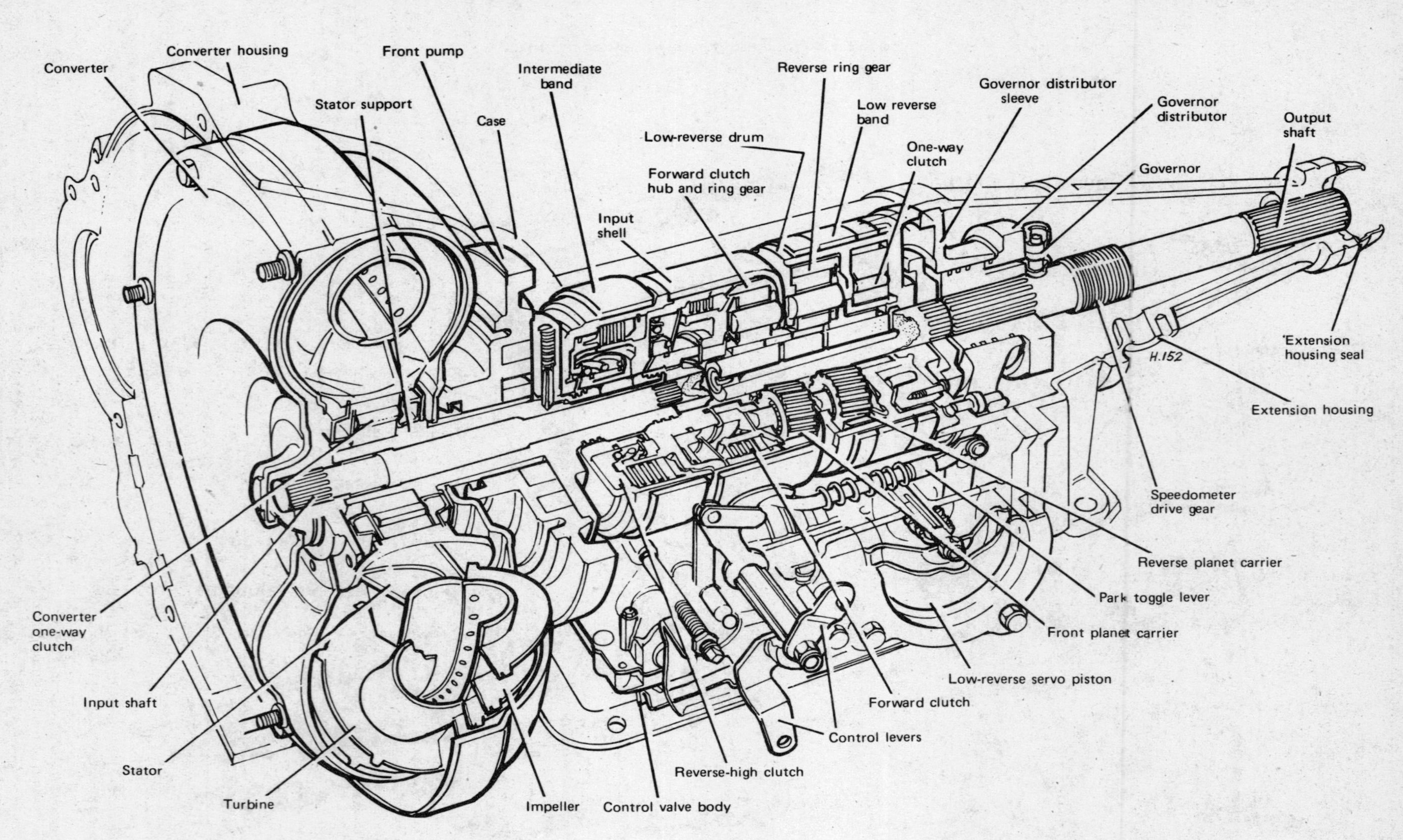
Converter
Converter housing
Front pump
Stator support
Case
Intermediate band
Input shell
Forward clutch hub and ring gear
Low-reverse drum
Reverse ring gear
Low reverse band
One-way clutch
Governor distributor sleeve
Governor distributor
Governor
Output shaft
Extension housing seal
H.152
Extension housing
Speedometer drive gear
Reverse planet carrier
Park toggle lever
Front planet carrier
Low-reverse servo piston
Forward clutch
Control levers
Reverse-high clutch
Control valve body
Impeller
Turbine
Stator
Input shaft
Converter one-way clutch

Fig. 6.13. Sectional view of C4 automatic transmission

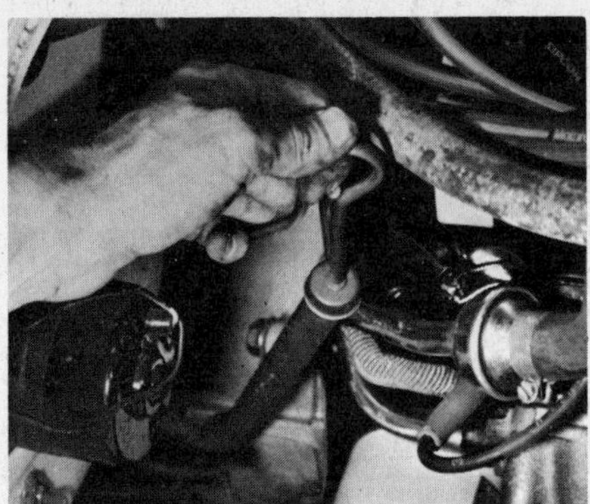

10.5 Automatic transmission dipstick and filler tube

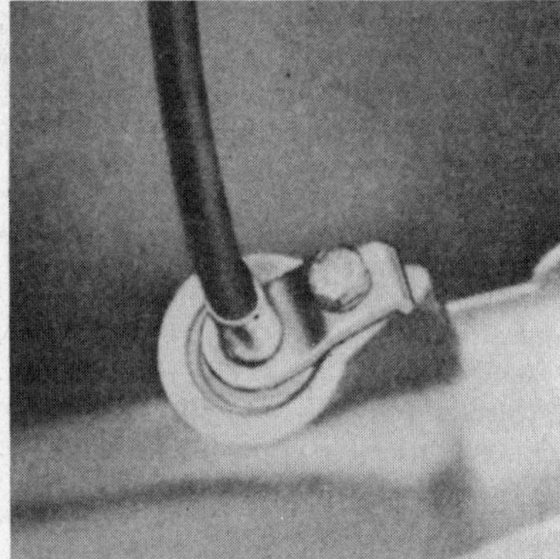

Fig. 6.14. Speedometer cable retaining clamp (Sec. 11)

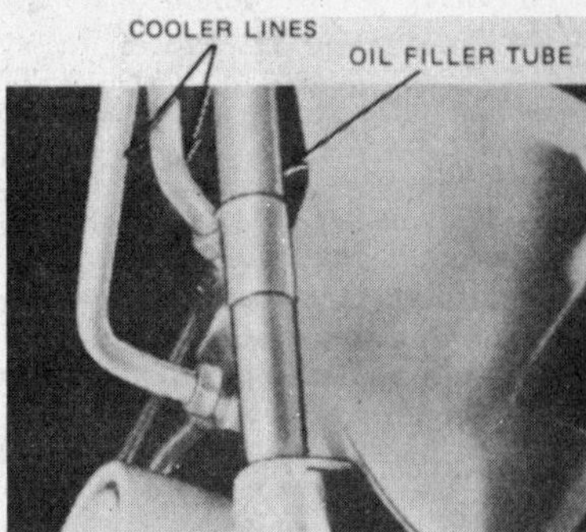

Fig. 6.15. Oil cooler lines and filler tube (Sec. 11)

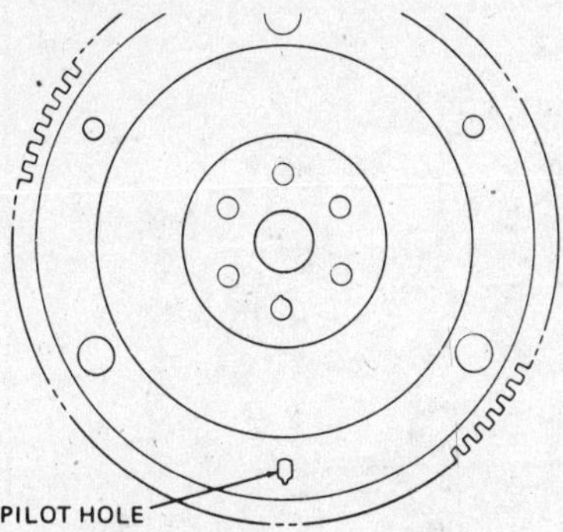

Fig. 6.16. Adapter plate pilot hole (Sec. 11)

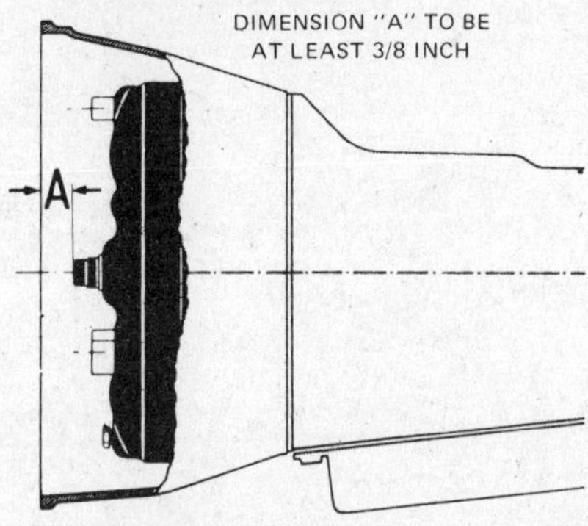

Fig. 6.17. Converter housing-to-hub flange position (Sec. 11)

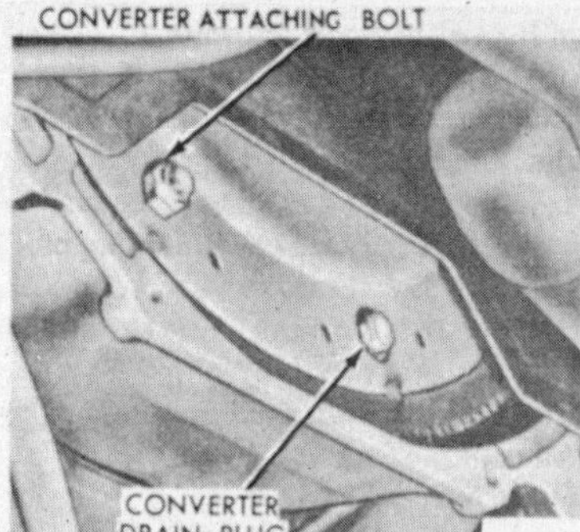

Fig. 6.18. Converter drain plug (Sec. 12)

away from the car.

20 Refitting the transmission is essentially the reverse of the removal procedure, but the following points should be noted:

a) Rotate the converter to align the bolt drive lugs and drain plug with their holes in the adapter plate.
b) Do not allow the transmission to take a 'nose-down' attitude as the converter will move forward and disengage from the pump gear.
c) When installing the three adapter plate-to-converter bolts position the adapter plate so that the pilot hole is in the six o'clock position (see Fig. 6.16). First install one bolt through the pilot hole and torque tighten it, followed by the two remaining bolts. Do not attempt to install it in any other way.
d) Adjust the downshift cable and selector linkage as necessary (see Sections 16 and 17).
e) When the car has been lowered to the ground, add sufficient fluid to bring the level up to the 'MAX' mark on the dipstick with the engine not running. Having done this, check and top-up the fluid level, as described in the previous Section.

12 Transmission - removal and refitting (C4)

Any suspected fault must be referred to the local Ford dealer or specialist before unit removal, as with this type of transmission the fault must be confirmed, using specialist equipment, before the unit has been removed from the car.

1 For safety reasons, disconnect the battery ground terminal.

2 Jack-up the car and support on firmly based stands if a lift or pit is not available.

3 Refer to Chapter 7, and remove the propeller shaft.

4 Wrap a polythene bag over the end of the transmission unit to prevent oil seeping out. Alternatively, drain out the oil. If the car has just been driven the oil will be very hot.

5 Undo and remove the two upper converter housing to engine securing nuts.

6 Undo and remove the bolt that secures the transmission fluid filler tube to the cylinder block. Lift away the filler tube.

7 Undo and remove the bolts securing the converter cover. This is located at the lower front side of the converter housing. Lift away the cover.

8 Remove the vacuum line hose from the transmission vacuum unit. Detach this vacuum line from the retaining clip.

9 Remove the speedometer cable from the extension housing.

10 Wipe the area around the oil cooler pipe unions on the side of the transmission unit and then detach the pipes. Plug the open ends to stop loss of fluid or dirt ingress.

11 Disconnect the transmission shift rod at the manual selector lever.

12 Disconnect the downshift rod and spring at the transmission downshift lever.

13 Make a note of and then disconnect the neutral start and back-up switch wires from the connectors and retaining clamps.

14 Undo and remove the four nuts securing the torque converter to the adapter plate. For this the engine will have to be rotated and the nuts removed working through the aperture left by removal of the converter cover (paragraph 7, see Fig. 6.18).

15 Support the weight of the transmission unit using a jack. It will also be necessary to have an assistant to hold the transmission unit.

16 Using an overhead hoist, crane or jack, support the weight of the engine.

17 Undo and remove the bolts securing the transmission unit crossmember to the body.

18 Undo and remove the bolts securing the rear engine support crossmember.

19 Remove the front exhaust pipe section between the manifold and the resonator box, (or converter). On V6 cars both front pipes will have to be removed.

20 Undo and remove the bolts securing the starter motor to the torque converter housing and withdraw the starter motor from its location.

21 Undo and remove the remaining bolts securing the torque converter housing to the rear of the engine.

22 Carefully draw the unit rearwards (take care because it is very heavy) and lower to the ground. Support on wooden blocks so that the selector lever is not damaged or bent.

23 To separate the converter housing from the transmission case, first lift off the converter from the transmission unit, taking suitable precautions to catch the fluid upon separation.
24 Undo and remove the bolts and spring washers which secure the converter housing to the transmission case. Lift away the converter housing.
25 Refitting the automatic transmission unit is the reverse sequence to removal, but there are several additional points which will assist:

a) *If the torque converter has been removed, before refitting it will be necessary to align the front pump drive tangs with the slots in the inner gear and then carefully replace the torque converter. Take care not to damage the oil seal.*
b) *Before mounting the transmission on the engine remove the two dowel pins from the converter housing flange and push them in the engine block. This is only applicable when dowels are fitted.*
c) *Adjust the manual selector linkage, the throttle downshift cable and the inhibitor switch. Full details of these adjustments will be found in subsequent Sections.*

13 Selector lever assembly - removal and replacement

1 Chock the front wheels, jack-up the rear of the car and support on firmly based axle stands.
2 Working under the car, undo and remove the manual lever control rod securing nut. Detach the rod from the stud.
3 Working inside the car, undo and remove the selector lever handle securing screw.
4 Undo and remove the screws securing the dial housing to the selector lever assembly. Lift away the dial housing (photos).

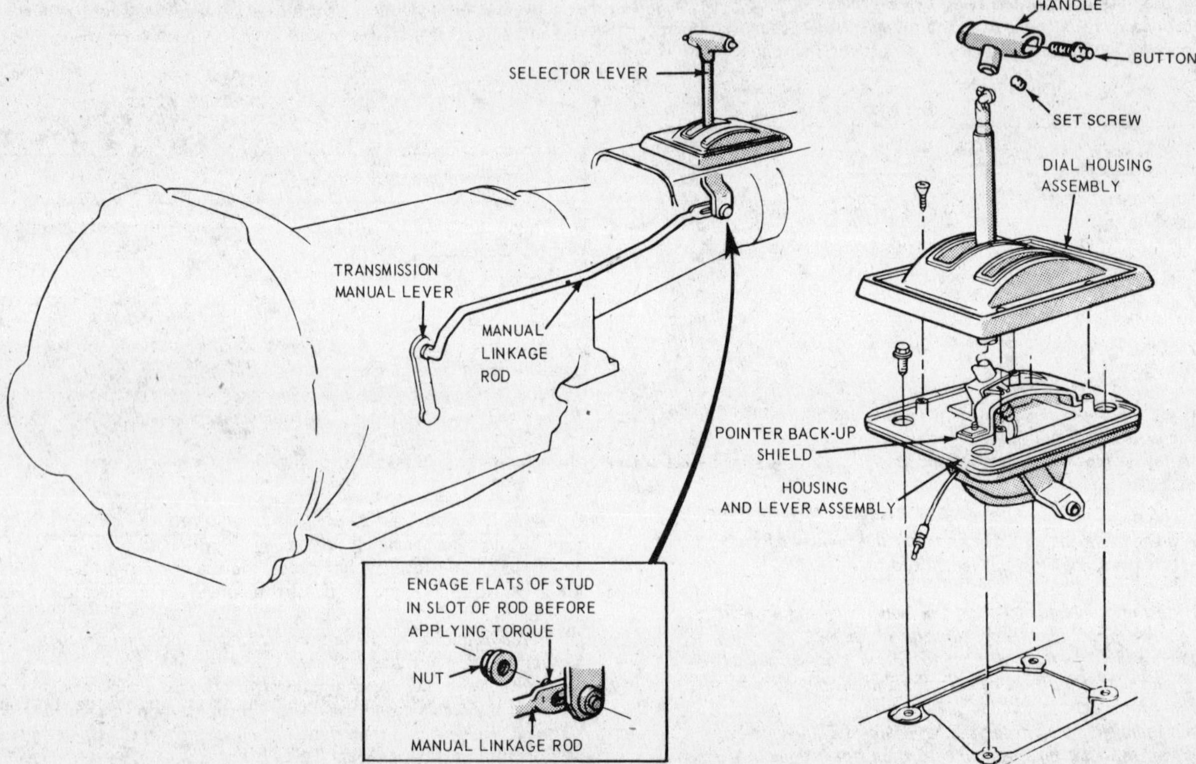

Fig. 6.19. Gear shift lever and linkage (Sec. 13)

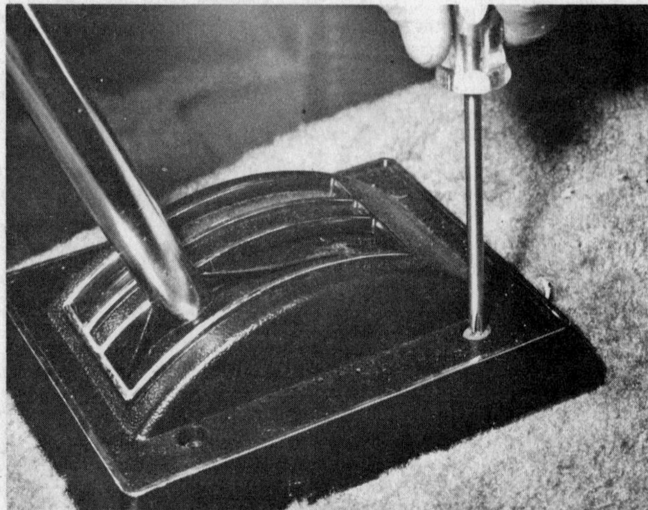
13.4A Removing the shift lever cover screws

13.4B Shift lever selector mechanism

5 Undo and remove the two screws securing the pointer back up shield to the selector lever assembly. Lift away the shield.
6 Undo and remove the two screws that secure the dial indicator light bulb retainer to the selector lever. Remove the retainer and bulb.
7 Undo and remove the selector housing and lever assembly securing bolts. Lift away the selector lever and housing.
8 If it is necessary to detach the selector lever from the housing undo and remove the one securing nut and detach the lever from the housing.
9 To reassemble first refit the selector lever to the housing and secure with the nut.
10 Fit the handle to the selector lever.
11 Check the clearance between the detent pawl and plate. The detent pawl when correctly adjusted should clear the highest point on the detent plate.
12 To adjust the pawl height, hold the adjustment screw stationary and turn the locknut until the correct clearance is obtained.
13 Remove the handle from the selector lever again.
14 Reassembly and refitting is now the reverse sequence to removal, and dismantling. It may be necessary to adjust the manual control linkage.

14 Neutral start switch - removal and replacement

1 Chock the front wheels, jack-up the rear of the car and support on firmly based axle stands.
2 Working under the car, disconnect the downshift linkage rod from the transmission downshift lever.
3 Apply a little penetrating oil to the downshift lever shaft and nut and allow to soak for a few minutes.
4 Undo and remove the transmission downshift outer lever retaining nut. Lift away the lever.
5 Undo and remove the two neutral start switch securing bolts.
6 Disconnect the multi-wire connector from the neutral switch and lift away the switch.
7 To refit the switch, place on the transmission unit and lightly secure with the two bolts.
8 Move the selector lever to the 'N' (neutral) position. Rotate the switch and fit a No 43 drill into the gauge pin hole. It must be inserted a full 0.48 in (12.30 mm) into the three holes of the switch. Tighten the switch securing bolts fully and remove the drill.
9 Refitting is now the reverse sequence to removal. Check that the engine only starts with the selector lever in the 'N' and 'P' positons.
Note: The neutral start switch on the C3 transmission is non-adjustable and any fault will be due to a malfunctioning switch, wear on the internal actuating cam or faulty wiring. If the switch is suspect, replace it with a new one. Always use a new 'O' ring seal and tighten to the specified torque.

15 Selector linkage - adjustment (C3)

1 First check that the selector lever is correctly adjusted. To do this, use feeler gauges to check the end-clearance between the lever pawl and the quadrant notch. This should be between 0.005 and 0.010 in (0.13 and 0.25 mm). If necessary, adjust the cable locknut which is accessible after removal of the selector lever housing plug.
2 Disconnect the shift rod from the shift lever at the base of the hand control lever (adjustable end of rod).
3 Place the hand control lever in 'D'.
4 Place the selector lever on the side of the transmission housing in 'D'. This can be determined by counting two 'clicks' back from the fully forward position.
5 Now attempt to reconnect the shift rod to the selector hand control lever by pushing in the clevis pin. The pin should slide in without any side stress at all. If this is not the case, release the locknut on the shift rod and adjust its effective length by screwing the adjusting link in, or out.

16 Selector linkage - adjustment (C4)

1 Chock the front wheels, jack-up the rear of the car and support on firmly based axle stands.
2 Move the transmission selector lever to the 'D' position.
3 Working under the car slacken the manual lever shift rod retaining nut.
4 Move the manual lever to the 'D' position. This is the fourth detent position from the rear of the transmission unit.
5 With transmission selector lever and manual lever in the 'D' positions tighten the retaining nut to a torque wrench setting of 10 - 12 lb f ft (1.38 - 2.77 kg f m).

17 Kick-down rod - adjustment

1 Disconnect the downshift rod return spring and hold the throttle shaft lever in the wide open position.
2 Hold the downshift rod against the through detent stop.
3 Adjust the downshift screw so as to provide a clearance of 0.050 - 0.070 in (1.27 - 1.78 mm) between the screw tip and the throttle shaft lever tab (photo).
4 Reconnect the downshift lever spring.

6

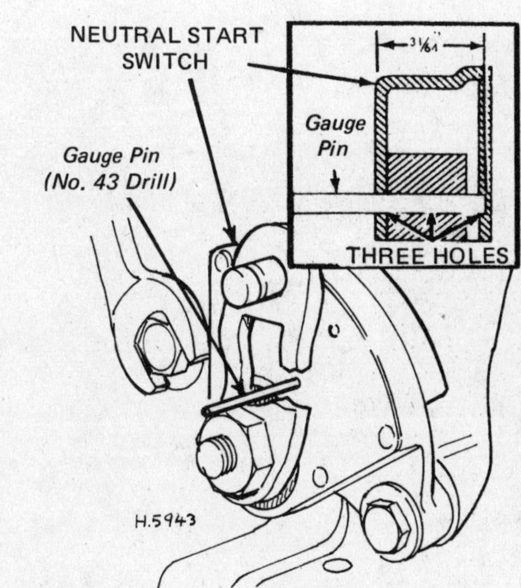

Fig. 6.20. Neutral start switch adjustment (Sec. 14)

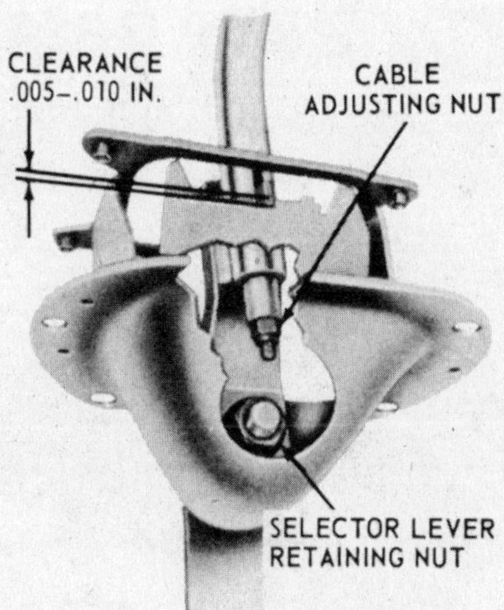

Fig. 6.21. Shift lever adjustment

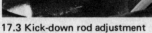

17.3 Kick-down rod adjustment

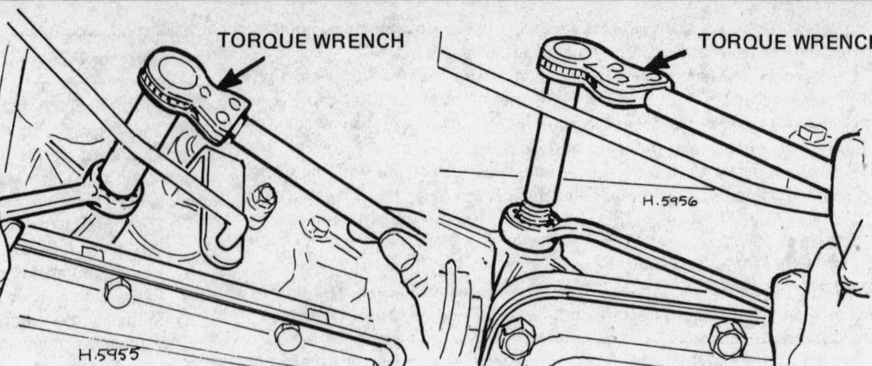

Fig. 6.22. Adjusting the intermediate transmission band (Sec. 18)

Fig. 6.23. Adjusting the low/reverse band (C4 transmission only) (Sec. 19)

18 Intermediate band (C4 and C3) - adjustment

The intermediate or front band is used to hold the sun gear stationary so as to give the second gear ratio. If it is not correctly adjusted there will be noticeable slip during first to second gearchange or from third to second gearchange. The first symptoms of these conditions will be a very sluggish gearchange instead of the usual crisp action.

To adjust the intermediate band, undo and remove the adjustment screw locknut located on the left-hand side of the transmission case. Tighten the adjusting screw using a torque wrench set to 10 lb f ft (1.4 kg f m) and then slacken off the adjustment screw 1½ turns (C3) or 1¾ turns (C4). A new locknut should be fitted and tighten to a torque wrench setting of 35 - 45 lb f ft (4.8 - 6.22 kg f m).

19 Low and reverse band (C4 only) - adjustment

The low and reverse band or rear band is in action when 'L' or 'R' position of the selector lever is obtained to hold the low and reverse pinion carrier stationary. If it is not correctly adjusted there will be a noticeable malfunction of the automatic transmission unit, whereby there will be no drive with the selector lever in the 'R' position, also associated with no engine braking on first gear when the selector lever is in the 'L' position.

To adjust the rear band undo and remove the adjusting screw locknut located on the left-hand side of the transmission case. Tighten the adjusting screw using a torque wrench set to 10 lb f ft (1.4 kg fm) and then slacken off the adjustment screw exactly 3 turns. A new locknut should be fitted and tightened to a torque wrench setting of 35 - 45 lb f ft (4.8 - 6.22 kg fm) - Fig. 6.23.

20 Fault diagnosis - automatic transmission

As has been mentioned elsewhere in this Chapter, no service repair work should be considered by anyone without the specialist knowledge and equipment required to undertake this work. This is also relevant to fault diagnosis. If a fault is evident carry out the various adjustments previously described and if the fault still exists consult your Ford dealer or specialist.

Chapter 7 Driveshaft

Contents

Specifications

Type ...	One piece tubular with single Cardan type universal joint at each end	
Torque wrench settings	**lb f ft**	**kg f m**
U-bolt nuts ...	8 to 15	1 to 2.07

1 General description

Drive is transmitted from the gearbox to the rear axle by means of a finely balanced tubular driveshaft. Fitted at each end is a universal joint which allows for vertical movement of the rear axle. Each universal joint comprises a four legged center spider, four needle roller bearings and two yokes.

Fore and aft movement of the rear axle is absorbed by a sliding spline in the front of the driveshaft which slides over a mating spline on the rear of the gearbox mainshaft.

All models are fitted with the sealed type of universal joint which requires no maintenance.

The propeller shaft is a relatively simple component and is fairly easy to overhaul and repair provided that spare parts are readily to hand.

2 Driveshaft - removal and replacement

1 Chock the front wheels, jack up the rear of the car or position the rear of the car over or on a ramp.
2 If the rear of the car is jacked up supplement the jack with support blocks so that danger is minimised should the jack fail.
3 If the rear wheels are off the ground place the car in gear and apply the parking brake to ensure that the driveshaft does not turn when an attempt is made to loosen the four nuts securing the propeller shaft 'U' bolts to the rear axle pinion flange.
4 Mark the pinion flange, 'U' bolts and driveshaft so that it may be refitted in its original position.
5 Undo and remove the four nuts securing the two 'U' bolts to the pinion flange and remove the 'U' bolts.

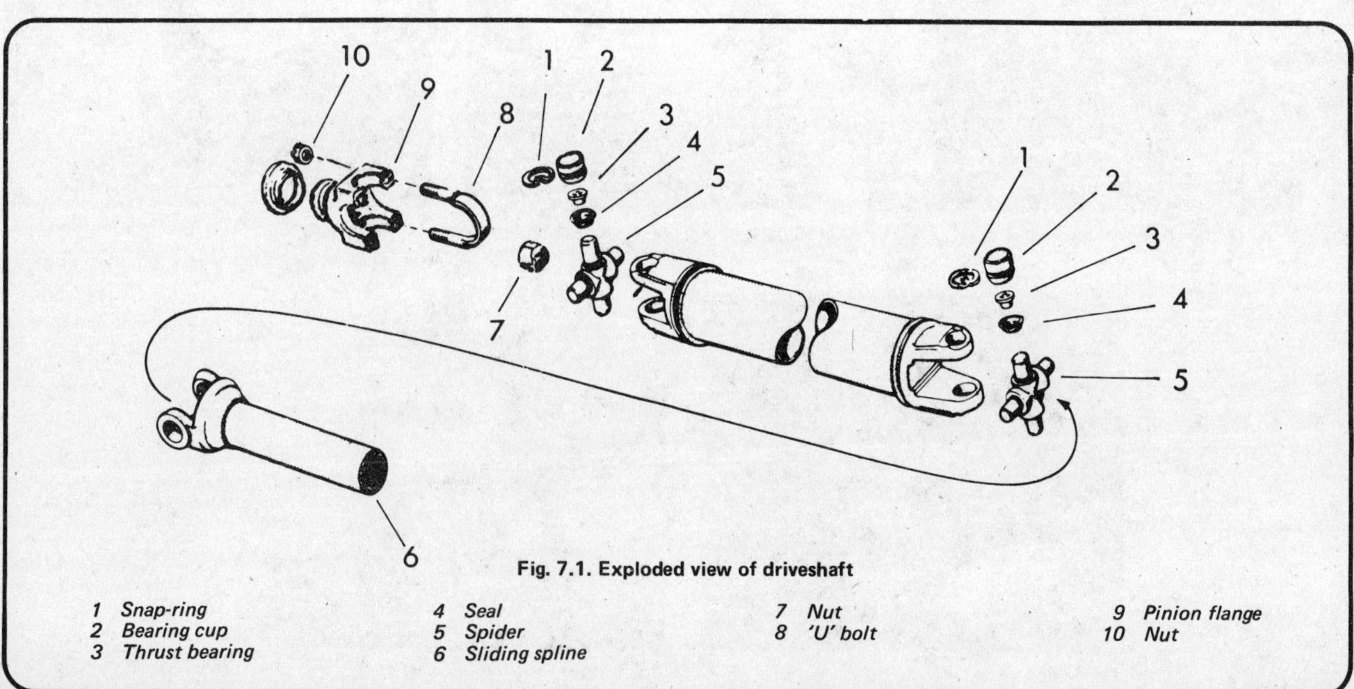

Fig. 7.1. Exploded view of driveshaft

1 Snap-ring
2 Bearing cup
3 Thrust bearing
4 Seal
5 Spider
6 Sliding spline
7 Nut
8 'U' bolt
9 Pinion flange
10 Nut

6 Slightly push the driveshaft forward to separate the spider assembly from the pinion flange, then lower the end of the shaft and pull it rearwards to disengage the gearbox mainshaft splines.
7 Place a large can or tray under the rear of the gearbox extension to catch any oil which is likely to leak from the end when the driveshaft is removed.
8 Replacement of the driveshaft is a reversal of the above procedure. Ensure that the previously made mating marks are lined up.
9 On later models, the rear end of the driveshaft is connected to the rear axle pinion by means of a flanged type coupling (Fig. 7.2). When disconnecting this type of coupling, mark the alignment of the two halves and when refitting, tighten the bolts to the specified torque and use new self-locking nuts if there is any doubt as to their efficiency.

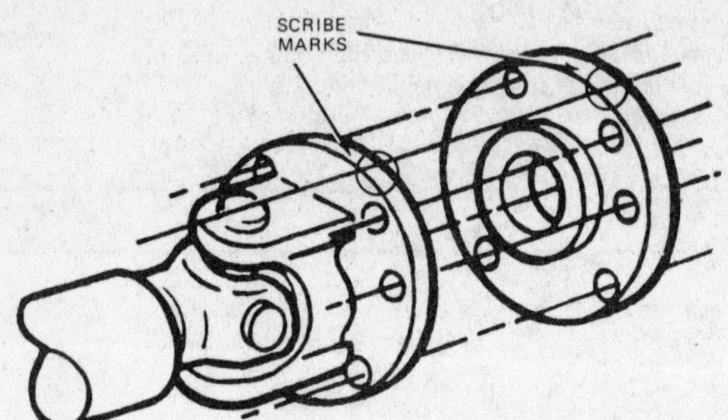

Fig. 7.2. Later model driveshaft coupling

3 Universal joints - inspection and repair

1 Wear in the needle roller bearings is characterised by vibration in the drive-line, 'clonks' on taking up the drive, and in extreme cases of lack of lubrication, metallic squeaking, and ultimately grating and shrieking.
2 It is easy to check if the needle roller bearings are worn with the driveshaft in position, by trying to turn the shaft with one hand, the other hand holding the rear axle pinion flange when the rear universal joint is being checked, and the front half coupling when the front universal is being checked. Any movement between the driveshaft and the front and the rear half couplings is indicative of considerable wear. If worn, the old bearings and spiders will have to be discarded and a repair kit, comprising new universal joint spiders, bearings, oil seals, and retainers purchased. Check also by trying to lift the shaft and noticing any movement in the joints.
3 Examine the driveshaft splines for wear. If worn it will be necessary to purchase a new front coupling, or if the yokes are badly worn, an exchange driveshaft. It is not possible to fit oversize bearings and journals to the trunnion bearing holes.

4 Front universal joint - dismantling, overhaul and reassembly

1 Clean away all traces of dirt and grease from the snap-rings located on the ends of the bearing cups, refer to the photo and remove the snap-rings by pressing their open ends together with a pair of pliers, and lever them out with a screwdriver. **Note:** If they are difficult to remove tap the bearing cup face resting on the top of the spider with a soft-faced hammer which will ease the pressure on the snap-ring.
2 Take off the bearing cups on the driveshaft yoke. To do this select two sockets from a socket set, one large enough to fit completely over the bearing cup and the other smaller than the bearing cup (photo).
3 Open the jaws of the vise and with the sockets opposite each other and the universal joint in between, tighten the vise and so force the narrower socket to move the opposite cup partially out of the yoke into the larger socket (photo).
4 Remove the cup with a pair of pliers. Remove the opposite cup, and then free the yoke from the driveshaft (photo).
5 To remove the remaining two cups now repeat the instructions in paragraph 3 or use a socket and hammer (photo).
6 Recover the thrust bearing from inside each cup and remove the seal from the base of each spider journal.
7 Before reassembling, using new parts as necessary, thoroughly clean out the yokes and journals.
8 Fit new oil seals to the spider journals and then assemble the needle rollers in the bearing cups with the assistance of some grease.
9 Fill each bearing cup about one third full with a universal grease, not forgetting to refit the thrust bearings first.

4.1 Removing the U-joint snap-rings

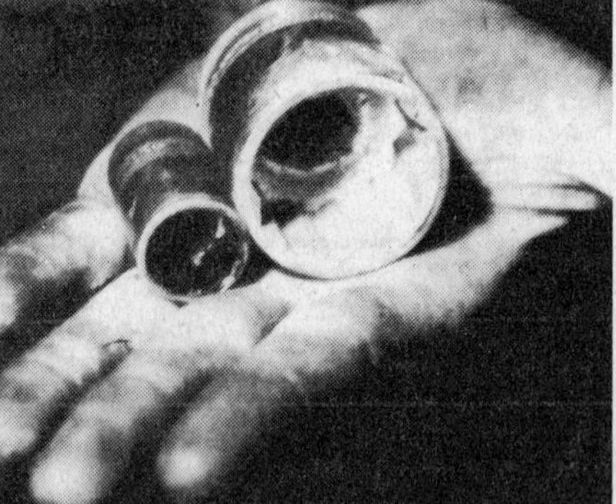

4.2 Two sockets of the correct size are required

4.3 Pressing the first cup inward using a vise

4.4 Pulling out a cup

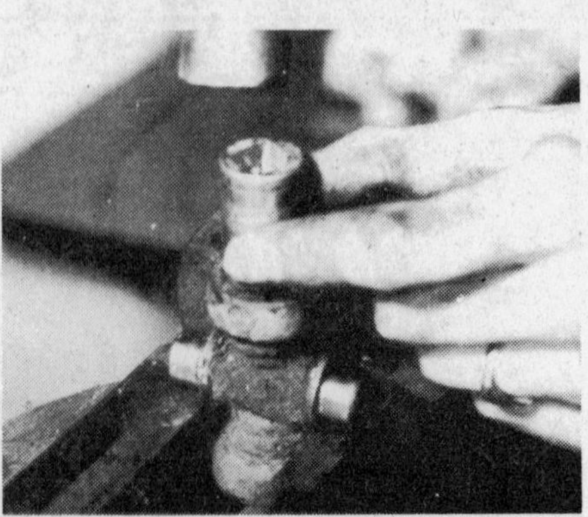

4.5 Tapping out the last two cups

10 Refit the bearing cups on the spider and tap the bearings home so that they lie squarely in position. Replace the snap-rings and settle the cups by tapping the whole assembly with a soft faced hammer.
11 Check that angular movement of the universal joint is free throughout its full range without signs of stiffness.

5 Rear universal joint - dismantling, overhaul and reassembly

This is easier than for the front universal joint as only two spider cups have to be removed as described in the previous Section. The remaining cups simply slide off the spider journals, these being held in position by the two 'U'bolts and small lips on the pinion flange cup locations.

6 Driveshaft - balance

1 If the vibration from the drive-line has been traced to the driveshaft and yet there are no traces of wear, then the driveshaft is probably out of balance. This can also occur after overhaul.
2 First detach the driveshaft from the drive pinion flange and refit having rotated the shaft through 180°, if this does not cure the trouble then the following sequence should be followed:
3 Suitably support the rear of the car so thatthe wheels are clear of the ground. Chock the front wheels so that there is no chance of the car moving off the supports.
4 Start the engine and with top gear selected run at a speed of 40-50 mph (reading on speedometer).
5 An assistant should now place a crayon or piece of chalk so that it *just* contacts the rear end of the driveshaft. Obviously great care must be taken to avoid injury (Fig. 7.3).
6 Fit two worm-drive type hose clips on the driveshaft so that the heads are 180° from the chalk mark. Tighten the clips (Fig. 7.4).
7 Start the engine again and run at a speed of 65-70 mph (reading on speedometer). If no vibration is felt, lower the car and road test.
8 Should, however, a vibration still exist rotate the clips approximately 45° away from each other and retest (Fig. 7.5).
9 Continue to rotate the clips apart in smaller amounts until the vibration has been eliminated.

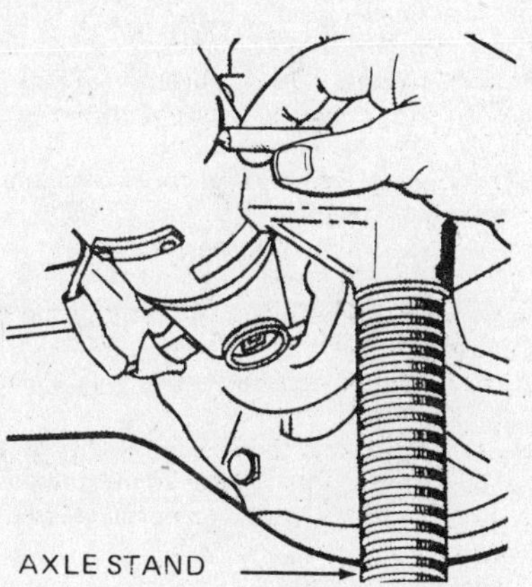

Fig. 7.3. Marking the driveshaft (Sec. 6)

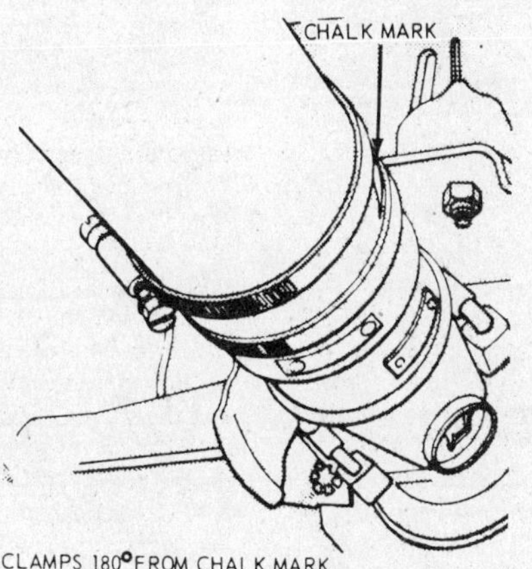

Fig. 7.4. Fitting the worm drive type hose clips (Sec. 6)

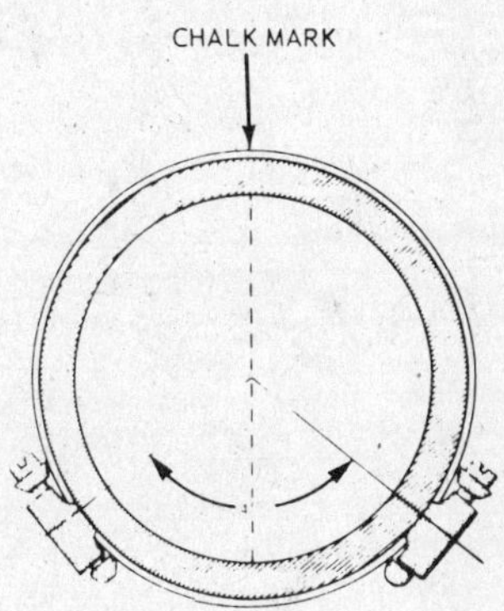

Fig. 7.5. Movement limit of clips (Sec. 6)

7 Fault diagnosis - driveshaft

Symptom	Reason/s
Vibration	Wear in sliding sleeve splines. Worn universal joint bearings. Driveshaft out of balance. Distorted driveshaft.
Knock or 'clunk' when taking up drive	Worn universal joint bearings. Worn rear axle drive pinion splines. Loose rear drive flange bolts. Excessive backlash in rear axle gears.

7

Chapter 8 Rear axle and differential

For modifications, and information applicable to later models, see Supplement at end of manual

Contents

Specifications

Type	Semi-floating hypoid with removable differential carrier	
Ratios:		
Pre 1975	3.55 : 1	
Post - 1975	3.0 : 1	
Crownwheel diameter	8 inches	
Axle oil capacity	4.0 US pints (2 liters)	
Oil type:		
Conventional axle	ESW-M2C-105-A	
Limited slip axle	ESW-M2C-119-A	
Torque wrench settings	**lb f ft**	**kg f m**
Bearing cap bolts	70 to 85	9.5 to 11.6
Adjusting nut lock bolts	12 to 25	1.7 to 3.5
Carrier to housing nuts	25 to 40	3.5 to 5.4
Pinion retainer to carrier bolts	30 to 45	4.2 to 6.1
Crownwheel attaching bolts	70 to 85	9.5 to 11.6
Axle shaft bearing retainer nuts	20 to 40	2.7 to 5.4
Pinion bearing preload (new bearing)	17 to 27	2.4 to 3.9

1 General description

The rear axle fitted to the Mustang II models is a semi-floating hypoid gear type and is attached to the chassis by longitudinal leaf springs and telescopic shock absorbers.

The differential assembly may be of removable carrier type or of integral carrier design according to model, year of production and manufacturing source.

Vehicles having the Traction-Lok limited slip option will automatically be fitted with the removable type carrier.

Refer to Chapter 13 for details of the integral type differential carrier rear axle.

The Traction-Lok limited slip differential is offered as an optional fitment on all Mustang II cars and provides improved traction in ice or snow conditions and also during hard acceleration. The procedure for removing and refitting the limited slip differential is exactly the same as that used for the conventional type.

Unless the necessary tools and gauges are available, it is not recommended that the rear axle is overhauled, although the procedure is described later in this Chapter for those who have the necessary equipment.

With the detachable differential type axle, it is recommended that the differential unit is either renewed on an exchange basis, or the original unit taken to your Ford dealer for reconditioning.

2 Axle shaft - removal and replacement

1 Place the car on level ground, chock the front wheels, loosen the rear wheel nuts on the side to be worked on, or both sides if both axle shafts are to be removed, then jack up the rear of the car and remove the wheels. Fit axle stands underneath the car.

2 Release the handbrake, then remove the brake drum securing screw and take off the brake drum.

3 Undo and remove the four bolts retaining the axle shaft bearing housing to the axle casing. These bolts are accessible with a socket on an extension through the holes in the axle shaft flange (Fig. 8.3).

4 Use a slide hammer or two setscrews (see Fig. 8.4) to remove the axle shaft. It is useless to pull on the axle flange in the hope of withdrawing it, you will only succeed in pulling the car off the jacks.

5 The axle shaft seals are made out of a synthetic material and are easily damaged. When withdrawing the shaft take care that the splined end does not cut the inner lip of the seal.

6 Replacement is the reversal of the removal procedure but again, care must be taken to avoid damaging the seal. If a taper roller bearing is fitted, the outer bearing should be removed from the axle housing using a slide hammer and refitted onto the taper bearing before installing the shaft.

3 Oil seal - renewal (ball bearing type)

1 Remove the axle shaft as described in the previous Section.

2 The seal fits just inside the outer end of the axle shaft housing and ideally a slide hammer should be used to extract it. However, it can be removed using a hammer and chisel, but great care should be taken not to damage the axle housing, otherwise oil will seep past the outside of the new seal.

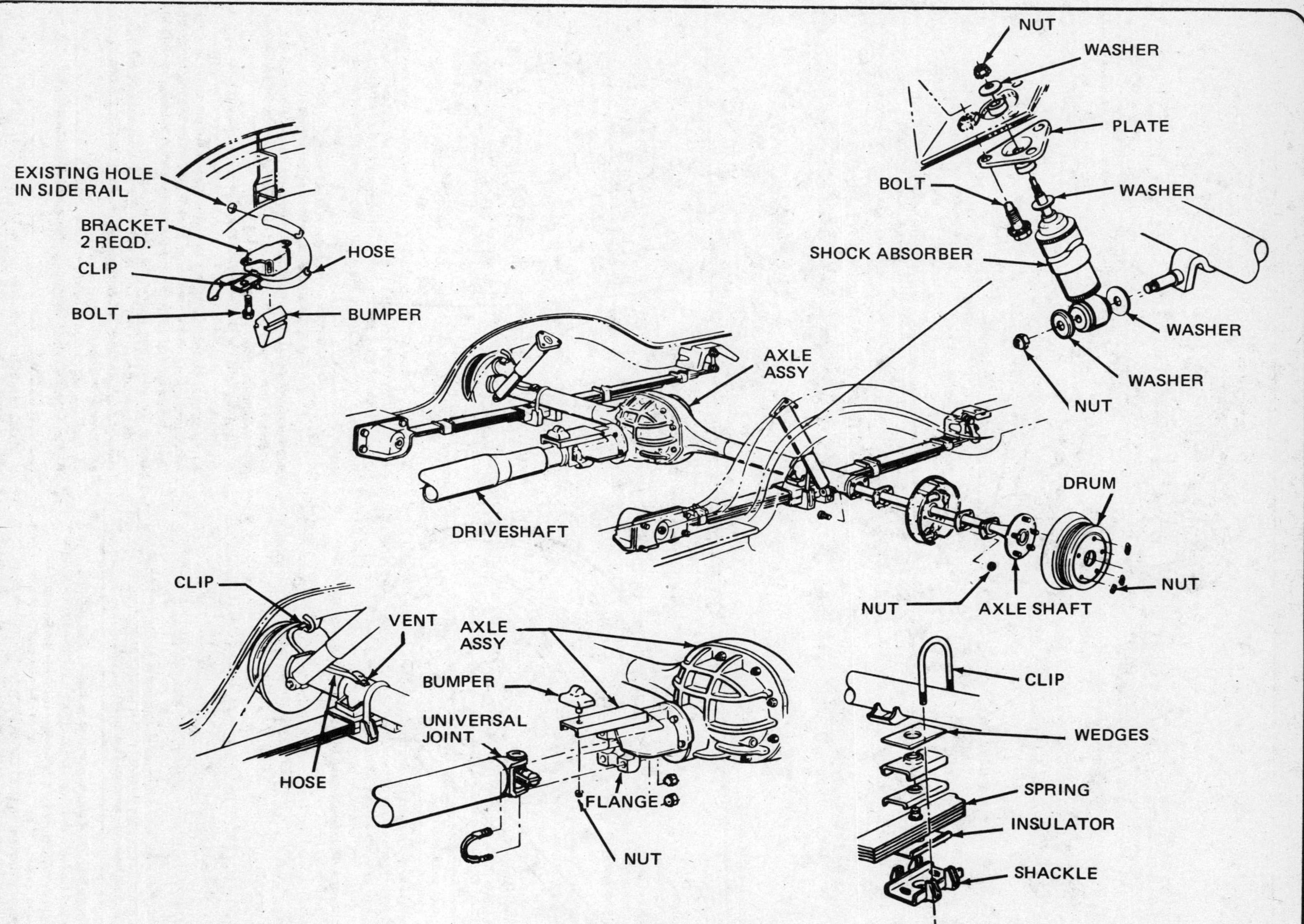

Fig. 8.1. Location of rear axle assembly

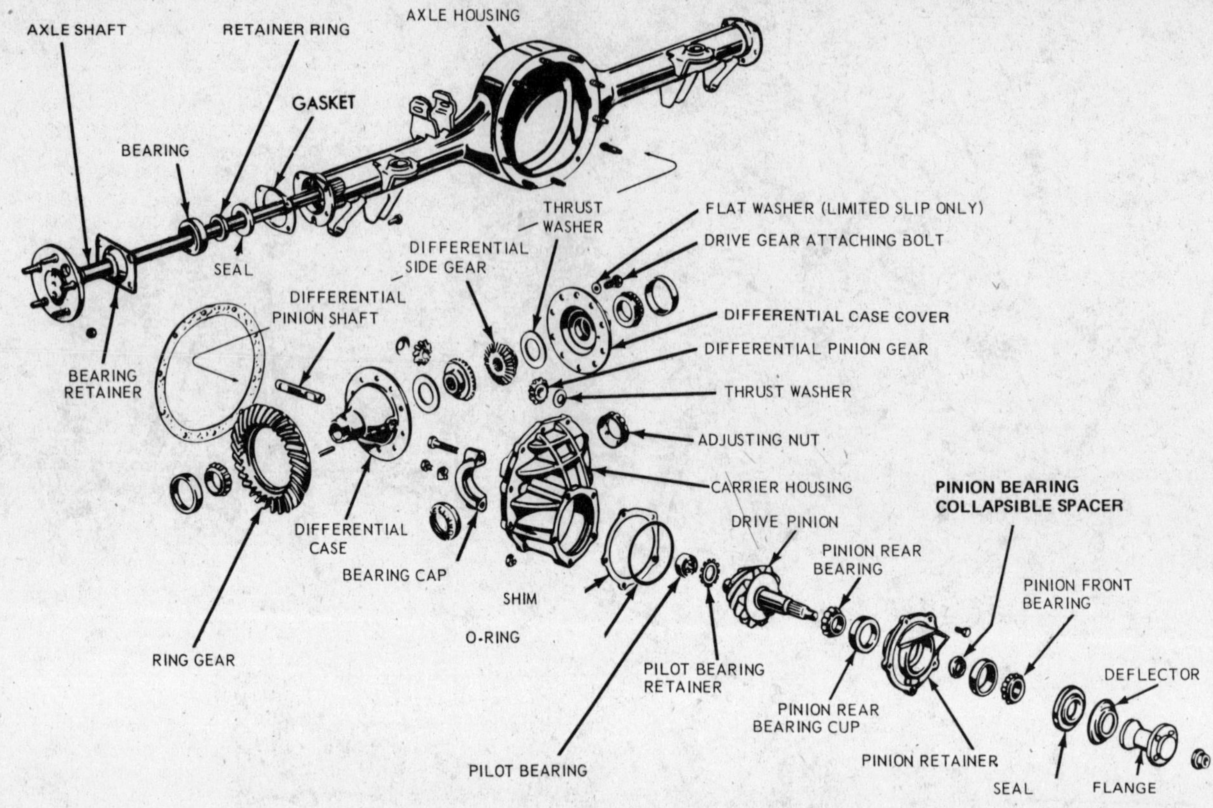

Fig. 8.2. Exploded view of axle components

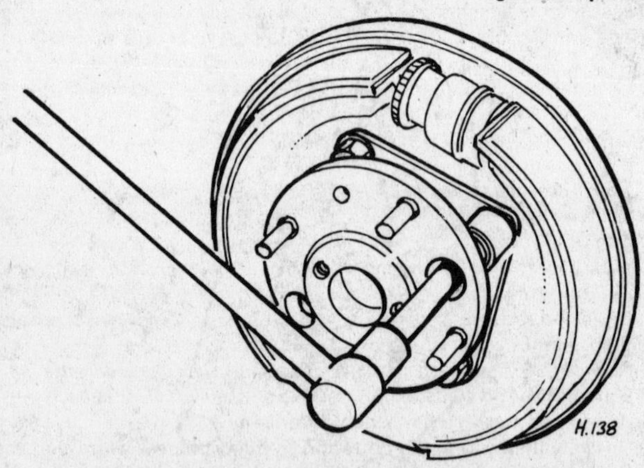

Fig. 8.3. Removing the axle shaft retaining nuts (Sec. 2)

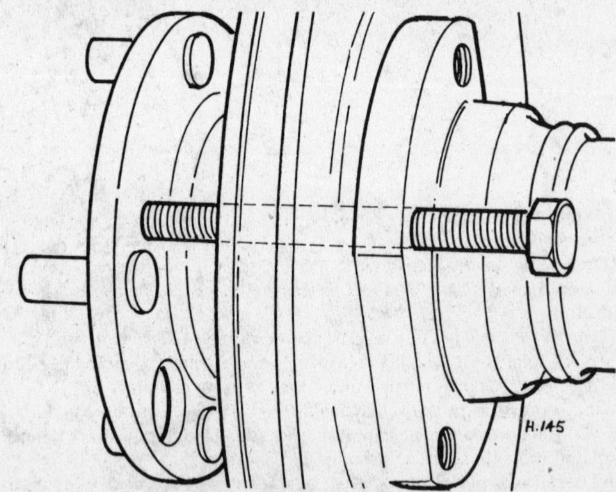

Fig. 8.4. Method of extracting axle shaft

3 Make a note of which way round the seal is located in the housing before removing it, usually the metal clad side of the seal faces toward the roadwheel.
4 Smear some gasket sealer around the outside casing of the new seal and drive it evenly into place using a block of wood or a tubular drift having the same outside diameter as the seal.
5 Replace the axle shaft as described in Section 2.

4 Axle shaft bearing - renewal (ball bearing type)

1 Refer to Section 2 and remove the axle shaft assembly.
2 Using a hammer and sharp chisel make several deep nicks in the bearing retainer ring. This will release its grip on the axle shaft and allow it to be slid off the shaft. If it is tight however, drill a hole in it and split with a sharp chisel. Take care not to damage the shaft.
3 Place the axle shaft up-side-down in a vise so that the bearing retainer is on the top of the jaws and the axle shaft flange is under them and using a soft faced hammer drive the axle shaft through the bearing. If this proves difficult it will be necessary to use a garage press. Note which way round the bearing is fitted.
4 Place the retainer plate and new bearing (correct way round) on the axle shaft.
5 Place the axle shaft vertically between the jaws of a bench vise - flange uppermost, so that the inner track is resting on the top of the vise jaws. Using a soft-faced hammer drive the axle shaft through the bearing until it is seating fully against the shaft shoulder.
6 The bearing retainer should next be refitted, the sequence for this being the same as for the bearing. Do not attempt to fit the bearing and retainer at one go.
7 Pack the bearing with a little multi-purpose grease.
8 Refit the axle shaft assembly as described in Section 2.

5 Axle shaft bearing/oil seal - renewal (taper roller bearing type)

1 Withdraw the axle shaft, as described in Section 2.

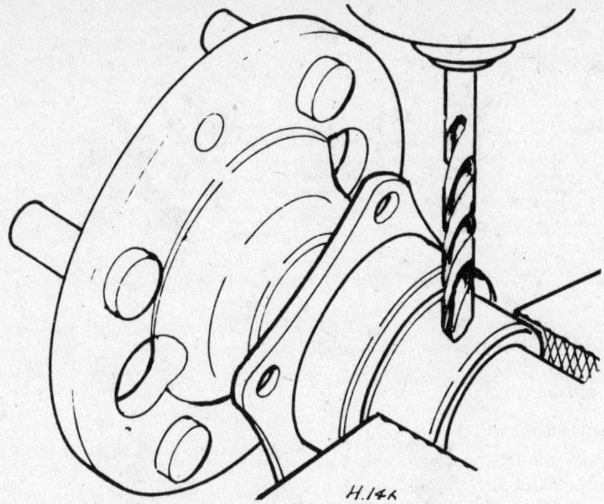

Fig. 8.5. Drilling bearing retainer, ball-bearing type (Sec. 4)

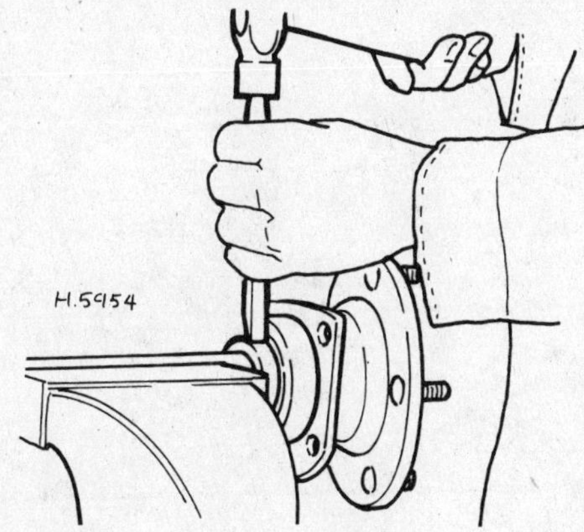

Fig. 8.6. Loosening the bearing retainer with a chisel (Secs. 4 and 5)

2 Secure the assembly in a vise, the jaws of which have been fitted with soft metal protectors.
3 Drill a hole in the bearing retainer and then remove by splitting it with a cold chisel. Take care not to damage the shaft during these operations.
4 Using a suitable press, draw off the combined bearing/oil seal.
5 To the axle shaft install the bearing retainer plate, the new bearing (seal side towards differential) and a new bearing retainer.
6 Apply pressure to the retainer only, using a press or bearing puller, and seat the components against the shoulder of the axle shaft flange.
7 Install the axle shaft, as described in Section 2.
Note: because a special press **has** to be used to remove and re-install this type of bearing, it is recommended that the complete shaft assembly is taken to a Ford dealer who will have the proper equipment to carry out the job.

6 Differential carrier - removal and refitting

1 To remove the differential carrier assembly, jack-up the rear of the vehicle, remove both roadwheels and brake drums and then partially withdraw both axle shafts as described in Section 2.
2 Disconnect the driveshaft at the rear end, as described in Chapter 7.
3 Undo the self-locking nuts holding the differential carrier assembly to the axle casing. Pull the assembly slightly forward and allow the oil to drain into a drain pan. The carrier complete with the differential unit can now be lifted clear with the gasket.
4 Before refitting, carefully clean the mating surfaces of the carrier and the axle casing and always fit a new gasket. Replacement is then a direct reversal of the above instructions. The nuts retaining the differential carrier assembly to the axle casing should be tightened to the specified torque.

7 Rear axle - removal and replacement

1 Chock the front wheels, jack up the rear of the car and support it on axle stands placed under the rear frame member.
2 Remove the wheels, brake drums and axle shafts as described in Section 2.
3 Remove the driveshaft as described in Chapter 7.
4 Disconnect the lower end of the shock absorbers from the axle housing.
5 Remove the brake vent tube (if fitted) from the brake pipe junction and retaining clamp (see Chapter 9).
6 Remove the brake pipes from the clips that retain them to the axle, but do not disconnect any of the pipe unions.
7 Remove the brake linings and brake back plates and support them with wire to avoid straining the hydraulic brake lines which are still attached (see Chapter 9).
8 Support the weight of the axle on a trolley jack and remove the nuts from the spring retaining U-bolts. Remove the bottom clamping plates.
9 Lower the axle assembly on the jack and withdraw it from the rear of the car.
10 The axle assembly is refitted using the reverse procedure to that of removal. Tighten the U-bolt and shock absorber nuts to the torque figures given in Chapter 9, Specifications.

8 Differential - overhaul (conventional type)

Most professional garages will prefer to renew the complete differential carrier assembly as a unit if it is worn, rather than to dismantle the unit to renew any damaged or worn parts. To do the job correctly 'according to the book' requires the use of special and expensive tools which the majority of garages do not have.

The primary object of these special tools is to enable the mesh of the crown wheel to the pinion to be very accurately set and thus ensure that noise is kept to a minimum. If any increase in noise cannot be tolerated (provided that the rear axle is not already noisy due to a defective part) then it is best to purchase an exchange built up differential unit.

The differential assembly should be stripped as follows:-

1 Remove the differential assembly from the rear axle, as described in Section 6.
2 With the differential assembly on the bench begin dismantling the unit.
3 Undo and remove the bolts, spring washers and lock plates securing the adjustment cups to the bearing caps.
4 Release the tension on the bearing cap bolts and unscrew the differential bearing adjustment cups. Note from which side each cup originated and mark with a punch or scriber.
5 Unscrew the bearing cap bolts and spring washers. Ensure that the caps are marked so that they may be fitted in their original positions upon reassembly.
6 Pull off the caps and then lever out the differential unit complete with crown wheel and differential gears.
7 Recover the differential bearing outer tracks and inspect the bearings for wear or damage. If evident, the bearings will have to be renewed.
8 Using a universal puller and suitable thrust block draw off the old bearings.
9 Undo and remove the bolts and washers that secure the crown wheel to the differential cage. Mark the relative positions of the cage and crown wheel, if new parts are not to be fitted, and lift off the crown wheel.
10 Clamp the pinion flange in a vise and then undo the nut. Any damage caused to the edge of the flange by the vise should be carefully filed smooth.
11 With the nut removed, pull off the splined pinion flange. Tap the end of the pinion shaft, if the flange appears to be stuck.
12 The pinion, complete with spacer and rear bearing cone, may now be extracted from the rear of the housing.
13 Using a drift carefully tap out the pinion front bearing and oil seal.
14 Check the bearings for signs of wear and if evident the outer tracks must be removed using a suitable soft metal drift.
15 To dismantle the pinion assembly detach the bearing spacer and remove the rear bearing cone using a universal puller. Recover any shims

8

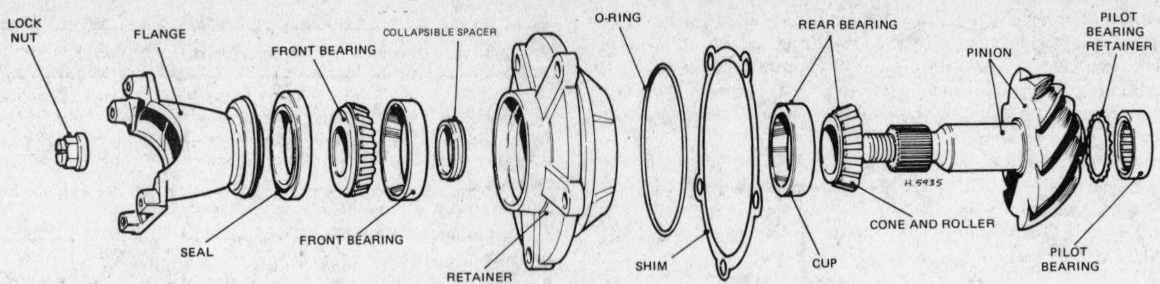

Fig. 8.7. Pinion gear and associated components (Sec. 8)

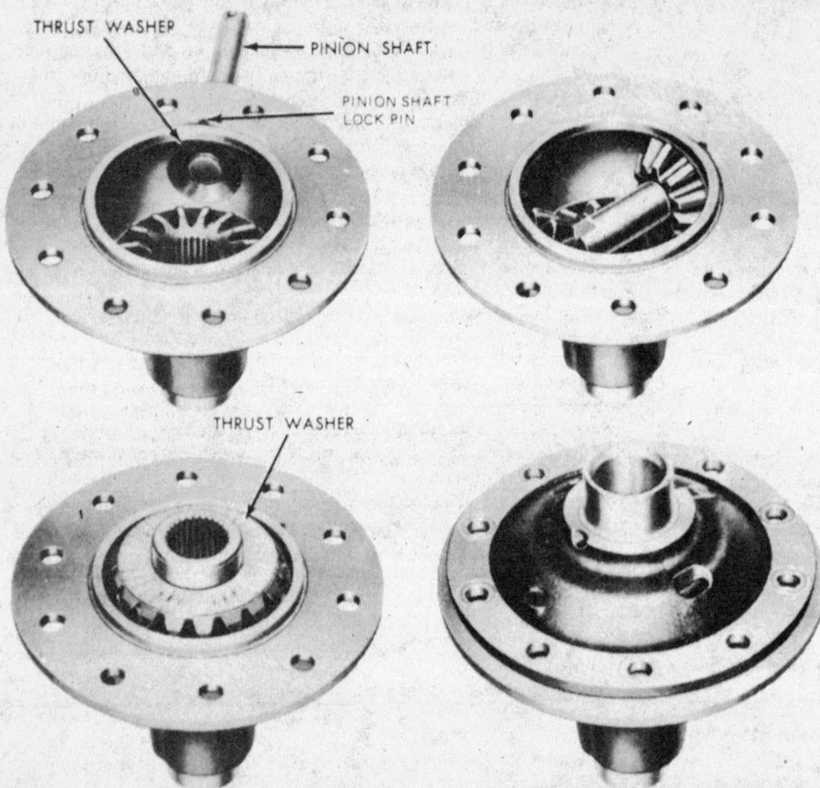

Fig. 8.8. Assembling the differential casing (Sec. 8)

Fig. 8.9. Refitting the pinion gear and retainer (Sec. 8)

found between the rear bearing and pinion head.

16 Tap out the differential pinion shaft locking pin which is tapered at one end and must be pushed out from the crown wheel side of the case.

17 Push the differential pinion shaft out of the case and rotate the pinions around the differential gears, so that they may be extracted through the apertures in the case. Cupped thrust washers are fitted between the pinions and the case and may be extracted after the pinions have been removed.

18 Remove the differential gears and thrust washers from the differential case.

19 Wash all parts and wipe dry with a clean lint-free cloth.

20 Again check all bearings for signs of wear or pitting and if evident a new set of bearings should be obtained.

21 Examine the teeth of the crown wheel and pinion for pitting, score marks, chipping and general wear. If a crown wheel and pinion is required a mated crown wheel and pinion must be fitted and under no circumstances may only one part of the two be renewed.

22 Inspect the differential pinions and side gears for signs of pitting, score marks, chipping and general wear. Obtain new gears as necessary.

23 Inspect the thrust washers for signs of wear or deep scoring. Obtain new thrust washers as necessary.

24 Once the pinion oil seal has been disturbed it must be discarded and a new one obtained.

25 Commence reassembly by lubricating the differential gear thrust washers and then positioning a flat washer on each differential side gear. Position the two gears in the case.

26 Position the cupped thrust washers on the machined faces in the case and retain in position with a smear of grease.

27 Locate the pinion gears in the case diametrically opposite each other and rotate the gears to move the pinion gears in line with the holes in the shaft.

28 Check that the thrust washers are still in place and push the spider shaft through the case, thrust washers and pinions. If the pinions do not line up they are not diametrically opposite each other, and should be extracted and repositioned. Measure the play of the gears and, if necessary select new thrust washers to obtain 0.005 - 0.007 in. (0.12 - 17 mm) play.

29 Insert the locking pin (tapered end first) and lightly peen the case to prevent the pin working out.

30 Examine the bearing journals on the differential case for burrs, and refit the differential bearing cones onto the differential case using a suitable diameter tubular drift. Make sure they are fitted the correct way round.

31 Examine the crown wheel and differential case for burrs, score marks and dirt. Clean as necessary and then refit the crown wheel. Take care to line up the bolt holes and any previously made marks if the original parts are being refitted.

32 Refit the crown wheel to differential case securing bolts and tighten in a diagonal manner to the specified torque wrench setting.

33 Using a suitable diameter drift carefully drive the pinion bearing cups into position in the final drive housing. Make sure they are the correct way round.

34 Slide the shim onto the pinion shaft and locate behind the pinion head and then fit the inner cone and race of the rear bearing. It is quite satisfactory to drift the rear bearing on with a piece of tubing 12 to 14 inches long with sufficient internal diameter to just fit over the pinion shaft. With one end of the tube bearing against the race, tap the top end

of the tube with a hammer, so driving the bearing squarely down the shaft and hard up against the underside of the thrust washer.
35 Slide a new collapsible type spacer over the pinion shaft and insert the assembly into the differential carrier.
36 Fit the pinion front bearing outer track and race, followed by a new pinion oil seal.
37 Fit the pinion drive flange and screw on the pinion self-locking nut and torque it to a figure of 175 lb f ft (24.1 kg f m) and check the pinion turning torque using either a suitable torque gauge or a spring balance and length of card wrapped round the pinion drive flange. The correct pinion turning torque should be:

Original bearings		
Torque wrench	*12 to 18 lbf in.*	*(0.14 to 0.216 kgfm)*
Pull on spring balance	*12 to 18 lb*	*(5 to 8 kg)*
New bearings		
Torque wrench	*20 to 26 lbf in.*	*(0.24 to 0.31 kgfm)*
Pull on spring balance	*20 to 26 lb*	*(9 to 11 kg)*

38 To the foregoing figures add 3 lbf in. (0.035 kgfm) if a new pinion oil seal has been fitted.
39 Throughout the nut tightening process, hold the pinion flange quite still with a suitable tool.
40 If the pinion nut is overtightened, the nut cannot be unscrewed to correct the adjustment as the pinion spacer will have been over-compressed and the assembly will have to be dismantled and a new collapsible type spacer fitted.
41 Fit the differential cage to the differential carrier and refit the two bearing caps, locating them in their original positions.
42 Tighten the bearing cap bolts finger-tight and then screw in the two adjustment cups.
43 It is now necessary to position the crown wheel relative to the pinion. If possible mount a dial indicator gauge and with the probe resting on one of the crown wheels determine the backlash. Backlash may be varied by moving the whole differential assembly using the two adjustment cups until the required setting is obtained.
44 Tighten the bearing cap securing bolts and recheck the backlash setting.
45 The best check the D-I-Y motorist can make to ascertain the correct meshing of the crownwheel and pinion is to smear a litte engineer's blue onto the crownwheel and then rotate the pinion. The contact mark should appear right in the middle of the crownwheel teeth. If the mark appears on the toe or the heel of the crownwheel then the crownwheel must be moved either nearer or further away from the pinion. The various tooth patterns that may be obtained are illustrated (Fig.8.11).
46 When the correct meshing between the crownwheel and pinion has been obtained refit the adjustment cup lock plates, bolts and spring washers.
47 The differential unit can now be refitted to the axle casing.

9 Differential - overhaul (Limited slip type)

1 The Traction-Lok limited slip differential is fitted to some cars as an option to the conventional type. This type of differential is considerably more complicated than the conventional type having a clutch mechanism fitted to the crownwheel, the springs of which are pre-loaded to 1,500 lb (3306 kg). It is not therefore advisable for the home mechanic to attempt stripping and repairing this type of unit.
2 To check the operation of the limited slip facility the following tests can be carried out.
3 If the proper tool cannot be obtained, make up a torque wrench adaptor as shown in Fig. 8.12.
4 Jack up one wheel and support that side of the car on an axle stand.
5 Remove the hub cap and attach the adaptor plate as shown in Fig. 8.12.
6 Make sure the transmission is in neutral and the handbrake off and, using the torque wrench attempt to turn the wheel.
7 The wheel should not start to turn until at least 40 lb f ft (5.5 kg f m) is showing on the torque wrench. Once the wheel is turning the torque required to keep it rotating may be lower than the initial breakaway torque figure but this is acceptable.
8 The wheel should turn with an even pressure throughout the check without slipping or binding.
9 If the initial rotation figure is below 40 lb f ft (5.5 kg f m) the limited slip facility is not operating to its full capability and, although it will not effect the normal running of the car, if maximum rear wheel traction is a necessity it should be replaced.
WARNING: Never start the car and put it in gear with one wheel jacked up as, unlike the conventional differential the limited slip type will cause the wheel still on the ground to turn with possibly disastrous results.

PAINT MARKING INDICATES POSITION IN WHICH GEARS WERE LAPPED

Fig. 8.10. Crownwheel and pinion indexing marks (Sec. 8)

8

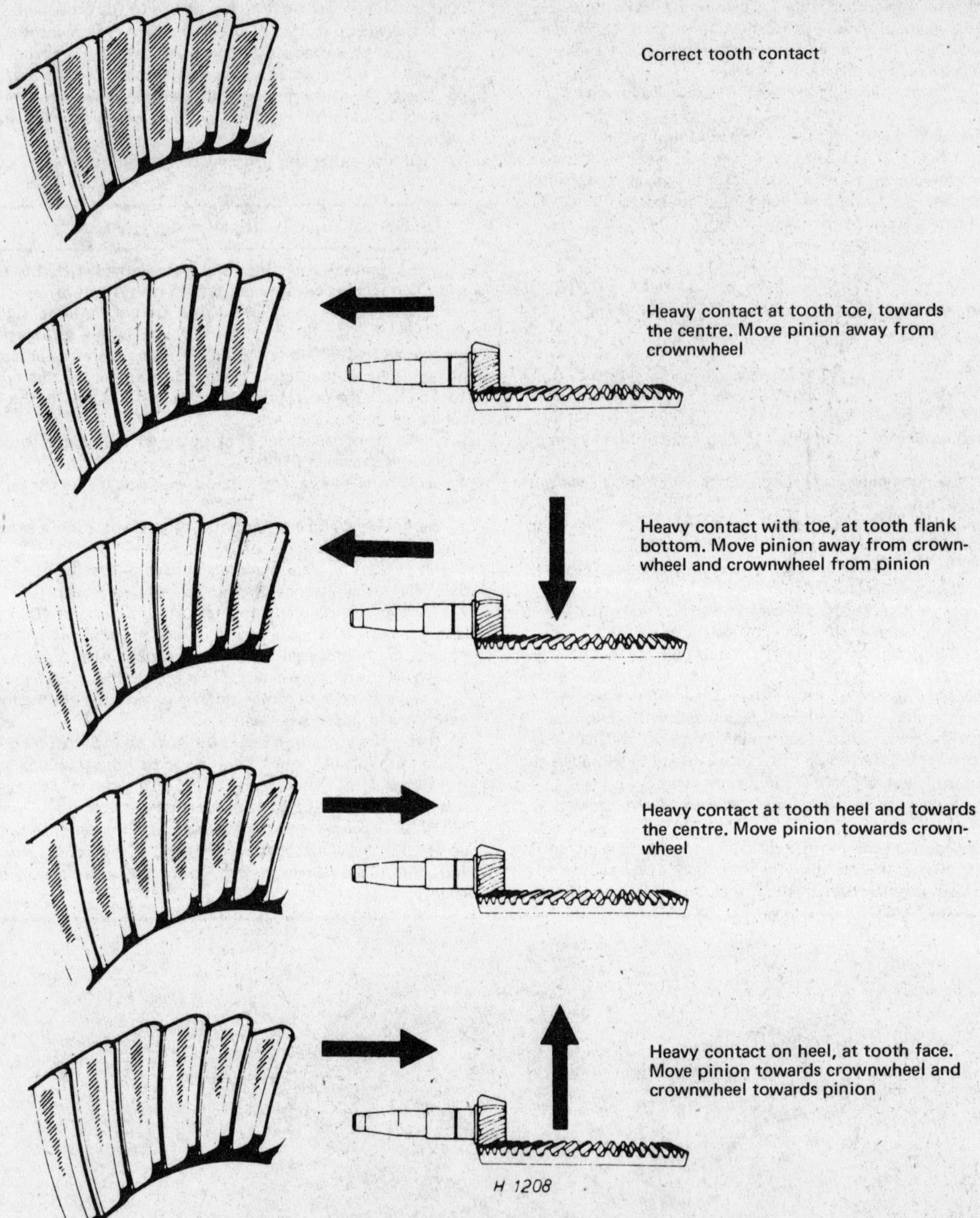

Correct tooth contact
Heavy contact at tooth toe, towards the centre. Move pinion away from crownwheel
Heavy contact with toe, at tooth flank bottom. Move pinion away from crownwheel and crownwheel from pinion
Heavy contact at tooth heel and towards the centre. Move pinion towards crownwheel
Heavy contact on heel, at tooth face. Move pinion towards crownwheel and crownwheel towards pinion
H 1208

Fig. 8.11. Correct meshing of crownwheel and pinion, and repositioning guide for incorrect tooth marking (Sec. 8)

10 Pinion oil seal - renewal

CAUTION: Care must be taken not to overtighten the pinion nut during this operation. If the pinion nut is overtightened, the differential assembly will have to be dismantled and a new collapsible spacer fitted.

1 Jack-up the rear of the car and secure on stands under the body-frame and axle casing.
2 Remove the roadwheels and brake drums.
3 Disconnect the driveshaft from the pinion drive flange (refer to Chapter 7, if necessary).
4 Using either a spring balance and a length of cord wrapped round the drive pinion or a torque wrench (lb in) check and record the turning torque of the pinion.
5 Hold the drive pinion quite still with a suitable tool and unscrew and remove the pinion self-locking nut.
6 Remove the washer, drive flange and dust deflector, and then prise out the oil seal. Do not damage or lever against the pinion shaft splines during this operation.
7 Tap in the new oil seal using a piece of tubing as a drift. Do not inadvertently knock the end of the pinion shaft.
8 Repeat the operations described in paragraphs 37 to 40 Section 8, but ensuring that the final pinion turning torque figure agrees with that recorded before dismantling.
9 Refit the brake drums, driveshaft and roadwheels and lower the car.

11 Wheel stud - removal and replacement

1 The usual reasons for renewal of a wheel stud are that either the

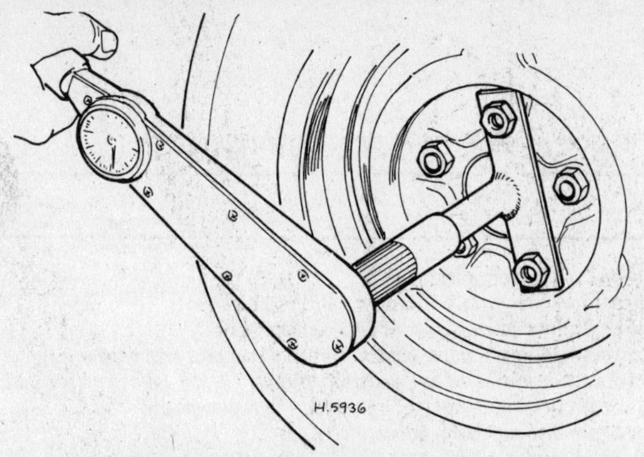

Fig. 8.12. Checking the operation of the limited slip facility on Traction Lok differential (Sec. 9)

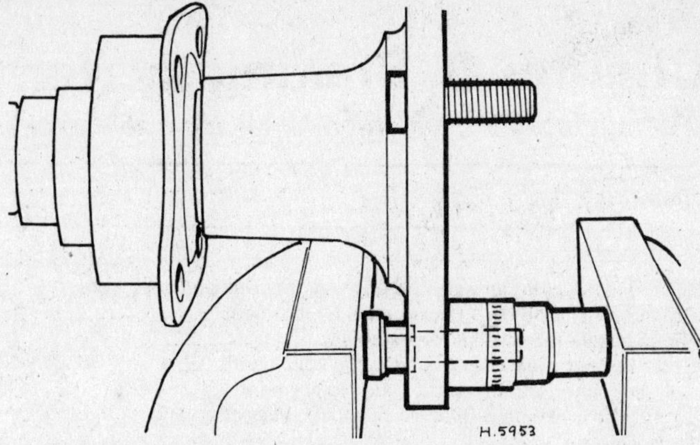

Fig. 8.13. Inserting a new stud into the axle shaft flange (Sec. 11)

threads have been damaged or the stud has broken, this usually being caused by overtightening of the wheel nuts. To renew a wheel stud, remove the axle shaft assembly as described in Section 2. Using a parallel pin punch of suitable diameter drive the old stud through the flange towards the bearing.

2 To fit a new stud place it in its hole from the rear of the flange and using a bench vise with a socket placed in front of the stud press it fully home in the flange (Fig. 8.13).

12 Fault diagnosis - Rear axle

Symptom	**Reason/s**
Vibration	Worn axle shaft bearings. Loose drive flange bolts. Out of balance driveshaft. Wheels require balancing.
Noise	Insufficient lubricant. Worn gears and differential components generally.
'Clunk' on acceleration or deceleration	Incorrect crownwheel and pinion mesh. Excessive backlash due to wear in crownwheel and pinion teeth. Worn axle shaft or differential side gear splines. Loose drive flange bolts. Worn drive pinion flange splines.
Oil leakage	Faulty pinion or axle shaft oil seals. May be caused by blocked axle housing breather.

Chapter 9 Braking system

For modifications, and information applicable to later models, see Supplement at end of manual

Contents

Specifications

Type of system	Disc at front, drum at rear	
Footbrake	Hydraulic on all four wheels	
Parking brake	Mechanical to rear wheels only	
Front brake layout	Trailing calipers	
Hydraulic system	Dual line, tandem master cylinder and servo assisted	
Front disc brakes		
Type	Single cylinder, sliding caliper	
Disc diameter	9.3 in (236.22 mm)	
Thickness:		
Standard	0.870 in	
Reground	0.810 in	
Caliper cylinder bore	2.6 in (66.0 mm)	
Lining size:		
Outer	5.0 x 1.4 in (12.6 x 3.6 cm)	
Inner	5.0 x 1.4 in (12.6 x 3.6 cm)	
Minimum lining thickness	1/8 in (3.175 mm)	
Rear drum brakes		
Drum diameter:		
Standard	9.00 in (228.6 mm)	
Reground	9.06 in (230.124 mm) - maximum	
Maximum ovality	0.007 in (0.1778 mm)	
Linings:		
Primary	1.75 x 6.12 in (44.45 x 155.45 mm)	
Secondary	1.75 x 8.63 in (44.45 x 219.2 mm)	
Minimum lining thickness	See text	
Wheel cylinder bore	0.875 in (22.23 mm)	
Master cylinder		
Type	Tandem	
Bore	0.938 in (23.813 mm)	
Vacuum servo diameter	7.5 in (190.5 mm)	
Brake pedal	**Max**	**Min**
Free height (power brakes)	7.4 in (164 mm)	6.6 in (144 mm)
Free height (standard brakes)	8.0 in (203 mm)	7.5 in (175 mm)
Pedal travel (power brakes)	2.25 in (57.65 mm)	—
Pedal travel standard brakes	2.75 in (69.85 mm)	—
Torque wrench settings	**lb f ft**	**kg f m**
Bleed valves (screws)	2.5 to 5.5	0.35 to 0.78
Hydraulic pipes:		
Brake hoses	12 to 20	1.6 to 2.8
Brake pipe	10 to 15	1.4 to 2.1
Upper anchor plate bolt (disc)	90 to 120	12.4 to 16.6
Lower anchor plate bolt (disc)	55 to 75	7.6 to 10.2
Parking brake assembly bolts	13 to 25	1.8 to 3.4
Master cylinder bolts	13 to 25	1.8 to 3.4

Torque wrench settings

	lb f ft	kg f m
Wheel cylinder bolts	5 to 7	0.7 to 1.0
Pressure differential valve mounting nuts and bolts	7 to 11	1.0 to 1.5
Front backplate nuts and bolts	9 to 14	1.1 to 2.5
Rear backplate nuts and bolts	20 to 40	2.8 to 5.5
Servo unit to dashpanel	13 to 25	1.6 to 3.4
Parking brake securing bolts	20 to 25	2.8 to 3.4

1 General description

The standard braking system on all Mustang II models comprises disc brakes on the front wheels and self-adjusting drum brakes on the rear. A vacuum brake booster which provides servo assistance to both front and rear brakes is an optional fit on some models, standard on others.

The rear drum brake system is of the single anchor, internal expanding and self-adjusting brake assembly type. To expand the shoes a dual piston single cylinder is used.

The self-adjuster mechanism comprises a cable, cable guide, adjusting lever, adjusting screw assembly and an adjuster spring. The cable is hooked over the anchor pin at the top and is connected to the lever at the bottom and is passed along the web of the secondary brake shoe by means of the cable guide. The adjuster spring is hooked onto the primary brake shoe and also to the lever.

The automatic adjuster operates only when the brakes are applied and the car is backing up. Also only when the secondary brake shoe is able to move towards the drum beyond a certain limit.

A dual master cylinder braking system is used on all models and comprises a dual master cylinder, pressure differential valve assembly and a switch. The switch is located on the differential valve and operates a dual brake warning light which is located on the instrument panel.

The self-centering pressure differential valve assembly body has a stepped bore to accommodate a sleeve and seal which is fitted over the piston and into the large valve body bore in the front brake system area.

The brake warning light switch is located at the center of the valve body and the spring loaded switch plunger fits into a tapered shoulder groove in the center of the piston. When in this condition the electric circuit through the switch is broken and the warning light on the instrument panel is extinguished.

The disc brake assembly comprises a ventilated disc and a caliper. The caliper is of the single piston, sliding caliper design and mounted on an anchor plate which is attached to the spindle arms.

The cylinder bore contains one piston with a square sectioned rubber seal located in a groove in the cylinder bore to provide sealing between the cylinder and piston.

An independent parking brake system is provided, and is operated by a lever mounted in the tunnel between the front seats. The parking brake operates the rear wheel brakes only, through a system of cables. The equaliser rod is connected directly to the parking brake lever and an equaliser.

The brake cables are routed from the equaliser to brackets mounted on the tunnel and then pass rearwards through clips welded to the floor panel, then through clips that attach the cables under the rear springs and through the rear brake backing plates. Finally they are connected to the parking brake levers on the rear brake secondary shoes.

2 Bleeding the hydraulic system

This is not a routine operation and it will normally only be required if the hydraulic circuit has been disconnected or when renewing the hydraulic fluid at 30 000-mile service interval.

1 Removal of all the air from the hydraulic fluid in the braking system is essential to the correct working of the braking system. Before undertaking this task, examine the fluid reservoir cap to ensure that the vent hole is clear, also check the level of fluid in the reservoir and top-up if necessary.

2 Check all brake line unions and connections for possible leakage, and at the same time check the condition of the rubber hoses which may be perished.

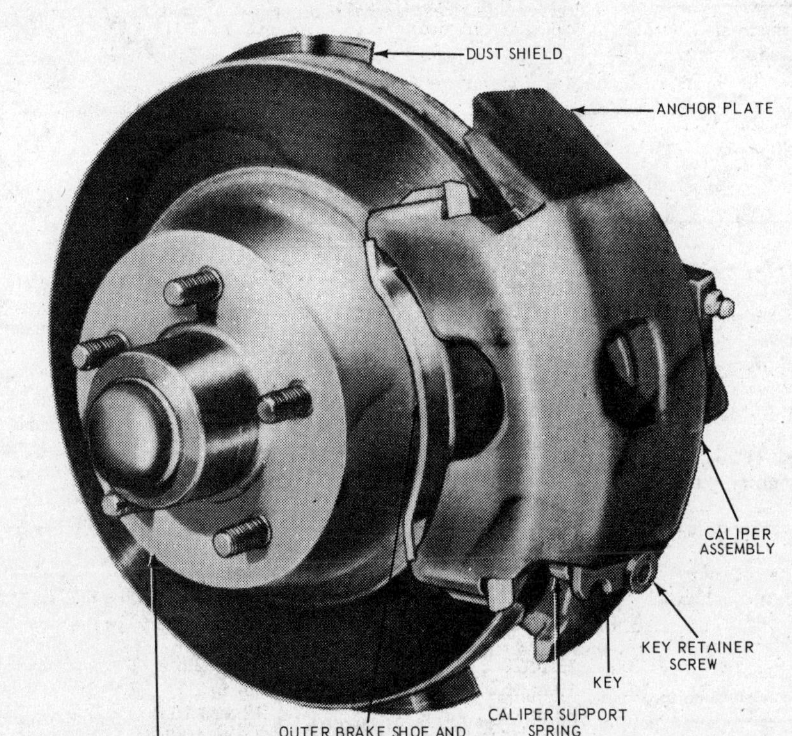

Fig. 9.1. Front disc brake rotor and caliper

9

3 If the condition of a caliper or wheel cylinder is in doubt, check for signs of fluid leakage.
4 If there is any possibility that incorrect fluid has been used in the system, drain all the fluid out and flush through with denatured alcohol. Renew all piston seals and cups as they will be affected and could possibly fail under pressure.
5 Gather together a clean jar, a 12 inch (304 mm) length of rubber tubing which fits tightly over the bleed valves and a tin of the correct grade of brake fluid.
6 The primary (front) and secondary (rear) hydraulic brake systems are individual systems and are therefore bled separately. Always bleed the longest line first.
7 To bleed the secondary system (rear) clean the area around the bleed valves and start at the rear right-hand wheel cylinder by first removing the rubber cap over the end of the bleed valve.
8 Place the end of the tube in the clean jar which should contain sufficient fluid to keep the end of the tube submerged during the operation.
9 Open the bleed valve approx ¾ turn with a wrench and depress the brake pedal slowly through its full travel.
10 Close the bleed valve and allow the pedal to return to the released position.
11 Continue this sequence until no more air bubbles issue from the bleed tube. Give the brake pedal two more strikes to ensure that the line is completely free of air, and then re-tighten the bleed valve - ensuring that the bleed tube remains submerged until the valve is closed.
12 At regular intervals during the bleeding sequence, make sure that the reservoir is kept topped-up, otherwise air will enter again at this point. **Do not re-use fluid bled from the system.**
13 Repeat the whole procedure on the rear left-hand brake line.
14 To bleed the primary system (front), start with the front right-hand side and finish with the front left-hand side cylinder. The procedure is identical to that previously described.

Note: Some models have a bleed valve incorporated in the master cylinder. Where this is the case, the master cylinder should be bled before the brake lines. The bleeding procedure is identical to that already described.

15 Top-up the master cylinder to within 0.25 inch (6 mm) of the top of the reservoirs, check that the diaphragm type gasket is correctly located in the cover and then refit the cover.

3 Pressure differential valve - centralization

1 After any repair or bleed operations it is possible that the dual brake warning light will come on due to the pressure differential valve remaining in an off center position.
2 To centralize the valve, first turn the ignition switch to the 'ON' or 'ACC' position.
3 Depress the brake pedal several times and the piston will center itself again causing the warning light to go out.
4 Turn the ignition off.

4 Flexible hoses - inspection, removal and replacement

1 Inspect the condition of the flexible hydraulic hoses leading to each of the front disc brake calipers and the one at the front of the rear axle. if they are swollen, damaged or chafed, they must be renewed.
2 Wipe the top of the brake master cylinder reservoir and unscrew the cap. Place a piece of polythene sheet over the top of the reservoir and refit the cap. This is to stop hydraulic fluid syphoning out during subsequent operations.
3 To remove a flexible hose wipe the union and any supports free from dust, pry out the clip from the bracket and undo the union nuts from the metal pipe ends.
4 Undo and remove the locknuts and washers securing each flexible hose end to the support and lift away the flexible hose.
5 Refitting is the reverse sequence to removal. It will be necessary to bleed the brake hydraulic system as described in Section 2. If one hose has been removed it is only necessary to bleed either the front or rear brake hydraulic system.

5 Front disc brake pads (linings) - removal, inspection and replacement

1 It is not necessary to remove the anchor plate assembly in order to fit new disc pads.
2 Chock the rear wheels, apply the parking brake, loosen the front wheel nuts, jack-up the front of the car and support on firmly based axle stands. Remove the roadwheel.
3 Remove the retaining screw from the caliper retaining key (Fig. 9.2).
4 Using a hammer and drift carefully tap the caliper retaining key and spring either inwards or outwards, from the anchor plate. It is important that the key is not damaged (Fig. 9.3).
5 Press the caliper inwards and upwards against the action of the caliper support springs and lift the assembly away from the anchor plate (Fig. 9.4).
6 Take care that the brake flexible hose is not stretched or twisted. Suspend the caliper assembly from the upper suspension arms with string or wire.
7 If the pads are to be re-used mark them so that they may be refitted in their original positions. They must not be interchanged.
8 The pad may now be removed from the anchor plate. It will probably be found that the anti-rattle clips will come out of place when the pad is removed.
9 Clean down the caliper, anchor plate and disc (rotor) assembly and generally inspect for fluid leakage, wear or damage.
10 Measure the thickness of the pad linings and if the lining has worn down to 0.03125 in (0.7937 mm) above the rivet heads the pads must be renewed.
11 If new pads are to be fitted push the piston into the bore using a block of wood 1.75 x 1 in (44.45 mm x 25.4 mm) and a 'G' clamp.
12 Refit the pad anti-rattle clips and insert the pads onto the anchor plate.
13 If the old pads are being refitted they must be replaced in their original positions. When new pads are being used they are interchangeable.
14 Remove the 'G' clamp and wooden block and detach the caliper from its supporting string or wire.
15 Position the caliper to the anchor plate so that the lower bevelled edge of the caliper is on the top of the rear caliper support spring.
16 Carefully slide the caliper on and over the pads with a pivoting motion until the caliper upper bevelled edge can be pushed over the forward caliper support spring.
17 Use a large and strong screwdriver to hold the caliper over the upper caliper support spring against the anchor plate.
18 Carefully insert the caliper retaining key and spring.
19 Remove the screwdriver and lightly tap the caliper key into position.
20 Refit the caliper key retaining screw.
21 Press the brake pedal several times to seat the pads and centralize the caliper.
22 Refit the roadwheel, lower the car and take it for a short test run to check the operation of the brakes.

6 Caliper anchor plate - removal and replacement

1 Place chocks behind the rear wheels, apply the parking brake, loosen the front wheel nuts, jack-up the front of the car and support it on axle stands. Remove the roadwheel.
2 Remove the disc caliper and pads as described in Section 5.
3 Remove the upper and lower anchor plate bolts and remove the anchor plate (photos).
4 Before refitting the anchor plate ensure that the mating surfaces of the plate and suspension spindle are clean and free from grit.
5 Because of the shear force they are subject to, the old anchor plate retaining bolts should be discarded and new ones fitted.
6 To avoid distorting the anchor plate, the upper bolts should be tightened to the specified torque figure followed by the lower bolts. Note that different torque figures are used for the upper and lower bolts (see Specifications).

7 Front disc brake caliper - inspection and overhaul

If hydraulic fluid is leaking from the caliper it will be necessary to fit new seals. Should brake fluid be found running down the side of the wheel, or if it is noticed that a pool of fluid forms alongside one wheel or the level in the master cylinder drops excessively, it is also indicative of seal failure.

1 Refer to Section 5 and remove the caliper, and remove the flexible hose (see Section 4).
2 Wrap a cloth around the caliper and using compressed air at the

Fig. 9.2. Removing the screw retaining the caliper locking key (Sec. 5)

Fig. 9.3. Driving out the caliper locking key (Sec. 5)

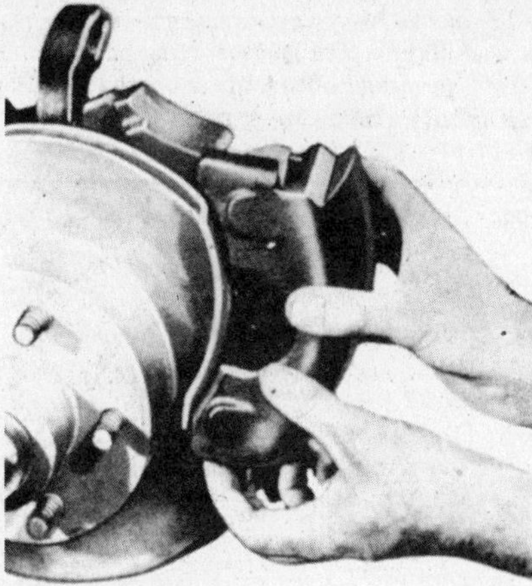
Fig. 9.4. Withdrawing the caliper assembly (Sec. 5)

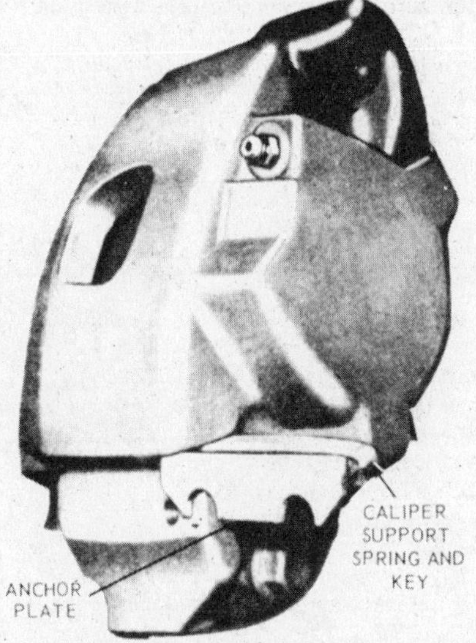

Fig. 9.5. Inserting the caliper retaining key and spring (Sec. 5)

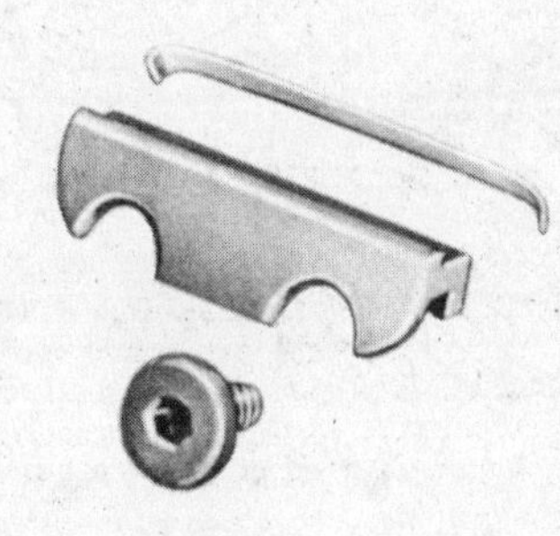
Fig. 9.6. Caliper key, spring and retaining screw (Sec. 5)

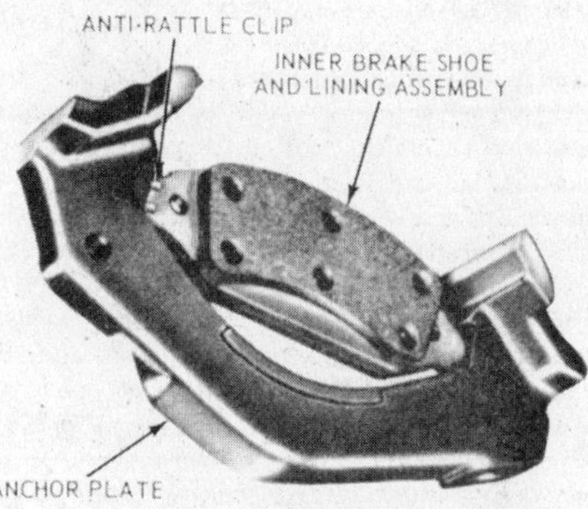

Fig. 9.7. Brake anchor plate and inner lining (pad) (Sec. 6)

6.3A Removing the upper anchor plate retaining bolt

6.3B Removing the lower anchor plate retaining bolt

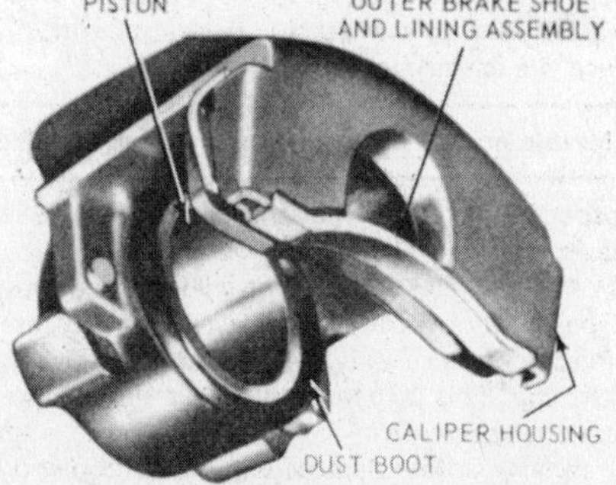

Fig. 9.8. Caliper assembly and outer brake pad (Sec. 7)

hydraulic fluid port carefully eject the pistons.

3 If the piston has seized in the bore carefully tap around the piston whilst applying air pressure. Remember the piston may come out with some force.

4 Remove the rubber dust boot from the caliper assembly.

5 Carefully remove the rubber piston seal from the cylinder bore with an old plastic knitting needle or something similar. Do not use a screwdriver as it could damage the bore.

6 Thoroughly wash all parts in denatured alcohol or clean hydraulic fluid. During reassembly new rubber seals must be fitted and these should be well lubricated with clean hydraulic fluid before fitment.

7 Inspect the piston and bore for signs of wear, score marks or other

damage: if evident a new caliper assembly will be necessary.
8 To reassemble, first place the new caliper piston seal into its groove in the cylinder bore. The seal must not become twisted.
9 Fit a new dust boot and ensure that the flange seats correctly in the outer groove of the caliper bore.
10 Carefully insert the piston into the bore. When it is about three-quarters of the way in, spread the dust boot over the piston. Seat the dust boot in the piston groove and push the piston fully into the bore.
11 Reassembly is now complete and the unit is ready for refitting to the car.

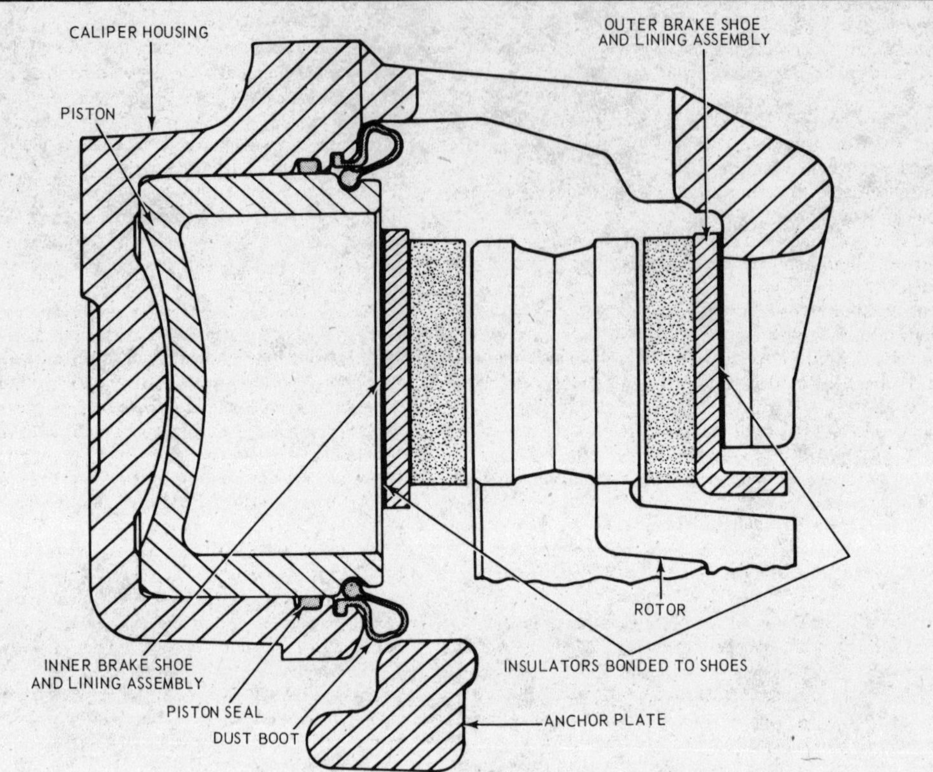

Fig. 9.9. Cross-sectional view of front brake caliper assembly (Sec. 7)

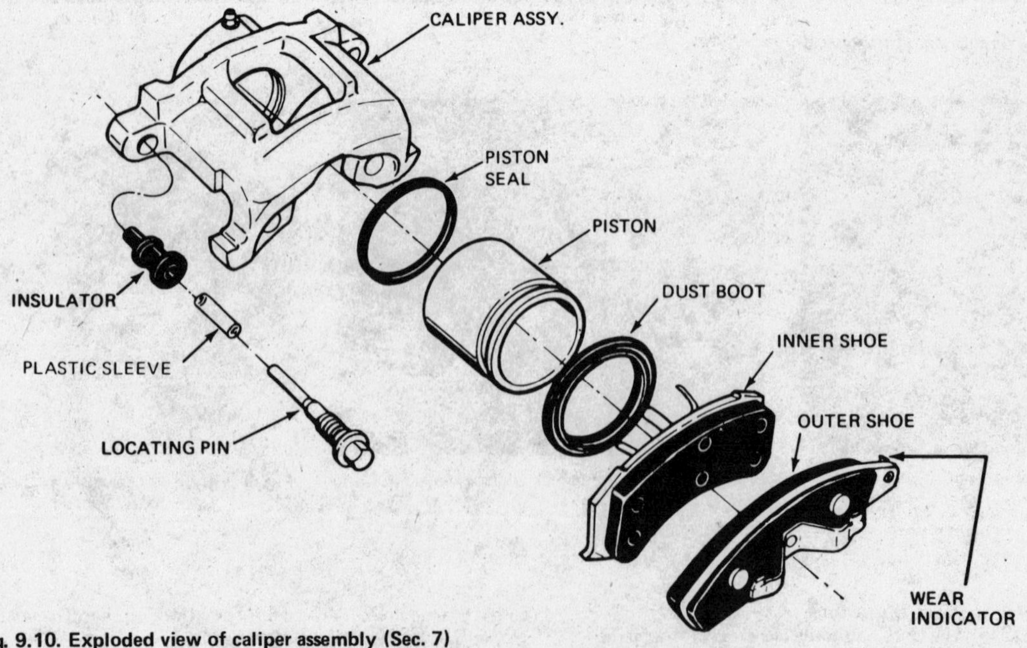

Fig. 9.10. Exploded view of caliper assembly (Sec. 7)

8 Front disc brake disc and hub - removal and replacement

1 Refer to Sections 5 and 6, and remove the caliper and anchor plate assembly. To save extra work and time, if the caliper and anchor plate are not requiring attention, it is not necessary to disconnect the flexible brake hose from the caliper. Suspend the assembly with string or wire from the upper suspension arm.
2 Carefully remove the grease cap from the wheel spindle.
3 Withdraw the cotter pin and nut lock from the wheel bearing adjusting nut.
4 Undo and remove the wheel bearing adjusting nut from the spindle.
5 Grip the hub and disc assembly and pull it outwards far enough to loosen the washer and outer wheel bearing.
6 Push the hub and disc back onto the spindle and remove the washer and outer wheel bearing from the spindle.
7 Grip the hub and disc assembly and pull it from the wheel spindle.
8 Carefully pry out the grease seal and lift away the inner tapered bearing from the back of the hub assembly.
9 Clean out the hub and wash the bearings with gasoline making sure that no grease or oil is allowed to get onto the brake disc.
10 Thoroughly clean the disc and inspect for signs of deep scoring or excessive corrosion. If these are evident the disc may be reground but the minimum thickness of the disc must not be less than the figure given in the Specifications. It is desirable however, to fit a new disc if at all possible.
11 To reassemble, first work a suitable grease well into the bearings; fully pack the bearing cages and rollers.
12 To reassemble the hub fit the inner bearing and then gently tap the grease seal back into the hub. A new seal must always be fitted as, during removal, it was probably damaged. The lip must face inward to the hub.
13 Replace the hub and disc assembly onto the spindle keeping the assembly centered on the spindle to prevent damage to the inner grease seal or the spindle threads.
14 Place the outer wheel bearing and flat washer on the spindle.
15 Screw the wheel bearing adjusting nut onto the spindle and tighten finger tight so that the hub and disc will still rotate freely.
16 Detach the caliper and anchor plate from the upper suspension arm and guide the assembly towards the disc. Be careful not to stretch or twist the brake flexible hose.
17 Start by sliding the caliper and anchor plate assembly onto the disc at the lower part of the caliper and continue refitting the assembly as described in Sections 5 and 6.

9 Rear drum brake shoes - inspection, removal and replacement

1 Chock the front wheels, jack-up the rear of the car and support on firmly based axle stands. Remove the roadwheel.
2 Remove the three Tinnerman nuts and remove the brake drum (photos).
3 If the drum will not come off, remove the rubber cover from the brake backplate and insert a narrow screwdriver through the slot. Disengage the adjusting lever from the adjusting screw.
4 Whilst holding the adjusting lever away from the screw, back off the adjusting screw with either a second screwdriver or shaped piece of metal as shown in Fig. 9.12. Take care not to burr, chip or damage the notches in the adjusting screw.
5 The brake linings should be renewed if they are so worn that the lining is only proud of the rivets by about 0.03 in (0.79 mm) or will be before the next routine check. If bonded linings are fitted they must be renewed when the lining material has worn down to 0.06 in (1.59 mm) at its thinnest part.
6 To remove the brake shoes detach and remove the secondary shoe to anchor spring and lift away the spring (photo).
7 Detach the primary shoe to anchor spring and lift away the spring.
8 Unhook the adjusting cable eye from the anchor pin.
9 Remove the shoe hold down springs (photo) followed by the shoes, adjusting screw, pivot nut, socket and automatic adjustment parts.
10 Remove the parking brake link and spring. Disconnect the parking brake cable from the parking brake lever (photo).
11 After the secondary shoe has been removed, the parking brake lever should be detached from the shoe.
12 It is recommended that only one brake assembly is overhauled at a time unless the parts are kept well apart. This is because the brake shoe adjusting screw assemblies are not interchangeable and, if interchanged, would in fact operate in reverse, thereby increasing the drum to lining clearance every time the car is backed up.
13 To prevent any mix up the socket end of the adjusting screw is stamped with an 'R' or 'L'. The adjusting pivot nuts can be identified by the number of grooves machined around the body of the nut. Two grooves on the nut indicate a right-hand thread and one groove indicates a left-hand thread (photo).
14 If the shoes are to be left off for a while, place a warning on the steering wheel as accidental depression of the brake pedal will eject the pistons from the wheel cylinder.
15 Thoroughly clean all traces of dust from the shoes, backplate and brake drums using a stiff brush. Excessive amounts of brake dust can

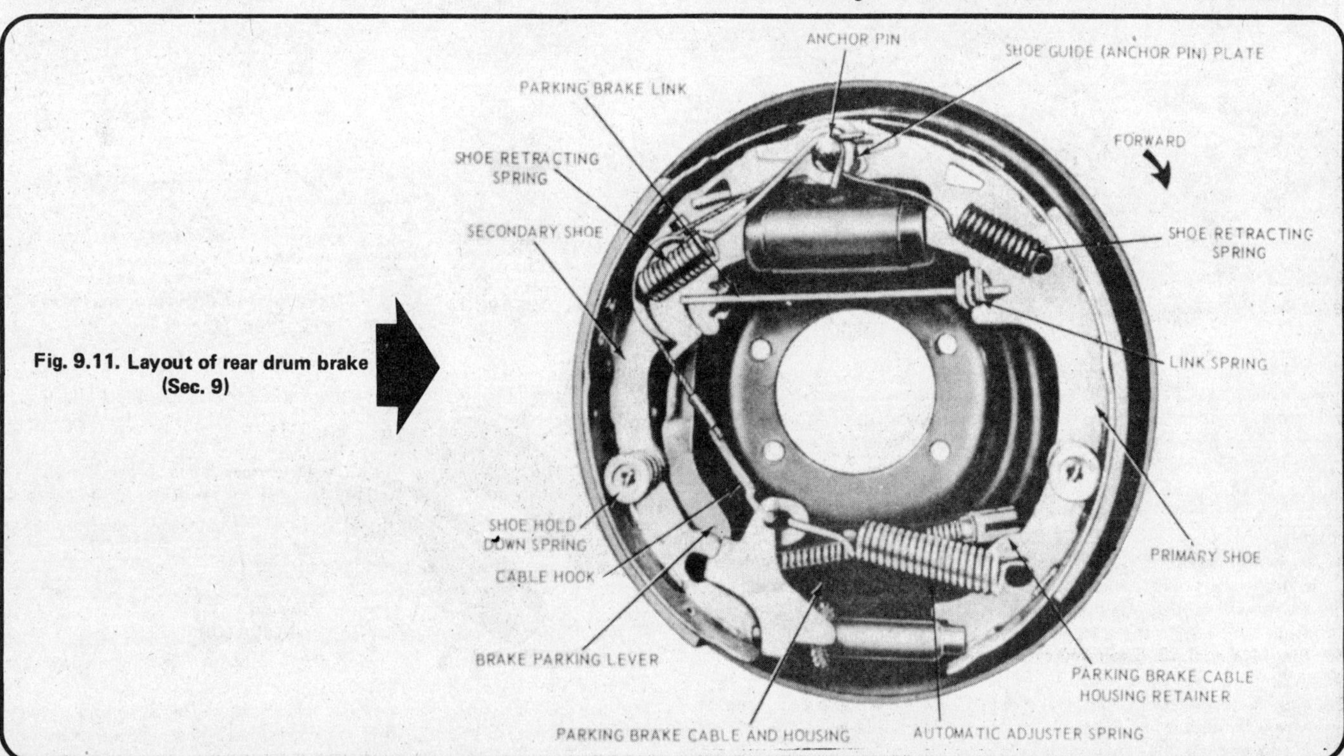

Fig. 9.11. Layout of rear drum brake (Sec. 9)

9

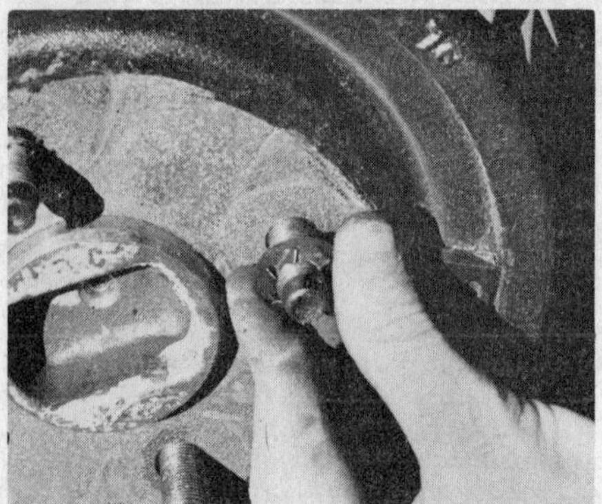
9.2A Removing the brake drum Tinnerman nuts

9.2B Lifting off the brake drum

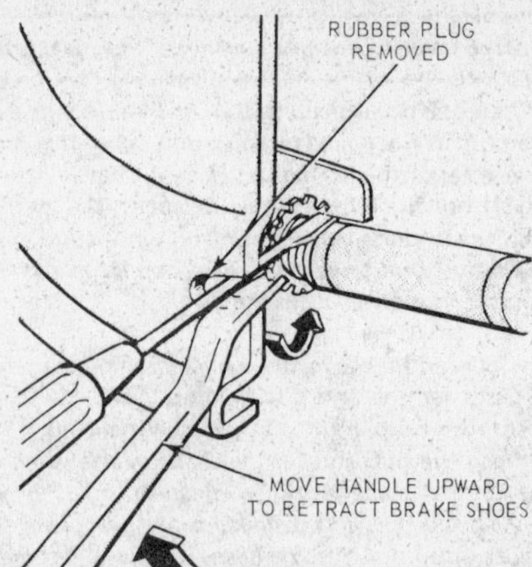

Fig. 9.12. Component parts of rear brake adjuster (Sec. 9)

9.6 Remove the secondary shoe spring

9.9 Removing the shoe retaining spring and lock washer

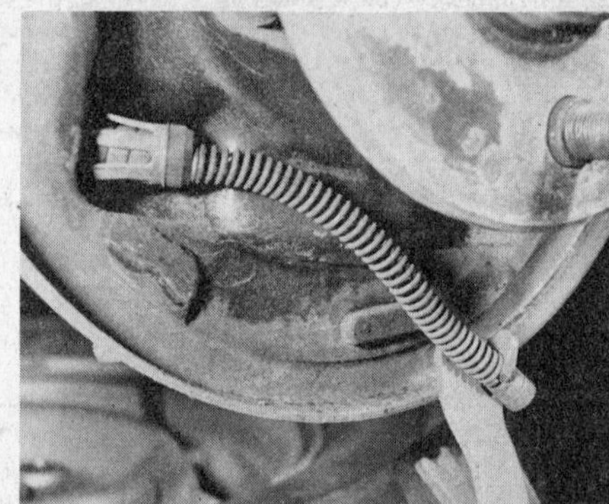
9.10 Parking brake cable and lever

9.13 Brake adjuster assembly

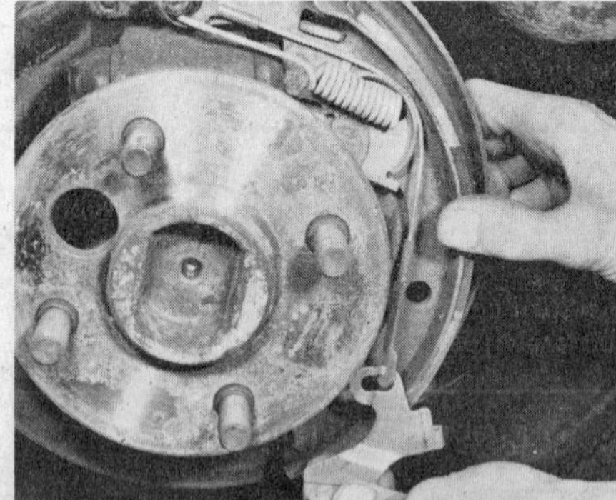
9.29 Cable end hooked into adjustment lever hole

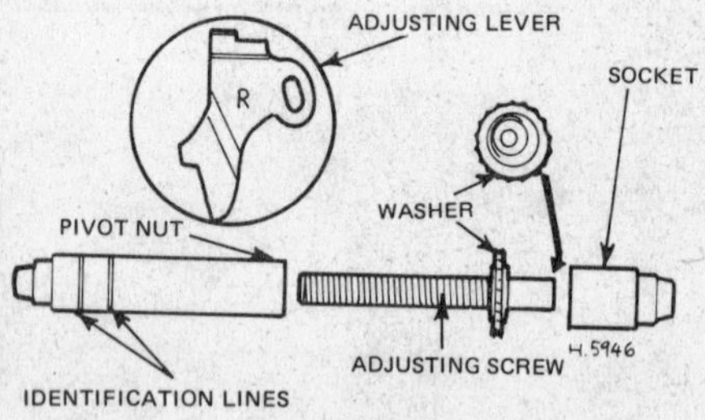

Fig. 9.13. Method of slackening rear brake shoes (Sec. 9)

cause judder or squeal and it is therefore important to remove all traces. It is recommended that compressed air is *not* used for this operation as this increases the possibility of the dust being inhaled. The dust contains asbestos, which is dangerous to health.

16 Check that the pistons are free in the cylinder, that the rubber dust covers are undamaged and in position, and that there are no hydraulic fluid leaks.

17 Prior to assembly smear a trace of brake grease on the shoe support pads, brake shoe pivots and on the ratchet wheel face and threads.

18 To reassemble first fit the parking brake lever to the secondary shoe and secure with the spring washer and retaining clip.

19 Place the brake shoes on the backplate and retain with the hold down springs.

20 Fit the parking brake link and spring. Slacken off the parking brake adjustment and connect the cable to the parking brake lever.

21 Fit the shoe guide (anchor pin) plate on the anchor pin (when fitted).

22 Place the cable eye over the anchor pin with the crimped side towards the backplate.

23 Replace the primary shoe to anchor spring.

24 Fit the cable guide into the secondary shoe web with the flanged hole fitted into the hole in the secondary shoe web. Thread the cable around the cable guide groove. It is very important that the cable is positioned in this groove and not between the guide and the shoe web.

25 Fit the secondary shoe to anchor spring.

26 Check that the cable eye is not twisted or binding on the anchor pin when fitted. All parts must be flat on the anchor pin.

27 Apply some brake grease to the threads and socket end of the adjusting screw. Turn the adjusting screw into the adjusting pivot nut fully and then back off by ½ turn.

28 Place the adjusting socket on the screw and fit this assembly between the shoe ends with the adjusting screw toothed wheel nearest to the secondary shoe.

29 Hook the cable hook into the hole in the adjusting lever. The adjusting levers are stamped with an 'R' or 'L' to show their correct fitment to the left or right brake assembly (photo).
30 Position the hooked end of the adjuster spring completely into the large hole in the primary shoe web. The last coil of the spring must be at the edge of the hole.
31 Connect the loop end of the spring to the adjuster lever holes.
32 Pull the adjuster lever, cable and automatic adjuster spring down and towards the rear to engage the pivot hook in the large hole in the secondary shoe web (photos).

9.32A Adjustment lever correctly fitted

9.32B Location of springs on anchor post

33 After reassembly check the action of the adjuster by pulling the section of the cable between the cable guide and the anchor pin towards the secondary shoe web far enough to lift the lever past a tooth on the adjusting screw wheel.
34 The lever should snap into position behind the next tooth and releasing the cable should cause the adjuster spring to return the lever to to its original position. This return motion of the lever will turn the adjusting screw one tooth.
35 If pulling the cable does not produce the desired action, or if the lever action is sluggish instead of positive and sharp, check the position of the lever on the adjusting screw toothed wheel. With the brake unit in a vertical position (the anchor pin at the top), the lever should contact the adjusting wheel 0.1875 in (4.763 mm) $\pm$ 0.0313 in (0.794 mm) above the center line of the screw.
36 Should the contact point be below this centerline the lever will not lock on the teeth in the adjusting screw wheel, and the screw will not be turned as the lever is actuated by the cable.
37 Incorrect action should be checked as follows:

a) Inspect the cable and fittings. They should completely fill or extend slightly beyond the crimped section of the fittings. If this is not so, the cable assembly should be renewed.
b) Check the cable length. The cable should measure 8.4063 in (213.519 mm) from the end of the cable anchor to the end of the cable hook.
c) Inspect the cable guide for damage. The cable groove should be parallel to the shoe web, and the body of the guide should lie flat against the web. Renew the guide if it is damaged.
d) Inspect the pivot hook on the lever. The hook surfaces should be square to the body of the lever for correct pivoting action. Renew the lever if the hook shows signs of damage.
e) Check that the adjustment screw socket is correctly seated in the notch in the shoe web.

38 Refit the brake drum and roadwheel, lower the car to the ground and take it for a short test run to check the operation of the parking brake and footbrake.

10 Rear drum brake wheel cylinder - removal and replacement

1 Refer to Section 9, and remove the brake shoes as described in paragraphs 1 to 11 inclusive.
2 Unscrew the brake pipe union from the rear of the wheel cylinder. Do not pull the metal tube from the cylinder as it will bend, making refitting difficult.
3 Undo and remove the two bolts securing the wheel cylinder to the brake backplate assembly.
4 Lift away the rear wheel cylinder assembly.
5 Plug the end of the hydraulic pipe to stop loss of too much hydraulic fluid.
6 Refitting the wheel cylinder is the reverse sequence to removal. It will be necessary to bleed the brake hydraulic system as described in Section 2.

9

11 Rear drum brake wheel cylinder - inspection and overhaul

1 Remove the wheel cylinder as described in the previous Section.
2 To dismantle the wheel cylinder, first remove the rubber boot from each end of the cylinder and push out the two pistons, cup seals and return spring (see Fig. 9.14).

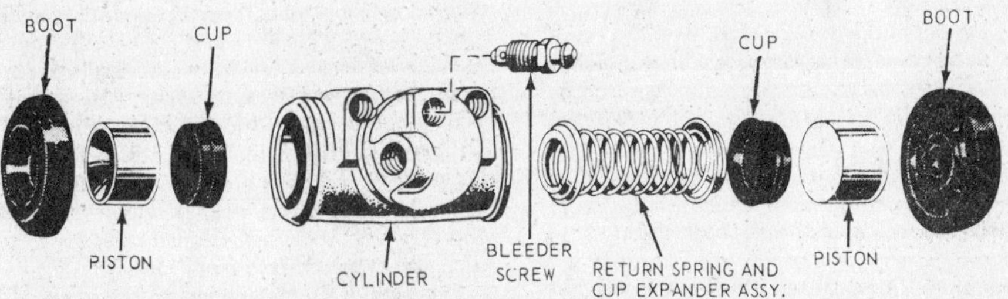

Fig. 9.14. Exploded view of rear brake wheel cylinder (Sec. 11)

3 Inspect the pistons for signs of scoring or scuff marks; if these are present the pistons should be renewed.
4 Examine the inside of the cylinder bore for score marks or corrosion. If these conditions are present the cylinder should be renewed.
5 If the cylinder is sound, thoroughly clean it out with fresh hydraulic fluid.
6 Remove the bleed screw and check that the hole is clean.
7 The old rubber cups will probably be swollen and visibly worn. Smear the new rubber cups and insert one into the bore followed by one piston.
8 Place the return spring inthe bore and push up until it contacts the rear of the first seal.
9 Refit the second seal and piston into the cylinder bore.
10 Replace the two rubber boots.
11 The wheel cylinder is now ready for refitting to the brake backplate.

12 Rear drum brake backplate - removal and replacement

1 Refer to Section 10, and remove the brake shoes and wheel cylinder from the backplate.
2 Disconnect the parking brake lever from the cable.
3 Refer to Chapter 8 and remove the axle shaft.
4 Disconnect the parking brake cable retainer from the backplate.
5 The backplate and gasket may now be lifted away from the end of the axle housing.
6 Refitting the brake backplate is the reverse sequence to removal. It will be necessary to bleed the brake hydraulic system as described in Section 2. Do not forget to top-up the rear axle oil level if necessary.

13 Rear drum brake shoes - adjustment

Automatic adjusters are fitted to the rear drum brakes and these operate when the car is backed-up and stopped. Should car use be such that it is not backed-up very often and the pedal movement has increased then it will be necessary to adjust the brakes as follows:
1 Drive the car rearwards and apply the brake pedal firmly. Now drive it forwards, and again, apply the brake pedal firmly.
2 Repeat the cycle until a desirable pedal movement is obtained. Should this not happen, however, it will be necessary to remove the drum and hub assemblies and inspect the adjuster mechanism as described in Section 9, paragraphs 33 to 37 inclusive.

14 Brake master cylinder - removal and replacement

1 For safety reasons, disconnect the battery.
2 Withdraw the hairpin retainer and slide the stoplight switch off the brake pedal pin just sufficiently for the switch outer hole to clear the pin. Lower the switch away from the pin. Lift the switch straight up from the pin taking great care not to damage the switch.
3 Slide the master cylinder pushrod and the nylon washers and bushing from the brake pedal pin.
Note: If the car is fitted with a brake booster servo it is most necessary to remove the stoplight switch, or the pushrod, from the brake pedal.
4 Unscrew the brake pipes from the primary and secondary outlet parts of the master cylinder (photo). Plug the ends of the pipes to stop dirt ingress. Take suitable precautions to catch the hydraulic fluid as the unions are detached from the master cylinder body.
5 Undo and remove the two screws securing the master cylinder to the dashpanel (or servo unit).
6 Pull the master cylinder forwards and lift it upwards from the car. Do not allow brake fluid to contact any paintwork as it acts as a solvent.
7 Refit the master cylinder using the reverse procedure to removal. It will be necessary to bleed the hydraulic system as described in Section 2.

15 Brake master cylinder - dismantling, examination and reassembly

If a replacement master cylinder is to be fitted, it will be necessary to lubricate the seals before fitting to the car as they have a protective coating when originally assembled. Remove the blanking plugs from the hydraulic pipe union seatings. Inject some clean hydraulic fluid into the master cylinder and operate the pushrod several times so that the fluid spreads over all the internal working surfaces.

If the master cylinder is to be dismantled after removal proceed as follows:
1 Clean the exterior of the master cylinder and wipe dry with a non-fluffy rag.
2 Remove the filler cover and diaphragm (sometimes called gasket) from the top of the reservoir and pour out any remaining hydraulic fluid.
3 Undo and remove the secondary piston stop bolt from the bottom of the master cylinder body.
4 Undo and remove the bleed screw.
5 Depress the primary piston and remove the snap-ring from the groove at the rear of the master cylinder bore (Fig. 9.15).
6 Remove the pushrod and the primary piston assembly.
7 *Do not* remove the screw that retains the primary return spring retainer, return spring, primary cup and protector on the primary piston. This is factory set and must not be disturbed.
8 Remove the secondary piston assembly.
9 *Do not* remove the outlet pipe seats, outlet check valves and outlet check valve springs from the master cylinder body.
10 Examine the bore of the cylinder carefully for any signs of scores or ridges. If this is found to be smooth all over new seals can be fitted. If however, there is any doubt of the condition of the bore then a new master cylinder must be fitted.
11 If the seals are swollen, or very loose on the pistons, suspect oil contamination in the system. Oil will swell these rubber seals and if one is found to be swollen it is reasonable to assume that all seals in the braking system will need attention.

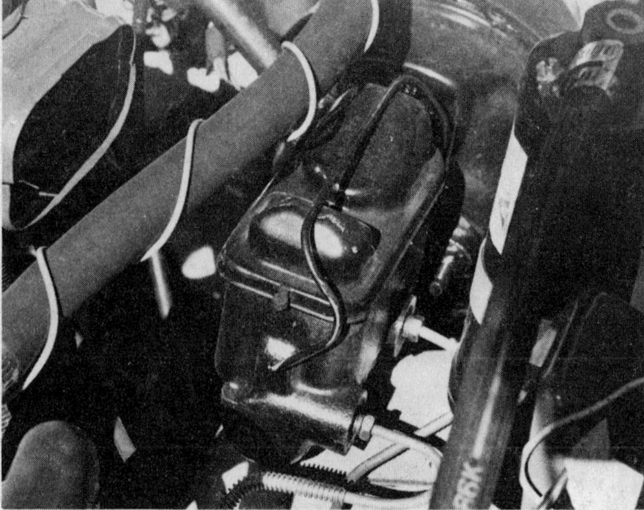
14.4 Location of master cylinder

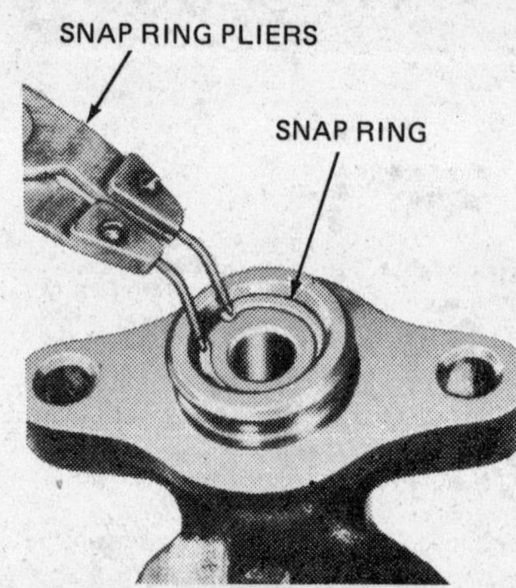

Fig. 9.15. Removing master cylinder snap-ring (Sec. 15)

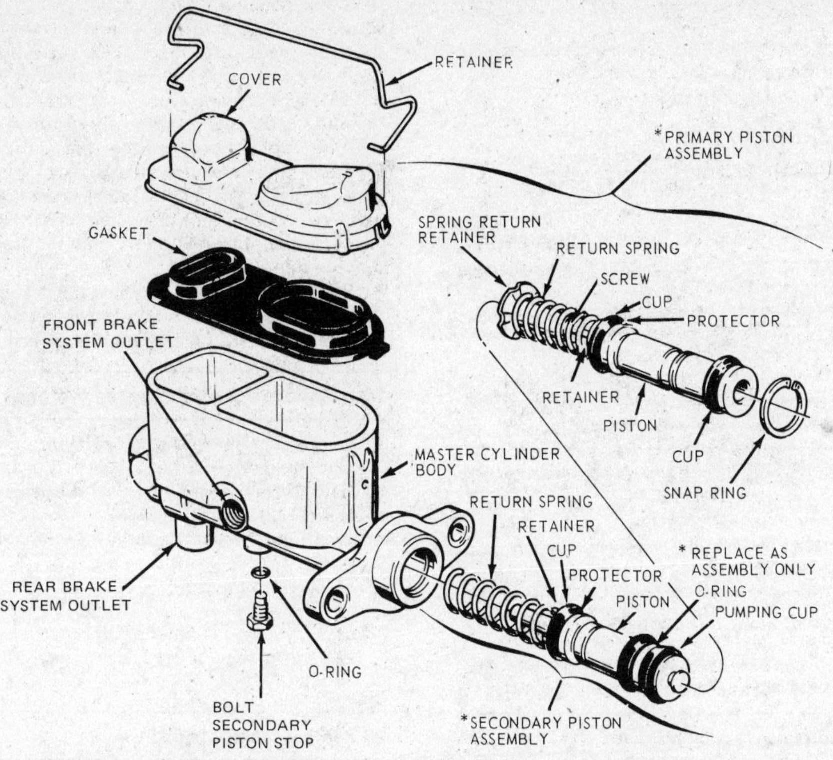

Fig. 9.16. Exploded view of brake master cylinder (Sec. 15)

12 Thoroughly clean all parts in clean hydraulic fluid or denatured alcohol. Ensure that the ports are clear.
13 All components should be assembled wet after dipping in fresh brake fluid.
14 Carefully insert the complete secondary piston and return spring assembly into the master cylinder bore, easing the seals into the bore, taking care that they do not roll over. Push the assembly fully home.
15 Insert the primary piston assembly into the master cylinder bore.
16 Depress the primary piston and fit the snap-ring into the cylinder bore groove.
17 Refit the pushrod, boot and retainer onto the pushrod and fit the assembly into the end of the primary piston. Check that the retainer is correctly seated and holding the pushrod securely.
18 Place the inner end of the pushrod boot in the master cylinder body retaining groove.
19 Fit the secondary piston stop bolt and 'O' ring into the bottom of the master cylinder body.
20 Refit the diaphragm into the filler cover making sure it is correctly seated and replace the cover. Secure in position with the spring retainer.

16 Brake pedal - removal and replacement

Manual gearbox models

1 Remove the clutch cable retaining clip and remove the cable from the clutch pedal.
2 Disconnect the stoplight switch wires at the connector.
3 Remove the switch retainer and slide the stoplight switch from the brake pedal pin just sufficiently for the switch outer hole to clear the pin. Lower the switch away from the pin.
4 Slide the master cylinder pushrod, nylon washers and bush from the brake pedal pin.
5 Remove the self-locking nut and washer from the brake and clutch pedal shaft.
6 Remove the clutch pedal and shaft assembly. Follow this with the brake pedal assembly and bushings from the pedal support bracket.
7 Refitting the brake pedal is the reverse sequence to removal but the following additional points should be noted:

a) Check and if necessary adjust the clutch pedal free-play as described in Chapter 5.
b) Check and if necessary adjust the brake pedal free-play as described in Section 18.
c) Lubricate all moving parts with a little grease.

Automatic transmission models

1 Disconnect the stoplight switch wires at the connector.
2 Withdraw the hairpin retainer and slide the stoplight switch off the brake pedal pin just sufficiently for the switch outer hole to clear the pin. Lower the switch away from the pin.
3 Slide the master cylinder pushrod, nylon washers and bushing from the brake pedal pin.
4 Remove the self-locking nut and washer from the brake pedal shaft.
5 Remove the shaft, the brake pedal and bushings from the pedal support bracket.
6 Refitting the brake pedal is the reverse sequence to removal.

a) Check and if necessary adjust the brake pedal free-play as described in Section 18.
b) Lubricate all moving parts with a little grease.

17 Pressure differential valve assembly - removal and replacement

1 Disconnect the brake warning light connector from the warning light switch.
2 Disconnect the front inlet and rear outlet pipe unions from the valve assembly. Plug the ends of the pipes to prevent loss of hydraulic fluid or dirt ingress.
3 Undo and remove the two nuts and bolts securing the valve bracket to the underside of the wing apron.
4 Lift away the valve assembly and bracket taking care not to allow any brake fluid to contact paintwork as it acts as a solvent.
5 The valve assembly cannot be overhauled or repaired, so if its performance is suspect a new unit will have to be obtained and fitted.
6 Refitting the pressure differential valve assembly and bracket is the

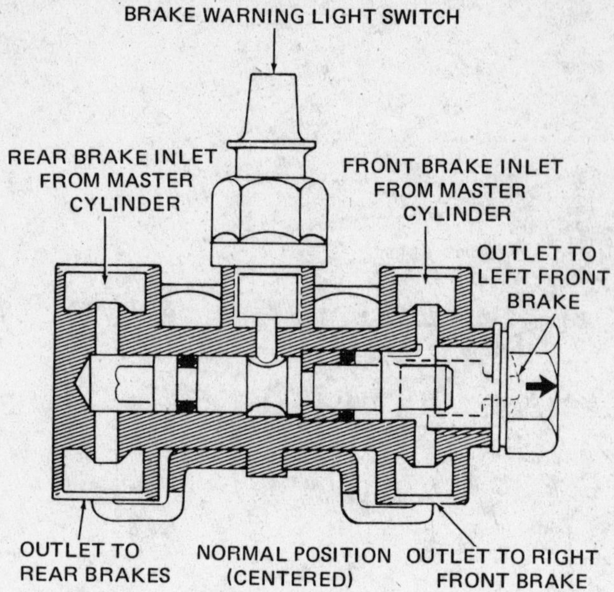

Fig. 9.17. Cross-section of brake differential valve (Sec. 17)

reverse sequence to removal. It will be necessary to bleed the brake hydraulic system as described in Section 2.

18 Brake pedal travel - measurement and adjustment

1 When the parking brake is fully released measure the brake pedal free height by first inserting a needle through the carpet and sound deadening felt until it contacts the metal dashpanel.
2 Measure the distance from the brake pedal to the metal dashpanel. This should be within the pedal height limits given in the Specifications.
3 If the measurement obtained is not within the specified limit check

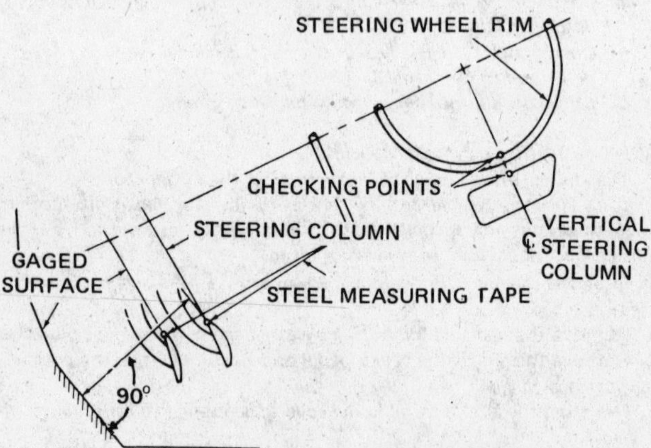

Fig. 9.18. Brake pedal free-travel and height measurement (Sec. 18)

the brake pedal linkage for missing, worn or damaged bushes or loose securing bolts. Rectify as necessary.
4 If the measurement is still incorrect then the master cylinder should be checked to see if it has been correctly reassembled after overhaul.
5 To check the brake pedal travel measure and record the distance from the pedal free height position to the datum point which is the six o'clock position on the steering wheel rim.
6 Depress the brake pedal and take a second reading. The differences between the brake pedal free-height and the depressed pedal measurement should be within the pedal travel figure given in the Specifications.
7 If the pedal travel is more than that specified, adjust the brakes as described in Section 13.
8 Should this still not produce the desired results the drums will have to be removed to check that the linings are not badly worn and the automatic adjusters are operating correctly. Rectify any faults found.

19 Parking brake assembly - removal and replacement

1 Undo and remove the adjustment nut from the equaliser rod.
2 Undo and remove the screws that secure the parking brake assembly to the floor tunnel and lift away the assembly.
3 Refitting the parking brake assembly is the reverse sequence to removal. The following additional points should be noted:

a) Tighten the securing screws to the specified torque wrench setting.
b) Lubricate all moving parts with a little grease.
c) Adjust the linkage as described in Section 20.

20 Parking brake - adjustment

The parking brake is normally self-adjusting and the following work will only be required to remove slack from the cables after a high mileage.

1 Refer to Section 13, and adjust the brakes.
2 Chock the front wheels, jack-up the rear of the car and support on firmly based stands.
3 Release the parking brake fully and move the shift to the neutral position.
4 Slowly tighten the adjustment nut on the equaliser rod at the parking brake lever assembly until the rear brakes are just applied.
5 Back-off the adjusting nut until the rear brakes are just fully released.
6 Lower the car and check parking brake lever free-movement.

21 Parking brake cable - removal and replacement

1 Chock the front wheels, jack-up the rear of the car and support on firmly based axle stands. Remove the wheels.
2 Refer to Section 9, and remove the brake drums.
3 Release the parking brake and back off the adjusting nut.
4 Remove the cable from the equalizer.
5 Compress the retainer prongs and pull the cable rearwards through the cable brackets by a sufficient amount to release the cable.
6 Remove the clips retaining each cable to the top of the rear springs (Fig. 9.20).

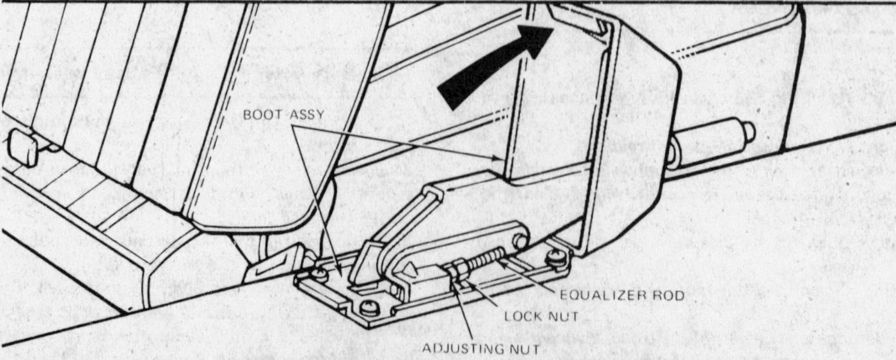

Fig. 9.19. Parking brake boot removal (Sec. 20)

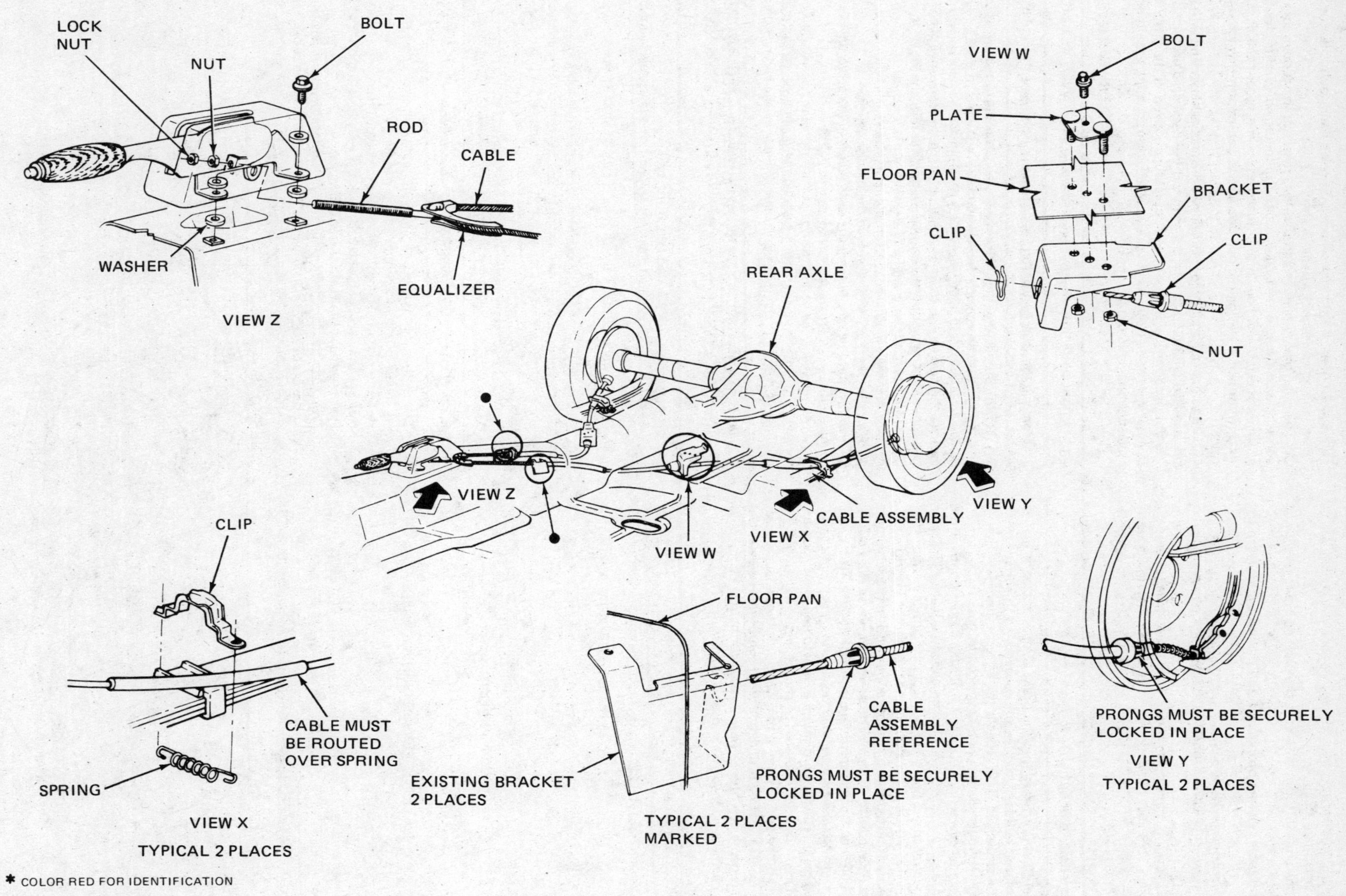
LOCK NUT
NUT
BOLT
ROD
CABLE
WASHER
EQUALIZER
VIEW Z
VIEW W
BOLT
PLATE
FLOOR PAN
BRACKET
CLIP
CLIP
NUT
REAR AXLE
VIEW Z
VIEW W
VIEW X
CABLE ASSEMBLY
VIEW Y
CLIP
CABLE MUST
BE ROUTED
OVER SPRING
SPRING
VIEW X
TYPICAL 2 PLACES
FLOOR PAN
EXISTING BRACKET
2 PLACES
CABLE
ASSEMBLY
REFERENCE
PRONGS MUST BE SECURELY
LOCKED IN PLACE
TYPICAL 2 PLACES
MARKED
PRONGS MUST BE SECURELY
LOCKED IN PLACE
VIEW Y
TYPICAL 2 PLACES
* COLOR RED FOR IDENTIFICATION

Fig. 9.20. Layout of parking brake and cable (Sec. 21)

7 Remove the self-adjuster springs and remove the cable retainers from the brake backplate.
8 Disconnect the ends of the cables from the parking brake levers on the secondary brake shoes.
9 Compress the cable retainer prongs and pull the cable ends from the backplates.
10 Undo and remove the nuts and bolts from the cable retainers on the rear springs. Lift away the cable from the retainers and remove from under the car.
11 Refitting the parking brake cable is the reverse sequence to removal. It will be necessary to adjust the parking brake as described in Section 20.

22 Vacuum servo unit - description

1 A vacuum servo unit is fitted into the brake hydraulic circuit in series with the master cylinder, to provide assistance to the driver when the brake pedal is depressed. This reduces the effort required by the driver to operate the brakes under all braking conditions.
2 The unit operates by vacuum obtained from the induction manifold and comprises basically a booster diaphragm and check valve. The servo unit and hydraulic master cylinder are connected together so that the servo unit piston rod acts as the master cylinder pushrod. The driver's braking effort is transmitted through another pushrod to the servo unit piston and its built in control system. The servo unit piston does not fit tightly into the cylinder, but has a strong diaphragm to keep its edges in constant contact with the cylinder wall, so assuring an air tight seal between the two parts. The forward chamber is held under the vacuum conditions created in the inlet manifold of the engine, and during periods when the brake pedal is not in use, the controls open a passage to the rear chamber, so placing it under vacuum conditions as well. When the brake pedal is depressed, the vacuum passage to the rear chamber is cut off and the chamber opened to atmospheric pressure. The consequent rush of air pushes the servo piston forward in the vacuum chamber and operates the main pushrod to the master cylinder.
3 The controls are designed so that assistance is given under all conditions and, when the brakes are not required, vacuum in the rear chamber is established when the brake pedal is released. All air from the atmosphere entering the rear chamber is passed through a small air filter.
4 Under normal operating conditions the vacuum servo unit will give trouble-free service for a very long time. If however, it is suspected that the unit is faulty, ie, increase in foot pressure is required to apply the brakes, it must be exchanged for a new unit. No attempt should be made to repair the old unit as it is not a serviceable item.

23 Vacuum servo unit - removal and replacement

1 Remove the stoplight switch and actuating rod from the brake pedal as described in Section 16.
2 Working under the hood, remove the air cleaner from the carburetor and the vacuum hose from the servo unit.
3 On four cylinder engines only (2.3 liter), it will be necessary to remove the two screws securing the throttle cable bracket to the engine and move the bracket in toward the engine. Remove the water inlet hose from the automatic choke house and move it out of the way. Also detach the vacuum hose from the EGR reservoir if necessary.
4 Refer to Section 14 and remove the master cylinder.
5 From inside the car, remove the nuts securing the servo unit to the dashpanel.
6 Working inside the engine compartment, move the servo unit forward until the actuating rod is clear of the dashpanel, rotate it through 90° and lift the unit upward until clear of the engine compartment.
7 Refitting a new servo unit is the reverse sequence to removal. If will be necessary to bleed the brake hydraulic system as described in Section 2.

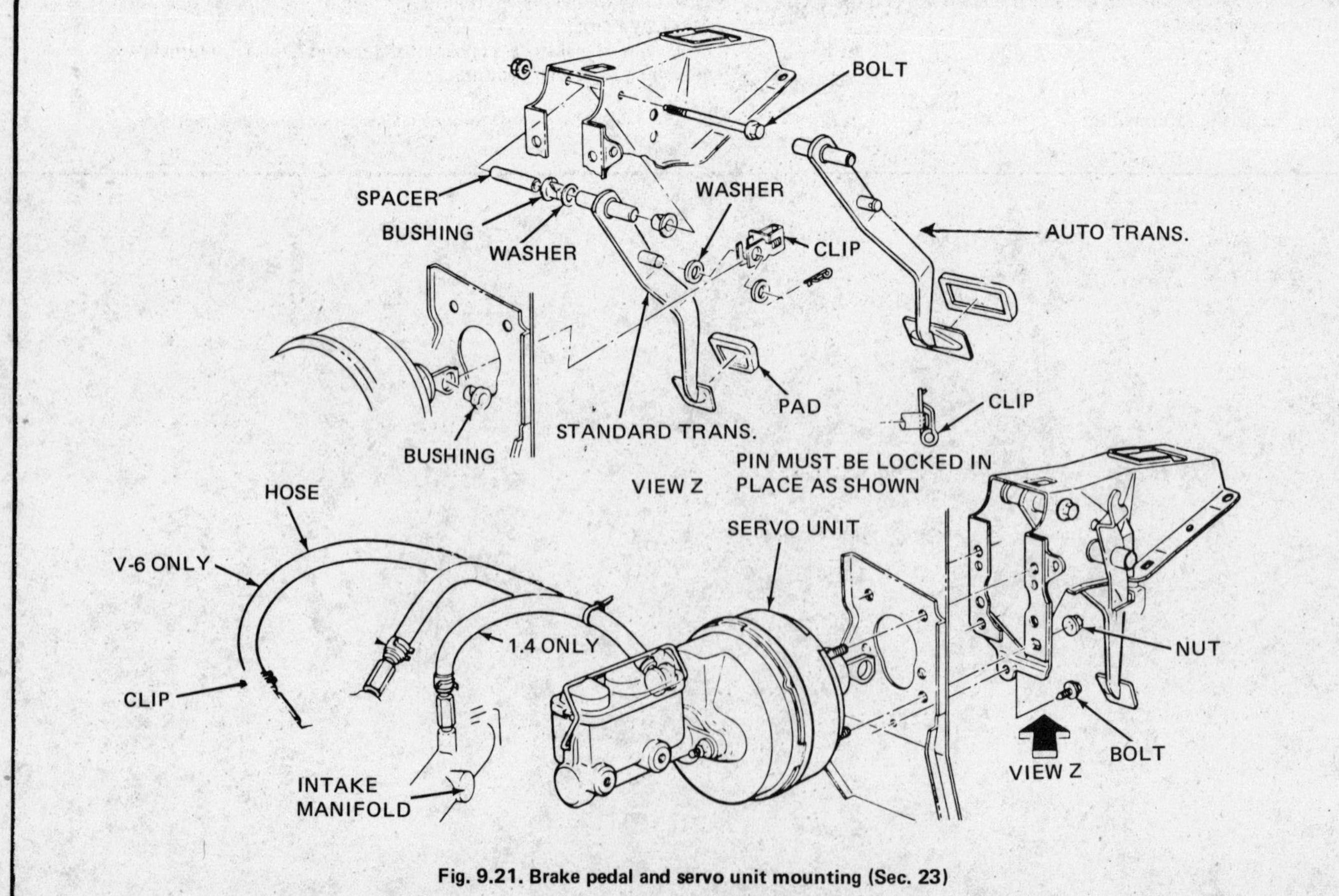

Fig. 9.21. Brake pedal and servo unit mounting (Sec. 23)

24 Fault diagnosis - Braking system

Before diagnosing faults from the following chart, check that any braking irregularities are not caused by:

1 *Uneven and incorrect tire pressures.*
2 *Incorrect 'mix' of radial and crossply tires.*
3 *Wear in the steering mechanism.*
4 *Defects in the suspension and dampers.*
5 *Misalignment of the bodyframe.*

Symptom	Reason/s
Pedal travels a long way before the brakes operate	Brake shoes set too far from the drums (auto.adjusters seized).
Stopping ability poor, even though pedal pressure is firm	Linings, discs or drums badly worn or scored. One or more wheel hydraulic cylinders seized, resulting in some brake shoes not pressing against the drums (or pads against discs). Brake linings contaminated with oil. Wrong type of linings fitted (too hard). Brake shoes wrongly assembled. Servo unit not functioning.
Car veers to one side when the brakes are applied	Brake pads or linings on one side are contaminated with oil. Hydraulic wheel cylinder(s) on one side partially or fully seized. A mixture of lining materials fitted between sides. Brake discs not matched. Unequal wear between sides caused by partially seized wheel cylinders.
Pedal feels spongy when the brakes are applied	Air is present in the hydraulic system.
Pedal feels springy when the brakes are applied	Brake linings not bedded into the drums (after fitting new ones). Master cylinder or brake backplate mounting bolts loose. Severe wear in brake drums causing distortion when brakes are applied. Discs out of true.
Pedal travels right down with little or no resistance and brakes are virtually non-operative	Leak in hydraulic system resulting in lack of pressure for operating wheel cylinders. If no signs of leakage are apparent the master cylinder internal seals are failing to sustain pressure.
Binding, juddering, overheating	One or a combination of reasons given in the foregoing Sections.

Chapter 10 Electrical system

For modifications, and information applicable to later models, see Supplement at end of manual

Contents

Specifications

Battery

Type	Lead acid
Grounded terminal	Negative (—ve)
Plates per cell/capacity:	
54	45 amp/hr
66	55 amp/hr
66	70 amp/hr
78	80 amp/hr

Starter motor

Type	Autolite
Diameter	4 in (101.6 mm)
Current draw (normal load)	150 - 200 amps
Cranking speed	180 - 250 rpm
Minimum still torque	9.0 lb f ft (1.2 kg f m)
Maximum load current	460 amps
No load current	70 amps
Brush length:	
New length	0.50 in (12.7 mm)
Minimum length	0.25 in (6.35 mm)
Spring tension	40 oz
Maximum commutator run-out	0.005 in (0.127 mm)

Alternator

Type	Ford
Color code	Purple, orange, red and green
Rating (at 15v):	
Purple	38 amps
Orange	42 amps
Red	55 amps
Green	61 amps
Output (at 15v):	
Purple	570 watts
Orange	630 watts
Red	825 watts
Green	915 watts
Field current (at 12v)	2.9 amps
Cut-in speed	400 rpm
Rated output speed (engine rpm):	
Cold	2000 rpm
Hot	2900 rpm
Slip ring diameter (minimum)	1.22 in (30.988 mm)
Slip ring maximum runout	0.0005 in (0.0127 mm)
Brush length:	
New length	0.5 in (12.7 mm)
Minimum length	0.3125 in (7.9375 mm)

Alternator regulator

Type	Autolite, electro mechanical, or transistorized
Voltage limiter (temperature 50° - 125°F/10° - 51°C)	Set to 13.5 - 15.3 volts
Field relay closing volts	2.0 - 4.2 volts

Fusible link identification

Color	**Wire gauge**
Red	18
Orange	16
Green	14

Fuses

Application	**Rating (amps)**
Instrument panel illumination lamps	4
Oil, brake, belts, indicator lamps, seat belt buzzer, throttle solenoid positioner, emission control solenoid	7.5
Windshield washer motor, door ajar warning lamp, heated backlight control and indicator lamp, anti-theft module, fuel economy indicator lamp	15
Radio/Tape player power	7.5
Horn, cigar lighter	20
Dome lamp, glove box lamp, map lamp, trunk compartment lamp, door and instrument panel courtesy lamps, key and 'Headlight on' warning buzzers; clock, anti-theft module and horn feed; seat belt warning system feed; 'Headlights on' indicator lamp	15
Rear stop and hazard flasher lamps	15
(With standard heater) heater motor power feed	15
(With optional A/C) A/C motor power feed	30
Back-up lamps, turn signal lamp	15

Bulb specifications

	Rating (CP or watts)
Headlights	40 - 50
Front parking/turn signal	3 - 32
Rear stop and turn	3 - 32
Back-up light	32
License plate light	4
Dome light	6
Side marker	2
Instrument panel illumination	2 cp
Main beam indicator	2 cp
Turn signal warning light	2 cp
Sundry warning lights	2 cp
Speedometer	2 cp
Fuel gauge	2 cp
Radio pilot light	1.9 cp
Automatic transmission selector	1.5 cp
Clock	3

Torque wrench settings

	lbf ft	**kg f m**
Alternator pulley nut	60 to 100	8.3 to 13.8
Starter motor through-bolts	55 to 75	7.6 to 10.2
Starter mounting bolts	15 to 20	2.1 to 2.8

1 General description

The major components of the 12 volt negative ground system comprise a 12 volt battery, an alternator (driven from the crankshaft pulley), and a starter motor.

The battery supplies a steady amount of current for the ignition, lighting and other electrical circuits and provides a reserve of electricity when the current consumed by the electrical equipment exceeds that being produced by the alternator.

The alternator has a separate regulator which ensures a high output if the battery is in a low state of charge and the demand from the electrical equipment is high, and a low output if the battery is fully charged and there is little demand from the electrical equipment.

When fitting electrical accessories to cars with a negative ground system it is important, if they contain silicone diodes or transistors, that they are connected correctly, otherwise serious damage may result to the components concerned. Items such as radios, tape recorders, electronic ignition system, electric tachometer, automatic dipping etc, should all be checked for correct polarity.

It is important that the battery positive lead is always disconnected if the battery is to be boost charged, also if body repairs are to be carried out using electronic welding equipment - the alternator must be disconnected, otherwise serious damage can be caused. Whenever the battery has to be disconnected it must always be reconnected with the negative terminal grounded.

2 Battery - removal and replacement

1 The battery is on a carrier fitted to the left-hand wing apron of the engine compartment. It should be removed once every three months for cleaning and testing. Disconnect, the positive and then the negative leads from the battery terminals by undoing and removing the plated nuts and bolts (photo).

2 Unscrew and remove the nut and plain washer that secures the clamp plate to the bodywork, remove the two nuts securing the battery clamp. Lift away the clamp plate. Carefully lift the battery from its carrier holding it vertically to ensure that none of the electrolyte is spilled.

3 Replacement is a direct reversal of this procedure. **Note**: Replace the negative lead before the positive lead and smear the terminals with petroleum jelly to prevent corrosion. **Never use** ordinary grease.

3 Battery - maintenance and inspection

1 Normal weekly battery maintenance consists of checking the electrolyte level of each cell to ensure that the separators are covered by ¼ inch of electrolyte. If the level has fallen, top-up the battery using distilled water only. Do not overfill. If a battery is overfilled or any electrolyte spilled, immediately wipe away and neutralize, as electrolyte attacks and corrodes any metal it comes into contact with very rapidly.

2 On later models, maintenance-free batteries are fitted which require no topping-up.

3 As well as keeping the terminals clean and covered with petroleum jelly, the top of the battery, and especially the top of the cells, should be kept clean and dry. This helps prevent corrosion and ensures that the battery does not become partially discharged by leakage through dampness and dirt.

4 Once every three months remove the battery and inspect the battery securing bolts, the battery clamp plate, tray, and battery leads for corrosion (white fluffy deposits on the metal which are brittle to touch). If any corrosion is found, clean off the deposits with ammonia and paint over the clean metal with an anti-rust anti-acid paint.

5 At the same time inspect the battery case for cracks. If a crack is found, renew the battery. Cracks are frequently caused to the top of the battery case by pouring in distilled water in the middle of winter *after* instead of *before* a run. This gives the water no chance to mix with the electrolyte and so the former freezes and splits the battery case.

6 If topping-up the battery becomes excessive and the case has been inspected for cracks that could cause leakage, but none are found, the battery is being overcharged and the voltage regulator will have to be checked and reset.

7 With the battery on the bench at the three monthly interval check, measure its specific gravity with a hydrometer to determine the state of charge and conditions of the electrolyte. There should be very little variation between the different cells and if a variation in excess of 0.025 is present it will be due to either:

a) Loss of electrolyte from the battery at sometime caused by spillage or a leak resulting in a drop in the specific gravity of the electrolyte, when the deficiency was replaced with distilled water instead of fresh electrolyte.

b) An internal short circuit caused by buckling of the plates or a similar malady pointing to the likelihood of total battery failure in the near future.

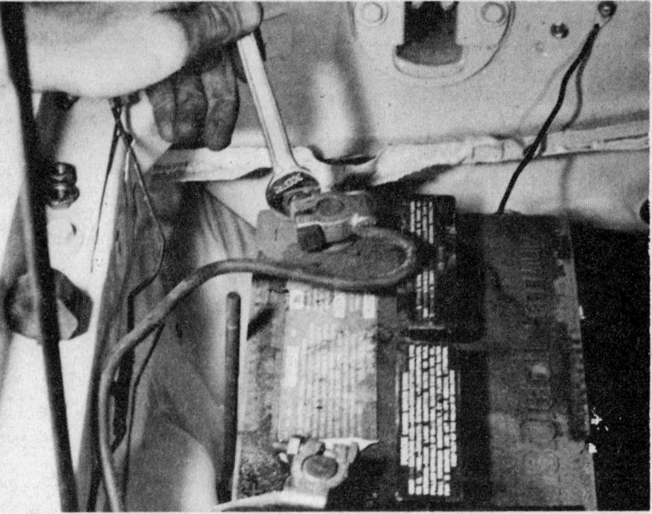

2.1 Removing battery terminal

8 The specific gravity of the electrolyte for fully charged conditions at the electrolyte temperature indicated, is listed in Table A. The specific gravity of a fully discharged battery at different temperatures of the electrolyte is given in Table B.

Table A

Specific gravity - Battery fully charged

1.268 at 100°F or 38°C electrolyte temperature
1.272 at 90°F or 38°C electrolyte temperature
1.276 at 80°F or 27°C electrolyte temperature
1.280 at 70°F or 21°C electrolyte temperature
1.284 at 60°F or 16°C electrolyte temperature
1.288 at 50°F or 10°C electrolyte temperature
1.292 at 40°F or 4°C electrolyte temperature
1.296 at 30°F or-1.5°C electrolyte temperature

Table B

Specific gravity - Battery fully discharged

1.098 at 100°F or 38°C electrolyte temperature
1.102 at 90°F or 32°C electrolyte temperature
1.106 at 80°F or 27°C electrolyte temperature
1.110 at 70°F or 21°C electrolyte temperature
1.114 at 60°F or 16°C electrolyte temperature
1.118 at 50°F or 10°C electrolyte temperature
1.122 at 40°F or 4°C electrolyte temperature
1.126 at 30°F or-1.5°C electrolyte temperature

4 Battery - electrolyte replenishment

1 If the battery is in a fully charged state and one of the cells maintains a specific gravity reading which is 0.025 or more lower than the others, and a check of each cell has been made with a voltmeter to check for short circuits (a four to seven second test should give a steady reading of between 12 to 18 volts) then it is likely that electrolyte has been lost from the cell with the low reading.

2 Have the battery checked out by your dealer and the electrolyte strength adjusted if necessary.

5 Battery - charging

1 In winter time when heavy demand is placed upon the battery, such as when starting from cold, and much electrical equipment is continually in use, it is a good idea occasionally to have the battery fully charged from an external source at the rate of 3.5 to 4 amps.
2 Continue to charge the battery at this rate until no further rise in specific gravity is noted over a four hour period.
3 Alternatively, a trickle charger charging at the rate of 1.5 amps can be safely used overnight.
4 Specially rapid 'boost' charges which are claimed to restore the power of the battery in 1 or 2 hours are to be avoided as they can cause serious damage to the battery plates through overheating.
5 While charging the battery, note that the temperature of the electrolyte should never exceed 100°F (37.8°C).

6 Alternator - general description

The main advantage of the alternator lies in its ability to provide a high charge at low revolutions. Driving slowly in heavy traffic with a dynamo invariably means no charge is reaching the battery. In similar conditions even with the wiper, heater, lights and perhaps radio switched on the alternator will ensure a charge reaches the battery.

The alternator is of rotating field, ventilated design. It comprises 3-phase output winding; a twelve pole rotor carrying the field windings - each end of the rotor shaft runs in ball race bearings which are lubricated for life; natural finish aluminium die cast end brackets, incorporating the mounting lugs; a rectifier pack for converting AC output of the machine to DC for battery charging, and an output control regulator.

The rotor is belt driven from the engine through a pulley keyed to the rotor shaft. A pressed steel fan adjacent to the pulley draws cooling air through the unit. This fan forms an integral part of the alternator specification. It has been designed to provide adequate air flow with minimum noise, and to withstand the high stresses associated with the maximum speed. Rotation is clockwise viewed on the drive end. Maximum continuous rotor speed is 12500 rpm.

Rectification of the alternator output is achieved by six silicone diodes housed in a rectifier pack and connected as a 3-phase full wave bridge. The rectifier pack is attached to the outer face of the slip ring end bracket and contains also three 'field' diodes. At normal operating speeds, rectified current from the stator output windings flows through these diodes to provide the self excitation of the rotor field, via brushes bearing on face type slip rings.

The slip rings are carried on a small diameter moulded drum attached to the rotor shaft outboard of the slip ring end bearing. The inner ring is centered on the rotor shaft axle, while the outer ring has a mean diameter of ¾ inch approximately. By keeping the mean diameter of the slip rings to a minimum, relative speeds between brushes and rings, and hence wear, are also minimal. The slip rings are connected to the rotor field windings by wires carried in grooves in the rotor shaft.

The brush gear is housed in a moulding fitted to the inside of the rear casing. This moulding thus encloses the slip ring and brush gear assembly, and together with the shielded bearing, protects the assembly against the entry of dust and moisture.

The regulator is located on the right-hand inner wing panel.

7 Alternator - maintenance

1 The equipment has been designed for the minimum amount of maintenance in service, the only items subject to wear being the brushes and bearings.
2 Brushes should be examined after about 75,000 miles (120,000 km) and renewed if necessary. The bearings are pre-packed with grease for life, and should not require further attention.
3 Check the fan belt at the specified service intervals for correct adjustment which should be 0.5 inch (13 mm) total movement at the center of the run between the alternator and water pump pulleys.

8 Alternator - special procedures

Whenever the electrical system of the car is being attended to, and external means of starting the engine is used, there are certain precautions that must be taken otherwise serious and expensive damage to the alternator can result.
1 Always make sure that the negative terminal of the battery is grounded. If the terminal connections are accidentally reversed or if the battery has been reverse charged the alternator diodes will be damaged.
2 The output terminal on the alternator marked 'BAT' or 'B+' must never be grounded but should always be connected directly to the positive terminal of the battery.
3 Whenever the alternator is to be removed or when disconnecting the terminals of the alternator circuit, always disconnect the battery ground terminal first.
4 The alternator must never be operated without the battery to alternator cable connected.
5 If the battery is to be charged by external means always disconnect both the battery cables before the external charger is connected.
6 Should it be necessary to use a booster charger or booster battery to start the engine always double check that the negative cable is connected to negative terminal and the positive cable to positive terminal.

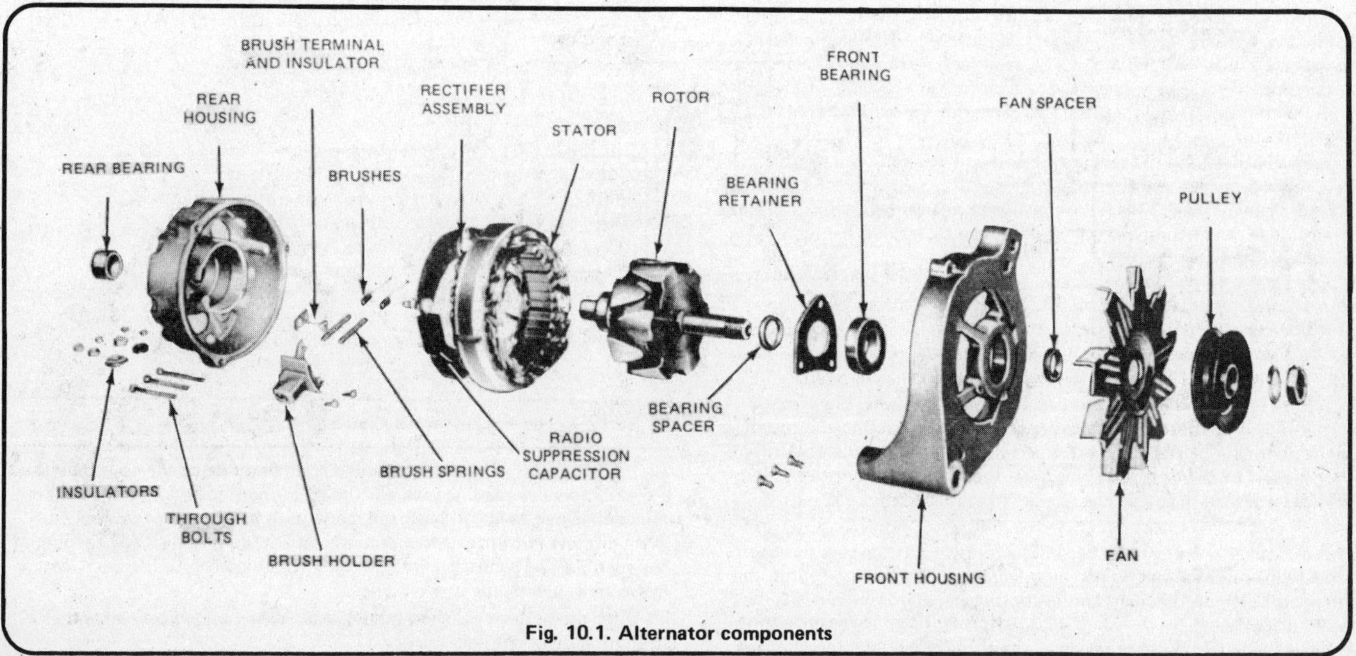

Fig. 10.1. Alternator components

10

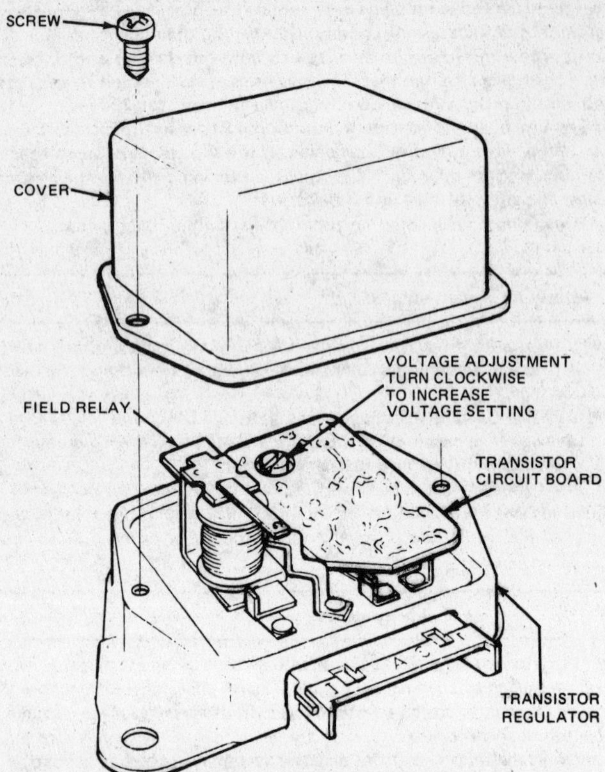

Fig. 10.2. Transistorized type voltage regulator. For adjustment procedure see Chapter 13

9 Alternator - removal and refitting

1 Disconnect the battery leads.
2 Note the terminal connections at the rear or side of the alternator and disconnect. (Fig. 10.4).
3 Undo and remove the alternator adjustment arm bolt, slacken the alternator mounting bolts and push the alternator inwards towards the engine. Lift away the fan belt(s) from the pulley.

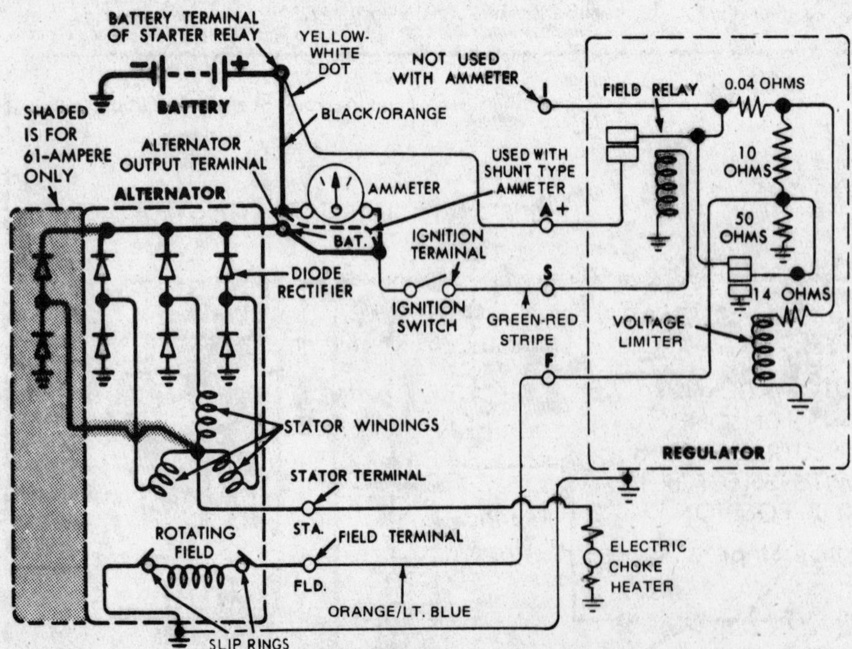

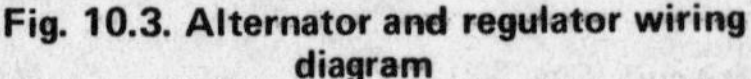

Fig. 10.3. Alternator and regulator wiring diagram

4 Remove the remaining two mounting bolts and carefully lift the alternator away from the car.
5 Take care not to knock or drop the alternator otherwise this can cause irreparable damage.
6 Refitting the alternator is the reverse sequence to removal.
7 Adjust the fan belt so that it has 0.5 inch (13 mm) total movement at the center of the run between the alternator and water pump pulleys.
Note: It may be necessary to remove other accessory drive belts before the alternator drive belt can be removed (see Chapter 2).

10 Alternator - fault diagnosis and repair

Due to the specialist knowedge and equipment required to test or service an alternator it is recommended that if the performance is suspect the car be taken to an automobile electrician who will have the facilities for such work. Because of this recommendation, information is limited to the inspection and renewal of the brushes.

The ammeter (ALT) gauge on the instrument panels indicates the charge (C) or discharge (D) current passing into, or out of the battery. With the electrical equipment switched on and the engine idling the gauge needle may show a discharge condition. However, at fast idle or normal driving speeds the needle should stay on the 'C' side of the gauge; just how far over will depend on the charged state of the battery.

If the gauge does not show a charge under these conditions there is a fault in the system and the following points should be checked before inspecting the brushes or, if necessary, renewing the alternator:

a) Check the fan belt tension, as described in Section 7.
b) Check the battery, as described in Section 3.
c) Check all electrical cable connections for cleanliness and security.

11 Alternator brushes - removal, inspection and replacement

1 Firstly remove the alternator as described in Section 9.
2 Scratch a line across the length of the alternator housing to ensure correct reassembly.
3 Remove the three housing thru-bolts, and the nuts and insulators from the rear housing. Make a careful note of all insulator positions.
4 Withdraw the rear housing section from the stator, rotor and front housing assembly.
5 Remove the brushes and springs from the brush holder assembly which is located inside the rear housing.

Fig. 10.4. Alternator wiring terminals (Sec. 9)

6 Check the length of the brushes against the wear dimension given in the Specifications at the beginning of this Chapter and renew if necessary.
7 Refit the springs and brushes into the holder assembly and retain them in place by inserting a piece of wire through the rear housing and brush terminal insulator as shown in Fig. 10.6. Make sure enough wire protrudes through the rear of the housing so that it may be withdrawn at a later stage.
8 Refit to the stator, the rear housing rotor and front housing assembly, making sure that the scribed marks line up.
9 Refit the three housing thru-bolts and rear end insulators and nuts, but do not tighten.
10 Carefully extract the piece of wire from the rear housing and ascertain as far as possible that the brushes are seated on the slip ring. Tighten the thru-bolts and rear housing nuts.
11 Refit the alternator as described in Section 9.

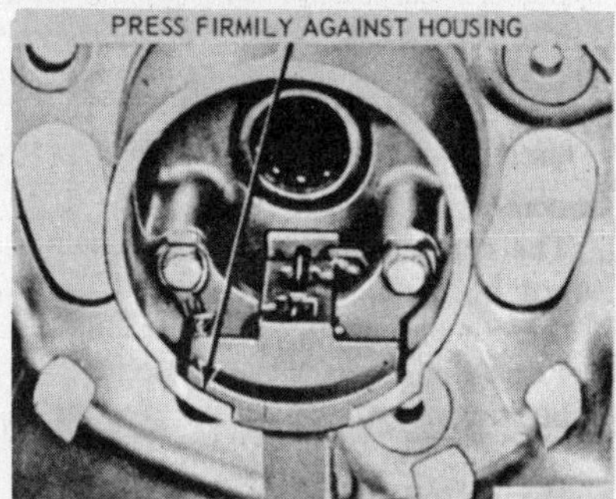

Fig. 10.5. Location of brushholder in the rear housing assembly (Sec. 11)

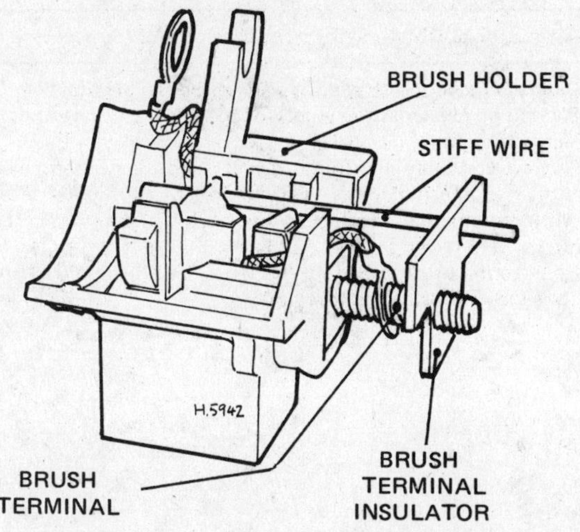

Fig. 10.6. Alternator brushholder assembly (Sec. 11)

12 Starter motor - general description

The starter motor system comprises a motor with an integral positive engagement drive, the battery, a remote control starter switch, a neutral start switch, the starter relay and the necessary wiring.

When the ignition switch is turned to the start position the starter relay is energised through the starter control circuit. The relay then connects the battery to the starter motor.

Cars fitted with an automatic transmission have a neutral start switch in the starter control circuit which prevents operation of the starter if the selector lever is not in the 'N' or 'P' positions.

With the starter in its rest position one of the field coils is connected directly to ground through a set of contacts. When the starter is first connected to the battery, a large current flows through the grounded field coil and operates a movable pole shoe. The pole shoe is attached to the starter drive plunger lever and so the drive is engaged with the ring gear on the flywheel.

When the movable pole shoe is fully seated, it opens the field coil grounding contacts and the starter is in a normal operational condition.

A special holding coil is used to maintain the movable pole shoe in the fully seated position whilst the starter is turning the engine.

13 Starter motor - testing on engine

1 If the starter motor fails to operate, then check the condition of the battery by turning on the headlights. If they glow brightly for several seconds and then gradually dim, the battery is in a discharged condition.
2 If the headlights continue to glow brightly and it is obvious that the battery is in good condition, check the tightness of the battery leads and all cables relative to the starting system. If possible, check the wiring with a voltmeter or test light for breaks or short circuits.
3 Check that there is current at the relay when the ignition switch is operated. If there is, then the relay should be suspect.
4 If there is no current at the relay, then suspect the ignition switch. On models with automatic transmission check the neutral start switch.
5 Should the above checks prove negative then the starter motor brushes probably need renewal or at the worst there is an internal fault in the motor.

14 Starter motor - removal and replacement

1 Chock the rear wheels, apply the parking brake, jack-up the front of the car and support on firmly based stands.
2 Disconnect the two battery terminals.
3 From beneath the car, remove the four bolts retaining the crossmember beneath the clutch housing, lower the crossmember to the ground.
4 Remove the flexible coupling from the steering gearbox, and remove

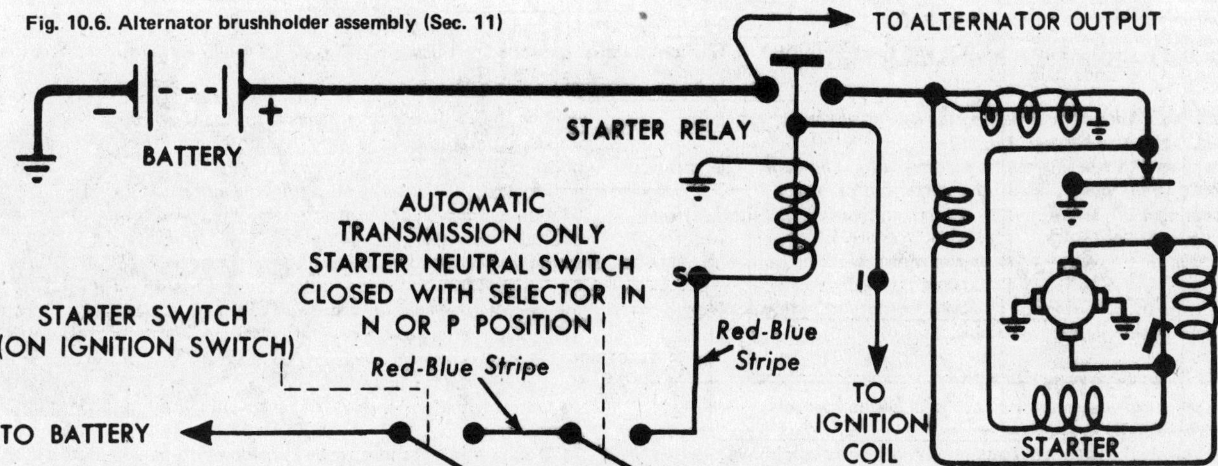

Fig. 10.7. Starter motor circuit (Sec. 12)

10

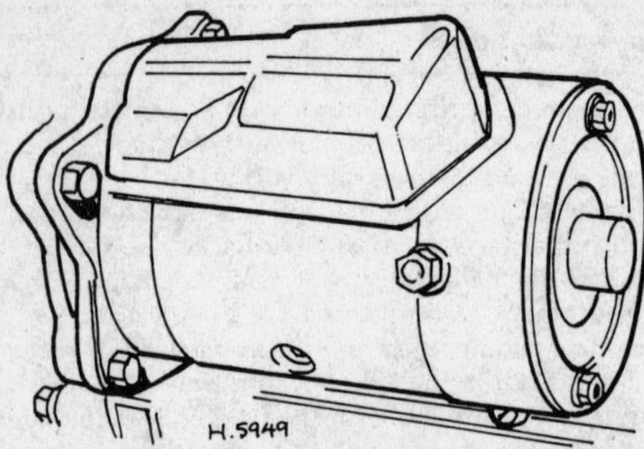

Fig. 10.8. Starter motor with side terminal (2.3 liter) (Sec. 14)

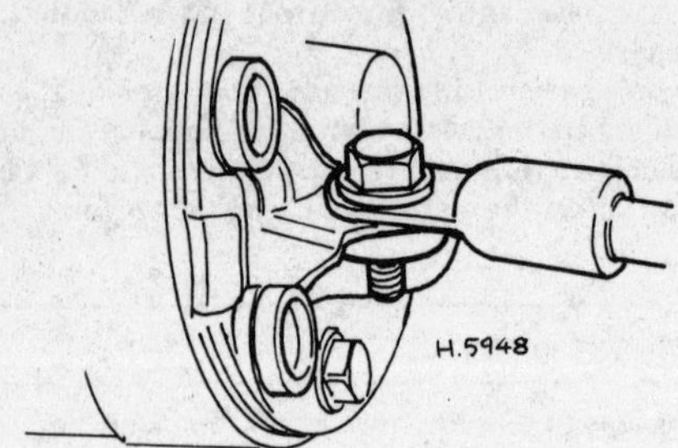

Fig. 10.9. Starter motor with end terminal (V6) (Sec. 14)

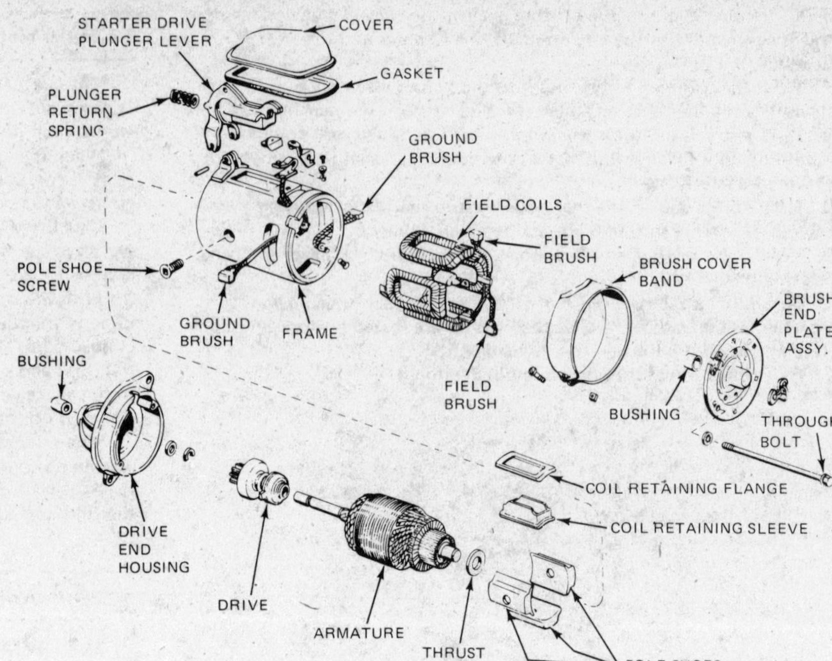

Fig. 10.10. Starter motor components (Sec. 15)

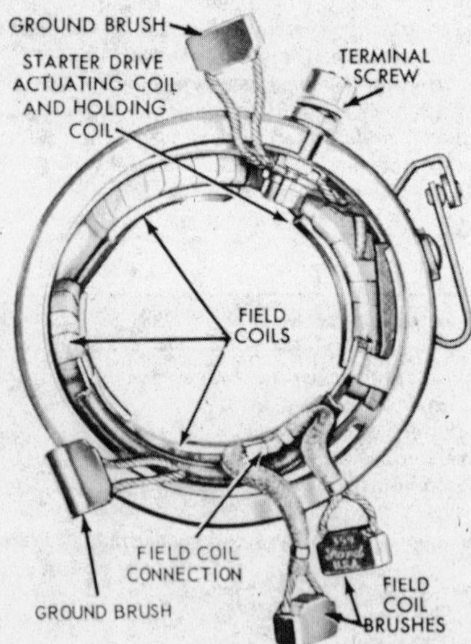

Fig. 10.11. Starter motor brushes and field coils (Sec. 15)

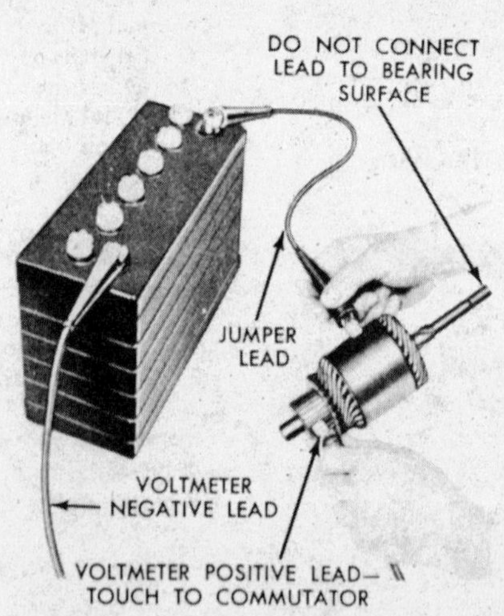

Fig. 10.12. Commutator grounded test using voltmeter and battery (Sec. 15)

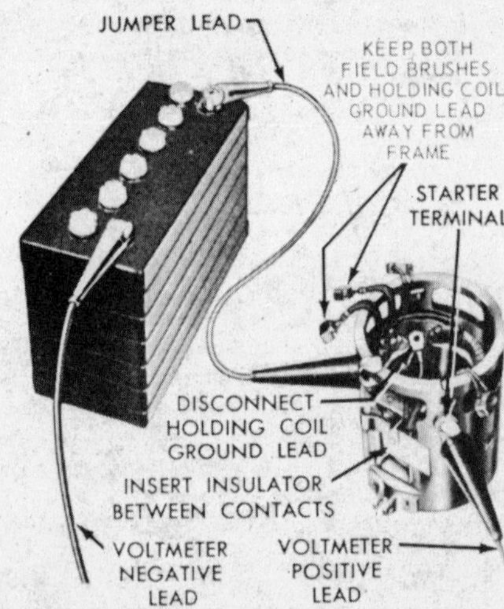

Fig. 10.13. Field coil grounded test (Sec. 15)

the three bolts that secure the steering gearbox to the chassis cross-member. (refer to Chapter 11).

5 Disengage the steering gearbox from the flexible coupling and pull it downward to provide access to the starter motor.

6 Disconnect the starter motor cable from the side (2.3 liter), or rear (V6) of the starter motor.

7 Undo and remove the three starter motor securing bolts and lift out the motor.

8 Refit the motor using the reverse procedure to removal. When replacing the steering gear assembly refer to Chapter 11.

15 Starter motor - dismantling, overhaul and reassembly

1 Slacken the brush cover band retaining screw and remove the brush cover band and starter drive plunger lever cover.

2 Note the positions of the leads to ensure correct reassembly and then remove the commutator brushes from the brush holder.

3 Undo and remove the long thru-bolts and lift off the drive end housing.

4 Remove the starter drive plunger lever return spring.

5 Remove the pivot pin that retains the starter gear plunger lever, using a suitable diameter pin punch.

6 Lift away the lever and withdraw the armature.

7 Remove the stop ring retainer followed by the stop ring that retains the starter drive gear onto the end of the armature shaft. The stop ring must be discarded and a new one obtained ready for reassembly.

8 Slide the starter drive assembly from the end of the armature.

9 Remove the brush endplate.

10 Unscrew the two screws that secure the ground brushes to the frame.

11 Dismantling should now be considered to be complete as removal of the field coils requires special equipment.

12 Clean the field coils, armature, commutator, armature shaft, brush

endplate and drive end housing using a non-fluffy cloth and brush. Other parts may be washed in a suitable solvent.
13 Carefully inspect the armature windings for broken or burned insulation and unsoldered connections.
14 Test the four field coils for an open circuit. Connect a 12 volt battery and 12 volt bulb to one of the leads between the field terminal post and the tapping point of the field coils to which the brushes are connected. An open circuit is proved by the bulb not lighting.
15 If the bulb lights it does not necessarily mean that the field coils are in order, as there is a possibility that one of the coils will be grounded to the starter yoke or pole shoes. To check this remove the lead from the brush connector and place it against a clean portion of the starter yoke. If the bulb lights, the field coils are grounding.
16 Replacement of the field coils calls for the use of a wheel operated screwdriver, a soldering iron, caulking and riveting operations, and is beyond the scope of the majority of owners. The starter yoke should be taken to a reputable electrical engineering works for new field coils to be fitted. Alternatively purchase an exchange starter motor.
17 If the armature is damaged this will be evident on inspection. Look for signs of burning, discoloration and for conductors that have lifted away from the commutator. Reassembly is a straightforward reversal of the dismantling procedure.
18 If a bearing is worn so allowing excessive side play of the armature shaft, the bearing bush must be renewed. Drift out the old bush with a piece of suitable diameter rod, preferably with a shoulder on it to stop the bush collapsing.
19 Soak a new bushing in engine oil for 24 hours or, if times does not permit, heat in an oil bath at 100°C (212°F) for two hours prior to fitting.
20 As a new bushing must not be reamed after fitting, it must be pressed into position using a small mandrel of the same internal diameter as the bushing and with a shoulder on it. Place the bushing on the mandrel and press into position using a bench vise.
21 If the brushes are renewed, their flexible connectors must be unsoldered and the connectors of new brushes soldered in their place. Check that the new brushes move freely in their holders as detailed above. If cleaning the commutator with gasoline fails to remove all the burnt areas and spots, then wrap a piece of glass paper around the commutator and rotate the armature.
22 If the commutator is very badly worn, remove the drive gear. Then mount the armature in a lathe and, with the lathe turning at high speed, take a very fine cut out off the commutator and finish the surface by polishing with glass paper. **Do not undercut the mica insulators between the commutator segments.**
23 Make sure that the drive moves freely on the armature shaft splines without binding or sticking.
24 To reassemble the starter motor is the reverse sequence to dismantling. The following additional points should be noted:

a) Fill the drive end housing approximately ¼ full with grease.
b) Always use a new stop ring.
c) Lightly lubricate the armature shaft splines with a Lubriplate 777 or thin oil.

16 Starter relay - removal and replacement

1 For safety reasons, disconnect the battery.
2 Make a note of and then disconnect the battery cables, ignition switch and coil wire from the relay (photo).
3 Undo and remove the two screws that secure the relay to the wing apron and lift away the relay.
4 Refitting the starter relay is the reverse sequence to removal.

17 Fusible link - testing, removal and replacement

1 A fusible link is used to protect the alternator from overload and is located in the wiring harness connecting the starter relay and 'BAT' terminal on the alternator.
2 If it is suspected that the alternator is not charging, first check that the battery is fully charged and the terminals are clean.
3 Using a voltmeter, check that there is voltage at the 'BAT' terminal at the rear of the alternator. No reading indicates that the fusible link has probably burned out. Check the fuse visually for swelling of the insulating sleeve.

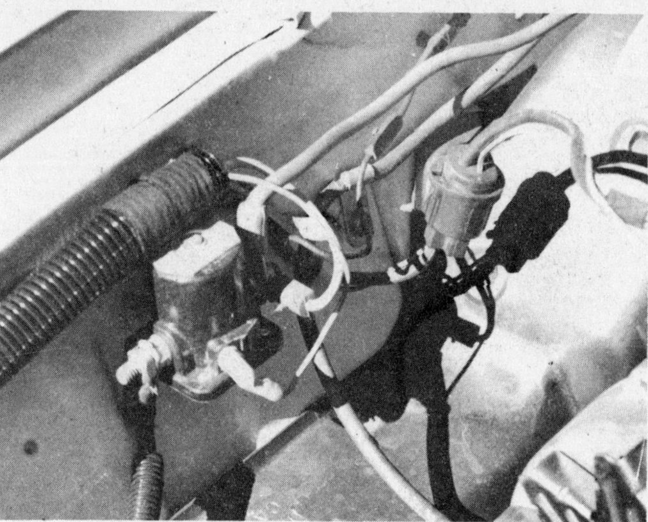

16.2 Location of starter relay

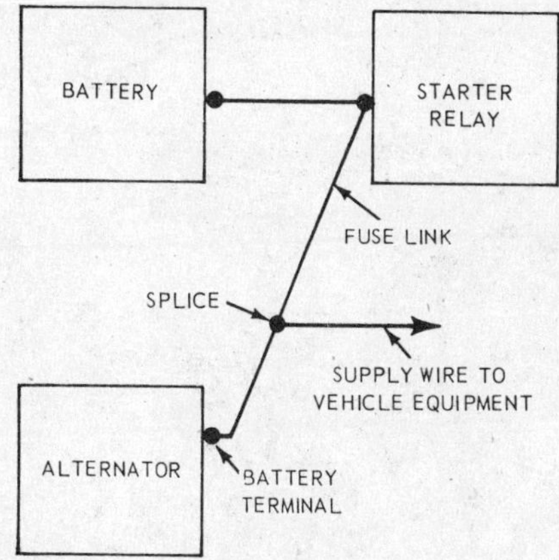

Fig. 10.14. Location of fuse link (Sec. 17)

4 To fit a new fusible link disconnect the battery ground terminal first.
5 Disconnect the fusible link eyelet terminal from the battery terminal of the starter relay.
6 Cut the fusible link and the splice(s) from the wire(s) to which it is attached.
7 Splice and solder the new fusible link to the wire from which the old link was cut. Protect the splice with insulation tape.
8 Securely connect the eyelet terminal to the battery stud on the starter relay.
9 Reconnect the battery ground terminal.

18 Headlight unit - removal and replacement

1 Undo and remove the two screws that secure the headlight rim to the front wing. Lift away the headlight rim (photos).
2 Remove the three screws that secure the sealed beam unit retaining ring to the adjusting ring (photo).
3 Rotate the retaining ring so as to disengage the ring from the adjusting screws.
4 Pull the sealed beam unit and disconnect the multi-pin connector to the rear of the sealed beam unit (photo).
5 Lift away the sealed beam unit.
6 Refitting is the reverse sequence to removal. It is recommended that whenever the sealed beam unit is changed the headlight alignment be checked. Further information will be found in Section 19.

19 Headlight alignment

1 It is always advisable to have the headlights aligned on proper optical beam setting equipment but if this is not available the following

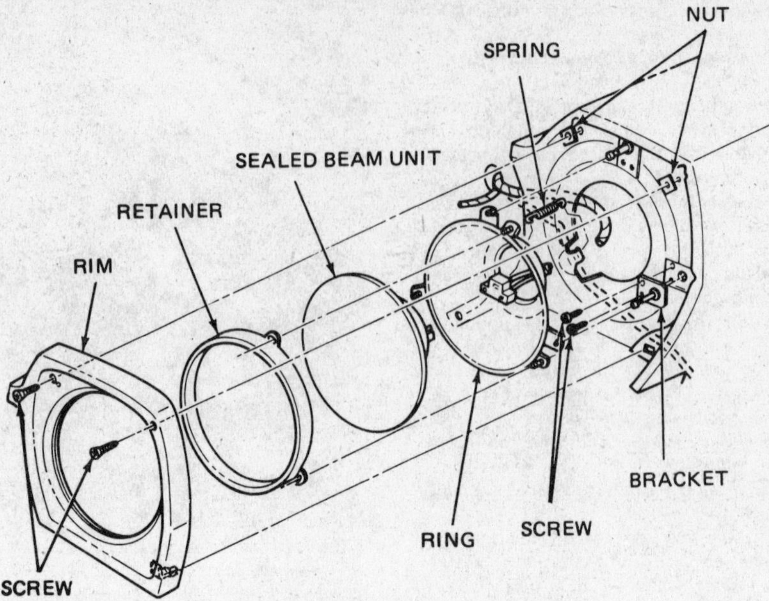

Fig. 10.15. Front headlight assembly - typical (Sec. 18)

18.1A Removing the headlight rim retaining screws

18.1B Lifting away the headlight rim

18.2 Removing the headlight unit retaining screws (the screw above is the adjusting screw)

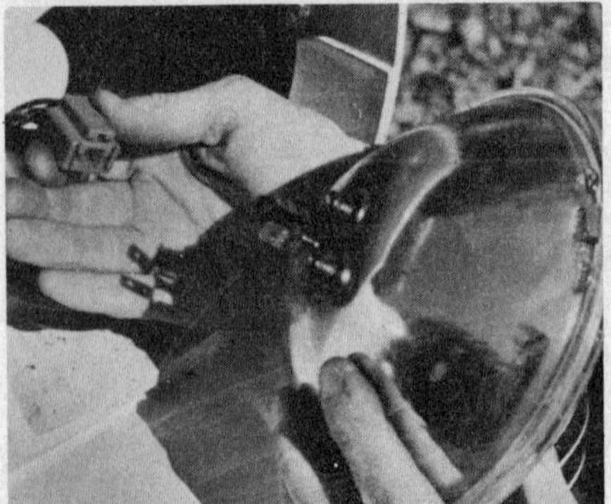

18.4 Disconnecting the headlight electrical connector

19.7 Position of headlight adjusting screws

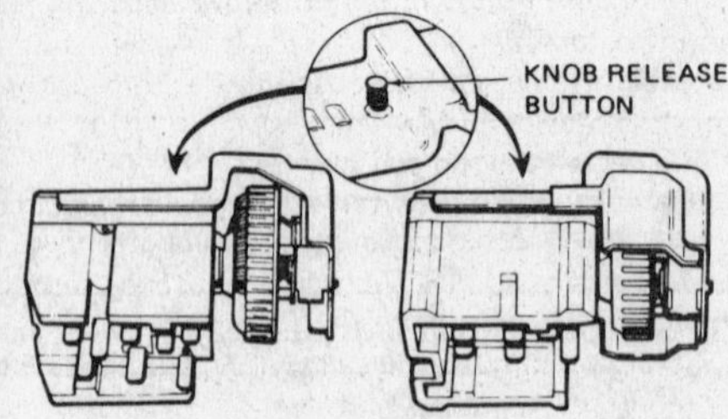

Fig. 10.16. Lighting knob removal button (Sec. 20)

procedure may be used.

2 Position the car on level ground 10 ft (3.048 metres) in front of a dark wall or board. The wall or board must be at right-angles to the center-line of the car.

3 Draw a vertical line on the board or wall in line with the center-line of the car.

4 Bounce the car on its suspension to ensure correct settlement and then measure the height between the ground and the center of the headlights.

5 Draw a horizontal line across the board or wall at this measured height. On this horizontal line mark a cross on either side of the vertical center-line, the distance between the center of the light unit and the center of the car.

6 Remove the headlight rims and switch the headlights onto full beam.

7 By careful adjusting of the horizontal and vertical adjusting screws on each light (photo), align the centers of each beam onto the crosses which were previously marked on the horizontal line.

8 Bounce the car on its suspension again and check that the beams return to the correct positions. At the same time check the operation of the dip switch. Replace the headlight rims.

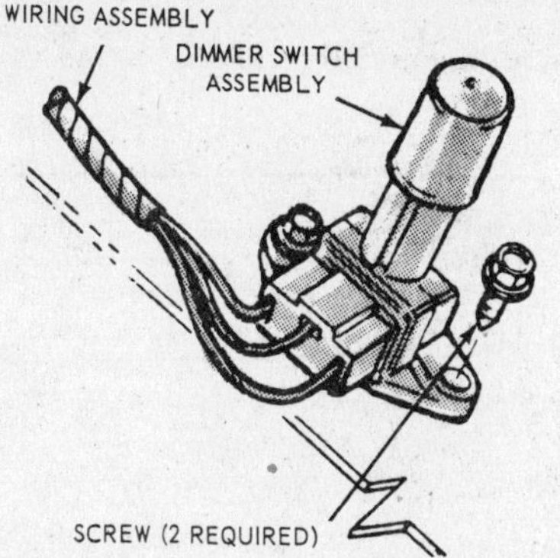

Fig. 10.17. Dimmer switch assembly (Sec. 22)

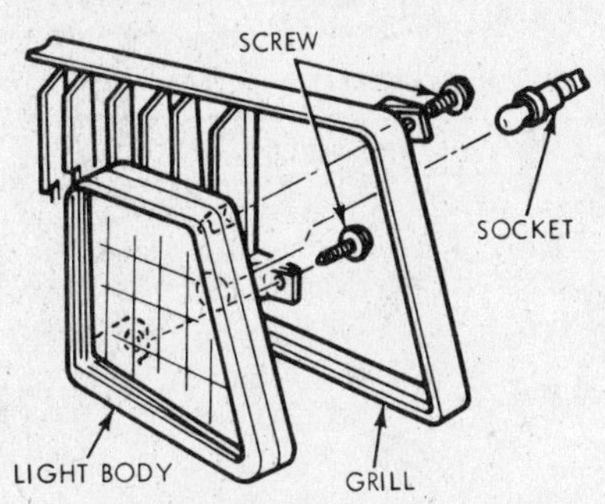

Fig. 10.18. Front parking/turn light assembly (Sec. 23)

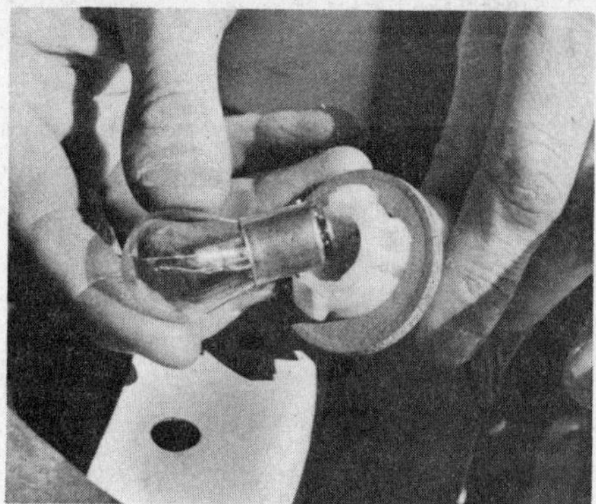
23.2 Removing parking/turn signal bulb

20 Headlight switch - removal and replacement

1 Disconnect the battery ground cable.
2 Working through the access hole in the underside of the instrument panel, press the release button using a small screwdriver (Fig. 10.16) and remove the switch knob and shaft.
3 Remove the bezel nut and lift out the switch body from behind the instrument panel. Disconnect the wiring harness connector.
4 Replace the switch using the reverse procedure to removal.

21 Headlight warning buzzer - removal and replacement

1 If the driver's door is opened while the headlights are on, a warning buzzer will sound and a warning lamp is illuminated.
2 The buzzer and relay assembly are located on a panel fitted to the right-hand side instrument panel endplate, just left of the glovebox.
3 To remove the buzzer and relay, refer to Chapter 12 and remove the glove box.
4 Remove the screws securing the buzzer and relay unit, disconnect the wiring terminals and lift the assembly out.
5 Neither component can be repaired, and if faulty must be replaced with a new unit.
6 Replace the buzzer and relay using the reverse procedure to removal.

22 Headlight dimmer switch - removal and replacement

1 Disconnect the battery ground cable.
2 Carefully pull back the carpet from around the dimmer switch, removing the scuff plate and cowl trim screws if necessary.
3 Undo and remove the two screws securing the dip switch to the mounting bracket.
4 Draw the switch forwards and disconnect the multi-pin connector from the rear of the switch.
5 Lift away the dip switch.
6 Refitting the dip switch is the reverse sequence to removal.

23 Front parking and turn signal lights - removal and replacement

Bulb renewal

1 To renew a light bulb it is not necessary to remove the light body.
2 Withdraw the socket from the rear of the light body and remove the bulb (photo).
3 Refitting the bulb and socket is the reverse sequence to removal.

Light body - removal and replacement

1 To remove the light assembly first disconnect the battery ground terminal.
2 Withdraw the bulb and socket assembly from the rear of the light body.
3 Undo and remove the two screws that secure the light body to the grille and lift away the light body.
4 Refitting the light assembly is the reverse sequence to removal.

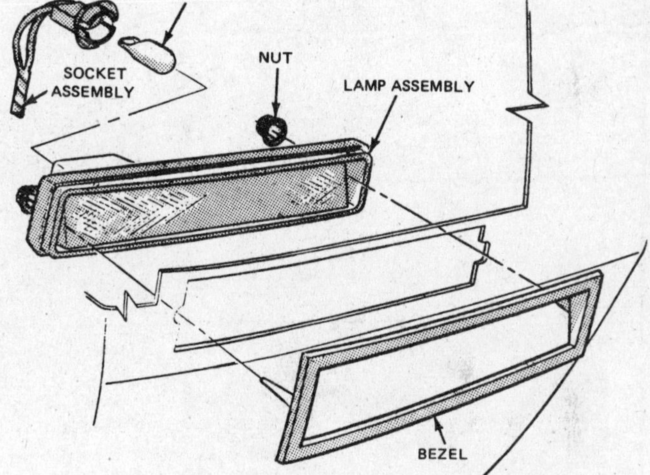

Fig. 10.19. Side marker light assembly (Sec. 24)

24 Front and rear side marker lights - removal and replacement

Front light - bulb renewal

1 To renew a bulb reach under the fender and disengage the light bulb socket from the light body.
2 Remove the bulb from the socket.
3 Refitting the bulb and socket is the reverse sequence to removal.

10

Front light assembly - removal and replacement

1 Disengage the light bulb socket from the rear of the light body.
2 Undo and remove the two nuts securing the light body to the fender.
3 Remove the light body bezel and working from the rear of the wing remove the light body assembly.
4 Refitting the light body assembly is the reverse sequence to removal.

Rear light - bulb renewal

1 Working inside the trunk remove the trim panel and disengage the light bulb socket from the light body.
2 Remove the bulb from the socket.
3 Refitting the bulb and socket is the reverse sequence to removal.

Rear light assembly - removal and replacement

1 Disengage the light bulb socket from the rear of the light body.
2 Undo and remove the two nuts securing the light body assembly to the rear fender.
3 Remove the light body bezel and working inside the trunk remove the light body assembly.
4 Refitting the light body assembly is the reverse sequence to removal.

25 Rear light cluster - removal and replacement

Bulbs - renewal

1 Working inside the trunk remove the trim panel (if fitted) and then disengage the relevant light bulb socket from the rear of the light cluster body (photo).

2 To remove the bulb from the socket turn anti-clockwise and lift it away from the socket.

3 Refitting the bulb and socket is the reverse sequence to removal.

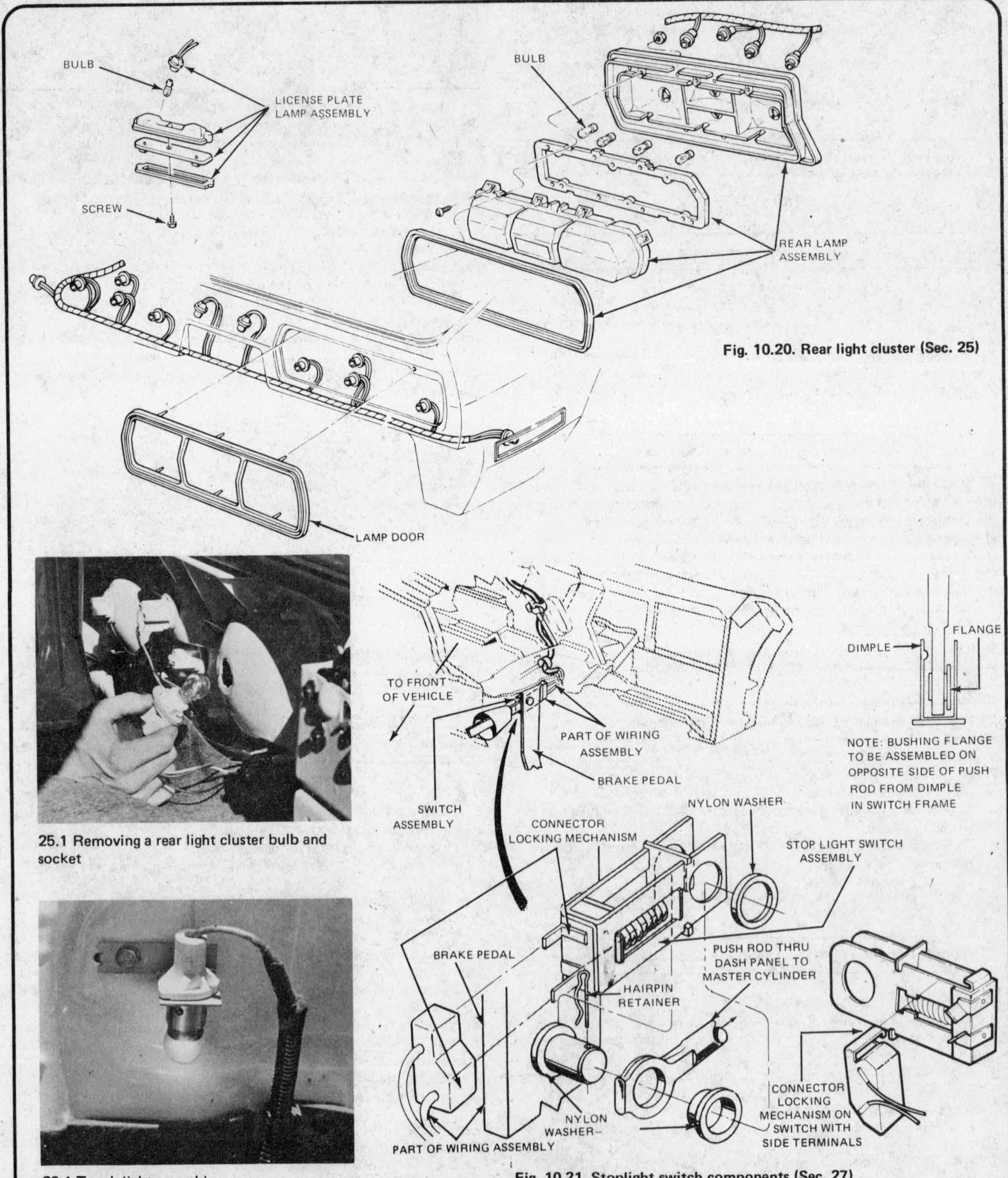

Fig. 10.20. Rear light cluster (Sec. 25)

25.1 Removing a rear light cluster bulb and socket

26.1 Trunk light assembly

Fig. 10.21. Stoplight switch components (Sec. 27)

Cluster assembly - removal and replacement

1 Working inside the trunk remove the two trim panels (if fitted) and then withdraw the four light bulb sockets from the rear of the light cluster body.
2 Undo and remove the six light body to back-panel securing nuts from the studs.
3 Carefully prise off the door from the body and lens.
4 If only the door is to be renewed, position the body and lens onto the new door.
5 If the light body is being renewed transfer the lens to the new body and fit a new lens gasket.
6 Reassembly is now the reverse sequence to removal.

26 Rear license plate and trunk light - removal and replacement

Bulb - renewal (license plate)

1 Undo and remove the screw securing the lens and lift away the lens.
2 Remove the bulb from its holder.
3 Refitting the bulb and lens is the reverse sequence to removal.

Light assembly - removal and replacement (license plate)

1 Disconnect the light body lead from inside the luggage compartment.
2 Carefully push the grommet out of the back-panel.
3 Undo and remove the two light body securing screws and lift away the light body assembly.
4 Refitting the light body assembly is the reverse sequence to removal.

Trunk light

1 Remove the retaining bolt and lift away the bracket (photo).

27 Stop light switch - removal and replacement

1 For safety reasons, disconnect the battery.
2 Disconnect the wires at the switch connector.
3 Withdraw the hairpin retainer, slide the stoplight switch, the push-rod, nylon washers and bushings away from the brake pedal.
4 The switch may now be lifted away.
5 Refitting the stop light switch is the reverse sequence to removal.

28 Back-up light switch - removal and replacement

Manual transmission models

1 Disconnect the wires from the back-up light switch.
2 Unscrew the switch from the gearbox extension housing.
3 Refitting the back-up light switch is the reverse sequence to removal.

Automatic transmission models

The back-up light switch is part of the neutral start switch on models fitted with automatic transmission. Refer to Chapter 6 for full information.

29 Turn signal lights switch - removal and replacement

1 For safety reasons, disconnect the battery.
2 Undo and remove the two screws from the back of the steering wheel horn pad. Lift off the complete pad and hornswitch assembly and disconnect the wires.
3 Remove the center steering wheel securing nut and pull the wheel off the shaft.
4 On 1974 and early 1975 cars, remove the turn signal arm by unscrewing from the side of the steering column. Remove the lower steering column shroud.
5 Late 1975 and 1976 cars have the windshield wiper and washer switch as an integral part of the turn signal arm. To remove the arm, first remove the two screws securing the upper and lower steering column shrouds and lift off the shrouds.
6 Remove the two screws securing the lower section of the instrument panel and lift away the panel (see Fig. 10.23).
7 Pull off the wiring cover from the bottom of the steering column.
8 Using a screwdriver as shown in Fig. 10.23 push in the retaining

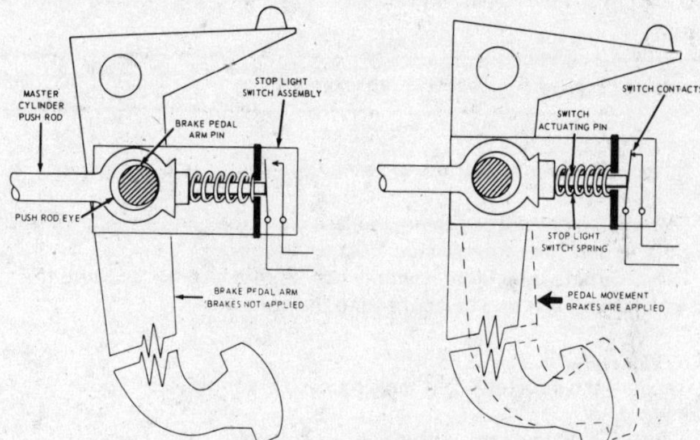

Fig. 10.22. Operation of stoplight switch (Sec. 27)

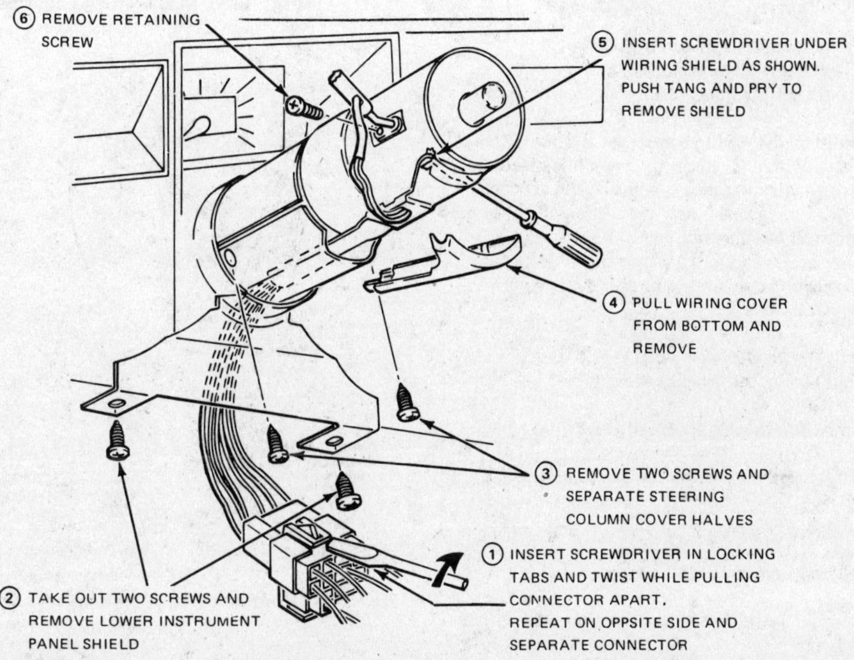

Fig. 10.23. Removal of steering column shrouds and later type turn signal/wiper arm (Sec. 29)

10

tang on the wiring shield and remove the shield.
9 Separate the wiring harness connector by inserting a screwdriver into the locking tabs and pulling the connector apart at the same time.
10 Using an Allen wrench, remove the securing screw from the base of the switch and remove the switch arm and wiring harness.
11 On all models, remove the screws that retain the direction indicator switch to the steering column, remove the cable retaining clamp, disconnect the turn switch connector and remove the switch and wiring harness.
12 Refitting the turn/wiper switch(es) is the reverse procedure to removal.

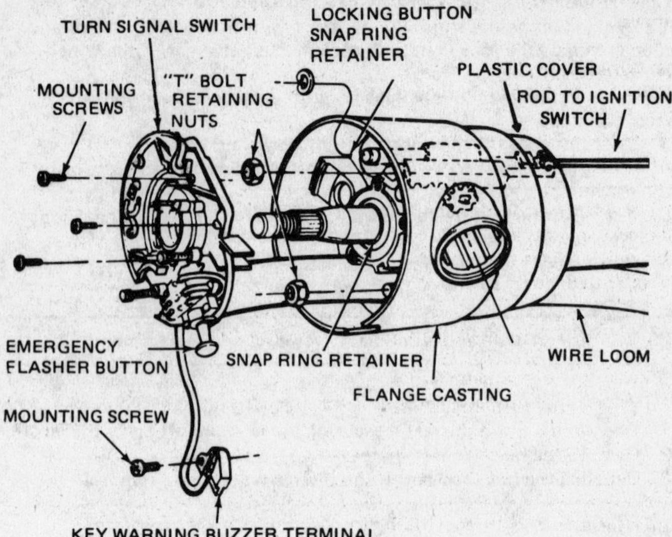

Fig. 10.24. Removal of turn switch assembly (Sec. 29)

30 Turn signal flasher unit - removal and replacement

1 The turn signal flasher unit is fitted on the main fuse panel which is located on the dash panel above the accelerator pedal.
2 The flasher unit simply plugs into the fuse panel and is retained by a spring clip.
3 To remove, grip firmly and pull straight out, taking care not to bend the connector tabs.
4 Replace using the reverse procedure.

31 Hazard warning lights flasher unit - removal and replacement

1 The hazard warning flasher unit is fitted adjacent to the turn signal unit and the removal and replacement procedure is the same as that described in the previous Section.

32 Interior lights - removal and replacement

Map light

1 Release the retaining clip and swing the light assembly outward. (See Fig. 10.25).
2 To replace the bulb, unscrew the lens from the end of the arm, push the bulb in and turn counterclockwise to remove.
3 The complete map light assembly can be removed by undoing the two securing screws and disconnecting the feed wire.

Courtesy light

1 Remove the courtesy light lens, squeeze in the sides and pull downward.
2 Lift the courtesy light bulb out of its retainers.
3 Replace the bulb and lens using the reverse procedure.

Courtesy light switch

1 The courtesy light switch is located in the door pillar.
2 Unscrew the hexagonal sleeve nut from the pillar.
3 Withdraw the switch and detach the multi-pin connector from the rear of the switch.
4 The new switch is locked onto the wiring connector by one of three tabs located 120° apart on the switch. If, when the switch is disconnected from the multi-pin connector the locking tabs break off, the switch should be rotated through 120° to engage a new tab. When all three tabs have been broken the switch must be renewed.
5 Refitting the switch is the reverse sequence to removal. Make sure that the courtesy light and ignition key warning buzzer systems are functioning correctly.

Automatic transmission control selector light

1 Undo and remove the four screws that secure the selector lever cover and dial indicator.
2 Lift the lever cover assembly up to gain access to the bulb.
3 Remove the bulb.
4 Refitting the bulb and cover assembly is the reverse sequence to removal.

Glove compartment lamp

1 The glove compartment lamp, (when fitted) is located inside the top of the compartment.
2 To remove the lamp assembly, push down the retaining tabs with a screwdriver and lift out the lamp.
3 To replace the bulb, push it out of the socket.

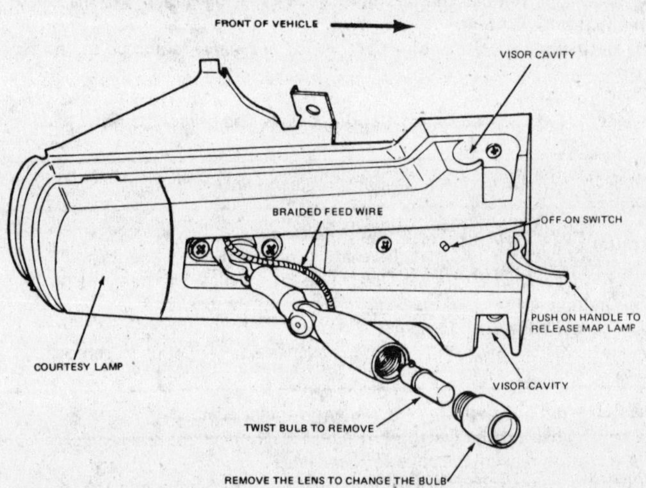

Fig. 10.25. Map light and courtesy lamp (Sec. 32)

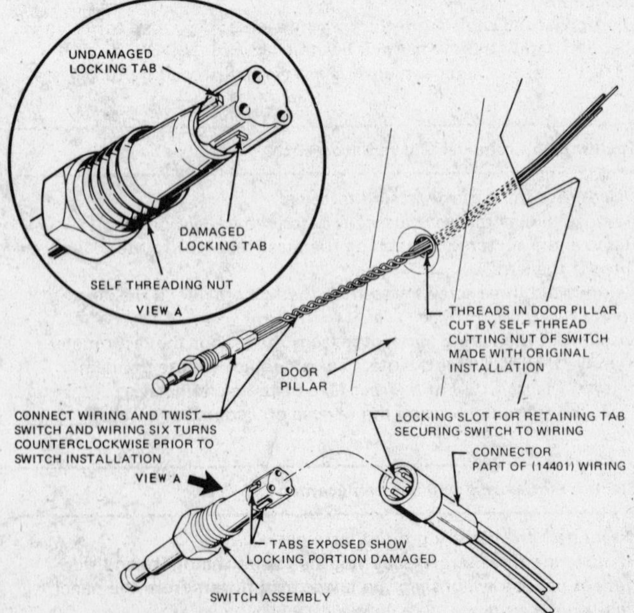

Fig. 10.26. Door operated light switch (Sec. 32)

4 Replace the bulb and lamp assembly using the reverse procedure to removal.

Instrument cluster lights

For full information refer to Section 39.

33 Speedometer head - removal and replacement

1 For safety reasons, disconnect the battery.
2 Working under the instrument panel disconnect the speedometer cable quick release connector.
3 Refer to Section 38 and remove the instrument cluster assembly.
4 Working at the rear of the cluster undo and remove the six screws that secure the mask and lens to the rear cover.
5 Undo and remove the two screws securing the speedometer head. Lift away the speedometer head.
6 Refitting the speedometer head is the reverse sequence to removal.

34 Speedometer cable - removal and replacement

Inner cable

1 Working behind the instrument panel disconnect the speedometer cable from the rear of the speedometer head (see Fig. 10.27).
2 Carefully pull the speedometer inner cable out from the upper end of the speedometer cable outer casing.
3 If the inner cable is broken, raise the car and working underneath undo and remove the bolt that secures the speedometer cable mounting clip to the transmission.
4 Remove the speedometer cable shaft and driven gear from the transmission.
5 Remove the driven gear retainer and the driven gear and shaft from the cable.
6 Remove the lower part of the broken inner cable from the end of the outer casing.
7 Refitting the new speedometer inner cable is the reverse sequence to removal.
8 Lightly lubricate the inner cable and insert into the outer casing. When the cable has nearly all been inserted turn the end to ensure that the squared end is engaged with the speedometer driven gear.

Outer cable

1 Working behind the instrument panel disconnect the speedometer cable from the rear of the speedometer head.
2 Push the outer cable and grommet through the opening in the dashboard panel.
3 Raise the car and working underneath detach the cable from all its retaining clips.
4 Disconnect the cable from the transmission as described earlier in this Section and withdraw from under the car (Fig. 10.28).
5 Refit the speedometer cable using the reverse procedure to removal.

35 Tachometer - removal and replacement

1 Disconnect the battery ground terminal.
2 Remove the instrument cluster as described in Section 38.
3 Remove the six screws attaching the mask and lens to the rear cover and lift off the lens.
4 Remove the three screws attaching the tachometer to the cluster backplate.
5 Disconnect the wiring connector from the rear of the tachometer and remove the instrument. **Note:** Take care not to lose the high-beam jewel that is fitted in the rear face of the tachometer.
6 Refit the tachometer using the reverse procedure to removal.

36 Electric clock - removal and replacement

1 Disconnect the battery ground terminal.
2 Remove the three screws securing the top of the right-hand side instrument panel trim, unsnap the lower trim fingers from the panel and remove the trim.
3 Undo and remove the three screws that secure the clock to the

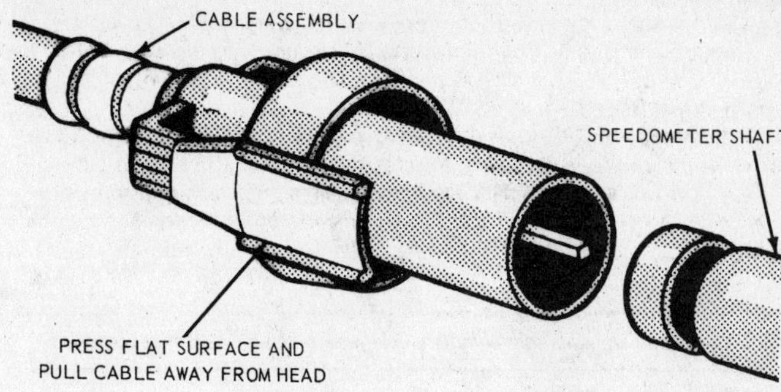

Fig. 10.27. Speedometer cable connector at Speedometer (Sec. 34)

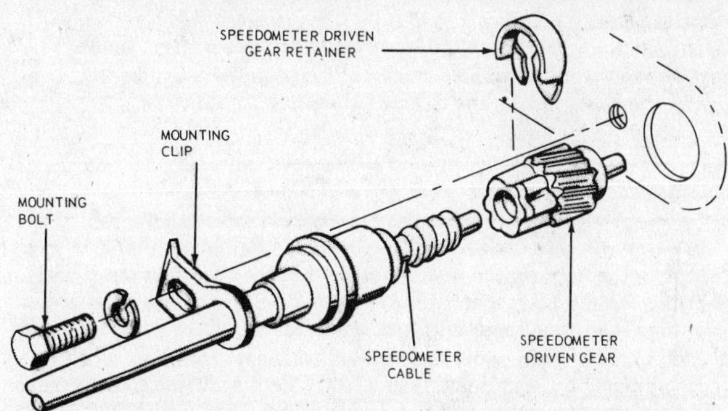

Fig. 10.28. Attachment of speedometer cable to transmission (Sec. 34)

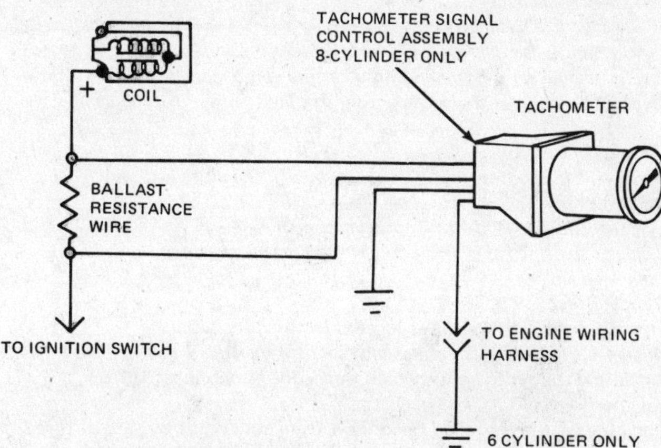

Fig. 10.29. Tachometer wiring diagram (Sec. 35)

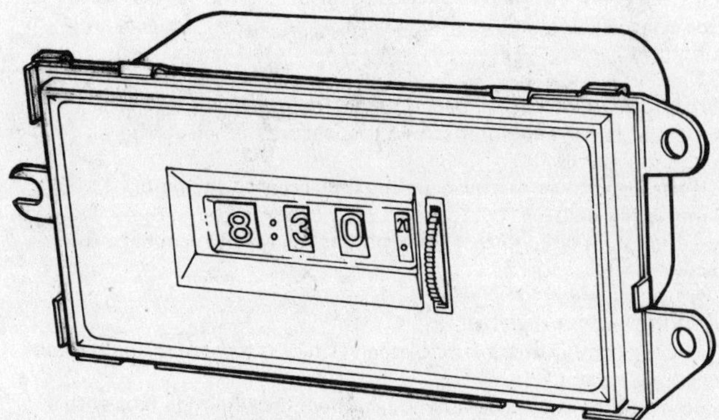

Fig. 10.30. Clock assembly (Sec. 36)

instrument panel.
4 Lift out the clock and disconnect the feed wire and bulb socket.
5 Replace the clock using the reverse procedure to removal.

Clock adjustment

Adjustment of the clock is automatic. Should the clock run too fast or too slow it is only necessary to reset the clock to the correct time. This action will automatically reset the adjuster. Turn the knob in a clockwise direction if the clock is slow or counterclockwise if the clock is fast.

37 Fuel, ammeter and temperature gauges - removal and replacement

1 Disconnect the battery ground terminal.
2 Remove the instrument cluster as described in Section 38.
3 Remove the six screws securing the mask and lens to the cover and remove the lens.
4 Remove the nuts retaining the gauges to the cover, (two on each gauge) and remove the gauges.
5 Refit the gauges using the reverse procedure to removal.

38 Instrument panel cluster - removal and replacement

1 For safety reasons, disconnect the battery ground terminal.
2 Remove the light switch and windshield wiper switch as described in Sections 20 and 50 respectively.
3 Remove the three upper and four lower screws that retain the instrument cluster trim panel and remove the panel (photos).
4 Disconnect the speedometer cable from the rear of the speedometer.
5 Remove the two upper and two lower screws that secure the instrument cluster to the instrument panel.
6 Pull the instrument panel forward and disconnect the large printed circuit wiring connector and the tachometer connector from the cluster backplate assembly.
7 Carefully lift out the instrument cluster assembly.
8 Refit the instrument cluster using the reverse procedure to removal.

39 Instrument cluster printed circuit - removal and replacement

1 Refer to the previous Section and remove the instrument cluster.
2 Unsnap the voltage regulator and radio choke assembly from the rear of the cover.
3 Remove the nuts retaining the gauges to the circuit board and remove the gauges.
4 Remove all the indicator and illumination bulb holders from the rear of the housing by turning them counterclockwise.
5 Refit the printed circuit assembly and instrument cluster, using the reverse procedure to removal.

40 Ignition switch - removal and replacement

1 The ignition switch is located on the upper side of the steering column under the shroud, and is operated by a rod connected to the key actuated lock cylinder.
2 To remove the switch, first remove the shrouding from the steering column (see Section 29).
3 Disconnect the battery ground terminal.
4 Pull apart the multi-plug electrical connector.
5 Remove the bolts securing the steering column to the brake support bracket and carefully lower the column.
6 Remove the two screws securing the ignition switch to the column.
7 Remove the pin that connects the switch plunger to the actuating rod and lift away the switch.
8 To adjust the switch during installation, first make sure that the locking mechanism at the top of the column and the switch itself are in the 'LOCK' position.

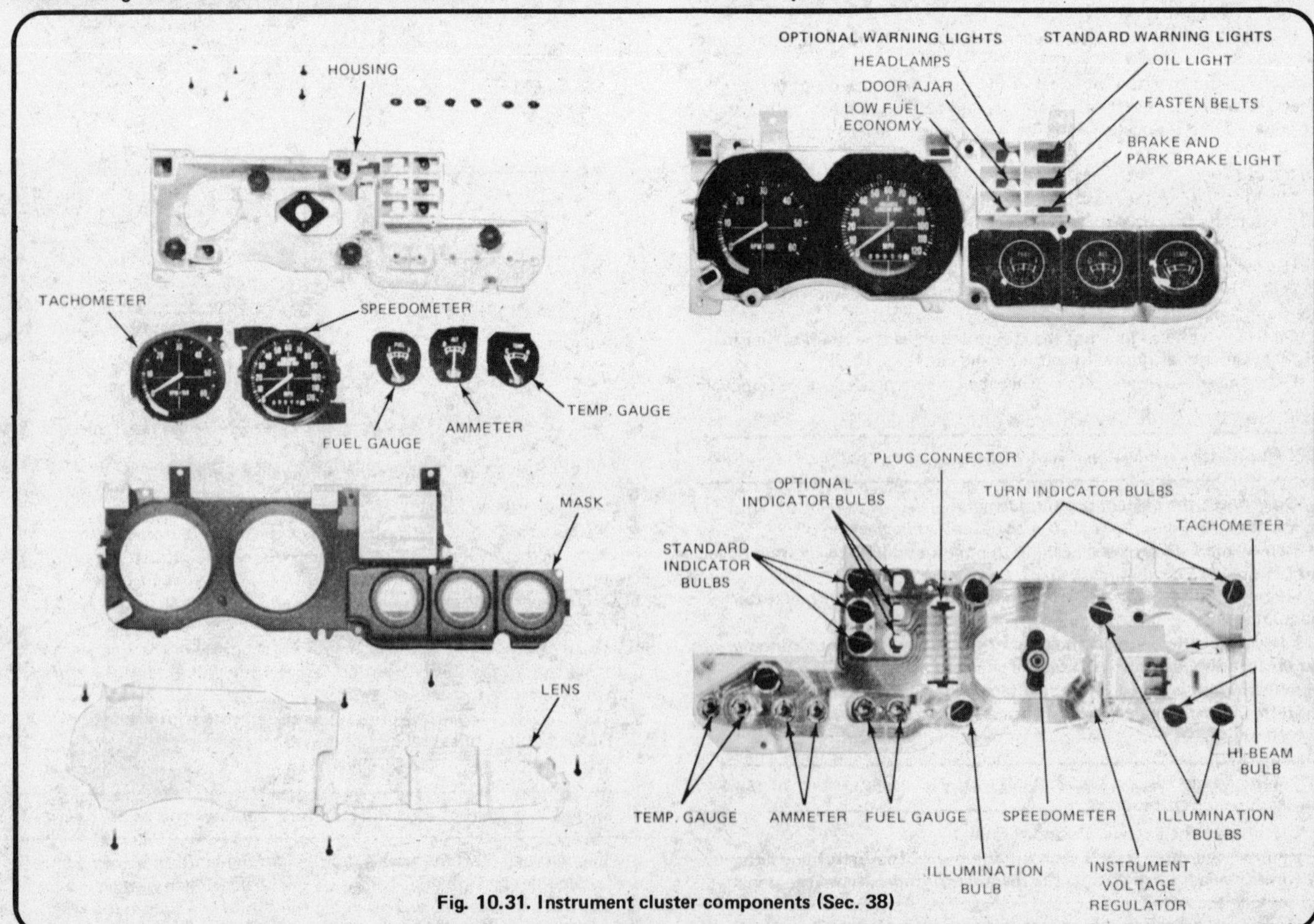

Fig. 10.31. Instrument cluster components (Sec. 38)

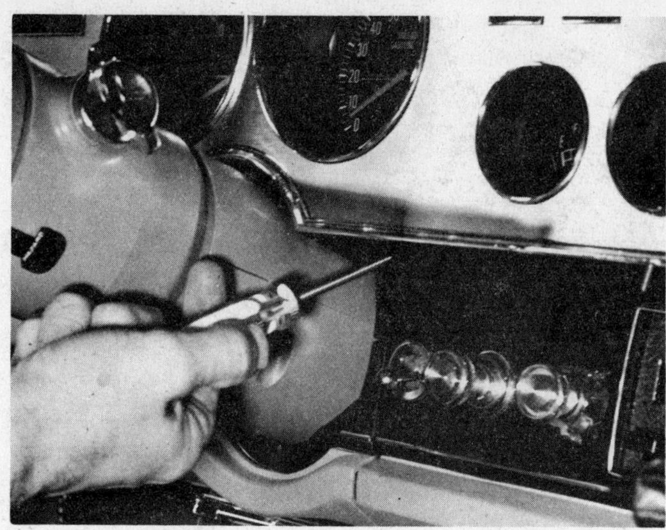

38.3A Removing lower instrument panel retaining screws

38.3B Removing upper instrument panel retaining screws

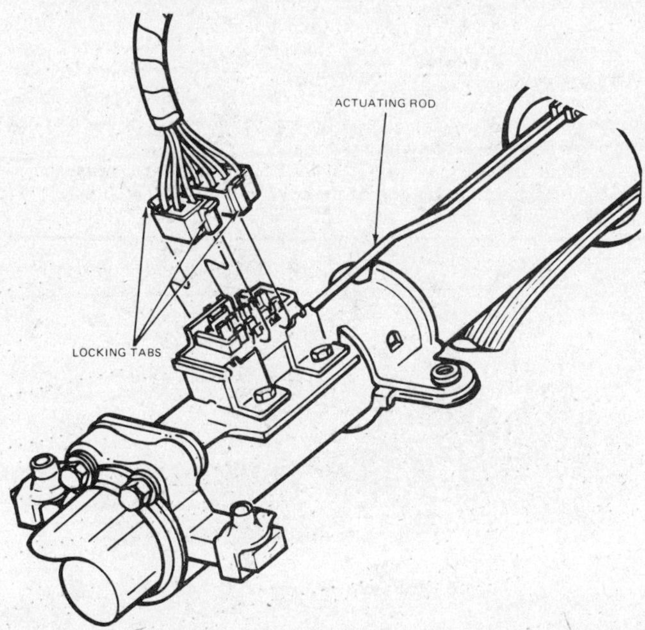

Fig. 10.32. Ignition switch and multi-pin wiring connector (Sec. 40)

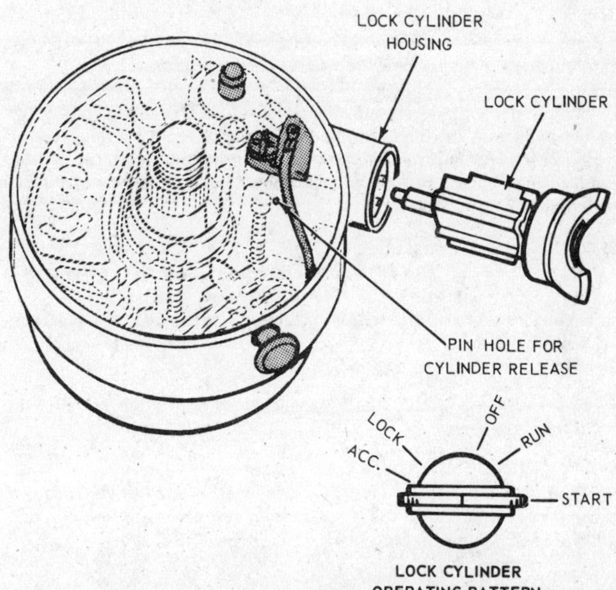

Fig. 10.33. Ignition lock cylinder (Sec. 41)

9 To hold the mechanical parts of the column in the 'LOCK' position move the selector lever to 'PARK' (automatic transmission) or to the reverse position (manual gearbox), turn the key to the 'LOCK' position and remove the key.
10 New replacement switches are supplied pinned in the 'LOCK' position by a plastic pin inserted in a locking hole on top of the switch.
11 Position the hole in the end of the switch up to the hole in the actuator, and install the connecting pin.
12 Position the switch on the column and replace the retaining nuts which should only be tightened finger tight at this stage.
13 Move the switch up and down along the column to locate the mid-position of the rod movement. Tighten the two retaining nuts.
14 Remove the plastic locking pin, reconnect the multi-plug and battery and check for correct starting in 'PARK' or 'NEUTRAL'.
15 Replace the column shrouds and support bracket using the reverse procedure to removal.

41 Ignition switch lock cylinder - removal and replacement

1 For safety reasons, disconnect the battery ground terminal.
2 Remove the horn pad and steering wheel as described in Chapter 11.
3 Insert a wire pin in the hole located inside the column halfway down the lock cylinder housing.
4 Move the selector lever to the 'PARK' position (automatic transmission) or the reverse position (manual gearbox) and turn the lock cylinder with the ignition key inserted to the 'RUN' position.
5 To remove the lock cylinder press the wire pin whilst pulling up on the lock cylinder.
6 To fit the lock cylinder insert it into its housing in the flange casing. Turn the key to the 'OFF' position. This action will extend the cylinder retaining pin into the cylinder housing.
7 Turn the key to ensure correct operation in all positions.
8 Refit the steering wheel and horn pad.

42 Seat belt and ignition warning buzzers - removal and replacement

1 The seat belt warning buzzer, and key-in-the ignition warning buzzer are located behind the right-hand side of the instrument panel.
2 Remove the three screws retaining the top of the right-hand side trim panel, unclip the lower fingers, and lift off the panel.

3 For safety reasons, remove the battery ground terminal.
4 Remove the buzzer retaining clips, lift out the buzzer unit and unplug the wiring connectors.
5 Refit the buzzer units using the reverse procedure.

43 Seat belt/starter interlock system

1 This system is installed on North American cars (not Canada) and is designed to prevent operation of the car unless the front seat belts have been fastened.
2 If either of the front seats is occupied and the seat belts have not been fastened, then, as the ignition key is turned to the 'II' (ignition on) position, a warning lamp will flash and a buzzer will sound.
3 If the warning is ignored, further turning of the key to the start position will not actuate the starter motor.
4 If a fault develops in the system, first check the fuse and then the security of all leads and connections.

44 Fuses

1 The fuse panel is located on the right-hand side of the steering column on a bracket attached to the pedal support (photo).
2 Most of the electrical circuits are protected by fuses and fuse identification is given in the caption to Fig. 10.34. If a fuse blows always trace the cause and rectify before renewing the fuse.

44.1 Location of fuse panel

45 Windshield wiper blades - removal and replacement

The windshield wiper blades fitted can be one of two types. With the bayonet type the blade saddle slides over the end of the arm and is engaged by a locking stud. With the side saddle pin type a pin on the arm indexes into the side of the blade saddle and engages a spring loaded clip in the saddle.

Bayonet type - 'TRICO'

1 To remove a 'TRICO' blade press down on the arm to disengage the top stud.
2 Depress the tab on the saddle to release the top stud and pull the blade from the arm.

Bayonet type - 'ANCO'

To remove an 'ANCO' blade press inwards on the tab and pull the blade from the arm.

Saddle pin type - 'TRICO'

To remove a pin type 'TRICO' blade insert a screwdriver into the spring release opening of the blade saddle, depress the spring clip and pull the blade from the arm.

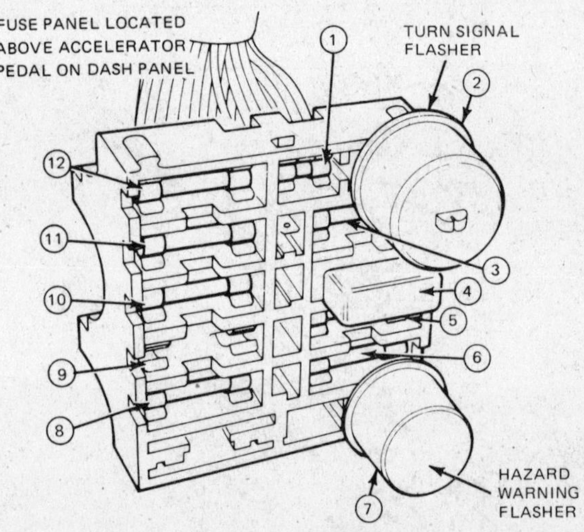

Fig. 10.34. Fuse panel assembly (Sec. 44)

1 (4 amp fuse) Cluster, heater or air conditioner control, radio, ashtray, and clock illumination lamps.
2 Turn signal flasher.
3 (7.5 amp fuse) Oil, brake, belts indicator lamps, seat belt, buzzer, throttle solenoid positioner, emission control solenoid.
4 (6.0 amp circuit breaker) Windshield wiper motor.
5 (15 amp fuse) Windshield washer motor, door ajar warning light, heater backlite control indicator lamp and anti-theft module, fuel-monitor indicating lamp.
6 (7.5 amp fuse) Radio/tape player.
7 Hazard flasher.
8 (20 amp fuse) Horn and cigar lighter.
9 (15 amp fuse) Dome light, glove box lamp, map lamp, trunk lamp, door, instrument panel, courtesy, key, headlamp-on warning buzzer and lamp, clock feed, anti-theft module, horn feed and seat belt warning system feed.
10 (15 amp fuse) Stop and hazard warning lamps.
11 (15 amp fuse) Heater motor power feed (with standard heater).
(30 amp fuse) Air conditioner motor power feed.
12 (15 amp fuse) Back-up lamps, turn signal lamps.

46 Windshield wiper arm - removal and replacement

1 Before removing a wiper arm, turn the windshield wiper switch on and off to ensure the arms are in their normal parked position parallel with the bottom of the windshield.
2 To remove the arm, swing the arm away from the windshield, depress the spring clips in the wiper arm boss and pull the arm off the spindle.
3 When replacing the arm, position it in the parked position and push the boss onto the spindle.

47 Windscreen wiper mechanism - fault diagnosis and rectification

1 Should the windscreen wipers fail, or work very slowly, then check the terminals on the motor for loose connections, and make sure the insulation of all the wiring is not cracked or broken, thus causing a short circuit. If this is in order then check the current the motor is taking by connecting an ammeter in the circuit and turning on the wiper switch. Consumption should be between 2.3 to 3.1 amps.
2 If no current is passing through the motor, check that the switch is operating correctly.
3 If the wiper motor takes a very high current check the wiper blades for freedom of movement. If this is satisfactory check the gearbox cover

and gear assembly for damage.
4 If the motor takes a very low current ensure that the battery is fully charged. Check the brush gear and ensure the brushes are bearing on the commutator. If not, check the brushes for freedom of movement and, if necessary, renew the tension springs. If the brushes are very worn they should be replaced with new ones. Check the armature by substitution if this unit is suspect.

48 Windshield wiper motor - removal and replacement

1 Slacken the two nuts and disconnect the wiper pivot shaft and link assembly from the motor drive arm ball.
2 Undo and remove the three bolts securing the motor to the underside of the left-hand side of the instrument panel.
3 Disconnect the multi-pin connector from the main wiring harness and lift away the motor.
4 Refitting the windshield wiper motor is the reverse sequence to removal.

49 Windshield wiper pivot shaft and link assembly - removal and replacement

1 Refer to Section 46, and remove the wiper arms and blades from the pivot shafts.
2 Slacken the two nuts securing the wiper pivot shaft and link assembly to the motor drive arm ball.
3 Undo and remove the three screws securing each pivot shaft assembly to the cowl inner plate.
4 Remove the pivot shaft and link assembly from under the left hand side of the instrument panel.
5 Refitting the wiper pivot shaft and link assembly is the reverse sequence to removal. Lubricate all moving parts with a little engine oil. The gaskets should be cemented to the pivots to stop any water leaks.

50 Windshield wiper switch - removal and replacement

1 Refer to Section 29 for removal and replacement of later type column mounted wiper switch. For instrument panel mounted switches, proceed as follows.
2 Insert a thin bladed screwdriver into the slot in the wiper switch knob and depress the spring. Then pull the knob from the wiper switch shaft.
3 Undo and remove the wiper switch bezel nut.
4 Make a note of and then unplug the wires from the rear of the switch. Lift away the switch.
5 Refitting the windshield wiper switch is the reverse sequence to removal.

51 Windshield wiper motor - dismantling, inspection and reassembly

1 Undo and remove the gear cover securing screws and lift away the ground terminal and cover (Fig. 10.37).
2 Carefully remove the idler gear and pinion retainer.
3 Lift away the idler gear and pinion and recover the thrust-washer.
4 Undo and remove the two long motor thru-bolts, and separate the housing, switch terminal insulator sleeve and armature.
5 Suitably mark the position of the output arm relative to the shaft to ensure correct reassembly.
6 Undo and remove the output arm retaining nut, output arm, spring washer, flat washer, output gearshaft assembly, thrust washer and parking switch lever and washer in that order.
7 Remove the brushes and brush springs.
8 Remove the brushplate and switch assembly and finally remove the switch contact to parking lever pin from the gear housing.
9 Thoroughly clean all parts and then inspect the gear housing for signs of cracks, distortion, or damage.
10 Carefully check all shafts, bushes and gears for signs of scoring or damage.
11 If the brushes are worn they should be renewed.
12 Any serious fault with the armature such as a breakdown in insulation necessitates a new motor assembly.
13 Reassembly of the windshield wiper motor is the reverse sequence to dismantling and will present no problems provided that care is taken.

52 Windshield washer nozzles - adjustment

1 To adjust the washer nozzles use a pair of thin-nosed pliers and carefully bend the nozzle in the required direction.
2 Do not squeeze the nozzle too hard otherwise it will be crimped closed.

53 Windshield washer reservoir and pump - removal and replacement

1 Remove the wiring connector plug and washer hose.
2 Undo and remove the retaining screws and lift the washer and motor assembly away from the left-hand side fender apron.
3 To remove the pump motor from the reservoir, pry out the retaining ring and carefully pull the motor out of the reservoir recess (See Fig. 10.38).
4 The motor and pump assembly cannot be repaired, and if faulty must be replaced with a new unit.
5 When refitting the motor into the reservoir, make sure the projection on the motor body is lined up with the slot in the reservoir.
6 Press on the motor retaining ring and refit the reservoir assembly to the car using the reverse procedure to removal.

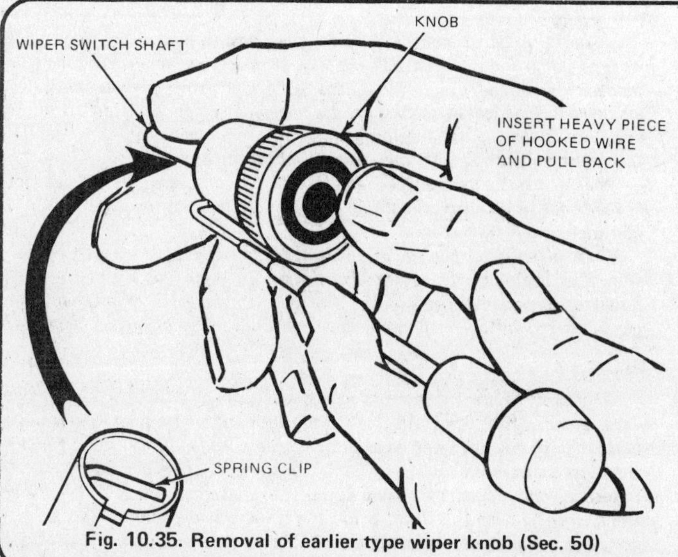

Fig. 10.35. Removal of earlier type wiper knob (Sec. 50)

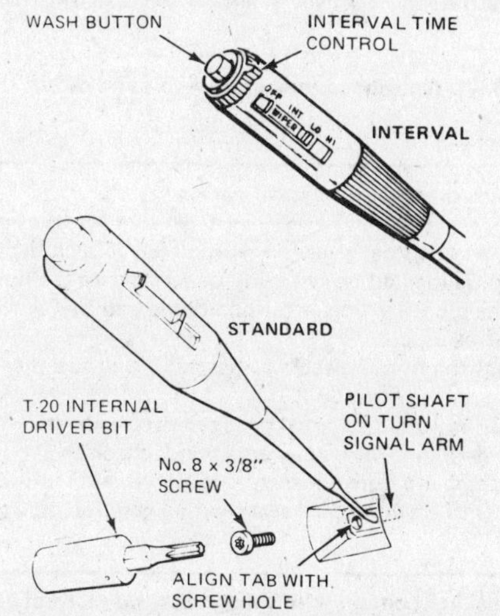

Fig. 10.36. Later type of wiper switch (Sec. 50)

10

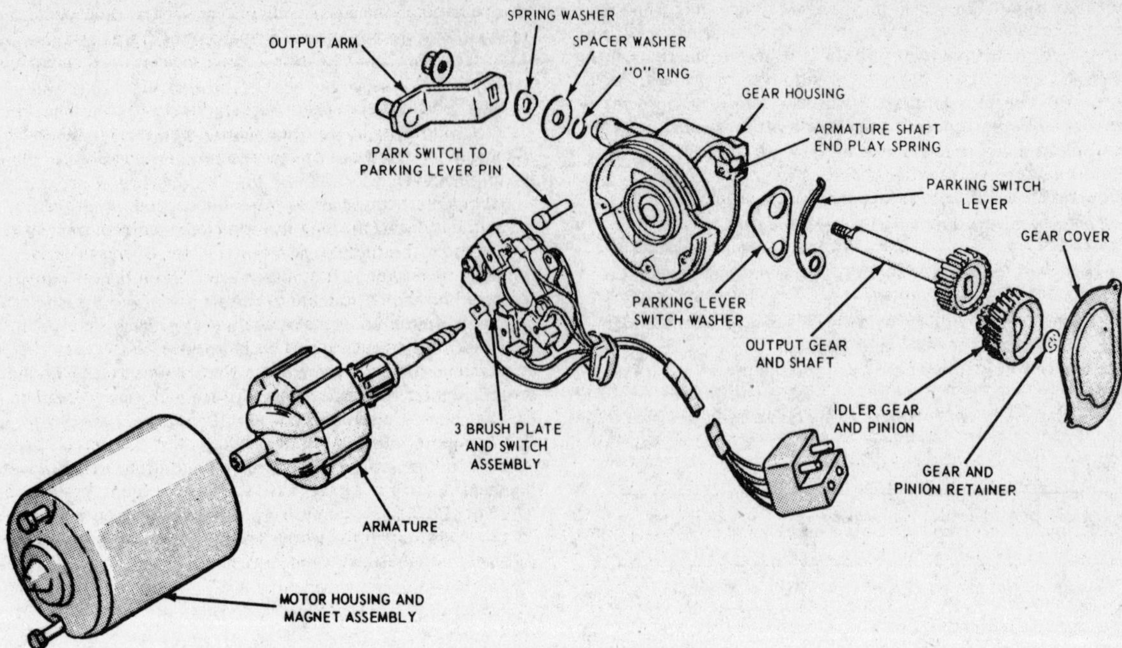

Fig. 10.37. Windshield wiper motor components (Sec. 51)

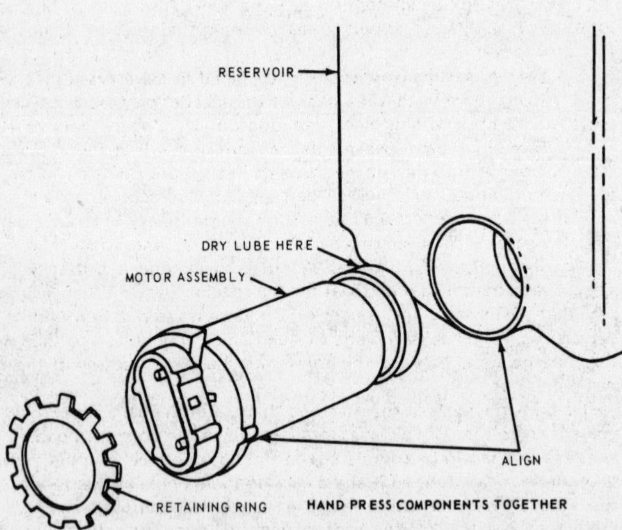

Fig. 10.38. Windshield washer reservoir and motor (Sec. 53)

54 Horn - fault diagnosis and rectification

1 If the horn works badly or fails completely, check the wiring leading to the horn plug located on the body panel next to the horn itself. Also check that the plug is properly pushed home and is in a clean condition free from corrosion etc.

2 Check that the horn is secure on its mounting and that there is nothing lying on the horn body.

3 If the fault is not an external one, remove the horn cover and check the leads inside the horn. If they are sound, check the contact breaker contacts. If these are burnt or dirty clean them with a fine file and wipe all traces of dirt and dust away with a gasoline moistened rag.

55 Turn signal light circuit - fault diagnosis and rectification

Should the flasher unit fail to operate, or work very slowly or rapidly, check out the turn signal circuit as detailed below, before assuming that there is a fault in the unit.

1 Examine the turn signal light bulbs, both front and rear, for broken filaments.

2 If the external flashers are working but either of the internal flasher warning lights have ceased to function, check the filaments in the warning light bulbs and replace with a new bulb if necessary.

3 If a flasher bulb is sound but does not work check all the flasher circuit connections with the aid of the relevant wiring diagram at the end of this Chapter.

4 With the ignition switched on check that the correct voltage is reaching the flasher unit by connecting a voltmeter between the 'plus' terminal and ground. If it is found that voltage is correct at the unit connect the two flasher unit terminals together and operate the turn signal switch. If one of the flasher warning lights comes on this proves that the flasher unit itself is at fault and must be renewed as it is not possible to dismantle and repair it.

56 Radios and tape players - fitting (general)

A radio or tape player is an expensive item to buy and will only give its best performance if fitted properly. It is useless to expect concert hall performance from a unit that is suspended from the dash panel on string with its speaker resting on the back seat or parcel shelf! If you do not wish to do the installation yourself there are many in-car entertainment specialists' who can do the fitting for you.

Make sure the unit purchased is of the same polarity as the car, and ensure that units with adjustable polarity are correctly set before commencing installation.

It is difficult to give specific information with regard to fitting, as final positioning of the radio/tape player, speakers and aerial is entirely a matter of personal preference. However, the following paragraphs give guidelines to follow, which are relevant to all installations.

Radios

Most radios are a standardised size of 7 inches wide, by 2 inches deep - this ensures that they will fit into the radio aperture provided in most cars. If your car does not have such an aperture, then the radio must be fitted in a suitable position either in, or beneath, the dashpanel. Alternatively, a special console can be purchased which will fit between the dashpanel and the floor, or on the transmission tunnel These consoles can also be used for additional switches and instrumentation if required. Where no radio aperture is provided, the following points should be borne in mind before deciding exactly where to fit the unit:

a) *The unit must be within easy reach of the driver wearing a seat belt.*
b) *The unit must not be mounted in close proximity to an electric tachometer, the ignition switch and its wiring or the flasher unit and associated wiring.*
c) *The unit must be mounted within reach of the aerial lead, and in such a place that the aerial lead will not have to be routed near the components detailed in the preceding paragraph 'b'.*
d) *The unit should not be positioned in a place where it might cause injury to the car occupants in an accident; for instance, under the dashpanel above the driver's or passengers' legs.*
e) *The unit must be fitted really securely.*

Some radios will have mounting brackets provided together with instructions: others will need to be fitted using drilled and slotted metal strips, bent to form mounting brackets - these strips are available from most accessory shops. The unit must be properly grounded, by fitting separate grounding leads between the casing of the radio and the vehicle frame.

Use the radio manufacturers' instructions when wiring the radio into the vehicle's electrical system. If no instructions are available refer to the relevant wiring diagram to find the location of the radio 'feed' connection in the vehicle's wiring circuit. A 1- 2 amp 'in-line' fuse must be fitted in the radio's 'feed' wire - a choke may also be necessary (see next Section).

The type of aerial used, and its fitted position is a matter of personal preference. In general the taller the aerial, the better the reception. It is best to fit a fully retractable aerial - especially, if a mechanical car-wash is used or if you live in an area where cars tend to be vandalized. In this respect electric aerials which are raised and lowered automatically when switching the radio on or off are convenient, but are more likely to give trouble than the manual type.

When choosing a site for the aerial the following points should be considered:

a) *The aerial lead should be as short as possible - this means that the aerial should be mounted at the front of the car.*
b) *The aerial must be mounted as far away from the distributor and HT leads as possible.*
c) *The part of the aerial which protrudes beneath the mounting point must not foul the roadwheels, or anything else.*
d) *If possible the aerial should be positioned so that the coaxial lead does not have to be routed through the engine compartment.*
e) *The plane of the panel on which the aerial is mounted should not be so steeply angled that the aerial cannot be mounted vertically (in relation to the 'end-on' aspect of the car). Most aerials have a small amount of adjustment available.*

Having decided on a mounting position, a relatively large hole will have to be made in the panel. The exact size of the hole will depend upon the specific aerial being fitted, although, generally, the hole required is of ¾ inch (19 mm) diameter. On metal bodied cars, a 'tank-cutter' of the relevant diameter is the best tool to use for making the hole. This tool needs a small diameter pilot hole drilled through the panel, through which, the tool clamping bolt is inserted. When the hole has been made the raw edges should be de-burred with a file and then painted, to prevent corrosion.

Fit the aerial according to the manufacturer's instructions. If the aerial is very tall, or if it protrudes beneath the mounting panel for a considerable distance it is a good idea to fit a stay between the aerial and the vehicle frame. This stay can be manufactured from the slotted and drilled metal strips previously mentioned. The stay should be securely screwed or bolted in place. For best reception it is advisable to fit a ground lead between the aerial and the vehicle frame.

It will probably be necessary to drill one or two holes through bodywork panels in order to feed the aerial lead into the interior of the car. Where this is the case ensure that the holes are fitted with rubber grommets to protect the cable, and to stop possible entry of water.

Positioning and fitting of the speaker depends mainly on its type. Generally, the speaker is designed to fit directly into the aperture already provided in the car (usually in the shelf behind the rear seats, or in the top of the dashpanel). Where this is the case, fitting the speaker is just a matter of removing the protective grille from the aperture and screwing or bolting the speaker in place. Take great care not to damage the speaker diaphragm whilst doing this. It is a good idea to fit a 'gasket' between the speaker frame and the mounting panel, in order to prevent vibration - some speakers will already have such a gasket fitted.

If a 'pod' type speaker was supplied with the radio, the best acoustic results will normally be obtained by mounting it on the shelf behind the rear seat. The pod can be secured to the mounting panel with self-tapping screws.

When connecting a rear mounted speaker to the radio, the wires should be routed through the vehicle beneath the carpets or floor mats - preferably the middle, or along the side of the floorpan, where they will not be trodden on by passengers. Make the relevant connections as directed by the radio manufacturer.

By now you will have several yards of additional wiring in the car, use PVC tape to secure this wiring out of harm's way. Do not leave electrical leads dangling. Ensure that all new electrical connections are properly made (wires twisted together will not do) and completely secure.

The radio should now be working, but before you pack away your tools it will be necessary to 'trim' the radio to the aerial. If specific instructions are not provided by the radio manufacturer, proceed as follows. Find a station with a low signal strength on the medium-wave band, slowly, turn the trim screw of the radio in, or out, until the loudest reception of the selected station is obtained - the set is then trimmed to the aerial.

Tape players

Fitting instructions for both cartridge and cassette stereo tape players are the same and in general the same rules apply as when fitting a radio. Tape players are not usually prone to electrical interference like radio - although it can occur - so positioning is not so critical. If possible the player should be mounted on an 'even-keel'. Also, it must be possible for a driver wearing a seat belt to reach the unit in order to change or turn over tapes.

For the best results from speakers designed to be recessed into a panel, mount them so that the back of the speaker protrudes into an enclosed chamber within the car (eg, door interiors or the boot cavity).

To fit recessed type speakers in the front doors, first check that there is sufficient room to mount the speakers in each door without it fouling the latch or window winding mechanism. Hold the speaker against the skin of the door, and draw a line around the periphery of the speaker. With the speaker removed draw a second 'cutting' line, within the first, to allow enough room for the entry of the speaker back, but at the same time providing a broad seat for the speaker flange. When you are sure that the 'cutting-line' is correct, drill a series of holes around its periphery. Pass a hacksaw blade through one of the holes and then cut through the metal between the holes until the center section of the panel falls out.

De-burr the edges of the hole and then paint the bare metal to prevent corrosion. Cut a corresponding hole in the door trim panel - ensuring that it will be completely covered by the speaker grille. Now drill a hole in the door edge and a corresponding hole in the door surround. These holes are to feed the speaker leads through - so fit grommets. Pass the speaker leads through the door trim, door skin and out through the holes in the side of the door and door surround. Refit the door trim panel and then secure the speaker to the door using self-tapping screws. **Note:** If the speaker is fitted with a shield to prevent water dripping on it, ensure that this shield is at the top.

Pod type speakers can be fastened to the shelf behind the rear seat, or anywhere else offering a corresponding mounting point on each side of the car. If the pod speakers are mounted on each side of the shelf behind the rear seat, it is a good idea to drill several large diameter holes through to the boot cavity beneath each speaker - this will improve the sound reproduction. Pod speakers sometimes offer a better reproduction quality if they face the rear window - which then acts as a reflector - so it is worthwhile to do a little experimenting before finally fixing the speaker.

57 Radios and tape players - suppression of interference (general)

To eliminate buzzes and other unwanted noises, costs very little and is not as difficult as sometimes thought. With a modicum of common sense and patience and following the instructions in the following paragraphs, interference can be virtually eliminated.

The first cause for concern is the generator. The noise this makes over the radio is like an electric mixer and the noise speeds up when you rev up (if you wish to prove the point, you can remove the drive-belt and try it). The remedy for this is simple; connect a 1.0 uf -3.0 uf capacitor between ground, probably the bolt that holds down the generator base and the *large* terminal on the alternator. This is most important for if you connect it to the small terminal you will probably damage the generator permanently (See Fig. 10.39).

A second common cause of electrical interference is the ignition system. Here a 1.0 ohm capacitor must be connected between ground and the 'SW' or '+' terminal on the coil (see Fig. 10.40). This may stop the tick-tick-tick sound that comes over the speaker. Next comes the spark itself.

There are several ways of curing interference from the ignition HT system. One is to use carbon film HT leads but these have a tendency to 'snap' inside and you don't know then, why you are firing on only half your cylinders. So the second, and more successful method is to use resistive spark plug caps (see Fig. 10.41) of about 10,000 ohm to 15,000 ohm resistance. If, due to lack of room, these cannot be used, an alternative is to use 'in-line' suppressors (Fig. 10.41). - if the interference is not too bad, you may get away with only one suppressor in the coil to distributor line. If the interference does continue (a 'clacking' noise) then doctor all HT leads.

At this stage it is advisable to check that the radio is well earthed, also the aerial, and to see that the aerial plug is pushed well into the set and that the radio is properly trimmed (see preceding Section). In addition, check that the wire which supplies the power to the set is as short as possible and does not wander all over the car. At this stage it is a good idea to check that the fuse is of the correct rating. For most sets this will be about 1 to 2 amps.

At this point the more usual causes of interference have been suppressed. If the problem still exists, a look at the causes of interference may help to pinpoint the component generating the stray electrical discharges.

The radio picks up electromagnetic waves in the air; now some are made by radio stations and other broadcasters and some, not wanted, are made by the car. The home made signals are produced by stray electrical discharges floating around the car. Common producers of these signals are electric motors; ie, the windshield wipers, electric screen washers, electric window winders, heater fan or an electric aerial if fitted. Other sources of interference are electric fuel pumps, flashing turn signals, and instruments. The remedy for these cases is shown in Fig. 10.42 for an electric motor whose interference is not too bad and Fig. 10.43 for instrument suppression. Turn signals are not normally suppressed. In recent years, radio manufacturers have included in the line (live) of the radio, in addition to the fuse, an 'in-line' choke.

All the foregoing components are available from radio shops or accessory shops. If you have an electric clock fitted this should be suppressed by connecting a 0.5 uf capacitor directly across it as shown for a motor in Fig. 10.42.

If after all this, you are still experiencing radio interference, first assess how bad it is, for the human ear can filter out unobtrusive unwanted noises quite easily. But if you are still adamant about eradicating the noise, then continue.

As a first step, a few 'experts' seem to favor a screen between the radio and the engine. This is O.K. as far as it goes, literally! - for the

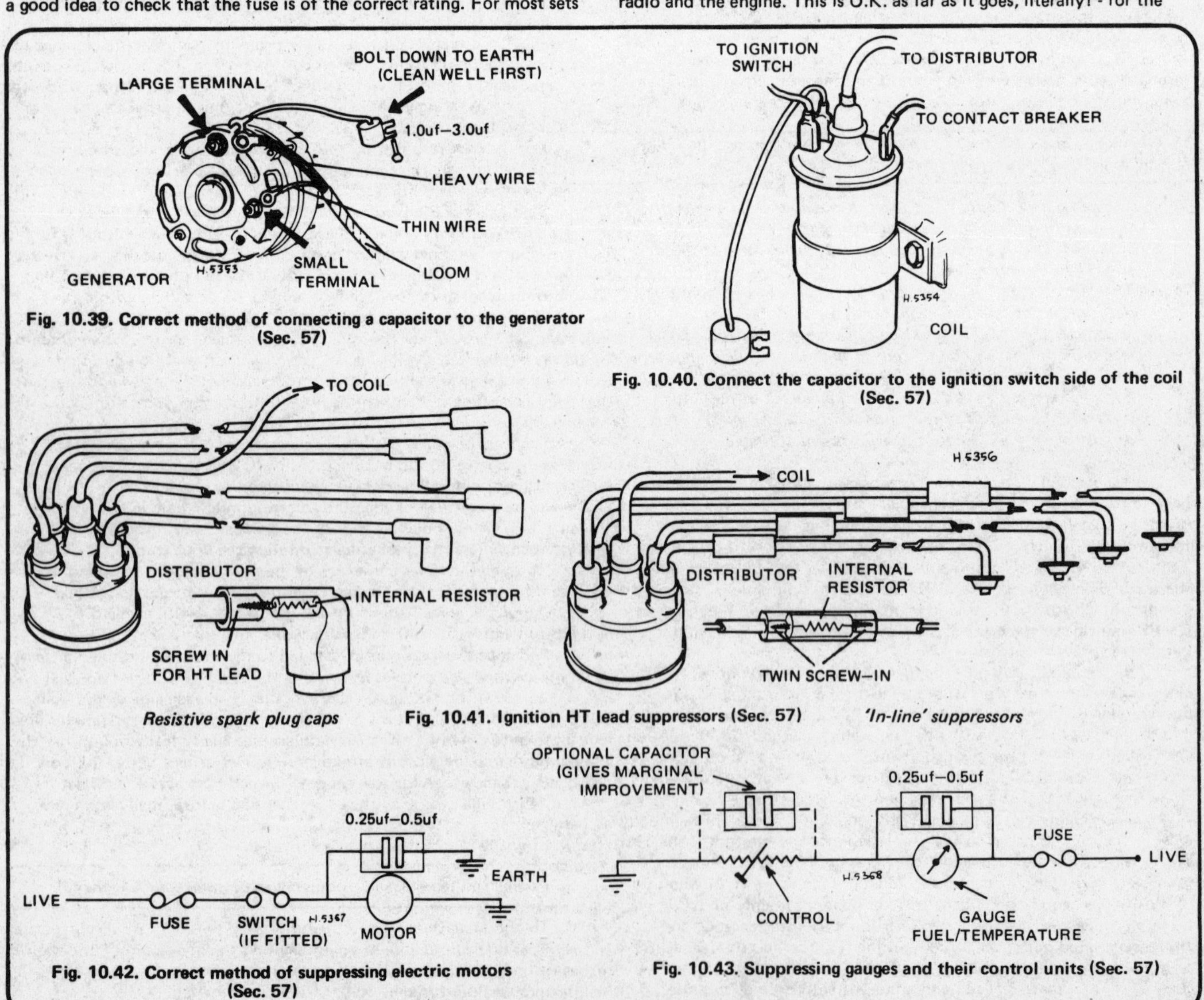

Fig. 10.39. Correct method of connecting a capacitor to the generator (Sec. 57)

Fig. 10.40. Connect the capacitor to the ignition switch side of the coil (Sec. 57)

Resistive spark plug caps **Fig. 10.41. Ignition HT lead suppressors (Sec. 57)** *'In-line' suppressors*

Fig. 10.42. Correct method of suppressing electric motors (Sec. 57)

Fig. 10.43. Suppressing gauges and their control units (Sec. 57)

whole set is screened and if interference can get past that then a small piece of aluminum is not going to stop it.

A more sensible way of screening is to discover if interference is coming down the wires. First, take the live lead, interference can get between the set and the choke (hence the reason for keeping the wires short). One remedy here is to screen the wire and this is done by buying screened wire and fitting that. The loudspeaker lead could be screened also to prevent 'pick-up' getting back to the radio - although this is unlikely.

Without doubt, the worst source of radio interference comes from the ignition HT leads, even if they have been suppressed. The ideal way of supressing these is to slide screening tubes over the leads themselves. As this is impractical, we can place an aluminium shield over the majority of the lead areas. In a vee - or twin-cam engine, this is relatively easy but for a straight engine the results are not particularly good.

Now for the really impossible cases, here are a few tips to try out. Where metal comes into contact with metal, an electrical disturbance is caused which is why good clean connections are essential. To remove interference due to overlapping or butting panels you must bridge the join with a wide braided ground strap (like that from the frame to the engine/transmission). The most common moving parts that could create noise and should be strapped are, in order of importance:

a) Muffler to frame.
b) Exhaust pipe to engine block and frame.
c) Air cleaner to frame.
d) Front and rear bumpers to frame.
e) Steering column to frame.
f) Hood and trunk lids to frame.
g) Hood frame to frame on soft tops.

These faults are most pronounced when (a) the engine is idling, (b) labouring under load. Although the moving parts are already connected with nuts, bolts, etc, these do tend to rust and corrode, thus creating a high resistance interference source.

If you have a 'ragged' sounding pulse when mobile, this could be wheel or tire static. This can be cured by buying some anti-static powder and sprinkling it liberally inside the tires.

If the interference takes the shape of a high pitched screeching noise that changes its note when the car is in motion and only comes now and then, this could be related to the aerial, especially if it is of the telescopic or whip type. This source can be cured quite simply by pushing a small rubber ball on top of the aerial (yes, really) as this breaks the electric field before it can form; but it would be much better to buy yourself a new aerial of a reputable brand. If, on the other hand, you are getting a loud rushing sound every time you brake, then this is brake static. This effect is most prominent on hot dry days and is cured only by fitting a special kit, which is quite expensive.

In conclusion, it is pointed out that it is relatively easy, and therefore cheap to eliminate 95 per cent of all noises, but to eliminate the final 5 per cent is time and money consuming. It is up to the individual to decide if it is worth it. Please remember also, that you will not get concert hall performance from a cheap radio.

Finally at the beginning of this Section are mentioned tape players; these are not usually affected by interference but in a very bad case, the best remedies are the first three suggestions plus using 3 - 5 amp choke in the 'live' line and in incurable cases screen the live and speaker wires.

Note: If your car is fitted with electronic ignition (1976 on) then it is not recommended that either the spark plug resistors or the ignition coil capacitor be fitted as these may damage the system. Most electronic ignition units have built-in suppression and should, therefore, not cause interference.

58 Fault diagnosis - electrical system

Symptom	Reason/s
No voltage at starter motor	Battery discharged. Battery defective internally. Battery terminal leads loose or ground lead not securely attached to body. Loose or broken connections in starter motor circuit. Starter motor switch or solenoid faulty.
Voltage at starter motor: faulty motor	Starter brushes badly worn, sticking, or brush wires loose. Commutator dirty, worn or burnt. Starter motor armature faulty. Field coils grounded.
Electrical defects	Battery in discharged condition. Starter brushes badly worn, sticking, or brush wires loose. Loose wires in starter motor circuit.
Dirt or oil on drive gear	Starter motor pinion sticking on the screwed sleeve.
Mechanical damage	Pinion or flywheel gear teeth broken or worn.
Lack of attention or mechanical damage	Pinion or flywheel gear teeth broken or worn. Starter drive main spring broken. Starter motor retaining bolts loose.
Wear or damage	Battery defective internally. Electrolyte level too low or electrolyte too weak due to leakage. Plate separators no longer fully effective. Battery plates severely sulphated.
Insufficient current flow to keep battery charged	Fan belt slipping. Battery terminal connections loose or corroded. Alternator not charging properly. Short in lighting circuit causing continual battery drain. Regulator unit not working correctly.
Alternator not charging *	Fan belt loose and slipping, or broken. Brushes worn, sticking, broken or dirty. Brush springs weak or broken.

* *If all appears to be well but the alternator is still not charging, take the car to an automobile electrician for checking of the alternator and regulator.*

Symptoms	Reason/s
Battery will not hold charge for more than a few days	Battery defective internally. Electrolyte level too low or electrolyte too weak due to leakage. Plate separators no longer fully effective. Battery plates severely sulphated. Fan/alternator belt slipping. Battery terminal connections loose or corroded. Alternator not charging properly. Short in lighting circuit causing continual battery drain. Regulator unit not working correctly.
Ignition light fails to go out, battery runs flat in a few days	Fan belt loose and slipping or broken. Alternator faulty.

Failure of individual electrical equipment to function correctly is dealt with alphabetically, below.

Symptoms	Reason/s
Fuel gauge gives no reading	Fuel tank empty! Eelctrical cable between tank sender unit and gauge grounded or loose. Fuel gauge case not grounded. Fuel gauge supply cable interrupted. Fuel gauge unit broken.
Fuel gauge registers full all the time	Electric cable between tank unit and gauge broken or disconnected.
Horn operates all the time	Horn push either grounded or stuck down. Horn cable to horn push grounded.
Horn fails to operate	Blown fuse. Cable or cable connection loose, broken or disconnected. Horn has an internal fault.
Horn emits intermittent or unsatisfactory noise	Cable connections loose. Horn incorrectly adjusted.
Lights do not come on	If engine not running, battery discharged. Light bulb filament burnt out or bulbs broken. Wire connections loose, disconnected or broken. Light switch shorting or otherwise faulty.
Lights come on but fade out	If engine not running battery discharged.
Lights give very poor illumination	Lamp glasses dirty. Reflector tarnished or dirty. Lamps badly out of adjustment. Incorrect bulb with too low wattage fitted. Existing wiring too thin not allowing full current to pass.
Lights work erratically - flashing on and off, especially over bumps	Battery terminals or ground connection loose. Lights not grounding properly. Contacts in light switch faulty.
Wiper motor fails to work	Blown fuse. Wire connections loose, disconnected or broken. Brushes badly worn Armature worn or faulty. Field coils faulty.
Wiper motor works very slowly and takes excessive current	Commutator dirty, greasy or burnt. Drive to spindles too bent or unlubricated. Drive spindle binding or damaged. Armature bearings dry or unaligned. Armature badly worn or faulty.
Wiper motor works slowly and takes little current	Brushes badly worn. Commutator dirty, greasy or burnt. Armature disengaged or faulty.
Wiper motor works but wiper blades remain static	Linkage disengaged or faulty. Drive spindle damaged or worn. Wiper motor gearbox parts badly worn.

Key to wiring diagrams, models thru 1976 (Figs. 10.44 thru 10.52 on pages 168 thru 185). For later models see Chapter 13

Components	Location		Components	Location		Components	Location		Components	Location	
Actuator			Dual brake warning			Modulator			Switch		
Horn warning	6	B7	indicator	2	B13	Breakerless ignition	2	C10	A/C mode	8	A13
Alternator	2	A1	Engine compartment	6	B3	Motor			Ambient temperature		
Alternator	2	B4	Glove box switch	7	C6	Blower	8	E10	sensor	8	C15
61 Amp	2	B3	Headlamp "ON"			Blower	8	E13	Anti-theft deck lid	7	D1
Ammeter	3	C8	warning indicator	6	D5	Starter	2	B7	Back window		
Backlite			Heated backlight			W/S washer pump	7	F9	Heater control	3	C10
Heated	3	D14	warning indicator	3	E12	W/S washer pump	7	D16	Backup lamp	5	A16
Battery			Heater controls			W/S wiper	7	E11	Backup lamp	5	A15
12 volt	1	B3	illumination	9	C6	W/S wiper	7	E14	Courtesy lamp	6	C9
12 volt	2	B5	Hi beam indicator	4	E1	Panel			Courtesy lamp	6	E16
Buzzer			I/P ash tray illumination	9	D3	Fuse	1	A1	Door open warning		
Key reminder	6	E4	L.H. backup	5	D4	Receiver			lamp	6	E1
Capacitor			L.H. front door			AM radio	8	B1	Door open warning		
Radio ignition			courtesy	6	D11	AM radio	9	D9	lamp	6	E2
interference	2	F3	L.H. front side marker	4	D11	AM/FM monaural radio	8	B2	Door lock cylinder	6	E6
Choke			L.H. license	5	D8	AM/FM monaural radio	9	D10	Door lock cylinder	6	E7
Electric	2	C3	L.H. Lo beam head	4	D9	AM/FM/MPX radio	8	B4	Dual brake warning	2	E13
Radio receiver			L.H. rear side marker	5	D1	AM/FM/MPX radio	9	D11	Gear shift neutral	3	D2
Suppression	3	D6	L.H. T/S	5	D5	Stero tape AM/FM/MPX			Gear shift neutral	5	A13
Clock	7	C6	L.H. front park and T/S	4	D10	radio	8	B6	Headlamp	1	C7
Coil			L.H. I/P courtesy	6	E13	Stero tape AM/FM/MPX			Headlamp	4	C1
Ignition	2	E11	L.H. stop and park	5	D2	radio	9	D12	Headlamp	6	B5
Distributor			L.H. stop and park	5	D6	Regulator			Headlamp dimmer	4	D1
2.3 liter breakerless	2	D5	L.H. turn indicator	4	E4	Alternator	2	E1	Heater blower	8	C10
2.8 liter breakerless	2	E4	Luggage compartment	7	D2	Instrument cluster			Heater mode	8	B10
8 cyl. 302 breakerless	2	F5	Oil pressure			voltage	3	D6	Horn	8	B8
Flasher			warning indicator	2	C14	Relay			Ignition	1	D4
Emergency warning	4	C7	PRNCL illumination			Back window heat			Ignition	3	C4
Turn signal	4	C6	(floor)	9	C15	control	3	A13	Ignition key warning	6	F4
Gauge			R.H. backup	5	D13	Headlamp on warning	6	D3	Oil pressure	2	E14
Fuel	3	B6	R.H. front door			Starter motor	1	A4	Park brake signal		
Governor			courtesy	6	E15	Resistor			lamp	3	D7
W/S wiper	7	C10	R.H. front side marker	4	D15	Blower motor	8	D9	Rear hatch		
Heater			R.H. license	5	D9	Blower motor	8	D12	courtesy lamp	7	C3
Engine block	3	D16	R.H. Lo beam head	4	D13	Sender			Seat belt retractor	7	E8
Horn			R.H. rear side marker	5	D16	Fuel gauge	3	D5	Seat belt warning		
Low pitch	8	E8	R.H. T/S	5	D12	Solenoid			indicator	7	C7
Lamp			R.H. front park & T/S	4	D14	A/C clutch	8	E15	Stop lamp	4	C3
A/C & heater			R.H. I/P courtesy	6	E14	Carb. throttle			Turn and emergency		
controls illumination	9	C7	R.H. stop and park	5	D10	Emission control	2	C11	signal	4	C4
Clock illumination	9	D1	R.H. stop and park	5	D14	Speaker			W/S/W washer	7	A15
Clock illumination	9	D4	R.H. turn indicator	4	E5	Radio receiver	8	E2	W/S/W washer	7	B10
Cluster illumination (4)	9	C13	Seat belts warning			Radio receiver			Water temperature	2	E15
Dome	6	E10	indicator	7	E7	rear seat	8	F4	A/C control	8	C12
Dome/map switches	7	D4	Water temp. warning ind.	2	C15	Radio receiver			Tachometer		
Door open warning			Lighter			rear seat	8	F6	Solid state	3	F2
indicator	6	B1	Cigar	6	C2						

Wiring color key (primary colors)

BK	Black	P	Purple	W	White	DG	Dark Green
BR	Brown	PK	Pink	Y	Yellow	LG	Light Green
GY	Gray	R	Red	DB	Dark Blue	(D)	Dot
O	Orange	T	Tan	LB	Light Blue	(H)	Hash

Stripe is understood

Fig. 10.44. Wiring diagram - Power distribution (continued on page 169). See page 167 for 'Key'

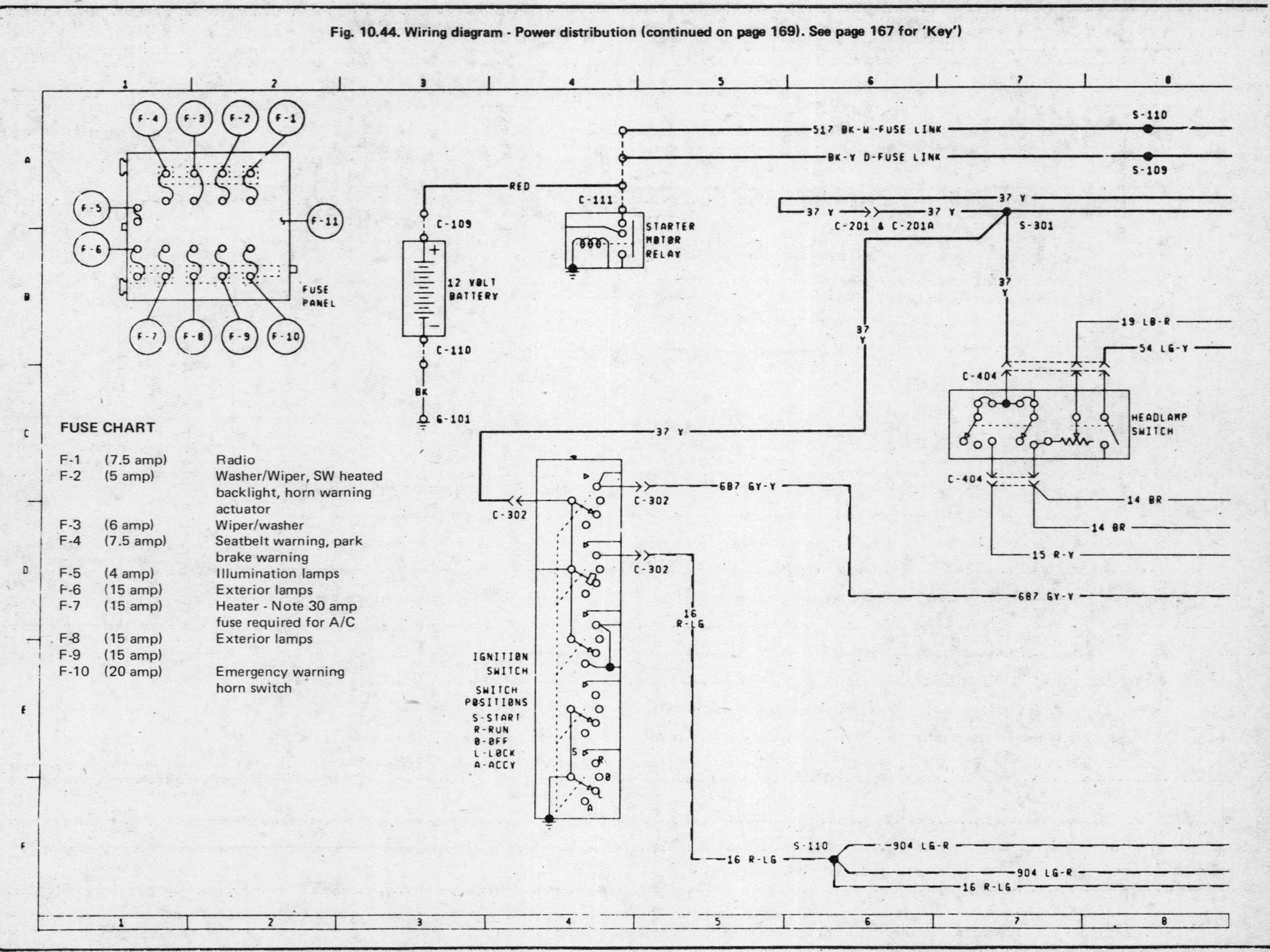

FUSE CHART

F-1	(7.5 amp)	Radio
F-2	(5 amp)	Washer/Wiper, SW heated backlight, horn warning actuator
F-3	(6 amp)	Wiper/washer
F-4	(7.5 amp)	Seatbelt warning, park brake warning
F-5	(4 amp)	Illumination lamps
F-6	(15 amp)	Exterior lamps
F-7	(15 amp)	Heater - Note 30 amp fuse required for A/C
F-8	(15 amp)	Exterior lamps
F-9	(15 amp)	
F-10	(20 amp)	Emergency warning horn switch

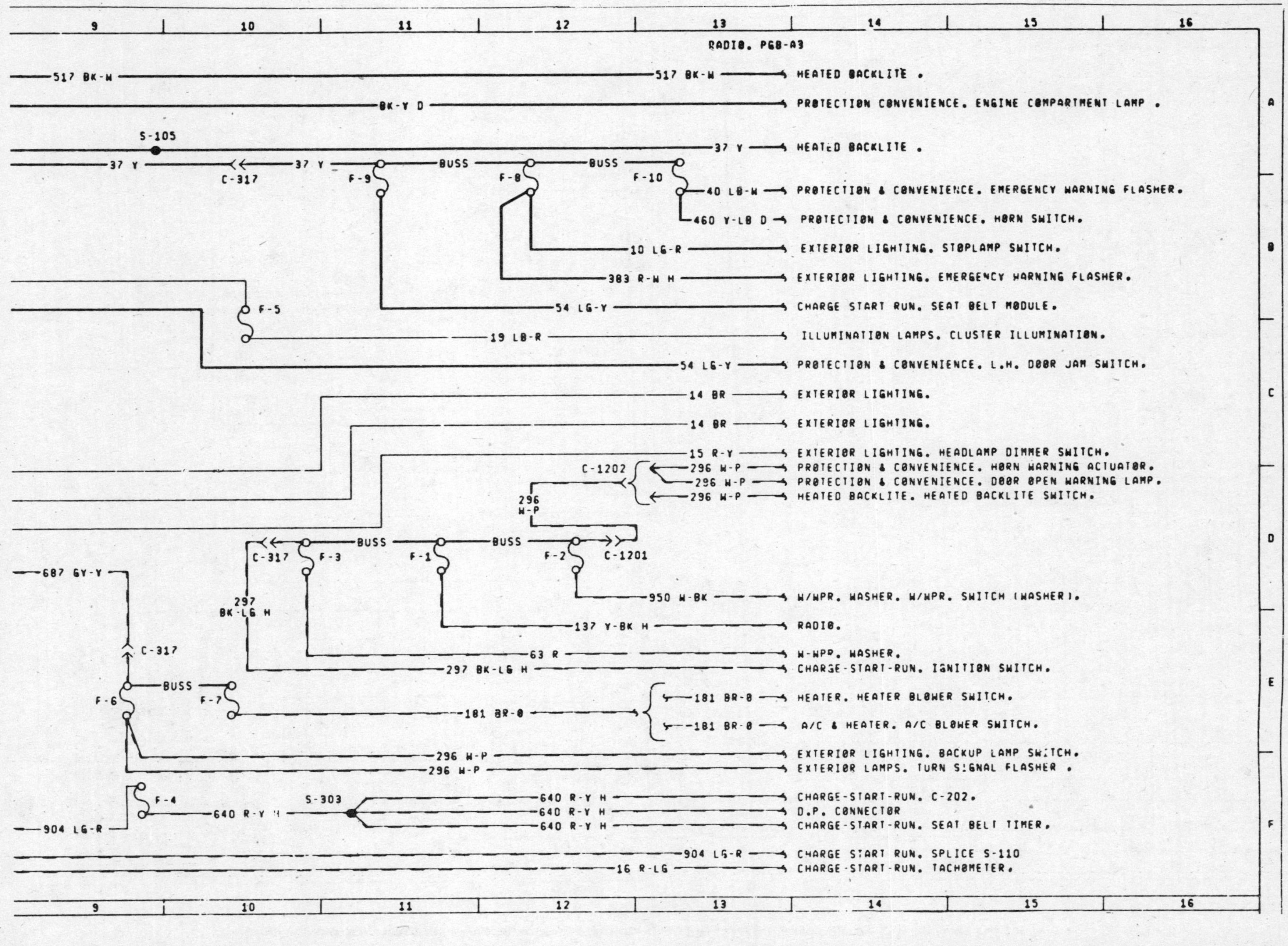

9 10 11 12 13 14 15 16
RADIO. PG8-A3
517 BK-W
517 BK-W HEATED BACKLITE .
BK-Y D PROTECTION CONVENIENCE. ENGINE COMPARTMENT LAMP .
S-105
37 Y HEATED BACKLITE .
37 Y
C-317
37 Y
F-9
BUSS
F-8
BUSS
F-10
40 LB-W PROTECTION & CONVENIENCE. EMERGENCY WARNING FLASHER.
460 Y-LB D PROTECTION & CONVENIENCE. HORN SWITCH.
10 LG-R EXTERIOR LIGHTING. STOPLAMP SWITCH.
383 R-W H EXTERIOR LIGHTING. EMERGENCY WARNING FLASHER.
F-5
54 LG-Y CHARGE START RUN. SEAT BELT MODULE.
19 LB-R ILLUMINATION LAMPS. CLUSTER ILLUMINATION.
54 LG-Y PROTECTION & CONVENIENCE. L.H. DOOR JAM SWITCH.
14 BR EXTERIOR LIGHTING.
14 BR EXTERIOR LIGHTING.
15 R-Y EXTERIOR LIGHTING. HEADLAMP DIMMER SWITCH.
C-1202
296 W-P PROTECTION & CONVENIENCE. HORN WARNING ACTUATOR.
296 W-P PROTECTION & CONVENIENCE. DOOR OPEN WARNING LAMP.
296 W-P HEATED BACKLITE. HEATED BACKLITE SWITCH.
296 W-P
C-317
F-3
BUSS
F-1
BUSS
F-2
C-1201
687 GY-Y
297 BK-LG H
950 W-BK W/WPR. WASHER. W/WPR. SWITCH (WASHER).
137 Y-BK H RADIO.
C-317
63 R W-WPR. WASHER.
297 BK-LG H CHARGE-START-RUN. IGNITION SWITCH.
BUSS
F-6
F-7
181 BR-O
181 BR-O HEATER. HEATER BLOWER SWITCH.
181 BR-O A/C & HEATER. A/C BLOWER SWITCH.
296 W-P EXTERIOR LIGHTING. BACKUP LAMP SWITCH.
296 W-P EXTERIOR LAMPS. TURN SIGNAL FLASHER .
F-4
S-303
640 R-Y H
640 R-Y H CHARGE-START-RUN. C-202.
640 R-Y H D.P. CONNECTOR
640 R-Y H CHARGE-START-RUN. SEAT BELT TIMER.
904 LG-R
904 LG-R CHARGE START RUN. SPLICE S-110
16 R-LG CHARGE-START-RUN. TACHOMETER.
A B C D E F
9 10 11 12 13 14 15 16

Fig. 10.45. Wiring diagram - Charging, starting and running circuits (1) (continued on page 171. See page 167 for 'Key')

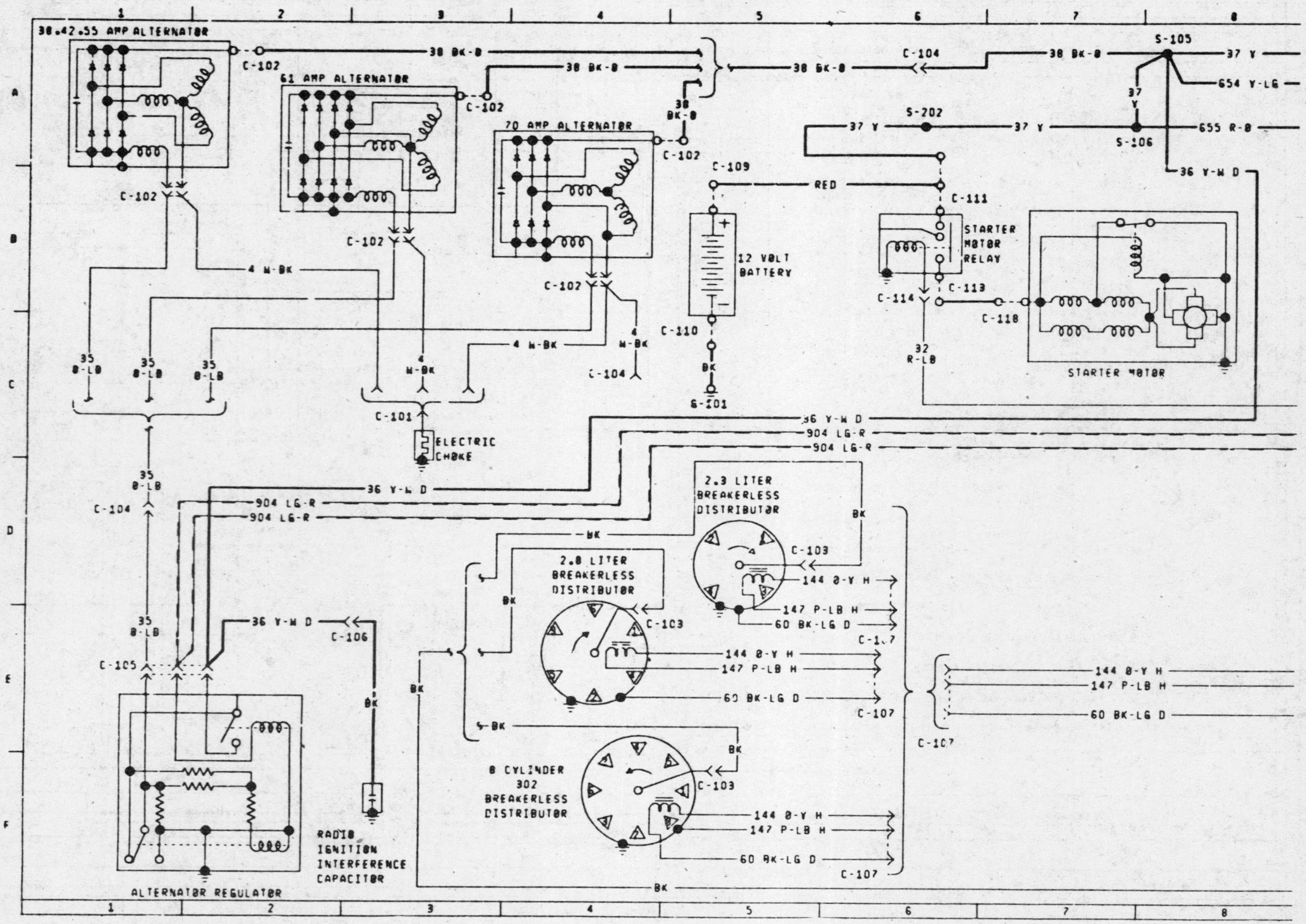

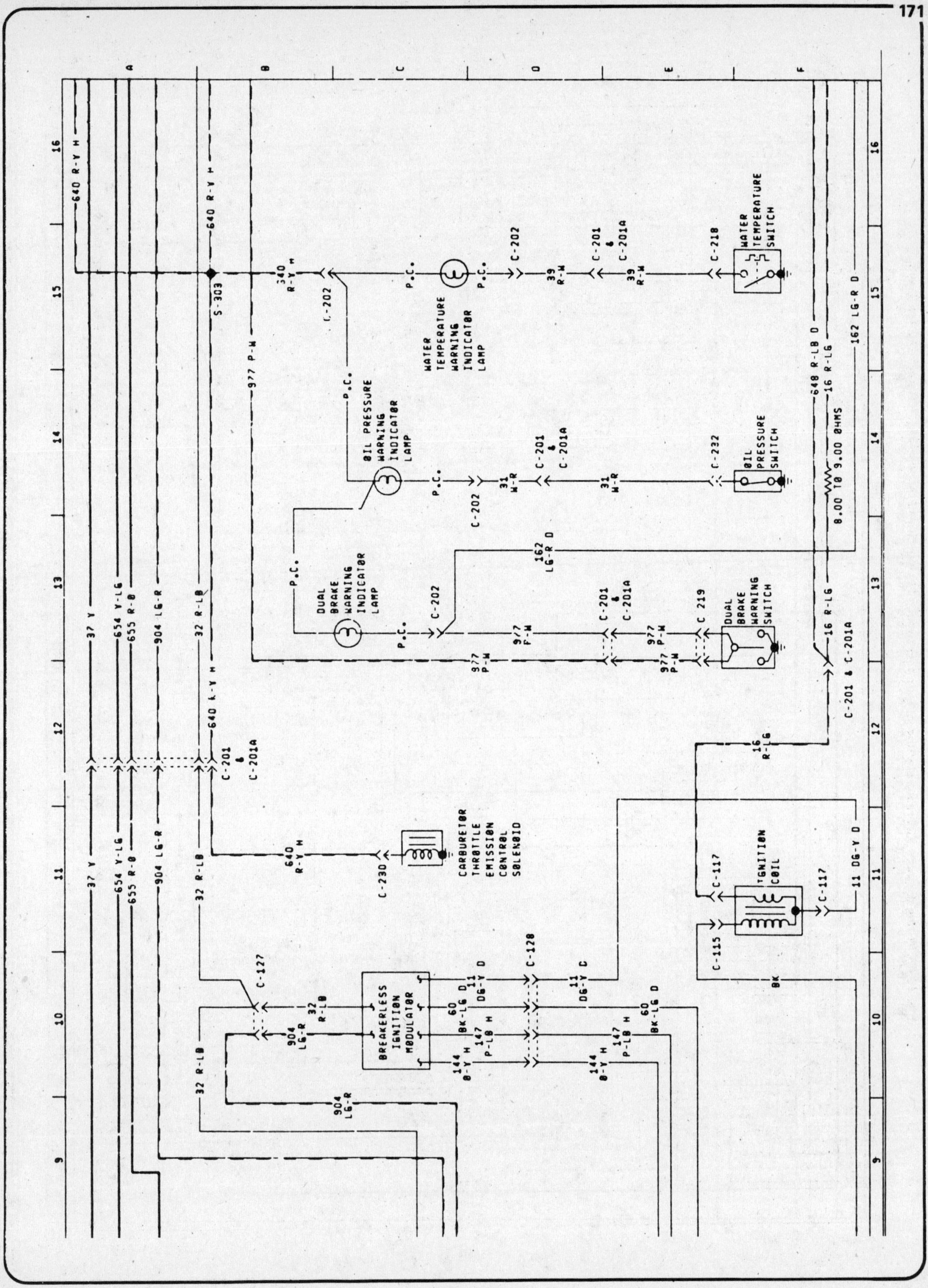

A
B
C
D
E
F

9
10
11
12
13
14
15
16

640 R-Y W
S-303
977 P-W
340 R-Y W
C-202
P.C.
WATER TEMPERATURE WARNING INDICATOR LAMP
39 R-W
C-201 & C-201A
C-218
WATER TEMPERATURE SWITCH
OIL PRESSURE WARNING INDICATOR LAMP
31 W-R
C-232
OIL PRESSURE SWITCH
648 R-LB D
16 R-LG
162 LG-R D
8.00 TO 9.00 OHMS
DUAL BRAKE WARNING INDICATOR LAMP
C 219
DUAL BRAKE WARNING SWITCH
C-201 & C-201A
37 Y
654 Y-LG
655 R-O
904 LG-R
32 R-LB
640 R-Y W
C-230
CARBURETOR THROTTLE EMISSION CONTROL SOLENOID
IGNITION COIL
C-117
C-115
11 DG-Y D
BK
C-127
BREAKERLESS IGNITION MODULATOR
C-128
11 DG-Y D
60 BK-LG D
147 P-LB W
144 O-Y W
11 DG-Y C

Fig. 10.46. Wiring diagram - Charging, starting and running circuits (2) (continued on page 173. See page 167 for 'Key')

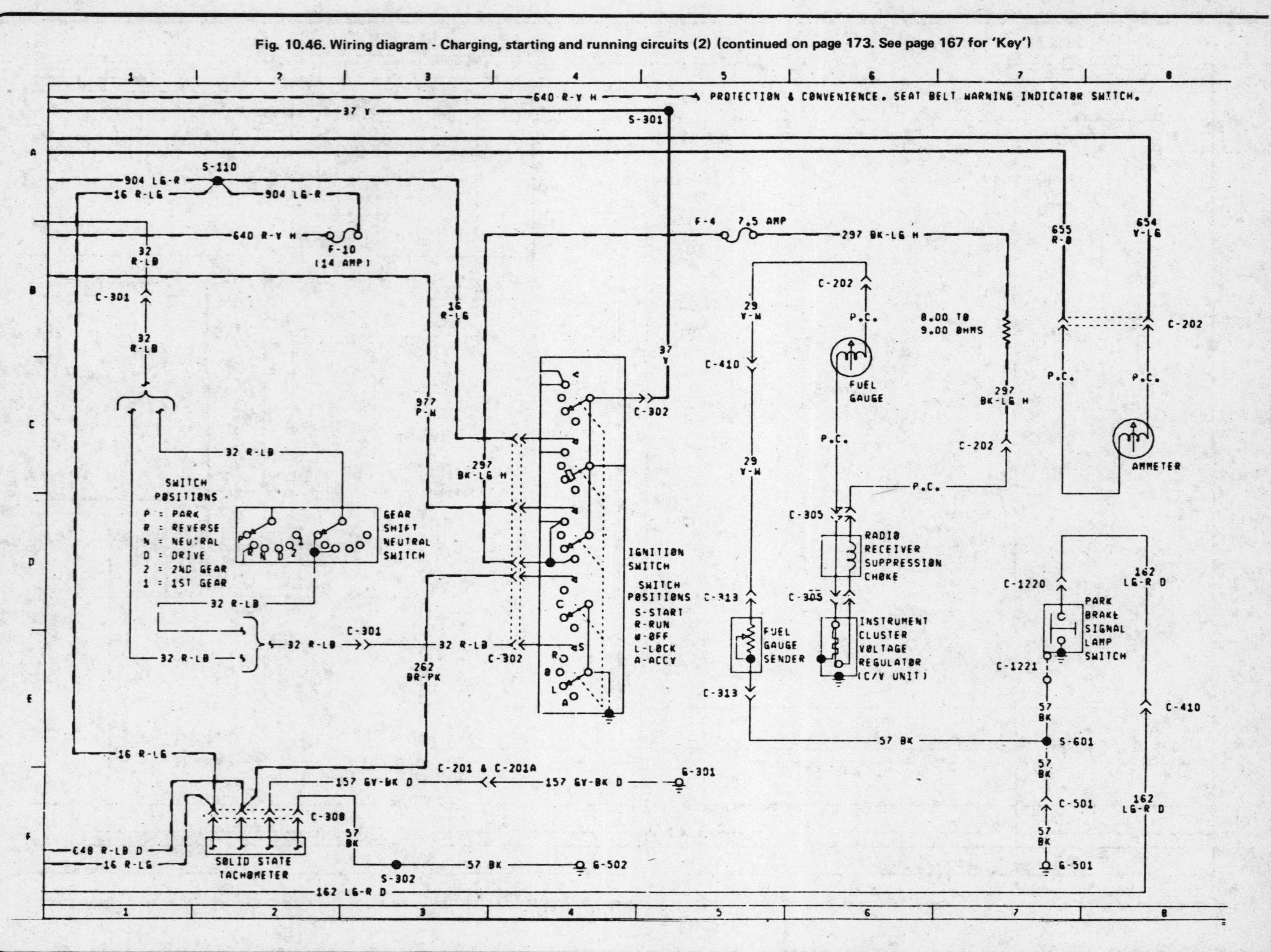

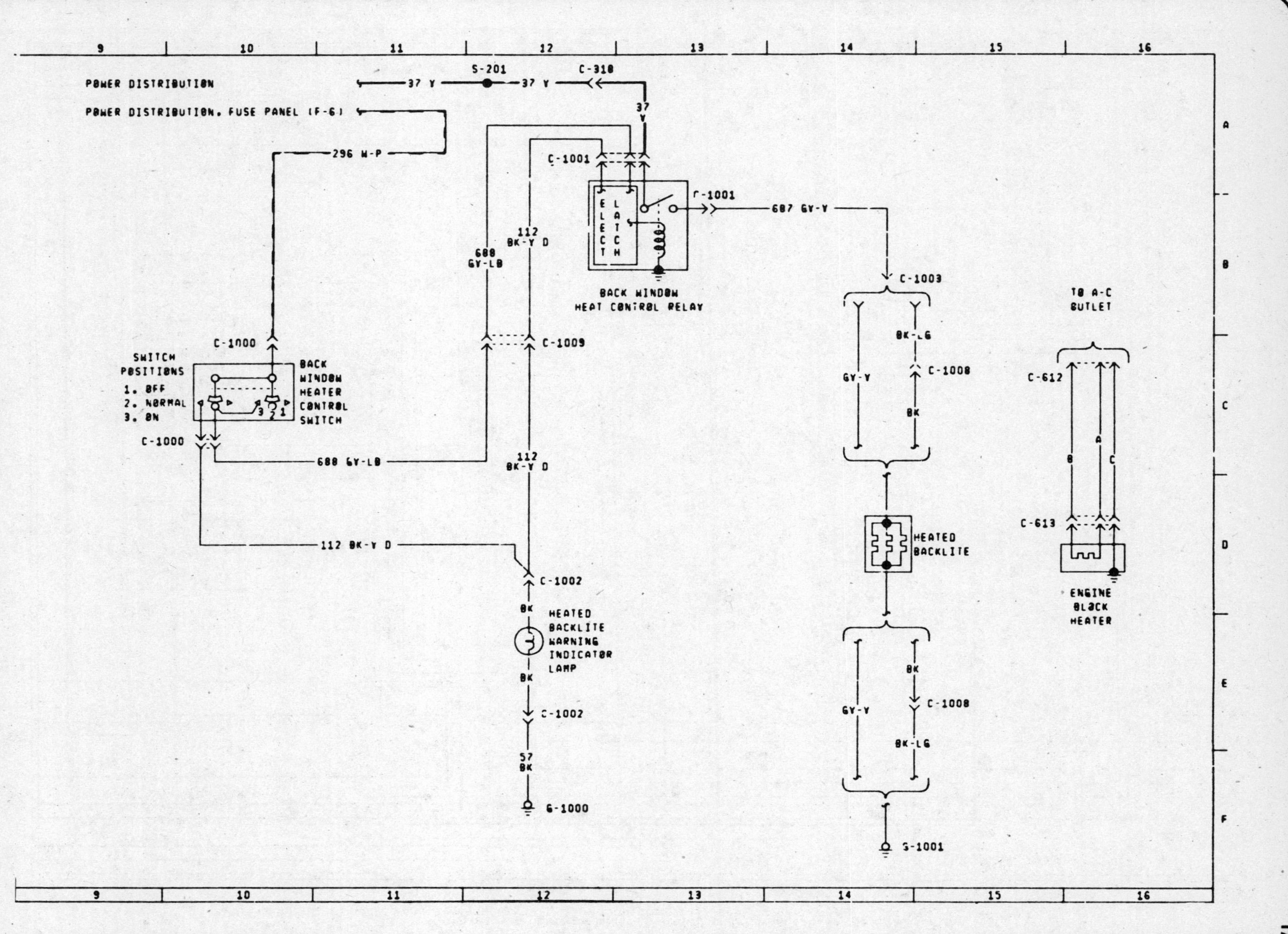
POWER DISTRIBUTION
POWER DISTRIBUTION, FUSE PANEL (F-6)
37 Y
S-201
C-318
296 W-P
C-1001
C-1000
SWITCH POSITIONS
1. OFF
2. NORMAL
3. ON
BACK WINDOW HEATER CONTROL SWITCH
688 GY-LB
112 BK-Y D
C-1009
ELECT
LATCH
BACK WINDOW HEAT CONTROL RELAY
687 GY-Y
C-1003
BK-LG
C-1008
GY-Y
BK
HEATED BACKLITE
G-1001
C-1002
HEATED BACKLITE WARNING INDICATOR LAMP
57 BK
G-1000
TO A-C OUTLET
C-612
C-613
ENGINE BLOCK HEATER

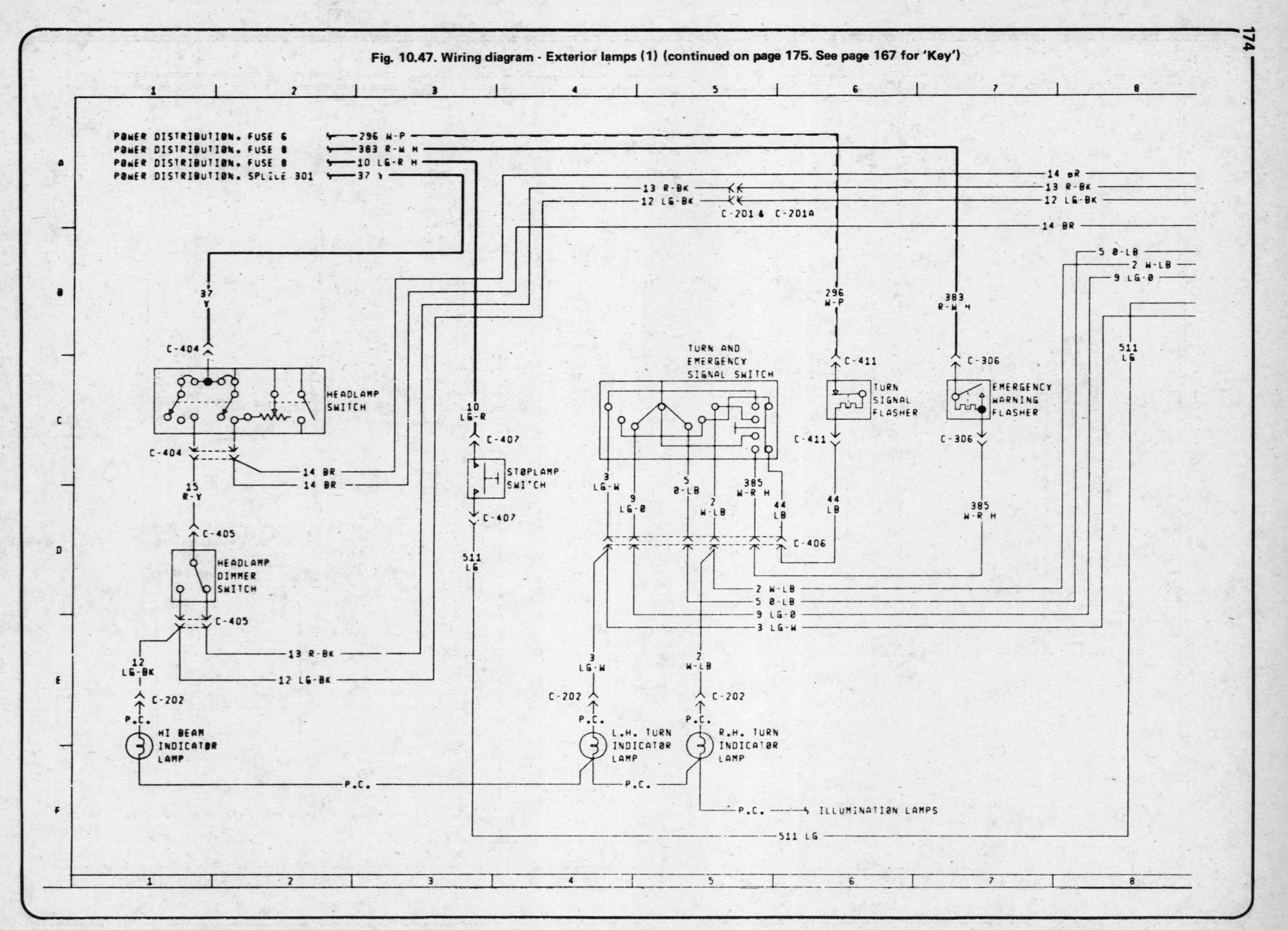

Fig. 10.47. Wiring diagram - Exterior lamps (1) (continued on page 175. See page 167 for 'Key')

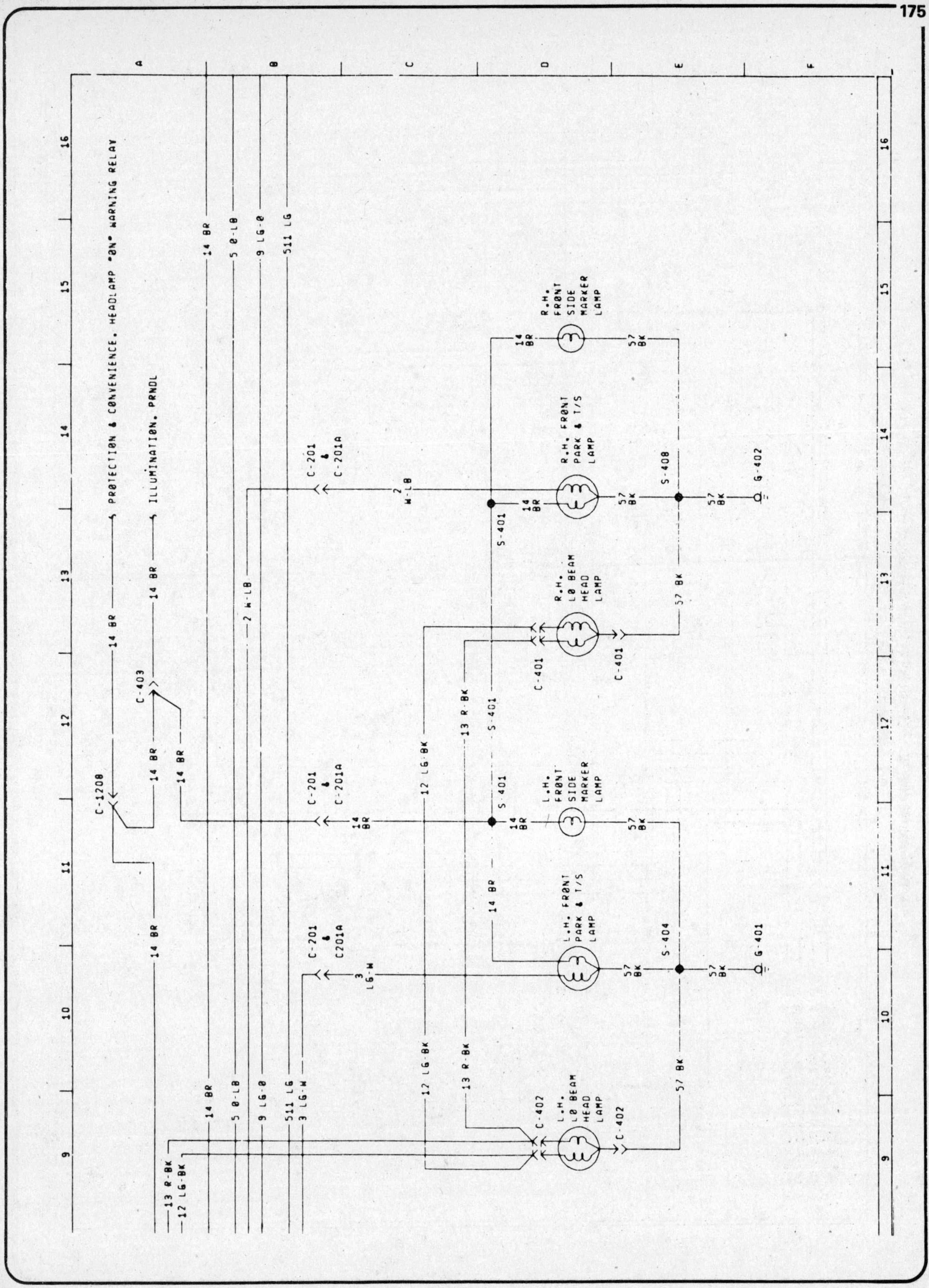

9 10 11 12 13 14 15 16

C-1208
14 BR
PROTECTION & CONVENIENCE. HEADLAMP "ON" WARNING RELAY
14 BR
14 BR
C-403
14 BR
ILLUMINATION. PRNDL
14 BR
13 R-BK
12 LG-BK
14 BR
5 O-LB
2 W-LB
9 LG-O
511 LG
3 LG-W
14 BR
5 O-LB
9 LG-O
511 LG

A
B
C
D
E
F

C-201 & C201A
3 LG-W
C-201 & C-201A
14 BR
C-201 & C-201A
2 W-LB
12 LG-BK
12 LG-BK
13 R-BK
13 R-BK
14 BR
S-401
S-401
S-401
14 BR
14 BR
14 BR
C-402
L.H. LO BEAM HEAD LAMP
C-402
L.H. FRONT PARK & T/S LAMP
L.H. FRONT SIDE MARKER LAMP
C-401
R.H. LO BEAM HEAD LAMP
C-401
R.H. FRONT PARK & T/S LAMP
R.H. FRONT SIDE MARKER LAMP
57 BK
57 BK
S-404
57 BK
57 BK
57 BK
57 BK
S-408
57 BK
57 BK
57 BK
G-401
G-402

9 10 11 12 13 14 15 16

10

Fig. 10.48. Wiring diagram - Exterior lamps (2) (continued on page 177. See page 167 for 'Key')

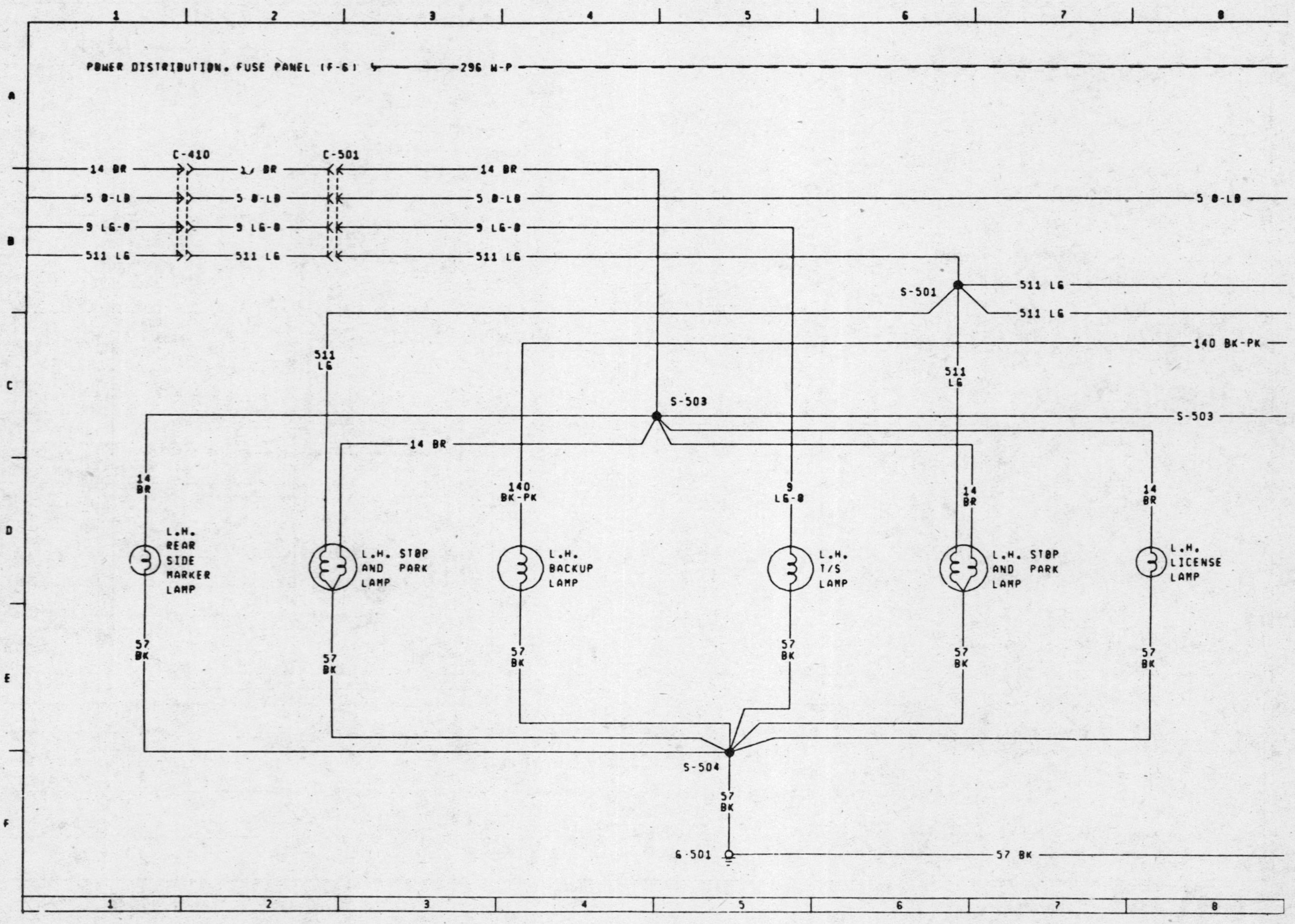

1 2 3 4 5 6 7 8

A B C D E F

POWER DISTRIBUTION, FUSE PANEL (F-6) — 296 W-P

C-410 C-501

14 BR — 14 BR — 14 BR

5 B-LB — 5 B-LB — 5 B-LB — 5 B-LB

9 LG-B — 9 LG-B — 9 LG-B

511 LG — 511 LG — 511 LG

S-501 511 LG 511 LG

140 BK-PK

511 LG

S-503 S-503

14 BR

511 LG

14 BR — L.H. REAR SIDE MARKER LAMP — 57 BK

L.H. STOP AND PARK LAMP — 57 BK

140 BK-PK — L.H. BACKUP LAMP — 57 BK

9 LG-B — L.H. T/S LAMP — 57 BK

14 BR — L.H. STOP AND PARK LAMP — 57 BK

14 BR — L.H. LICENSE LAMP — 57 BK

S-504

57 BK

G-501 — 57 BK

1 2 3 4 5 6 7 8

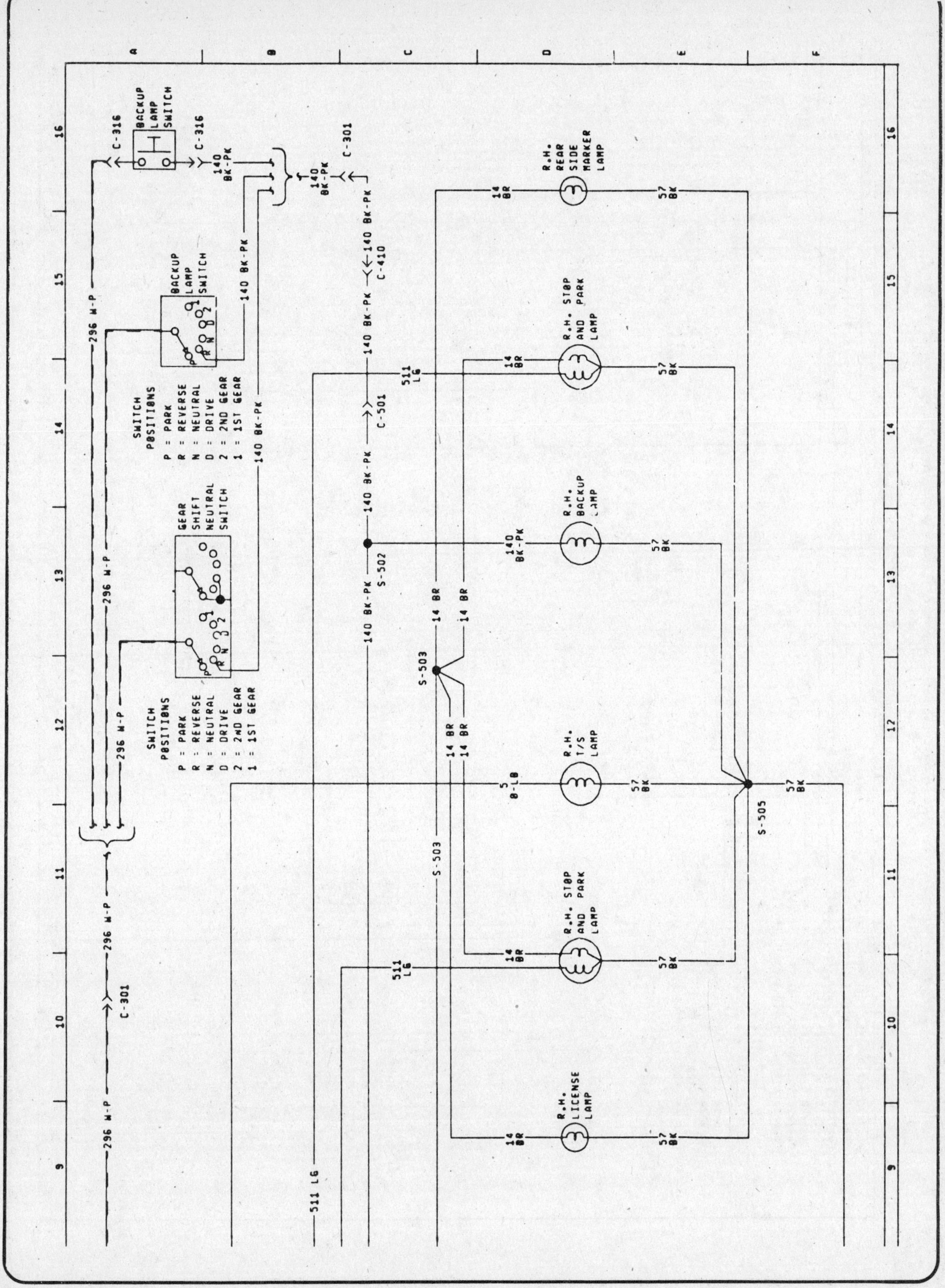

A
B
C
D
E
F
9
10
11
12
13
14
15
16
C-316
BACKUP
LAMP
SWITCH
C-316
140
BK-PK
C-301
140
BK-PK
140 BK-PK
C-410
296 W-P
BACKUP
LAMP
SWITCH
SWITCH
POSITIONS
P = PARK
R = REVERSE
N = NEUTRAL
D = DRIVE
2 = 2ND GEAR
1 = 1ST GEAR
140 BK-PK
C-501
511
LG
GEAR
SHIFT
NEUTRAL
SWITCH
296 W-P
S-502
140
BK-PK
14 BR
S-503
SWITCH
POSITIONS
P = PARK
R = REVERSE
N = NEUTRAL
D = DRIVE
2 = 2ND GEAR
1 = 1ST GEAR
296 W-P
5
O-LB
S-505
C-301
511 LG
R.H.
REAR
SIDE
MARKER
LAMP
R.H. STOP
AND PARK
LAMP
R.H.
BACKUP
LAMP
R.H.
T/S
LAMP
R.H. STOP
AND PARK
LAMP
R.H.
LICENSE
LAMP
14
BR
57
BK

10

Fig. 10.49. Wiring diagram - Warning and convenience lamps circuits (continued on page 179. See page 167 for 'Key')

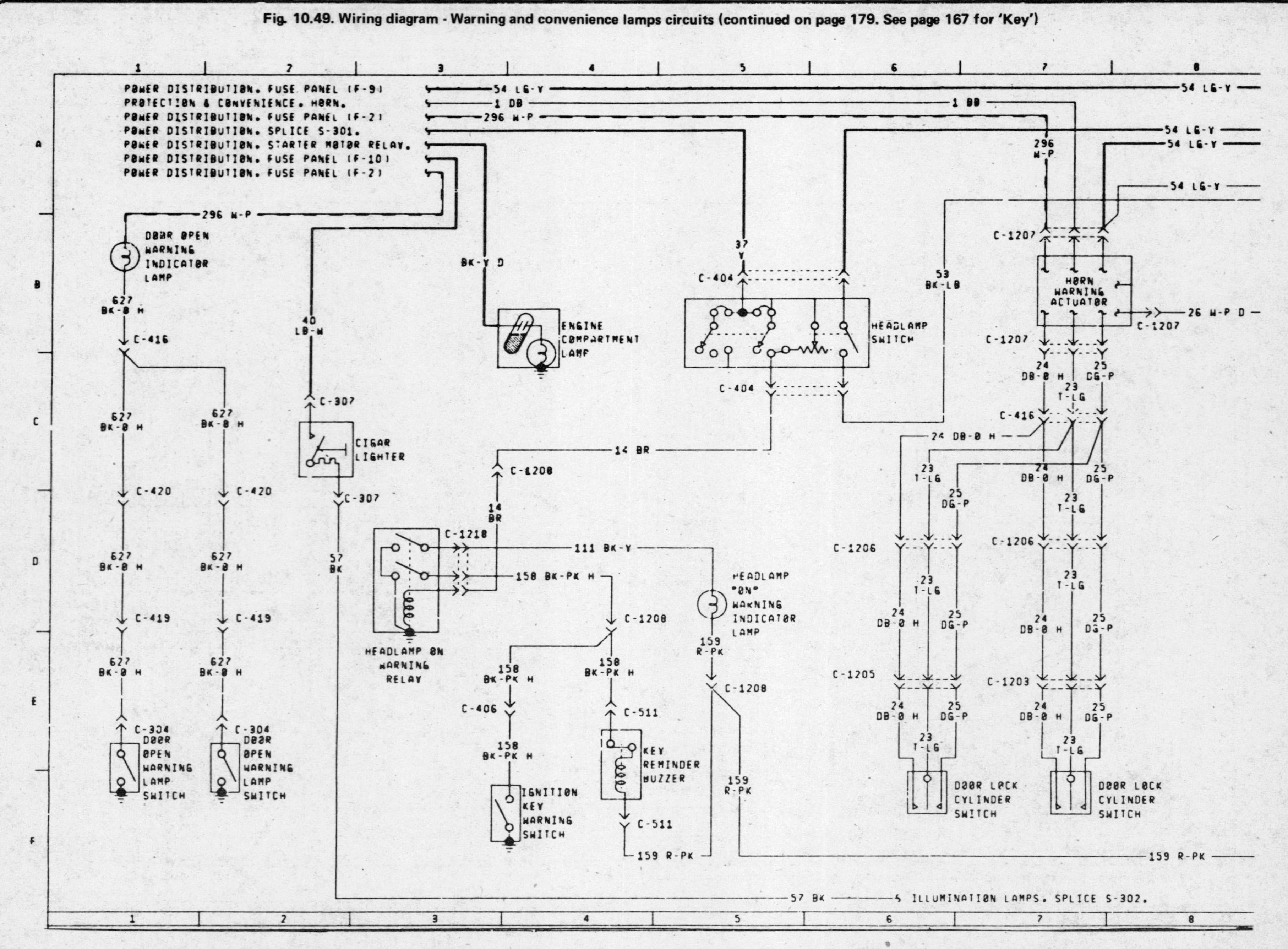

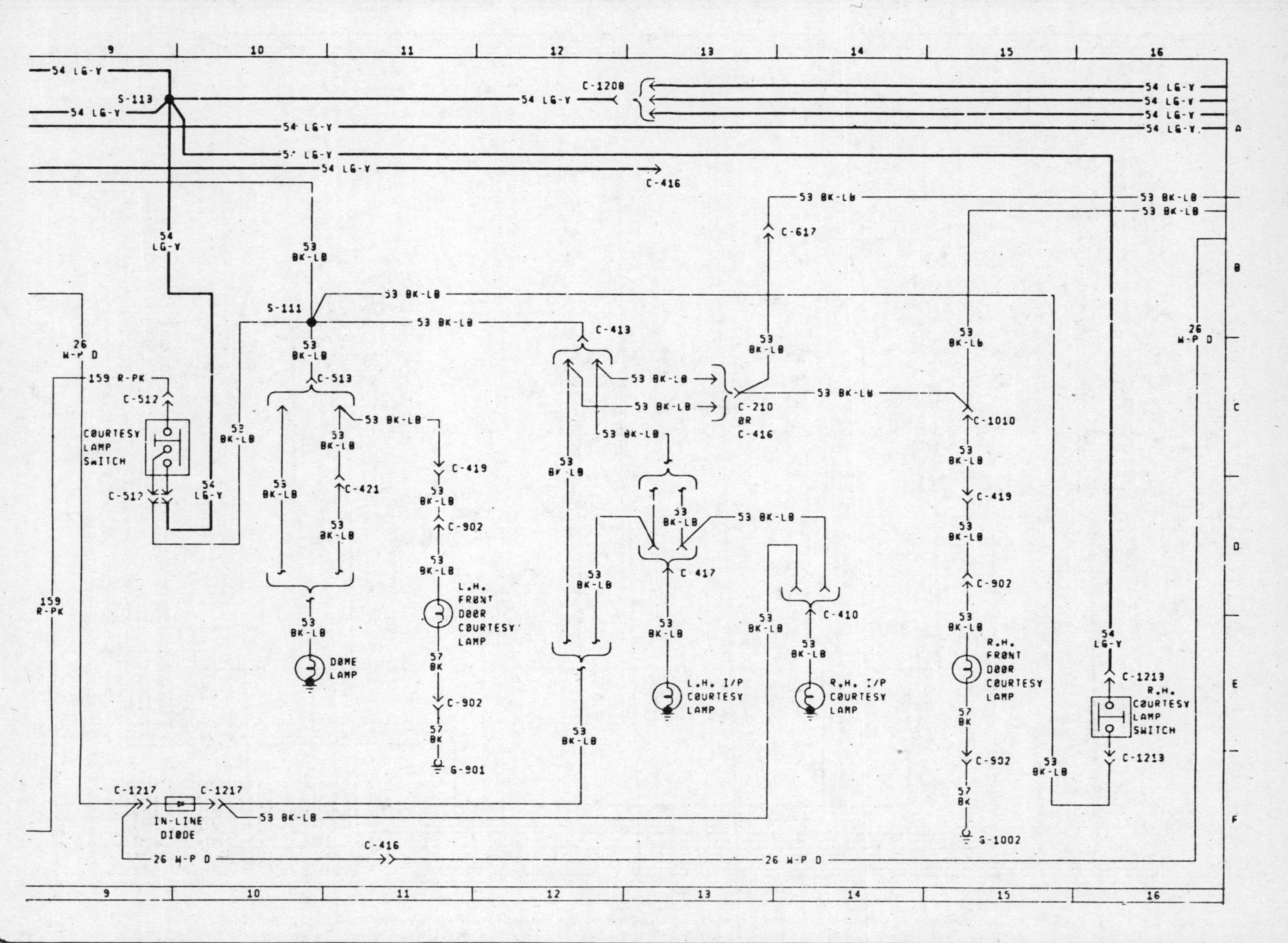

S-113
54 LG-Y
C-1208
S-111
53 BK-LB
C-416
C-617
C-513
C-512
159 R-PK
26 W-P D
COURTESY LAMP SWITCH
C-512
C-421
C-419
C-902
L.H. FRONT DOOR COURTESY LAMP
57 BK
G-901
DOME LAMP
C-413
C-210 OR C-416
C-417
L.H. I/P COURTESY LAMP
C-410
R.H. I/P COURTESY LAMP
C-1010
R.H. FRONT DOOR COURTESY LAMP
G-1002
C-1213
R.H. COURTESY LAMP SWITCH
C-1217
IN-LINE DIODE

Fig. 10.50. Wiring diagram - Warning, convenience and windshield wiper circuits (continued on page 181. See page 167 for 'Key').

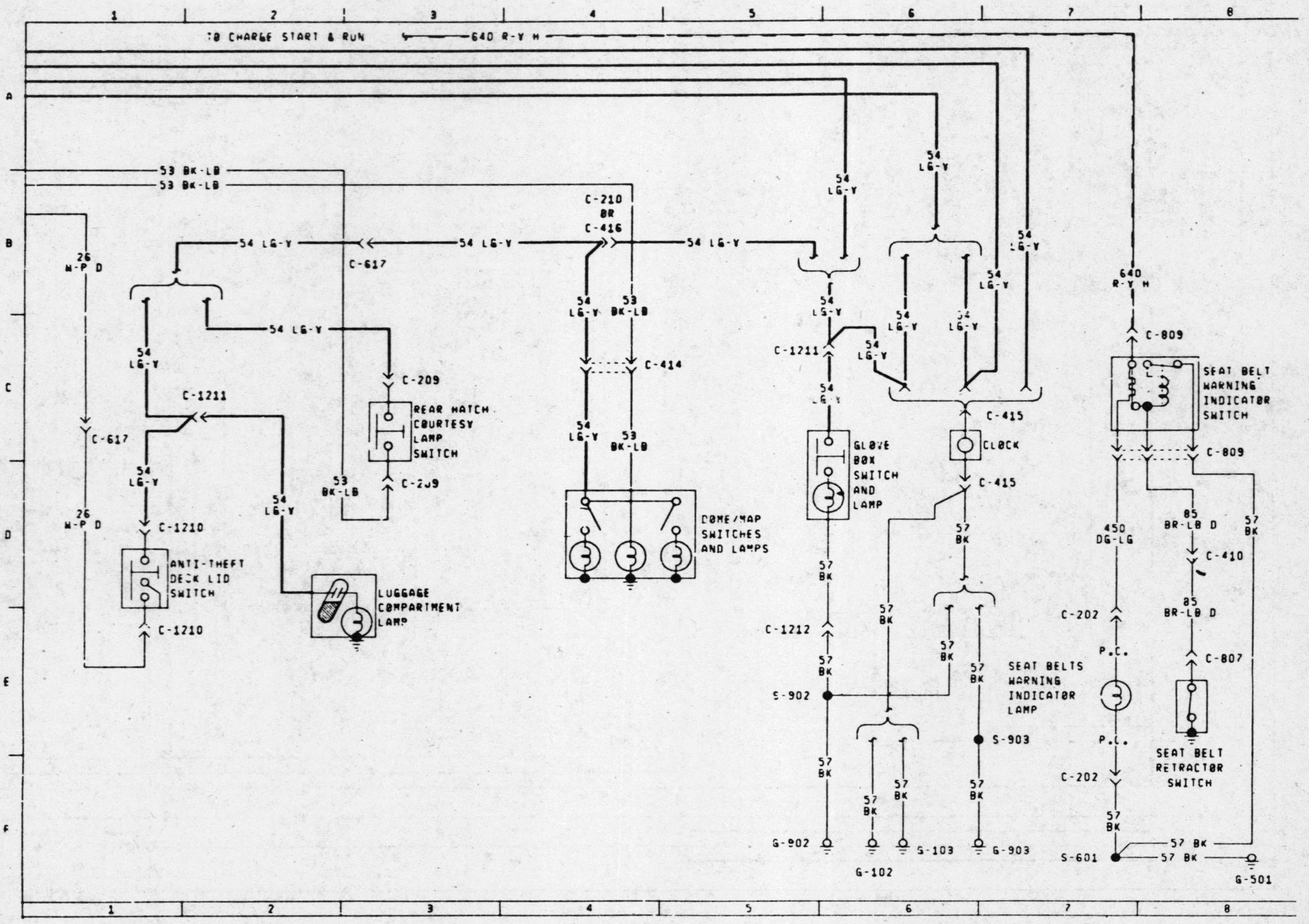

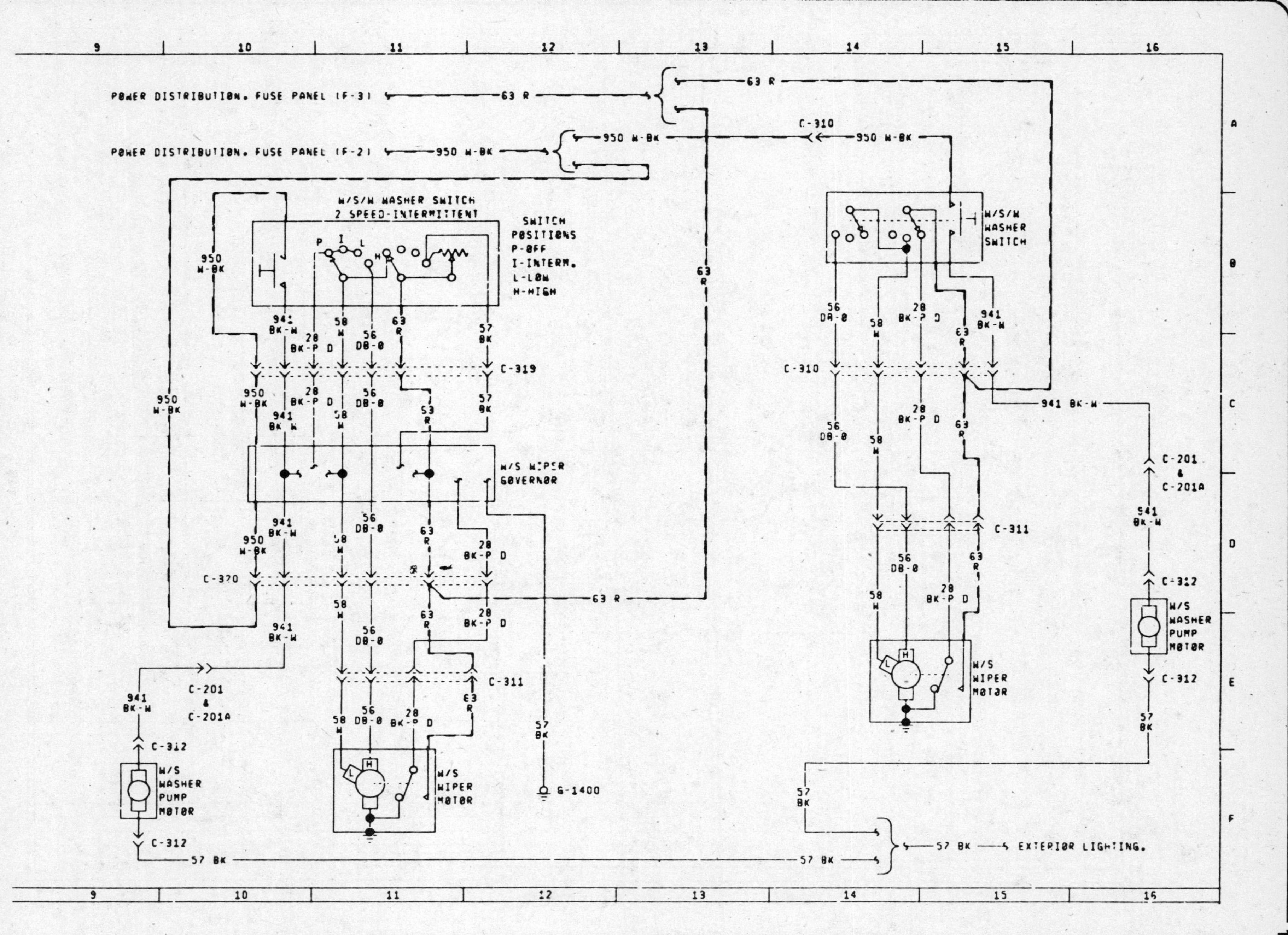
POWER DISTRIBUTION. FUSE PANEL (F-3)
63 R
POWER DISTRIBUTION. FUSE PANEL (F-2)
950 W-BK
W/S/W WASHER SWITCH
2 SPEED-INTERMITTENT
SWITCH POSITIONS
P-OFF
I-INTERM.
L-LOW
H-HIGH
941 BK-W
28 BK-P D
58 W
56 DB-O
63 R
57 BK
C-319
W/S WIPER GOVERNOR
C-320
C-311
C-201 & C-201A
C-312
W/S WASHER PUMP MOTOR
W/S WIPER MOTOR
G-1400
C-310
W/S/W WASHER SWITCH
57 BK
EXTERIOR LIGHTING.

Fig. 10.51. Wiring diagram - Radio and heater/air-conditioning circuits (continued on page 183. See page 167 for 'Key')

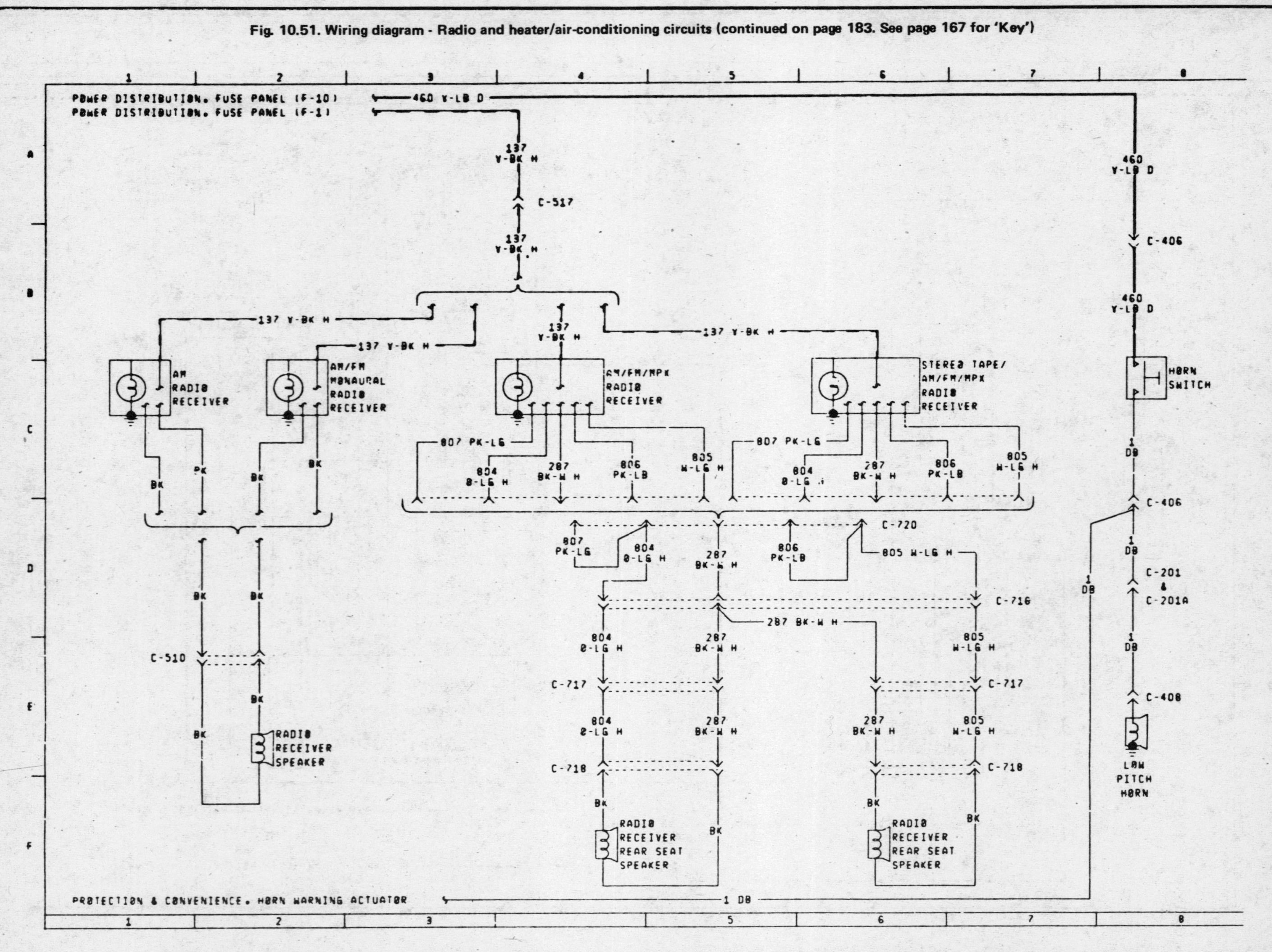

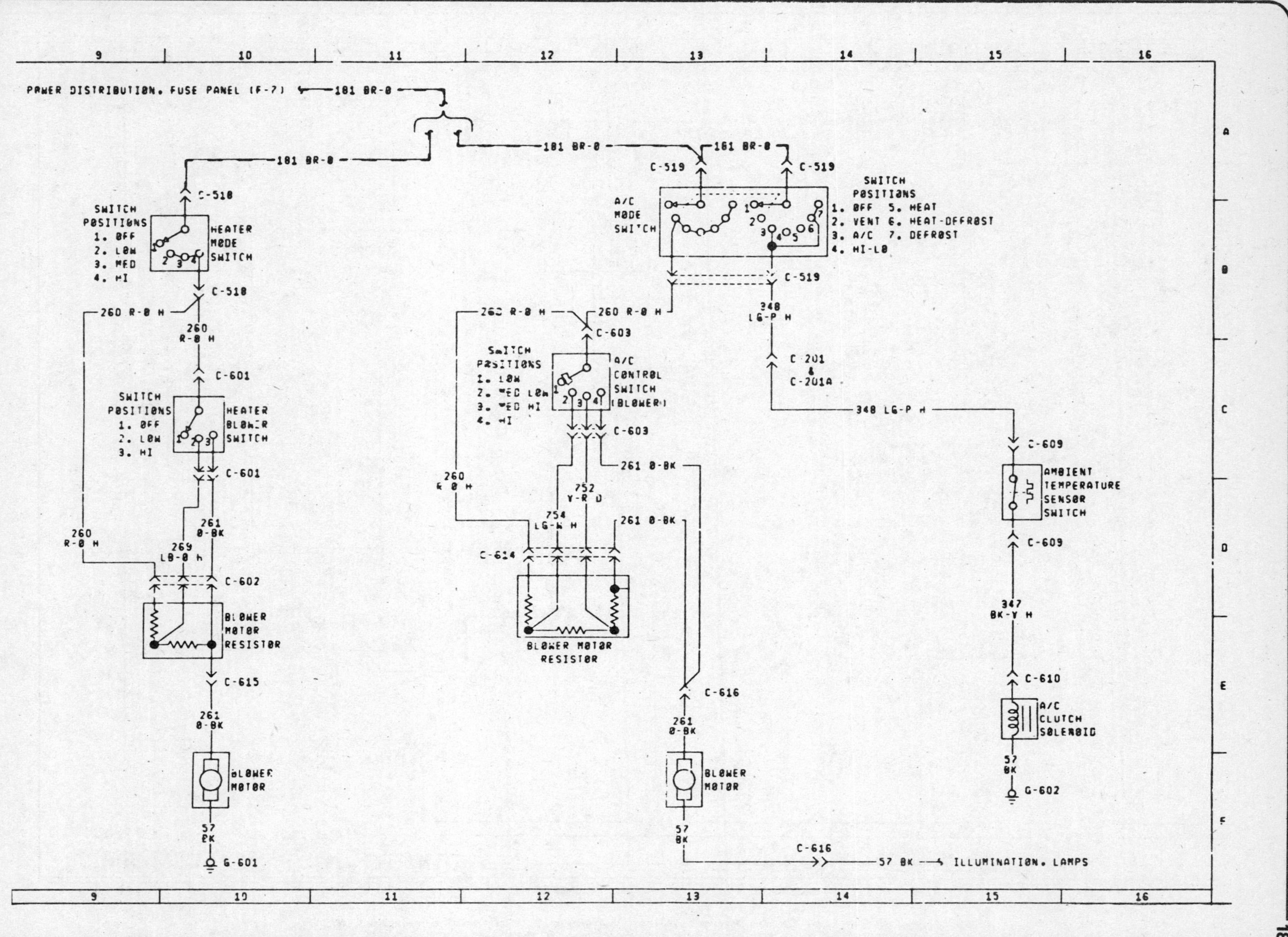

POWER DISTRIBUTION. FUSE PANEL (F-7)
181 BR-O
C-518
SWITCH POSITIONS
1. OFF
2. LOW
3. MED
4. HI
HEATER MODE SWITCH
260 R-O H
260 R-O H
C-601
SWITCH POSITIONS
1. OFF
2. LOW
3. HI
HEATER BLOWER SWITCH
261 O-BK
269 LB-O H
C-602
BLOWER MOTOR RESISTOR
C-615
BLOWER MOTOR
57 BK
G-601
C-519
A/C MODE SWITCH
SWITCH POSITIONS
1. OFF 5. HEAT
2. VENT 6. HEAT-DEFROST
3. A/C 7. DEFROST
4. HI-LO
348 LG-P H
C-201 & C-201A
C-603
SWITCH POSITIONS
1. LOW
2. MED LOW
3. MED HI
4. HI
A/C CONTROL SWITCH (BLOWER)
752 Y-R D
754 LG-W H
261 O-BK
C-614
BLOWER MOTOR RESISTOR
C-616
C-609
AMBIENT TEMPERATURE SENSOR SWITCH
347 BK-Y H
C-610
A/C CLUTCH SOLENOID
G-602
57 BK — ILLUMINATION. LAMPS

Fig. 10.52. Wiring diagrams - Instrument panel lighting circuits (continued on page 185. See page 167 for 'Key')

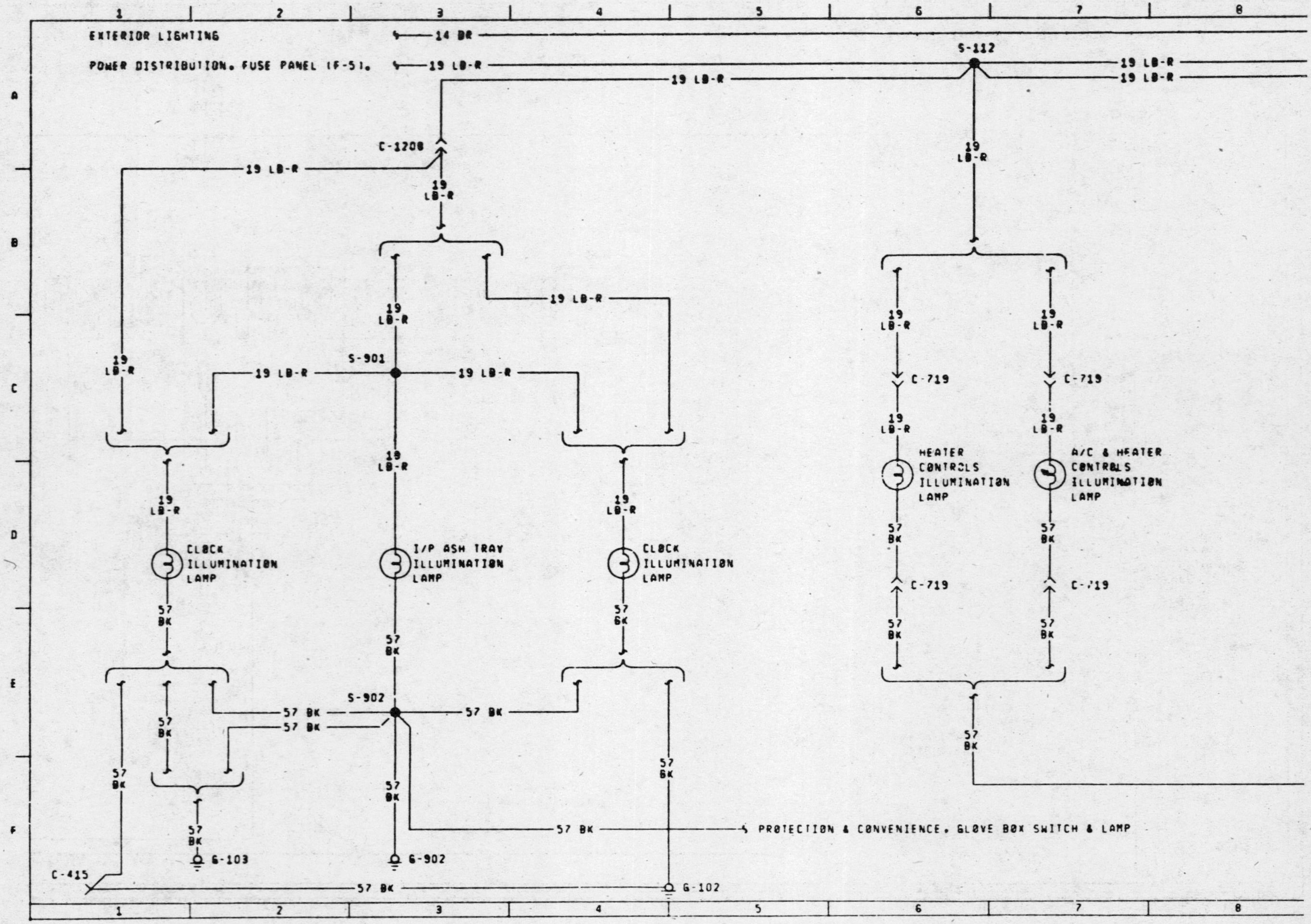

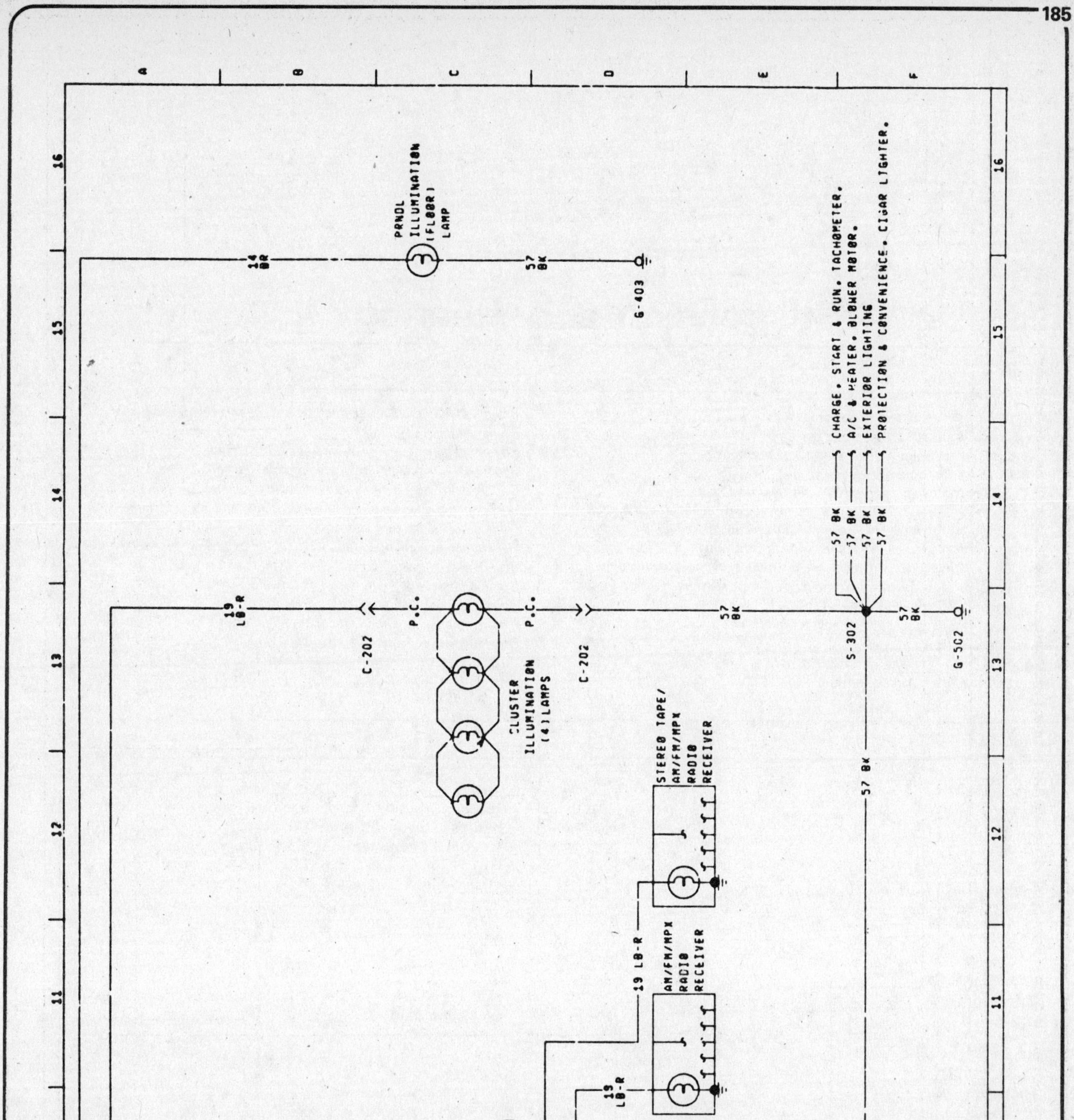

9 10 11 12 13 14 15 16

A B C D E F

19 LB-R

C-517

13 LB-R

19 LB-R

C-202

P.C.

CLUSTER ILLUMINATION (4) LAMPS

P.C.

C-202

14 BR

PRNDL ILLUMINATION (FLOOR) LAMP

57 BK

G-403

19 LB-R

19 LB-R

19 LB-R

19 LB-R

AM RADIO RECEIVER

AM/FM MONAURAL RADIO RECEIVER

AM/FM/MPX RADIO RECEIVER

STEREO TAPE/ AM/FM/MPX RADIO RECEIVER

57 BK

S-302

57 BK

57 BK — CHARGE, START & RUN, TACHOMETER.

57 BK — A/C & HEATER, BLOWER MOTOR.

57 BK — EXTERIOR LIGHTING

57 BK — PROTECTION & CONVENIENCE, CIGAR LIGHTER.

57 BK

G-502

9 10 11 12 13 14 15 16

Chapter 11 Suspension and steering

Contents

Specifications

Front suspension

Type	Independent, coil spring, upper and lower arms. Double acting, hydraulic telescopic shock absorbers.
Toe-in	0.125 in (3 mm) + or – 0.125 in (3 mm)
Castor	0.875° (min 0.125°, max 1.625°)
Camber	+0.5° (min 0.25°, max 1.25°)
Toe out on turns:	
Inner wheel	20°
Outer wheel	18.84°

Rear suspension

Type	Half elliptical leaf springs. Double acting, hydraulic telescopic shock absorbers.

Steering (Manual)

Type	Rack and pinion
Ration	
Straight-ahead	24.2 : 1
At full turn	18.34 : 1
Number of turns (lock-to-lock)	4 : 15
Oil capacity	Approx 7 oz
Steering wheel play	0.375 in (9.52 mm)
Steering wheel turning effort (static)	34.0 lbs

Steering (Power assisted)

Type	Rack and pinion with integral control valve and piston.
Pump type	Ford-Thompson, with integral reservoir, belt driven from the engine.
Ratio:	
Straight-ahead	19.03 : 1
Full lock	16.24 : 1
Number of turns (lock-to-lock)	3.3
Oil capacity (total)	2.44 U.S pints
Steering wheel turning effort (static)	5.0 lbs
Fluid type	Automatic transmission fluid type D2AZ-19582-A

Tires

Size	Refer to the tire information decal located on the front of the L.H door puller.
Pressures	

Torque wrench settings

	lb f ft	kg f m
Front suspension		
Shock absorber upper attachment	20 to 28	2.8 to 3.9
Shock absorber lower attachment	60 to 80	8.3 to 11.1
Strut to chassis member	60 to 80	8.3 to 11.1
Strut to lower arm	30 to 45	4.2 to 6.2
Lower arm to underbody	75 to 110	10.2 to 15.2
Brake backplate to spindle	20 to 35	2.8 to 4.8
Ball joint to spindle (upper and lower)	60 to 90	8.3 to 12.4
Upper arm and inner shaft to body	75 to 105	10.2 to 14.2
Wheel bearing adjusting nut	17 to 25	2.4 to 3.4
Rear suspension		
Shackle nut	20 to 26	2.8 to 3.5
Shock absorber to upper bracket	14 to 26	1.9 to 3.5
Shock absorber to spring clip plate	14 to 26	1.9 to 3.5
Shackle hanger to underbody	30 to 50	4.2 to 6.9
Spring to axle 'U' bolt nut	30 to 50	4.2 to 6.9
Wheel lug nut	70 to 115	9.7 to 15.9
Spring to front hanger (bolt or nut)	100 to 140	13.8 to 19.7
Universal joint 'U' bolt nut	8 to 15	1.1 to 2.1
Shock absorber bracket to underbody	18 to 30	2.5 to 4.2
Steering		
Support yoke cover to housing	6 to 8	0.8 to 1.1
Pinion cover to housing	12 to 15	1.6 to 2.1
Steering gear assembly to crossmember	50 to 65	6.9 to 9.0
Connecting rod end to spindle arm	35 to 47	4.8 to 6.2
Connecting rod end to inner tie rod	35 to 50	4.8 to 6.9
Steering gear to crossmember bolts	80 to 100	13.8 to 11.1
Flex coupling lockscrew	72 to 120	9.6 to 16.6
Flex coupling to steering shaft bolts	20 to 37	2.8 to 5.1
Upper column attaching bracket nuts	8 to 20	1.1 to 2.8
Steering wheel nut	30 to 40	4.2 to 5.5
Upper 'U' joints nuts	20 to 37	2.8 to 5.1
Power steering pump bracket - to - engine bolts	30 to 45	4.2 to 6.3
Power steering pump - to - bracket	30 to 45	4.2 to 6.3
Pump pressure hose	12 to 24	1.6 to 3.2
Steering gear pressure hose	16 to 25	2.1 to 3.5
Return hose	25 to 39	3.5 to 5.5

1 General description

The front suspension system fitted to the Mustang II models thru' 1978 is of the conventional independent front suspension type with upper and lower control arms and coil springs. A double action telescopic shock absorber is located inside each coil spring.
spring.

Each front wheel rotates on a spindle, the upper and lower ends of which are mounted on ball joints attached to the upper and lower control arms.

The upper arm pivots on a bush and shaft assembly which is bolted to the bodyframe. The lower arm pivots on a bolt located in the front crossmember.

The coil spring seats between the lower arm and the top of the spring housing. The shock absorber is bolted to the lower arms and the top of the spring housing.

Each rear wheel, hub and brake drum assembly is bolted to the rear axle shaft flange and the wheel and axle shaft rotates in the rear axle housing.

Two spring parts, integral with the axle housing, rest on two leaf spring assemblies. The rear axle housing is attached to the center of the springs by 'U' bolts, retainers, insulators and nuts.

Each spring assembly is suspended from the underbody main longitudinal member by hanger and shackle assemblies located at the front and rear of the spring.

The mounting stud at the top and bottom of the shock absorber is attached, via insulators, to a bracket bolted to the underside of the body. The lower end is mounted, via insulators, to the 'U' bolt plate.

The steering gear is the rack and pinion type with power assistance available as an optional fit. The steering wheel is connected to the gear through a collapsable shaft and flexible couplings.

A tie-rod is attached to each end of the rack joint which allows the tie-rod to move with any deflection in the front suspension unit. The rack and pinion assembly ends are sealed by rubber bellows.

Couplings attached to the tie-rods are retained on the rack and pinned. They cannot be dismantled once assembled. This means that replacement of the inner tie-rods, rack, housing, or upper pinion bearing necessitates the fitting of a new steering gear assembly.

The steering column is of the safety type. A locking mechanism is actuated by depressing the push button located below the turn signal switch lever. This prevents inadvertent locking of the steering wheel by blocking the actuator out of the lock position.

The outer column tube terminates just below the attachment to the brake support bracket. Energy absolution is accomplished by the lower column mounting bracket. There is no shift tube in this assembly.

The steering shaft has a machined bar with grooves in the lower half designed to accept two plastic anti-rattle clips. The lower shaft comprises an upper section that is a formed tube to fit into the upper shaft.

The column is secured to the brake support brackets bolted to flanges on the brake support. The lower column attaching collar contains a sintered iron ring with internal protrusions. These protrusions act as a guide which deforms the outer tube as the column collapses.

2 Front wheel bearings - removal and replacement

1 Chock the rear wheels, apply the parking brake, loosen the front wheel nuts, jack-up the front of the car and support on firmly based axle stands. Remove the roadwheel.
2 Refer to Chapter 9 and detach the disc brake caliper.
3 Carefully remove the grease cap from the hub.
4 Withdraw the cotter pin and lift away the nut lock, adjusting nut and plain washers from the spindle.
5 Lift away the outer bearing cone and roller assembly.
6 Remove the disc from the wheel spindle.

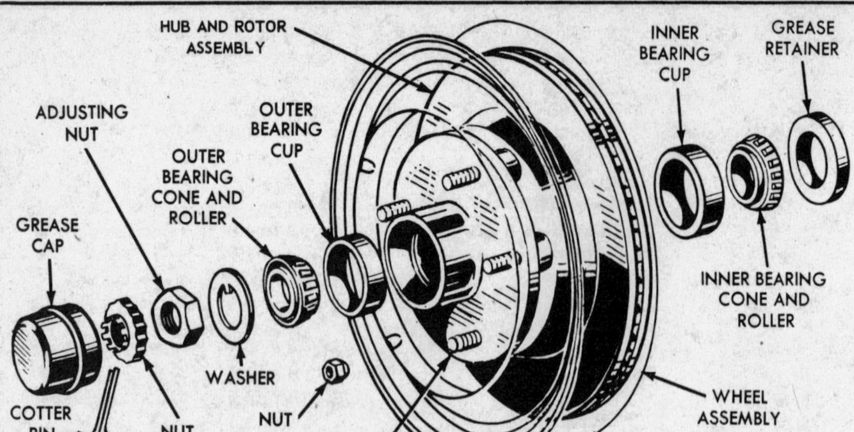

Fig. 11.1. Exploded view of front wheel bearings (Sec. 2)

7 Using a screwdriver or tapered drift remove the grease seal. This must not be used again but always renewed.
8 Remove the inner bearing cone and roller assembly from the hub.
9 Remove grease from the inner and outer bearing cups and inspect for signs of wear, scratching or pitting. Damage of this kind means that the bearings must be renewed, using a tapered drift. The outer bearing cups can be removed.
10 Clean the inner and outer bearing cone and roller assemblies and wipe dry with a clean non-fluffy rag.
11 Carefully inspect the cone and roller assemblies for signs of wear or damage which, if evident, means that complete race assemblies must be obtained. Do not use a new cone and roller assembly in an old cup.
12 Clean down the spindle and lubricate with fresh grease.
13 If the inner and/or outer bearing cups were removed the new cups should be fitted using a suitable diameter drift. Make sure they are replaced the correct way round and also correctly seated.
14 Pack the inside of the hub with fresh grease until it is flush with the inside diameter of both bearing cups.
15 With each bearing cone and roller assembly clean off old grease, pack with fresh grease taking care to work the grease well in between the rollers.
16 Place the inner bearing cone and roller assembly in the inner cup.
17 Apply a smear of grease to the lip of the grease seal and replace using a suitable diameter drift. Ensure the seal is correctly seated.
18 Refit the disc onto the wheel spindle taking care to keep the hub in a central position so that the grease retainer is not damaged.
19 Replace the outer bearing cone and roller assembly. Follow this with the plain washer and adjustment nut.
20 Adjust the wheel bearing as described in Section 3.
21 Fit a new cotter pin and bend the ends around the castellations of the nut lock to prevent interference with the radio static collector in the grease cap.
22 Replace the grease cap, tapping in position with a soft faced hammer.
23 Refer to Chapter 9 and replace the caliper.
24 Refit the wheel and secure. Lower the car to the ground.

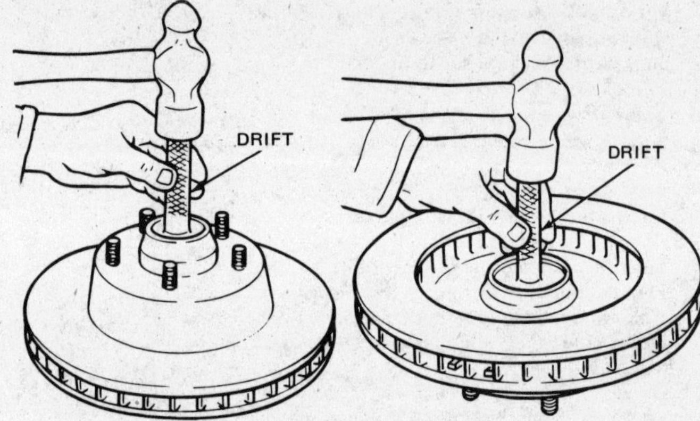

Fig. 11.2. Fitting the outer and inner bearing cups (Sec. 2)

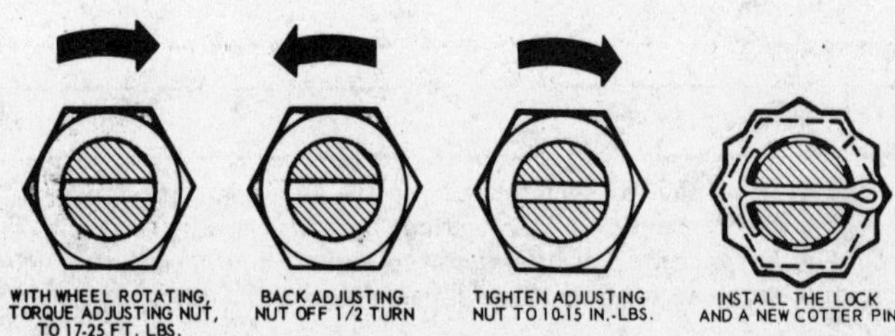

Fig. 11.3. Correct method of adjusting the front wheel bearing (Sec. 3)

3 Front wheel bearings - adjustment

1 Front wheel bearings should be adjusted if the wheel is loose on the spindle or if the wheel does not rotate freely.
2 Chock the rear wheels and apply the parking brake. Jack-up the front of the car and support on firmly based stands.
3 Remove the hub cap and ease off the grease cap from the hub.
4 Wipe the excess grease from the end of the spindle. Remove the cotter pin and nut lock.
5 Slowly rotate the wheel and hub assembly and tighten the adjusting nut to the specified torque wrench setting to seat the bearings.
6 Using a box spanner back off the adjustment nut by one half of a turn and then retighten the adjusting nut to a torque wrench setting of 10 - 15 lb f in or finger tight.
7 The castellations on the nut lock on the adjusting nut must be aligned with the cotter pin hole in the spindle.
8 Fit a new cotter pin and bend the ends of the cotter pin around the castellated flange of the nut to prevent interference with the radio static collector in the grease cap.
9 Check that the wheel rotates freely and then replace the grease cap and hub cap. Lower the car to the ground.

4 Front suspension lower balljoint - removal and replacement

1 Chock the rear wheels, apply the parking brake, jack-up the front of the car: leave the lower arm free to drop as the coil spring tension is eased.
2 Using a 1/8 inch (3.1 mm) drill, drill a pilot hole completely through each rivet. Now drill off the rivet head through the pilot hole using a 3/8 inch (9.5mm) drill.
3 Using a suitable diameter parallel pin punch, drive out both rivets.
4 Place a jack or stand under the lower arm and lower the car by about 6 inches (152 mm) so as to offset the coil spring tension.
5 Withdraw the balljoint stud cotter pin and remove the nut.
6 Using a universal balljoint separator tension the stud and then tap the spindle near to the lower stud. Do not release the stud using tension alone.
7 Remove the balljoint.
8 Clean the end of the arm, and remove all burrs from the hole edges

using a scraper.

9 Carefully inspect the arm especially in the area around the holes for cracks. If evident a new arm must be fitted.

10 Place the stand of the balljoint in the spindle bore and replace the securing nut which should be tightened finger tight at this stage.

11 Attach the balljoint to the lower arm and secure with high tensile steel nuts and bolts. **Do not** attempt to rivet the new balljoint to the arm. Tighten the nuts fully.

12 Tighten the balljoint stud nut to the specified torque wrench setting, and align to the nearest cotter pin hole.

13 Insert a new cotter pin.

14 Lower the car to the ground.

15 It is recommended that the steering angles and wheel track be checked by the local Ford dealer and adjusted if necessary.

5 Front suspension lower arm strut - removal and replacement

1 To give better working access jack-up the front of the car and support on firmly based stands.

2 Undo and remove the nut, washer and bushing from the lower arm strut at the frame sidemember.

3 Undo and remove the two nuts and bolts securing the strut to the lower arm.

4 Carefully pull the strut from the frame sidemember.

5 To refit, first position the front sidemember washer and bushing onto the strut and locate the strut in the sidemember and on the lower arm.

6 Refit the two nuts and bolts securing the strut to the lower arm. Tighten the nuts to the specified torque wrench setting.

7 Tighten the strut to sidemember securing nut to the specified torque wrench setting.

6 Front suspension lower arm - removal and replacement

1 Chock the rear wheels, apply the parking brake, jack-up the front of the car and support on firmly based axle stands. Remove the wheel to provide better access.

2 Refer to Section 2, and remove the disc and hub assembly from the spindle.

3 Undo and remove the dust shield securing bolts and lift away the backplate or dust shield.

4 Disconnect the lower end of the shock absorber and contract it into the spring.

5 Withdraw the cotter pins from the upper and lower balljoint stud nuts.

6 Undo and remove the two bolts and nuts securing the strut to the lower arm.

7 Remove the lower balljoint stud nut and then using a universal balljoint separator tension the stud. Tap the spindle near the lower stud

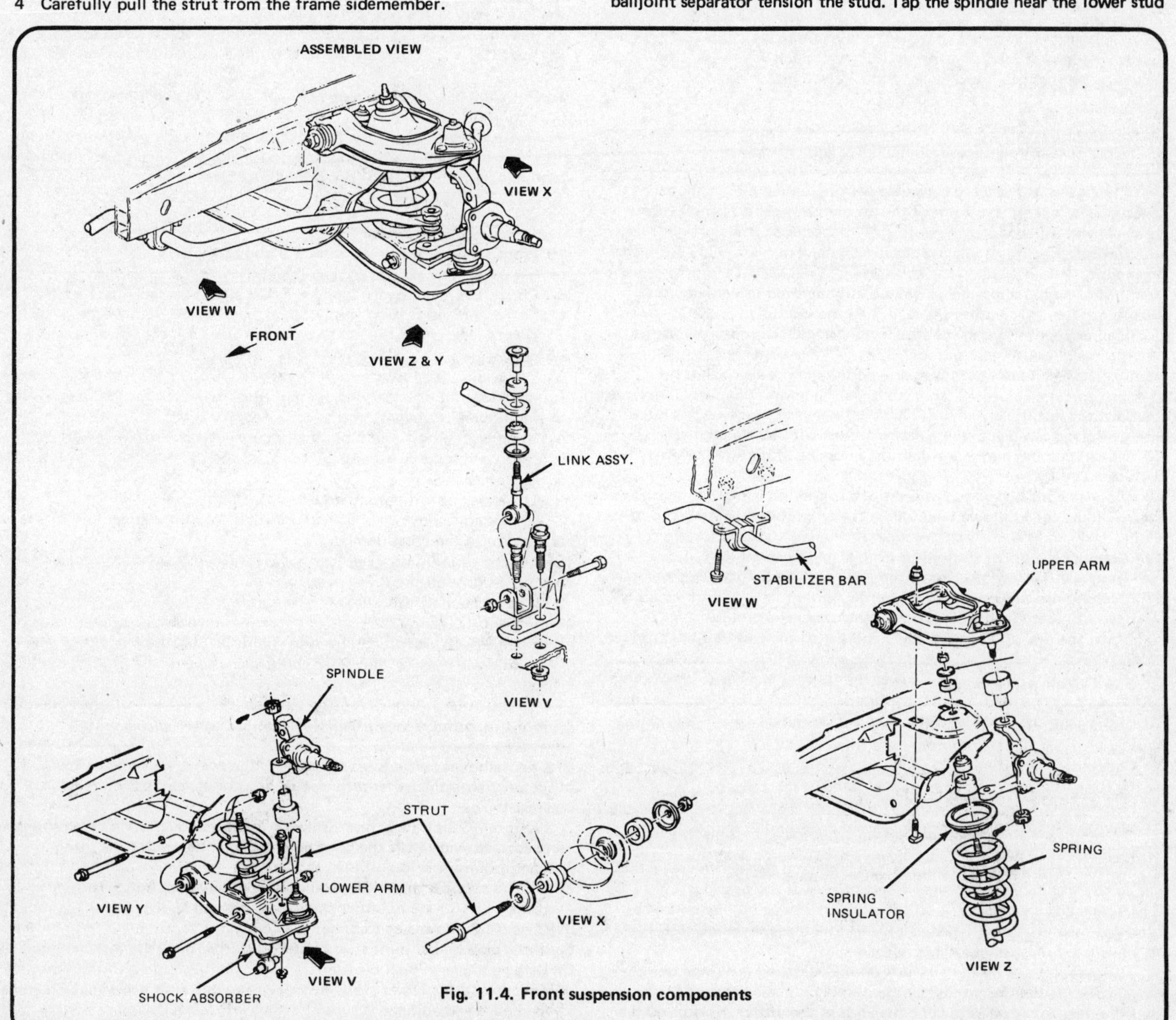

Fig. 11.4. Front suspension components

11

with a hammer to loosen the stud in the spindle. **Do not** attempt to loosen the stud using tension only.
8 Place a jack under the lower arms and then remove the lower balljoint stud nut.
9 Lower the jack and lift away the spring and insulator.
10 Undo and remove the one nut and bolt attaching the lower control arm to the no. 2 crossmember. Lift away the lower arm.
11 To refit, first position the lower arm to the no. 2 crossmember and loosely fit the securing nut and bolt.
12 Place the spring and insulator up onto the upper spring pad and then position on the lower arm.
13 Using a jack compress the spring whilst at the same time guiding the lower balljoint stud into the spindle hole.
14 Fit the balljoint stud securing nut and tighten to the specified torque wrench setting. Continue to tighten the nut until the cotter pin hole is in line with the nut slots.
15 Fit a new cotter pin to the upper and lower balljoint studs.
16 Draw the shock absorber down and connect it to the lower arm.
17 Position the strut to the lower arm and fit the securing bolts and nuts. Tighten the nuts to the specified torque wrench setting.
18 Tighten the lower arm to no. 2 crossmember securing bolt and nut to the specified torque wrench setting.
19 Place the dust shield onto the spindle and secure with the bolts which should be tightened to the specified torque wrench setting.
20 Refit the disc and hub assembly and adjust the bearings as described in Section 3.
21 Replace the roadwheel and lower the front of the car to the ground.
22 It is recommended that the steering angles and wheel track be checked by the local Ford dealer and adjusted if necessary.

7 Front suspension upper arm - removal and replacement

1 Chock the rear wheels, apply the parking brake, loosen the front wheel nuts, jack-up the front of the car and support on firmly based axle stands. Remove the wheel to provide better access.
2 Refer to Section 2 and remove the disc and hub assembly from the spindle.
3 Withdraw the upper balljoint stud nut and then using a universal balljoint separator tension the stud. Tap the spindle near the lower stud with a hammer to loosen the stud in the spindle. **Do not** attempt to loosen the stud using tension only.
5 Place a jack under the lower arm and then raise the jack until spring pressure is released from the upper balljoint stud nut. Undo and remove the nut.
6 Undo and remove the upper arm inner shaft securing bolts.
7 The upper arm and inner shaft may now be lifted away as an assembly.
8 To reassemble, first position the upper arm inner shaft to the frame side rail and refit the two securing bolts and washers. Tighten the bolts fully.
9 Connect the upper balljoint stud to the spindle and install the securing nut. Tighten the nut to the specified torque wrench setting.
10 Continue to tighten the nut until the cotter pin hole in the stud is in line with the nut slots. Fit a new cotter pin.
11 Refit the disc and hub assembly and adjust the bearings as described in Section 3.
12 Replace the roadwheel and lower the front of the car to the ground.
13 It is recommended that the steering angles and wheel track be checked by the local Ford dealer and adjusted if necessary.

8 Front suspension upper arm bushes - removal and replacement

To remove the bushings requires the use of special tools to avoid damage to the upper arm. If the bushings require renewal the upper arm should be taken to the local Ford dealer for renewal.

9 Front spindle - removal and replacement

1 Chock the rear wheels, apply the parking brake, loosen the front wheel nuts, jack-up the front of the car and support on firmly based axle stands. Remove the wheel.
2 Refer to Section 2, and remove the disc and hub assembly from the spindle.
3 Undo and remove the dust shield.
4 Remove the steering connecting rod from the spindle arm.
5 Withdraw the cotter pins from both balljoint stud nuts.
6 Remove the stud nuts and then using a universal balljoint separator tension the stud. Tap the spindle near the stud with a hammer to loosen the stud in the spindle. **Do not** attempt to loosen the stud tension only.
7 Place a jack under the lower control arm.
8 Undo and remove the balljoint stud nuts and lower the jack, thereby lowering the lower control arm, and lift away the spindle.
9 To refit the spindle, first position the spindle onto the lower balljoint stud and replace the securing nut which should be tightened to the specified torque wrench setting.
10 Continue to tighten the nut until the cotter pin hole is in line with the slots in the nut. Lock with a new cotter pin.
11 Jack-up the lower arm and carefully guide the upper balljoint stud into the spindle hole. Refit the securing nut and tighten to the specified torque wrench setting.
12 Continue to tighten the nut until the cotter pin hole is in line with the slots in the nut. Lock with a new cotter pin.
13 Lower the jack under the lower control arm.
14 Attach the steering connecting rod to the spindle and refit the nut and tighten to the specified torque wrench setting. Continue to tighten the nut until the cotter pin hole is in line with the slots in the nut. Lock with a new cotter pin.
15 Place the brake backplate/dust shield on the spindle and secure with the nuts and bolts. Tighten the nuts to the specified torque wrench setting.
16 Refit the disc and hub assembly and adjust the bearings as described in Section 3.
17 Replace the roadwheel and lower the front of the car to the ground.
18 It is recommended that the steering angles and wheel track be checked by the local Ford dealer and adjusted if necessary.

10 Front suspension spring - removal and replacement

1 Chock the rear wheels, apply the parking brake, jack-up the front of the car and support on firmly based axle stands. Remove the wheel.
2 Place a jack under the lower arm and raise until the lower arm is supported.
3 Disconnect the lower end of the shock absorber from the lower arm. It may be found necessary to use a pry bar to detach the 'T' shaped end of the shock absorber from the lower end.
4 Undo and remove the bolts that secure the strut to the lower arm.
5 Undo and remove the nut that secures the shock absorber to the crossmember.
6 The shock absorber may now be lifted away.
7 Undo and remove the nut and bolt that secure the inner end of the lower arm to the crossmember.
8 The jack should now be slowly and carefully lowered so relieving spring pressure on the lower arm.
9 When free of tension lift away the spring.
10 Inspect the spring for signs of excessive corrosion or broken coils. If evident a new pair of springs must be fitted because the one on the other side will have settled. This could cause adverse steering characteristics.
11 To refit the spring, first position it on the lower arm so that the lower end of the spring seats correctly against the corner of the spring pilot on the lower arm.
12 To maintain correct vehicle height the lower end of the spring must face rearwards on the right-hand side and forwards on the left-hand side of the car.
13 Carefully raise the lower arm with the jack whilst guiding the inner end so as to align with the bolt hole in the crossmember.
14 Slide the securing bolt into the front of the crossmember and through the lower arm. Refit the nut and tighten to the specified torque wrench setting.
15 Secure the lower end of the shock absorber to the lower arm with the nut and bolt which should be tightened to the specified torque wrench setting.
16 Secure the strut to the lower suspension arm with the two nuts and bolts and tighten to the specified torque wrench setting.
17 Refit the wheel and lower the car to the ground.

11 Front shock absorber - removal and replacement

1 Chock the rear wheels, apply the parking brake, loosen the front wheel nuts, jack-up the front of the car and support on firmly based axle stands. Remove the wheel.
2 Undo and remove the nut, washer and bushing from the top end of the shock absorber.
3 Undo and remove the nut and bolt securing the bottom end of the shock absorber to the lower suspension arm.
4 It may be found necessary to use a pry bar to detach the 'T' shaped end of the shock absorber from the lower end.
5 Examine the shock absorber for signs of damage to the body, distorted piston rod, loose mounting or hydraulic fluid leakage which, if evident, means a new unit should be fitted.
6 To test for shock absorber efficiency hold the unit in the vertical position and gradually extend the contract the unit between its maximum and minimum limits ten times. It should be apparent that there is equal resistance on both directions of movement. If this is not apparent a new unit should be fitted - always renew the shock absorbers in pairs.
7 Refitting the shock absorbers is the reverse sequence to removal but the following two additional points should be noted:

a) Tighten the shock absorber lower attachment to the specified torque wrench setting.
b) Tighten the shock absorber upper attachment to the specified torque wrench setting.

12 Rear suspension leaf spring - removal and replacement

1 Chock the front wheels, jack-up the rear of the car and support on firmly based axle stands. Also support the weight of the rear axle.
2 Disconnect the lower end of the shock absorber from the 'U' bolt spring plate and push it out of the way of the spring.
3 Undo and remove the spring plate nuts from the 'U' bolts and then lift away the plate.
4 Raise the rear axle slightly until its weight is taken from the spring.
5 Undo and remove the rear shackle bar securing nuts. Lift away the shackle bar and the two shackle inner bushes.
6 Remove the rear shackle assembly and recover the two outer bushings.
7 Undo and remove the front hanger bolt and nut from the eye at the front end of the spring.
8 Lift away the spring assembly.
9 If the front bushing is to be renewed it is best to leave this part of the job to the local Ford dealer as a special tool is required to draw out the old bushing and insert the new one. If one is ambitious, however, the job can be done using a large bench vise and a selection of tubular drifts.
10 The manufacturer's recommend that when a rear spring is being renewed all old nuts and bolts should be discarded and new ones obtained. Always renew rear springs in pairs.
11 To refit the rear spring, first position it under the rear axle and insert the shackle assembly with the two shackle bushings into the rear hanger bracket and the rear eye of the spring.
12 Fit the shackle inner bushings, the shackle plate and the locknuts. These should be tightened finger tight at this stage.
14 Refit the locknut on the hanger bolt and tighten finger tight at this stage.
15 Assemble the insulators and retainer to the spring.
16 Lower the rear axle until it rests on the spring. Place the spring plate on the insulator center locator.
17 Replace the 'U' bolts and secure with the nuts which should be tightened to the specified torque wrench setting.
18 Reconnect the lower end of the shock absorber to the spring plate and assemble the insulator, washer and new nut.
19 Place stands under the rear axle and lower the car until the spring is in its approximate normal position.
20 Tighten the front hanger locknut to the specified torque wrench setting.
21 Tighten the rear shackle locknuts to the specified torque wrench setting.
22 Refit the wheel and lower the car to the ground.

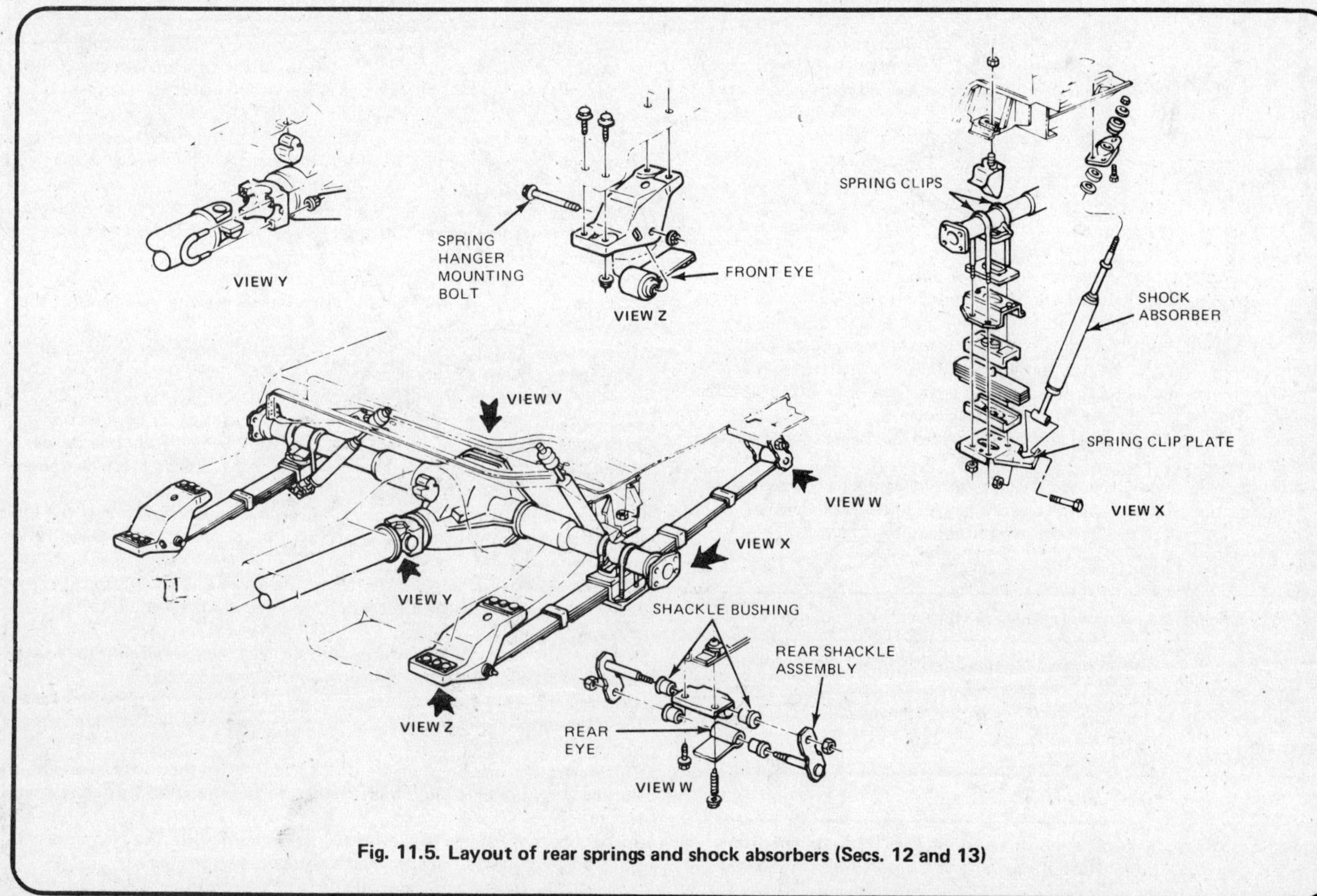

Fig. 11.5. Layout of rear springs and shock absorbers (Secs. 12 and 13)

11

13 Rear suspension shock absorber - removal and replacement

1 Chock the front wheels, jack-up the rear of the car and support on firmly based axle stands. Remove the wheel to give better access.
2 Disconnect the lower end of the shock absorber from the 'U' bolt spring plate.
3 Undo and remove the three bolts securing the mounting bracket located at the upper end of the shock absorber.
4 Compress the shock absorber and remove it from the car.
5 Remove the securing bracket, nut, bushing and washers from the shock absorber studs.
6 Examination and testing of the rear shock absorber is similar to that for the front shock absorber. Refer to Section 11, paragraphs 5 and 6 for full information.
7 Refitting the rear shock absorber is the reverse sequence to removal but the following additional points should be noted:

a) *Tighten the shock absorber to bracket securing nut to the specified torque wrench setting.*
b) *Tighten the shock absorber to 'U' bolt spring plate securing nut to the specified torque wrench setting.*
c) *Tighten the shock absorber upper bracket to body to the specified torque wrench setting.*

14 Steering assembly - removal and replacement

1 Move the steering wheel to the 'straight-ahead' position, and lock the steering with the ignition key.
2 Chock the rear wheels, apply the parking brake, loosen the front wheel nuts, jack-up the front of the car and support on firmly based axle stands. Remove the roadwheels.
3 Undo and remove the bolts securing the flexible coupling to the pinion shaft.
4 Withdraw the cotter pins and remove the nuts securing the connecting rod ends to the spindle arms.
5 Using a universal balljoint separator detach the connecting rod ends from the spindle arms.
6 To gain access to the steering gear retaining bolts, it will be necessary to remove the bolts securing the secondary (No. 2A) crossmember located at the rear of the main (No. 2) crossmember to which the steering gear is attached.
7 Support the steering gear and remove the three nuts, washers and long bolts that retain the steering gear to the front crossmember (see Fig. 11.6).
8 The steering assembly may now be removed from the left-hand side of the car.
9 To refit the steering assembly, first check that the front wheels (steering wheel) are in the 'straight-ahead' position.
10 Inspect the steering assembly and guide into position working from the left-hand side of the car.
11 Align the mating splines on the flexible coupling and the pinion shaft.
12 Line up the steering gear and crossmember mounting holes, fit the insulating washers and insert the three securing bolts. Screw on the nuts and tighten to the specified torque setting.
13 Refit the No. 2A crossmember at the rear of the main front crossmember.
14 Fit the connecting rod ends to the spindle arms. Replace the castellated nuts and tighten them to the specified torque wrench setting.
15 Tighten the nut to align to the nearest cotter pin slot and lock with a new cotter pin.
16 Tighten the flexible coupling to pinion shaft bolts to the specified torque wrench setting.
17 Refit the roadwheels and lower the car to the ground.
18 Whenever the steering gear assembly is removed or refitted it is recommended that the front wheel alignment be checked. Further information will be found in Section 28.

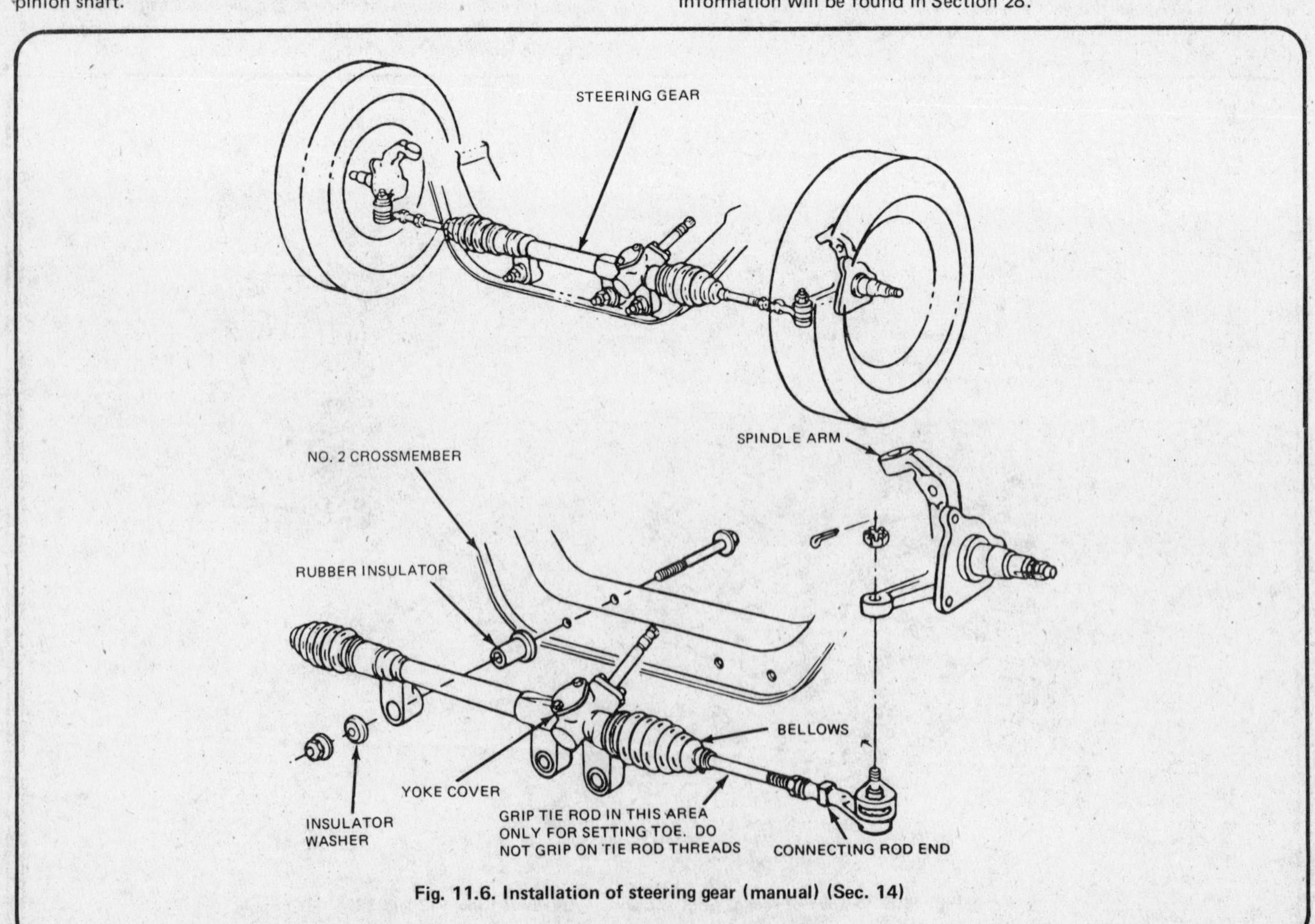

Fig. 11.6. Installation of steering gear (manual) (Sec. 14)

15 Manual steering assembly - repair - general

1 Whenever it is found necessary to repair the steering gear it must always be removed from the car first.
2 Due to the special skill and tools required to remove and refit the rack ball sockets, repair operations should be restricted to those given in the following Sections.

16 Bellows seal - removal and replacement

1 Mount the steering gear assembly in a bench vise. Use the mounting pads for this.
2 Slacken both clips that secure the ends of the bellows and remove the bellows.
3 Be sure to keep the gear body below the level of the bellows as this will avoid spilling lubricant. Empty the lubricant into a clean container.
4 Hold the gear assembly in a vertical position. Move the rack between the two locks to remove any remaining lubricant.
5 To fit the new bellows mount the gear assembly vertically in a bench vice.
6 Move the rack until the upper rod is fully extended.
7 Carefully fit the new bellows and tighten the larger diameter clip. (See paragraph 10).
8 Refill with 7 ounces of gear lubricant (obtainable from Ford dealers (type: 'C6AZ - 19580-B'). A squirt oil can is best for this purpose.
9 Move the rack to-and-fro to distribute the lubricant.
10 The clips must now be positioned so that the tightening screws are in the same plane as the pinion shaft. The screw ends must point upwards.
11 Tighten the clips and refit the clip screw caps.

17 Input shaft seal - removal and replacement

1 Thoroughly clean the input shaft and area around the shaft.
2 Using a small screwdriver prise out the old pinion seal from its bore.
3 Well lubricate a new pinion seal and fit the seal over the shaft.
4 Using a piece of suitable diameter tube engage the outer flange of the seal and press or tap the seal into its bore until the flange is flush with the shoulder of the bore. Should the outer edge of the seal not be engaged during assembling the seal will be damanged.

18 Rack support yoke assembly - removal and replacement

1 Thoroughly clean the exterior of the gear assembly and mount in a bench vise.
2 Remove the yoke cover securing bolts and lift away the cover, gasket, shims and yoke spring.
3 The old gasket must not be re-used.
4 Reassembly is the reverse sequence to removal. Should it be necessary to adjust the yoke to rack spring tension refer to Section 19, for further information. Always use a sealer on the cover bolt threads and tighten to the specified torque wrench setting.

19 Support yoke to rack - adjustment

1 Refer to Section 18, and follow the instructions given in paragraphs 1 - 3, inclusive.
2 Refit the yoke and cover but leave out the gasket, shims and the spring.
3 Tighten the cover bolts to the specified torque wrench setting, until the cover just touches the yoke.
4 Measure the gap between the cover and the housing flange with feeler gauges.
5 The thickness of the shim pack and gasket must give a combined rack thickness of 0.0005 - 0.0006 in (0.0127 - 0.0152 mm) greater than the measured gap.
6 Remove the cover again, and fit the new gasket next to the housing flange. Follow this with the selected shims, spring and cover.
7 Always use a sealer on the cover bolt threads and tighten the bolts to the specified torque wrench setting.

20 Pinion shaft cover assembly - removal and replacement

1 Thoroughly clean the exterior of the gear assembly and mount in a bench vise.
2 Slacken the bolts of the rack support cover to relieve the yoke spring tension on the rack.
3 Move the rack to either lock and note the relative position of the flat on the input shaft. It is very important that when subsequent reassembly of the pinion shaft is made, the flat be aligned in the same position. Should the pinion not be reassembled in the same original position steering wheel alignment will be incorrect.
4 Remove the pinion cover, shims and gasket.
5 The old gasket must not be re-used.
6 Withdraw the pinion lower bearing and the pinion shaft. Recover the spacer.
7 Inspect the pinion shaft, seal, bearing and rack teeth for damage and renew any worn or suspect parts.
8 To reassemble, first well lubricate the spacer, pinion shaft and bearing with steering gear lubricant and the internal diameter of the pinion seal with chassis grease.
9 Place the gear assembly in the vise with the pinion shaft cover flange upwards.
10 Fit the spacer into position against the bearing face.
11 With the rack moved to one full lock position assemble the pinion. The flat on the shaft must be in the same relative position as was noted before dismantling (paragraph 3).
12 Reassemble the bearing aligning the shaft with the internal diameter of the bearing by rotating the shaft and applying side pressure.
13 Tap the bearing evenly into its bore until it is recessed below the shoulder of the bore.
14 If the bearing preload needs to be adjusted or a new shim pack to be fitted refer to Section 21 for further information.
15 Assemble the shim pack with the thinnest shim (or shims) first and then follow with the 0.093 in (2.362 mm) shim next to the cover (Fig. 11.8).
16 Fit a new gasket, and the cover.
17 Always use a sealer on the cover bolt threads and tighten the bolts to the specified torque wrench setting.

21 Pinion bearing preload - adjustment

1 Refer to Section 20 and follow the instructions given in paragraphs 1 and 2.
2 Remove the pinion cover and clean the cover flange area thoroughly.
3 Remove the gasket and shims. Discard the old gasket.

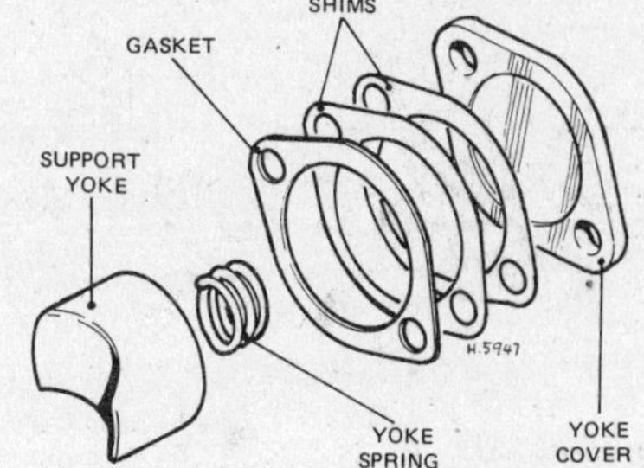

Fig. 11.7. Rack support yoke components (Sec. 19)

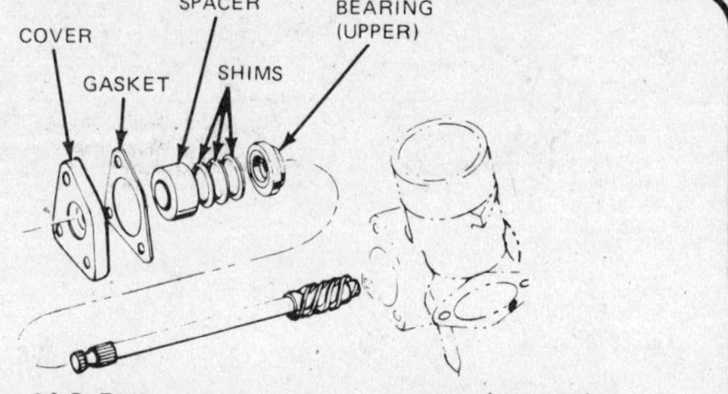

Fig. 11.8. Pinion bearing cover and shims (Sec. 20)

4 Fit a new gasket and shims until the shim pack is flush with the gasket. Use a straight edge and feeler gauge for this.
5 Build up the shim pack in the following order: Fit the thinnest shim first and then the 0.093 in (2.362 mm) shim and cover.
6 Add a further 0.005 in (0.127 mm) shim to the pack to preload the bearings.
7 The thickest shim should always be fitted next to the cover.
8 Refit the cover. Always use a sealer on the cover bolt threads and tighten the bolts to the specified torque wrench setting.

22 Power steering - general description

1 The power steering system available on Mustang II cars has a pulley-driven Ford Thompson type pump. This pump delivers fluid to a servo assisted rack and pinion gear assembly (photo).
2 Servo assistance is obtained through a piston mounted on the rack and running in the rack tube. The degree of assistance is controlled by a spool valve mounted concentrically with the input and pinion shaft.

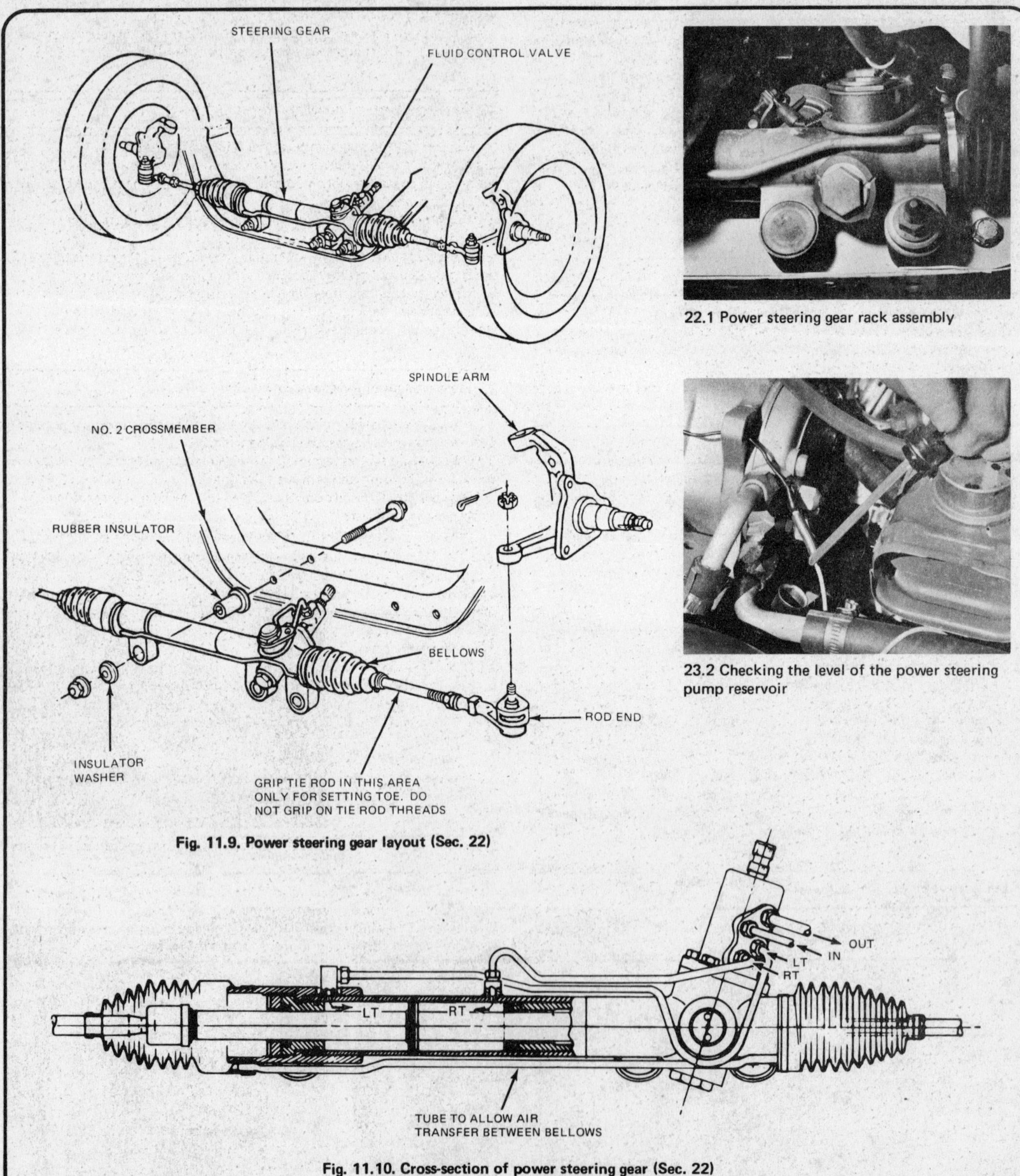

22.1 Power steering gear rack assembly

23.2 Checking the level of the power steering pump reservoir

Fig. 11.9. Power steering gear layout (Sec. 22)

Fig. 11.10. Cross-section of power steering gear (Sec. 22)

3 The power steering pump incorporates an integral fluid reservoir.
4 Owing to the complexity of the power steering system it is recommended that servicing etc., is limited to that given in the following Sections. In the event of a fault occurring it is recommended that repair or overhaul is entrusted to a specialist in this type of work.

23 Power steering - bleeding

1 The power steering system will only need bleeding in the event of air being introduced into the system ie, where pipes have been disconnected or where a leakage has occurred. To bleed the system proceed as described in the following paragraphs.
2 Open the hood and check the fluid level in the pump reservoir (photo). Top up if necessary using the specified type of fluid.
3 If fluid is added, allow two minutes then run the engine at approximately 1500 rpm. Slowly turn the steering wheel from lock-to-lock, whilst checking and topping-up the fluid level until the level remains steady, and no more bubbles appear in the reservoir.
4 Clean and refit the reservoir cap, and close the hood.

24 Power steering pump - removal and refitting

1 Slacken the pump adjusting bolt and retaining bolts.
2 Push the pump in toward the engine, and remove the drive belt.
3 Disconnect the power system fluid lines from the pump and drain the fluid into a suitable container.
4 Plug, or tape over, the end of the lines to prevent dirt ingress.
5 If necessary, remove the alternator drive belt(s) as described in Chapter 10.
6 Remove the bolts attaching the pump to the engine bracket and remove the pump. **Note:** On some engine installations it may be necessary to remove the pump complete with bracket.
7 Refitting is a direct reversal of the removal procedure. Ensure that the fluid lines are tightened to the specified torque, top-up the system with an approved fluid, adjust the alternator drivebelt tension (see Chapter 10), then bleed the system, as described in Section 23.

25 Power steering gear - removal and refitting

1 The procedure for removing the power steering gear is similar to that described in Section 14 for the manual steering gear with the additional task of disconnecting the pump lines. When refitting, ensure that the fluid lines are tightened to the specified torque, top-up the system with an approved fluid, adjust the alternator drivebelt tension (see Chapter 10), then bleed the system, as described in Section 23.

26 Steering wheel - removal and refitting

1 Disconnect the negative terminal from the battery.
2 Remove the two screws from the underside of the horn pad, remove the complete horn pad assembly and disconnect the horn wiring terminals (photos).
3 Using a socket wrench, remove the steering wheel retaining nut (photo).
4 Remove the wheel by knocking it upward using the palms of the hand only. Do not strike the wheel with a hammer or mallet.
5 When refitting the steering wheel ensure the front wheels are in a straight-ahead position, and line up the mark on the end of the steering column center shaft with the mark on the steering wheel.

27 Steering column - removal and replacement

1 For safety reasons, disconnect the battery negative cable. Remove the steering wheel as described in Section 26.
2 Remove the screws retaining the section of instrument panel below the steering column and remove the panel.
3 Remove the trim shrouds that cover the steering column adjacent to the instrument panel.
4 Pull out the rubber boot from the base of the steering column at

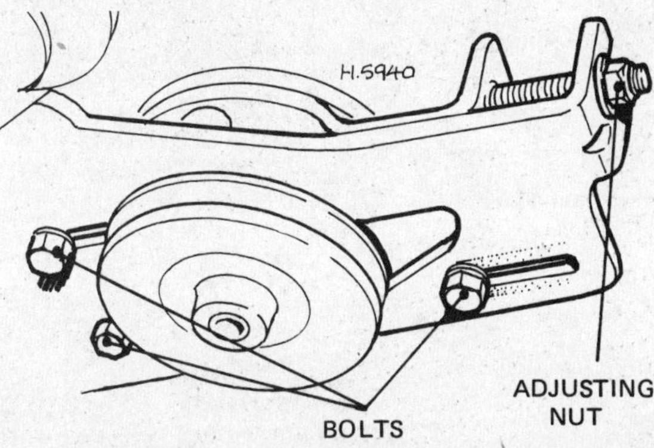

Fig. 11.11. Power steering pump retaining and adjuster nuts (V6 shown) (Sec. 24)

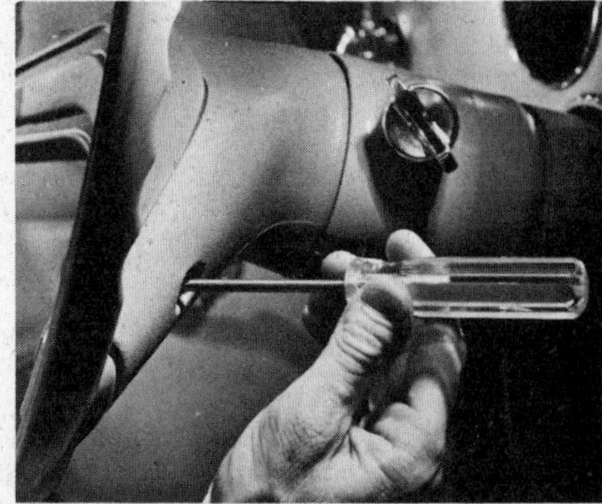
26.2A Removing the horn pad retaining screws

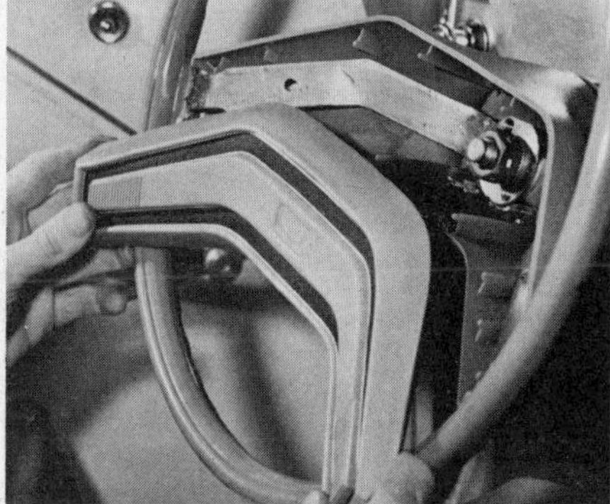
26.2B Lifting away the horn pad.....

26.2C .....and disconnecting the wiring terminals

26.3 Steering wheel retaining nut

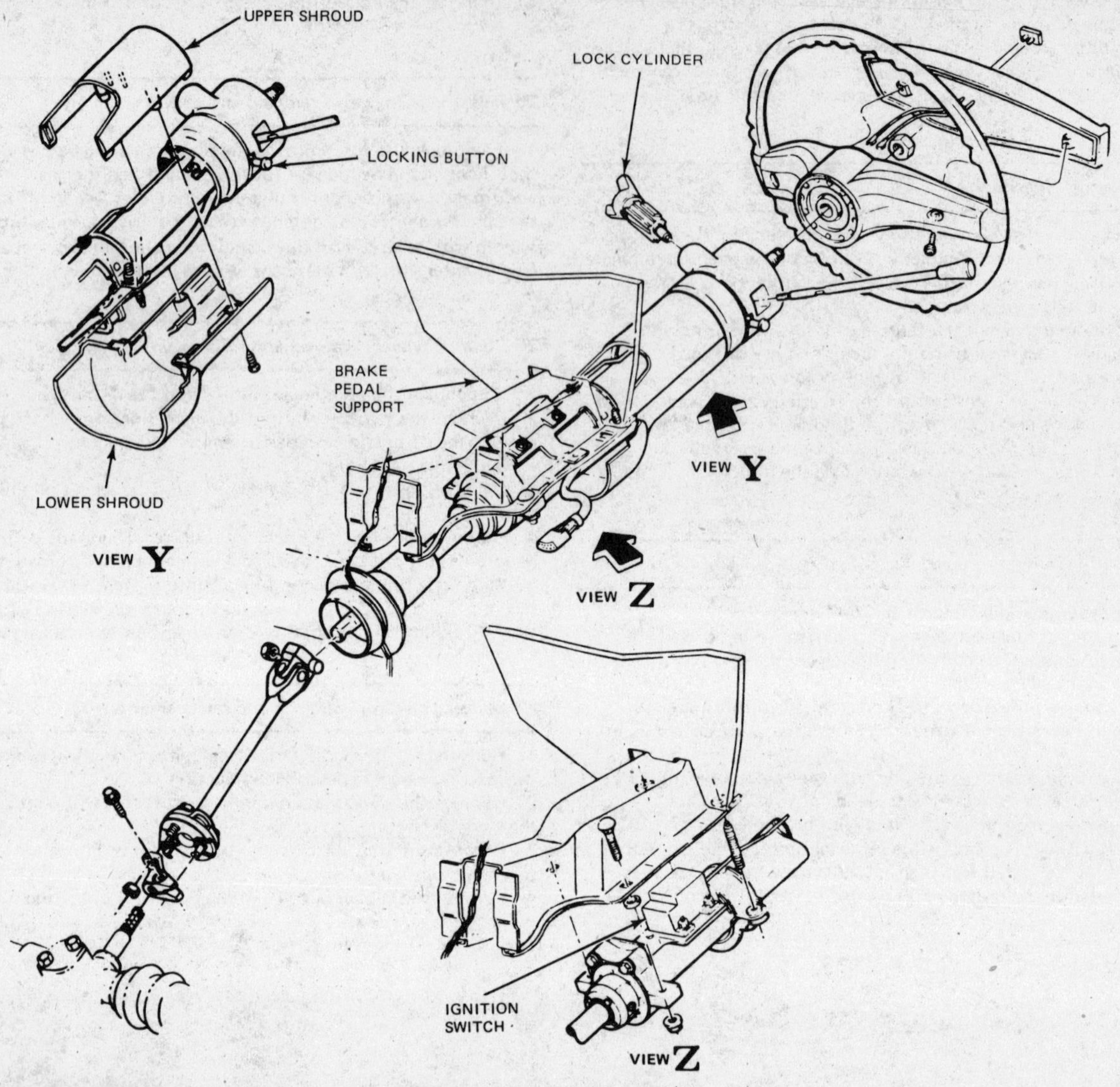

Fig. 11.12. Steering column layout (Sec. 27)

the dash panel aperture.

5 Remove the two nuts that secure the steering column lower shaft and 'U' coupling assembly to the flange on the input shaft.

6 Disengage the bolt and safety strap from the flange.

7 Remove the four nuts that attach the steering column support bracket to the brake pedal housing.

8 Carefully lower the column assembly and disconnect the electrical coupling from the column (see Chapter 10).

9 Withdraw the complete steering column assembly from beneath the instrument panel.

10 Refer to Chapter 10 and remove the turn signal switch.

11 Undo and remove the turn signal switch screws and lift the switch over the upper shaft.

12 Carefully remove the snap-ring from the top of the steering shaft.

13 Make a note of their relative jointings and disconnect the ignition switch, turn signal and horn wire connections.

14 Undo and remove the four nuts securing the steering column to the brake support bracket.

15 Suitably support the column assembly and raise the column whilst tapping the steering shaft lightly with a soft faced hammer to free the upper bearing from the steering shaft.

16 Once the upper bearing has been removed continue to raise the column assembly until it is free of the steering shaft.

17 Undo and remove the two screws holding the lower bearing retainer assembly to the end of the column tube.

18 Remove the lower bearing retainer assembly.

19 The lower bearing can now be snapped out of the plastic retainer.

20 Examine the bearings and shaft for wear and replace if necessary.

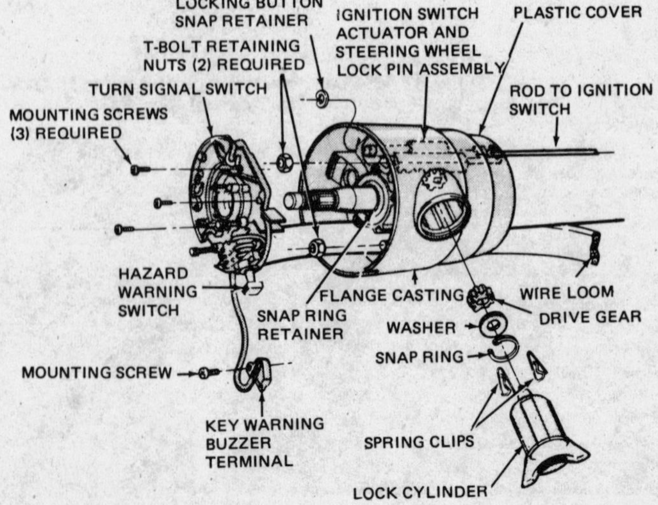

Fig. 11.13. Steering column lock and switch components (Sec. 27)

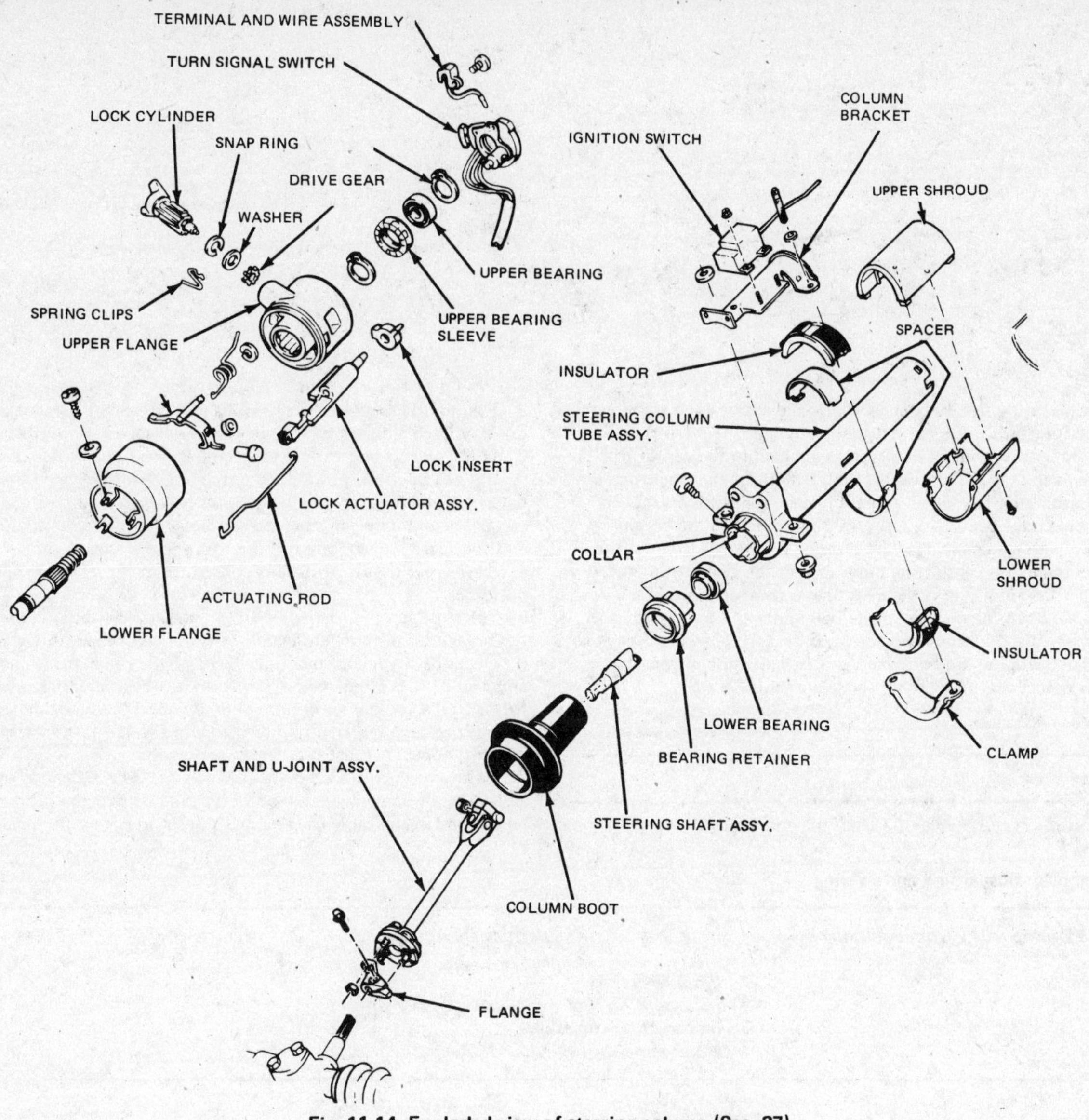

Fig. 11.14. Exploded view of steering column (Sec. 27)

21 To remove the ignition lock and switch refer to Chapter 10.
22 Reassemble the steering column using the reverse procedure to dismantling.
23 Before refitting the column assembly into the car do not forget to fit the rubber boot over the lower end of the column.
24 When refitting the steering column lower shaft 'U' joint to the steering gear input shaft make sure the safety strap is correctly positioned to prevent metal-to-metal contact after the nuts are tightened to the specified torque wrench setting.
25 The remainder of the refitting procedure is the reverse of the removal procedure.

28 Steering angles and front wheel alignment

1 Accurate front wheel alignment is essential for good steering and tire wear. Before considering the steering angle, check that the tires are correctly inflated, that the front wheels are not buckled, the hub bearings are not worn or incorrectly adjusted and that the steering linkage is in good order, without slackness or wear at the joints.
2 Wheel alignment consists of four factors:

Camber which is the angle at which the front wheels are set from the vertical when viewed from the front of the car. Positive camber is the amount (in degrees) that the wheels are tilted outwards at the top from the vertical.

Castor is the angle between the steering axis and a vertical line when viewed from each side of the car. Positive castor is when the steering axis is inclined rearwards.

Steering axis inclination is the angle when viewed from the front of the car, between the vertical and an imaginary line drawn between the upper and lower knuckle pivots.

Toe is the amount by which the distance between the **front** inside edges of the roadwheels (measured at hub height) differs from the distance measured between the **rear** inside edges.

3 The angles of camber, castor and steering axis require special equipment to set up and the job should be left to a Ford dealer.
4 Front wheel alignment (toe-in) checks are best carried out with modern setting equipment but a reasonably accurate alternative is by means of the following procedure.
5 Place the car on level ground with the wheels in the 'straight-ahead' position.
6 Obtain or make a toe-in gauge. One may easily be made from a length of rod or tubing, cranked to clear the sump or bellhousing and having a setscrew and locknut at one end.
7 With the gauge, measure the distance between the two inner wheel rims at hub height at the front of the wheel.
8 Rotate the roadwheel through 180° (half a turn) by pushing or pulling the car and then measure the distance again at hub height between the inner wheel rims at the rear of the roadwheel. This measurement should either be the same as the one just taken or greater by not more than 0.28 in (7 mm).
9 Where the toe-in is found to be incorrect slacken the locknuts on

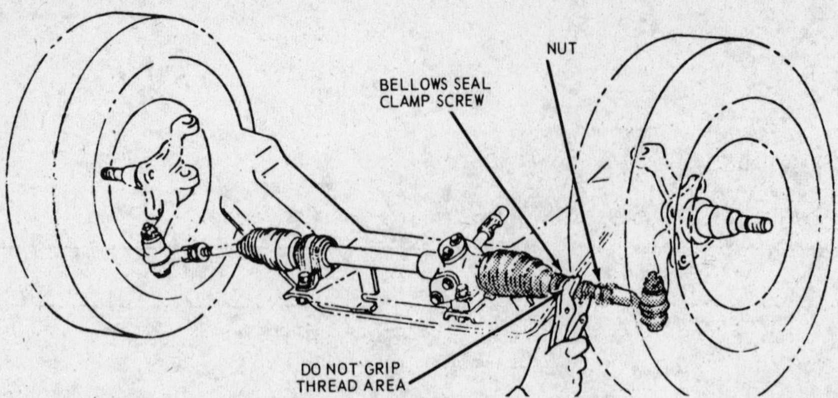

Fig. 11.15. Adjusting the front wheel alignment

each trackrod, also the flexible bellows clips and rotate each trackrod by an equal amount until the correct toe is obtained. Tighten the trackrod-end locknuts while the ball joints are held in the center of their arcs of travel. It is imperative that the lengths of the trackrods are always equal otherwise the wheel angles on turns will be incorrect. If new components have been fitted, set the roadwheels in the 'straight-ahead' position and also centralise the steering wheel. Now adjust the lengths of the trackrods by turning them so that the tierod-end ball joint studs will drop easily into the eyes of the steering arms. Measure the distances between the centers of the ball joints and the grooves on the inner ends of the trackrods and adjust, if necessary, so that they are equal. This is an initial setting only and precise adjustment must be carried out as described in earlier paragraphs of this Section.

29 Wheels and tires

1 Check the tire pressures weekly (when they are cold).

2 Frequently inspect the tire walls and treads for damage and pick out any large stones which have become trapped in the tread pattern.

3 If the wheels and tires have been balanced on the car then they should not be moved to a different axle position. If they have been balanced off the car then, in the interests of extending tread life, they can be moved between the front and rear on the same side of the car and the spare incorporated in the rotational pattern.

4 Never mix tires of different construction or very dissimilar tread patterns.

5 Always keep the roadwheels tightened to the specified torque and if the bolt holes become elongated or flattened, renew the wheel.

6 Occasionally, clean the inner faces of the roadwheels and if there is any sign of rust or corrosion, paint them with metal preservative paint. **Note:** Corrosion on aluminium alloy wheels may be evidence of a more serious problem which could lead to wheel failure. If corrosion is evident, consult your Ford dealer for advice.

7 Before removing a roadwheel which has been balanced on the car, always mark one wheel stud and bolt hole so that the roadwheel may be refitted in the same relative position to maintain the balance.

30 Fault diagnosis - Suspension and steering

Before diagnosing faults from the following chart, check that any irregularities are not caused by:

1 *Binding brakes.*
2 *Incorrect 'mix' of radial and crossply tires.*
3 *Incorrect tire pressures.*
4 *Misalignment of the bodyframe.*

Symptom	Reason/s
Steering wheel can be moved considerably before any sign of movement of the roadwheels is apparent	Wear in the steering linkage, gear and column coupling.
Vehicle difficult to steer in a consistent straight line - wandering	As above. When alignment incorrect (indicated by excessive or uneven tire wear). Front wheel hub bearings loose or worn. Worn ball joints.
Steering stiff and heavy	Incorrect wheel alignment (indicated by excessive or uneven tire wear). Excessive wear of seizure in one or more of the joints in the steering linkage or suspension. Excessive wear in the steering gear. Failure of power steering gear pump.
Wheel wobble and vibration	Roadwheels out of balance. Roadwheels buckled. Wheel alignment incorrect. Wear in the steering linkage, suspension ball joints or track control arm pivot. Broken front spring.
Excessive pitching and rolling on corners and during braking	Defective shock absorbers and/or broken spring.

Chapter 12 Bodywork and fittings

For modifications, and information applicable to later models, see Supplement at end of manual

Contents

1 General description

The Mustang II is available in two basic body styles, the two-door sedan and the three-door hatchback. The Mustang II Mach 1 has the same body style as the hatchback but has lower front and rear bumpers and a black finish around the lower body sections. The Ghia model has a vinyl covered roof and rear opera windows as standard, plus a host of luxury features too numerous to mention.

All models have a combined body and underframe of all steel welded construction, making a very strong and torsionally rigid shell.

Large impact-absorbing bumpers are fitted to all models as standard and bumper guards are available as optional extras.

The front door windows have a conventional winding mechanism. On certain models opening rear quarter windows are fitted. These are hinged at the forward edge and are operated from an 'over-center' type latch. A heated rear window is available as an optional extra throughout the range.

All vehicles have individual reclining front bucket seats. On hatchback models the rear seat folds down to provide luggage space. The standard seat and panel upholstery is a vinyl material but a cloth fabric trim is available for all models.

A padded facia crash panel is standard equipment together with deep pile wall-to-wall carpeting. Inertia reel seatbelts are fitted to all models.

All models are fitted with a heating and ventilating system which operates by ram air when the car is moving, or by a blower when stationary or for increased airflow. The heater is operated from a central control panel and airflow is directed to the windshield or car interior according to the control lever settings. A heavy duty heater is available for some markets, and all models can be supplied with an optional air conditioning system.

2 Maintenance - bodywork and underframe

1 The general condition of a car's bodywork is the thing that significantly affects its value. Maintenance is easy but needs to be regular. Neglect, particularly after minor damage, can lead quickly to further deterioration and costly repair bills. It is important also to keep watch on those parts of the car not immediately visible, for instance the underside, inside all the wheel arches and the lower part of the engine compartment.

2 The basic maintenance routine for the bodywork is washing - preferably with a lot of water, from a hose. This will remove all the loose solids which may have stuck to the car. It is important to flush these off in such a way as to prevent grit from scratching the finish. The wheel arches and underframe need washing in the same way to remove any accumulated mud which will retain moisture and tend to encourage rust. Paradoxically enough, the best time to clean the underframe and wheel arches is in wet weather when the mud is thoroughly wet and soft. In very wet weather the underframe is usually cleaned of large accumulations automatically and this is a good time for inspection.

3 Periodically, it is a good idea to have the whole of the underframe of the car steam cleaned, engine compartment included, so that a thorough inspection can be carried out to see what minor repairs and renovations are necessary. Steam cleaning is available at many garages and is necessary for removal of the accumulation of oily grime which sometimes is allowed to become thick in certain areas. If steam cleaning

facilities are not available, there are one or two excellent grease solvents available which can be brush applied. The dirt can then be simply hosed off.

4 After washing paintwork, wipe off with a chamois leather to give an unspotted clear finish. A coat of clear protective wax polish will give added protection against chemical pollutants in the air. If the paintwork sheen has dulled or oxidised, use a cleaner/polisher combination to restore the brilliance of the shine. This requires a little effort, but such dulling is usually caused because regular washing has been neglected. Always check that the door and ventilator opening drain holes and pipes are completely clear so that water can be drained out. Bright work should be treated in the same way as paintwork. Windscreens and windows can be kept clear of the smeary film which often appears, by adding a little ammonia to the water. If they are scratched a good rub with a proprietary metal polish will often clear them. Never use any form of wax or other body or chromium polish on glass.

3 Maintenance - upholstery and carpets

1 Mats and carpets should be brushed or vacuum cleaned regularly to keep them free of grit. If they are badly stained remove them from the car for scrubbing or sponging and make quite sure they are dry before refitting. Seats and interior trim panels can be kept clean by a wipe over with a damp cloth. If they do become stained (which can be more apparent on light coloured upholstery) use a little liquid detergent and a soft nail brush to scour the grime out of the grain of the material. Do not forget to keep the head lining clean in the same way as the upholstery. When using liquid cleaners inside the car do not over-wet the surfaces being cleaned. Excessive damp could get into the seams and padded interior causing stains, offensive odours or even rot. If the inside of the car gets wet accidentally it is worthwhile taking some trouble to dry it out properly, particularly where carpets are involved. *Do not leave oil or electric heaters inside the car for this purpose.*

4 Maintenance - PVC external roof covering

Under no circumstances try to clean any external PVC roof covering with detergents, caustic soaps or spirit cleaners. Plain soap and water is all that is required, with a soft brush to clean the dirt that may be ingrained. Wash the covering as frequently as the rest of the car.

5 Minor body damage - repair

The photographic sequences on pages 206 and 207 illustrate the operations detailed in the following sub-sections.

Repair of minor scratches in the car's bodywork

If the scratch is very superficial, and does not penetrate to the metal of the bodywork, repair is very simple. Lightly rub the area of the scratch with a paintwork renovator, or a very fine cutting paste, to remove loose paint from the scratch and to clear the surrounding bodywork of wax polish. Rinse the area with clean water.

Apply touch-up paint to the scratch using a fine paintbrush; continue to apply thin layers of paint until the surface of the paint in the scratch is level with the surrounding paintwork. Allow the new paint at least two weeks to harden: then blend it into the surrounding paintwork by rubbing the scratch area with a paintwork renovator or a very fine cutting paste. Finally, apply wax polish.

Where the scratch has penetrated right through to the metal of the bodywork, causing the metal to rust, a different repair technique is required. Remove any loose rust from the bottom of the scratch with a penknife, then apply rust inhibiting paint to prevent the formation of rust in the future. Using a rubber or nylon applicator fill the scratch with bodystopper paste. If required, this paste can be mixed with cellulose thinners to provide a very thin paste which is ideal for filling narrow scratches. Before the stopper-paste in the scratch hardens, wrap a piece of smooth cotton rag around the top of a finger. Dip the finger in cellulose thinners and then quickly sweep it across the surface of the stopper-paste in the scratch; this will ensure that the surface of the stopper-paste is slightly hollowed. The scratch can now be painted over as described earlier in this Section.

Repair of dents in the car's bodywork

When deep denting of the car's bodywork has taken place, the first task is to pull the dent out, until the affected bodywork almost attains its original shape. There is little point in trying to restore the original shape completely, as the metal in the damaged area will have stretched on impact and cannot be reshaped fully to its original contour. It is better to bring the level of the dent up to a point which is about 1/8 in (3 mm) below the level of the surrounding bodywork. In cases where the dent is very shallow anyway, it is not worth trying to pull it out at all. If the underside of the dent is accessible, it can be hammered out gently from behind, using a mallet with a wooden or plastic head. Whilst doing this, hold a suitable block of wood firmly against the outside of the panel to absorb the impact from the hammer blows and thus prevent a large area of the bodywork from being 'belled-out'.

Should the dent be in a section of the bodywork which has double skin or some other factor making it inaccessible from behind, a different technique is called for. Drill several small holes through the metal inside the area – particularly in the deeper section. Then screw long self-tapping screws into the holes just sufficiently for them to gain a good purchase in the metal. Now the dent can be pulled out by pulling on the protruding heads of the screws with a pair of pliers.

The next stage of the repair is the removal of the paint from the damaged area, and from an inch or so of the surrounding 'sound' bodywork. This is accomplished most easily by using a wire brush or abrasive pad on a power drill, although it can be done just as effectively by hand using sheets of abrasive paper. To complete the preparation for filling, score the surface of the bare metal with a screwdriver or the tang of a file, or alternatively, drill small holes in the affected area. This will provide a really good 'key' for the filler paste.

To complete the repair see the Section on filling and respraying.

Repair of rust holes or gashes in the car's bodywork

Remove all paint from the affected area and from an inch or so of the surrounding 'sound' bodywork, using an abrasive pad or a wire brush on a power drill. If these are not available a few sheets of abrasive paper will do the job just as effectively. With the paint removed you will be able to gauge the severity of the corrosion and therefore decide whether to renew the whole panel (if this is possible) or to repair the affected area. New body panels are not as expensive as most people think and it is often quicker and more satisfactory to fit a new panel than to attempt to repair large areas of corrosion.

Remove all fittings from the affected area except those which will act as a guide to the original shape of the damaged bodywork (eg headlamp shells etc). Then, using tin snips or a hacksaw blade, remove all loose metal and any other metal badly affected by corrosion. Hammer the edges of the hole inwards in order to create a slight depression for the filler paste.

Wire brush the affected area to remove the powdery rust from the surface of the remaining metal. Paint the affected area with rust inhibiting paint; if the back of the rusted area is accessible treat this also.

Before filling can take place it will be necessary to block the hole in some way. This can be achieved by the use of zinc gauze or aluminium tape.

Zinc gauze is probably the best material to use for a large hole. Cut a piece to the approximate size and shape of the hole to be filled, then position it in the hole so that its edges are below the level of the surrounding bodywork. It can be retained in position by several blobs of filler paste around its periphery.

Aluminium tape should be used for small or very narrow holes. Pull a piece off the roll and trim it to the approximate size and shape required, then pull off the backing paper (if used) and stick the tape over the hole; it can be overlapped if the thickness of one piece is insufficient. Burnish down the edges of the tape with the handle of a screwdriver or similar, to ensure that the tape is securely attached to the metal underneath.

Bodywork repairs - filling and respraying

Before using this Section, see the Sections on dent, deep scratch, rust holes and gash repairs.

Many types of bodyfiller are available, but generally speaking those proprietary kits which contain a tin of filler paste and a tube of resin hardener are best for this type of repair. A wide, flexible plastic or nylon applicator will be found invaluable for imparting a smooth and well contoured finish to the surface of the filler.

Mix up a little filler on a clean piece of card or board – measure the hardener carefully (follow the maker's instructions on the pack) otherwise the filler will set too rapidly or too slowly.

Using the applicator apply the filler paste to the prepared area: draw the applicator across the surface of the filler to achieve the correct contour and to level the filler surface. As soon as a contour that approximates to the correct one is achieved, stop working the paste – if you carry on too long the paste will become sticky and begin to 'pick up' on the applicator. Continue to add thin layers of filler paste at twenty-minute intervals until the level of the filler is just proud of the surrounding bodywork.

Once the filler has hardened, excess can be removed using a metal plane or file. From then on, progressively finer grades of abrasive paper should be used, starting with a 40 grade production paper and finishing with 400 grade wet-and-dry paper. Always wrap the abrasive paper around a flat rubber, cork, or wooden block – otherwise the surface of the filler will not be completely flat. During the smoothing of the filler surface the wet-and-dry paper should be periodically rinsed in water. This will ensure that a very smooth finish is imparted to the filler at the final stage.

At this stage the 'dent' should be surrounded by a ring of bare metal, which in turn should be encircled by the finely 'feathered' edge of the good paintwork. Rinse the repair area with clean water, until all of the dust produced by the rubbing-down operation has gone.

Spray the whole repair area with a light coat of primer – this will show up any imperfections in the surface of the filler. Repair these imperfections with fresh filler paste or bodystopper, and once more smooth the surface with abrasive paper. If bodystopper is used, it can be mixed with cellulose thinners to form a really thin paste which is ideal for filling small holes. Repeat this spray and repair procedure until you are satisfied that the surface of the filler, and the feathered edge of the paintwork are perfect. Clean the repair area with clean water and allow to dry fully.

The repair area is now ready for final spraying. Paint spraying must be carried out in a warm, dry, windless and dust free atmosphere. This condition can be created artificially if you have access to a large indoor working area, but if you are forced to work in the open, you will have to pick your day very carefully. If you are working indoors, dousing the floor in the work area with water will help settle the dust which would otherwise be in the atmosphere. If the repair area is confined to one body panel, mask off the surrounding panels; this will help to minimise the effects of a slight mis-match in paint colours. Bodywork fittings (eg chrome strips, door handles etc) will also need to be masked off. Use genuine masking tape and several thicknesses of newspaper for the masking operations.

Before commencing to spray, agitate the aerosol can thoroughly, then spray a test area (an old tin, or similar) until the technique is mastered. Cover the repair area with a thick coat of primer; the thickness should be built up using several thin layers of paint rather than one thick one. Using 400 grade wet-and-dry paper, rub down the surface of the primer until it is really smooth. While doing this, the work area should be thoroughly doused with water, and the wet-and-dry paper periodically rinsed in water. Allow to dry before spraying on more paint.

Spray on the top coat, again building up the thickness by using several thin layers of paint. Start spraying in the centre of the repair area and then, using a circular motion, work outwards until the whole repair area and about 2 inches of the surrounding original paintwork is covered. Remove all masking material 10 to 15 minutes after spraying on the final coat of paint.

Allow the new paint at least two weeks to harden, then, using a paintwork renovator or a very fine cutting paste, blend the edges of the paint into the existing paintwork. Finally, apply wax polish.

6 Major body damage and repair

1 Because the body is built on the monocoque principle and is integral with the underframe, major damage must be repaired by competent technicians with the necessary welding and hydraulic straightening equipment.

2 If the damage has been serious it is vital that the body is checked for correct alignment as otherwise the handling of the car will suffer and many other faults such as excessive tire wear and wear in the transmission and steering may occur.

3 There is a special body jig which most large body repair shops have to ensure that all is correct. It is important that this jig be used for all major repair work.

7 Maintenance - hinges and locks

Once every 3000 miles (5000 km) or 3 months the door, hood and trunk or liftgate hinges and locks should be given a few drops of oil from an oil can. The door striker plates can be given a thin smear of grease to reduce wear and to ensure free movement.

8 Front door - removal and replacement

1 Using a pencil, accurately mark the outline of the hinge relative to the door. This will act as a datum for refitting.

2 An assistant should now be obtained to take the weight of the door.

3 Undo and remove the three bolts securing the upper hinge to the door.

4 Undo and remove the three bolts securing the lower hinge to the door.

5 Carefully lift the door away from the car and stand it on an old blanket to prevent the paint chipping.

6 Refitting the front door is the reverse sequence to removal. It will probably be necessary to re-align the door, especially if new hinges have been fitted. Refer to Section 10, for further information.

9 Front door hinges - removal and replacement

1 Refer to Section 8, and remove the door as described in paragraphs 1 to 5 inclusive.

2 Undo and remove the three bolts that secure the hinge(s) to the body and lift away the hinge(s). (Fig. 12.1).

3 Refitting the front door hinges and door is the reverse sequence to removal. It will probably be necessary to re-align the door, especially if new hinges have been fitted. Refer to Section 10, for further information.

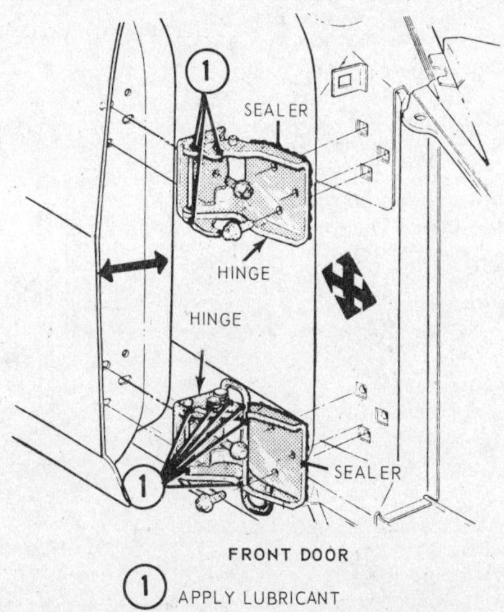

Fig. 12.1. Front door hinge assembly (Sec. 9)

10 Front door - alignment

1 The door hinges are designed to provide sufficient adjustment to correct most misalignment problems. The holes of the hinge and attaching points are elongated or enlarged to provide for correct alignment.

2 The fore and aft and up and down adjustments are made at the hinge to body attachment points. The in and out adjustment of the door is made at the hinge to door attachment points.

3 To align a door, first slacken the door latch striker stud. There is a special tool for this but a self-grip wrench may be used to unscrew the striker stud.
4 Check to see which hinge bolts must be slackened in order to move the door in the correct direction for alignment.
5 Slacken the hinge bolts and move the door in the required direction for correct alignment.
6 Retighten the door hinge bolts.
7 Reset the door latch striker to give correct engagement with the door latch. Further information will be found in Section 13.

11 Front door weatherstrip - removal and replacement

1 Remove the screws retaining the two mouldings at the front and rear of the door (see Fig. 12.2) and remove the two mouldings.
2 Remove the door trim panel as described in Section 13.
3 Pull out the old weatherstrip complete with retaining pins.
4 Position the new weatherstrip around the door and push the weatherstrip retaining pins into the associated holes in the door.
5 Replace the trim panel and fittings as described in Section 13.
6 Screw on the moulding plates at each end of the door.

12 Front door latch striker - removal, replacement and adjustment

1 Using either the special tool (T7OP 2100-A) or a self-grip wrench, remove the door latch striker stud.
2 Refitting the striker stud is the reverse sequence to removal.
3 The striker stud may be adjusted vertically and laterally as well as fore-and-aft.
4 The latch striker must not be used to counteract any door sag.
5 The latch striker may also be shimmed to obtain the correct clearance between the striker and latch as shown in Fig. 12.3.
6 To check the clearance, clean the latch jams and the striker area. Apply a thin layer of dark grease to the striker.
7 Close and open the door and note the pattern in the grease.
8 Move the striker assembly laterally to provide a flush fit at the door and pillar or quarter panel.
9 Ideally the stud should be tightened to a torque wrench setting of 40-60 lb f ft (5.5 - 8.3 kg fm) but without the special tool the tightness must be judged.

13 Front door trim panel - removal and replacement

1 Unscrew the door lock pushbutton.
2 Remove the two screws from the armrest after pulling back the trim cover (photo). Remove the two bolts from below the armrest.
3 Undo and remove the screw securing the window glass winding handle to its shaft. Lift away the handle and plastic washer (photos).
4 Undo and remove the screw securing the door lock handle to its shaft. Lift away the handle.
5 Using a wide bladed screwdriver release the clips securing the trim panel to the door inner panel. Lift away the door trim panel.
6 Carefully remove the watershield from the door inner panel.
7 Refitting the door trim panel is the reverse sequence to removal.
Note: When replacing the panel ensure that each of the trim panel retaining clips is firmly located in its hole by sharply striking the panel in the approximate area of each clip with the palm of the hand. This will make sure the trim is seated fully.

14 Front door latch remote control - removal and replacement

1 Raise the window and remove the door trim panel, as described in Section 13.
2 Disconnect the link from the remote control assembly.
3 Undo and remove the three nuts securing the remote control, from the door inner panel.
4 Refitting the door latch remote control is the reverse sequence to removal.

15 Front door outside handle - removal and replacement

1 Refer to Section 13 and remove the door trim panel.
2 Disconnect the door latch actuating rod from the door outside handle.

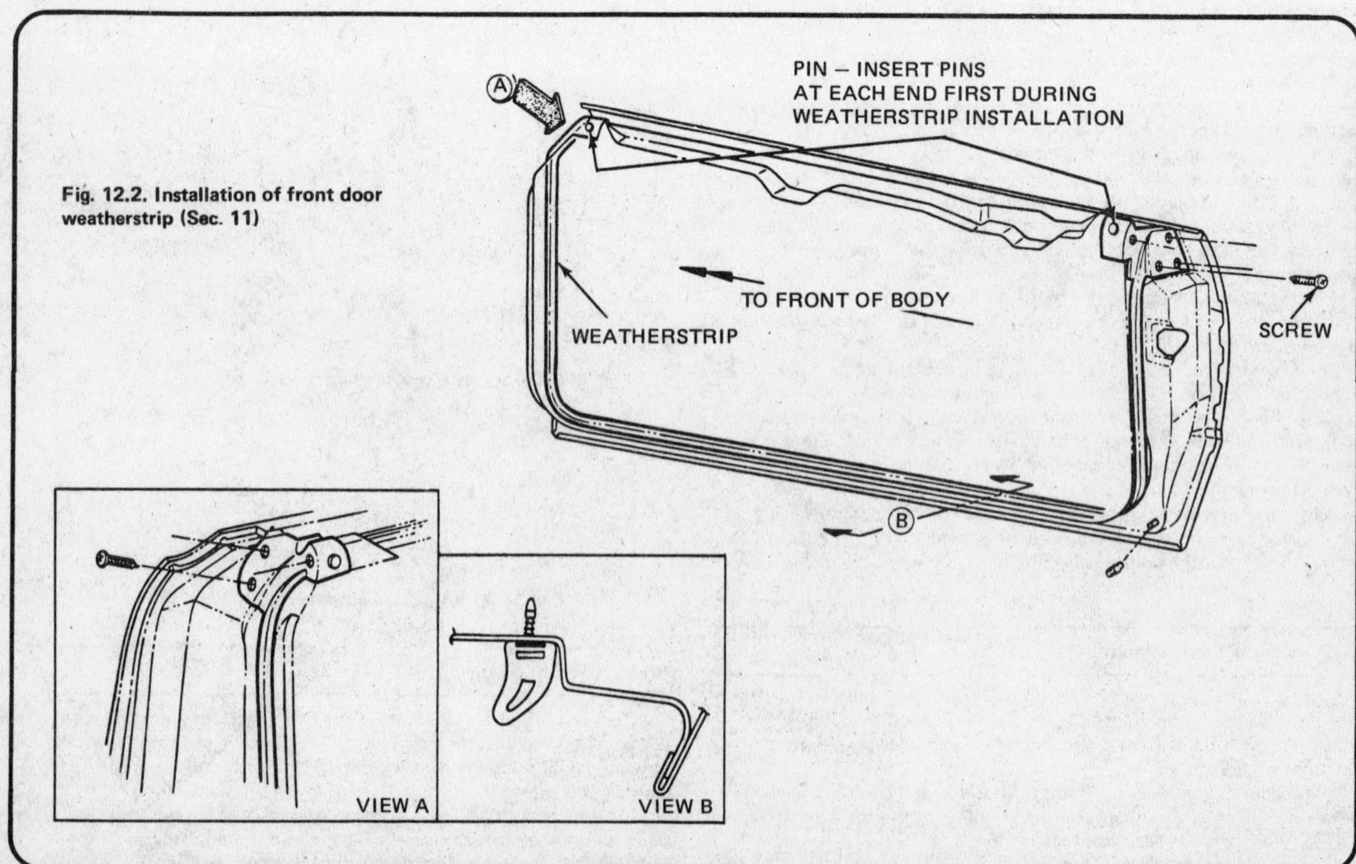

Fig. 12.2. Installation of front door weatherstrip (Sec. 11)

3 Undo and remove the two nuts securing the outside handle to the door.
4 Remove the handle and rod from the door.
5 Refitting the outside handle is the reverse sequence to removal.

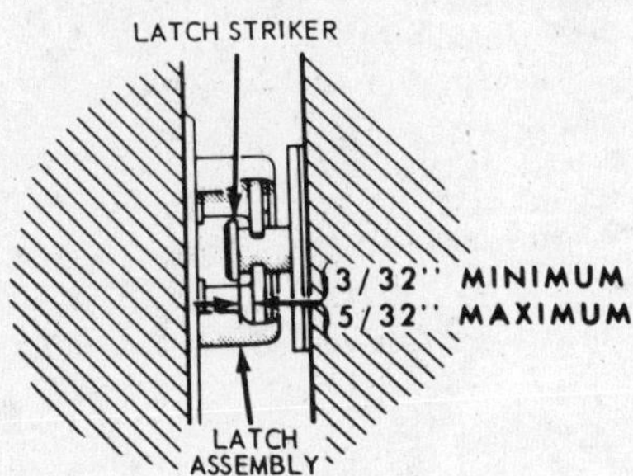

Fig. 12.3. Door latch striker adjustment (Sec. 12)

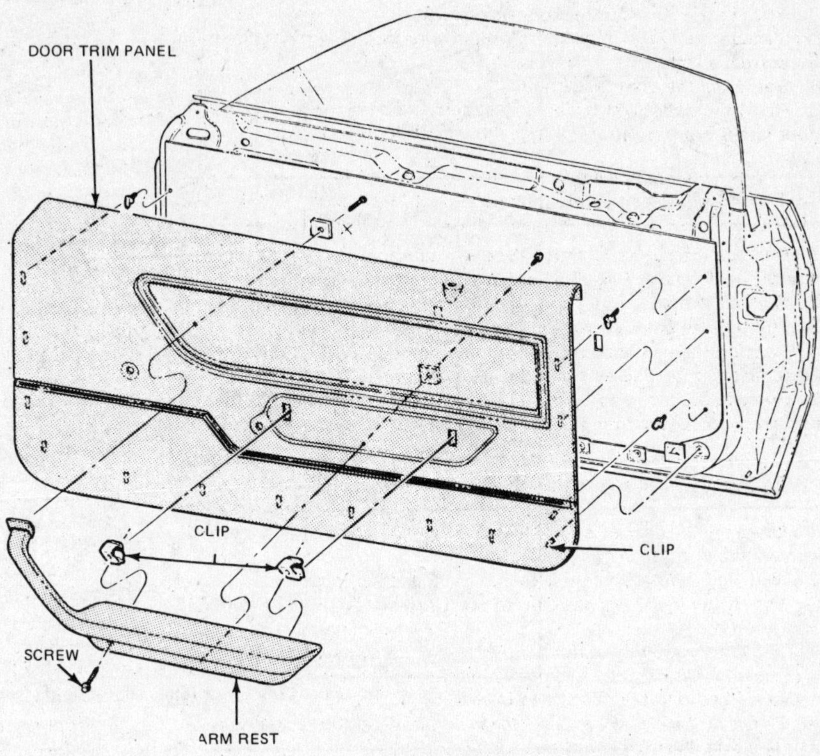

Fig. 12.4. Door trim panel (Sec. 13)

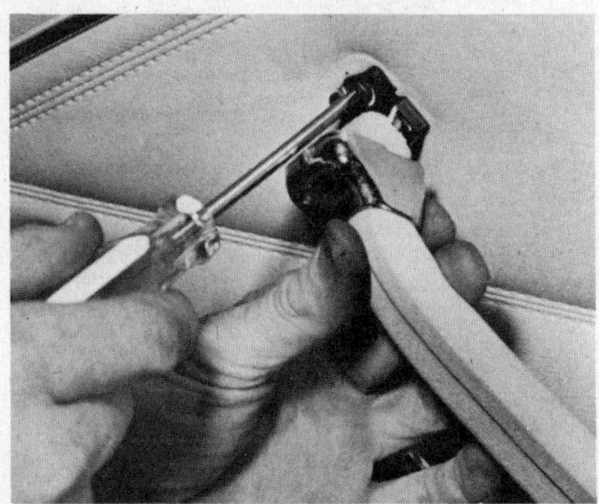

13.2 Removing armrest retaining screws

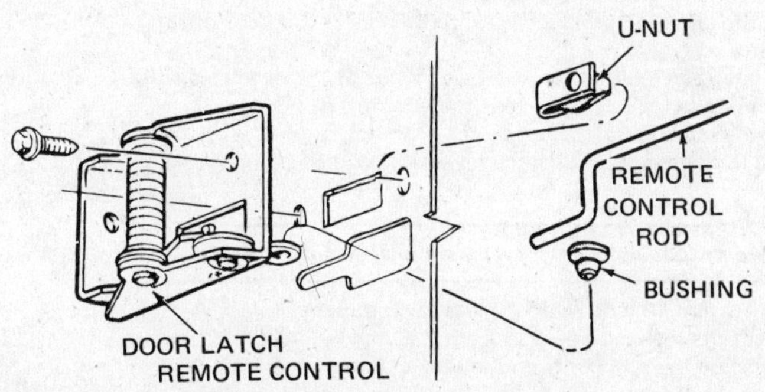

Fig. 12.5. Door latch remote control (Sec. 14)

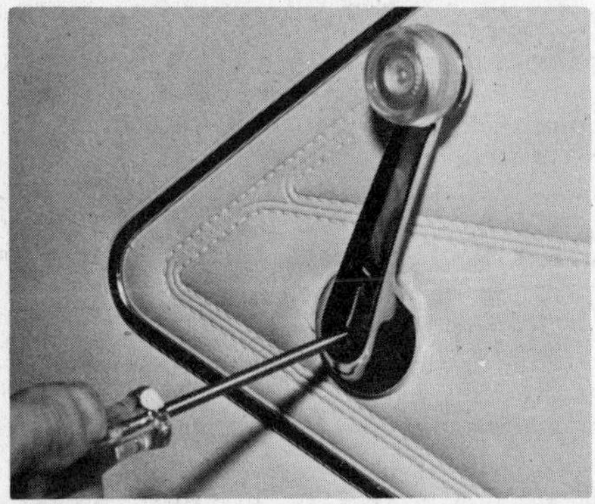

13.3A Removing window winder retaining screw

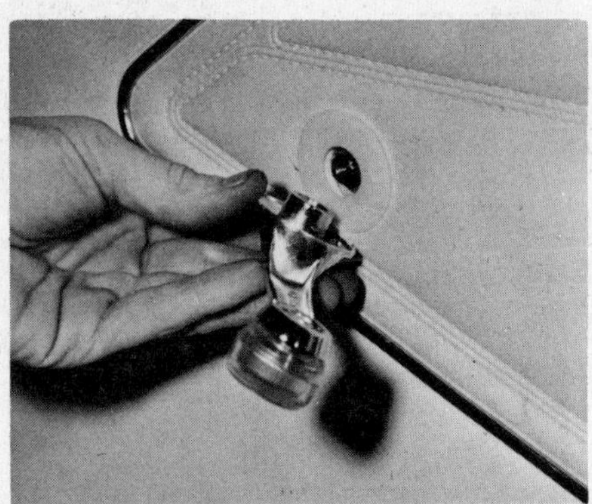

13.3B Lifting of the winder handle.....

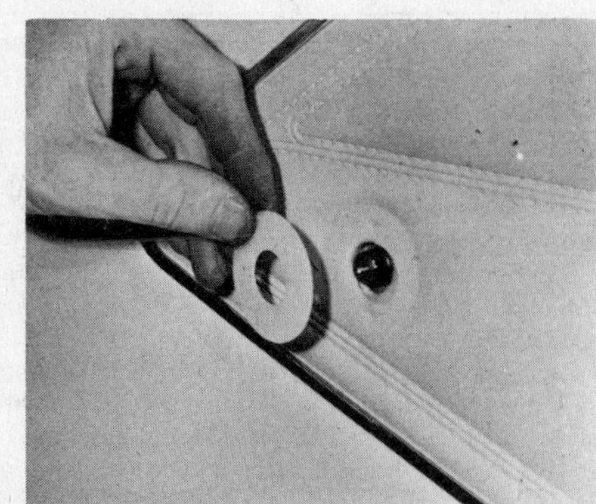

13.3C .....and washer

12

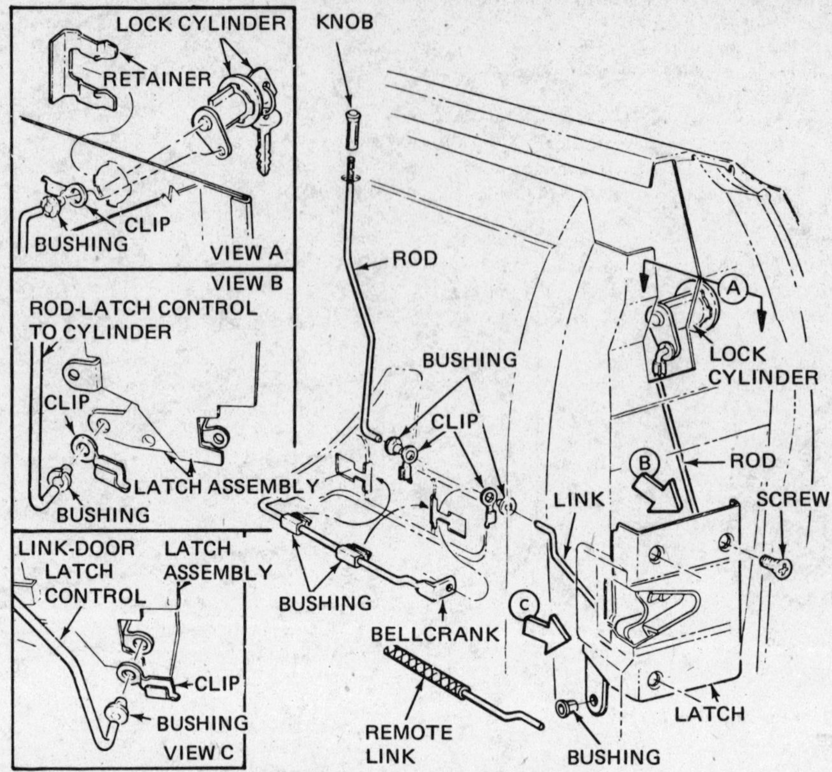

Fig. 12.6. Door latch components (Sec. 16)

16 Front door latch - removal and replacement

1 Refer to Section 13, and remove the door trim panel.
2 Wind the window to the fully up position.
3 Remove the latch retaining screws and disconnect the door-open indicator wire.
4 Lift the latch assembly as far as necessary out of the door to enable the remote link and lock cylinder rods to be removed.
5 Remove the latch and indicator switch from the door.
6 Refit the latch assembly using the reverse procedure to removal.

17 Front door lock cylinder - removal and replacement

1 Refer to Section 13, and remove the door trim panel.
2 Disconnect the lock cylinder rod from the lock cylinder.
3 Carefully slide the retainer from the lock cylinder.
4 The lock cylinder may now be lifted away from the door.
5 Refitting the door lock cylinder is the reverse sequence to removal.

18 Front door window glass - removal and replacement

1 Refer to Section 13 and remove the door trim panel.
2 Remove the screws from the front and rear glass stabilizers and remove the stabilizers (see Fig. 12.8).
3 Remove the upper front and rear glass stops (one screw on each stop).
4 Using a small pin punch, push the center pin from the rivets attaching the glass to the bracket.
5 Remove the rivets by drilling off the head using a ¼ in (6 mm) drill. Do not attempt to pry the rivets out without removing the heads as damage to the glass could result.
6 Support the glass and remove the rivets from the glass and bracket.
7 Move the glass forward inside the door until the rear upper stop is aligned with the access notch in the inner panel.
8 Lift the rear of the glass up and out of the door, then move the glass rearward until the front upper stop is aligned with the access hole. The glass can now be removed from the door.

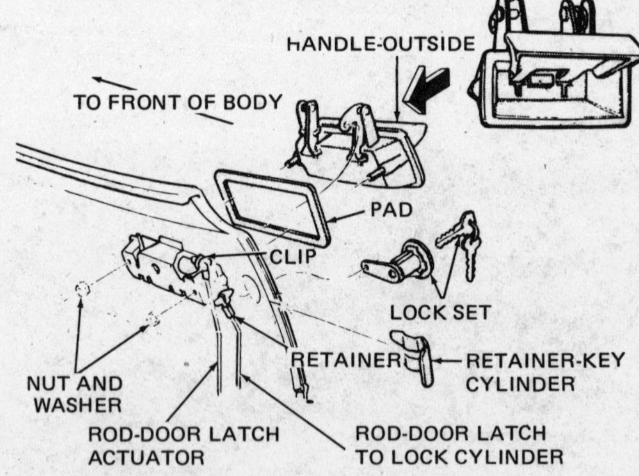

Fig. 12.7. Outside door handle and lock assembly (Sec. 17)

9 When replacing the window glass, use three ¼ in x 1 in (6 mm x 25 mm) bolts and nuts to attach the glass to the glass bracket.
10 For window glass adjustment refer to Section 20.

19 Front door window regulator - removal and replacement

1 Refer to Section 13, and remove the door trim panel.
2 Wind the window to the fully up position.
3 Remove the center pins from the regulator attaching rivets using a pin punch. (Fig. 12.9).
4 Using a ¼ in (6 mm) drill, remove the heads from the regulator attaching rivets.
5 Support the glass, disengage the regulator arm from the glass bracket and remove the regulator assembly from the door.

6 When replacing the regulator assembly use ¼ in x ½ in (6 mm x 12 mm) screws in place of the regulator attaching rivets.

20 Front door window glass - adjustment

1 Refer to Section 13 and remove the door trim panel.
2 To adjust the fore and aft position of the glass, slacken the upper guide retaining screw, move the glass to the required position and tighten the guide screw.
3 The upper and lower stops are used to limit the travel of the glass in the associated direction. To adjust the maximum wind-up height of the glass raise the window to the required height, slacken the upper stop brackets and position them against the glass stops. Tighten the stop brackets.
4 The lower stop controls the glass wind-down position which should be approximately ¼ in (6 mm) of glass protruding above the top of the door when fully wound down.
5 With the glass in the correct position, slacken the lower stop screw and push the stop against the glass bracket. Tighten the stop screw.
6 The two top glass stabilizers can be adjusted by winding the glass fully up, slackening the stabilizer retaining screws and pushing each stabilizer firmly against the glass. Tighten the stabilizer retaining screws.
7 To adjust the glass lean-in or lean-out, slacken the lower guide attaching screws (see Fig. 12.8).
8 Wind the window up and move the glass inward or outward to obtain a good seal against the doorway weatherstrip. Tighten the lower guide retaining screws.
9 Raise and lower the glass several times to check the position and travel, and if alright, refit the trim panel.

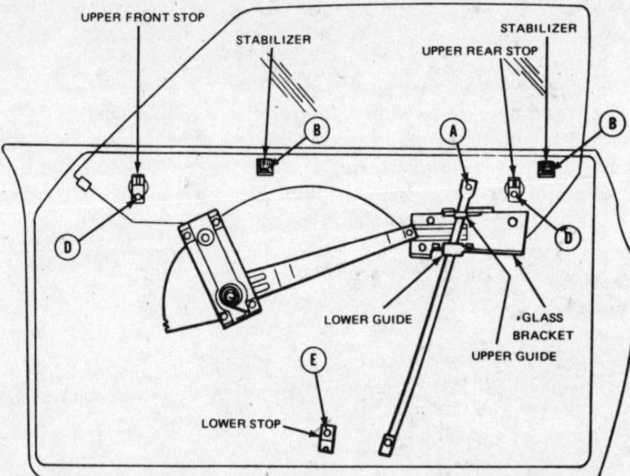

Fig. 12.8. Front door window glass adjustment points (Secs. 18 and 20)

21 Front door belt weatherstrip - removal and replacement

1 Lower the window glass fully.
2 Carefully prise out the nine weatherstrip retainers from the retainer holes in the glass opening flange. Take great care not to chip the paintwork on the glass opening flange.
3 Lift away the weatherstrip.
4 Refitting the weatherstrip is the reverse sequence to removal.

22 Pivoting quarter vent window (optional on hatchback models) - removal and replacement

1 Carefully remove the quarter window trim surround (see Fig. 12.10).
2 Remove the three upper window retaining screws (see Fig. 12.11).
3 Remove the three front retaining screws.
4 Remove the two lower retaining bolts and lift out the complete window and frame assembly from inside the car.
5 To remove the latch assembly, remove the two retaining screws from the frame, remove the pin from the glass retainer and remove the latch.
6 The glass and the frame can only be replaced as a complete assembly. Use the reverse procedure to removal.

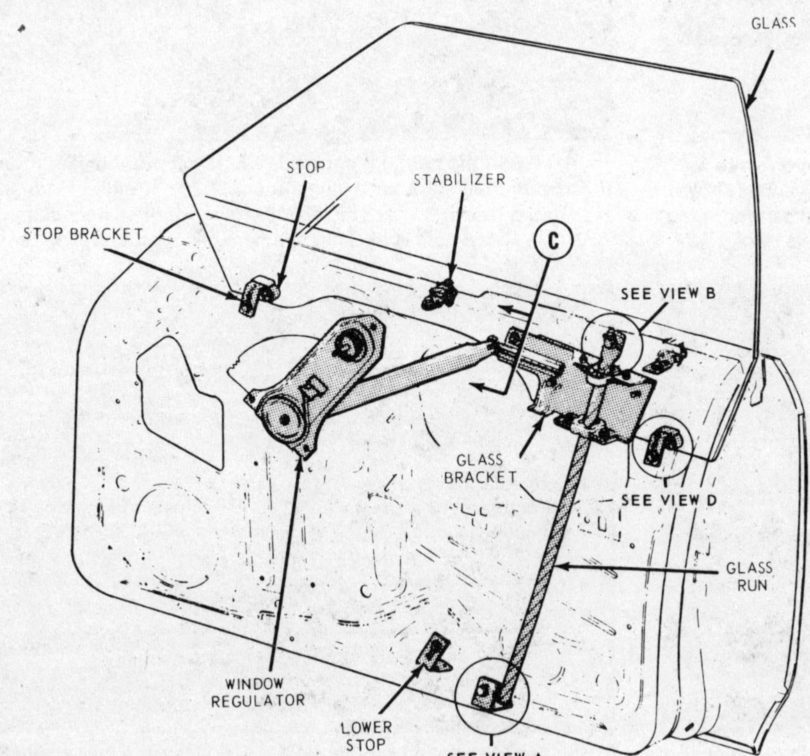

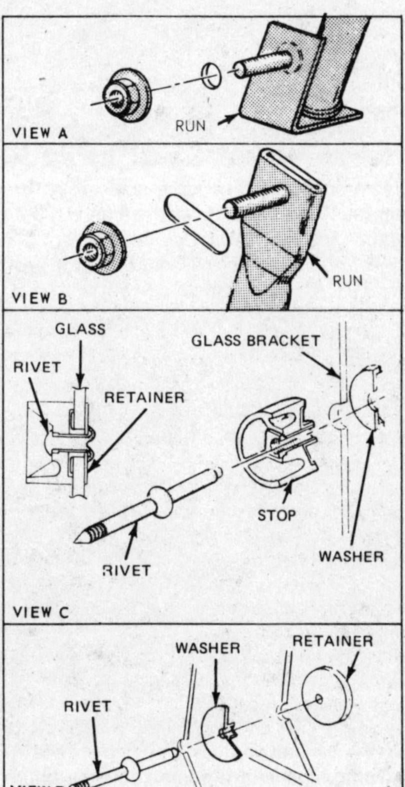

Fig. 12.9. Window regulator assembly (Sec. 19)

These photos illustrate a method of repairing simple dents. They are intended to supplement *Body repair - minor damage* in this Chapter and should not be used as the sole instructions for body repair on these vehicles.

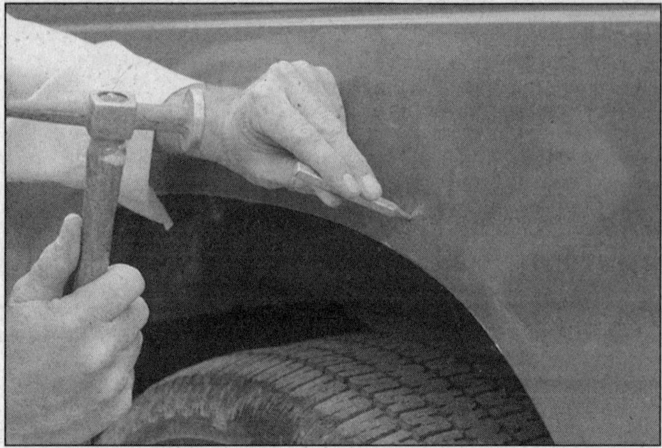

1 If you can't access the backside of the body panel to hammer out the dent, pull it out with a slide-hammer-type dent puller. In the deepest portion of the dent or along the crease line, drill or punch hole(s) at least one inch apart . . .

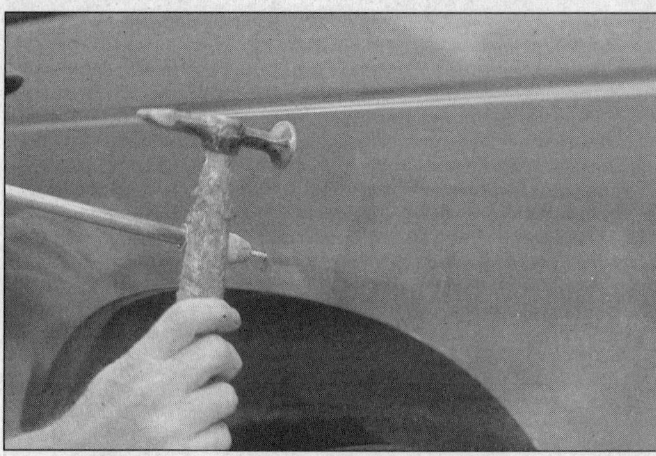

2 . . . then screw the slide-hammer into the hole and operate it. Tap with a hammer near the edge of the dent to help 'pop' the metal back to its original shape. When you're finished, the dent area should be close to its original contour and about 1/8-inch below the surface of the surrounding metal

3 Using coarse-grit sandpaper, remove the paint down to the bare metal. Hand sanding works fine, but the disc sander shown here makes the job faster. Use finer (about 320-grit) sandpaper to feather-edge the paint at least one inch around the dent area

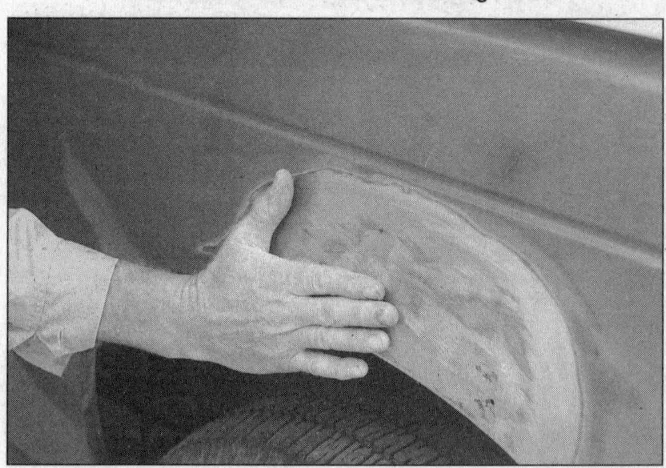

4 When the paint is removed, touch will probably be more helpful than sight for telling if the metal is straight. Hammer down the high spots or raise the low spots as necessary. Clean the repair area with wax/silicone remover

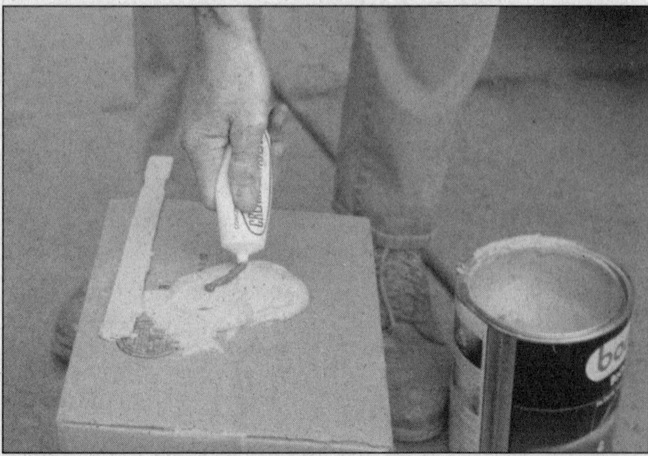

5 Following label instructions, mix up a batch of plastic filler and hardener. The ratio of filler to hardener is critical, and, if you mix it incorrectly, it will either not cure properly or cure too quickly (you won't have time to file and sand it into shape)

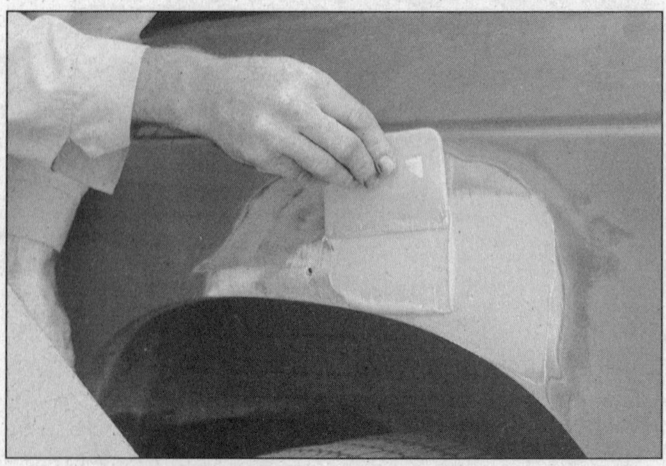

6 Working quickly so the filler doesn't harden, use a plastic applicator to press the body filler firmly into the metal, assuring it bonds completely. Work the filler until it matches the original contour and is slightly above the surrounding metal

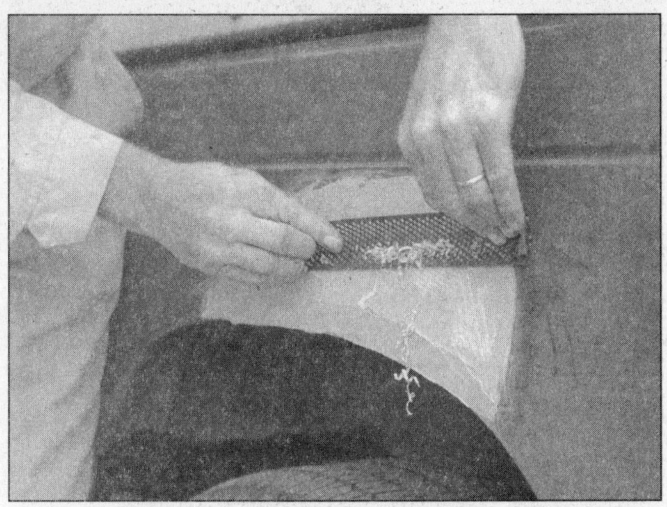

7 Let the filler harden until you can just dent it with your fingernail. Use a body file or Surform tool (shown here) to rough-shape the filler

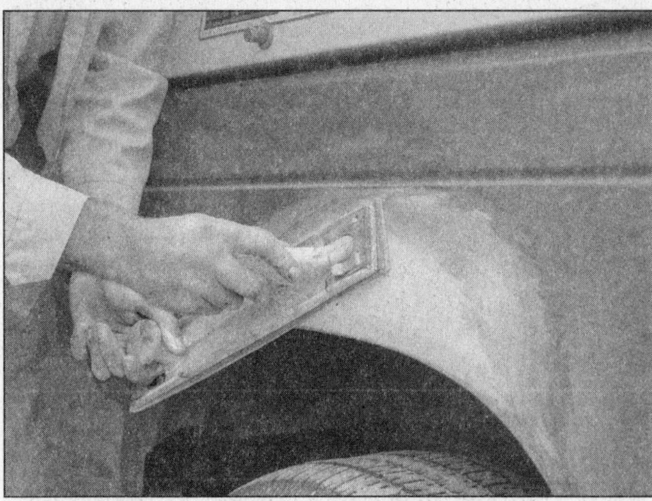

8 Use coarse-grit sandpaper and a sanding board or block to work the filler down until it's smooth and even. Work down to finer grits of sandpaper - always using a board or block - ending up with 360 or 400 grit

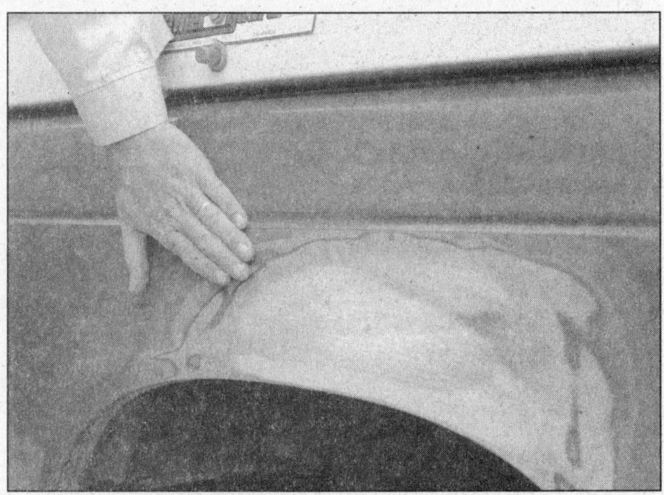

9 You shouldn't be able to feel any ridge at the transition from the filler to the bare metal or from the bare metal to the old paint. As soon as the repair is flat and uniform, remove the dust and mask off the adjacent panels or trim pieces

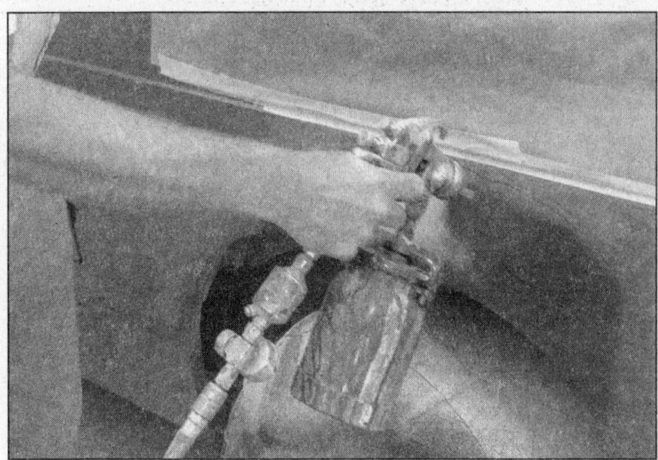

10 Apply several layers of primer to the area. Don't spray the primer on too heavy, so it sags or runs, and make sure each coat is dry before you spray on the next one. A professional-type spray gun is being used here, but aerosol spray primer is available inexpensively from auto parts stores

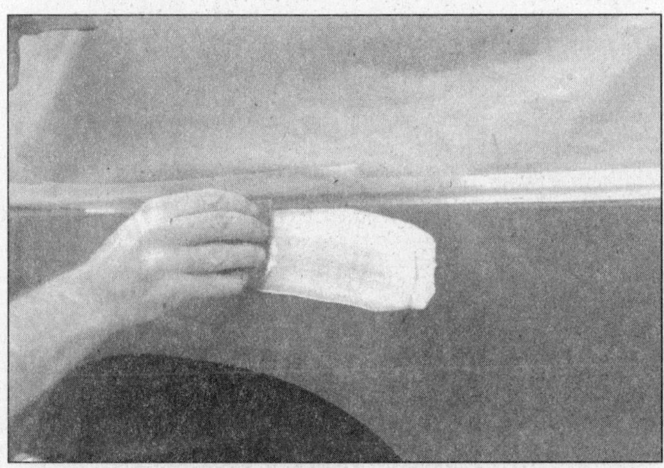

11 The primer will help reveal imperfections or scratches. Fill these with glazing compound. Follow the label instructions and sand it with 360 or 400-grit sandpaper until it's smooth. Repeat the glazing, sanding and respraying until the primer reveals a perfectly smooth surface

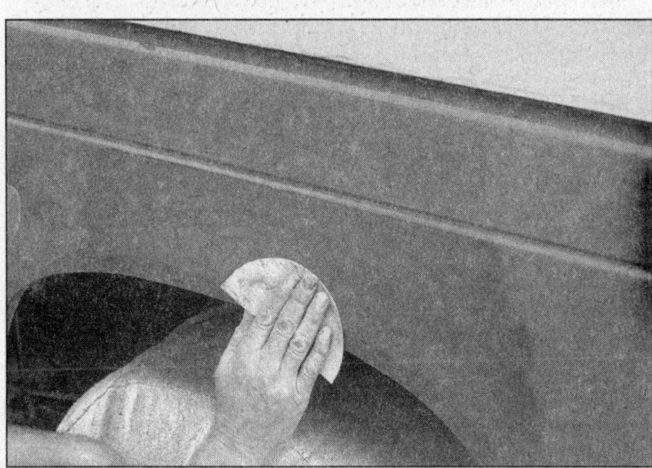

12 Finish sand the primer with very fine sandpaper (400 or 600-grit) to remove the primer overspray. Clean the area with water and allow it to dry. Use a tack rag to remove any dust, then apply the finish coat. Don't attempt to rub out or wax the repair area until the paint has dried completely (at least two weeks)

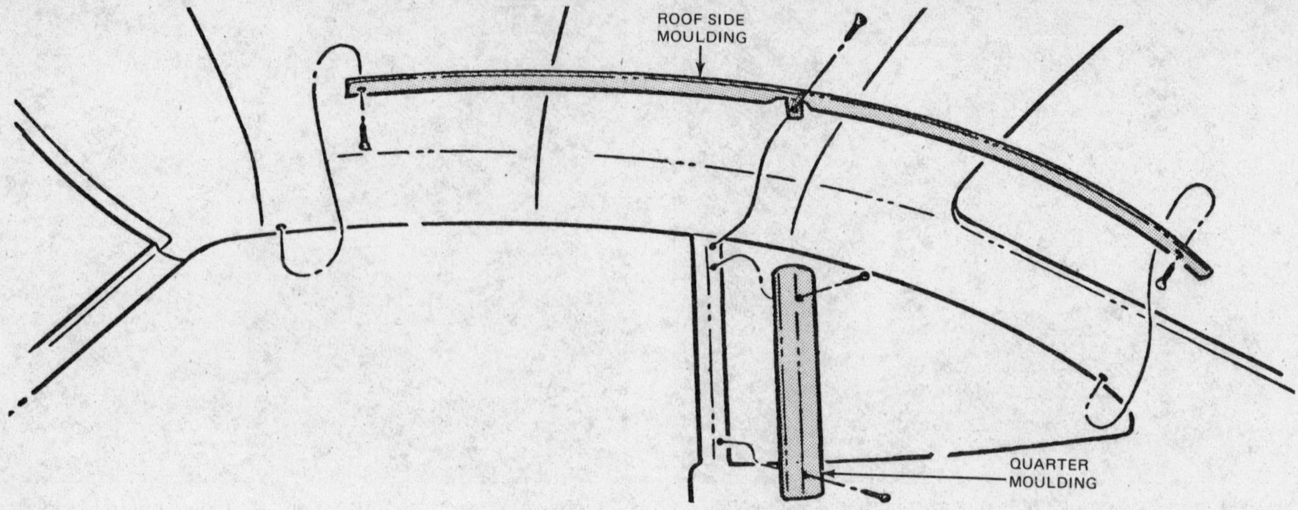

Fig. 12.10. Quarter window trim mouldings (Sec. 22)

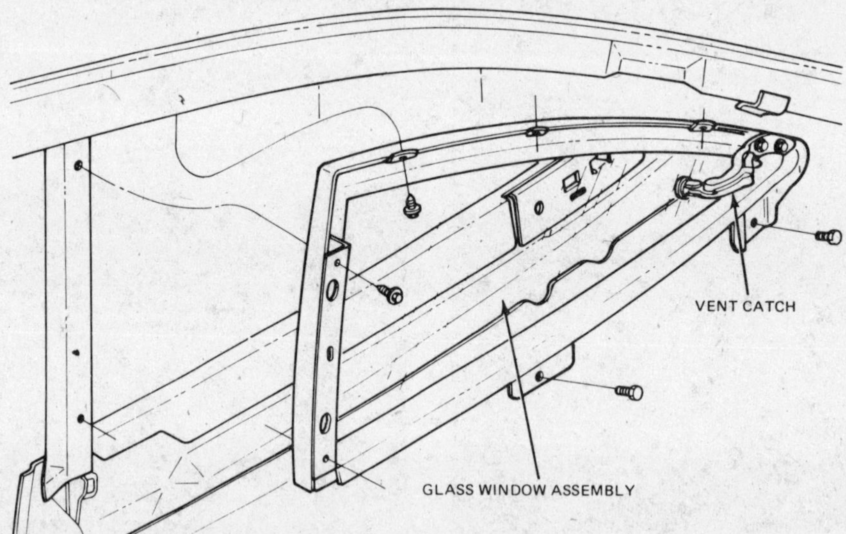

Fig. 12.11. Quarter window assembly, Hatchback pivot type (Sec. 22)

23 Fixed quarter vent window - removal and replacement

1 Remove the interior window surround mouldings.
2 Refer to Fig. 12.12 and remove the window and frame retaining screws.
3 Lift out the complete window and frame assembly from the inside of the car.
4 If required, remove the outside front moulding and pull off the sealing strip.
5 Replace the sealing strip using adhesive, and refit the window using the reverse procedure to removal.

24 Windshield and rear window glass - removal and replacement

The windshield and rear window glass on all Mustang II cars are sealed in place with a special Butyl compound. To remove the existing sealant requires the use of an electric knife specifically made for the task, and replacement of the glass is a complex operation.

In view of this it is not recommended that the owner attempts to replace the windshield or rear window. If replacement is necessary due to shattering or leakage, have the work carried out by a bodywork repair specialist.

25 Hood - removal and replacement

1 Open the hood and support in the open position.
2 Fit covers to the fenders and top cowl to prevent accidental damage to the paintwork.
3 Mark the outline of the hinges on the hood to assist refitting.
4 An assistant should now support the hood to prevent it moving when the hood hinges are detached.
5 Undo and remove the two bolts and washers that secure each hinge to the hood.
6 Lift the hood from over the front of the car.
7 Refitting the hood is the reverse sequence to removal. Provision for correct fitment of the hood in the aperture is made at the hinges.

26 Hood hinges - removal and replacement

1 Open the hood and support in the open position.
2 Fit covers to the fender and top cowl to prevent accidental damage to the paintwork.
3 Mark the outline of the hinge on the hood to assist refitting.
4 Undo and remove the two screws and washers securing the hinge to the hood.

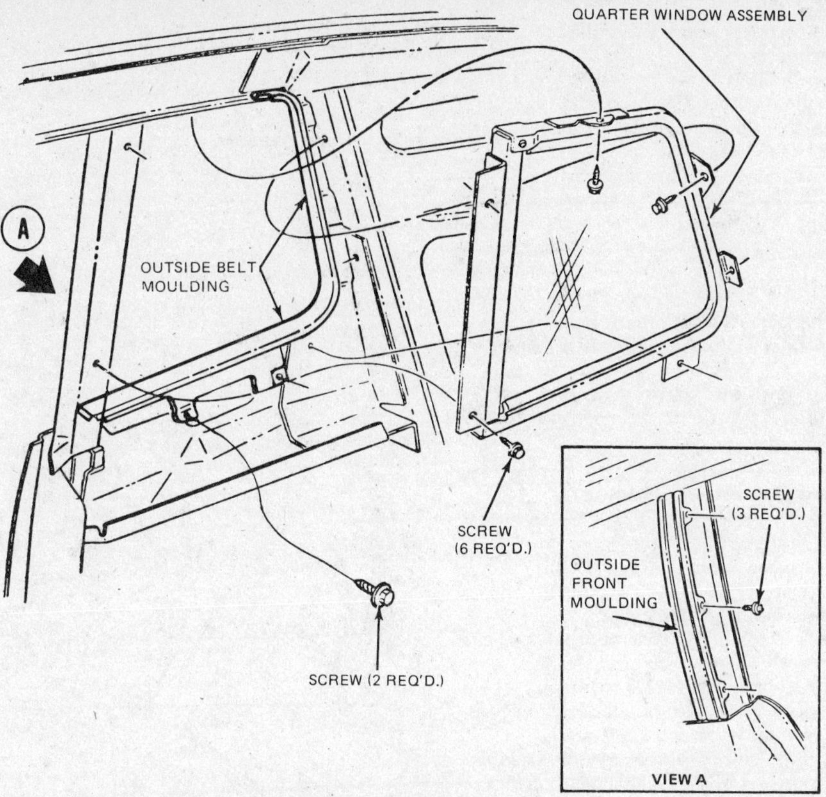

Fig. 12.12. Quarter window assembly, Sedan fixed type (Sec. 23)

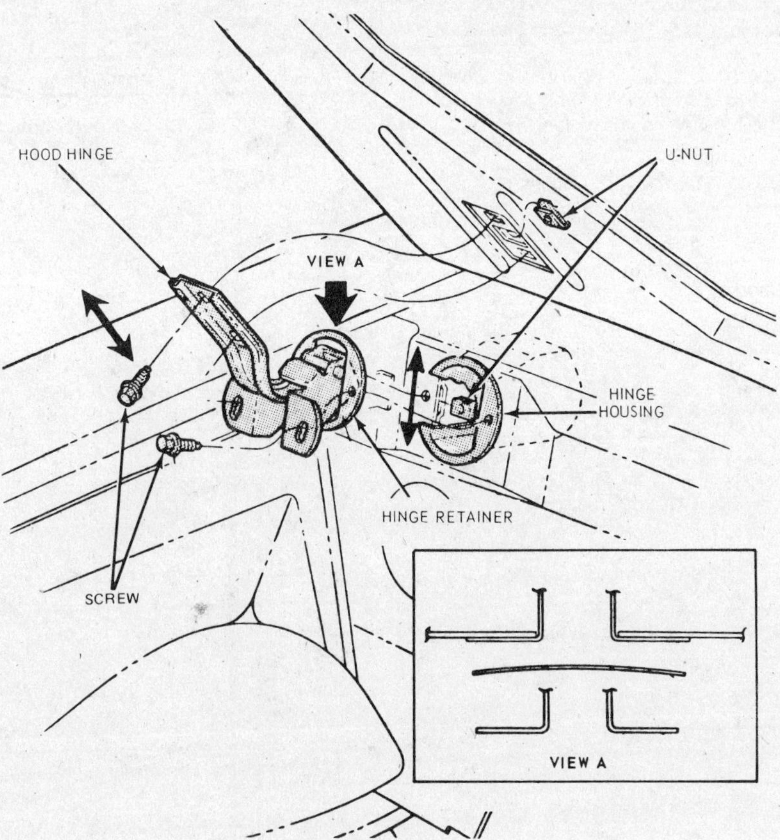

Fig. 12.13. Hood hinge assembly (Secs. 25 and 26)

5 Undo and remove the two screws and washers securing the hinge and hinge retainer to the hinge housing.
6 Pull the hinge from the hinge housing.
7 Refitting the hood hinge is the reverse sequence to removal. Provision for correct fitment of the hood in the aperture is made at the hinges.

27 Hood support rod - removal and replacement

1 Open the hood and support in the open position with a long piece of wood.
2 Detach the hood support rod from its stowed position.
3 Unsnap the rod from the retainer and pull the rod out of the hole in the retainer.
4 Remove the washers and anti-rattle spring from the support rod.
5 Refitting the hood support rod is the reverse sequence to removal.

28 Hood latch - removal, replacement and adjustment

1 Open the hood and support in the open position.
2 Undo and remove the two screws securing the latch to the reinforcement panel.
3 Lift the hood latch from the reinforcement panel.
4 To refit the hood latch, place on the reinforcement panel and refit the two screws. Do not tighten yet.
5 The hood latch can be adjusted from side-to-side to obtain alignment with the hood latch hook. It can also be adjusted up and down to obtain a flush fit between the hood and the fenders.
6 Slacken the hood latch reinforcement panel securing screws and move the reinforcement panel sideways to obtain alignment of the latch with the hood latch hook.
7 When correct alignment has been obtained tighten the reinforcement panel securing screws.
8 With the hood latch securing screws loose move the hood latch up, or down, as necessary, so as to obtain a flush fit between the hood and fender top surfaces.
9 Tighten the latch securing screws.
10 Adjust the rubber bumpers on each side of the radiator support so as to eliminate any looseness of the hood when latched.

29 Trunk lid (Sedan) - removal and replacement

1 Open the luggage compartment door and support in the open position.
2 Undo and remove the four screws that secure the hinges to the door.

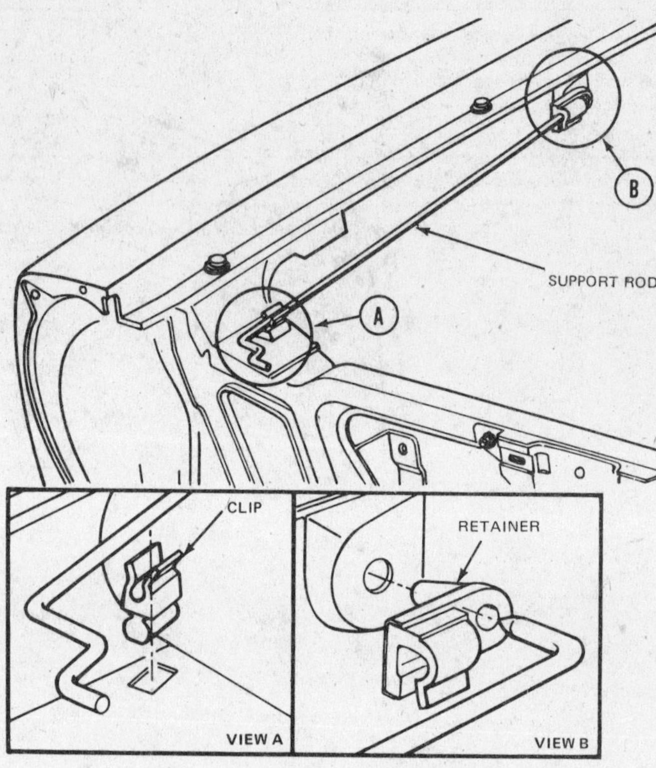

Fig. 12.14. Hood support rod (Sec. 27)

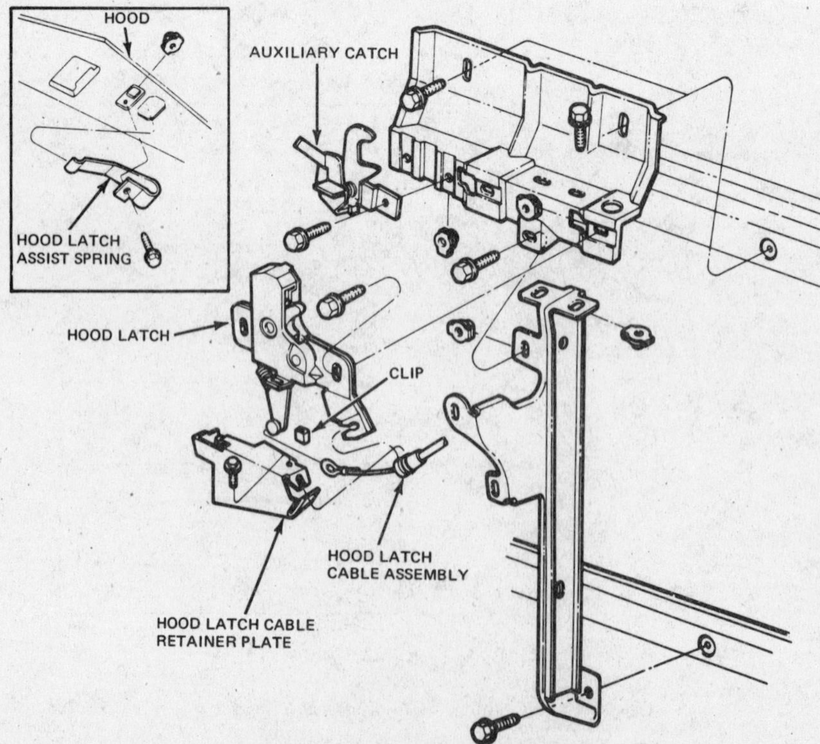

Fig. 12.15. Hood latch assembly (Sec. 28)

3 Lift away the door and shim(s).
4 Refitting the luggage compartment door is the reverse sequence to removal. It may be necessary to adjust the position of the luggage compartment door in the aperture. Refer to Section 30 for further information.

30 Trunk lid (Sedan) - adjustment

The luggage compartment door can be moved fore-and-aft by slackening the hinge to door securing screws. The up and down adjustment is obtained by adding or subtracting shims between the hinge and the door.

31 Trunk lid weatherstrip (Sedan) - removal and replacement

1 Open the luggage compartment door and carefully pull the weatherstrip from the opening.
2 Clean off any old adhesive from the weatherstrip mounting area.
3 Offer up the new weatherstrip in the opening and cut to the required length.
4 Apply a bead of adhesive around the entire weatherstrip mounting area.
5 Fit the weatherstrip to the body opening with the joint at the rear center.
6 Close the luggage compartment and leave closed until the adhesive has at least partially dried.

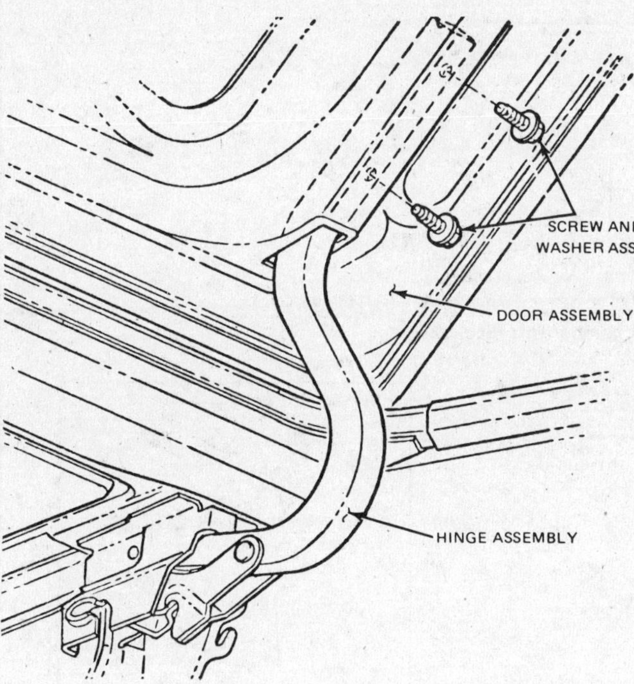

Fig. 12.16. Trunk lid hinge attachment point (Sec. 29)

32 Trunk latch (Sedan) - removal and replacement

1 Open the luggage compartment door.
2 Undo and remove the three latch securing screws and lift away the latch.
3 Refitting the latch is the reverse sequence to removal. It will be necessary to adjust the position of the latch by moving it up, or down, as necessary, to obtain a watertight fit between the luggage compartment door and the weatherstrip.
4 Once the latch has been correctly positioned the latch striker should be adjusted to give proper contact and alignment with the latch.

33 Trunk lid lock cylinder (Sedan) - removal and replacement

1 Open the luggage compartment door.
2 Working behind the latch remove the lock cylinder retaining clip.
3 Pull the lock cylinder, pad and extension from the back panel.
4 Refitting the lock cylinder is the reverse sequence to removal. If a new lock cylinder is being fitted it will be necessary to transfer the pad spring and extension to the new cylinder.

34 Trunk lid latch striker (Sedan) - removal and replacement

1 Open the luggage compartment door.
2 Undo and remove the screw securing the striker to the door and lift away the striker.
3 Refitting the striker is the reverse sequence to removal. Adjust the striker position to give correct alignment with the latch.

35 Liftgate (Hatchback) - removal and replacement

1 Using a pencil, mark the position of the hinge relative to the door to assist replacement.

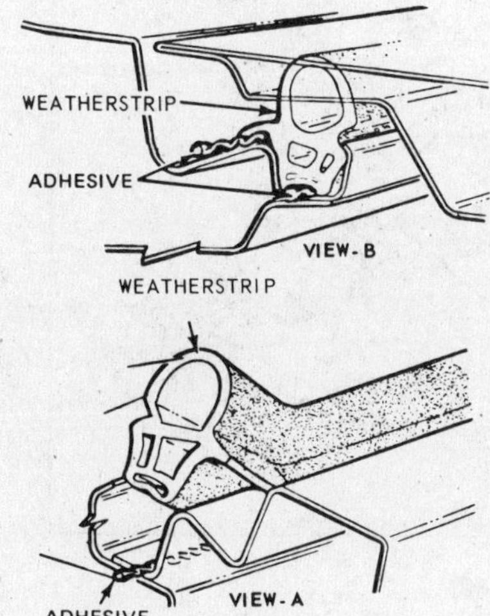

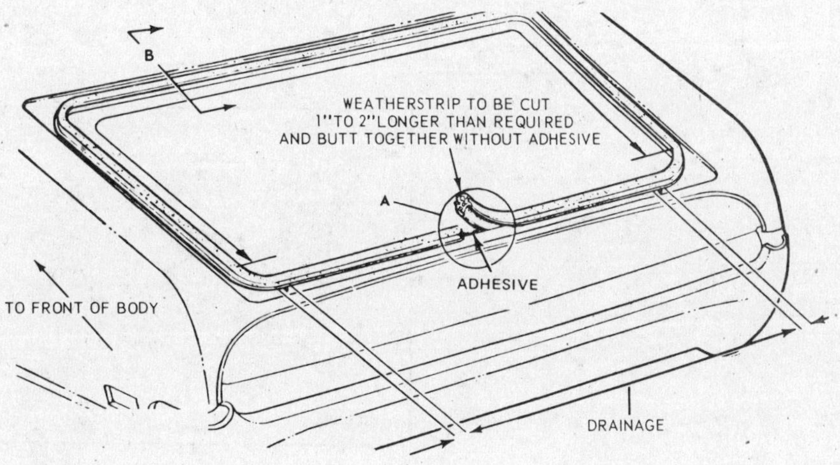

Fig. 12.17. Trunk weatherstrip (Sec. 31)

12

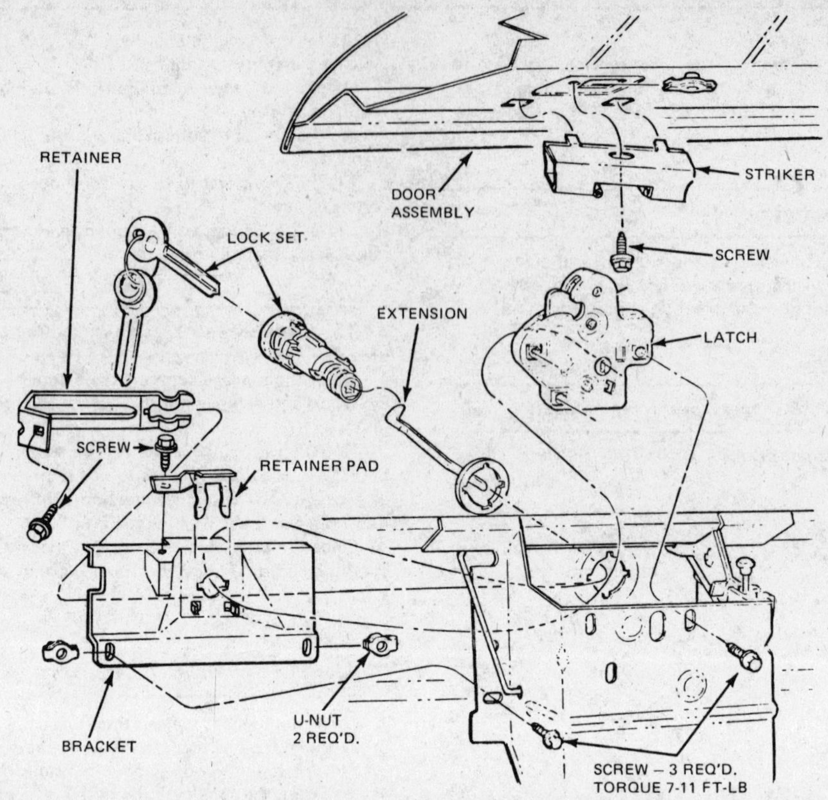

Fig. 12.18. Trunk latch and lock components (Sec. 32)

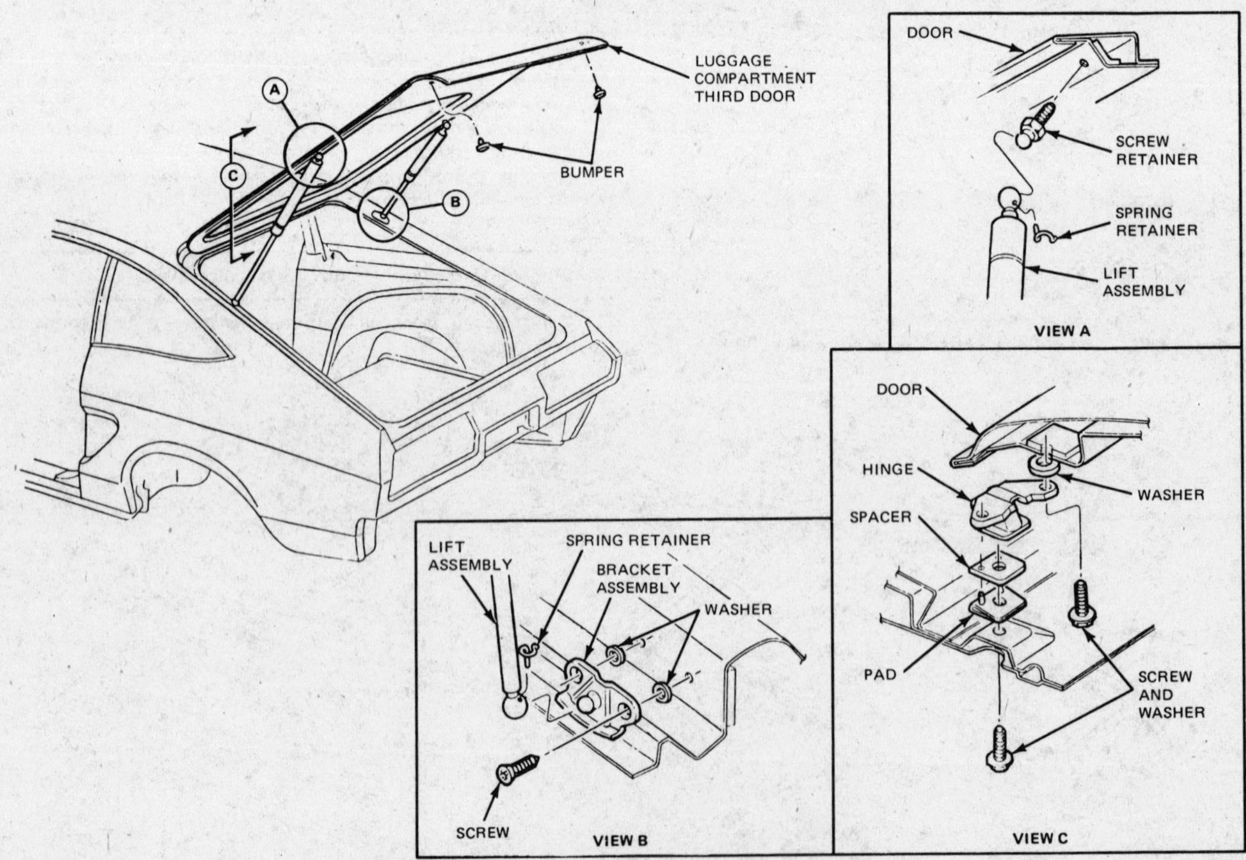

Fig. 12.19. Rear door lift assemblies (Hatchback) (Secs. 35 and 36)

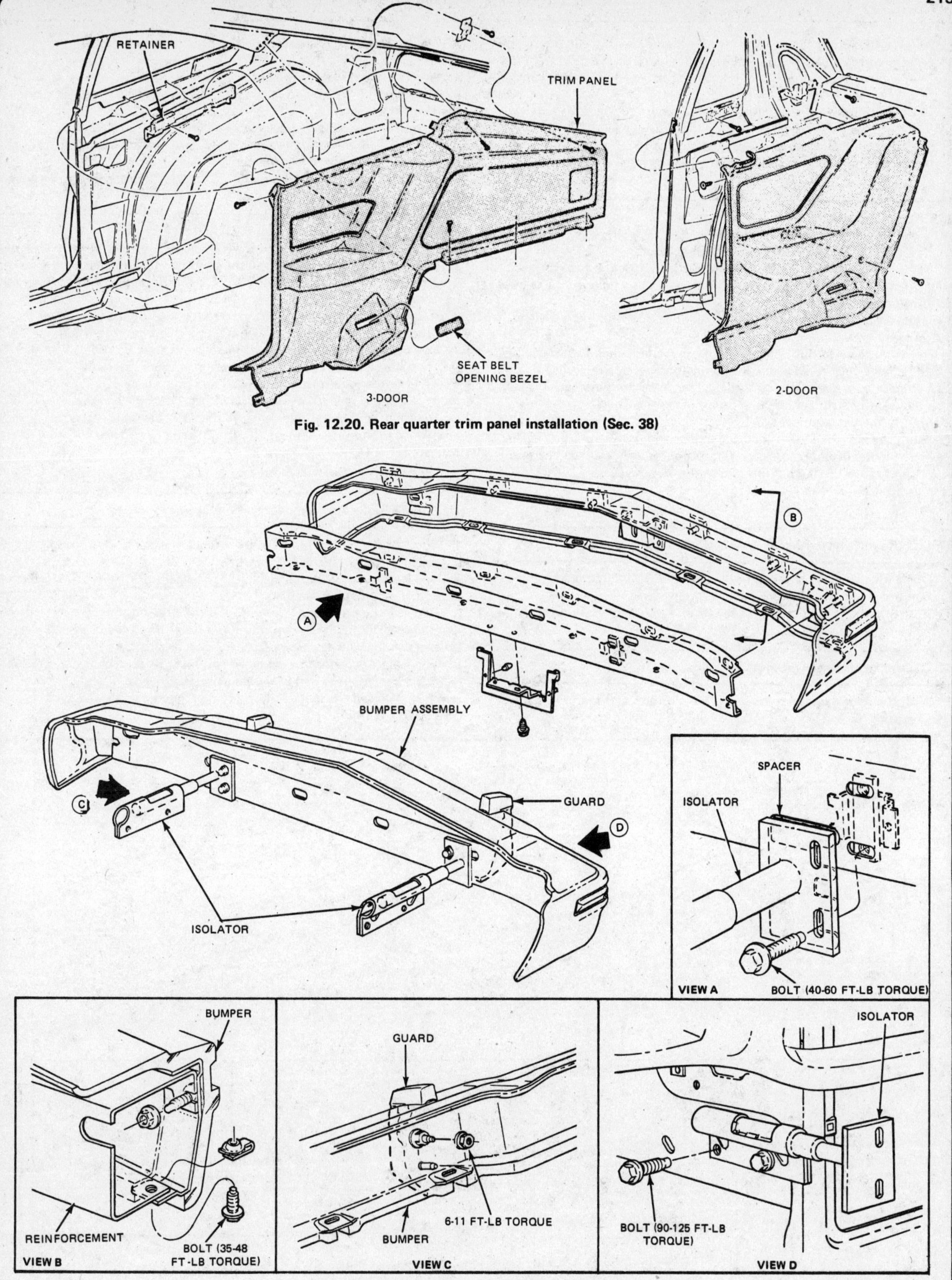

Fig. 12.20. Rear quarter trim panel installation (Sec. 38)

Fig. 12.21. Front bumper assembly (Sec. 39)

2 Release the spring clips and detach the supports from the door.
3 Pull down the weatherstrip across the top edge of the door opening.
4 The help of an assistant should now be enlisted to take the weight of the rear door.
5 Undo and remove the nuts securing the hinges to the door and carefully lift away the door.
6 Refitting the liftgate is the reverse sequence to removal. Align the liftgate to the hinges before fully tightening the nuts.

36 Liftgate hinges (Hatchback) - removal and replacement

1 Refer to Section 35 and remove the rear door.
2 Carefully pull down the weatherstrip from across the top of the door opening. Then peel back the headlining just sufficiently to expose the hinge nut access holes.
3 Using a socket, undo and remove the hinge nuts and lift away the two hinges.
4 Refitting the rear door hinges is the reverse sequence to removal. It will be necessary to stick the headlining back in position with a clear impact adhesive. Make sure that all wrinkles are removed. Finally glue the weatherstrip back in position.
5 Should the liftgate prove difficult to close, and is offset in the aperture, slacken the striker securing screws and reposition the striker. However, if the liftgate closes too far, or not enough, slacken the latch screws and move the latch either up, or down, as necessary, until the correct position is found.

37 Liftgate lock (Hatchback) - removal and replacement

1 Open the rear door and carefully move the retainer to one side.
2 Pull out the lock cylinder, pad and extension.
3 Refitting the rear door lock is the reverse sequence to removal.

38 Quarter trim panel - removal and replacement

1 With the Sedan model remove the seat cushion and rear seat back (see Sections 45 and 46).
2 On the Hatchback model, open the rear door and lower the rear seat.
3 Remove the door sill scuff plate.
4 Refer to Fig. 12.20 and remove the trim retaining screws (six on the Hatchback, two on the Sedan).
5 Remove the seatbelt opening bezel.
6 Lift the trim panel off the retaining clips, slide the seatbelt through the trim and lift away from the car.
7 Refitting the quarter trim panel is the reverse procedure to removal.

39 Front and rear bumpers - removal and replacement

1 Undo the four bolts retaining the bumper reinforcement plate to the isolators (see Fig. 12.21 and 12.22), and withdraw the bumper assembly from the car.
2 If a new bumper is being fitted, remove the bolts securing the reinforcement bar and guards to the bumper and remove them.
3 To remove the bumper rub strips, remove the two outer nuts and ease out the strip retaining clips from the bumper assembly.
4 The bumper guard mouldings can be removed by carefully easing them out of the guards using a screwdriver (see Fig. 12.25).
5 Replace the bumper and reinforcing plate assembly using the reverse procedure to removal. Torque the four retaining bolts to a setting of 35 - 50 lb f ft (4.85 - 7.0 kg fm).

40 Bumper isolators - removal and replacement

1 The front and rear bumpers are attached to the body through energy absorbing hydraulic isolators.
2 The isolators should be checked periodically for leaks and if oil is present they must be renewed.
3 Remove the bumper as described in the previous Section.
4 Remove the four bolts retaining the isolators to the chassis. (The isolators should always be replaced in matched pairs).
5 The isolators cannot be repaired and must be replaced with new ones.
6 Refit the isolators and bumpers using the reverse procedure to removal. Tighten the isolator bolts to a torque wrench setting of 35 - 50 lb f ft (4.85 - 7.0 kg fm).

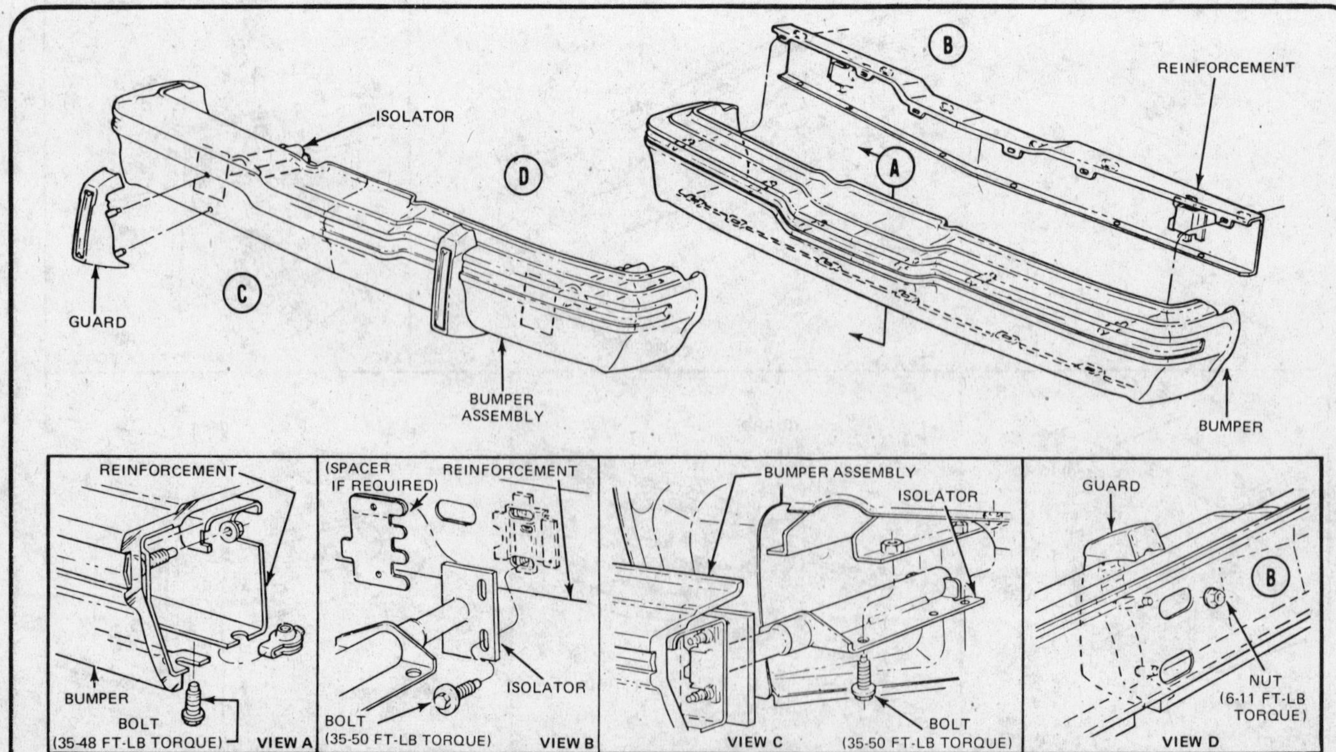

Fig. 12.22. Rear bumper assembly (Sec. 39)

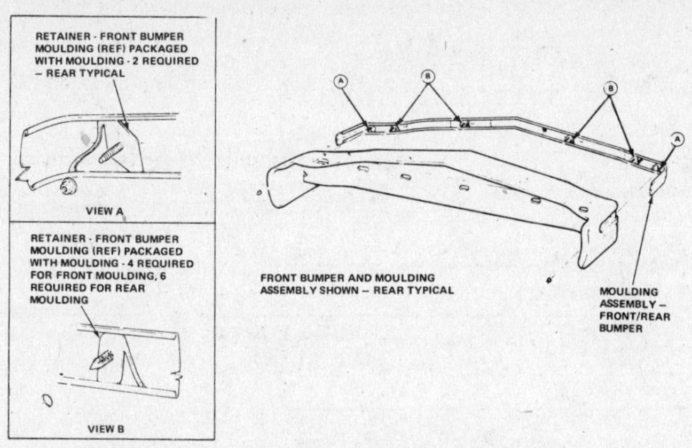

Fig. 12.23. Bumper rub strip attachment points (1975 models) (Sec. 39)

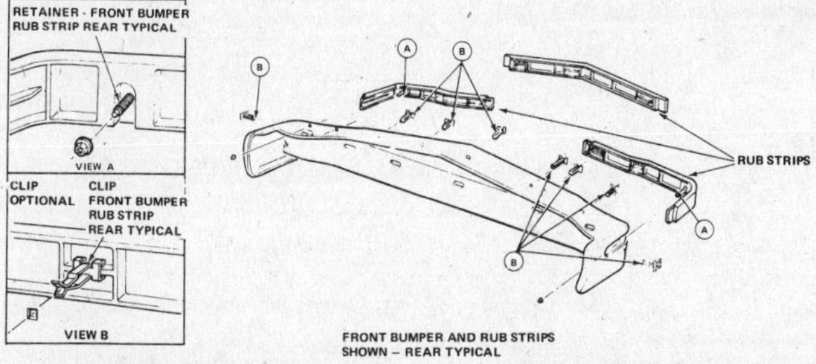

Fig. 12.24. Bumper rub strip attachment points (1976 models) (Sec. 39)

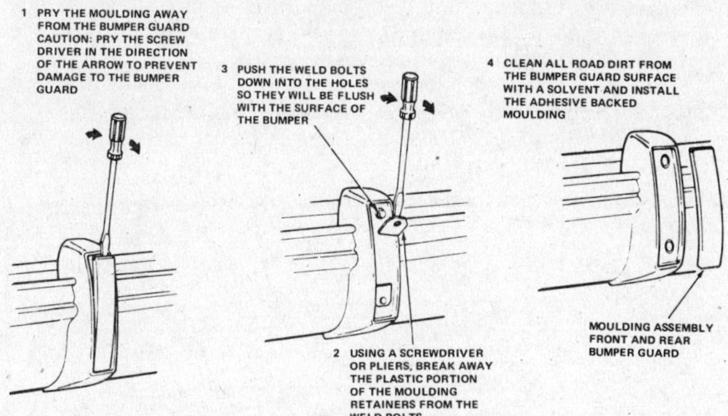

Fig. 12.25. Replacing the bumper guard mouldings (on later models the mouldings are clipped in) (Sec. 39)

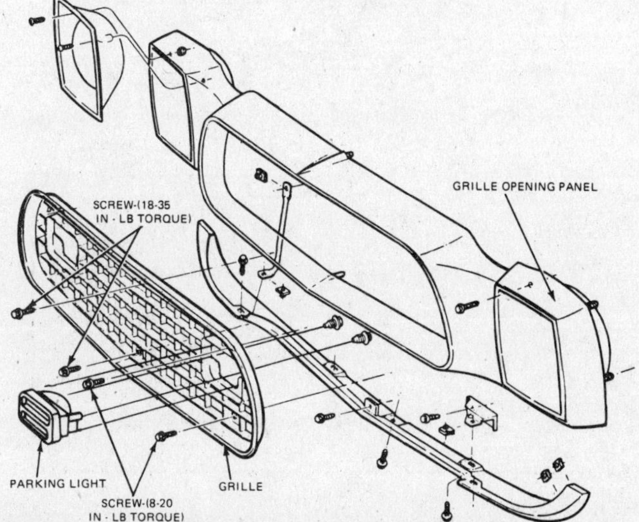

Fig. 12.26. Radiator grille assembly (Sec. 41)

41 Radiator grille - removal and replacement

1 Refer to Chapter 10, and remove the front (parking turn signal) light bulbs and sockets.
2 Undo and remove the seven screws that secure the grille to the front panels of the car.
3 Lift away the radiator grille.
4 Refitting the radiator grille is the reverse sequence to removal. Do not tighten any screws until all are in place.

42 Instrument panel trim pad - removal and replacement

1 Refer to Fig. 12.27 and remove the two screws from the windshield defroster openings on top of the instrument panel.
2 Remove the five screws from underneath the front of the trim pad.
3 Pull the pad and top finish panel away from the instrument panel.
4 Refit the trim pad using the reverse procedure to removal.

43 Sunroof panel - adjustment

1 First remove the inner trim panel by opening the sunroof approximately five inches and pulling out the seven clips holding the inner trim panel to the main sliding panel (see Fig. 12.29).
2 Slide the inner panel to the rear of the car and close the sunroof.
3 To adjust the front of the sunroof panel so that it is a flush fit with the roof, proceed as follows.
4 Loosen the two screws that attach the front slide assembly to the tapping plate (see Fig. 12.30).
5 Move the tapping plate forward to raise the panel and rearward to lower it. Have an assistant check the position of the panel from outside the car, and tighten the tapping plate screws when the sunroof panel is flush with the roof.
6 On Ghia models equipped with the glass (moonroof) panel the front of the panel can be raised or lowered by adding or removing shims beneath the tapping plate.
7 To adjust the height of the sunroof at the rear end, slacken the rear adjusting screws (see Fig. 12.31) on both sides of the panel and set the roof to the correct height. Tighten the adjusting screws.

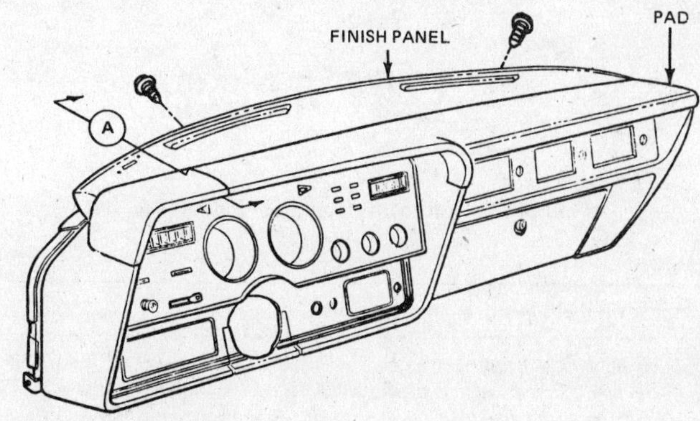

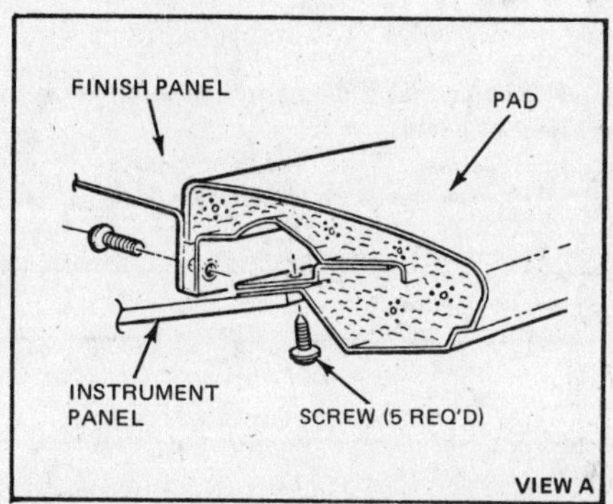

Fig. 12.27. Instrument panel pad installation

12

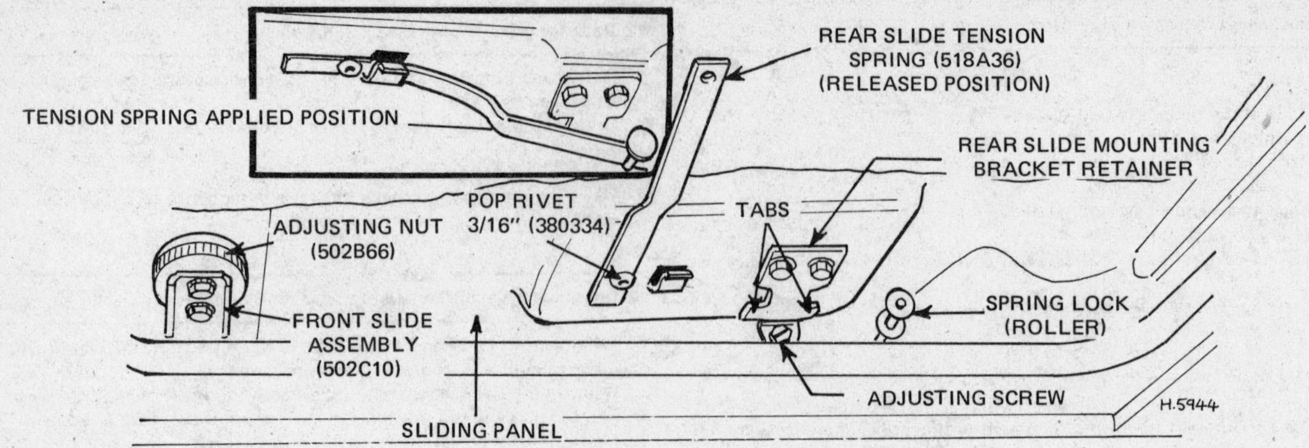

Fig. 12.28. Location of sliding roof attachment points (Sec. 44)

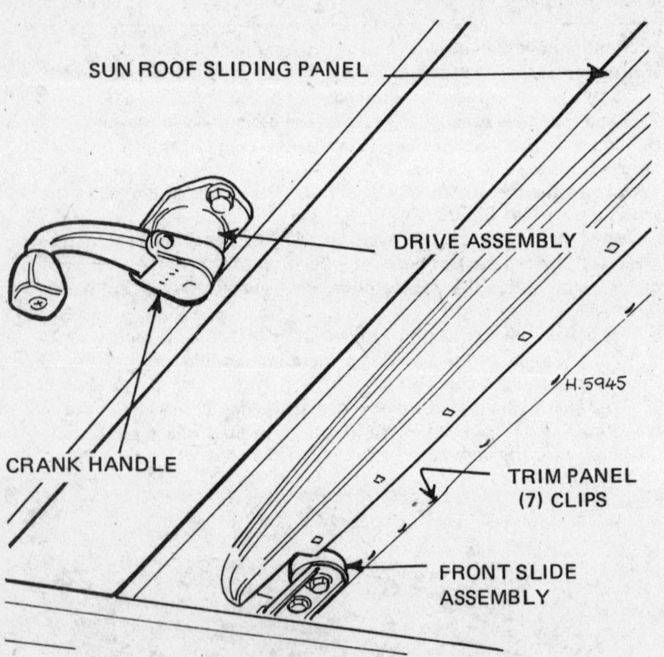

Fig. 12.29. Sliding roof trim attachment points (Sec. 43)

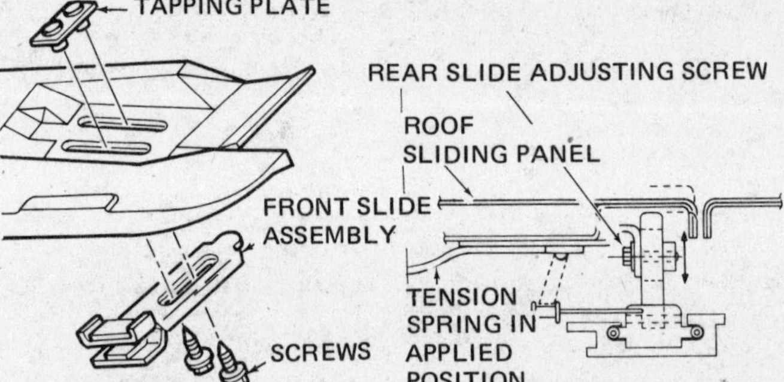

Fig. 12.30. Roof front slide assembly (Sec. 43)

Fig. 12.31. Roof rear slide assembly (Sec. 43)

44 Sunroof panel - removal and replacement

1 Open the sunroof approximately 5 inches and remove the inner trim panel as described in the previous Section.
2 Release the two slide tension springs by moving them in toward the center of the car (see Fig. 12. 28).
3 Remove the two screws securing each front slide assembly to the roof panel.
4 Remove the screws from the two rear slide assemblies and lift out the tabs from the slots in the roof panel.
5 Pull the roof panel forward and out of the roof aperture.
6 Refit the panel using the reverse procedure to removal.

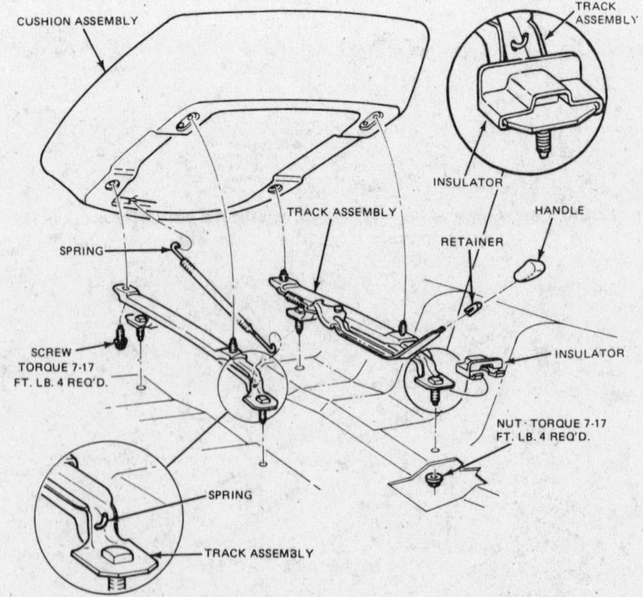

Fig. 12.32. Front seat attachment points (Sec. 45)

45 Front seat - removal and replacement

1 Open the door and disconnect the seat sensor switch wires from under the seat.
2 Working under the auto undo and remove the four nuts that secure the seat track studs to the floor panel.
3 The seat may now be lifted out of the car.
4 Should it be necessary to remove the tracks from the seat then on the driver's seat unhook and remove the seat return spring.
5 Undo and remove the four screws that secure the seat tracks to the underside of the seat.
6 Lift away the seat tracks.
7 Refitting the seat tracks and seat is the reverse sequence to removal. Lubricate the tracks with a little grease to ensure free movement.

46 Rear seat - removal and replacement

Fixed type

1 Undo and remove the two screws that secure the front edge of the seat cushion (Fig. 12.33).
2 Raise the seat cushion and draw forwards. Lift away from inside the car.
3 Undo and remove the two screws that secure the seat squab at its lower end to the body.
4 Carefully unhook the seat squab at the top and lift away from inside the car.
5 Refitting the rear seat cushion and squab is the reverse sequence to removal.

Fold down type

1 Remove the two screws retaining the rear seat back supports to the floor panel (Fig. 12.34).
2 Undo and remove the screws that secure the seat back and lift away from inside the car.
3 Undo and remove the two screws that secure the front edge of the seat cushion.
4 Raise the seat cushion and draw forwards. Lift away from inside the car.
5 Refitting the rear seat cushion and back is the reverse sequence to removal.

47 Center floor console - removal and replacement

1 Open the console glove box door and remove the four retaining screws (see Fig. 12.35).
2 Slide the console forward to clear the front retaining clip and lift the console out over the parking brake and gearshift lever.
3 Refit the console using the reverse procedure to removal.

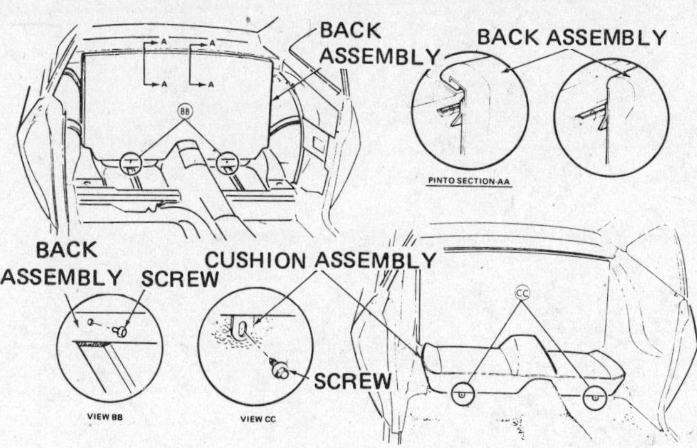

Fig. 12.33. Rear seat installation (fixed type) (Sec. 46)

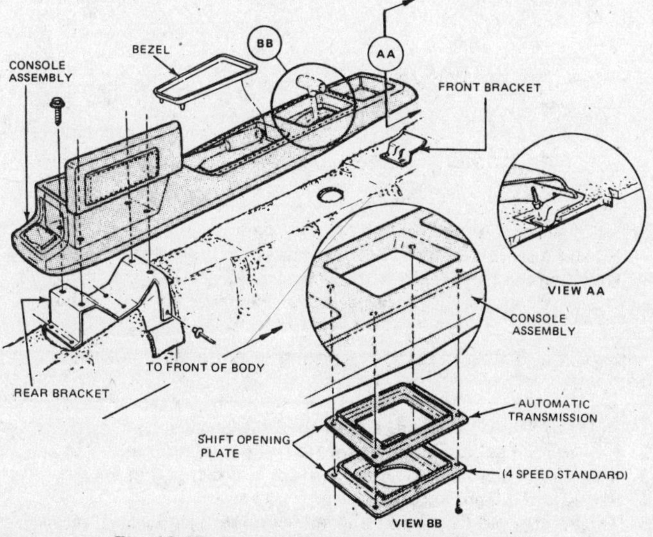

Fig. 12.35. Center console assembly (Sec. 47)

48 Interior ventilation system - general description

Fresh air enters the system by ram effect through the cowl top grille and flows into the left-hand and right-hand cowl vent ducts. The right vent is an integral part of the heater assembly whereas the left-hand vent is separate from the heater.

Both vents operate in a similar manner. Left to right and control knobs operate doors in the left and right vent ducts respectively to control the air flow into the car.

The control knobs have three positions:

a) Control knob pushed in. The cowl vent doors are closed.
b) Control knob is in mid position. About 75% of the air flows through the registers in the instrument panel and 25% to the floor.
c) Pulled out. The doors deflect all air to the floor.

When the right-hand vent door is closed all outside air flows into the heating system.

49 Vent duct - removal and replacement

Right-hand vent duct

1 From inside the car, disconnect the right-hand vent control from the instrument panel.
2 Remove the screws retaining the air duct to the instrument panel and

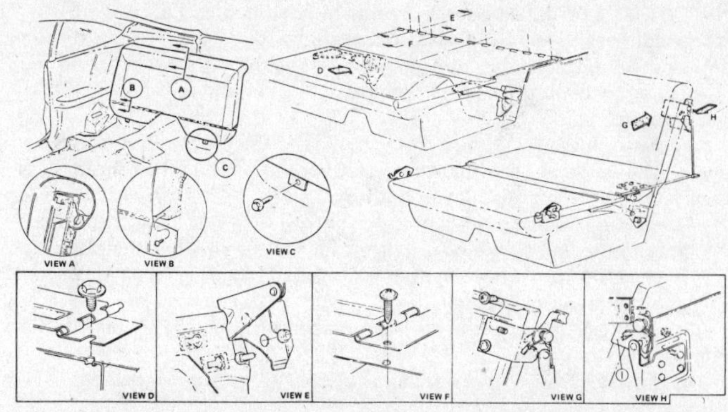

Fig. 12.34. Rear seat installation (folding type) (Sec. 46)

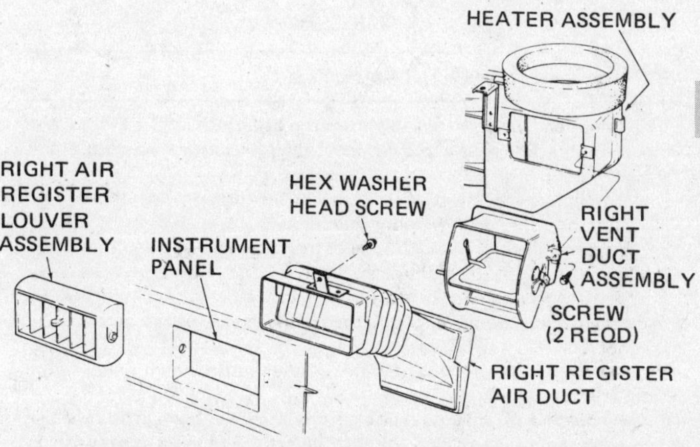

Fig. 12.36. Right-side ventilation duct assembly (Sec. 49)

12

the vent duct to the heater assembly.
3 Contract the duct and remove from under the dashboard.
4 Refitting the vent duct is the reverse sequence to removal.

Left-hand vent duct

1 Working inside the auto disconnect the left-hand vent control from the instrument panel.
2 Undo and remove the two left-hand vent to cowl top panel securing screws.
3 Compress the air duct and remove the vent and duct as one assembly.
4 Separate the air duct from the vent.
5 Refitting the vent duct is the reverse sequence to removal.

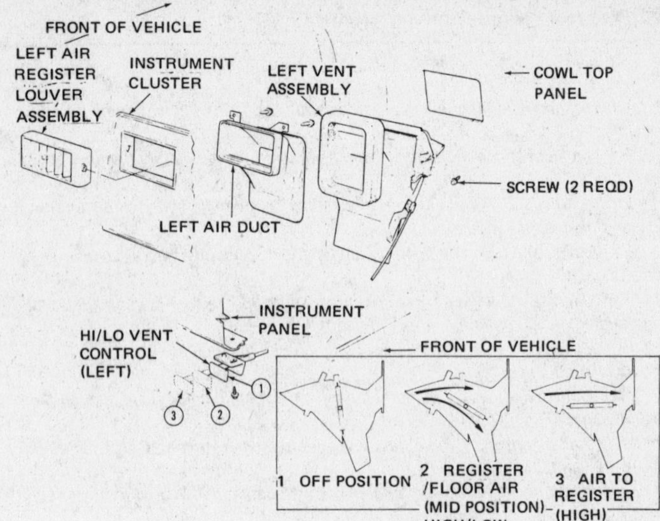

Fig. 12.37. Left-side ventilation duct assembly (Sec. 49)

50 Air registers - removal and replacement

1 Refer to Fig. 12.38 and using a screwdriver carefully pry in the end of the louver assembly which has the larger pivot.
2 When the pivot is clear of the hole, lift the louver outwards and sideways,
3 Refit the air register louver assembly using the reverse procedure to removal.

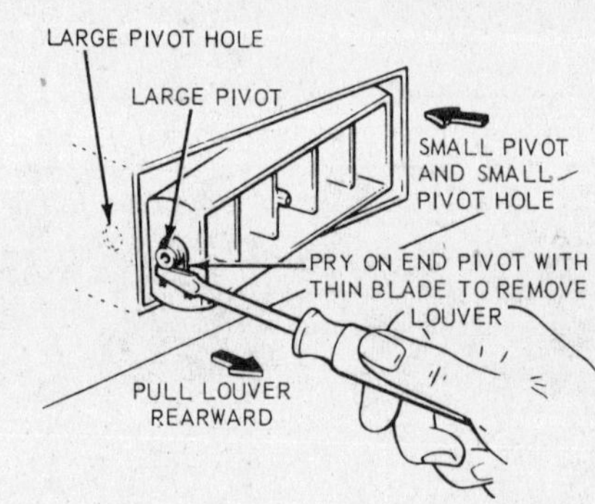

Fig. 12.38. Removing the ventilation louver assembly (Sec. 50)

51 Heater system - general description

Fresh air enters the right-hand duct of the heater assembly through the cowl opening. When the right-hand air vent is closed, air is drawn through the blend door opening(s), through and/or around the heater core into the blower housing. The blower then forces the air into the plenum chamber where it discharges either through the defroster nozzle or the air distribution duct to the floor.

When the upper lever (temperature control) is moved to the 'COOL' position the door shuts off the air passage to the heater core and bypasses it directly to the blower housing in an unheated condition.

When the temperature control lever is moved from the 'COOL' to the 'WARM' position the control cable moves the blend door from minimum heat to the full heat position to modulate the air flow through and/or around the heater core. The air passing through the core and the air passing through the bypass chamber is then mixed as it enters the blower housing.

At the full 'WARM' position the bypass to the blower is shut off, and all the air passes through the heater core to pick up maximum heat before entering the blower housing.

The lower control lever (function control) operates a control cable which is connected to the heat defrost door in the plenum chamber.

In the 'OFF' position, the door is closed so blocking all air passage through the plenum chamber.

In the 'FLOOR' position air is discharged through the air distribution duct to the floor area.

In the 'DEFROST' position, air is discharged to the windshield through the defroster nozzle.

Air flow can also be modulated in direct proportion to the control setting between 'FLOOR' and 'DEFROST' positions.

A single defrost nozzle which is connected to the top of the plenum chamber distributes air through two openings in the forward instrument panel to the windshield.

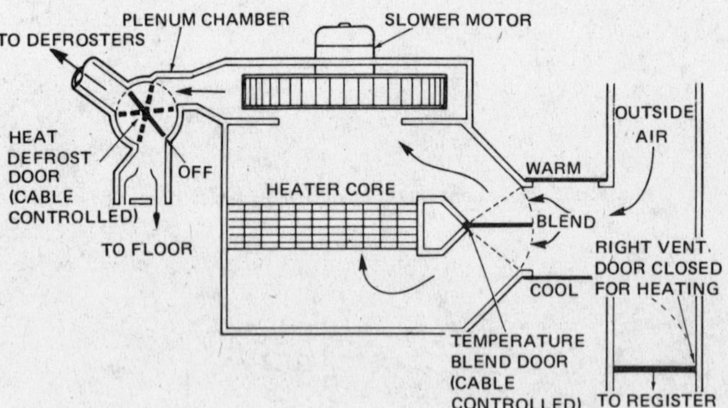

Fig. 12.39. Air flow through heater unit (Sec. 51)

52 Heater unit - removal and replacement

1 Disconnect the control cable from the heater assembly. Remove the mounting bracket clips and disconnect the cables from the door crank arms.
2 Remove the snap rivet which attaches the forward side of the defroster air duct to the plenum chamber.
3 Move the air duct back into the defroster nozzle so as to disengage it from the tabs on the plenum chamber.
4 Tilt the forward edge of the duct up and forwards to disengage it from the nozzle. Remove it from the left-hand side of the heater assembly.
5 Undo and remove the heater unit casing to instrument panel support bracket mounting screw.
6 The heater unit may now be carefully removed from inside the car. Place polythene sheeting on the floor and over the seats to prevent water from the heater staining the carpet and trim. If will be necessary to pull the heater hoses through the dash panel.
7 Finally disconnect the hoses from the heater core in the heater unit.
8 Refitting the heater unit is the reverse sequence to removal. It will be necessary to reset the controls as described later on in this Chapter.

53 Heater core - removal and replacement

1 Refer to Section 52, and remove the heater unit.
2 Remove the compression gasket from the cowl air inlet.
3 Release the eleven clips from the front and rear casing flanges.
4 Separate the front and rear halves of the casing.
5 The heater core may now be lifted from the front half of the case.
6 Refitting the heater core is the reverse sequence to removal.

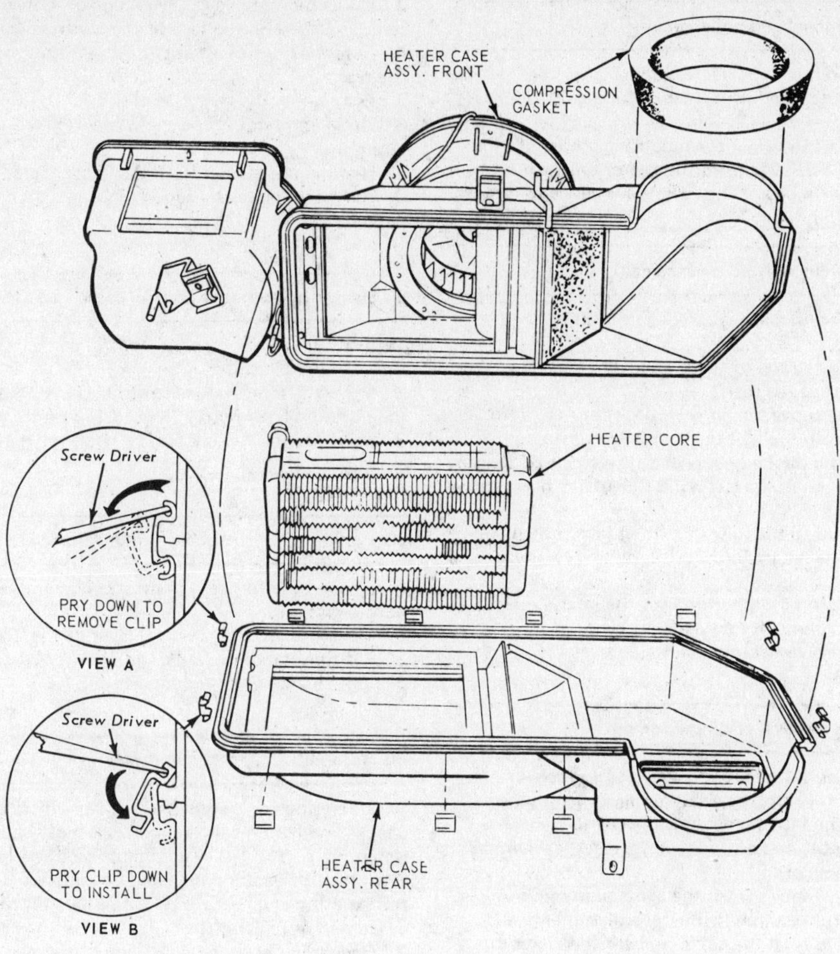

Fig. 12.40. Heater unit core assembly - removal (Sec. 53)

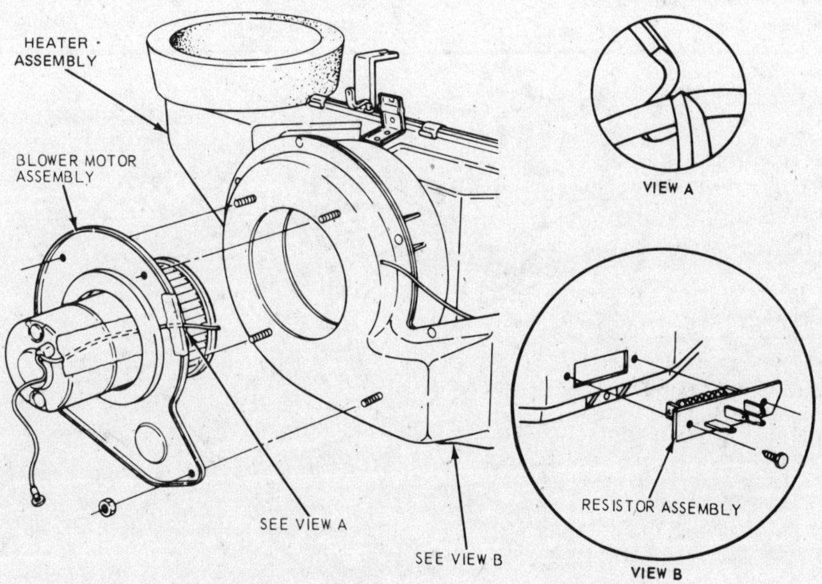

Fig. 12.41. Heater blower motor - removal (Sec. 54)

54 Heater blower motor - removal and replacement

1 Refer to Section 52, and remove the heater unit.
2 Disconnect the blower motor lead wire (colored orange) from the resistor.
3 Undo and remove the four blower motor mounting plate nuts and remove the motor and wheel assembly from the heater unit.
4 Refitting the heater blower motor is the reverse sequence to removal.

55 Heater defroster nozzle - removal and replacement

1 It is necessary for the defroster air duct to be removed before the nozzle can be removed.
2 The air duct is attached to the top of the plenum chamber by a snap rivet at the front and two tabs at the rear.
3 Remove the snap rivet and move the air duct back into the defroster nozzle so as to disengage it from the tabs on the plenum chamber.
4 Tilt the forward edge of the duct upwards and forwards to disengage it from the nozzle. Remove it from the left-hand side of the heater assembly.
5 The defroster nozzle is held to the four mounting tabs, which are integral with the instrument panel, by four corresponding retaining clips.
6 Carefully prise off the retaining clips and lower the nozzle rearwards to clear the plenum chamber. Now lift away the nozzle.
7 Refitting the nozzle is the reverse sequence to removal.

56 Heater control assembly - removal and replacement

1 Remove the control assembly support bracket securing screw.
2 Undo and remove the two control assembly to instrument panel mounted screws located on the face of the control assembly.
3 Lift out the control assembly and disconnect the electrical connectors from the switch and light terminals.
4 Disconnect the two control cables from the control assembly.
5 Refitting the heater control assembly is the reverse sequence to removal. It will be necessary to reset the cables as described later on in this Chapter.

57 Heater blower motor switch - removal and replacement

1 For safety reasons, disconnect the battery ground cable.
2 Pull the knob off the switch lever.
3 Undo and remove the two control to instrument panel mounting screws located on the face of the control assembly.
4 Ease the control assembly forwards out of the panel to give access to the rear.
5 Disconnect the switch lead wire.
6 Undo and remove the screw securing the switch to the control assembly.
7 Remove the switch from the forward side of the control assembly.
8 Refitting the heater blower motor switch is the reverse sequence to removal.

58 Heater temperature control cable - adjustment

1 Slacken the temperature control cable mounting clip located near to the door crank arm.
2 Move the temperature control lever to the full 'WARM' position and then bring it back by 0.125 in (3.175 mm).
3 Move the door crank arm towards the mounting bracket and tighten the clip.

59 Function control cable - adjustment

1 Slacken the function control cable mounting clip located near to the door crank arm.
2 Move the function control lever to the 'DEFROST' position.
3 Position the door crank arm midway between the two dots on the plenum chamber and tighten the clip.

60 Air-conditioning system - general

1 Where the car is equipped with an air-conditioning system, the checks and maintenance operations must be limited to the following items. No part of the system must be disconnected due to the danger from the refrigerant which will be released. Your Ford dealer or a refrigeration engineer must be employed if the system has to be evacuated or recharged.
2 Regularly check the condition of the system hoses and connections.
3 Inspect the fins of the condenser (located ahead of the radiator) and brush away accumulations of flies and dirt.
4 Check the compression drivebelt adjustment. There should be a total deflection of ½ in (12.7 mm) at the center of the longest run of the belt. Where adjustment is required, move the position of the idler pulley.
5 Keep the air-conditioner drain tube clear. This expels condensation

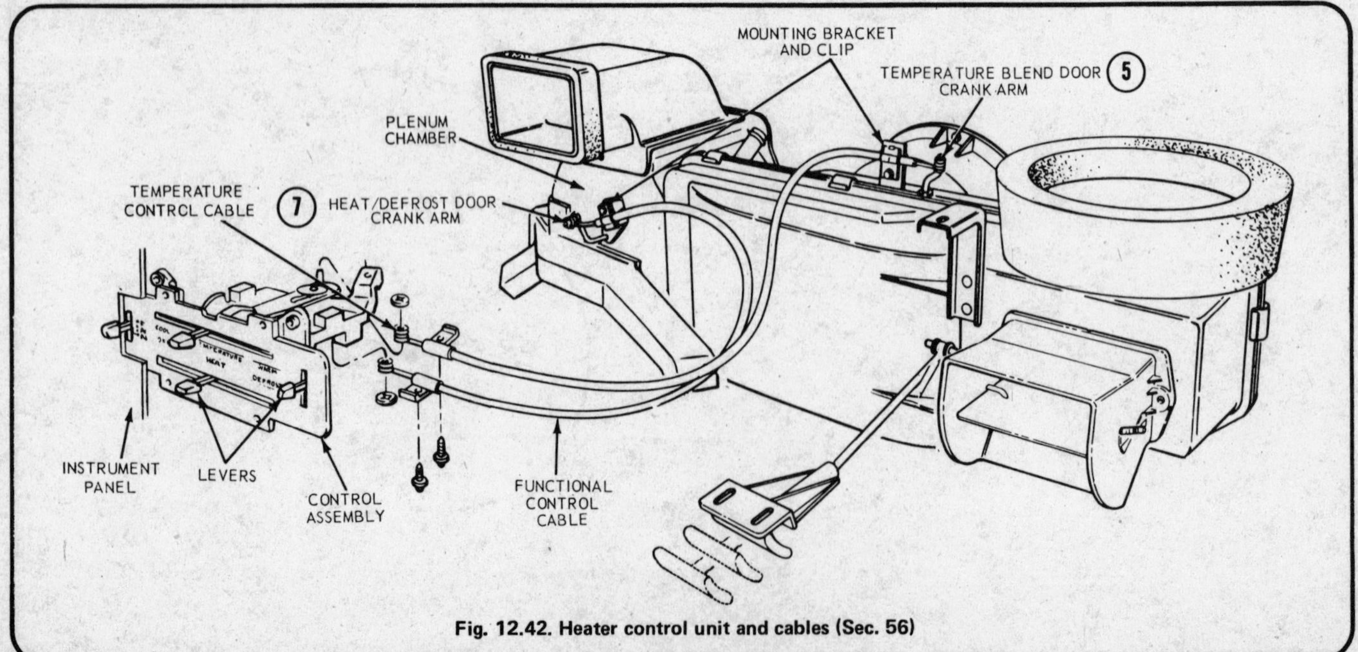

Fig. 12.42. Heater control unit and cables (Sec. 56)

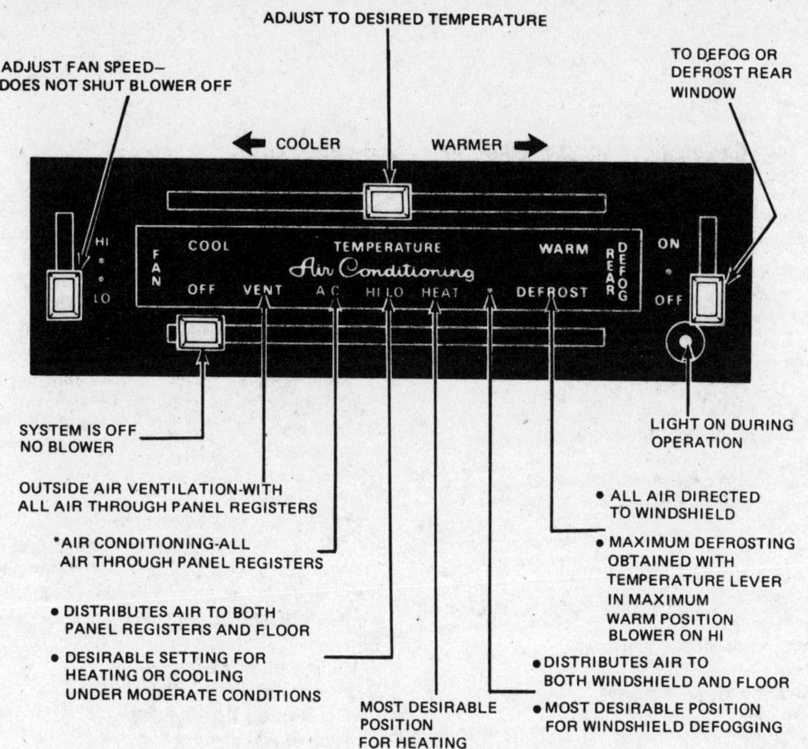
ADJUST TO DESIRED TEMPERATURE
ADJUST FAN SPEED–
DOES NOT SHUT BLOWER OFF
TO DEFOG OR
DEFROST REAR
WINDOW
COOLER
WARMER
HI
LO
FAN
COOL
TEMPERATURE
Air Conditioning
WARM
REAR
DEFOG
ON
OFF
OFF
VENT
A/C
HI LO
HEAT
DEFROST
SYSTEM IS OFF
NO BLOWER
LIGHT ON DURING
OPERATION
OUTSIDE AIR VENTILATION-WITH
ALL AIR THROUGH PANEL REGISTERS
• ALL AIR DIRECTED
TO WINDSHIELD
*AIR CONDITIONING-ALL
AIR THROUGH PANEL REGISTERS
• MAXIMUM DEFROSTING
OBTAINED WITH
TEMPERATURE LEVER
IN MAXIMUM
WARM POSITION
BLOWER ON HI
• DISTRIBUTES AIR TO BOTH
PANEL REGISTERS AND FLOOR
• DESIRABLE SETTING FOR
HEATING OR COOLING
UNDER MODERATE CONDITIONS
• DISTRIBUTES AIR TO
BOTH WINDSHIELD AND FLOOR
MOST DESIRABLE
POSITION
FOR HEATING
• MOST DESIRABLE POSITION
FOR WINDSHIELD DEFOGGING
*A/C COMPRESSOR WILL RUN CONTINUOSLY IN THIS MODE
EXCEPT AT LOW OUTSIDE AIR TEMPERATURE

Fig. 12.43. Air-conditioning controls (Sec. 60)

produced within the unit to a point under the car.

6 When the system is not in use, move the control to the 'OFF' position. During the winter period operate the unit for a few minutes every three or four weeks to keep the compressor in good order.

7 Every six months, have your Ford dealer check the refrigerant level in the system and the compressor oil level.

Chapter 13 Supplement

Contents

1 Introduction

General

The information contained in this Supplement covers modifications and additions which have been made to the Mustang range during 1977 and 1978.

If you have one of these later models, always read this Supplement before referring to the main Chapters of this Manual.

The radically changed 1979 Mustang cars which are based upon the Fairmont/Zephyr are not covered by this manual and they are the subject of separate Haynes Owners Workshop Manuals.

Routine Maintenance

The maintenance schedules have been revised for later models; a brief outline is given below. Comparison with the earlier maintenance schedules at the front of the manual will show that the mileage intervals for most tasks have been increased. The prudent owner may prefer to adopt shorter intervals for some tasks, especially where low annual mileages or severe operating conditions are involved.

The weekly checklist as given in the earlier schedules remains unchanged.

2.3 and 2.8 liter engines (Schedule A or B - see decal)

Every 10 000 miles (16 000 km):
- Renew engine oil and filter
- Check valve clearances (2.8 l)
- Check drivebelt tension and condition
- Check idle speed
- Check clutch pedal free play

Every 20 000 miles (32 000 km):
- Renew spark plugs
- Check automatic choke system
- Check Thermactor delay valve
- Clean or renew PCV valve (see decal)
- Check idle mixture
- Renew automatic transmission fluid (trailer to wing or severe service conditions only) and adjust brake bands

Every 30 000 miles (48 000 km):
- Renew air cleaner element
- Check exhaust system
- Check brake linings for wear
- Check brake hydraulic lines and hoses
- Lubricate and adjust front hub bearings
- Lubricate front syspension balljoints

Annually:
- Renew coolant
- Renew crankcase filter in air cleaner (2.8 l)

5 liter (V8) engine

Every 7500 miles (12 000 km):
- Renew engine oil and filter
- Check clutch pedal adjustment

Every 15 000 miles (24 000 km):
- Adjust automatic transmission brake bands (trailer towing or severe service conditions)

Every 22 500 miles (36 000 km):
- Renew spark plugs
- Renew PCV valve (only if specified on decal)
- Check fuel mixture adjustment
- Check automatic choke

Every 30 000 miles (48 000 km):
- Renwe air cleaner element
- Check exhaust system
- Lubricate front suspension and balljoints
- Check brake linings
- Check brake hydraulic lines and hoses
- Lubricate and adjust front hub bearings

Annually:
- Renew coolant and check system hoses
- Renew crankcase filter in air cleaner

2 Specifications

V8 engine (5 liter nominal)

1975 models

General	
Bore	4.00 in (101.6 mm)
Stroke	3.00 in (76.2 mm)
Displacement	302 cu in (4949 cc)
Firing order	1-5-4-2-6-3-7-8
Valves and valve gear	
Valve guide bore	0.3433 to 0.3443 in (8.72 to 8.75 mm)
Valve seat width	0.060 to 0.080 in (1.52 to 2.03 mm)
Valve seat angle	45°
Valve seat run-out	0.002 in (0.05 mm) maximum
Valve sequence (counting from timing gear end):	
Left-hand bank	Exhaust 1-3-5-7, Inlet 2-4-6-8
Right-hand bank	Exhaust 2-4-6-8, Inlet 1-3-5-7
Rocker arm stud bore	0.3680 to 0.3695 in (9.35 to 9.39 mm)
Pushrod run-out	0.015 in (0.38 mm) maximum
Valve lifter diameter	0.8740 to 0.8745 in (22.20 to 22.21 mm)
Lifter clearance in bore	0.0007 to 0.0027 in (0.0178 to 0.0686 mm)
Wear limit	0.005 in (0.127 mm)
Lifter leakdown ratio	5 to 50 seconds measured at 1/16 in (1.6 mm) plunger travel
Rocker arm-to-valve stem clearance (lifter collapsed)	0.090 to 0.206 in (2.29 to 5.23 mm)
Clearance adjustment method	Alternative length pushrods
Valve spring free length:	
Intake	1.94 in (49.28 mm)
Exhaust	1.85 in (46.99 mm)
Valve spring assembled height:	
Intake	1.67 to 1.70 in (42.42 to 43.18 mm)
Exhaust	1.59 to 1.61 in (40.39 to 40.89 mm)
Valve stem clearance in bore:	
Intake	0.0010 to 0.0027 in (0.025 to 0.069 mm)
Exhaust	0.0015 to 0.0032 in (0.038 to 0.081 mm)
Wear limit	0.005 in (0.127 mm)
Valve head diameter:	
Intake	1.773 to 1.791 in (45.03 to 45.49 mm)
Exhaust	1.442 to 1.460 in (36.63 to 37.08 mm)
Valve face angle	44°
Valve stem diameter:	
Intake	0.3416 in (8.68 mm)
Exhaust	0.3411 in (8.66 mm)
Oversizes available	+ 0.003, 0.015 and 0.030 in (0.076, 0.381 and 0.762 mm)
Camshaft	
Lobe lift:	
Intake	0.2303 in (5.850 mm)
Exhaust	0.2375 in (6.032 mm)
Maximum lobe lift loss	0.005 in (0.127 mm)
Endplay	0.001 to 0.007 in (0.0254 to 0.1778 mm)
Wear limit	0.009 in (0.2286 mm)
Camshaft bearing-to-journal clearance	0.001 to 0.003 in (0.0254 to 0.0762 mm)
Timing chain deflection (maximum)	0.5 in (12.7 mm)
Camshaft journal diameter:	
No 1	2.0805 to 2.0815 in (52.85 to 52.87 mm)
No 2	2.0655 to 2.0665 in (52.46 to 52.49 mm)
No 3	2.0505 to 2.0515 in (52.08 to 52.11 mm)
No 4	2.0355 to 2.0365 in (51.70 to 51.73 mm)
No 5	2.0205 to 2.0215 in (51.32 to 51.35 mm)
Camshaft bearing inside diameter:	
No 1	2.0825 to 2.0835 in (52.90 to 52.92 mm)
No 2	2.0675 to 2.0685 in (52.52 to 52.54 mm)

No 3	2.0525 to 2.0535 in (52.13 to 52.16 mm)
No 4	2.0375 to 2.0385 in (51.75 to 51.78 mm)
No 5	2.0225 to 2.0235 in (51.37 to 51.40 mm)
Cylinder block	
Bore diameter	4.0004 to 4.0052 in (101.61 to 101.73 mm)
Bore out-of-round (maximum)	0.0015 in (0.038 mm)
Bore taper (maximum)	0.001 in (0.025 mm)
Crankshaft	
Main bearing journal diameter	2.2482 to 2.2490 in (57.10 to 57.13 mm)
Maximum journal run-out	0.005 in (0.127 mm)
Maximum journal taper	0.0006 in per inch (0.006 mm per cm)
Connecting rod journal diameter	2.1228 to 2.1236 in (53.92 to 53.94 mm)
Maximum journal out-of-round	0.0006 in (0.0152 mm)
Maximum journal taper	0.0006 in per inch (0.006 mm per cm)
Crankshaft endplay	0.004 to 0.012 in (0.102 to 0.305 mm)
Main bearing running clearance	0.0001 to 0.0020 in (0.0025 to 0.051 mm)
Connecting rod bearing running clearance	0.0008 to 0.0015 in (0.0203 to 0.0381 mm)
Connecting rod and piston	
Piston pin bore diameter in connecting rod	0.9104 to 0.9112 in (23.12 to 23.15 mm)
Rod length (centre-to-centre)	5.0885 to 5.0915 in (129.25 to 129.32 mm)
Rod side clearance	0.010 to 0.023 in (0.254 to 0.584 mm)
Piston diameter (measured at piston pin bore centreline at 90° to pin bore):	
Red	3.9984 to 3.9990 in (101.56 to 101.58 mm)
Blue	3.9996 to 4.0002 in (101.59 to 101.61 mm)
Yellow	4.0020 to 4.0026 in (101.65 to 101.67 mm)
Oversize	+ 0.003 in (0.0762 mm)
Piston pin-to-piston clearance	0.0018 to 0.0026 in
Piston pin bore diameter in piston	0.9122 to 0.9126 in (23.170 to 23.180 mm)
Piston ring groove width:	
Top and second (compression)	0.080 to 0.081 in (2.032 to 2.057 mm)
Oil control	0.1880 to 0.1890 in (4.775 to 4.801 mm)
Piston pin length	3.010 to 3.040 in (76.454 to 77.216 mm)
Piston pin diameter	0.9120 to 0.9123 in (23.165 to 23.172 mm)
Oversize available	+ 0.001 in (0.0254 mm)
Piston pin-to-connecting rod clearance	Interference fit
Piston ring clearance in groove	0.002 to 0.006 in (0.0508 to 0.1524 mm)
Piston ring end gap:	
Compression	0.010 to 0.020 in (0.254 to 0.508 mm)
Oil control rail	0.015 to 0.055 in (0.381 to 1.397 mm)
Lubrication system	
Oil pan capacity	4 US qt (3½ Imp qt, 4½ liters) (add 1 US qt for filter change)
Oil pressure (hot @ 2000 rpm)	40 to 60 lbf/in^2 (2.8 to 4.2 kgf/cm^2)
Oil pump:	
Type	Rotor
Driveshaft-to-bearing clearance	0.0015 to 0.0029 in (0.0381 to 0.0737 mm)
Relief valve clearance	0.0015 to 0.0029 in (0.0381 to 0.0737 mm)
Rotor end clearances	0.001 to 0.004 in (0.0254 to 0.1016 mm)
Rotor-to-housing clearance	0.001 to 0.013 in (0.0254 to 0.3302 mm)

1976 thru 1977 models

Specifications as for 1975 models except for the following differences

Valve spring assembled height:	
Intake	1.66 to 1.72 in (42.16 to 43.69 mm)
Exhaust	1.56 to 1.63 in (39.62 to 41.40 mm)
Camshaft lobe lift:	
Intake	0.2373 in (6.027 mm)
Exhaust	0.2474 in (6.284 mm)
Piston pin diameter (standard)	0.9118 to 0.9124 in (23.160 to 23.175 mm)

1978 models

Specifications as for 1976/77 models except for the following differences

Valve head diameter:	
Intake	1.770 to 1.794 in (44.958 to 45.568 mm)
Exhaust	1.439 to 1.463 in (36.551 to 37.160 mm)
Valve stem diameter:	
Intake	0.3446 to 0.3453 in (8.753 to 8.771 mm)
Exhaust	0.3441 to 0.3448 in (8.740 to 8.758 mm)
Oversizes available	+ 0.015 and 0.030 in (0.381 to 0.762 mm)
Valve spring free length:	
Intake	2.04 in (51.82 mm)
Exhaust	1.85 in (46.99 mm)
Rocker arm-to-valve stem clearance (lifter collapsed)	0.071 to 0.193 in (1.803 to 4.902 mm)
Camshaft gear backlash	0.006 to 0.010 in (0.152 to 0.257 mm)
Main bearing running clearance:	
No 1	0.0001 to 0.0017 in (0.0025 to 0.0432 mm)
All others	0.0004 to 0.0021 in (0.0102 to 0.0533 mm)
Piston pin bore diameter in connecting rod	0.9096 to 0.9112 in (23.104 to 23.145 mm)

Piston pin diameter:	
Standard	0.9119 to 0.9124 in (23.162 to 23.175 mm)
Oversizes available	+ 0.001 and 0.002 in (0.0254 and 0.0508 mm)
Piston pin-to-piston clearance	0.0002 to 0.0004 in (0.0051 to 0.0102 mm)

Torque wrench settings (all V8 engines)	**lbf ft**	**Nm**
Cylinder head bolts:		
Stage 1	55	75
Stage 2	70	95
Intake manifold bolts	24	33
Exhaust manifold bolts	24	33
Flywheel bolts	80	109
Main bearing cap bolts	70	95
Oil drain plug	20	27
EGR valve-to-carburetor	16	22
Oil intake-to-oil pump	12	16
Camshaft gear bolt	40	54
Camshaft thrust plate bolts	12	16
Crankshaft vibration damper	85	115
Crankshaft pulley bolts	45	61
Connecting rod nuts	24	33
Rocker arm stud nuts (after nut contacts shoulder)	17 to 23	23 to 31
Alternator bracket bolts	20	27
Alternator pivot bolt	50	68
Thermactor pump bracket	20	27
Thermactor pump pivot bolt	30	41
Power steering pump pulley-to-damper	45	61
Fan fixing bolts	16	22
Cylinder front cover bolts	15	20
Oil pan bolts (5/16 in)	12	16
Oil pan bolts (¼ in)	8	10

Cooling system

Thermostat

Starts to open	193° to 200°F (89° to 93°C)
Fully open	221°F (105°C)

Torque wrench settings	**lbf ft**	**Nm**
Fan-to-pulley hub bolts	16	22
ATF cooler unions (at radiator)	12	16

Fuel system

Carburetor application

2.3 liter 4-cyl engine	Motorcraft 5200 2V or Holley Weber 6500 Feedback (later models only)
2.8 liter V6 and 5.0 liter V8 engines	Motorcraft 2150 2V or 2700 VV

Carburetor specification

5200 2V and 2150 2V - 1975/76

Primary throttle bore	32.0 mm (1.260 in)
Secondary throttle bore	36.0 mm (1.417 in)
Primary venturi diameter	26.0 mm (1.024 in)
Secondary venturi diameter	27.0 mm (1.063 in)
Float setting	11.7 ± 0.8 mm (0.46 ± 0.03 in)
Primary idle jet	0.90 mm
Secondary idle jet	0.50 mm
Primary main metering jet	1.42 to 1.32 mm depending on model
Secondary main metering jet	1.32 mm
Primary main well tube	14R-905
Secondary main well tube	14R-816 (F50)
Primary high speed bleed	1.35 to 1.99 mm depending on model
Secondary high speed bleed	1.95 mm
Accelerator pump lever hole setting	No 2
Choke pull-down setting at 75°F (24°C):	
D6ZE-LA and -SA	6.0 ± 0.5 mm (0.236 ± 0.020 in)
D6ZE-EA, -NA, -NB and -RA	7.0 ± 0.5 mm (0.276 ± 0.020 in)
Bimetal identification	°8
Automatic choke setting:	
D6ZE-LA	Index
D6ZE-AA, -AAA, -BA, -CA, -DA, -UA	3-NR
All other models	1-NL
Fast idle cam setting (at kickdown):	
D6ZE-EA, -NA and -NB	4.0 ± 0.5 mm (0.158 ± 0.020 in)
D6ZE-RA	5.0 ± 0.5 mm (0.197 ± 0.020 in)
D6ZE-BA	3.0 ± 0.5 mm (0.120 ± 0.020 in)
D6ZE-AAA, -CA, -DA and -UA	3.3 ± 0.5 mm (0.130 ± 0.020 in)

Dechoke (minimum)	6.5 mm (0.256 in)
2150 2V - 1976	
Throttle bore diameter	39.6 mm (1.56 in)
Venturi diameter	27.4 mm (1.08 in)
Float setting:	
Dry	11.1 mm (7/16 in)
Wet	20.6 mm (13/16 in)
Main jet:	
D5DE-AEA	51F
D5WE-FA, D6ZE-AA and -JA	50F
D6ZE-DA	49F
D6ZE-UA	48F
Enrichment valve:	
D5DE-AEA, D6ZE-AA and -DA	Green 7.5
D5WE-FA	Black 5.5
D6ZE-JA	Plain 8.5
D6ZE-UA	Violet 11.5
Accelerator pump hole	No 2
Choke cap setting	3-NR
Choke pull-down setting:	
D5DE-AEA and D5WE-FA	3.43 mm (0.135 in)
D6ZE-JA, -UA, -AA and -DA	3.56 mm (0.140 in)
Fast idle cam setting	4.06 mm (0.160 in)
5200 2V - 1977	
Primary throttle bore diameter	32.0 mm (1.260 in)
Secondary throttle bore diameter	36.0 mm (1.417 in)
Primary venturi diameter	26.0 mm (1.024 in)
Secondary venturi diameter	27.0 mm (1.063 in)
Float level setting	11.5 ± 0.8 mm (0.435 ± 0.03 in)
Primary idle jet	0.90 mm
Secondary idle jet	0.50 mm
Primary main jet	255
Secondary main jet	239
Primary main well tube	14R-905
Secondary main well tube	14R-816 (F50)
Primary high speed bleed	1.85 mm
Secondary high speed bleed	1.95 mm
Power valve timing	8.5 in (216 mm) Hg
Accelerator pump lever hole setting	No 2
Choke pull-down at 75°F (24°C)	6.0 ± 0.5mm (0.236 ± 0.020 in)
Bimetal identification	09
Automatic choke setting:	
D7EE-BGA and -BHA	Index
D7EE-BLA and -BMA	1-NR
Fast idle cam setting	3.0 mm (0.118 in) at kickdown
Dechoke (minimum)	6.0 mm (0.236 in)
2150 2V - 1977 (series D7YE-EA)	
Throttle bore diameter	39.6 mm (1.56 in)
Venturi diameter	27.4 mm (1.08 in)
Float setting:	
Dry	9.53 ± 0.8 mm (3/8 ± 1/32 in)
Wet	19.05 ± 1.6 mm (¾ ± 1/16 in)
Main jet	48F
Enrichment valve	7.5 green
Accelerator pump rod location	No 3
Choke bimetal identification	2-85 OD
Choke cap setting	2-NR
Choke pull-down setting	3.10 mm (0.122 in)
Fast idle cam setting	3.61 mm (0.142 in)
2150 2V - 1977 (series D7BE-YA)	
Throttle bore diameter	39.6 mm (1.56 in)
Venturi diameter	27.4 mm (1.08 in)
Float setting:	
Dry	11.1 ± 0.8 mm (7/16 ± 1/32 in)
Wet	20.6 ± 1.6 mm (13/16 ± 1/16 in)
Main jet	51F
Enrichment valve	Yellow 6.5
Accelerator pump rod location	No 2
Choke bimetal identification	2-65 OD
Choke cap setting	1-NR
Choke pull-down setting	3.73 mm (0.147 in)
Fast idle cam setting	4.24 mm (0.167 in)
5200 2V - 1978	
Primary throttle bore diameter	32.0 mm (1.260 in)
Secondary throttle bore diameter	36.0 mm (1.417 in)
Primary venturi diameter	22.0 mm (0.866 in)

Secondary venturi diameter	27.0 mm (1.063 in)
Float level setting	11.5 mm (29/64 in)
Primary idle jet	0.60 mm
Secondary idle jet	0.50 mm
Primary and secondary main jet	Varies according to application; for details consult manufacturer's literature
Primary main well tube	14R-905
Secondary main well tube	14R-1004
Primary high speed bleed:	
D8BE-FA	1.95 mm
All other models	1.85 mm
Secondary high speed bleed	1.70 mm
Power valve timing	8.5 in (216 mm) Hg
Accelerator pump rod location	No 2
Choke pull-down setting at 75°F (24°C):	
D8EE-ATA	5.0 ± 0.5 mm (0.197 ± 0.020 in)
All other models	6.0 ± 0.5 mm (0.236 ± 0.020 in)
Bimetal identification	No 10
Automatic choke cap setting:	
D8BE-HA, D8EE-CA and -KA, D8ZE-SA and -RA	1-NR
All other models	2-NR
Fast idle cam setting	3.0 ± 0.5 mm (0.118 ± 0.020 in) at kickdown
Dechoke (minimum)	6.0 mm (0.236 in)
2150 2V - 1978	
Throttle bore diameter	39.6 mm (1.56 in)
Venturi diameter	
D8BE-ACA, D8DE-HA, D8ZE-TA and -UA	30.7 mm (1.21 in)
All other models	27.4 mm (1.08 in)
Float setting (dry):	
D8OE-EA and D8KE-EA	40.5 mm (1.19/32 in)
D8ZE-TA and -UA and D8BE-MB	9.5 mm (3/8 in)
All other models	11.1 mm (7/16 in)
Float setting (wet)	19 to 20.6 mm (¾ to 13/16 in)
Main jet:	
D8ME-BA and D8OE-EA	51F
D8BA-ACA, D8ZE-TA and -UA	55F
D8DE-HA	59F
D8KE-EA and D8BE-MB	50F
All other models	49F
Enrichment valve:	
D8BE-ACA, D8ZE-TA and -UA	Red 9.5
D8OE-EA and D8BE-MB	Green 7.5
D8DE-HA	Orange 10.5
All other models	Black 5.5
Accelerator pump rod location:	
D8BE-ACA, D8ZE-TA and -UA	No 4
D8DE-HA and D8BE-MB	No 3
All other models	No 2
Choke cap setting:	
D8BE-AEA and -AFA	4-NR
D84E-EA, D8BE-ADA and D8KE-EA	3-NR
D8BE-ACA and D8DE-HA	2-NR
All other models	Index
Choke pull-down setting:	
D8DE-HA	4.57 mm (0.180 in)
D8BE-ACA	3.94 mm (0.155 in)
D8ME-BA, D80E-EA, D8KE-EA, D8ZE-TA and -UA	3.43 mm (0.135 in)
All other models	2.79 mm (0.110 in)
Fast idle cam setting	See text
2700 VV - 1978	
Throttle bore diameter	39.6 mm (1.56 in)
Venturi	Variable
Float setting (dry)	26.4 mm (1.04 in)
Float drop	37.1 mm (1.46 in)
Metering rod	No 163
Venturi valve limiter setting:	
D8BE-EB	18.5 to 19.6 mm (0.73 to 0.77 in)
D84E-DB	23.9 to 24.9 mm (0.94 to 0.98 in)
Wide open throttle stop setting	25.2 to 25.6 mm (0.99 to 1.01 in)
Internal vent setting	0.127 to 0.381 mm (0.005 to 0.015 in)
Bimetal identification:	
D8BE-EB	7-40 MF
D84E-DB	7-50 MF
Choke cap setting	Index
Fast idle cam setting	1-NR/3rd step
Cold enrichment rod setting	3.05 to 3.30 mm (0.120 to 0.130 in) at index

Tune-up specifications

1977 models

Fuel decal valve timing:	
2300 cc	3 to 4½ seconds
2800 cc	2 seconds minimum
Fast idle speed:	
2300 cc (manual)	1800 rpm California, 1600 rpm others
2300 cc (auto)	1800 to 2000 rpm
2800 cc (manual)	1700 rpm
2800 cc (auto)	1800 rpm California, 1600 rpm others
302 cu in (manual)	2100 rpm
302 cu in (automatic)	1900 rpm California, 2000 rpm others
TSP-OFF idle speed:	
2300 cc	550 rpm
All other models	500 rpm
Automatic choke pull-down gauge setting:	
2300 cc	6 mm (0.236 in)
2800 cc	0.6 to 2.4 mm (0.025 to 0.093 in)
302 cu in:	
High Altitude models	3.6 to 3.8 mm (0.14 to 0.15 in)
Other models	3.3 to 3.6 mm (0.13 to 0.14 in)
Choke plate rotational period to vertical:	
2300 cc	240 seconds max
2800 cc	100 to 200 seconds
302 cu in	180 seconds max
Electric choke heater resistance:	
2300 cc (high altitude)	2 to 3 ohms
2300 cc (other models)	6 to 9 ohms
2800 cc	0.8 to 4 ohms
302 cu in	0.8 to 4 ohms
Time for choke rod to move down to seated position (2700 VV carburetor only)	60 to 100 seconds
Time for fast idle cam to drop (5200 carburetor only)	5 minutes

1978 models	Refer to individual vehicle decal

Torque wrench settings

	lbf ft	Nm
Fuel pump mounting bolts	26	35
Carburetor mounting nuts	20	27
EGR tube-to-exhaust manifold	10	14
EGR tube nut	10	14
EGR valve-to-spacer	20	27

Ignition system

General

System type	Dura Spark high energy breakerless
Firing order:	
2300 cc	1-3-4-2
2800 cc	1-4-2-5-3-6
302 cu in	1-5-4-2-6-3-7-8
Distributor rotation:	
2300 cc and 2800 cc	Clockwise
302 cu in	Counterclockwise

Distributor

Shaft endplay:	
2300 cc and 2800 cc	0.56 to 0.84 mm (0.022 to 0.033 in)
302 cu in	0.61 to 0.89 mm (0.024 to 0.035 in)
Rotor air gap (voltage drop)	8.0 kV maximum

Coil

Primary resistance:	
Dura Spark I	0.71 to 0.77 ohms
Dura Spark II	1.13 to 1.23 ohms
Secondary resistance:	
Dura Spark I	7350 to 8250 ohms
Dura Spark II	7700 to 9300 ohms
Ballast resistor (Dura Spark I only)	1.05 to 1.15 ohms

Spark plugs*

Type:	
2300 cc	AGRF 52
2800 cc	AGR 42
302 cu in	ARF 52

Electrode gap:

2300 cc and 2800 cc	0.86 mm (0.034 in)
302 cu in	1.12 mm (0.044 in)

**Refer also to tune-up decal*

For all other ignition system specifications, including ignition timing, refer to engine compartment decal

Torque wrench settings

	lbf ft	Nm
Spark plugs:		
2300 cc	10	14
2800 cc and 302 cu in	15	20
Distributor clamp bolt	15	20
Distributor vacuum pipe tube-to-adapter (2300 cc)	8	11

Clutch (V8 engine)

General

Type	Single dry plate, diaphragm spring
Actuation	Cable
Disc diameter	10.0 in (25.4 cm)
Identification color	Pink
Number of springs	12 (6 pink, 6 orange)

Adjustment data

Clutch pedal free travel	1.3/8 to 1.5/8 in (35 to 41 mm)

Manual transmission

Gear ratios (Type RAD transmission)

2 - 3 l engine, 1977 on:		
1st	3.50 : 1	
2nd	2.21 : 1	
3rd	1.43 : 1	
4th	1.00 : 1	
Reverse	3.38 : 1	
2.8 l V6 engine:	**1977**	**1978**
1st	3.50 : 1	4.07 : 1
2nd	2.21 : 1	2.57 : 1
3rd	1.43 : 1	1.66 : 1
4th	1.00 : 1	1.00 : 1
Reverse	3.38 : 1	3.95 : 1
5.0 l V8 engine:		
1st	2.64 : 1	
2nd	1.89 : 1	
3rd	1.34 : 1	
4th	1.00 : 1	
Reverse	2.56 : 1	

Revised torque wrench settings

	lbf ft	Nm
Input shaft bearing retainer-to-case bolts	15	20
Extension housing-to-case bolts	25	34
Access cover screw	10	14
Filler plug	25	34
Detent setscrew	12	16
Reverse pivot bolt	25	34
Offset assembly nut	20	27
Back-up lamp switch	12	16
Seat belt sensing switch	12	16

Rear axle

General

Type	Integral differential carrier (C2)
Ring gear diameter	6¾ in (171.45 mm)

Ratios

1975-76:	
WGF-AA, -U and -R2	3.18 : 1
WGF-H and -K	3.40 : 1
WGF-N and -R	3.55 : 1
1977-78:	
WGF-AJ	2.73 : 1
WGF-AA, -K1 and -U1	3.18 : 1

Dimensions and clearances

Maximum run-out of rear face of crownwheel	0.003 in (0.0762 mm)
Differential side gear thrust washer thickness	0.030 to 0.032 in (0.762 to 0.8128 mm)
Differential pinion gear thrust washer thickness	0.030 to 0.032 in (0.762 to 0.8128 mm)

Pinion locating shim:	
Nominal size	0.030 in (0.762 mm)
Available pinion locating shims	0.008 to 0.024 in (0.2032 to 0.3048 mm) in steps of 0.001 in (0.254 mm)
Crownwheel/pinion backlash	0.008 to 0.012 in (0.2032 to 0.3048 mm)
Maximum backlash variation between teeth	0.003 in (0.0762 mm)
Maximum radial runout of pinion flange	0.010 in (0.254 mm)
Minimum torque for pinion flange nut	140 lbf ft (190 Nm)
Pinion bearing preload:	
Original bearings	6 to 12 lbf in (0.68 to 1.36 Nm)
New bearings	17 to 32 lbf in (1.92 to 3.62 Nm)
Lubricant capacity	3 US pints (1.4 liters, 2½ Imp pints)

Torque wrench settings	lbf ft	Nm
Differential bearing cap bolts	50	68
Differential bearing adjustment nut lockbolts	20	27
Crownwheel securing bolts	55	75
Rear cover securing bolts	30	41
Oil filler plug	45	61
Axleshaft bearing retainer bolt nuts	40	54
Shock absorber nuts	25	34
Spring U-bolt nuts	35	48
Rear universal joint U-bolt nuts	15	20
Rear universal joint flange bolts	70	95

Electrical system

Alternator (side terminal type)

Rating (Amps):	
70 Amp type	1050 W at 15V
90 Amp type	1350 W at 15V
Field current	4.0 Amps
Slip ring minimum diameter	1.22 in (30.988 mm)
Brush length (new)	½ in (12.7 mm)
Wear limit	5/16 in (7.9 mm)

Starter motor (1977 on)

Current draw	150 to 200 Amps
Engine cranking speed	180 to 250 rpm
Brush length	½ in (12.7 mm)
Wear limit	¼ in (6.4 mm)

Fuses, circuit breakers and fusible links

For fuse arrangement, see text

Circuit breakers:	
Number	2
Rating	18A (headlamps) and 15A (other exterior lamps)
Location	In lighting switch
Fusible links:	
Number	4
Circuits protected	Heated rear window, electric choke, engine compartment light, main load circuit

Torque wrench settings	lbf ft	Nm
Alternator (70 - 90 Amp) pulley nut	90	122
Starter thru bolts	60	82
Starter mounting bolts	20	27

Roadwheels and tires

Wheels

Size	13 x 5 or 14 x 5.5 according to model, 4-bolt fixing

Tires

Tire size	B78, C78, BR78, CR78, X13 or X14 according to model
Tire pressure	Refer to vehicle decal

3 Engine (5 liter nominal - 302 cu in) - V8

Description

1 This engine was available as an option from 1975 on. It is of V8 type with overhead valves operated by pushrods from a chain-driven camshaft.

2 The crankshaft is supported in five main bearings. The bearing shells of No 3 main bearing incorporate thrust flanges to control the crankshaft endfloat.

3 Hydraulic valve lifters are used in this engine.

Major operations possible with engine in vehicle

4 The following operations can be carried out without having to remove the engine from the vehicle:

(a) Removal and refitting of engine supports
(b) Removal and refitting of intake manifold
(c) Removal and refitting of valve lifter(s)
(d) Removal and refitting of cylinder heads
(e) Removal and refitting of timing cover and chain
(f) Removal and refitting of camshaft
(g) Renewal of crankshaft front oil seal
(h) Removal and refitting of oil pan and oil pump

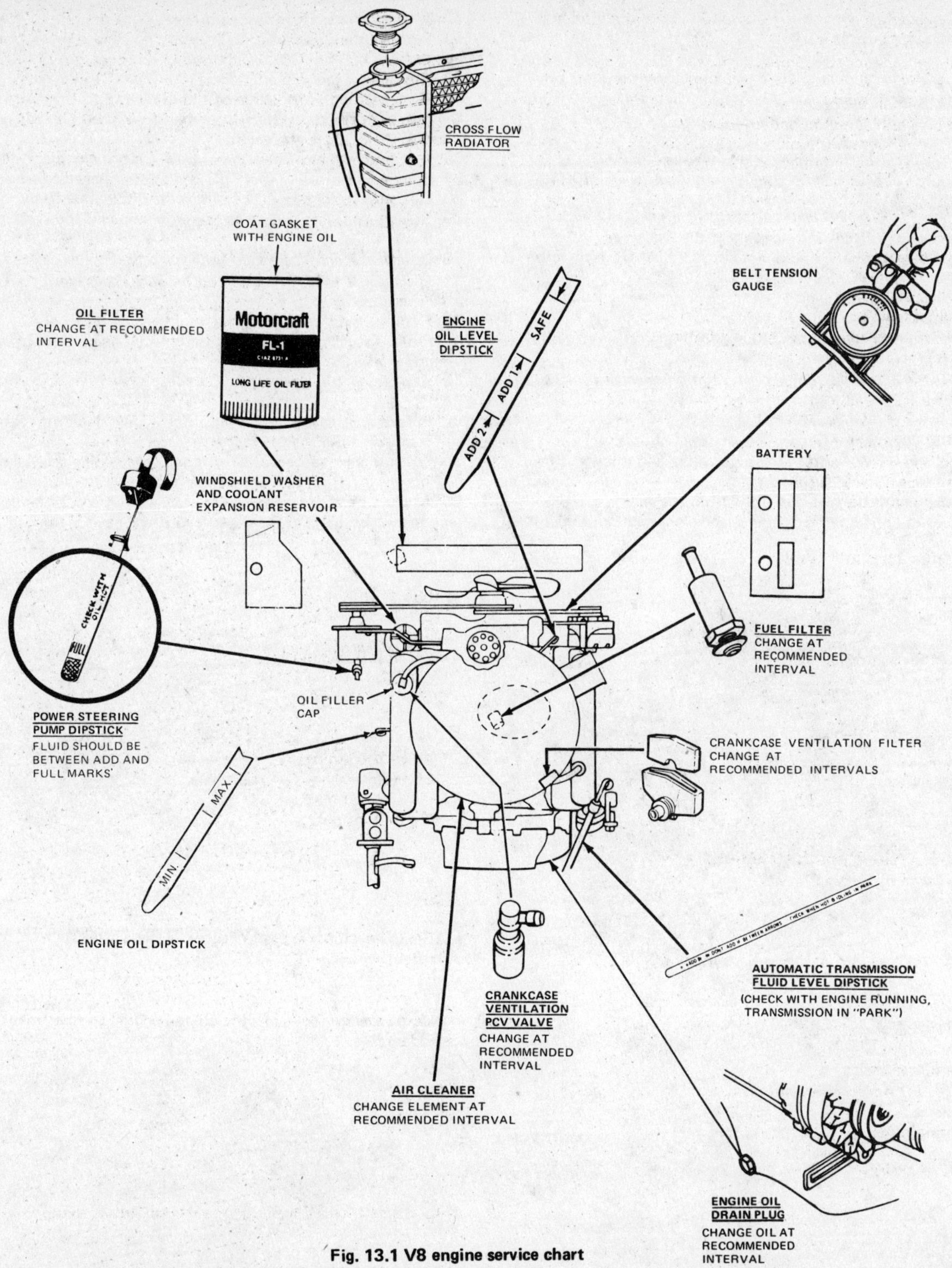

Fig. 13.1 V8 engine service chart

(j) *Renewal of main bearing shells (see below)*
(k) *Renewal of connecting rod bearing shells (see below)*
(m) *Removal and refitting of pistons/connecting rods*

5 Although it is possible for the main and connecting rod bearings to be renewed without lifting the engine from the vehicle, this is not recommended but should be carried out at time of major overhaul when the engine has been removed.

Major operations only possible (or recommended) after removal of engine from vehicle

6 The following components can only be removed and refitted with the engine out of the vehicle:

(a) *Crankshaft*
(b) *Flywheel (or adapter plate - automatic transmission)*

Engine supports - removal and refitting (engine in vehicle)

Front supports

7 Release the radiator fan shroud by extracting the securing screws.
8 Support the weight of the engine using a jack and wooden block as an insulator under the oil pan.
9 Unscrew and remove the nut and through bolt which hold the support insulator to the frame crossmember.

10 Raise the engine just enough to be able to remove the insulator and heat shield (where fitted).

Rear support

11 To renew the rear support, place a jack under the transmission and unbolt the crossmember from the frame of the vehicle and from the rear support. Remove the support.

All supports

12 Refitting is a reversal of removal, but where self-locking nuts are used, they should be renewed and all nuts tightened to specified torque.

Intake manifold - removal and refitting (engine in vehicle)

13 Drain the cooling system and disconnect the battery.

14 Disconnect the automatic choke hot air inlet hose from the tube adjacent to the right-hand rocker cover.

15 Remove the air cleaner together with the crankcase ventilation hose and the intake duct.

16 Disconnect the throttle control linkage from the carburetor and manifold brackets.

17 Disconnect the brake vacuum and automatic transmission vacuum hoses from the intake manifold.

18 Disconnect the wires from the coil terminals.

19 Remove the Thermactor bypass and air supply hoses.

20 Disconnect the HT wires from the spark plugs and disengage the wires from the rocker cover clips.

21 Remove the distributor cap and lift it from the engine compartment with wires disconnected from the spark plugs and ignition coil.

22 Remove the EGR vacuum amplifier from the rear of the manifold.

23 Remove the carburetor fuel supply pipe and the automatic choke heat tube.

24 Disconnect the vacuum hoses from the distributor.

25 Mark the relative position of the rotor arm to the distributor and the distributor body to the intake manifold, then unbolt and remove the distributor from the engine.

26 Disconnect the radiator upper hose from the coolant outlet

27 Disconnect the wire from the coolant temperature sender unit.

28 Disconnect the heater hose from the intake manifold.

29 Release the water pump bypass hose clip and slide the hose from the outlet housing.

30 Detach the crankcase vent hose from the rocker cover.

31 Disconnect the EGR valve and vacuum hoses from the back pressure transducer.

32 Remove the intake manifold complete with carburetor. If the manifold is stuck, tap it with a plastic-faced hammer to break the seal, do not pry it off.

33 Remove all old gaskets and bolt sealing washers and obtain new items.

34 Before refitting the manifold, thoroughly clean the mating surfaces of manifold and block.

35 Position new gaskets and front and rear sealing strips so that the gaskets are interlocked with the seal tabs.

36 Apply a bead of silicone (RTV) sealer to the outer ends of each sealing strip so that it runs the full width of each sealing strip.

Fig. 13.2 Right side view of V8 engine

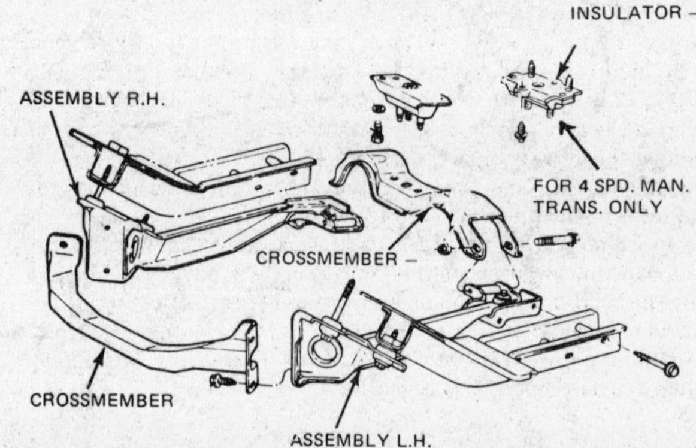

Fig. 13.3 Engine crossmember mounting components

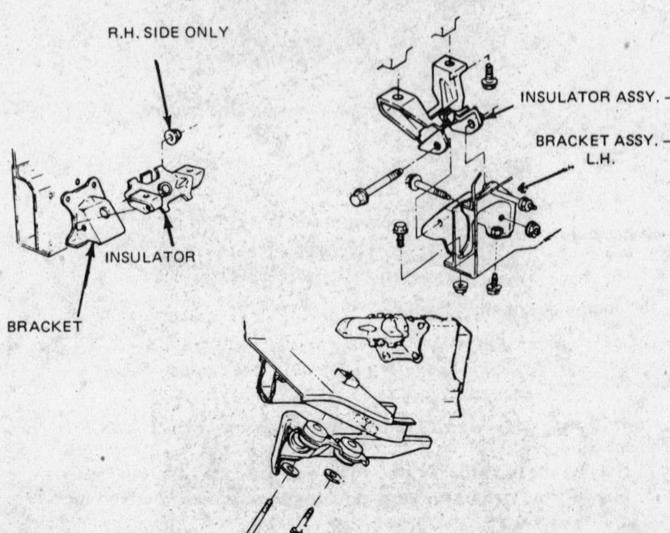

Fig. 13.4 Engine mounting brackets (note direction of bolt heads)

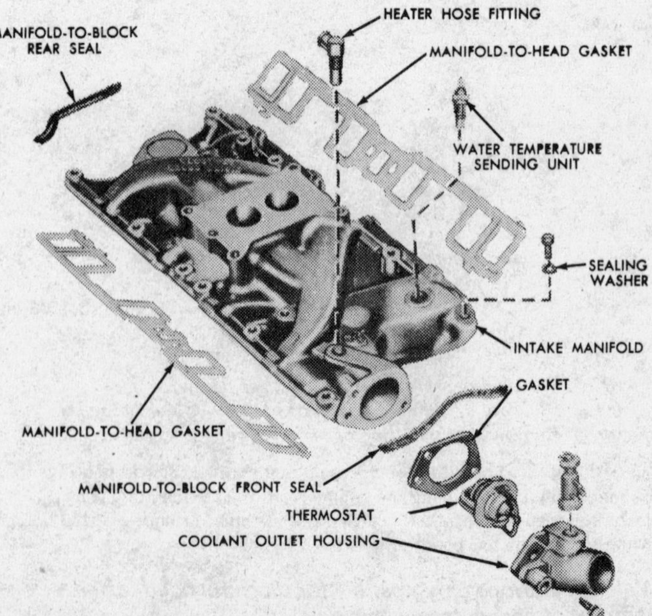

Fig. 13.5 Intake manifold details

1/8" DIA. BEAD SEALER
CYLINDER HEAD
SEAL MOUNTING SURFACE OF CYLINDER BLOCK
INTAKE MANIFOLD GASKET
INTAKE MANIFOLD SEAL
1/16" DIA. BEAD SEALER

Fig. 13.6 Intake manifold sealant diagram

37 Lower the manifold into position on the block and check that the sealing strips are not displaced. Check that the holes in the manifold and the gasket are in alignment.
38 Refit the manifold bolts and tighten to the specified torque in the sequence shown (Fig. 13.7).
39 On 1975 models only, the torque of these units and bolts must be checked after the engine has been run up to normal operating temperature.
40 Refitting of all remaining components is a reversal of removal.
41 Refill the cooling system.

Valve lifter(s) - removal and refitting

42 The need to remove a valve lifter is normally due to noisy operation but before taking this step, make sure that the noise is not caused by incorrect rocker arm-to-valve stem clearance (see paragraphs 225 thru 236) or worn rocker arms or pushrods.
43 Remove the intake manifold as described in the paragraphs above.
44 Remove the valve rocker cover.
45 Release the rocker arm nuts and swivel the arm aside so that the pushrod can be withdrawn.
46 Use a magnet to remove the valve lifter. It may be necessary to clean the deposits away before the lifter can be widhrawn. If more than one pushrod or lifter is being removed, identify them as to location as they must not be mixed up.
47 Refitting is a reversal of removal. Oil the lifter before installing and adjust the valve clearance as described in paragraphs 225 thru 236.

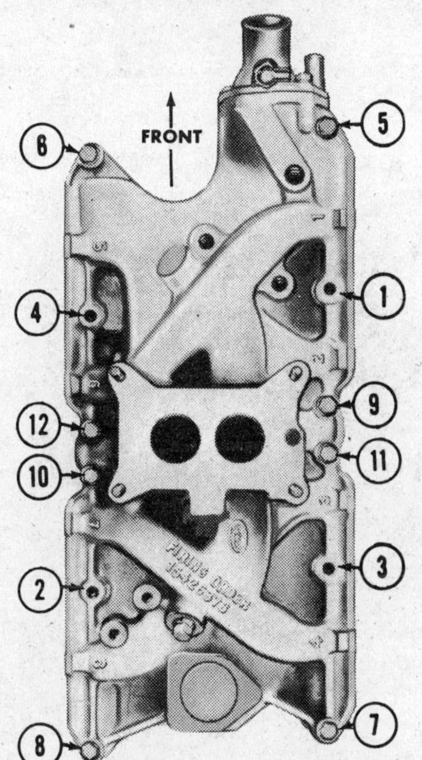

Fig. 13.7 Intake manifold bolt tightening sequence

Cylinder head - removal and refitting

48 Drain the cooling system, disconnect the battery and then remove the intake manifold complete with carburetor as described in paragraphs 13 thru 32.
49 Remove the rocker arm cover.
50 If the left-hand cylinder head is to be removed, on vehicles with an air conditioner, unbolt the compressor and move it to one side. *Do not disconnect the refrigerant pipelines.* On vehicles with power-assisted steering, unbolt the power steering pump and move it to one side.
51 If the right-hand cylinder head is to be removed, the alternator will have to be unbolted, also the air cleaner inlet duct from the cylinder head.
59 Disconnect the exhaust pipe from the exhaust manifold.
53 Release the rocker arm stud nuts, swivel the arms aside and remove the pushrods. Keep the rods in their originally fitted sequence. A piece of card with holes punched in it and numbered is useful for this.
54 Take off the exhaust valve stem caps.

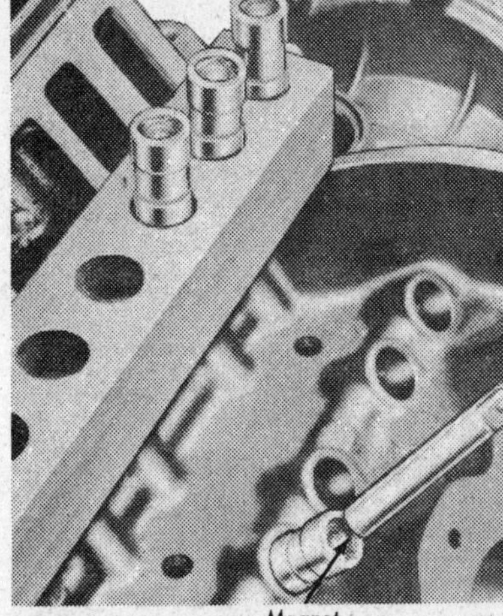

Fig. 13.8 Removing valve lifter with a magnet

Fig. 13.9 Removing a valve push rod

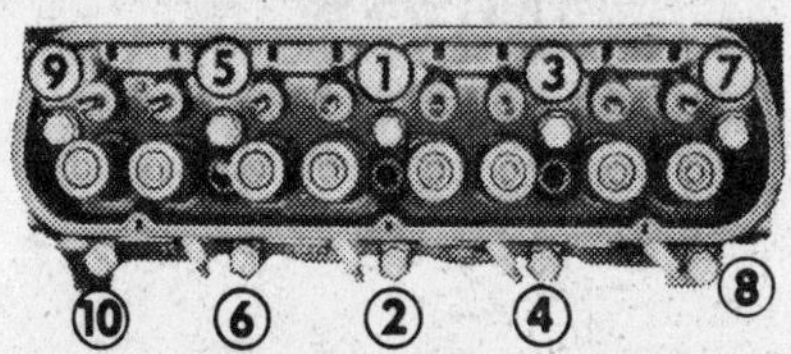

Fig. 13.10 Cylinder head bolt tightening sequence

13

55 Unscrew and remove the cylinder head bolts and with the help of an assistant, lift the head from the engine block. If it is stuck, use the exhaust manifold as a lever to rock the head and break the seal.
56 Peel off the cylinder head gasket and discard it.
57 Refitting is a reversal of removal, but observe the following:

(a) *Make sure that the head and block mating surfaces are absolutely clean*
(b) *Fit the gasket, without jointing compound, over the positioning dowels on the block*
(c) *Tighten the cylinder head bolts in three stages to the specified torque and in the sequence shown*
(d) *Check the valve clearance as described in paragraphs 225 thru 236.*
(e) *Refill the cooling system and connect the battery*

Timing cover and timing chain - removal and refitting

58 On vehicles equipped with a fan shroud, unbolt the shroud and hang it over the fan. Drain the cooling system.
59 Unbolt and remove the fan and its spacer from the coolant pump. Withdraw the shroud.
60 If an air conditioner is fitted, remove the compressor drivebelt and idler pulley.
61 Remvoe the alternator drivebelt.
62 If power steering is fitted, remove the pump drivebelt, unbolt the pump and move it to one side.
63 Remove the coolant pump pulley and disconnect all coolant hoses from the pump.
64 Drain the engine oil.
65 Unbolt and remove the pulley from the crankshaft vibration damper.
66 Remove the damper fixing bolt and using a suitable puller, remove the damper.
67 Disconnect the fuel pump outlet pipe, unbolt the pump and remove it as far as possible without disconnecting the flexible fuel inlet pipe.
68 Withdraw the engine oil dipstick.
69 Extract the bolts which hold the oil pan to the timing cover.
70 Use a very sharp knife to cut the oil pan gasket flush with the face of the cylinder block before removing the timing cover.
71 Unbolt and remove the timing cover complete with coolant pump.
72 Discard the timing cover gasket.
73 Remove the crankshaft front oil slinger.
74 If the timing gears or chain must be renewed, continue with the following operations.
75 Rotate the crankshaft (using the starter motor, or by temporarily refitting the damper bolt and applying a wrench to it) until the timing marks are aligned as shown (Fig. 13.11).
76 Extract the screw from the center of the fuel pump operating eccentric and remove the eccentric and washers.
77 Remove the two gears and the chain together as an assembly. Do not move the position of the crankshaft or camshaft.
78 Refitting is a reversal of removal, but observe the following:

(a) *Refit the timing gears and chain simultaneously, adjusting the chain as necessary to ensure that the timing marks are again in alignment as the gears engage with the shaft keys*
(b) *Renew the oil seal in the cover*
(c) *Cut a section from a new oil pan gasket to replace the old piece. Apply a bead of sealer at the corners to provide a leakproof joint*
(d) *Oil the new chain and apply grease to the lips of the oil seal*

79 Refill the engine with oil and coolant.
80 Check and if necessary adjust the ignition timing.

Fig. 13.11 Timing mark alignment

Fig. 13.12 Fuel pump eccentric

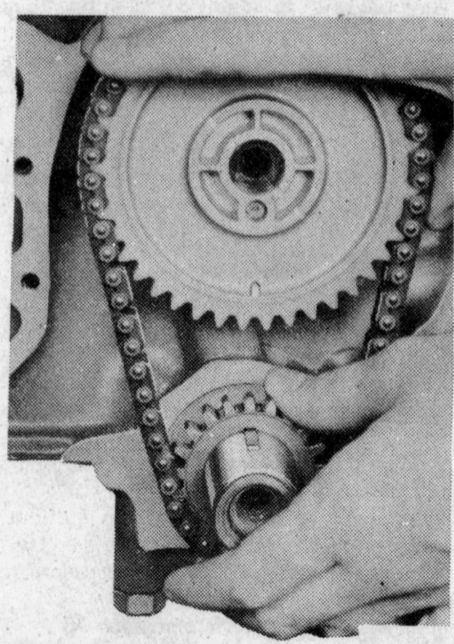

Fig. 13.13 Installing timing chain and gears

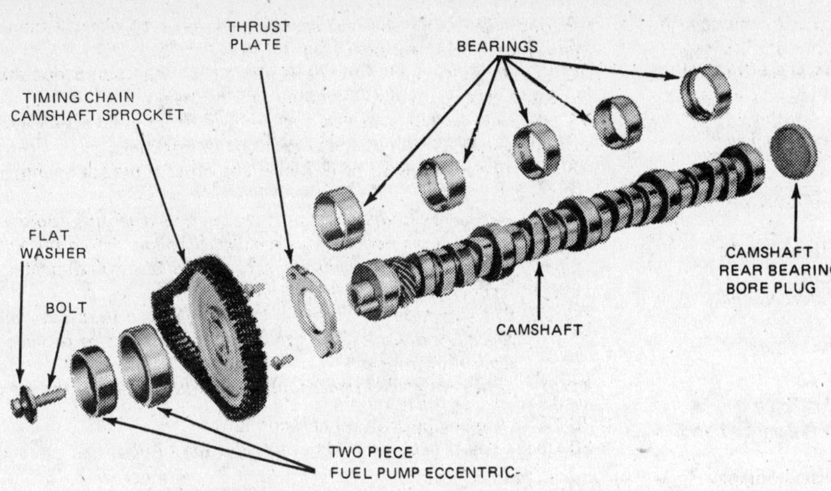

Fig. 13.14 Camshaft and associated components

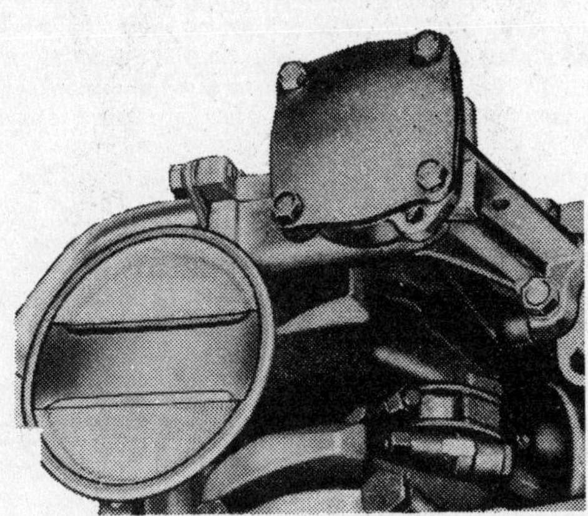

Fig. 13.15 Oil pump and pick-up tube

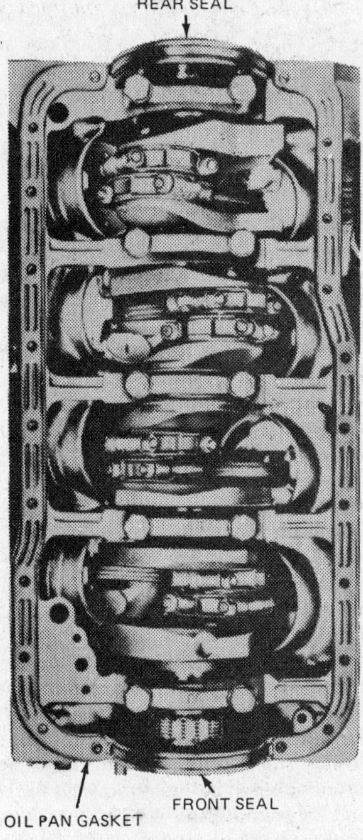

Fig. 13.16 Oil pan gaskets and seals in position

Camshaft - removal and refitting

81 Drain the cooling system.
82 Disconnect the transmission fluid cooler lines from the radiator (if applicable).
83 Unbolt the fan shroud and hang it over the fan.
84 Unbolt and remove the radiator.
85 On vehicles equipped with air conditioning, unbolt the condenser and move it aside but without disconnecting the refrigerant lines.
86 Remove the timing cover, gears and chain as described above.
87 Remove the intake manifold as described in paragraphs 13 thru 32.
88 Remove the rocker covers.
89 Release the rocker arm stud nuts and swivel the arms aside so that the pushrods can be withdrawn. Keep the rods in their originally fitted sequence.
90 Mark the position of the distributor body in relation to the cylinder block, disconnect the vacuum pipe, distributor cap and primary wire, unbolt the clamp and withdraw the distributor from the engine.
91 Withdraw the valve lifters, again keeping them in their originally fitted sequence. A magnet is useful for withdrawing the lifters.
92 Remove the camshaft thrust plate, noting the groove in the plate is towards the cylinder block.
93 Taking great care not to damage the camshaft bearings, withdraw the camshaft from the front of the engine.
94 Refitting is a reversal of removal, but oil the camshaft bearings before installing the camshaft.
95 Once the camshaft is installed, check it for endfloat. If this exceeds specified tolerance, renew the thrust plate. Use a dial indicator to check the endfloat and fit the thrust plate so that its groove is nearer the cylinder block.
96 Refit the timing gear as described in paragraph 78.
97 Refit the radiator and connect the transmission fluid cooler lines (if applicable).
98 Reposition the condenser (air conditioned vehicles).
99 Fit the fan shroud.
100 Fill the cooling system.
101 Refit the intake manifold.
102 Adjust the rocker arm clearances (see paragraphs 225 thru 236).
103 Refit the distributor and check and if necessary adjust the ignition timing.

Crankshaft front oil seal - renewal

104 The oil seal can be renewed if the timing cover is first withdrawn as previously described.

Engine oil pan and oil pump - removal and refitting

105 Disconnect the battery.
106 Unbolt the fan shroud and hang it over the fan.
107 Raise and support the front end of the vehicle and drain the engine oil.
108 Unscrew the four bolts and remove the crossmember from under the oil pan.
109 Release and remove the pinch-bolt from the steering shaft flexible coupling.
110 Unbolt the steering gear from its crossmember.
111 Extract the four bolts which hold the stabilizer bar to the body-frame members and pull the bar downwards.
112 Disconnect the wires from the starter motor and unbolt and remove the starter motor.
113 Unbolt and remove the oil pan and gasket.
114 Remove the oil pump inlet pipe and filter screen.
115 Unbolt the oil pump and withdraw it with the gasket and drive-shaft.
116 If a new oil pump is being fitted, prime it first by pouring

13

engine oil into the inlet or outlet port of the pump. Turn the pump shaft to distribute the oil.
117 Insert the driveshaft. It should seat firmly with its stop washer in contact with the crankcase. Adjust the position of the stop if necessary.
118 Bolt the pump into position using a new gasket and fit the pick-up tube and filter screen.
119 Using contact adhesive, stick new oil pan seals and gaskets into position so that the gaskets overlap the seal ends.
120 Locate the oil pan, screw in the fixing screws and tighten to the specified torque.
121 Refit the steering gear and crossmember and bolt up the stabilizer bar.
122 Reconnect the battery and refill the engine with oil.

Main bearing shells - renewal

123 It is possible to renew the main bearing shells with the engine still in the vehicle provided the following operations are carefully carried out.
124 Drain the engine oil, remove the oil pan and oil pump as previously described.
125 Release the bolts from the first main bearing cap and tap off the cap, discard the bearing shell and fit the new one. Make quite sure that the shell is of exactly the same size as the one being discarded, either standard or of correct undersize. The backs of the shells will be marked.
126 In the absence of the special tool (6331) a cotter pin of suitable size can be inserted in the crankshaft oil hole and the crankshaft rotated using a socket wrench on the damper bolt. The head of the cotter pin will push the upper shell round and out of its crankcase seat.
127 Oil the bearing shells and refit the cap, tightening the bolts to the specified torque.
128 Repeat the operations on the remaining four main bearings. *Only release one bearing cap at a time.*
129 When working on the rear main bearing, renew the oil seal (semi-circular sections). To renew the upper section, insert a small screw into the cut face of the seal and pull it from its recess. When refitting the seal, refer to Fig. 13.17 and set the seal projection as indicated.
130 When renewing No 3 main bearing shells which incorporate thrust flanges, fit the cap bolts only finger tight and then pry the crankshaft towards the front of the engine while the main bearing cap is pressed to the rear. Tighten the bolts to the specified torque while the pressures just described are maintained.
131 Complete reassembly by refitting the items removed.
132 Fill the engine with oil and operate the engine at reduced speed for the first 500 miles (800 km) to allow the new components to bed in.

Connecting rod (big-end) bearing shells - renewal

133 The operations are very similar to those described for the main bearing shells. Work on one rod at a time and make sure that you are renewing the shell with one of similar thickness. Do not push the piston/connecting rod up the cylinder bore more than is necessary to extract the upper shell and always disconnect the cap when the rod and crankpin are at their lowest points.
134 Tighten the cap nuts to the specified torque.

Piston(s)/connecting rod(s) - removal and refitting

135 Drain the cooling system and the engine oil.
136 Refer to previous paragraphs and remove the intake manifold, the cylinder head(s), oil pan and oil sump.
137 Using a scraper or suitable cutter, remove the wear ridge from the top of the cylinder bores.
138 Check that the connecting rods and their caps are numbered and note which side the numbers face so that they will be installed in their original positions at reassembly.
139 Unbolt and remove the bearing cap nuts, remove the cap and push the piston/rod up and out of the top of the cylinder bore. If the original shells are to be used again, tape them to the shell and cap.
140 When installing the piston/rod, make sure that the ring end gaps are correctly positioned as shown in Fig. 13.19 and that the notch on the piston crown is facing the timing cover end of the engine.
141 Fit a ring compressor to the piston, which should have been well lubricated, and insert the rod into its bore so that the compressor sits squarely on the block. Drive the piston/rod assembly into the cylinder bore by applying the wooden handle of a hammer to the piston crown.
142 Fit the bearing shells and cap and connect the rod to the crankshaft while the crankpin is at its lowest point. Tighten the nuts to the specified torque.
143 Refit the removed components by reversing the removal operations and then fill the engine with oil and the cooling system with antifreeze mixture.

Engine - removal and installation

144 The engine should be removed on its own, leaving the transmission in the vehicle.
145 Drain the cooling system.
146 Drain the engine oil.
147 With the help of an assistant, remove the hood by unbolting the hinges.
148 Disconnect the battery and alternator ground cables from the engine block.
149 Remove the air cleaner and the intake duct.
150 Disconnect the upper and lower radiator hoses.

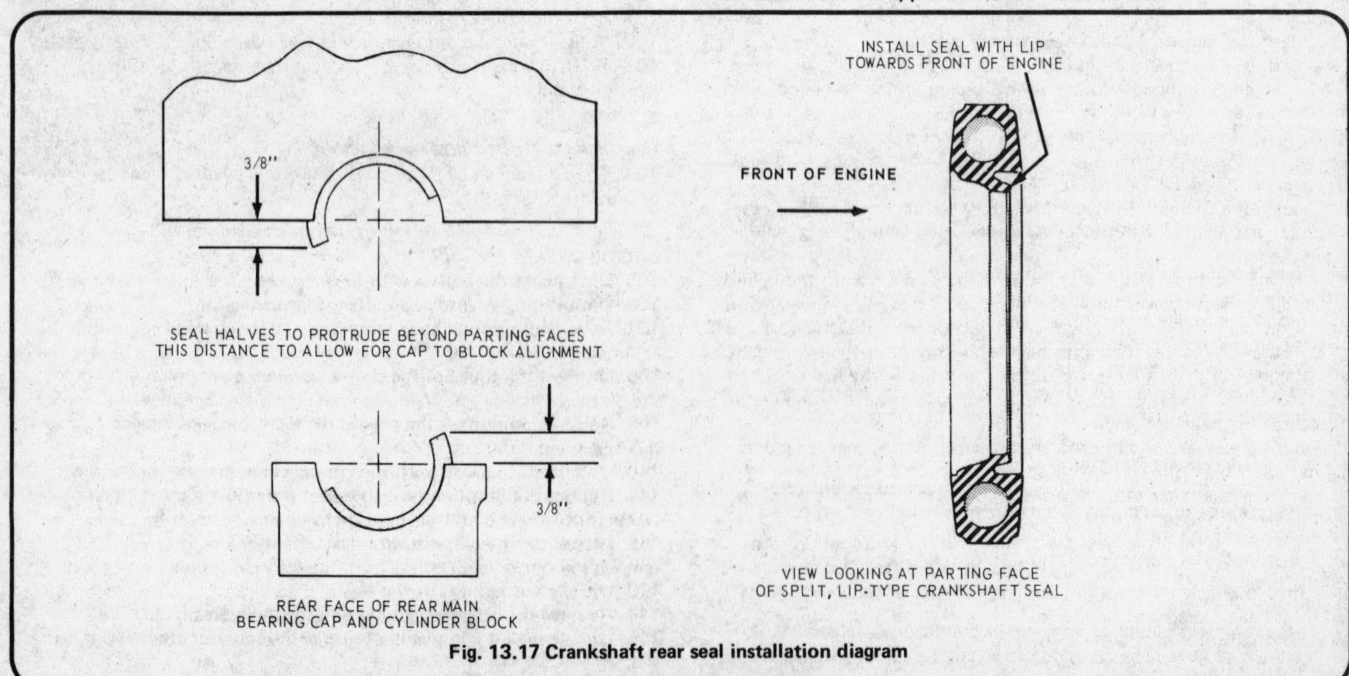

Fig. 13.17 Crankshaft rear seal installation diagram

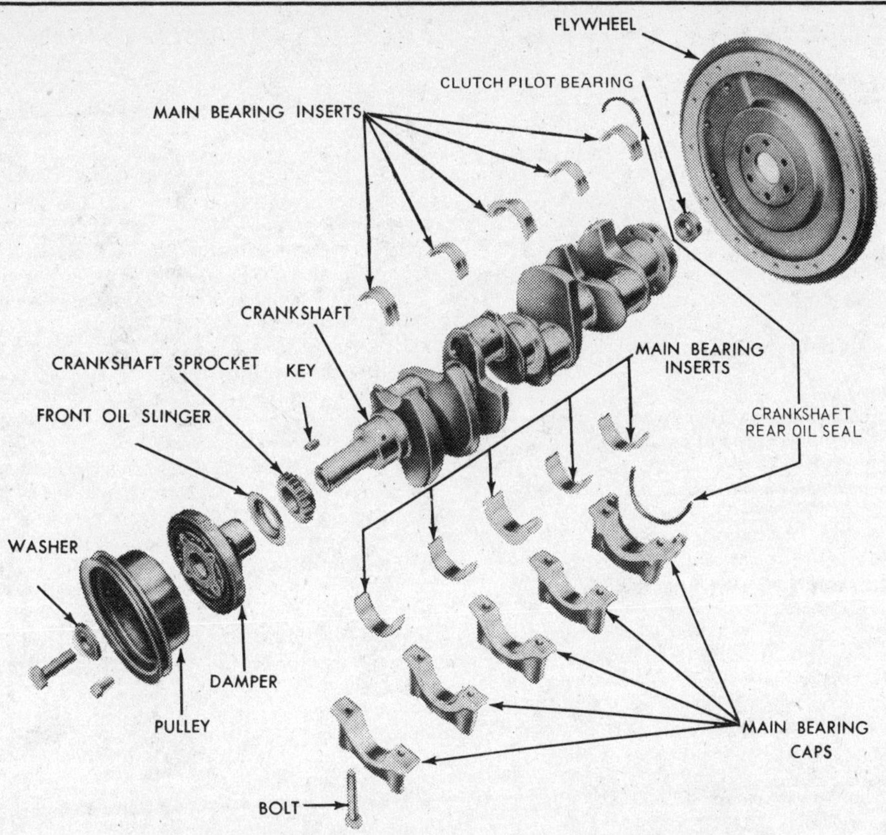

Fig. 13.18 Crankshaft, main bearings and associated components

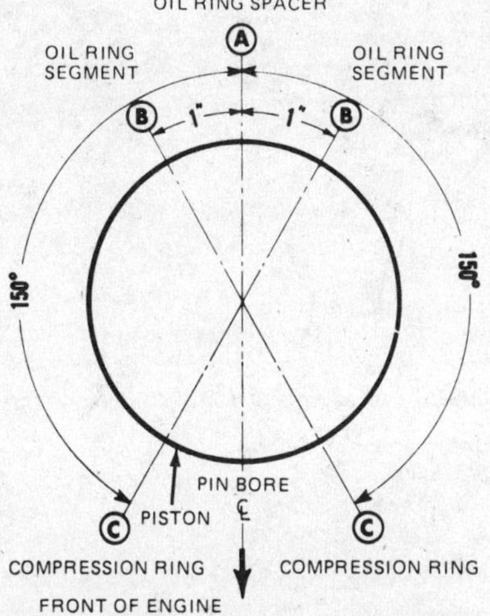

Fig. 13.19 Piston ring spacing diagram

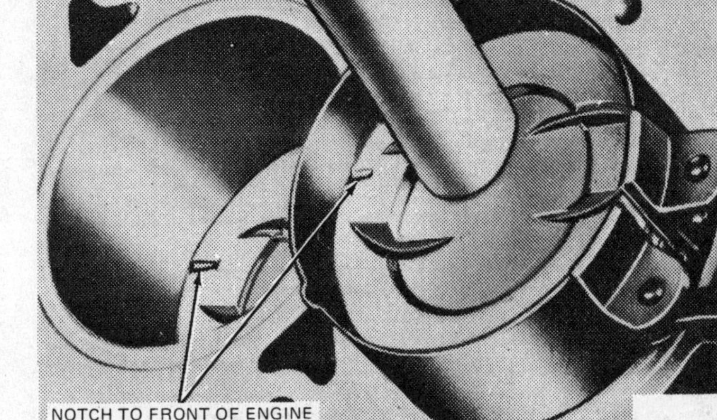

Fig. 13.20 Installing piston/connecting rod

151 On cars equipped with automatic transmission, disconnect the fluid cooler lines from the radiator and cap the openings.
152 Unbolt the radiator fan shroud and hang it over the fan.
153 Unbolt and remove the radiator.
154 Remove the fan, spacer, belt pulley and the shroud.
155 Disconnect the wire from the oil pressure sender unit.
156 Disconnect the fuel inlet line from the fuel pump and plug the line.

Cars with automatic transmission

157 Disconnect the throttle control from the carburetor and the transmission throttle vacuum valve line from the intake manifold.
158 Disconnect the shift rod.
159 Disconnect the transmission fluid filler tube bracket from the cylinder block.

All vehicles

160 If the vehicle is equipped with an air conditioner, release the compressor and move it to one side of the engine compartment. If the compressor cannot be moved sufficiently far to clear the engine, *do not disconnect the refrigerant lines until the system has to be discharged by your dealer,* otherwise personal injury may result.
161 If the vehicle is equipped with power steering, disconnect the power steering pump from the cylinder head, slip off the drivebelt and tie the pump to one side of the engine compartment.
162 If the vehicle is equipped with power-assisted braking, disconnect the booster vacuum line from the intake manifold.
163 Disconnect the heater coolant hoses.
164 Disconnect the wire from the coolant temperature sender unit.
165 Unscrew and remove the bolts from the upper part of the flywheel or torque converter housing-to-engine connecting flange.
166 Disconnect the primary wire from the ignition coil.
176 Unbolt the wiring harness from the left-hand rocker arm cover and move the harness out of the way.
168 Disconnect the ground strap from the cylinder block.
169 Raise the front end of the vehicle and disconnect the starter cable.
170 Unbolt the starter motor.
171 Unbolt and disconnect the exhaust pipes from the manifolds.

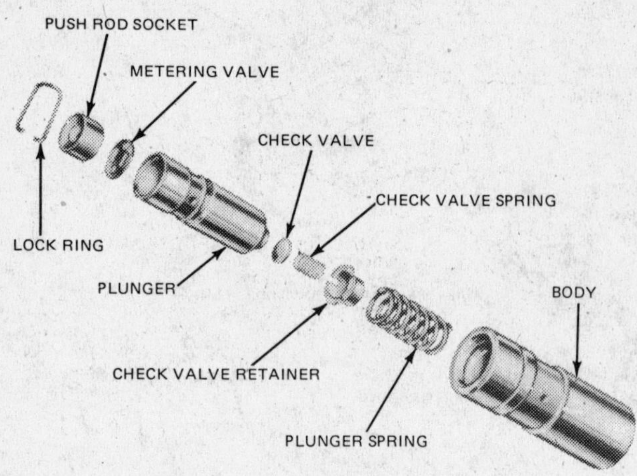

Fig. 13.21 Hydraulic valve lifter

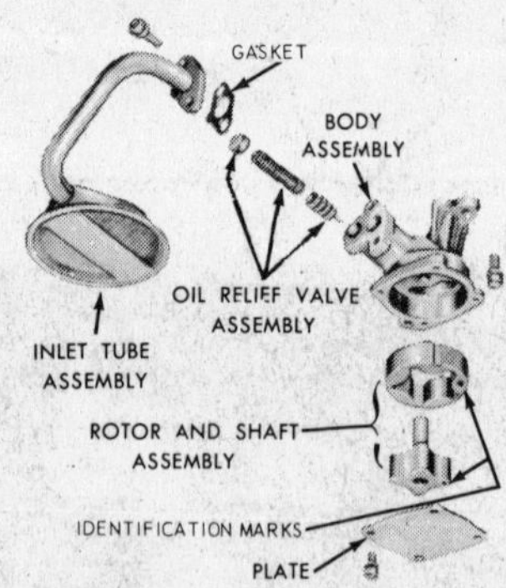

Fig. 13.23 Exploded view of oil pump

172 Support the weight of the engine on a suitable hoist and disconnect the engine insulator mounts from their frame brackets.
173 Extract the remaining lower flywheel or torque converter housing bolts.
174 Remove the cover from the lower front face of the flywheel or torque converter housing.
175 On cars with automatic transmission, use a socket to unscrew the bolts which hold the adapter plate to the torque converter. These will have to be brought into view in sequence by rotating the crankshaft by applying a socket wrench to the pulley bolt.
176 Support the transmission on a jack, raise the engine slightly by means of a hoist, pull it forward and lift it from the engine compartment. During this operation, on cars with automatic transmission, keep the torque converter pressed fully towards the transmission to keep the converter in engagement with the oil pump and to prevent damage to the oil seal. The help of an assistant will make the job easier.
177 Installation is a reversal of removal but on cars equipped with automatic transmission, align the adapter plate and torque converter all the time in its fully rearward position.
178 On cars with manual transmission, centralise the clutch if it has been disturbed (refer to Chapter 5).
179 Fill the engine with oil and coolant.
180 Check and adjust the transmission shift control (automatic transmission).

Engine - complete dismantling

181 Most of the operations have been described above with the engine still in the vehicle.
182 The following dismantling sequence is recommended:

(a) Intake manifold with carburetor
(b) Valve lifters
(c) Cylinder heads

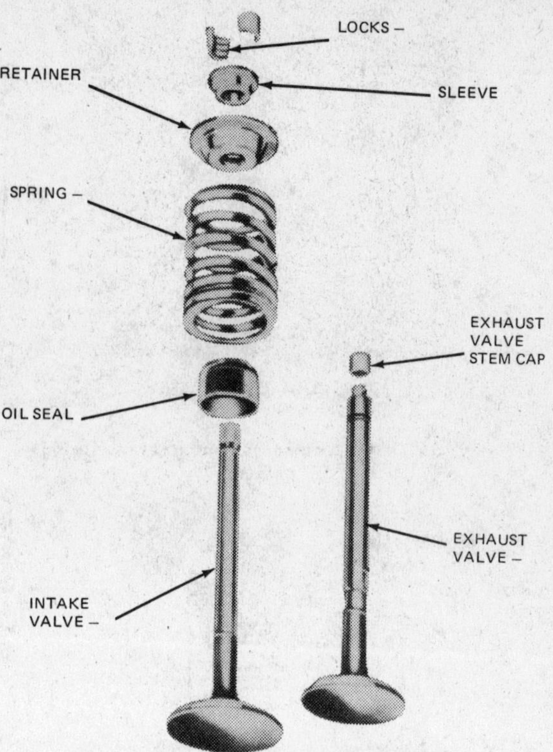

Fig. 13.22 Valve components

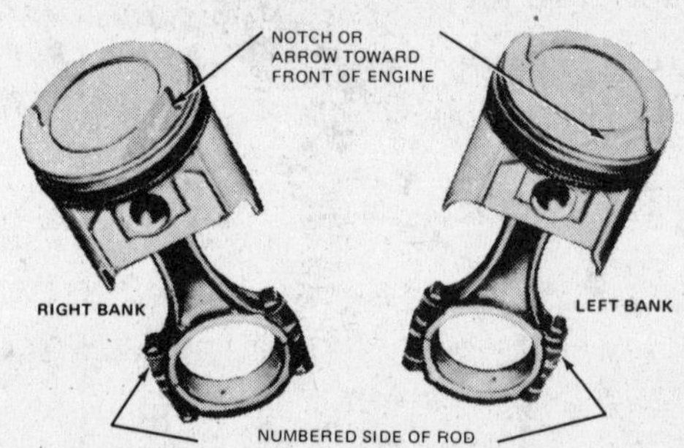

Fig. 13.24 Correct piston-to-connecting rod relationship

(d) Timing cover and chain
(e) Camshaft
(f) Oil pan and oil pump
(g) Pistons/connecting rods

183 To remove the flywheel or adapter plate, lock the starter ring gear teeth with a large screwdriver blade or chisel and unscrew the fixing bolts. The holes are offset so that the flywheel or adapter plate can only be installed one way.
184 To remove the crankshaft, first check that the main bearing caps are marked with a number and a forward-facing directional arrow. If they are not, mark them with punch marks or by filing.
185 As each cap is unbolted and removed, keep the bearing shell with its cap. Note that No 3 shell incorporates thrust flanges.
186 Lift the crankshaft from the crankcase and again keep the bearing shells in their originally installed order. If necessary, mark them with pieces of numbered adhesive tape to prevent any mix up.

Examination and renovation

187 With the engine completely dismantled, all components should be carefully cleaned and checked for wear essentially as described in Chapter 1.
188 Note the differences in some of the components and refer to the Specifications at the front of this Chapter for tolerances and clearances relative to the V8 engine.
189 If the timing chain has covered more than 50 000 miles (80 000 km) it should be renewed as a matter of routine.

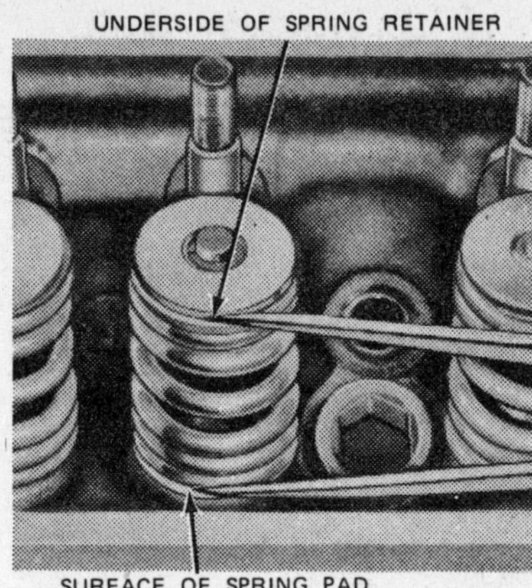

Fig. 13.25 Valve spring installed height measuring points

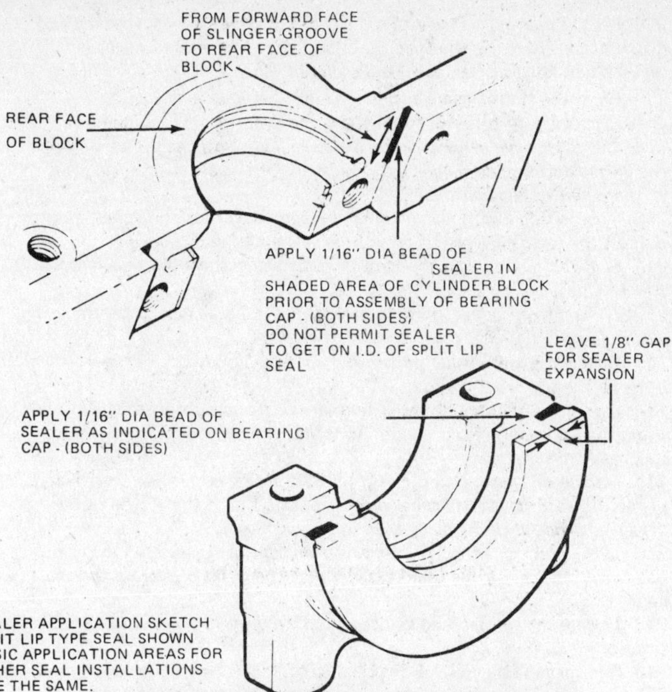

Fig. 13.26 Sealer application points at rear main bearing

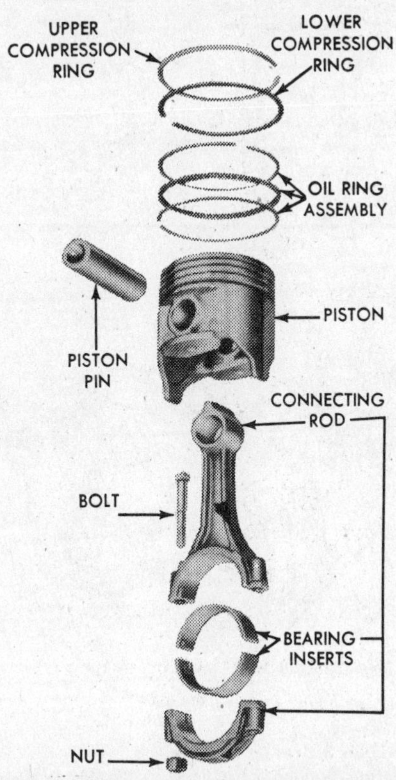

Fig. 13.27 Piston/connecting rod components

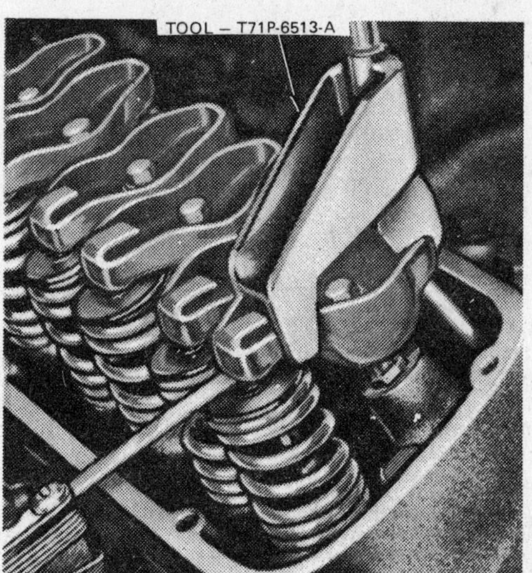

Fig. 13.28 Checking valve clearance

190 Check the valve spring installed height as shown (Fig. 13.25).
191 Obtain the necessary gasket kits and other items in advance of reassembly.

Engine - reassembly

192 With all components clean, stand the cylinder block (inverted) on the bench.
193 Lubricate the components with engine oil as they are refitted and observe strict cleanliness.
194 Clean the shell bearing recesses in the crankcase and fit the shells, noting that No 3 incorporates flanges to control end thrust.
195 Fit the bearing shells into the caps which must be scrupulously clean.
196 Clean out the rear oil seal grooves in the block and the bearing cap and having dipped the seal halves in oil, insert them into their grooves so that the undercut sides are towards the front of the engine and their ends are projecting by 3/8 in (9.5 mm).
197 Oil the bearing shells and lower the crankshaft into position in the crankcase.
198 Fit the main bearing caps the correct way round, and screw in the bolts finger tight. When fitting the rear cap, apply a bead ot RTV sealer as shown (Fig. 13.26).
199 Pry the crankshaft towards the front of the engine and tighten the main bearing cap bolts to the specified torque.
200 Check the crankshaft endfloat if the original bearing shells are being refitted.
201 Fit the bearing shells to the connecting rods and their caps.
202 Turn the crankshaft so that the first crankpin is at the lowest point of its throw.
203 Using a piston ring compressor to compress the piston ring, insert the first piston/rod into the cylinder bore so that the compressor stands squarely on the top of the cylinder block. Make sure that the notch in the piston crown is towards the front of the engine and the piston ring gaps are staggered as shown in Fig. 13.19.
204 Using the wooden handle of a hammer applied to the piston crown, drive the piston/rod into the cylinder bore and out of the compressor.
205 Carefully push the piston down the bore until the connecting rod seats on the crankpin.
206 Fit the cap and screw in and tighten the nuts to the specified torque.
207 Oil the camshaft bearings and carefully install the camshaft.

208 Fit the camshaft thrust plate and check for endfloat, renew the thrust plate if outside the specified tolerance. The groove in the thrust plate must be nearer to the cylinder block.
209 Refit the timing gears and chain simultaneously, adjusting the chain as necessary to ensure that the timing marks are in alignment once the gears have engaged with the shaft keys. Adjust the setting of the crankshaft and camshaft and reposition the gears within the loop of the chain to achieve this.
210 Fit the fuel pump eccentric to the camshaft gear and screw in and tighten the securing bolt.
211 Fit the oil slinger to the front face of the crankshaft gear (convex side to gear).
212 Fit the front cover, complete with new oil seal (lips greased), using a new gasket.
213 Install the crankshaft pulley and vibration damper. Tighten all bolts to the specified torque.
214 Install the flywheel or adapter plate (automatic transmission), using thread locking fluid on the bolts and tightening them to the specified torque.
215 Fit the oil pump and pick-up tube. If a new pump has been fitted, prime it by filling it with oil and rotating the pump shaft. The pump driveshaft should be firmly seated in the crankcase.
216 Using contact adhesive, stick new oil seals and gaskets for the oil pan into position on the crankcase so that the gaskets overlap the seal ends.
217 Locate the oil pan and tighten the fixing screws to the specified torque.
218 Support the partially assembled engine so it stands on its oil pan.
219 Refit the valve lifters, the pushrods and the assembled cylinder heads as described in earlier paragraphs.

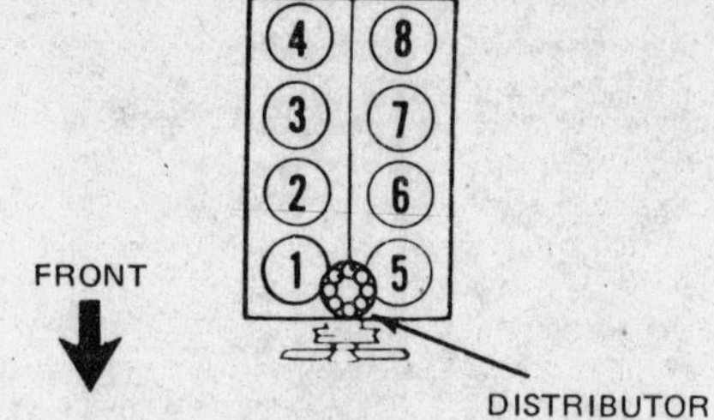
4
8
3
7
2
6
1
5
FRONT
DISTRIBUTOR

Fig. 13.29 V8 engine cylinder numbering

220 Install the intake and exhaust manifolds, the engine mounting brackets, fuel pump, alternator and emission control equipment also as described in earlier paragraphs.
221 Grease the sealing ring of a new oil filter and screw it into position using hand pressure only.
222 Refit the distributor as described in Section 6.
223 Fit the rocker covers.
224 Check that the engine oil drain plug is tight. Check the electrode gaps and fit the spark plugs.

Valve clearances - checking

225 As a result of grinding in the valves or re-cutting the valve seats, it is possible that the clearance between the rocker arm and the end of the valve stem may be outside the specified limits.
226 To check this condition, apply a wrench to the crankshaft pulley

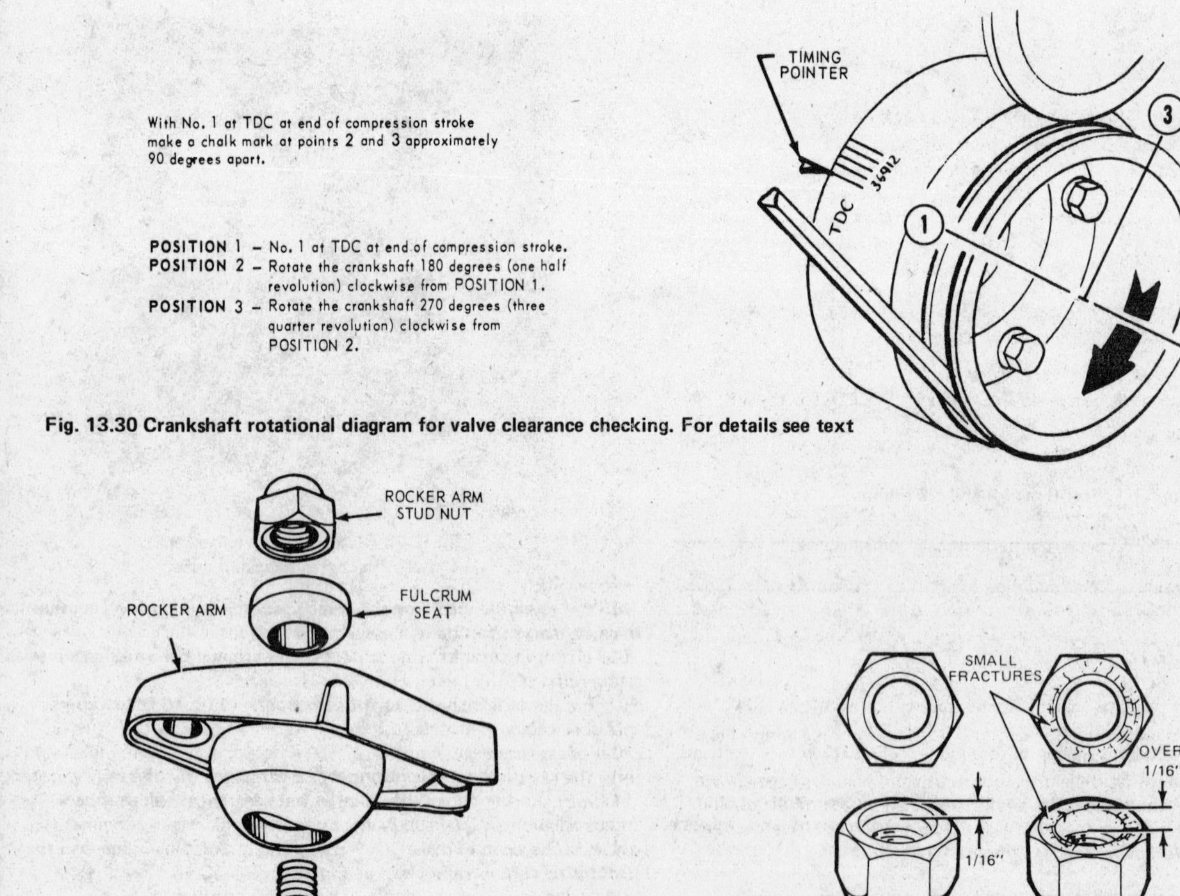
With No. 1 at TDC at end of compression stroke make a chalk mark at points 2 and 3 approximately 90 degrees apart.
POSITION 1 – No. 1 at TDC at end of compression stroke.
POSITION 2 – Rotate the crankshaft 180 degrees (one half revolution) clockwise from POSITION 1.
POSITION 3 – Rotate the crankshaft 270 degrees (three quarter revolution) clockwise from POSITION 2.
TIMING POINTER
TDC
1
2
3
ROCKER ARM STUD NUT
FULCRUM SEAT
ROCKER ARM
SMALL FRACTURES
OVER 1/16"
1/16"
GOOD
POOR

Fig. 13.30 Crankshaft rotational diagram for valve clearance checking. For details see text

Fig. 13.31 Valve rocker arm components (thru 1978)

Fig. 13.32 Rocker arm stud nut conditions

bolt and turn the crankshaft until No 1 piston is at TDC on its compression stroke. This setting is indicated when the crankshaft damper TDC mark is opposite the pointer and both valves of No 1 cylinder are closed (rocker cover removed).
227 The lash adjuster must now be compressed until it bottoms by applying pressure slowly with the special tool 6513-A, or a suitable substitute lever which will engage in the groove in the lash adjuster plunger.
228 Using a feeler gauge not exceeding 3/8 in (9.5 mm) in width, inserted between the rocker arm and the end of the valve stem, check that the clearance is within the specified limits. If the clearance is too small, change the pushrod for a shorter one. If the clearance is too great, change the rod for a longer one. Pushrods are available 0.060 in (1.52 mm) longer or shorter than the standard length.
229 The sequence of valves from the timing cover end of the engine is given in the Specifications.
230 With No 1 piston at TDC, check the clearances of the following valves:

Left cylinder bank	Right cylinder bank
6 (IN)	*1 (IN)*
1 (EX)	*2 (EX)*
8 (IN)	*8 (EX)*

231 Rotate the crankshaft through 180° (half a turn) in the normal direction of rotation and check the clearances of the following valves:

Left cylinder bank	Right cylinder bank
2 (IN)	*4 (EX)*
3 (EX)	*7 (IN)*

232 Rotate the crankshaft through 270° (¾ turn) and check the clearances of the following valves:

Left cylinder bank	Right cylinder bank
5 (EX)	*3 (IN)*
4 (IN)	*5 (IN)*
7 (EX)	*6 (EX)*

233 On some engines, positive stop type rocker arms are used. The nuts must be in good condition and correctly torqued.
234 At specified service intervals, when checking the valve clearances, follow the valve checking sequence given previously and also remove the nuts of the rockers concerned and examine them for fractures as shown in Fig. 13.32. Renew the nuts if they are not in good condition.
235 When fitting the stud nut, screw it onto the stud until it contacts the stop and then tighten it to the specified torque.
236 On very late models, the rocker arms are retained by a fulcrum and bolt which screws into the threaded pedestal.

Initial start-up after major overhaul

237 The procedure is as described in Chapter 1, Part B, for the V6 engine.

Fault diagnosis - V8 engine

238 Refer to Chapter 1, Part B, as for the V6 engine.

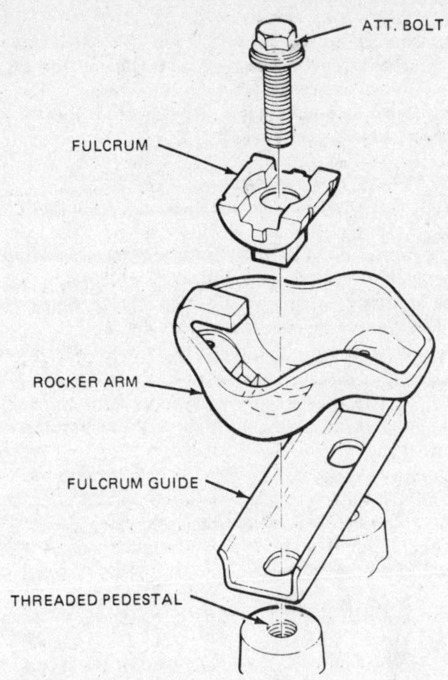

Fig. 13.33 Valve rocker arm components (very late 1978 models)

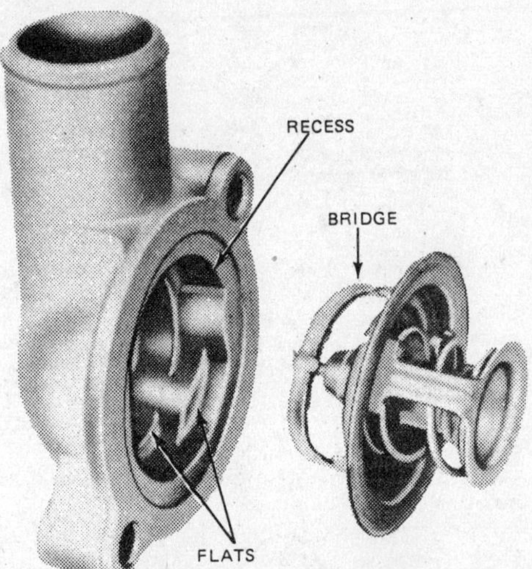

Fig. 13.34 Thermostat and cover

4 Cooling system

Thermostat (V8 engine)

1 The thermostat incorporates a locking tang which engages in a recess in the housing to prevent incorrect installation.

Flex-blade fan

2 Certain models are equipped with radiator cooling fans which have blades made of flexible material.
3 The fan blades adjust their pitch automatically according to engine speed and so vary the airflow depending upon the needs of the engine.
4 A supplementary benefit is that less power is used to drive the fan and a marginal fuel saving can be anticipated.

Constant-full cooling system

5 This system is fitted to cars equipped with a V8 engine. It comprises an expansion tank/reservoir which accepts displaced coolant when the engine is hot and provides a reservoir for this coolant until, when the engine cools down, the coolant is drawn back into the cooling system.
6 The valves in the radiator cap control the necessary pressure release and vacuum functions to operate the system.
7 No topping up should be required but if it is, only pour coolant into the reservoir until it reaches the level marked. **Do not** remove the radiator cap to top up and never remove it while the engine is running.
8 To fill this type of system after draining, check that the drain tap is closed and set the heater control lever to maximum.
9 Pour coolant into the radiator until it is full. Fit the radiator pressure cap.
10 Pour coolant (of similar antifreeze proportions as the main supply) into the reservoir until it reaches the HOT mark. Fit the reservoir cap.
11 Start the engine and run it at a moderate speed for a few minutes. If the level drops in the expansion tank/reservoir, this will be due to coolant replacing expelled air. Top up the reservoir to the HOT mark. Do not top up by removing the radiator cap.

5 Fuel system

Fuel tank

1 The fuel tank on later models differs in detail from earlier versions.
2 To remove the tank, refer to the relevant illustration for disconnection points.

Fuel pump (V8 engine) - description

3 The pump is bolted to the left side of the cylinder (timing) front cover and is operated by rocker arm which bears upon an eccentric bolted to the front of the camshaft.

4 The pump is not repairable and in the event of it becoming faulty it must be discarded and a new one fitted.

Fuel pump (V8 engine) - removal and refitting

5 Disconnect the fuel pipes from the pump and plug them to prevent loss of fuel.

6 Release the mounting bolts and then rotate the crankshaft by means of a socket wrench on the pulley bolt until the fuel pump is felt to become loose on its fixing bolts. This indicates that the cam lobe is exerting minimum pressure on the pump rocker arm.

7 Remove the bolts and the pump and clean away all traces of old gasket.

8 Apply jointing compound to both sides of a new gasket and position it on the engine.

9 Locate the fuel pump so that its rocker arm is below the cam eccentric with the cam lobe still positioned as described in paragraph 6.

10 Insert the fixing bolts, tighten to torque and reconnect the fuel hoses.

11 Start the engine and check for leaks.

Exhaust systems (later models)

12 The systems used on later models differ according to version and to operating territory.

13 Typical single catalytic converter systems are shown in Figs. 13.39 and 13.40. Removal and installation is similar to the operations described in Chapter 3.

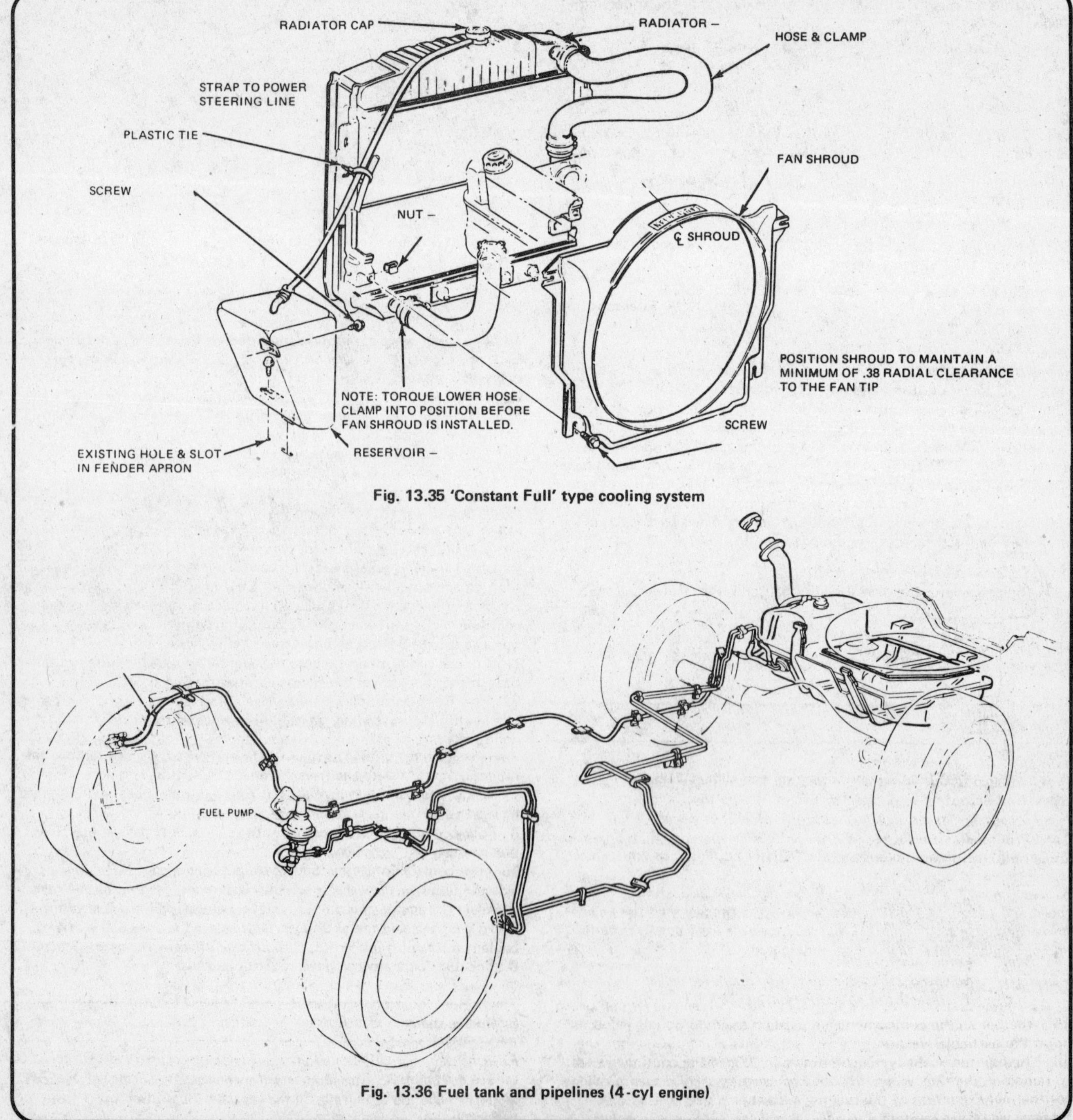

Fig. 13.35 'Constant Full' type cooling system

Fig. 13.36 Fuel tank and pipelines (4-cyl engine)

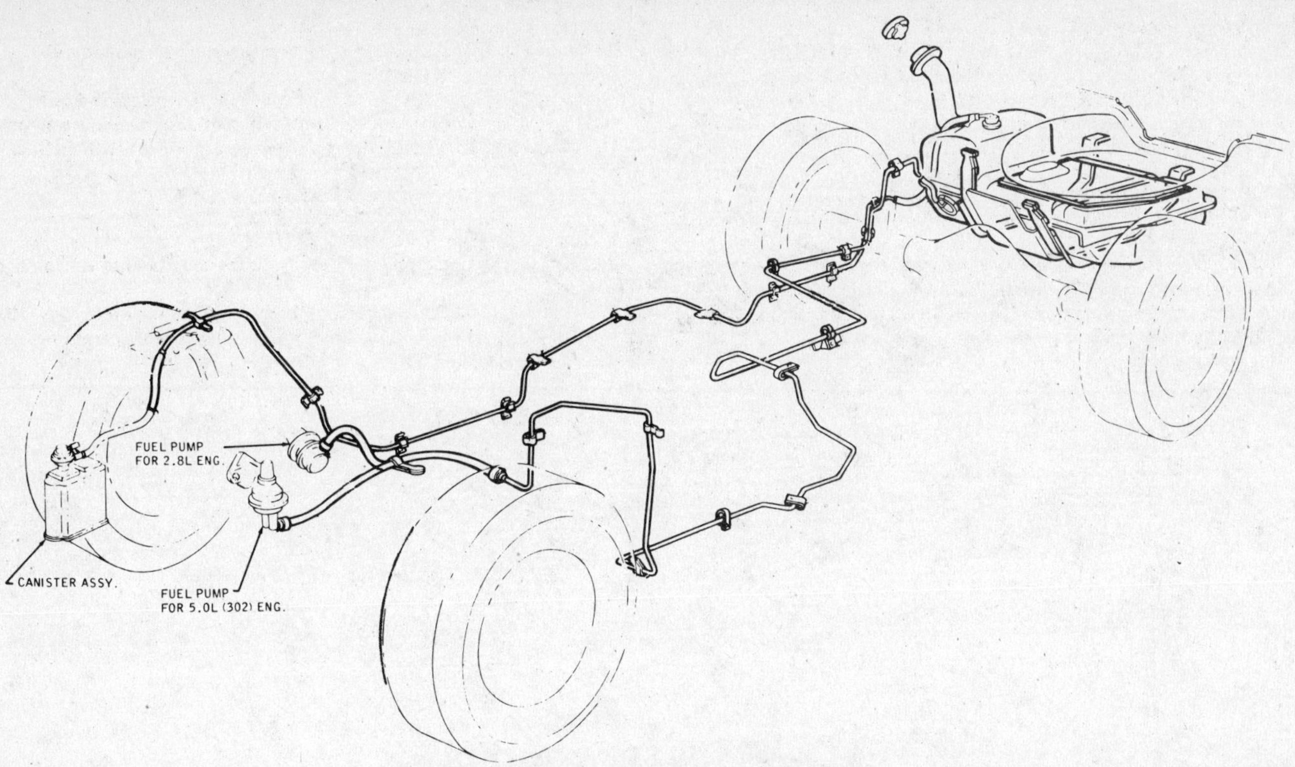

Fig. 13.37 Fuel tank and pipelines (V6 and V8 engines)

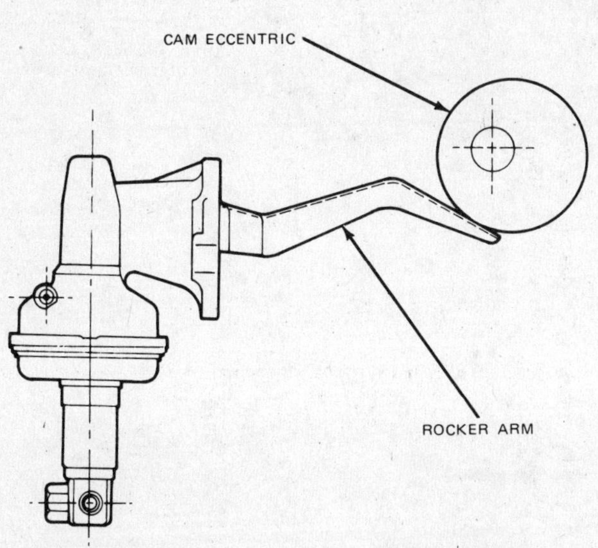

Fig. 13.38 Fuel pump rocker arm and cam (V8 engine)

Fuel vapor emission control system (1978 models)

14 Later models are equipped with a modified system which comprises some or all of the following components:

- *(a) Sealed fuel tank*
- *(b) Pressure/vacuum relief fuel cap*
- *(c) Fuel tank vapor valve*
- *(d) Carbon cannister*
- *(e) Purge control valve*
- *(f) Solenoid vent valve and purge regulator valve*
- *(g) Thermactor idle vacuum valve (TIV)*

15 Whether all the components are used on any one vehicle depends upon the particular version.

16 The fuel tank vent system allows for a 10 to 12 percent air space to remain in the tank when it is filled to capaciry. This space provides for thermal expansion of the fuel as well as being part of the tank internal vapor vent system.

17 The vapor valve assembly is mounted on the raised section of the tank's upper surface and incorporates a small orifice which permits only vapor and not fuel to pass into the line which runs to the vapor storage cannister. This vapor is stored in the cannister until the engine is started and purges the cannister by burning the vapor during the normal combustion cycle.

18 Fuel vapor from the carburetor is also vented and stored in the same or an additional carbon cannister.

19 A purge control valve is located on the carbon cannister and controls the flow of fuel vapor into or out of the cannister.

20 A fuel bowl solenoid vent valve is located in the vent line of the Motorcraft 2150 2V carburetor where the unit does not have an integral fuel bowl vent valve. The valve is closed when the engine is running and open when the ignition is switched off.

21 A thermal vent valve is located in the carburetor-to-cannister vent line and is shut when the engine compartment is cold. Its purpose is to prevent fuel tank vapors being vented through the fuel bowl under circumstances where the fuel tank warms up due to the heat of the sun and yet the engine compartment is cold.

22 The Thermactor idle vacuum valve (TIV) is used to improve the idle quality at hot starting. A rich mixture condition usually exists due to the purge valve not being actuated as it is delayed by the vacuum delay valve and the time required to evacuate the vacuum reservoir.

23 The TIV bleeds air into the PCV tube to weaken the idle fuel mixture until the purge valve is actuated when the TIV is then closed by common vacuum from the purge valve.

24 A purge regulator valve is located in the purge line between the purge control valve and its vacuum source to regulate the volume of air which is drawn into the intake manifold through the carbon cannister. This valve must always be mounted in the vertical plane.

25 If a ported vacuum switch (PVS) is used in the system, this may be of two- or four-post type. The purpose of the switch is to actuate the vacuum for the purge valve as the engine warms up.

26 The tank filler cap incorporates a pressure/vacuum relief valve. The normal function of the valve is to allow air to enter the fuel tank to replace the void left by usage of fuel and at the same time to restrict the escape of vapor.

27 On 2.3 l four-cylinder engines, a fuel vapor return system is used to reduce the amount of vapor entering the carburetor. The system comprises a return line from the fuel pump to the fuel return outlet of the sender unit on the fuel tank.

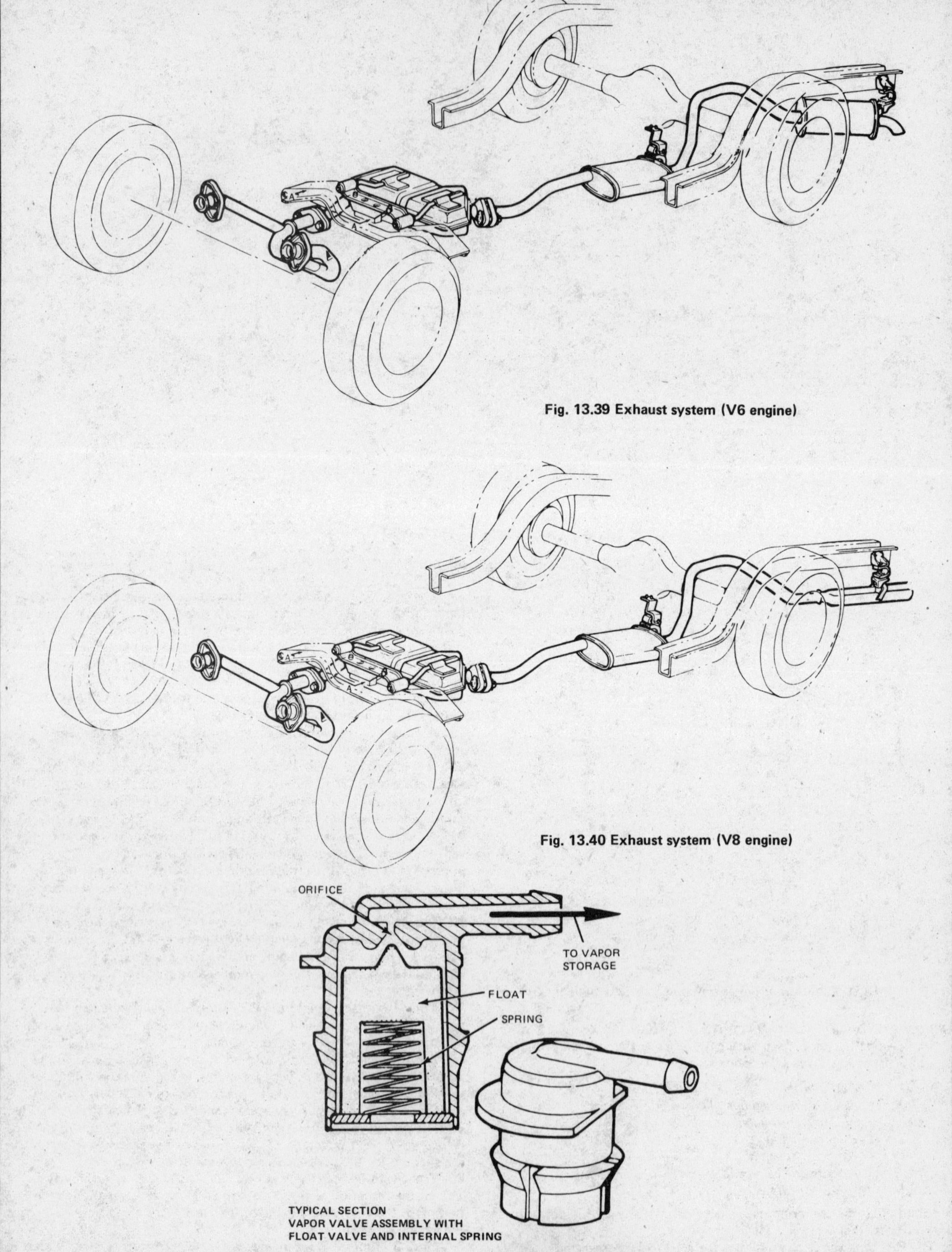

Fig. 13.39 Exhaust system (V6 engine)

Fig. 13.40 Exhaust system (V8 engine)

Fig. 13.41 Fuel tank vapor valve

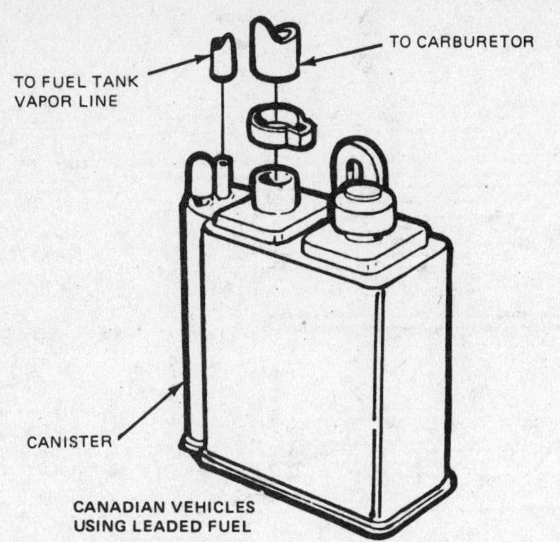

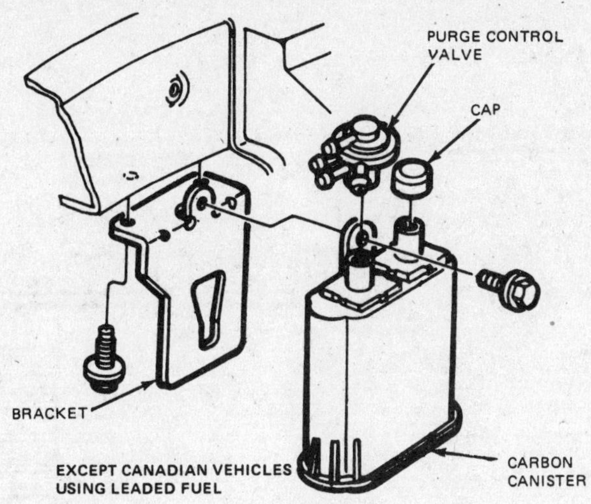

Fig. 13.42 Typical carbon canisters

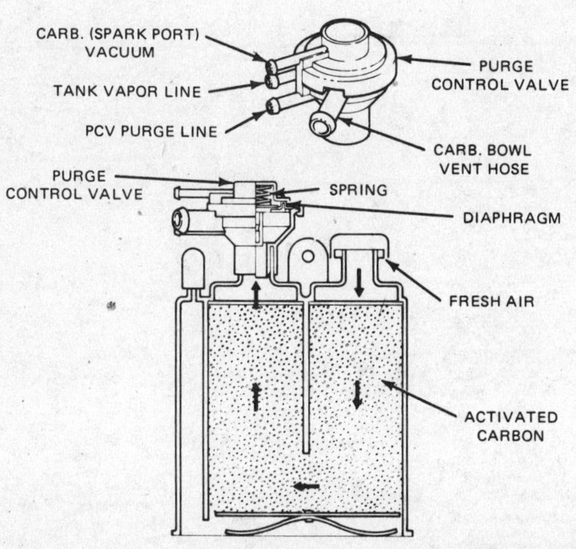

Fig. 13.43 Purge control valve

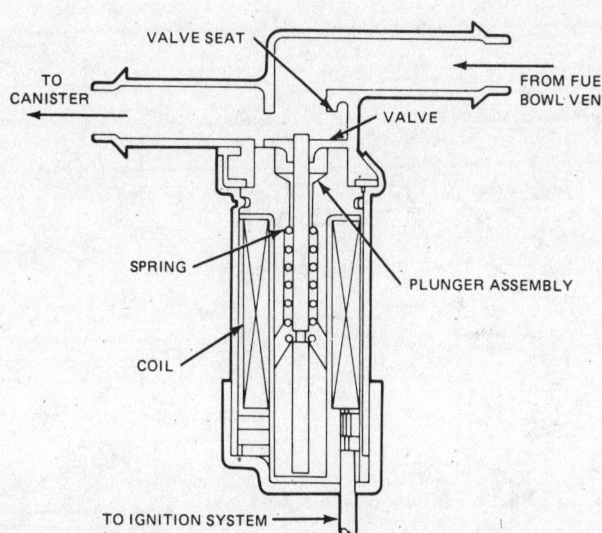

Fig. 13.44 Fuel bowl solenoid vent valve

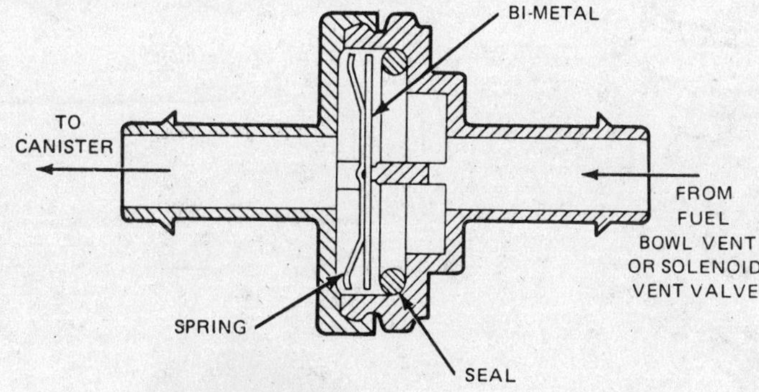

Fig. 13.45 Fuel bowl thermal vent valve

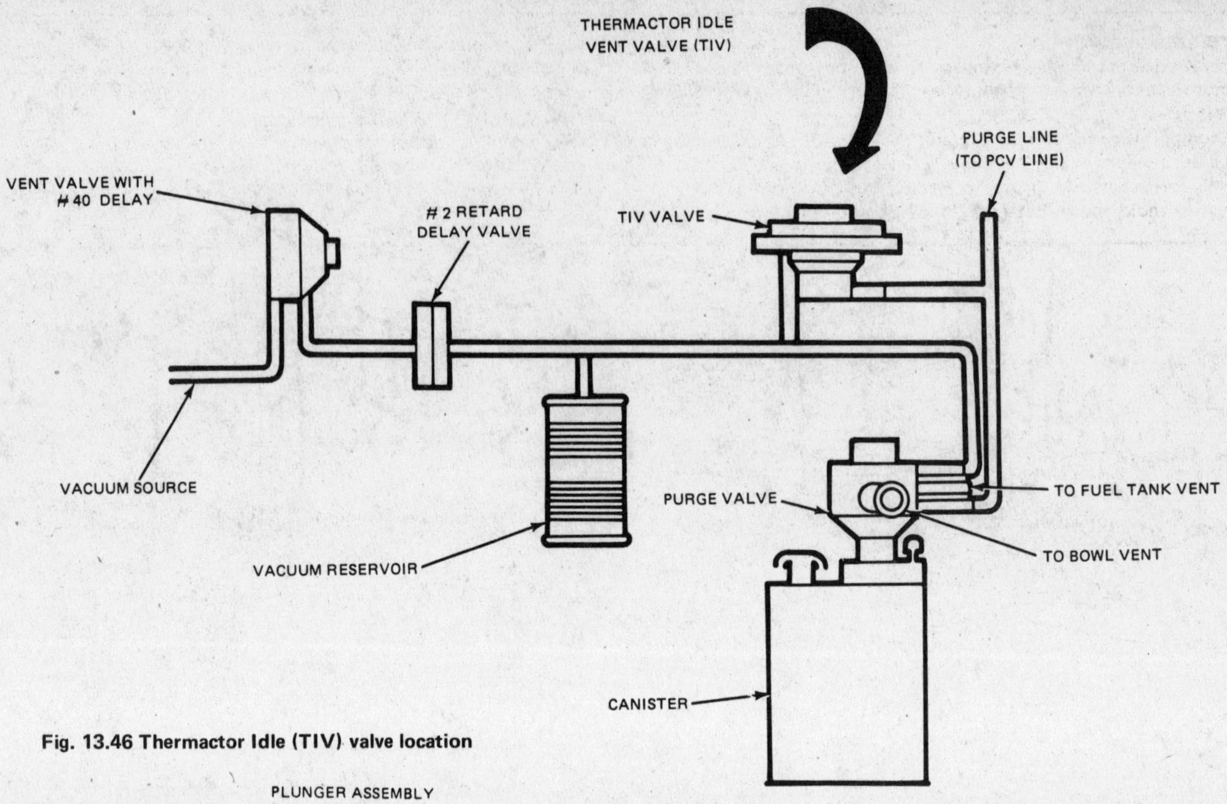

THERMACTOR IDLE
VENT VALVE (TIV)
VENT VALVE WITH
#40 DELAY
#2 RETARD
DELAY VALVE
TIV VALVE
PURGE LINE
(TO PCV LINE)
VACUUM SOURCE
TO FUEL TANK VENT
PURGE VALVE
TO BOWL VENT
VACUUM RESERVOIR
CANISTER

Fig. 13.46 Thermactor Idle (TIV) valve location

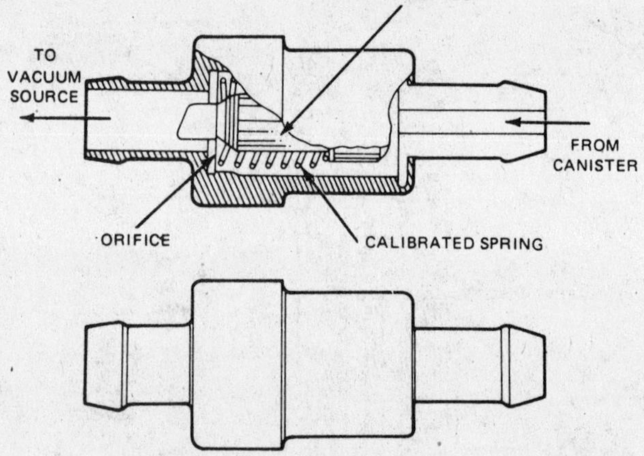

PLUNGER ASSEMBLY
TO
VACUUM
SOURCE
FROM
CANISTER
ORIFICE
CALIBRATED SPRING

Fig. 13.47 Purge regulator valve

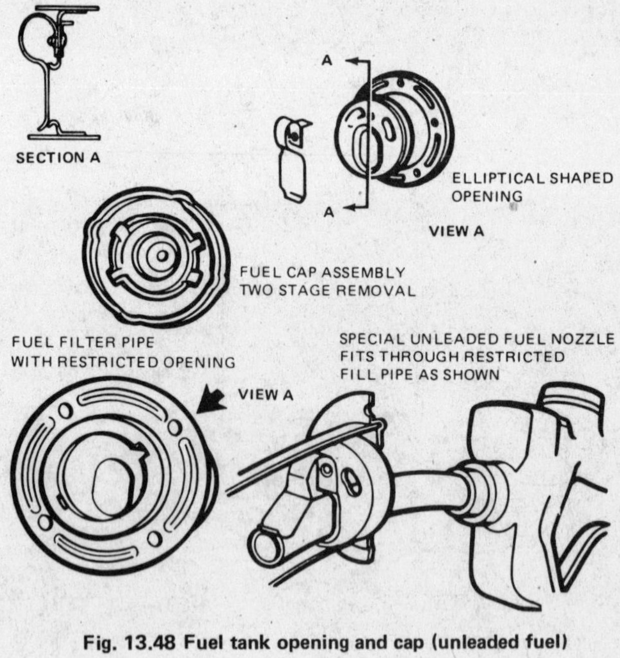

SECTION A
A
A
ELLIPTICAL SHAPED
OPENING
VIEW A
FUEL CAP ASSEMBLY
TWO STAGE REMOVAL
FUEL FILTER PIPE
WITH RESTRICTED OPENING
VIEW A
SPECIAL UNLEADED FUEL NOZZLE
FITS THROUGH RESTRICTED
FILL PIPE AS SHOWN

Fig. 13.48 Fuel tank opening and cap (unleaded fuel)

FUEL
PUMP
FUEL
RETURN
LINE
FUEL LINE

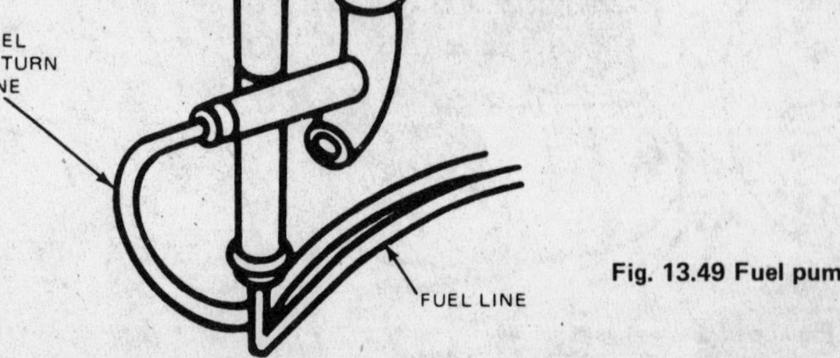

Fig. 13.49 Fuel pump vapor separator

Carburetors - description

28 Later models are fitted with one of several different types of carburetor depending upon engine type, capacity and operating territory.

Motocraft 5200 2V

29 Although this carburetor is covered in Chapter 3, the unit has been modified during later years. After 1976 the automatic choke is electrically-heated instead of coolant-heated and incorporates a fuel bowl vent solenoid and an external choke vacuum pull-down connection.

30 On vehicles equipped with air conditioning, a vacuum solenoid valve is provided at the carburetor to maintain the engine idle speed when the air conditioner compressor is switched on.

Motorcraft 2150 2V carburetor

31 The unit comprises two main assemblies, the air horn and the main body. The air horn contains the choke plate, the fuel bowl vent valve, the pull-over enrichment system and the fuel deceleration metering system.

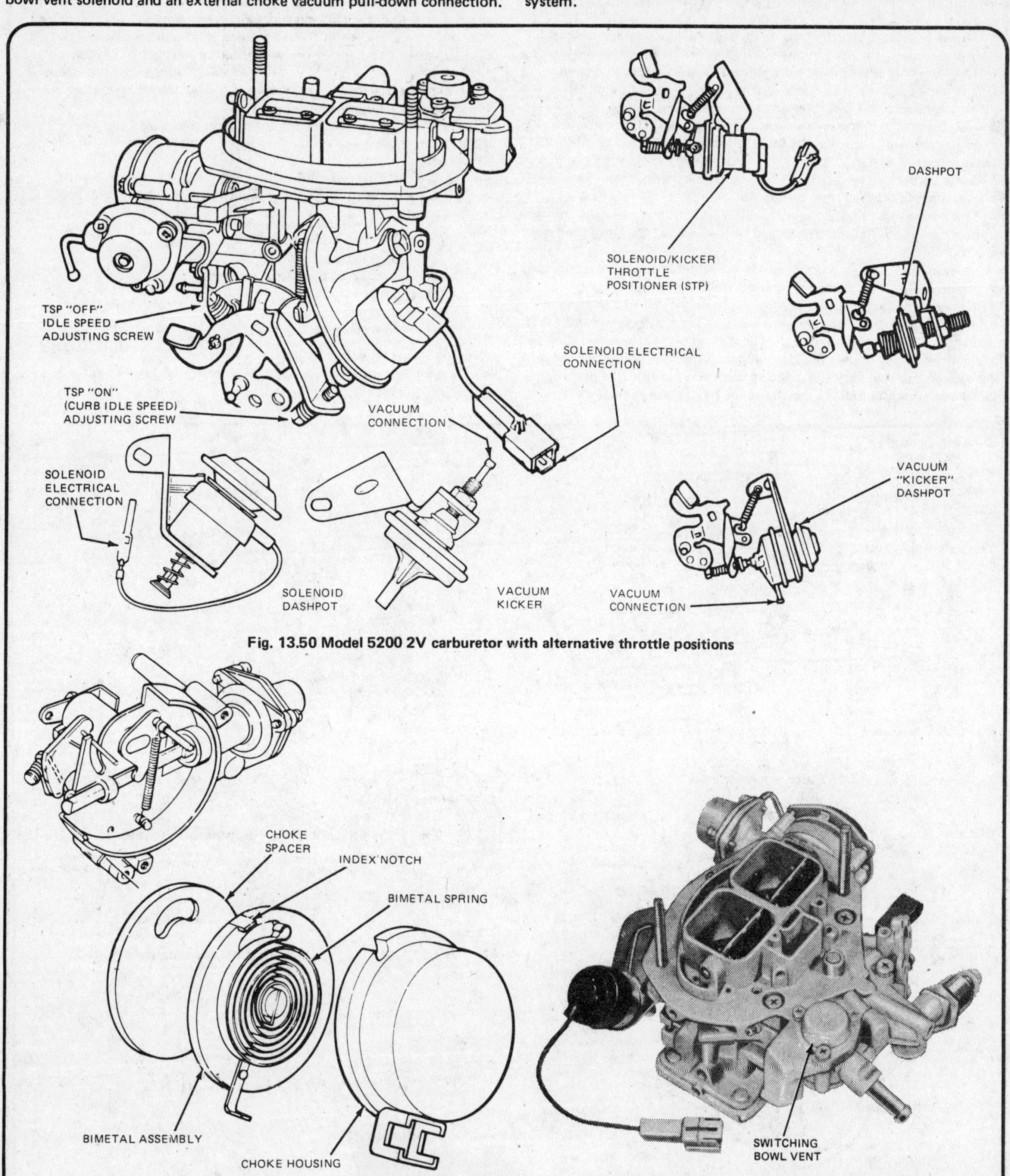

Fig. 13.50 Model 5200 2V carburetor with alternative throttle positions

Fig. 13.51 Fast idle cam latch (5200 2V carburetor)

Fig. 13.52 Model 5200 carburetor with switching bowl vent

13

32 Located in the main body are the throttle plate, the accelerator pump, the fuel bowl and the high speed bleed system.
33 Attached to the main body is the manifold (hot-air) heated choke, with an electrically-heated assister element powered from the alternator and controlled by a temperature-sensing switch.
34 A factory-set altitude compensator is fitted to certain carburetors.
35 Some carburetors are equipped with a throttle positioner, deceleration device or anti-dieseling solenoid cut-off valve.

Motorcraft Model 2700 VV carburetor

36 This is a variable venturi type carburetor using a dual element venturi valve controlled by engine vacuum and throttle position.
37 The fuel inlet system is of conventional suspended-float design.
38 The choke (cold start device) is actuated by exhaust manifold heat and connects to a fast idle cam.
39 An accelerator pump is built into the carburetor. The carburetor fuel vapor is vented into the carbon cannister which is part of the emission control system.
40 Some carburetors are fitted with an altitude compensator.

Holley/Weber 6500 feedback carburetor

41 This carburetor is basically a Model 5200 with an externally variable auxiliary fuel metering system instead of the enrichment valve used on the 5200 unit.
42 Vacuum and electrical connections are required for this carburetor which also features an electronic control unit in its circuit.
43 The system operates by metering the fuel according to the engine load (vacuum), throttle position, the coolant temperature and the exhaust gas CO content (mixture). These conditions are all signalled to the electronic control unit (ECU) which in turn then directs the vacuum solenoid regulator to vary the position of the carburetor fuel metering rod, so adjusting the fuel/air ratio to meet the precise engine requirements of the moment. This cycle is of course continuously variable all the time that the engine is running.

Curb idle speed adjustment (Model 5200 and 6500 carburetors

44 The fuel system is designed to comply with the USA Federal regulations covering emmissions of hydrocarbons and carbon monoxide. To achieve this, the ignition system must be accurately set before any attempt is made to adjust the carburetor or its controls. The fuel system may then be adjusted but special equipment will be required. The information given in these Sections is to assist the owner to clean, overhaul and adjust the various components but on completion, final setting must be left to your Ford dealer (unless you have access to an exhaust gas analyzer), otherwise the car may not comply with the prevailing regulations.
45 Refer to the Specifications for setting tolerances, but where these differ from those given on the particular vehicle decal, use the decal information.
46 Before carrying out any adjustment check the following for correct tune, good condition and security of attachment (as applicable):

- *(a) Vacuum hoses and ignition wires*
- *(b) Ignition settings*
- *(c) Spark plugs*
- *(d) Crankcase ventilation system*
- *(e) Valve clearances*
- *(f) Cylinder compression*
- *(g) Idle mixture*

Without throttle positioner device

47 The engine curb idle speed should always be kept to the speed shown on the individual vehicle decal.

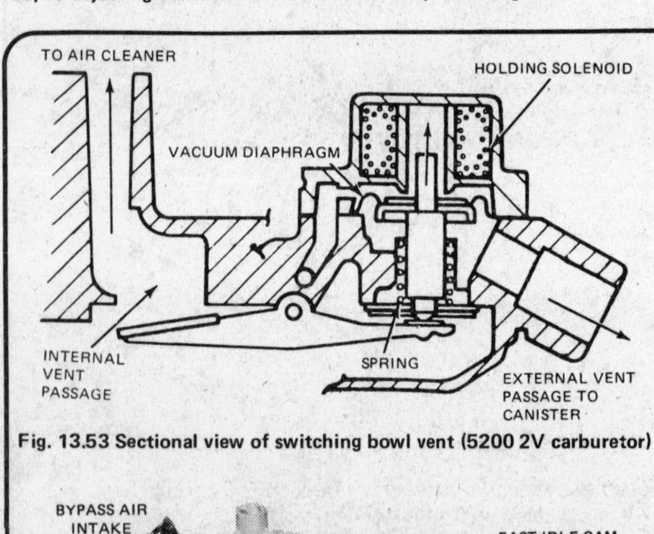

Fig. 13.53 Sectional view of switching bowl vent (5200 2V carburetor)

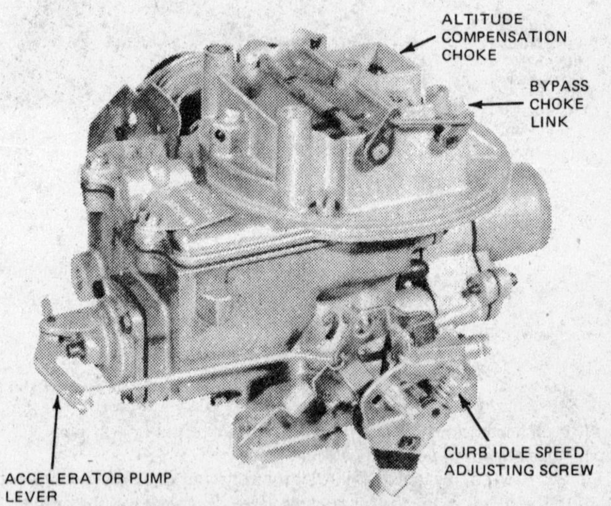

Fig. 13.54 Model 2150 2V carburetor (front view)

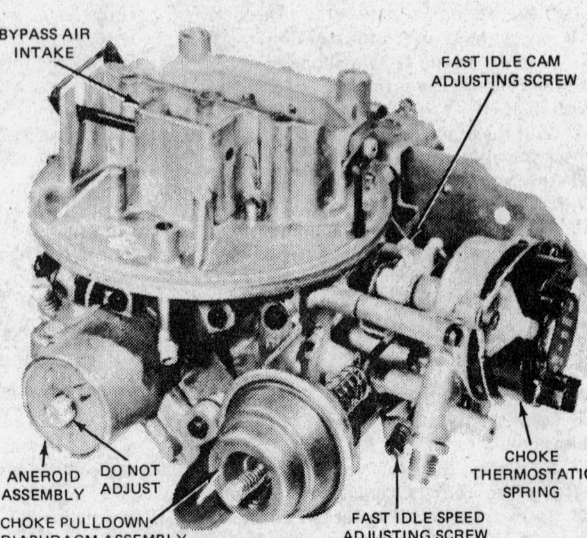

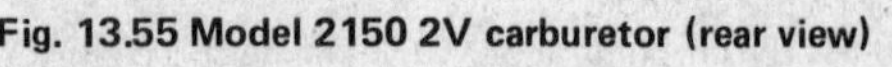

Fig. 13.55 Model 2150 2V carburetor (rear view)

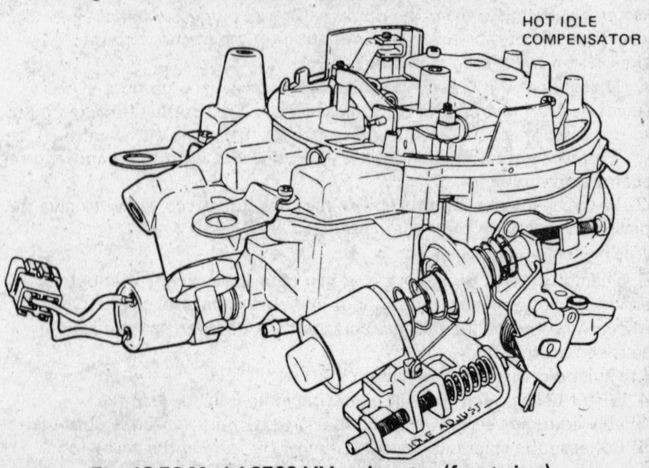

Fig. 13.56 Model 2700 VV carburetor (front view)

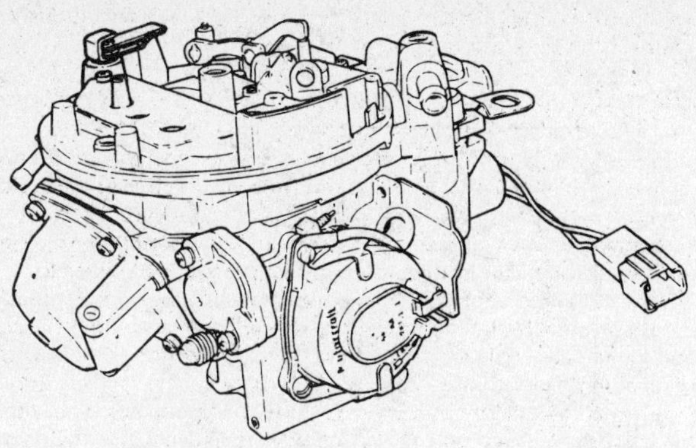

Fig. 13.57 Model 2700 VV carburetor (rear view)

With vacuum-operated throttle modulator (air conditioned cars only)

56 Release the locknut which secures the vacuum-operated throttle modulator. Rotate the modulator until there is just a slight clearance between the modulator stem and the throttle lever pad.

57 Adjust the curb idle to specification (see decal) by turning the throttle stop screw.

58 Adjust the position of the throttle modulator until the stem just makes contact with the throttle lever pad. Retighten the locknut.

With vacuum-operated throttle modulator and dashpot (air conditioned cars only)

59 With the engine at normal operating temperature, adjust the curb idle speed to specifications (see decal) by turning the throttle stop screw. If this speed cannot be set low enough, back off the TSP-ON screw until sufficient adjustment is available.

60 Now collapse the throttle modulator plunger and check the clearance between the end of the stem and the TSP-ON screw on the throttle lever pad. If adjustment is necessary, turn the TSP-ON screw to obtain the specified clearance.

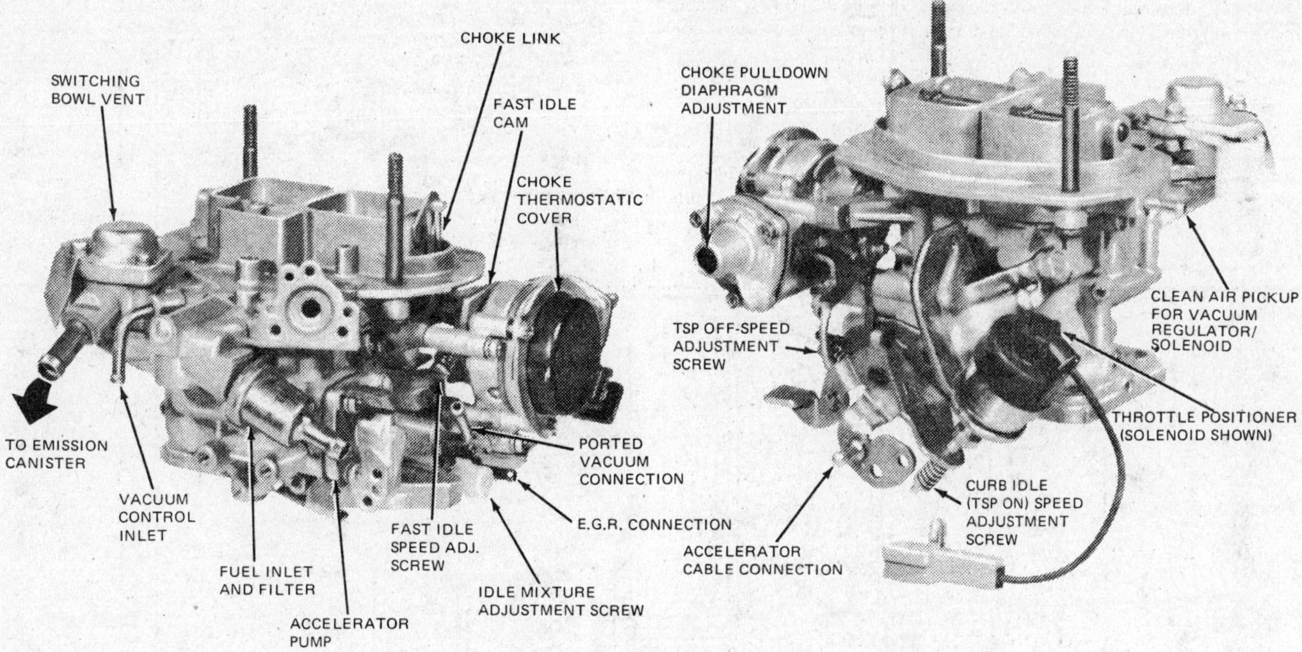

Fig. 13.58 Views of the Model 6500 feedback carburetor

48 With all accessories off, run the engine to normal operating temperature and then switch it off.

49 On 2.3 liter engines with Thermactor emission control, disconnect and plug the hoses from the air bypass valve. If the valve has only one hose at the top connected to the spark port in the carburetor, disconnect the hose from the dump valve and plug it. Connect a hose from the dump valve vacuum fitting to one of the vacuum take-offs on the intake manifold.

50 Disconnect the fuel evaporative purge valve vacuum hose at its tee connection nearest the carbon cannister. Cap or plug both openings. Do not disconnect the vacuum hose directly from the purge valve.

51 Connect a suitable tachometer in accordance with the manufacturer's recommendations.

52 With the engine running adjust the curb idle speed screw to give the specified reading on the tachometer.

With throttle delay dashpot

53 The adjustmént procedure is as just described except that before carrying it out, collapse the dashpot and check that the clearance between the end of the plunger and the throttle lever pad is within the specified tolerance.

With solenoid throttle positioner (TSP)

54 With the engine at normal operating temperautre, turn the TSP-ON adjusting screw until the specified curb idle speed is obtained.

55 Collapse the solenoid dashpot plunger by forcing the throttle lever pad against the plunger. Now turn the TSP-OFF adjusting screw until the specified TSP-OFF speed is obtained (see decal).

Curb idle speed adjustment - (Model 2150 carburetor)

Without dashpot or throttle positioner

61 With the engine at normal operating temperature, turn the throttle stop screw until the specified curb idle speed is obtained.

With dashpot

62 With the engine switched off, collapse the dashpot plunger and check the clearance between the plunger and the throttle lever pad. Where necessary, adjust to specification.

With anti-diesel throttle solenoid positioner (TSP)

63 Adjust the solenoid positioner by turning the hexagon head at the rear of the solenoid until the curb idle speed is at the specified level.

64 With the engine running, collapse the TSP plunger by forcing the throttle lever pad against the plunger. Turn the throttle stop screw until the specified TSP-OFF engine speed is obtained (refer to decal).

With air conditioner throttle solenoid positioner (TSP)

65 To adjust the air conditioner compressor-ON speed move the climate control selector to A/C ON.

66 Open the throttle to allow the TSP plunger to fully extend, then release the throttle.

67 Disconnect the air conditioner compressor clutch electrical connecting wire from the compressor terminal.

68 Check the air conditioner ON engine speed. If adjustment is required, adjust the solenoid positioner by turning the hexagon head at the rear of the solenoid.

69 To adjust the air conditioner OFF engine speed, turn the throttle stop screw as necessary.

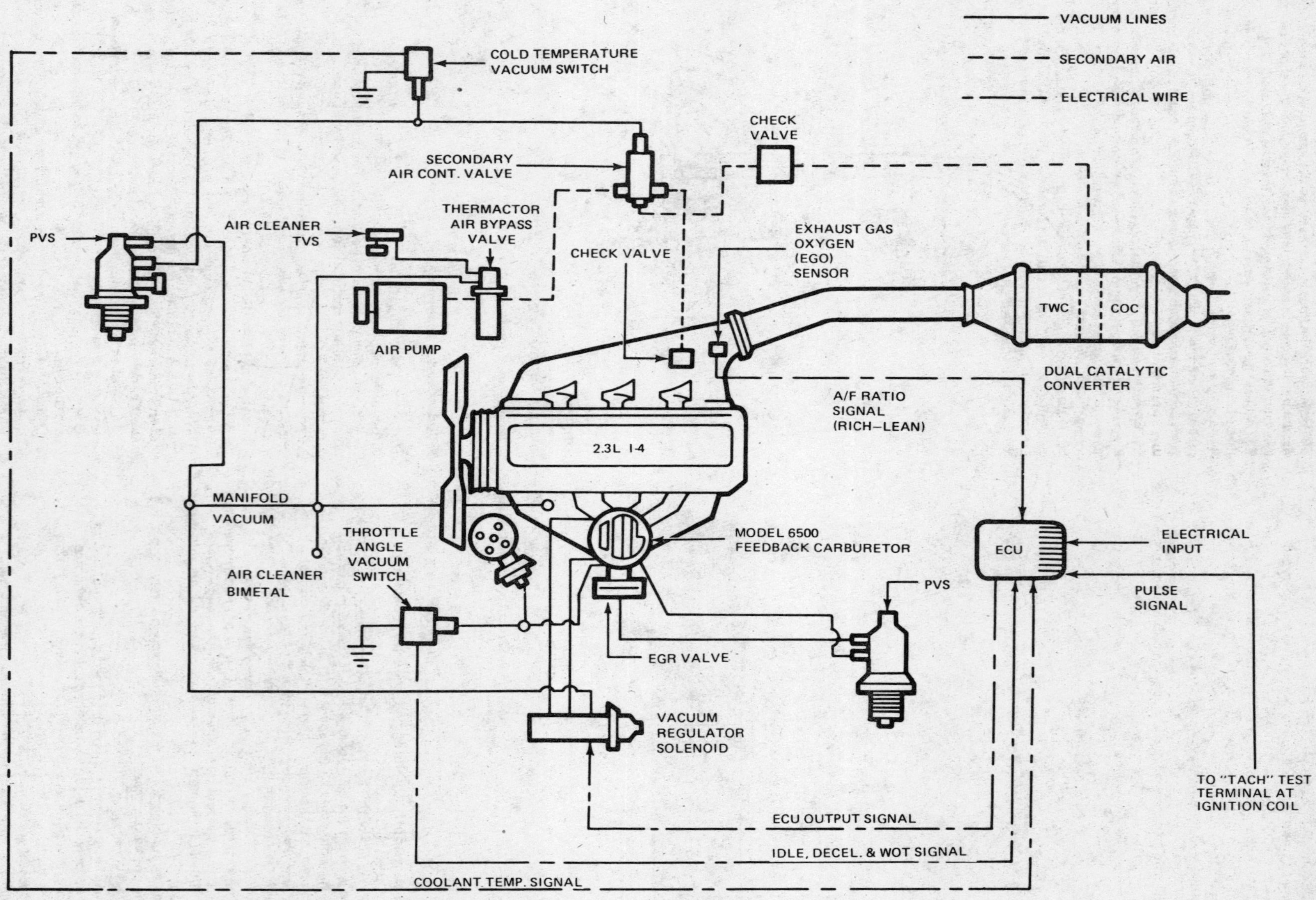

Fig. 13.59 Schematic layout of feedback carburetor electronic control system

Curb idle speed adjustment (Model 2700 VV carburetor)

Without throttle solenoid positioner (TSP)

70 Have the engine at normal operating temperature with the air cleaner in position but all accessories off.

71 Disconnect the fuel evaporative purge vacuum hose at the nearest tee connector from the carbon canister. Cap or plug the openings. Do not disconnect the hose directly from the purge valve.

72 Connect a suitable tachometer in accordance with the manufacturer's instructions.

73 Turn the throttle stop screw until the specified idle speed is obtained (see decal).

With throttle dashpot

74 Switch off the engine, collapse the dashpot and check and adjust if necessary, the clearance between the plunger and the throttle lever pad.

With anti-diesel throttle solenoid positioner (TSP)

75 Adjust the solenoid positioner by turning the hexagon head at the rear of the solenoid until the specified curb idle speed is obtained (see decal).

76 With the engine idling, collapse the TSP plunger by forcing the throttle lever pad against the plunger. Turn the throttle stop screw until the specified TSP-OFF speed is obtained as stated on the decal.

77 Re-make all hose connections and remove the tachometer

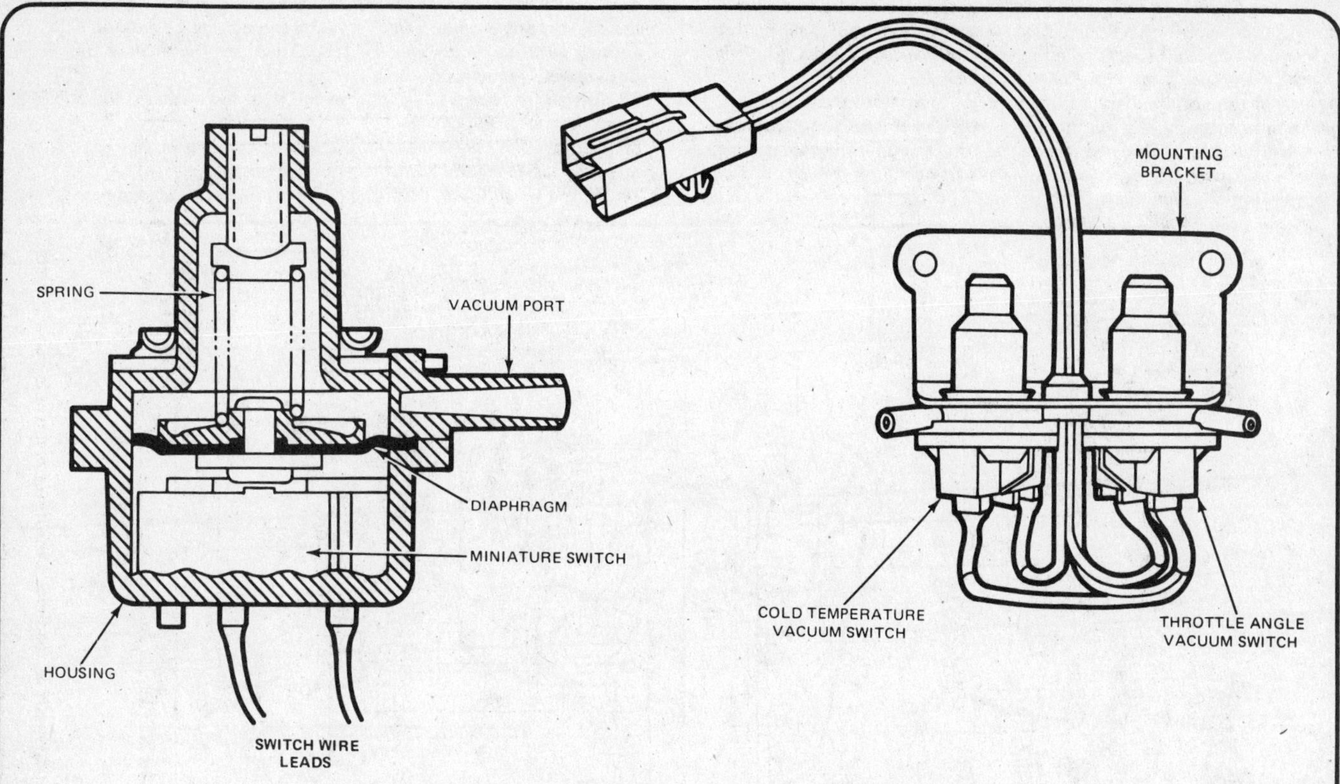

Fig. 13.60 Vacuum switches (feedback carburetor electronic control)

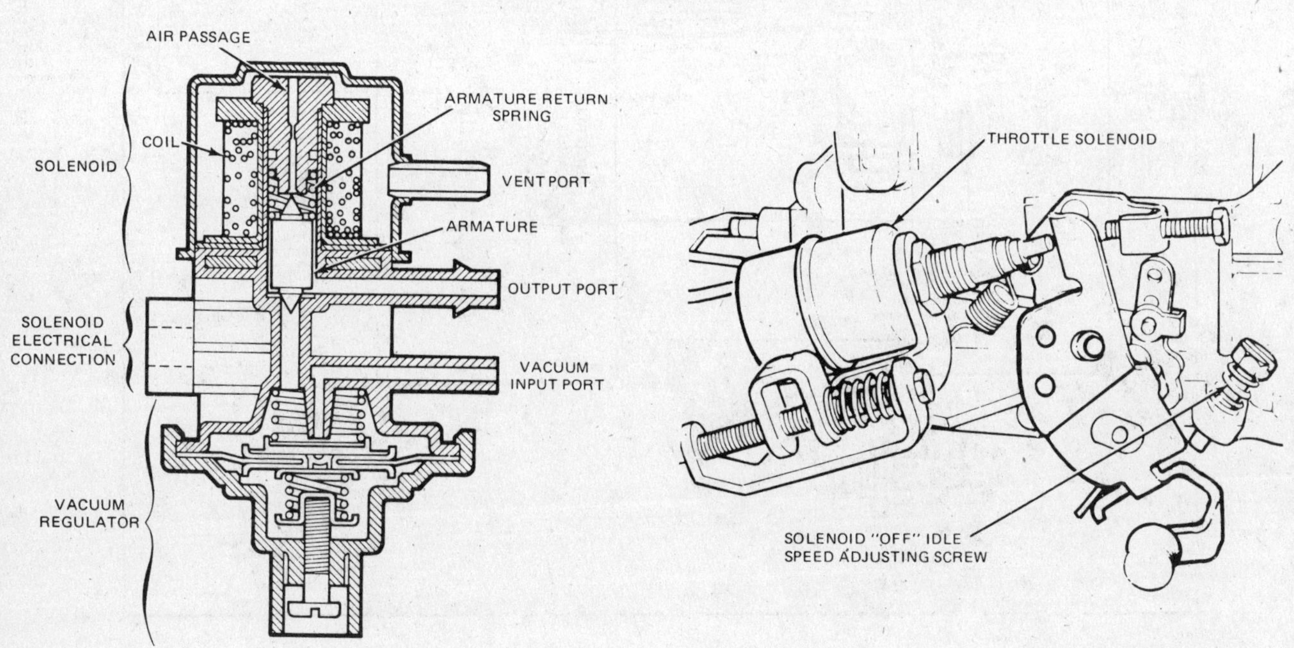

Fig. 13.61 Vacuum solenoid regulator

Fig. 13.62 Curb idle speed adjusting screws (Model 2150)

78 After curb idle speed adjustment has been carried out, check and adjust where necessary, the setting of the internal vent as described later in this Section.

Fuel mixture adjustment (Model 5200, 2150, 6500 carburetors)

79 The fuel (idle) mixture adjustment screws on all these carburetors are fitted with plastic limiter caps. The purpose of these caps is to prevent mixture adjustment being altered more than a small, pre-set amount, which may be required to take care of any slight need for a weaker or richer fuel/air mixture to offset engine changes due to wear, climate, loading etc.

80 If because of overhaul or repair, these screws must be removed, the limiter caps will have to be broken off. At reassembly, sophisticated gas enrichment and analysing equipment will be required to reset the mixture, in most cases a job for your dealer. Before removing the screws at time of overhaul, screw them gently in until they seat, at the same time counting the number of turns. Then at least, on reassembly you will be able to start the engine and run it to operating temperature before making final adjustments. Always fit new limiter caps on completion of adjustment, with the stops at the rich position.

81 Even when adjusting the fuel (idle) mixture screws within the limits of the travel permitted by their caps, it is preferable to adjust them in conjunction with an exhaust gas analyser rather than to attempt to judge their setting.

Service adjustments (Model 5200 2V carburetor)

Fast idle cam clearance

82 With the air cleaner removed, insert a twist drill or gauge rod of the specified diameter (see Specifications) between the lower edge of the choke plate and the wall of the air horn.

83 With the fast idle screw held on the bottom step of the fast idle cam, measure the clearance between the tang of the choke lever and the arm on the fast idle cam. The tang should just be making light contact with the arm. Bend the tang if necessary to achieve this.

Choke plate vacuum pull-down

84 Extract the screws and remove the ring which retains the choke thermostatic spring cover.

85 Remove the choke electric element assembly and then set the fast idle cam on its second step.

86 With a screwdriver, push the diaphragm stem back against its stop

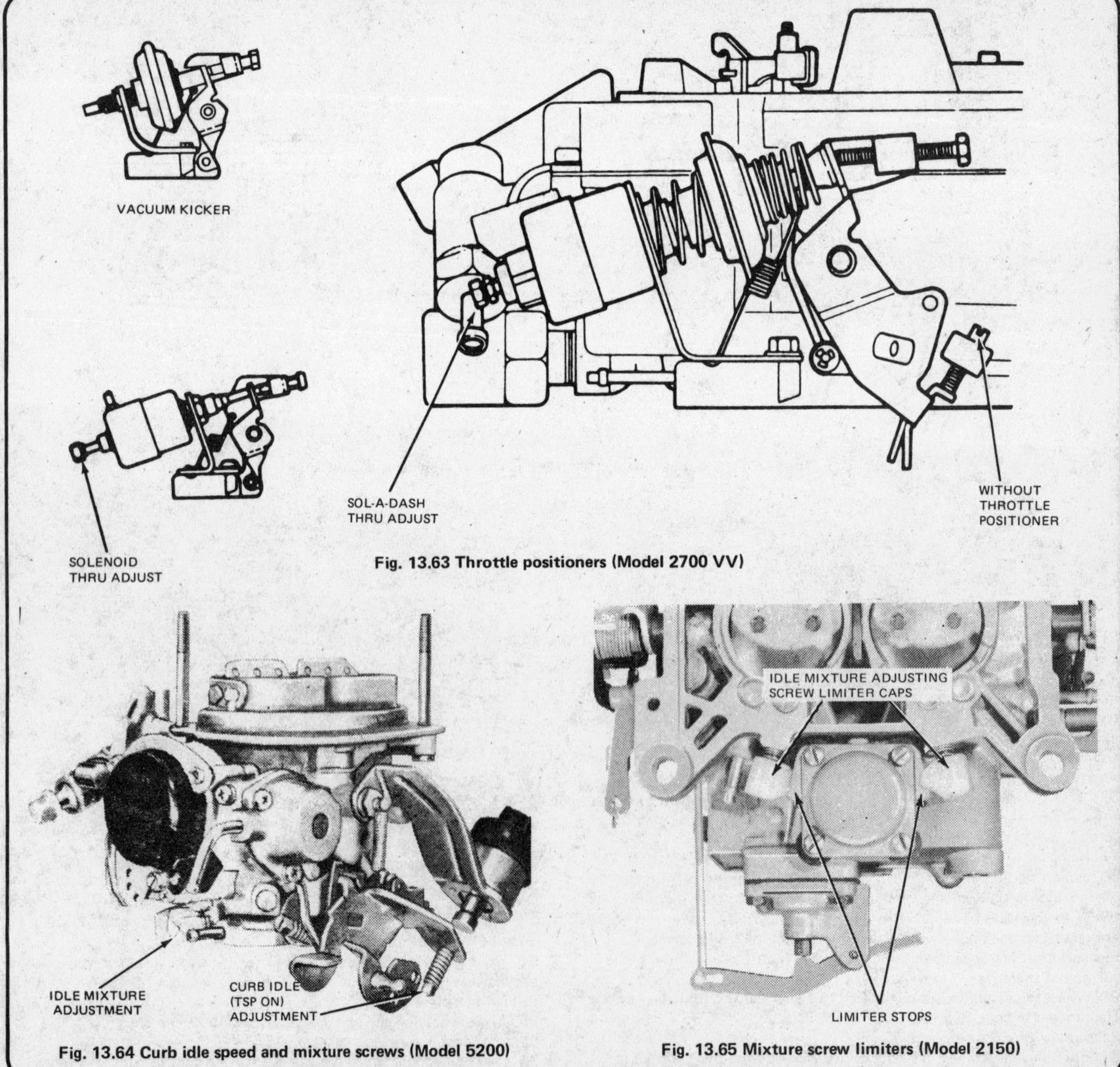

Fig. 13.63 Throttle positioners (Model 2700 VV)

Fig. 13.64 Curb idle speed and mixture screws (Model 5200)

Fig. 13.65 Mixture screw limiters (Model 2150)

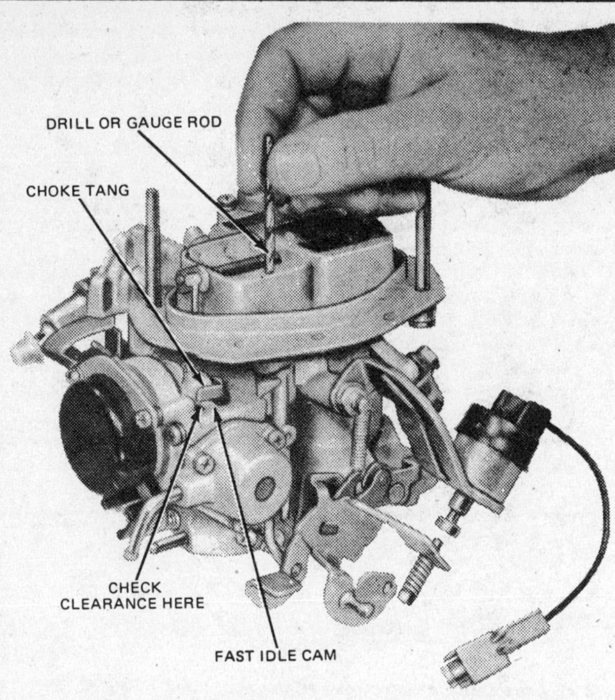

Fig. 13.66 Checking fast idle cam clearance (Model 5200)

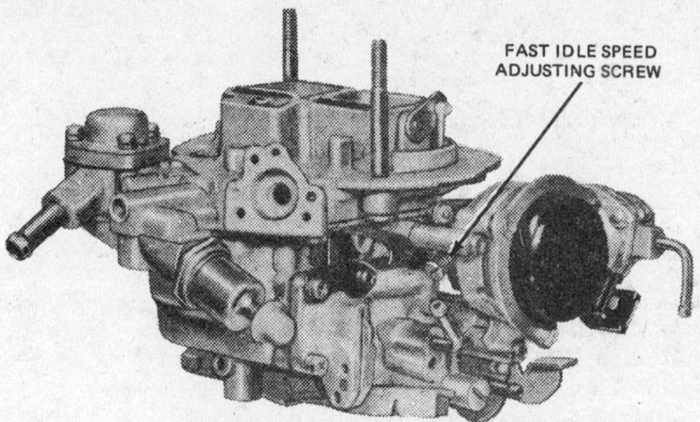

Fig. 13.67 Fast idle screw (Model 5200)

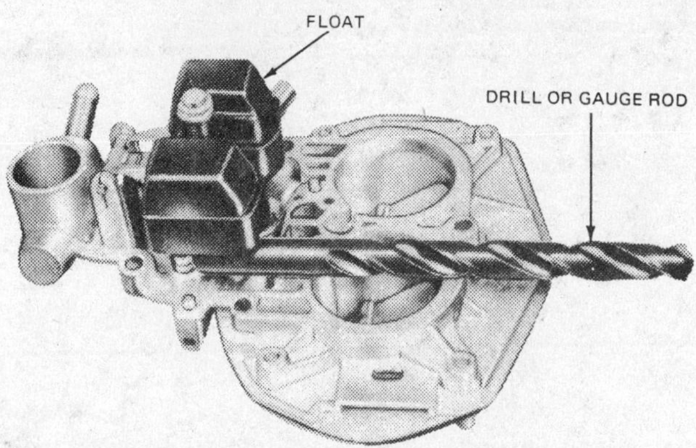

Fig. 13.69 Checking float setting (Model 5200)

Fig. 13.68 Checking choke plate pull-down (Model 5200)

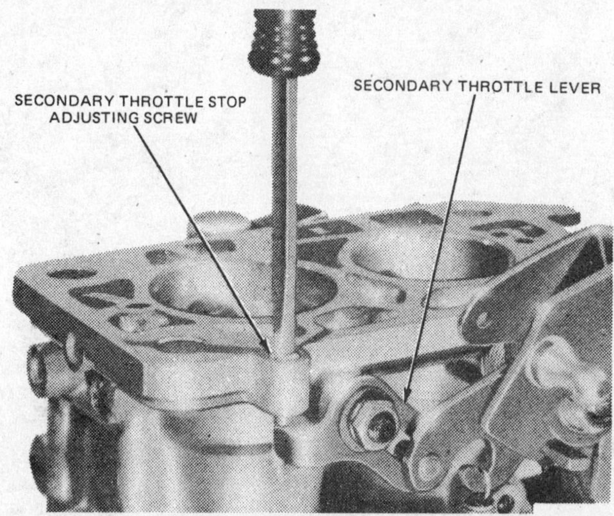

Fig. 13.70 Adjusting secondary throttle stop (Model 5200)

inside the choke housing. Using a twist drill or gauge rod of the specified diameter inserted between the lower edge of the choke plate and the wall of the air horn, check that the drill or gauge rod is a sliding fit. Slack in the choke linkage should be eliminated during this operation by using a rubber band attached to the choke lever as shown.

87 Turn the vacuum diaphragm adjusting screw as necessary to correct the choke plate opening. An Allen key will be necessary to turn the screw.

Float setting

88 For this adjustment, the carburetor must be removed from the engine and partially dismantled as described later in this Section.

89 With the float bowl cover removed and inverted, so that the floats are resting under their own weight on the fuel inlet needle valve, measure the clearance between the edge of the float and the metal surface of the cover.

90 Where necessary, bend both float tangs equally so that the clearance is as specified (see Specifications).

Secondary throttle stop screw

91 For this adjustment, the carburetor must be removed from the engine and partially dismantled as described later in this Section.

92 Back off the secondary throttle stop screw until the secondary throttle valve plate closes.

93 Turn the stop adjusting screw until it touches the tab on the secondary throttle lever. On 2.3 l engines, turn the screw in by an additional ¼ turn.

Service adjustments (Model 6500 carburetor)

94 The adjustments are as described for the Model 5200 carburetor except that when checking the choke plate vacuum pull-down, note the following differences.

95 After removing the choke screws, withdraw the choke cap, the bi-metal heater and the plastic shield.

96 Set the fast idle speed adjusting screw on the top step of the fast idle cam.

SCREWDRIVER
GAGE
RUBBER BAND

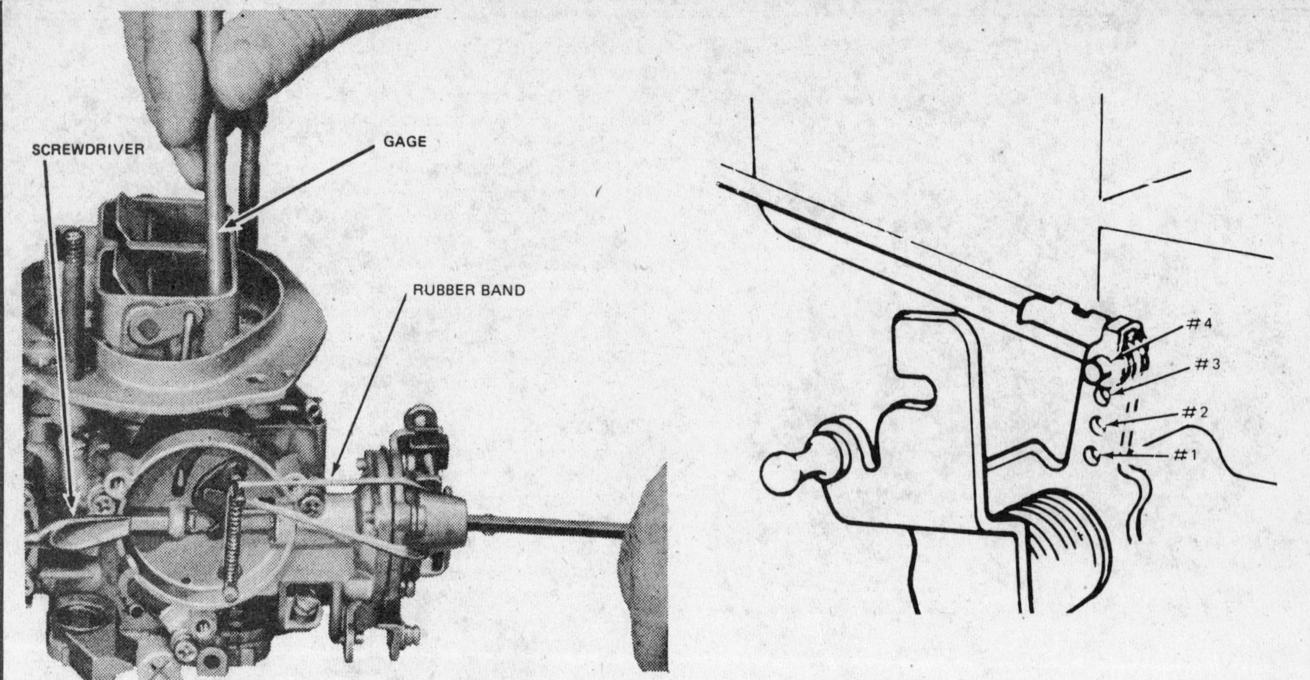

Fig. 13.71 Checking choke plate pull-down (Model 6500)

#4
#3
#2
#1

Fig. 13.72 Accelerator pump stroke adjustment holes (Model 2150)

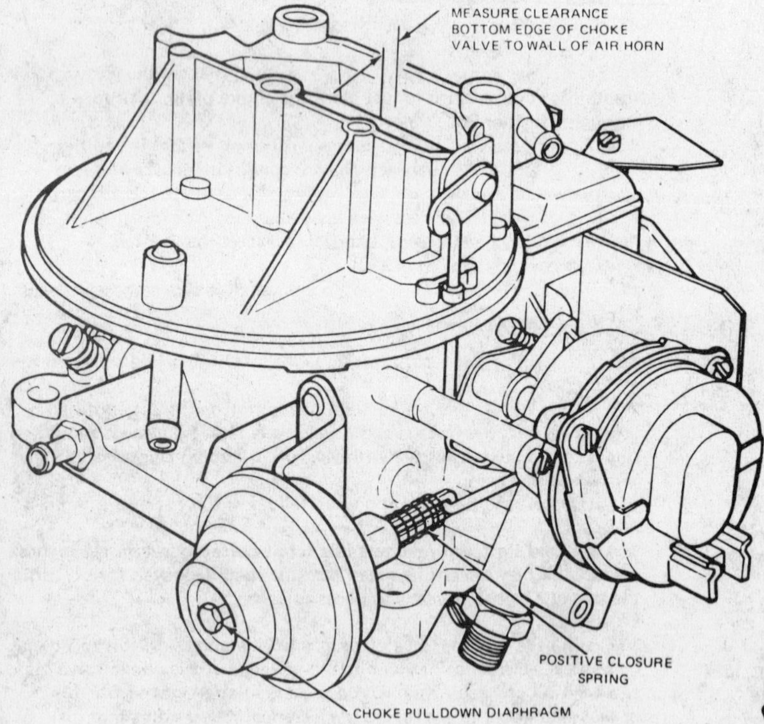

MEASURE CLEARANCE
BOTTOM EDGE OF CHOKE
VALVE TO WALL OF AIR HORN
POSITIVE CLOSURE
SPRING
CHOKE PULLDOWN DIAPHRAGM

Fig. 13.73 Choke plate pull-down (Model 2150, thru 1977)

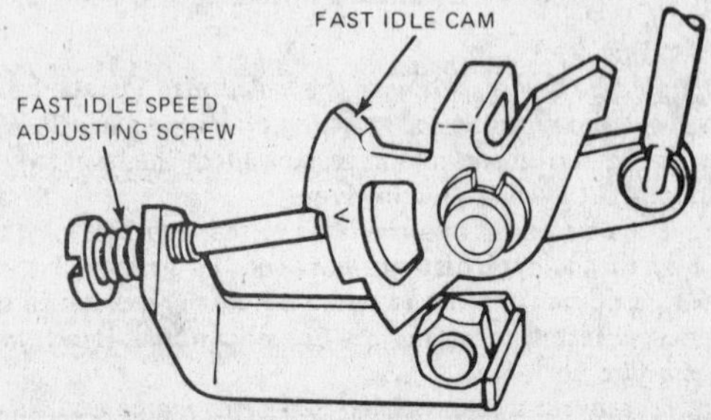

FAST IDLE CAM
FAST IDLE SPEED
ADJUSTING SCREW

Fig. 13.74 Fast idle screw (Model 2150 carburetor)

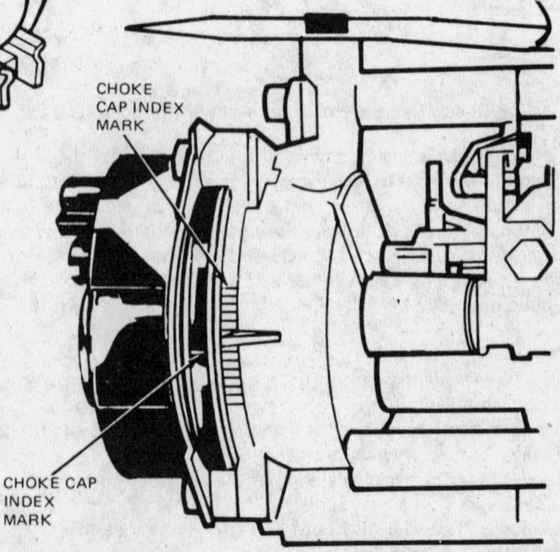

CHOKE
CAP INDEX
MARK
CHOKE CAP
INDEX
MARK

Fig. 13.75 Choke housing marks (Model 2150 carburetor)

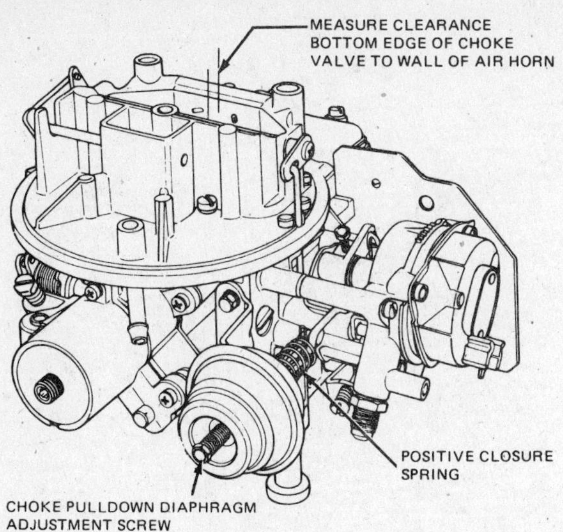

Fig. 13.76 Choke plate pull-down (Model 2150, 1978 on)

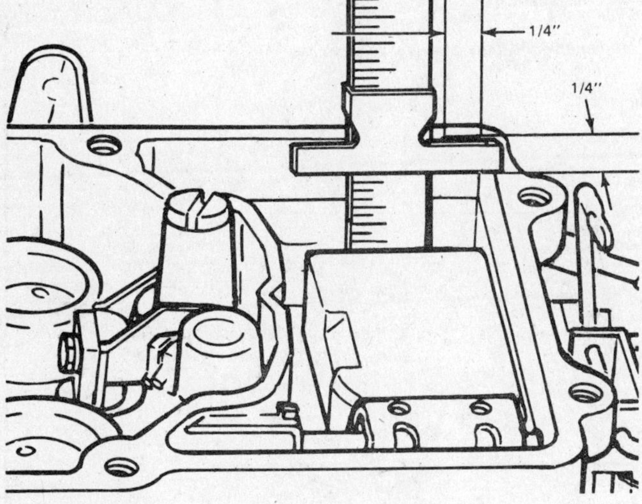

Fig. 13.77 Float setting (wet) on Model 2150 carburetor

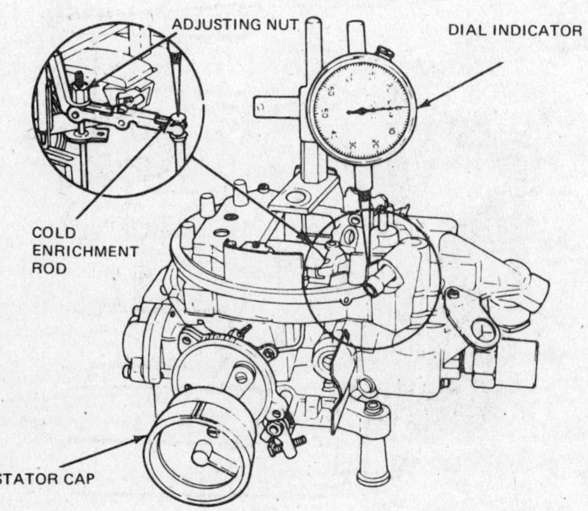

Fig. 13.78 Cold enrichment metering rod adjustment (Model 2700 VV)

Service adjustments (Model 2150 2V carburetor)

Accelerator pump stroke

97 This is pre-set during production and should not normally require alteration unless the pump has been dismantled for renewal of components.

98 Where adjustment is needed, release the rod from its retaining clip by lifting up the part of the clip which snaps over the rod.

99 Locate the rod in the specified hole in the overtravel lever (see Specifications) and secure with the clip.

Choke plate pull-down (thru 1977)

100 This is actuated by a remotely-mounted diaphragm unit.

101 Set the throttle so that the fast idle cam is on the top step and record the setting of the automatic choke cap pointer to the index.

102 Release the choke cap outer screws and turn the cap through 90° In the RICH direction.

103 Apply pressure to the diaphragm unit link and close the choke plate. Measure the clearance between the bottom edge of the choke plate and the wall of the air horn using a gauge rod or twist drill of suitable diameter. If the clearance (see Specifications) is incorrect, adjust the stop screw on the end of the diaphragm unit. Before this screw can be turned, its thread sealant must be released by careful application of heat from an electric soldering gun.

104 Once the choke pull-down adjustment is complete, reset the automatic choke housing cap to its original position and then check and adjust if necessary, the fast idle speed as described in the following paragraphs.

Fast idle cam clearance (thru 1977)

105 With the choke set in the cold start position, the fast idle adjusting screw should be against the top of the highest cam.

106 With a tachometer connected to the engine adjust the screw as necessary to give the specified fast idle speed (see Specifications).

Choke plate pull-down (1978)

107 Note the automatic choke cover setting. Release the screws and rotate the cover enough to just close the choke plate, then turn it through a further 90°.

108 Apply pressure to the vacuum unit link to retract it and then measure the clearance between the lower edge of the choke plate and the wall of the air horn. Use a twist drill or gauge rod for this of equivalent diameter to the clearance (see Specifications).

109 To adjust the clearance, bend the loop on the link rod.

Fast idle cam adjustment (1978)

110 This is necessary whenever the choke pull-down setting has been altered.

111 With the automatic choke housing cover still in its RICH + 90° position, depress the accelerator pedal to set the fast idle screw on the cam.

112 Apply pressure to the vacuum unit link to retract it and then actuate the throttle linkage and observe the fast idle cam. It should rotate to the kickdown step with the fast idle screw opposite to the V-mark on the cam.

113 If necessary, bend the rod which slides in the cut-out in the fast idle cam.

114 At cold start, with the fast idle screw correctly set on the highest cam, check that the engine speed is at the specified level. If not, turn the fast idle adjusting screw as necessary.

De-choke

115 Hold the throttle valve plate in the wide open position and then measure the clearance between the lower edge of the choke valve plate and the wall of the air horn. Use a twist drill or gauge rod for this, of diameter equal to the specified clearance. Where adjustment is required, bend the tang on the fast idle speed lever which is attached to the throttle shaft.

Float level setting

116 This should be carried out with the carburetor installed to the intake manifold and with the car standing on a level surface. Where the carburetor has been dismantled and reassembled, the level should first be provisionally set in the following way.

117 Remove the air horn, raise the float to seat the fuel inlet needle valve and then measure the distance between the surface of the main body (gasket removed) and the top of the float. The distance should be in accordance with that specified (see Specifications). Bend the float tab if necessary to correct it.

118 With the carburetor reassembled, start the engine and allow it to run for a few minutes until the float fuel level has stabilised. Ideally, the engine should be at normal operating temperature.

119 Remove the air horn and the gasket. Restart the engine and while

it is idling, measure the level of the fuel in the float bowl from the machined surface of the main body. Make sure that you take the measurement at least ¼ in (6.4 mm) away from the vertical surface of the fuel bowl. If the level is outside the specified tolerance, again bend the float tab to correct the setting.

Service adjustments (Model 2700 VV carburetor)

120 Before carrying out any adjustment to the venturi valve limiter, remove the carburetor. For other adjustments, leave the carburetor in position on the manifold.

Cold enrichment metering rod

121 A special tool will be required for this adjustment (No T77L-9848-A).

122 Remove the automatic choke cover cap and install the special tool, which acts as a weight to seat the cold enrichment rod.

123 Fit a dial indicator so that the tip of its stylus is in contact with the top surface of the enrichment rod and then adjust the dial gauge to zero. Lift the special tool slightly to make sure that the zero repeats.

124 Remove the special tool and refit it at the index position, when the dial gauge should indicate the specified rod height. If the rod height is outside specification, turn the adjusting nut as necessary to correct it.

125 Refit the choke cover cap to the specified setting.

Internal vent

126 Set the curb idle speed to the specified level.

127 Place an 0.010 in (0.254 mm) feeler gauge between the stem of the accelerator pump and the operating link and adjust the nylon nut until a slight drag can be felt when the blade is withdrawn.

Fast idle speed

128 With the engine idling, set the fast idle lever on the specified step of the fast idle cam. The EGR valve vacuum line should be disconnected and plugged. Check that the high cam speed positioner lever is disengaged and then turn the fast idle adjusting screw as necessary to bring the fast idle speed to the specified level.

Fast idle cam

129 Remove the cap from the automatic choke.

130 Set the fast idle lever into the corner of the specified step of the fast idle cam with the cam speed positioner retracted.

131 Hold the throttle lightly closed using a rubber band to maintain the cam position (this is not necessary if the adjustment is being carried out on the car).

132 Install the special tool (T77L-9848A) and turn it clockwise until the lever just contacts the fast idle adjusting screw.

133 Now turn the fast idle adjusting screw until the index mark on the stator cap lines up with the specified mark on the choke housing.

134 Remove the special tool and refit the cap to its specified setting.

Float level

135 Remove the carburetor upper body and invert it. Measure the distance between the metal surface of the upper body and the bottom of the float.

136 Where this is outside the specified limits, bend the float operating lever.

137 The float drop must now be checked by holding the upper body the correct way up and measuring between the lower metal surface of the body and the bottom of the float.

138 Where the dimension is outside that specified, bend the stop tab on the float lever.

Venturi valve limiter

139 The carburetor must be removed from the engine for this job.

140 Remove the venturi valve cover and roller bearings (see later dismantling operations).

141 Remove the expansion plug which is located at the rear of the main body on the throttle side of the carburetor.

142 Using an Allen wrench, remove the venturi valve (wide open) throttle stop screw.

143 Block the throttle plates in the wide open position.

144 Apply light pressure to close the venturi valve and check the gap between the valve and the wall of the air horn. If this is outside the specified limit, move the venturi valve to the wide open position and insert an Allen wrench into the hole from which the stop screw was removed. Turn the limiter type adjuster screw with the Allen wrench until on re-checking, the gap is correct.

145 Refit the venturi valve stop screw and screw it in until it just contacts the valve. Push the valve to the wide-open position and then check the gap between the valve and the wall of the air horn. Turn the screw until the gap is within specification.

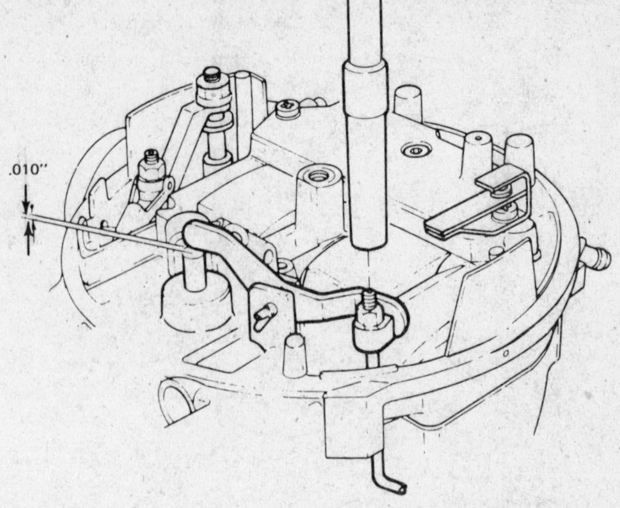

Fig. 13.79 Internal vent adjustment (Model 2700 VV)

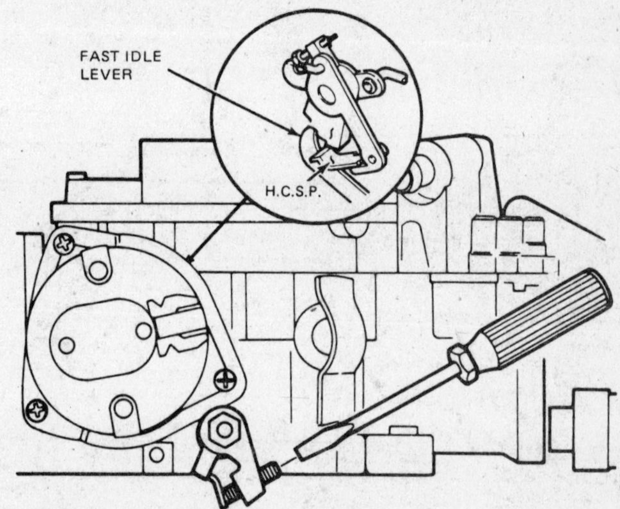

Fig. 13.80 Fast idle speed adjustment (Model 2700 VV)

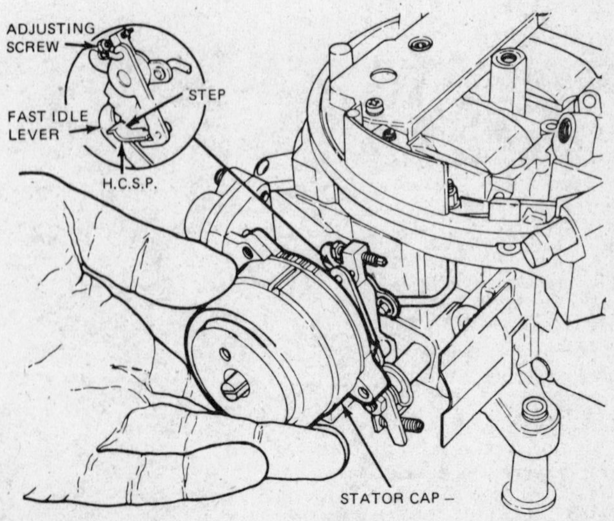

Fig. 13.81 Using special tool to adjust the fast idle cam (2700 VV)

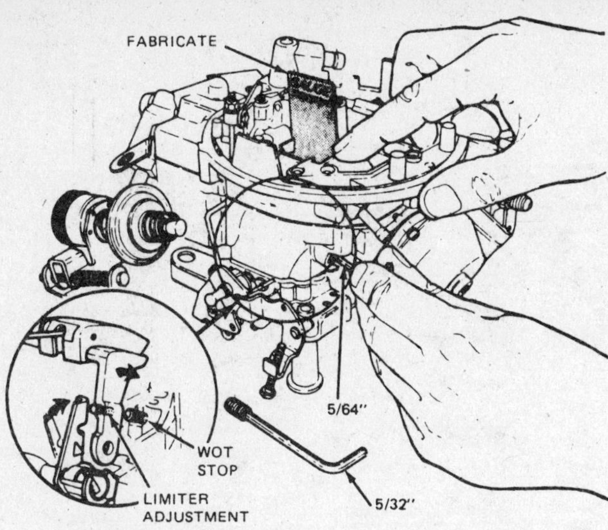

Fig. 13.82 Adjusting venturi valve limiter (Model 2700 VV)

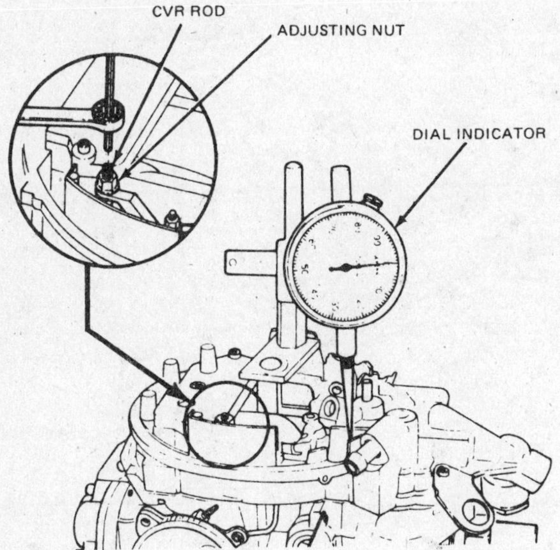

Fig. 13.83 Adjusting Control Vacuum Regulator (CVR) on Model 2700 VV carburetor

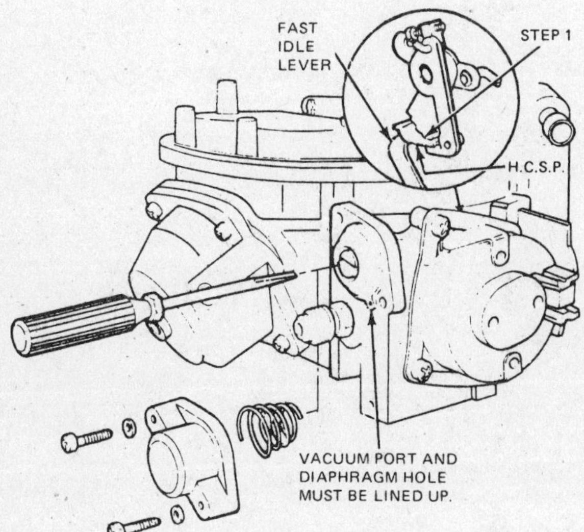

Fig. 13.84 Adjusting High cam Speed Positioner (HCSP) on Model 2700 VV carburetor

146 Fit a new expansion plug, refit the venturi valve cover and the roller bearings. Refit the carburetor to the engine.

Control vacuum regulator (CVR)

147 It is essential that the cold enrichment metering rod adjustment has been checked beforehand (refer to paragraph 121).

148 Leave the dial gauge in position, but not the special tool described earlier, and do not reset the dial gauge to zero after removing the tool.

149 Press down on the CVR rod until it seats and read the measurement on the dial gauge. If this is outside specification, hold the CVR adjusting nut with a box wrench and using a 3/32 in Allen wrench, turn the CVR rod as necessary.

High cam speed positioner (HCSP)

150 Set the HCSP in the corner of the specified cam step, then position the fast idle lever in the corner of the HCSP.

151 Hold the throttle firmly closed in order to retain these HCSP settings.

152 Remove the diaphragm cover and adjust the diaphragm in a clockwise direction until it lightly seats on the casting, then unscrew it between ½ and 1½ turns until the vacuum port and diaphragm holes line up.

153 Refit the diaphragm cover.

Carburetors - dismantling and reassembly - general

154 The need for complete dismantling of a carburetor seldom arises. When it is required, then usually the carburetor is so badly worn that a new or exchange unit is a more economical proposition.

155 Although complete dismantling is described in the following paragraphs, only those operations should be carried out which are necessary to remove the particular worn or damaged part.

156 Try to avoid removing components which have their fixing screws staked or sealed, and always use small wrenches and screwdrivers of the correct size to remove jets and other precision parts. Purchase the appropriate repair kit in advance of starting work.

Carburetor (Model 5200 2V) - dismantling and reassembly

157 There are differences in the automatic choke operating mechanism on later models. This will be apparent when comparing the exploded drawings in this Supplement with those in Chapter 3. The upper body, automatic choke and accelerator pump may be removed with the carburetor in position on the manifold. Further dismantling will require removal of the unit to the bench.

Carburetor (Model 6500) - dismantling and reassembly

158 This carburetor differs from the Model 5200 by having an internal choke pull-down vacuum passage rather than the external vacuum connection found on later Model 5200 units.

159 In other respects, dismantling and reassembly is as described for the Model 5200 in Chapter 3, except for the feedback fuel valve piston and diaphragm, the electrically-heated choke and additional solenoids and dashpots.

160 If it is essential to dismantle the feedback fuel valve piston and diaphragm, it is most important to follow the reassembly operations exactly as given in the subsequent paragraphs.

161 Apply a drop of thread locking compound to the threads of the three tapped holes in the piston assembly upper body. Hold the feedback fuel diaphragm and piston assembly over the spring so that the securing screw holes are in alignment. Check that one end of the spring is over the adjustment screw, with the other end centered within the cupped washer of the piston/diaphragm assembly.

162 Fit the screws and tighten to between 4 and 5 lbf in (0.5 and 0.6 Nm).

Carburetor (Model 2150 2V) - dismantling and reassembly

163 The following dismantling operations can be carried out with the carburetor in position on the manifold, provided the air cleaner is first removed:

(a) Removal of the air horn
(b) Removal of the float, fuel inlet valve and main jets (after withdrawal of the air horn)
(c) Removal of the accelerator pump and diaphragm valve (after withdrawal of air horn)

164 Complete dismantling of the carburetor should be carried out as follows, having first cleaned away all grease and external dirt.

165 Remove the air cleaner anchor screw and the automatic choke control rod retainer.

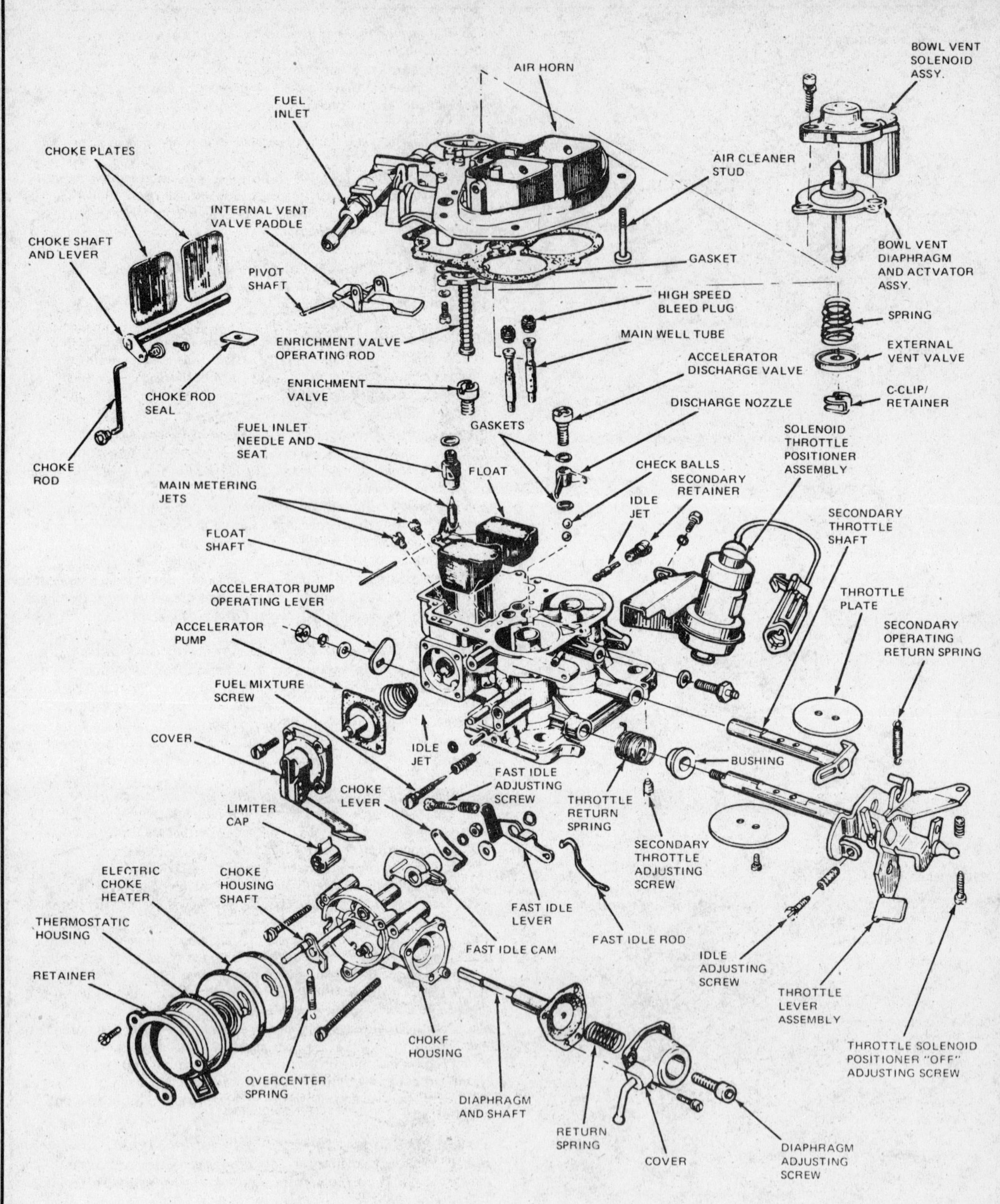

Fig. 13.85 Exploded view of Model 5200 carburetor

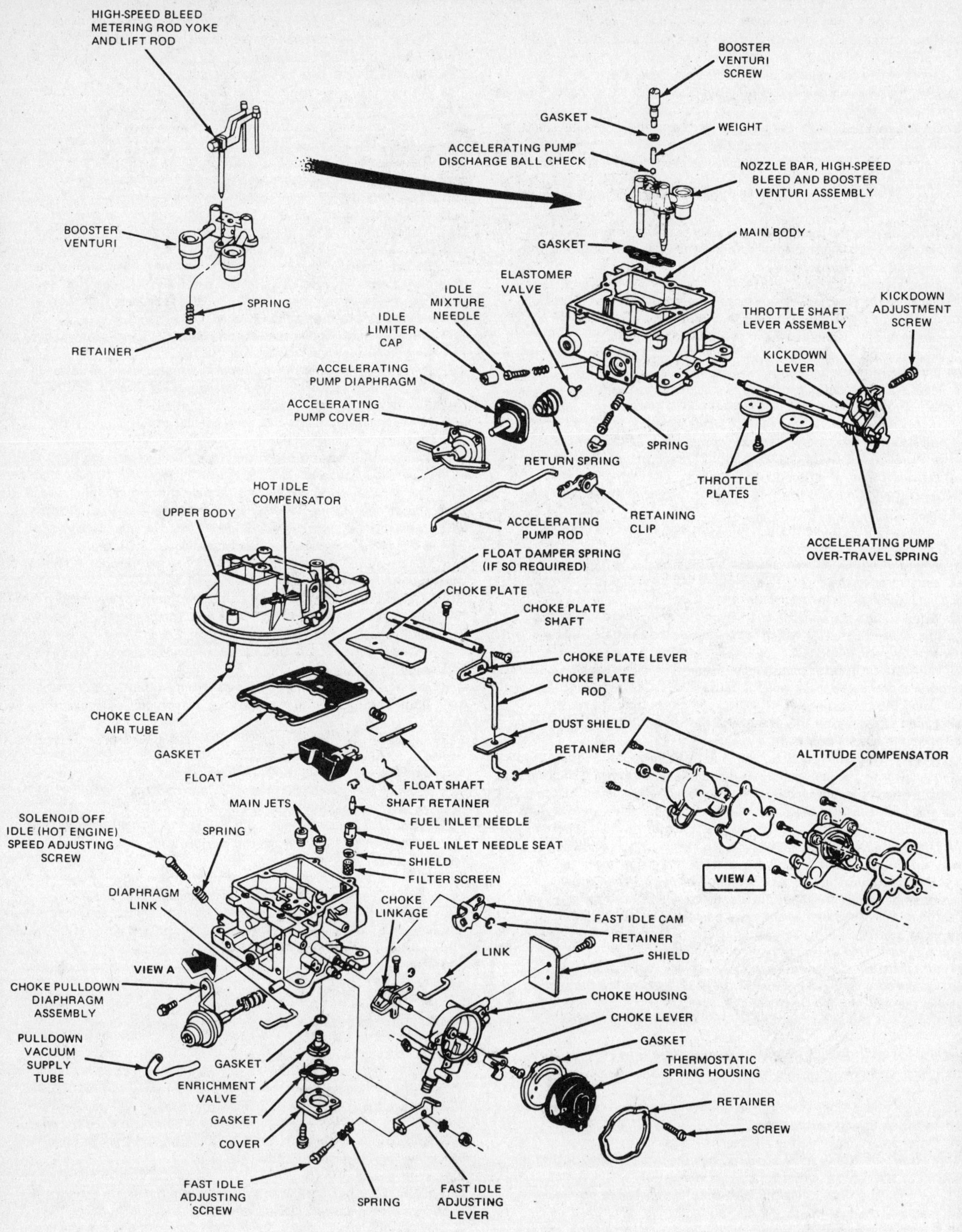

HIGH-SPEED BLEED METERING ROD YOKE AND LIFT ROD
BOOSTER VENTURI SCREW
GASKET
WEIGHT
ACCELERATING PUMP DISCHARGE BALL CHECK
NOZZLE BAR, HIGH-SPEED BLEED AND BOOSTER VENTURI ASSEMBLY
BOOSTER VENTURI
GASKET
MAIN BODY
ELASTOMER VALVE
IDLE MIXTURE NEEDLE
SPRING
IDLE LIMITER CAP
THROTTLE SHAFT LEVER ASSEMBLY
KICKDOWN ADJUSTMENT SCREW
RETAINER
KICKDOWN LEVER
ACCELERATING PUMP DIAPHRAGM
ACCELERATING PUMP COVER
SPRING
RETURN SPRING
THROTTLE PLATES
HOT IDLE COMPENSATOR
UPPER BODY
RETAINING CLIP
ACCELERATING PUMP ROD
ACCELERATING PUMP OVER-TRAVEL SPRING
FLOAT DAMPER SPRING (IF SO REQUIRED)
CHOKE PLATE
CHOKE PLATE SHAFT
CHOKE PLATE LEVER
CHOKE PLATE ROD
CHOKE CLEAN AIR TUBE
DUST SHIELD
GASKET
RETAINER
ALTITUDE COMPENSATOR
FLOAT
FLOAT SHAFT
SHAFT RETAINER
MAIN JETS
FUEL INLET NEEDLE
SOLENOID OFF IDLE (HOT ENGINE) SPEED ADJUSTING SCREW
SPRING
FUEL INLET NEEDLE SEAT
SHIELD
VIEW A
FILTER SCREEN
DIAPHRAGM LINK
CHOKE LINKAGE
FAST IDLE CAM
RETAINER
VIEW A
LINK
SHIELD
CHOKE PULLDOWN DIAPHRAGM ASSEMBLY
CHOKE HOUSING
CHOKE LEVER
GASKET
PULLDOWN VACUUM SUPPLY TUBE
GASKET
THERMOSTATIC SPRING HOUSING
ENRICHMENT VALVE
RETAINER
GASKET
SCREW
COVER
FAST IDLE ADJUSTING SCREW
SPRING
FAST IDLE ADJUSTING LEVER

Fig. 13.86 Exploded view of Model 2150 2V carburetor

166 Extract the screws and remove the air horn and gasket.
167 Remove the choke control rod from the air horn and slide the plastic air horn from it.
168 Remove the choke valve plate only if essential. Do so by unstaking the plate screws and sliding the plate out of the shaft. Remove the shaft from the air horn.
169 On V6 engines, invert the air horn, extract the three screws and remove the idle decel metering assembly.
170 Remove the fast idle cam retainer, the thermostatic choke spring housing, clamp and gasket.
171 Remove the choke housing, fast idle cam and rod, then the choke lever.
172 To dismantle the main body, use a screwdriver to pry the float shaft retainer from the fuel inlet seat and then remove the float, the fuel inlet and the filter screen.
173 Unscrew the main jets.
174 Remove the booster venturi screw, the booster venturi, the metering rod and the gasket. Invert the main body and catch the accelerator pump discharge weight and ball in the hand.
175 Remove the accelerator pump operating rod from the overtravel lever and the retainer.
176 Remove the accelerator pump cover, then the diaphragm assembly and spring.
177 If it is necessary to remove the Elastomer valve, grasp it firmly and pull it out. Always renew the Elastomer valve at reassembly. If during removal, the tip of the valve should break off, make sure that you retrieve it from the fuel bowl.
178 With the main body inverted, remove the enrichment valve cover and gasket.
179 If necessary, remove the fast idle adjusting lever from the throttle shaft.
180 Where so equipped, remove the dashpots and solenoids.
181 Only remove the throttle valve plates if essential and then always mark each plate as to location.
182 When sliding the throttle shaft from the main body, catch the high speed bleed actuator which is located on the throttle shaft between the throttle plates.
183 With the carburetor completely dismantled, clean each component and inspect for wear or damage.
184 Using the correct repair kit which will contain all the necessary gaskets and seals, reassembly is a reversal of dismantling, but observe the following special points.
185 When fitting the new Elastomer fuel inlet valve, lubricate its tip and insert it into the center hole of the accelerator pump. Using a pair of needle-nosed pliers, reach into the fuel bowl, grip the tip of the valve and pull it until it seats. Cut the tip from the valve just forward of the retaining shoulder and remove the tip from the fuel bowl.
186 If the idle mixture screws have been removed, screw them in gently until they just seat and then unscrew them 1½ turns to provide an initial setting to get the engine running. When the carburetor has been installed, the fuel mixture will have to be adjusted as described earlier and once correctly set, new limiter caps must be fitted to the screws. Soak the new caps in very hot water before fitting to make them more pliable.
187 When fitting the fast idle cam lever on the thermostatic choke shaft, make sure that the bottom of the fast idle cam lever adjusting screw is against the tang on the choke lever.
188 Carry out the adjustments described earlier in this Section.

Carburetor (Model 2700 VV) - dismantling and reassembly

189 Unscrew and remove the fuel inlet fitting, the filter, gasket and spring.
190 Pry off the E-rings from the accelerator pump and choke control rods and then disengage the rods.
191 Unscrew and remove the air cleaner stud.
192 Extract the fixing screws and remove the upper body, noting the location of the longer screws for correct reassembly.
193 Remove the float hinge pin, also the float and float bowl gasket.
194 Remove the fuel inlet valve components.
195 Remove the accelerator pump rod and seal, also the link and its pin and the swivel.
196 Remove the choke control rod, seal and retainer.
197 Pry off the choke hinge pin E-ring and slide the pin from the housing.
198 Remove the nut from the cold enrichment rod and remove the lever, swivel and vacuum regulator as an assembly.
199 Slide the cold enrichment rod from the upper body nylon seal.
200 Extract the venturi valve cover plate screws and remove the cover, gasket and roller bearings.
201 Remove the venturi air bypass screw.
202 A small clamp should now be used to push out the venturi pivot pins.
203 Slide the venturi valve to free it from the body and then remove the pivot pin bushings.
204 Remove the metering rod pivot pins, the metering rods and the springs. Mark the rods as to which side they are located to ensure correct reassembly.
205 Block the venturi valve in the wide open position and remove the jet plugs which are recessed into the upper body. These are brass plugs which can be carefully drilled and then pryed out.
206 Before the main metering jets are removed, their setting must be determined and recorded. To do this, carefully turn each jet clockwise, counting the exact number of turns until it is seated. Record the number of turns to the nearest ¼ turn.
207 Unscrew and remove the jets and O-rings, identifying them as to throttle and choke sides.
20 Remove the accelerator pump and dismantle it if necessary.
209 Remove the venturi valve limiter adjusting screw from the throttle side of the venturi valve.
210 If the fuel inlet needs cleaning, extract the pipe plug from the fuel inlet boss.
211 Turning your attention to the main body, remove the cranking enrichment solenoid and its O-ring seal.
212 Extract the fixing screws and remove the venturi valve diaphragm cover, guide and spring. Tap the cover off if necessary, do not pry it.
213 Loosen the diaphragm and slide it from the main body.
214 Extract the venturi valve diaphragm adjusting screw.
215 Center-punch the cover plug until loose and remove it so that the venturi valve limiter stop can be removed.
216 Withdraw the cranking fuel control assembly from the bottom of the fuel bowl only if essential. To do this, the bi-metal will have to be bent aside to expose the discharge port and then the jet plug removed.
217 Invert the main body and catch the accelerator pump check ball and weight.
218 Extract the five fixing screws which hold the throttle body to the main body and then remove the choke heat shield screw and the shield itself.
219 To dismantle the throttle body, remove the throttle control device according to type (dashpot, solenoid), also the kickdown return spring (automatic transmission).
220 Extract the choke thermostatic housing screws, retainer ring, housing and the gasket.
221 Remove the choke thermostatic lever screw and lever, slide the choke shaft and lever from the carburetor body and remove the fast idle cam.
222 Remove the high cam speed positioner assembly, including the cover and the return spring, also the diaphragm and the rod.
223 In the rare event of the choke housing bushing needing renewal, it will have to be unstaked and the casting supported while it is pressed out and a new one pressed in.
224 Remove the choke heat tube fitting and the throttle solenoid positioner off (TSP-OFF) idle speed screw.
225 Remove the throttle shaft retaining nut, the fast idle adjusting levers and the adjusting screw.
226 Only remove the throttle valve plates if absolutely essential and then mark them carefully before removing them to ensure correct refitting. Note that the fixing screws are staked in position. Grind off the staking to release the screws and use new screws at reassembly.
227 Before the throttle shaft can be removed, it will be necessary to drive the limiter lever stop pin down until it is flush with the shaft.
228 Slide the throttle shaft from its location and then remove the venturi valve limiter lever and bushing.
229 With the carburetor completely dismantled, clean all components and renew worn or damaged items. Obtain a repair kit which will contain all the necessary gaskets and other renewable parts.
230 Reassembly is a reversal of dismantling, but observe the following special points.
231 Renew the venturi valve limiter stop pin before reassembling the throttle shaft assembly.
232 Stake new screws to fix the throttle valve plates and make sure that the venturi valve limiter stop pin is exposed by 1/8 in (3.1 mm).
233 When assembling the upper body to the main body make sure

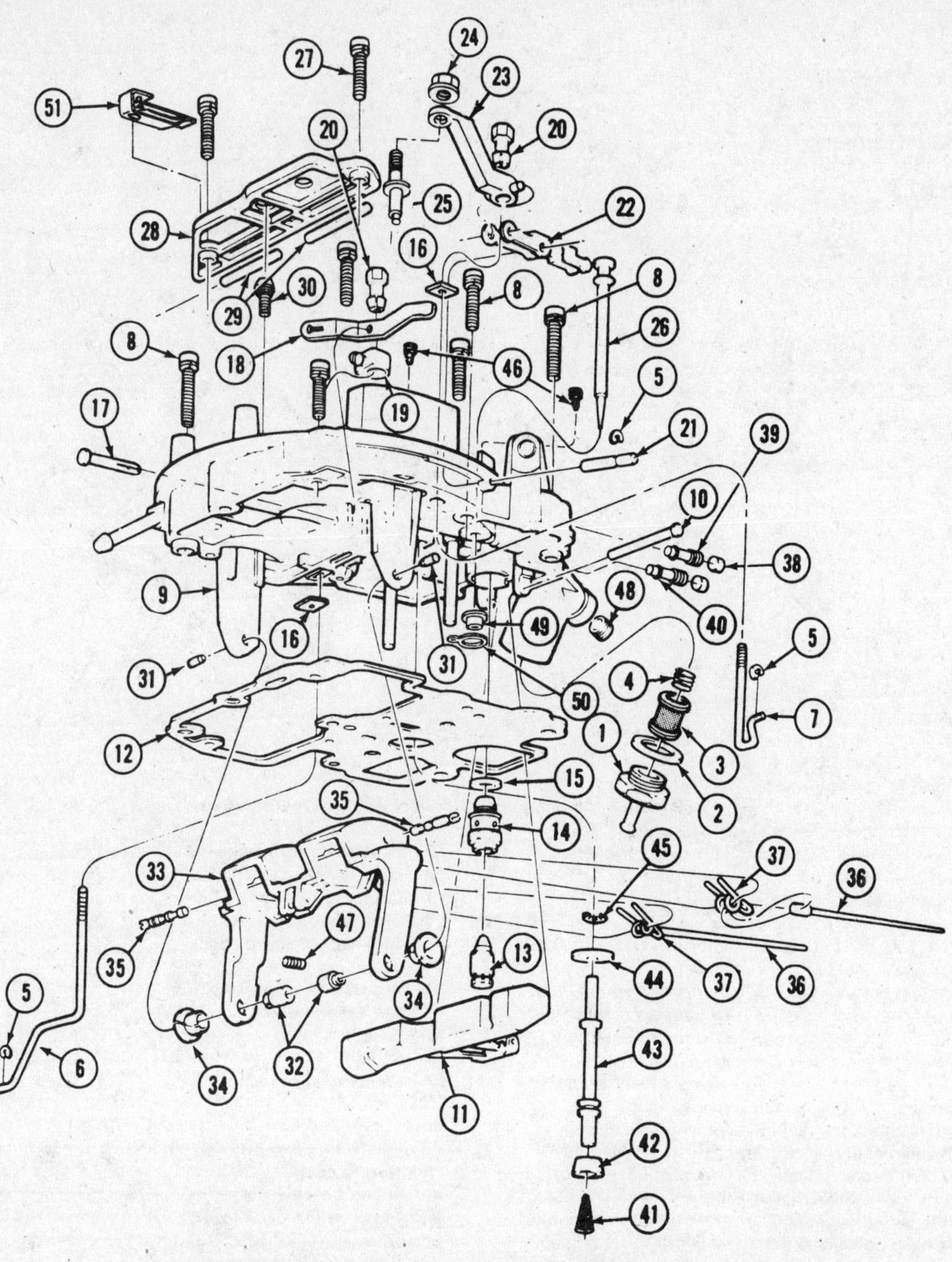

Fig. 13.87 Upper body components (Model 2700 VV carburetor)

1 Fuel inlet
2 Gasket
3 Filter
4 Spring
5 E-ring
6 Accelerator pump rod
7 Choke control rod
8 Screws
9 Upper body
10 Float hinge pin
11 Float
12 Gasket
13 Fuel inlet valve
14 Seat
15 Gasket
16 Dust excluder
17 Pin
18 Link
19 Swivel
20 Nylon nut
21 Choke hinge pin
22 Cold enrichment rod lever
23 Swivel
24 Vacuum regulator nut
25 Vacuum regulator
26 Cold enrichment rod
27 Screw
28 Venturi valve cover plate
29 Roller bearing
30 Air bypass screw
31 Pivot plug
32 Pivot pin
33 Venturi valve
34 Pivot pin bushing
35 Metering rod pivot pin
36 Metering rod
37 Spring
38 Plug
39 Main metering jet
40 O-ring
41 Pump return spring
42 Cup
43 Plunger
44 Internal vent valve
45 E-ring
46 Idle screw
47 Venturi valve limiter screw
48 Plug
49 Seal
50 Seal retainer
51 Hot idle compensator

13

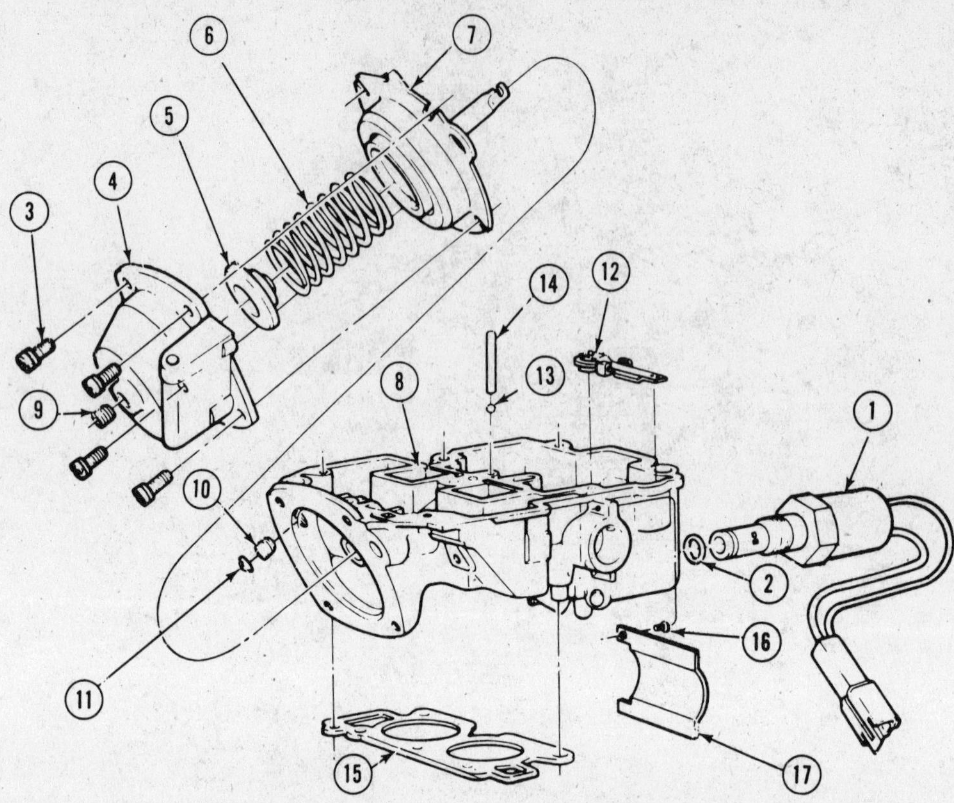

Fig. 13.88 Main body components (Model 2700 VV carburetor)

1 Cranking enrichment solenoid
2 O-ring
3 Screw
4 Venturi valve diaphragm cover
5 Diaphragm spring guide
6 Diaphragm spring
7 Diaphragm assembly
8 Main body
9 Venturi valve adjusting screw
10 Wide open stop screw
11 Plug
12 Cranking fuel control assembly
13 Accelerator pump check ball
14 Accelerator pump check ball weight
15 Gasket
16 Screw
17 Choke heat shield

that the venturi valve diaphragm stem engages with the venturi valve correctly.
234 Carry out the adjustments described earlier for this carburetor.
235 Adjustment of the curb idle speed must be carried out after the unit has been refitted to the vehicle as described earlier.
236 As there is no external means of mixture adjustment it will be appreciated how important it is to reset the position of the main metering jets exactly as set during production (refer to prragraph 206).

Electronic engine control system

237 Cars destined for operation in California and powered by a 2.3 liter engine are equipped with the following components and systems:

(a) Holley-Weber 6500 feedback carburetor
(b) Thermactor emission control
(c) Dual catalytic converter

238 More important is the engine control system which is used in conjunction with these devices. This system employs an electronic control unit (ECU) which monitors the composition of the exhaust gases by means of a sensor screwed into the exhaust manifold, which in turn varies the mixture to ensure the lowest exhaust emissions.
239 The dual type catalytic converter used in this arrangement incorporates two sections in one shell with a mixing chamber between them.

6 Ignition system

Dura Spark electronic ignition

1 Commencing with 1977 versions, a new high energy Dura Spark I or II ignition system is used.
2 The Dura Spark I differs from the earlier electronic system by having special primary wiring, a new ignition coil, electronic module and distributor cap in addition to modified secondary wiring and wide gap spark plugs.
3 When it is in operation, the Dura Spark I system senses current flow through the ignition coil and adjusts 'dwell' to ensure maximum spark intensity.
4 The coil-ON time is adjusted for best efficiency in relation to engine speed. If the electronic module senses that the ignition switch is ON but the distributor is not rotating, then it will automatically switch the coil current off after a period of one second. The module cycle can be re-established if the key is turned to the START position or to OFF/ON.
5 Dura Spark II is basically a development of the pre-1977 solid state breakerless system but with two major differences: the ballast resistor value has been changed to boost coil current, and a new design of rotor is used. In addition, a new distributor cap and wide-gap spark plugs are fitted in order to accept the new higher energy level.
6 It is important to appreciate that the Dura Spark II amplifier

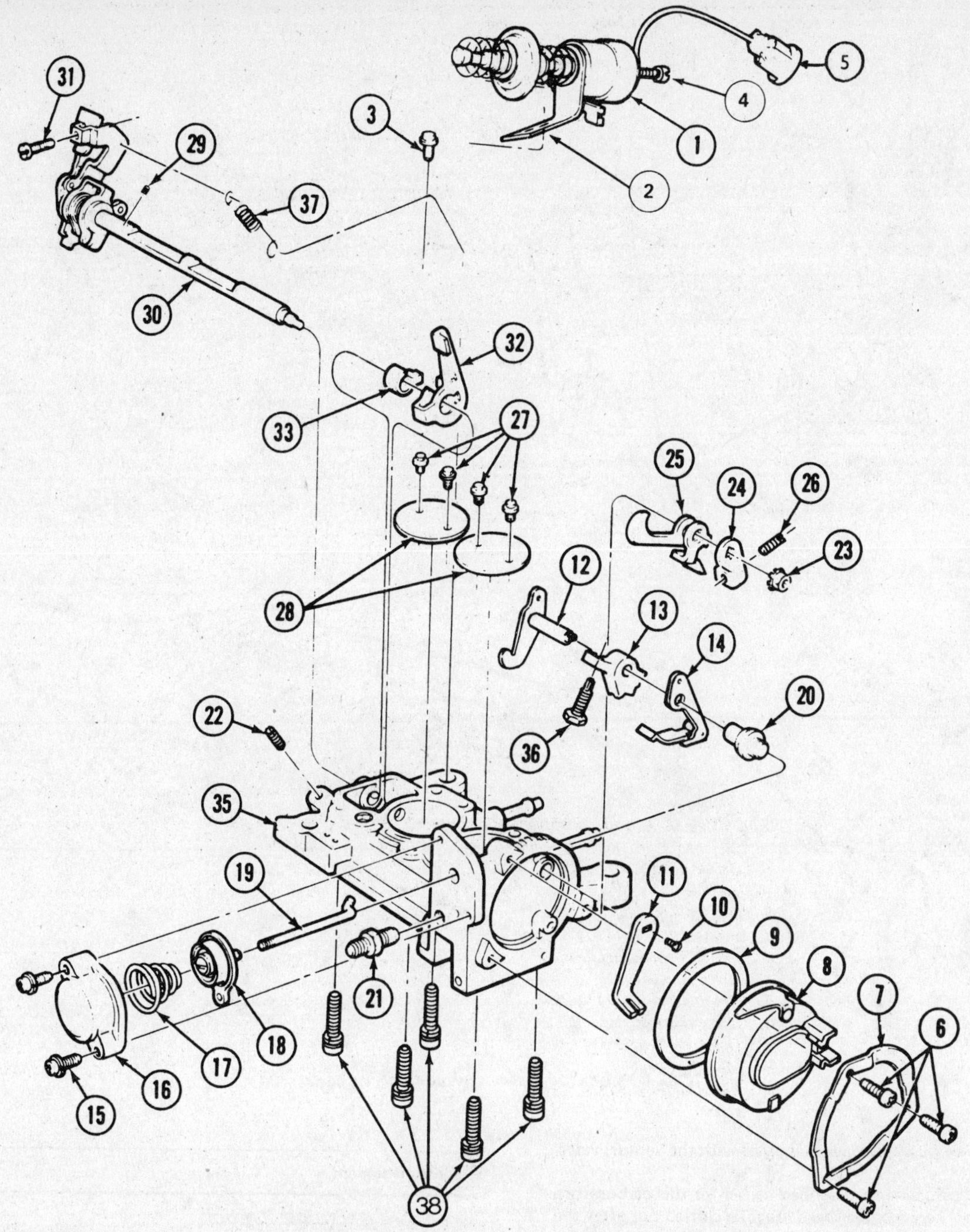

Fig. 13.89 Throttle body components (Model 2700 VV carburetor)

1 *Throttle return control device*
2 *Bracket*
3 *Mounting screw*
4 *TSP-ON screw*
5 *Connector*
6 *Screw*
7 *Choke housing retainer*
8 *Choke housing*
9 *Gasket*
10 *Screw*
11 *Choke thermostatic lever*
12 *Choke lever/shaft*
13 *Fast idle cam*
14 *High speed cam positioner*
15 *Screw*
16 *High speed cam positioner diaphragm cover*
17 *Diaphragm spring*
18 *Diaphragm assembly*
19 *High speed cam positioner rod*
20 *Choke housing bushing*
21 *Choke heat tube fitting*
22 *TSP-OFF adjusting screw*
23 *Nut*
24 *Fast idle adjusting lever*
25 *Fast idle lever*
26 *Fast idle adjusting screw*
27 *Throttle plate screws*
28 *Throttle plates*
29 *Venturi valve limiter stop pin*
30 *Throttle shaft assembly*
31 *Transmission kickdown screw*
32 *Venturi valve limiter lever*
33 *Venturi valve limiter bushing*
35 *Throttle body*
36 *Fast idle cam screw*
37 *Kickdown lever return spring*
38 *Screw*

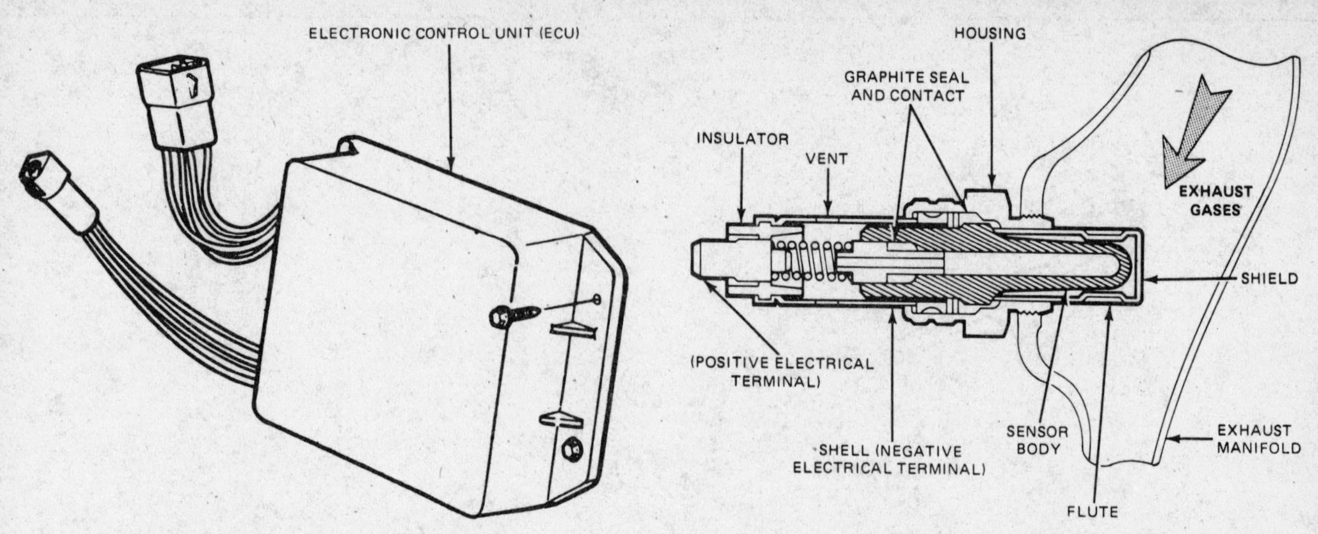

Fig. 13.90 Electronic Control Unit (ECU)

Fig. 13.91 Exhaust Gas Oxygen sensor (EGO)

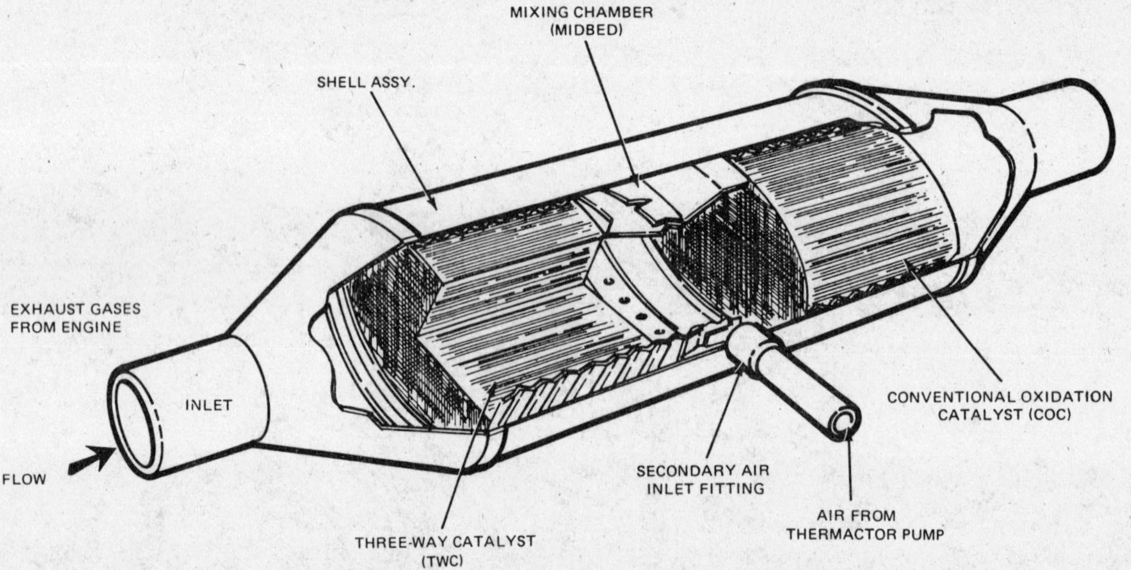

Fig. 13.92 Cutaway view of dual type catalytic converter

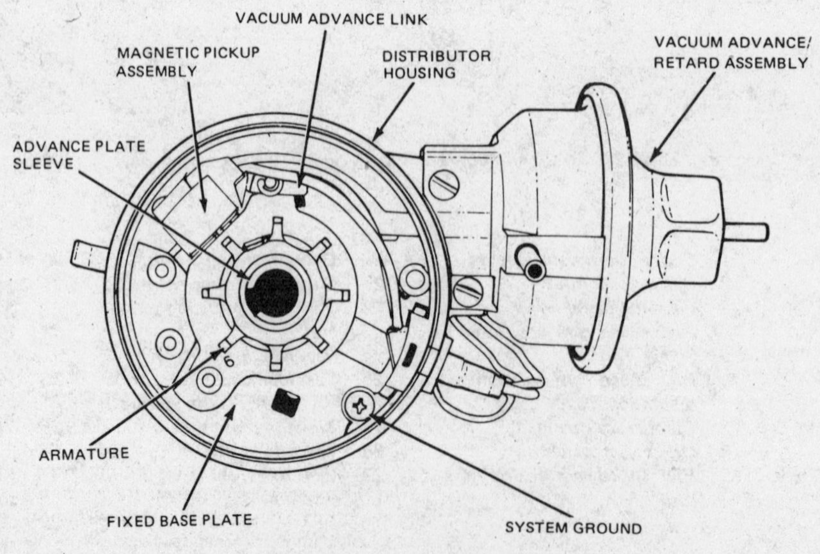

Fig. 13.93 V8 ignition distributor

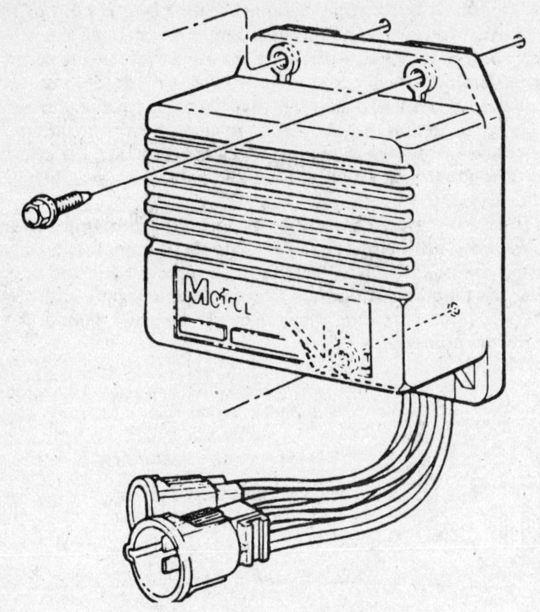

Fig. 13.94 Typical Dura Spark electronic module

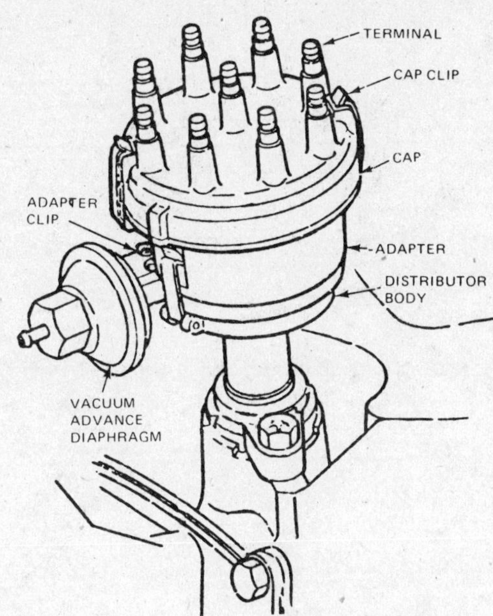

Fig. 13.95 V8 distributor installed

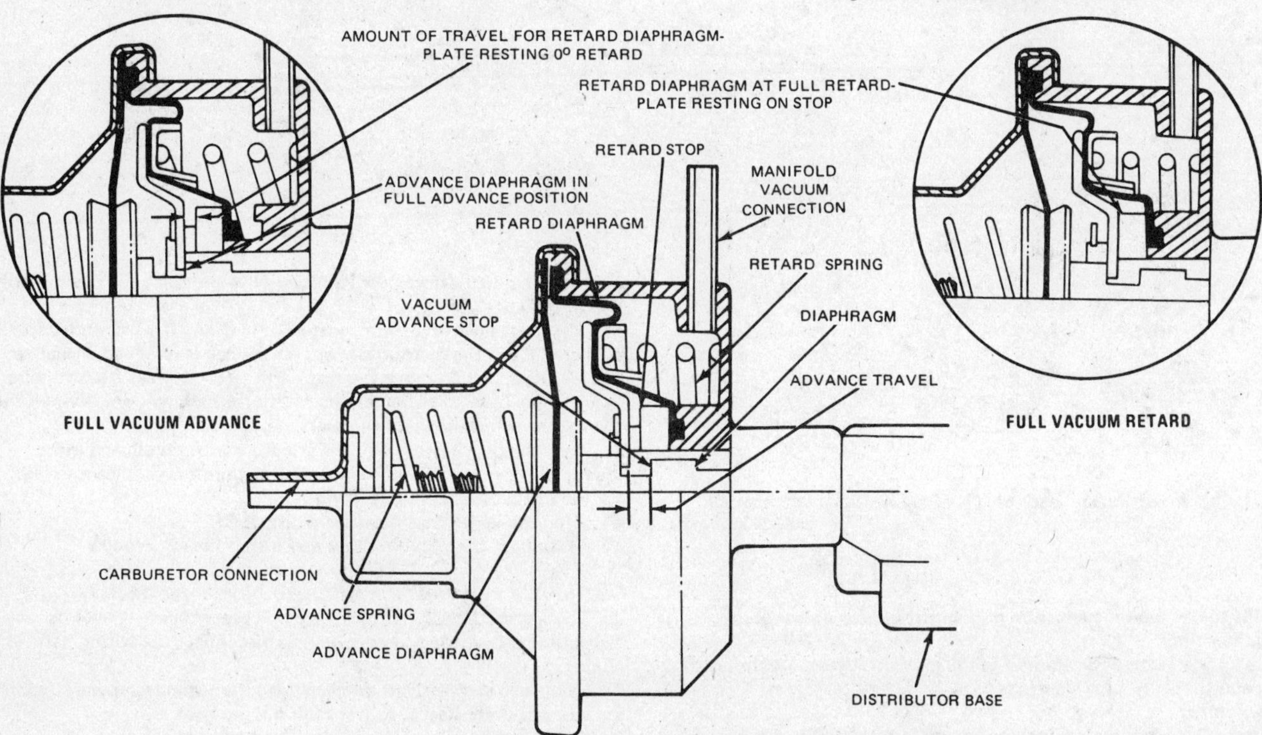

Fig. 13.96 Distributor dual diaphragm vacuum advance

13

module and coil are ON when the ignition switch is turned on. As a result of this, a spark is generated when the key is turned off. *Keep the key in the OFF position when carrying out under-hood operations.* Removing the distributor cap with the ignition on may cause the engine to fire.

7 The Dura Spark II module may be modified for certain applications by the inclusion of two additional devices described in the following paragraphs.

Altitude compensator

8 This is essentially a barometric switch which provides an automatic retard signal at varying altitudes to provide advanced timing at high levels and retarded timing for spark knock elimination at lower levels.

Economy calibration switch

9 This is a vacuum switch which senses manifold vacuum to provide an automatic retard signal to the distributor when operating under heavy engine load but still permitting spark advance under light to moderate engine loads.

10 A dual vacuum control unit is fitted to the distributor. The outer (primary) diaphragm senses the carburetor vacuum just upstream of the throttle butterflies to advance ignition timing; the inner (secondary) diaphragm senses manifold vacuum. When the manifold vacuum is high during deceleration or at curb idle, the secondary diaphragm retards the spark. As soon as the throttle is opened, the primary diaphragm takes control and causes the spark to advance. The purpose of the

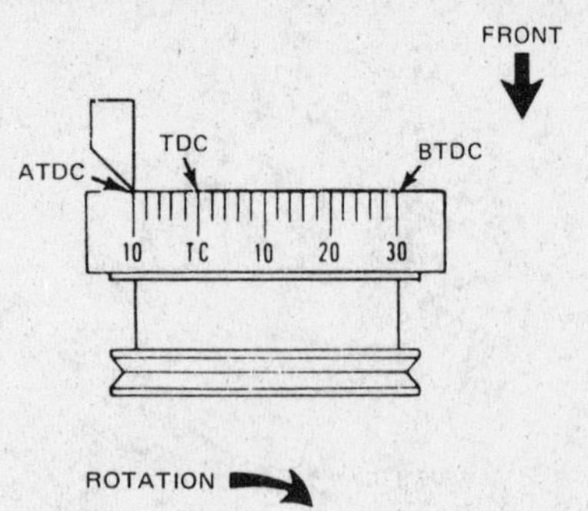

Fig. 13.97 Crankshaft damper timing marks (V8 engine)

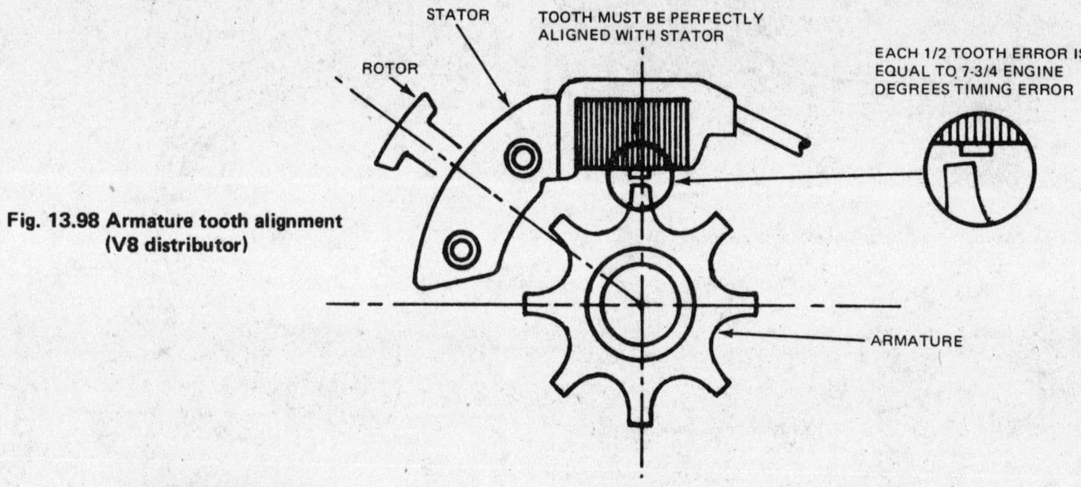

Fig. 13.98 Armature tooth alignment (V8 distributor)

Fig. 13.99 Distributor spark plug lead connections (V8 engine)

system is to decrease the emission of unburnt hydrocarbons at low throttle openings.

11 The only adjustments required to the ignition system are those for timing and the spark plug electrode gaps.

Ignition timing

12 Although the method of ignition timing is described in Chapter 4, Section 17, it should be noted that due to the high coil currents present in Dura Spark systems, the use of timing lights (stroboscopes) which have capacitive or direct connecting pick-ups should be avoided. The use of inductive type pick-ups is recommended, connected in accordance with the manufacturers' instructions.

Distributor (V8 engine) - removal and refitting

13 Remove the air cleaner and disconnect the distributor wiring harness plug.

14 Disconnect the vacuum hoses from the distributor.

15 Remove the distributor cap and place it to one side without disconnecting the high tension wires.

16 The distributor is mounted centrally on the engine above the coolant pump. The position of the rotor relative to the rim of the distributor body, and the relationship of the distributor body to the cylinder block, should be marked before the distributor clamp bolt is removed and the distributor lifted from the engine.

17 If the crankshaft is not rotated while the distributor is out of the car, then the distributor can be installed simply by aligning the marks made before removal. Anticipate the movement of the rotor during installation as it will turn as the drivegears mesh. Set the position of the rotor a few degrees in advance of its final alignment position before installing the distributor to allow for this rotation.

18 If the crankshaft has been rotated while the distributor is out of the car, or if the distributor was not marked before removal, install it in the following way.

19 Turn the crankshaft on the starter motor, or by applying a wrench to the pulley bolt, until No 1 piston is rising on its compression stroke. Compression can be felt if No 1 spark plug is removed and the finger placed over the plug hole. Continue to turn the crankshaft until the specified static timing mark on the crankshaft vibration damper is aligned with the pointer.

20 Hold the distributor over its recess with the cap clips positioned as shown in Fig. 13.99.

21 When installed, the rotor must align with the No 1 cylinder spark plug contact in the distributor cap. As the cap is removed, visualize this setting and then move the rotor arm a few degrees from its final required position to anticipate its rotation which will occur when the distributor is installed and the gears mesh.

22 Turn the distributor until the armature tooth is aligned quite square with the stator and then fit and tighten the distributor clamp.

23 Fit the distributor cap and wires.

24 Time the ignition as previously described.

25 Reconnect the vacuum pipes and install the air cleaner.

Distributor (V8 engine) - dismantling and reassembly

26 To remove the magnetic pick-up coil assembly, first take off the distributor cap, rotor and adapter and disconnect the wiring harness plug.

27 Using two screwdrivers as levers, pry the armature upward from the advance plate sleeve. Extract the roll pin.

28 Remove the large wire retaining clip from the groove in the baseplate.

29 Remove the map-ring that secures the vacuum advance link to the pick-up.

30 Extract the ground screw from the pick-up assembly and remove the assembly from the distributor.

31 Lift the vacuum advance arm off the post on the pick-up assembly and move it outwards against the distributor housing.

32 To remove the vacuum advance unit, the cap, rotor and adapter must first be withdrawn and the vacuum hoses disconnected.

33 Remove the spring clip that secures the diaphragm link to the movable advance plate.

34 Remove the diaphragm unit securing screws and withdraw the unit by tilting it downward to disengage the link from the post on the movable advance plate.

35 To remove the fixed baseplate, first withdraw the distributor cap, adapter and rotor and the vacuum advance diaphragm unit.

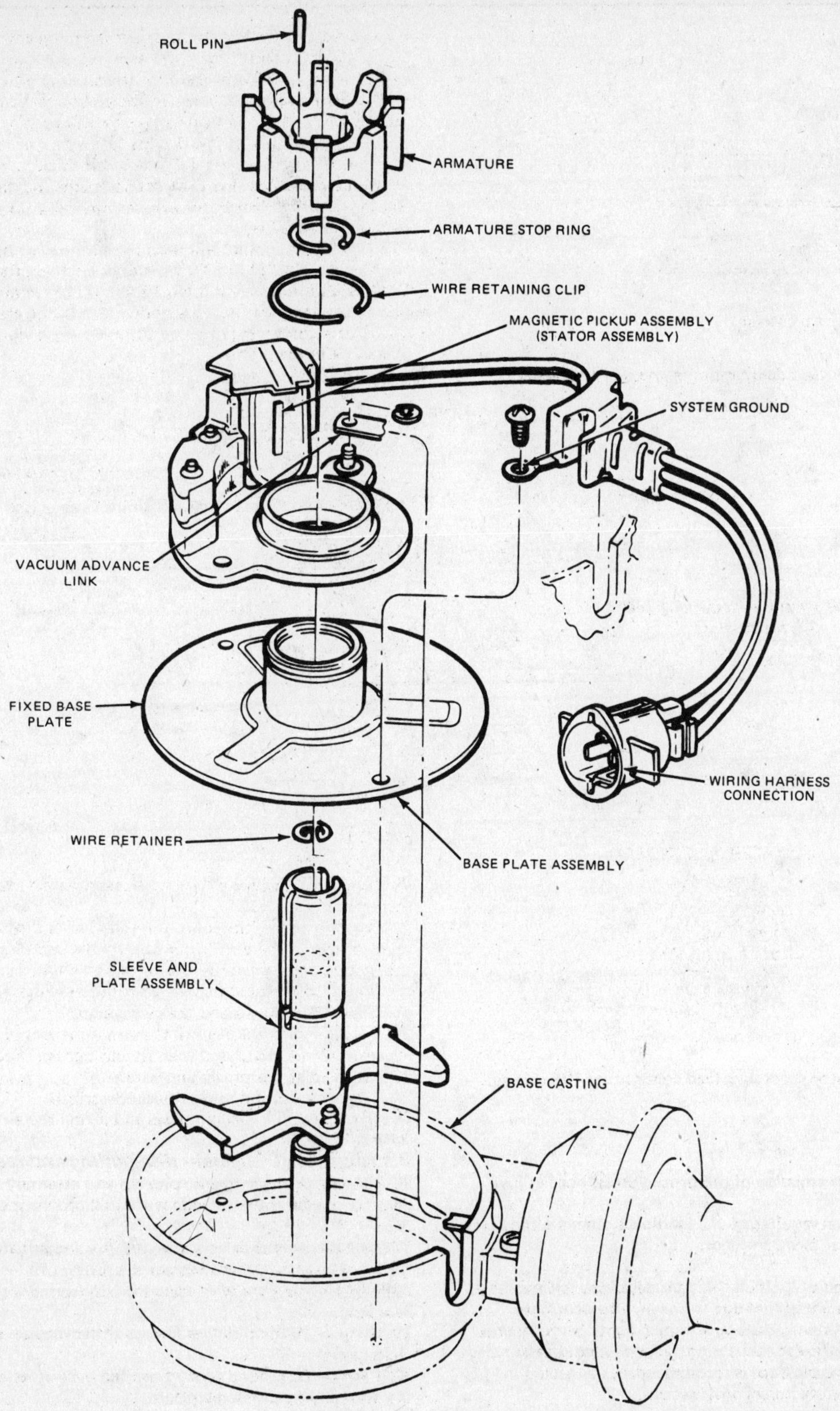

Fig. 13.100 Exploded view of Dura Spark distributor

Fig. 13.101 Typical Ported Vacuum Switch (PVS)

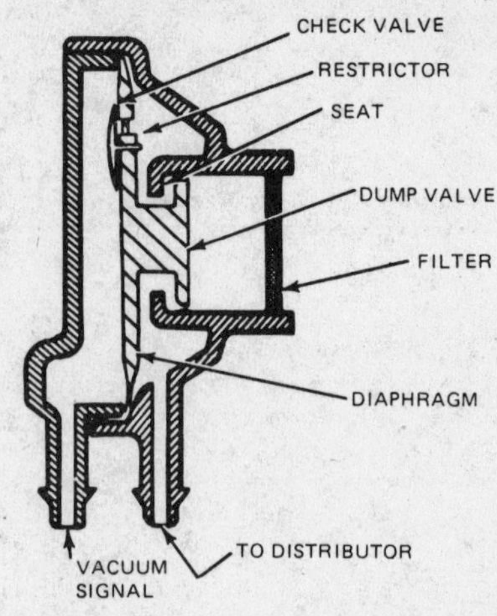

Fig. 13.102 Distributor vacuum vent valve

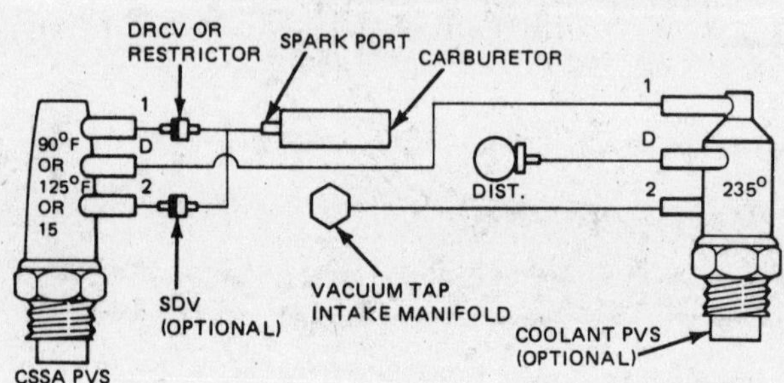

Fig. 13.103 Cold Start Spark Advance (CSSA) system

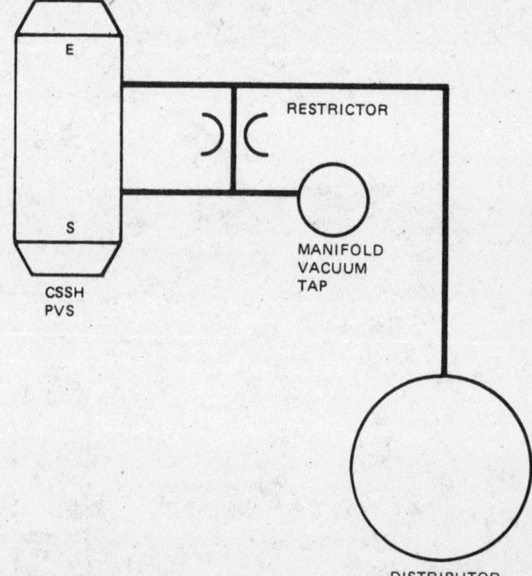

Fig. 13.104 Cold Start Spark Hold (CSSH) system

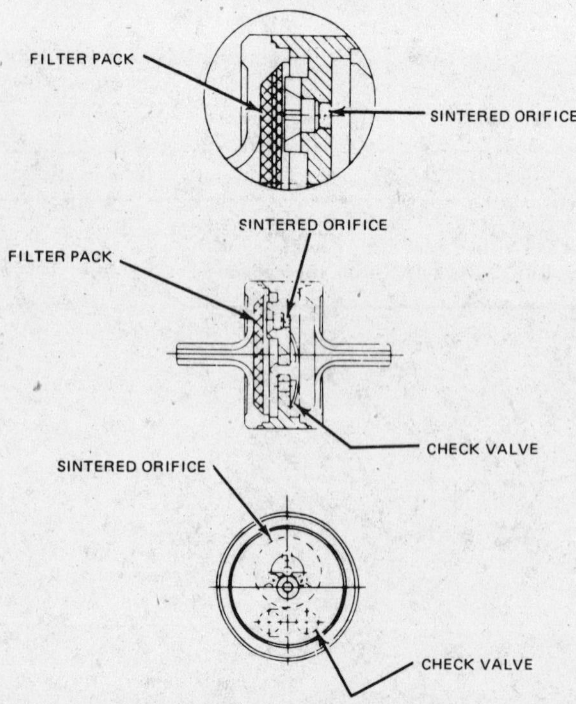

FIG. 13.105 Spark Delay Valve (SDV)

36 Remove the magnetic pick-up as previously described.
37 The baseplate will now be held in position by one screw only and once this is extracted, the baseplate can be removed. Do not attempt to dismantle further by removing the plate, counterweights or springs.
38 Reassembly of all components is a reversal of dismantling.

Emission control related spark regulating devices

39 Ported vacuum switches (PVS) are located in various places to vary the vacuum advance to the distributor according to coolant temperature and so increase or decrease the engine idle speed.
40 A distributor vacuum vent valve is fitted to some engines to prevent fuel seepage into the distributor vacuum diaphragm and also to act as a spark advance delay valve. The valve helps to reduce exhaust emission by delaying spark advance during periods of light acceleration and by eliminating advance vacuum during heavy acceleration or deceleration and when the engine is idling.
41 On some models, a cold start spark advance (CSSA) system is incorporated. Its purpose is to momentarily trap vacuum advance at the distributor diaphragm when coolant temperature is below 125°F (51.7°C) in order to retard the spark. At temperatures above this level, spark advance occurs normally, while at temperatures above 235°F (112.8°C), engine idle speed is increased, the intake manifold vacuum being applied directly to the distributor instead of being controlled from the carburetor as is the case at lower temperatures.
42 Cold start spark hold (CSSH) system, where fitted, provides momentary spark advance hold during acceleration when the engine is cold as a means of improving cold engine acceleration. When the engine coolant temperature is less than 128°F (53°C) the system remains closed and distributor vacuum is applied through the restrictor. At cold start, high vacuum acts on the distributor

diaphragm to give maximum spark advance. During cold acceleration, this high vacuum is bled slowly through the restrictor to modify the initial stage of acceleration.
43 Many engines are equipped with spark delay valves to provide closer control of vacuum-operated emission control equipment. These valves have an internal sintered orifice to reduce airflow in one direction and a check valve to permit free airflow in the opposite direction.

Fault diagnosis - electronic ignition systems

Symptom	Reason(s)
Engine fails to start	Incorrect air gap (wear in distributor shaft) Loose battery connections Discharged battery Disconnected wires Damp spark plug leads Damp distributor cap interior Faulty control unit Faulty pick-up unit Faulty anti-diesel solenoid
Engine starts and runs but misfires	Faulty spark plugs Cracked distributor cap Cracked rotor Incorrect air gap (wear in distributor shaft) Worn advance mechanism Incorrect plug gap Faulty coil Faulty control unit Faulty pick-up unit Incorrect timing Poor ground connections
Engine overheats, lacks power	Seized centrifugal weights Perforated vacuum pipe Incorrect ignition timing
Engine 'pings'	Timing too advanced Advance mechanism stuck in advanced position Broken counterweight spring Fuel octane rating too low

7 Clutch

Clutch pilot bearing

1 This is of needle roller type and differs in design according to engine capacity.
2 The bearing is located in the center of the flywheel mounting flange at the rear of the crankshaft.
3 If this bearing is worn and is to be renewed, it can be removed using a slide hammer engaged in the notches provided or at the front rim. An alternative method of removal is to fill the bearing two-thirds full of grease and then drive in a close-fitting rod. Hydraulic pressure will eject the bearing.

8 Rear axle and differential

Description (Integral type, 6¾ in ring gear)

1 This axle differs from the removable carrier type described in Chapter 8 by having a detachable cover at the rear of the axle

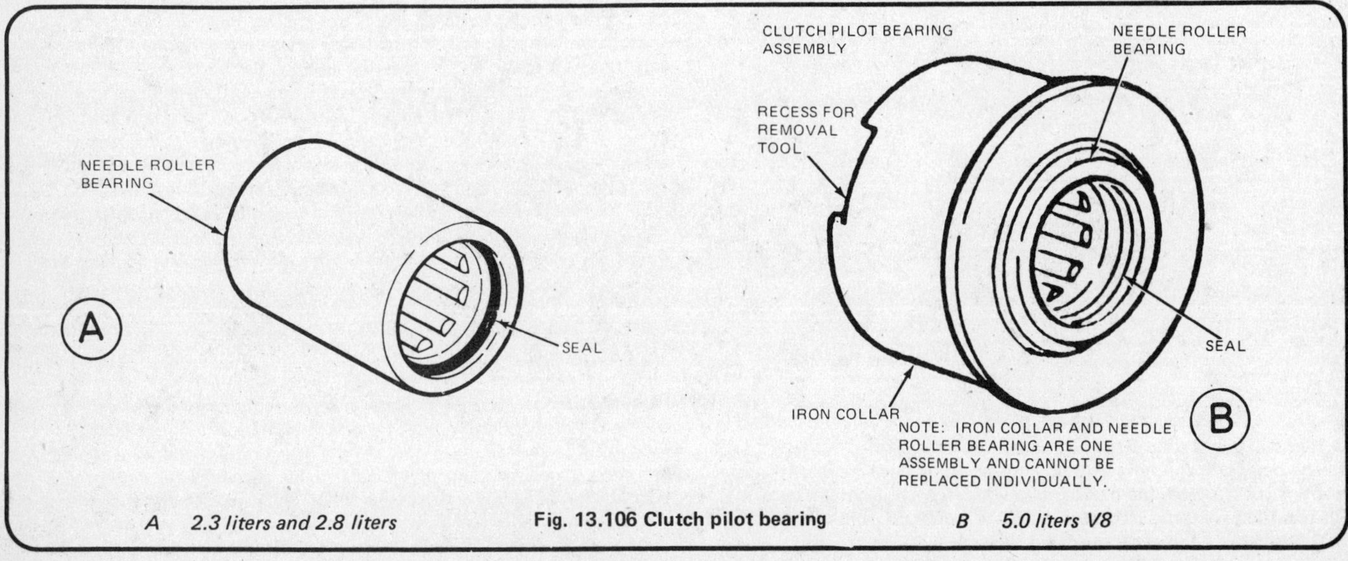

A 2.3 liters and 2.8 liters **Fig. 13.106 Clutch pilot bearing** *B 5.0 liters V8*

13

housing to provide access to the final drive gears and differential. A silicone type sealant is used for this cover instead of a conventional gasket.

2 Before deciding to overhaul a rear axle, owners are advised to check the availability and price of spare parts, and to compare the likely cost of overhaul with the cost of a new or reconditioned axle.

Rear axle - removal and installation

3 Raise the rear of the car and support it under the body sideframe members.

4 Remove the rear roadwheels.

5 Support the weight of the rear axle on (preferably) a trolley jack.

6 With a scriber or file mark the pinion driving flange and driveshaft so that they may be refitted together in their original positions.

7 Undo and remove the four U-bolt securing nuts, detach the rear of the driveshaft from the pinion driving flange and carefully lower the driveshaft. To give better access the driveshaft can be drawn rearwards from the gearbox, but remember to place a container under the gearbox end, to catch oil that will seep out.

8 Drain the lubricant by unbolting the rear cover and withdrawing it so that the oil can run out.

9 Disconnect the lower end of each shock absorber from the spring plate by undoing and removing the securing nut. Recover the lower washer and bush.

10 Refer to Chapter 8 and remove both axleshafts and oil seals.

11 Detach the differential ventilation tube from the top left hand side of the differential carrier.

12 Disconnect the brake line T-connector from the axle housing. Detaching the brake line rather than disconnecting it means that the system will not have to be bled on reassembly.

13 Detach the brake line from its clip on the axle housing.

14 Remove both brake backplate assemblies from the ends of the axle housing. Hang them from the body on string or wire. It should be noted that the brake lines and parking brake cable do not have to be disconnected.

15 Undo and remove the rear spring U-bolt nuts.

16 The complete rear axle assembly may now be withdrawn from the underside of the car.

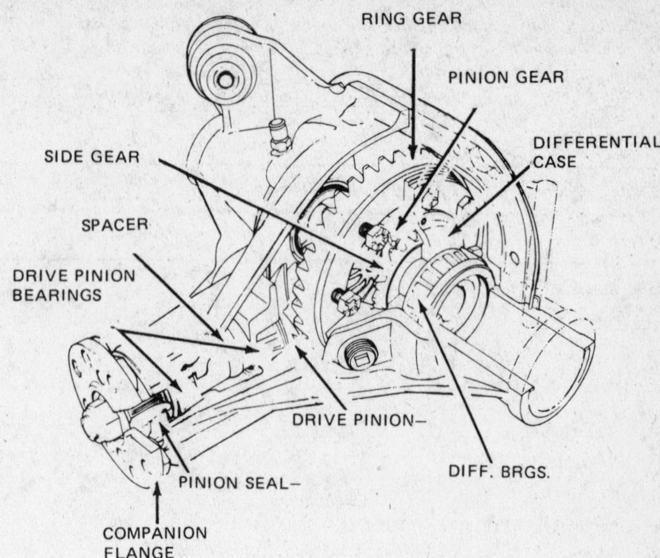

Fig. 13.107 Cutaway view of differential (integral 6¾ in type)

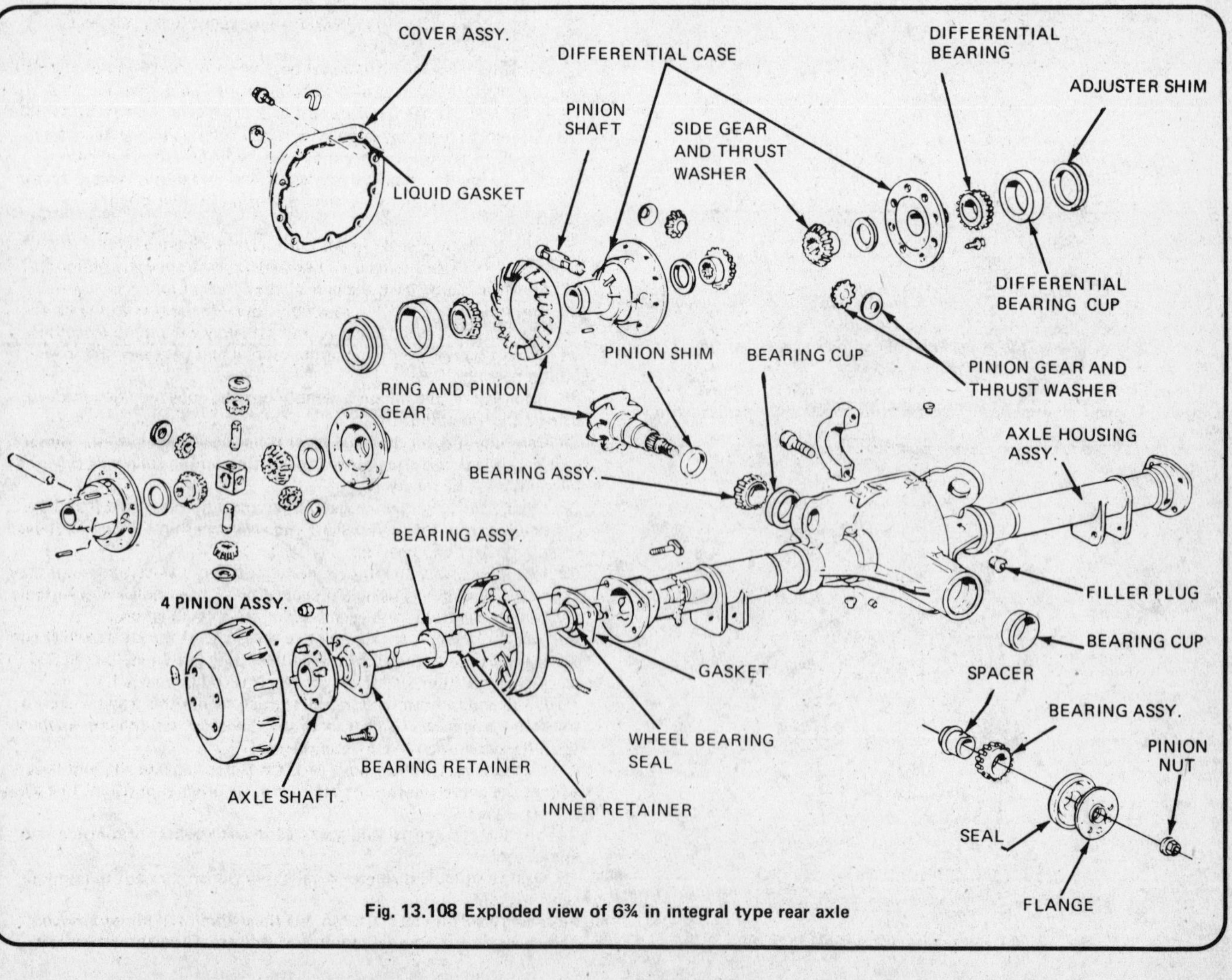

Fig. 13.108 Exploded view of 6¾ in integral type rear axle

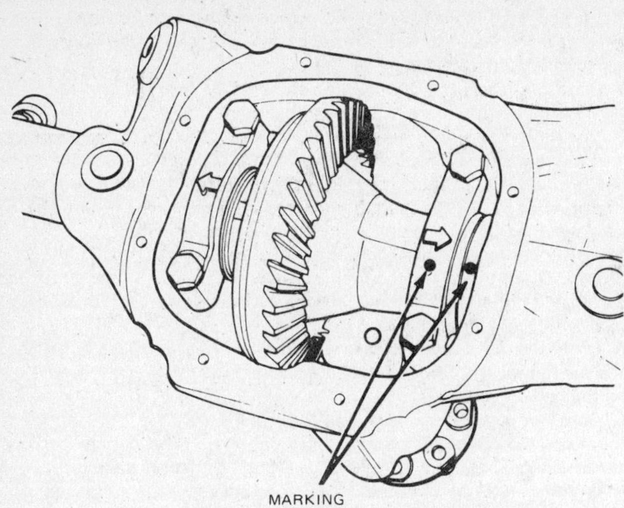

Fig. 13.109 Differential cap and case markings

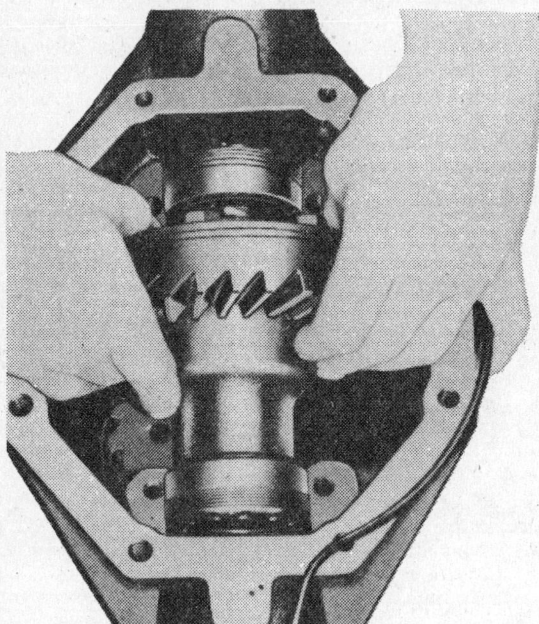

Fig. 13.110 Removing differential

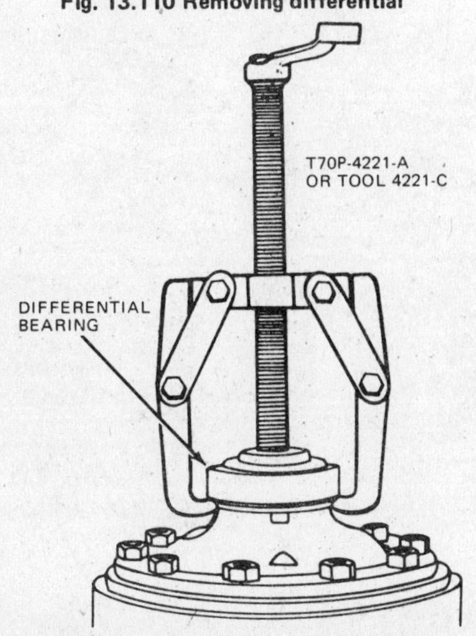

Fig. 13.111 Removing differential bearing

17 Refitting the rear axle is the reverse sequence to removal but the following additional points should be noted:

- *(a) Do not forget to refill the axle housing and gearbox (if necessary) with the correct amount and grade of oil.*
- *(b) Align the marks on the propeller shaft and pinion flange.*

Integral type final drive/differential - overhaul

18 Most dealers will prefer to fit a complete set of gears, bearings, spacers and thrust washers rather than renew individual parts which may have worn. To do the job properly requires the use of special and expensive tools which the majority of dealers do not have.

19 The primary object of these special tools is to enable the mesh of the crownwheel to the pinion to be very accurately set and thus ensure that noise is kept to a minimum. If any increase in noise cannot be tolerated (providing that the rear axle is not already noisy due to a defective part) then it is best to allow the local Ford dealer to carry out the repairs.

20 Rear axles have been rebuilt without the use of special tools so if the possibility of a slight increase in noise can be tolerated then it is quite possible for any do-it-yourself mechanic to successfully recondition the rear axle without special tools.

21 The axle can be dismantled without removing it from the car but it is easier if the unit is removed to the bench as described earlier and in Chapter 8.

22 Wash down the final drive housing area, to remove all traces of dirt and oil. Wipe dry with a non-fluffy rag.

23 Support the rear axle on wooden blocks.

24 Place a container of at least 3.5 pints (2 liters) capacity under the rear axle casing to catch the oil as the rear cover is released.

25 Undo and remove the bolts and spring washers that secure the rear cover to the final drive housing. Lift away the rear cover and its gasket.

26 Refer to Chapter 8 and remove the axleshafts if they are still in position.

27 Remove the differential bearing adjustment locks. These are located on the bearing caps.

28 Suitably mark the differential bearing caps and casing to ensure that the caps are refitted in their original position. Later caps are marked.

29 Undo and remove the differential bearing caps. Be careful to hold the differential assembly otherwise it will roll out of the axle casing.

30 The differential assembly may now be lifted out. Take care to recover the bearing cups (outer tracks) and also ensure that they are kept in such a way that they can be refitted in their original positions.

31 Hold the pinion shaft flange with a large adjustable type wrench or self-grip wrench and using a socket undo and remove the pinion nut.

32 Slide the flange from the end of the drive pinion.

33 Carefully tap the piston assembly towards the rear of the axle casing with a soft-faced hammer and lift away the pinion assembly.

34 Using a screwdriver remove the oil seal and lift away the front pinion bearing.

35 If necessary, the pinion assembly bearing cups may be removed using a shoft metal drift.

36 Carefully inspect the large taper roller bearing behind the pinion gear and if it shows signs of wear or pitting on the rollers or cage the bearings must be renewed.

37 Using a universal two-legged puller and suitable thrust pad draw the bearing from the pinion shaft. Recover the shims located between the pinion gear and bearing.

38 If it is necessary to remove the two differential case bearings they may next be removed using a universal two-legged puller and suitable thrust pad. Carefully ease each bearing from its location.

39 Using a scriber mark the relative positions of the crownwheel and differential case so that the crownwheel (ring gear) may be refitted in its original position, unless, of course, it is to be renewed.

40 Undo and remove the ten bolts which secure the crownwheel to the differential case. Using a soft-faced hammer, tap the crownwheel from its location on the differential case.

41 Mark the relative positions of the differential case and end-cover, so that the end-cover may be refitted in its original position. Lift away the end-cover.

42 Lift the differential side-gear and thrust washer from inside the end-cover.

43 Using a suitable diameter parallel pin punch, tap out the pinion shaft lockpin.

44 Using a soft metal drift, tap out the differential pinion gearshaft. Lift away the differential pinion and side gears and thrust washers,

taking care to ensure that the thrust washers are kept with their relative gears.

45 The final drive assembly is now dismantled and should be washed in kerosene or gasoline and dried with a clean non-fluffy rag ready for inspection.

46 Carefully inspect all the gear teeth for signs of pitting or wear. If these faults are evident, new parts must be obtained. The crownwheel and pinion are a matched pair so if one of the two requires renewal, a new matched pair must be obtained.

47 If wear is evident on one of the differential pinion gears or side-gears it is far better to obtain a complete set of new gears rather than just replace the worn one.

48 Inspect the thrust washers for signs of score marks or wear and if evident obtain new ones. Before the bearings were removed they should have been inspected for wear. If one bearing is worn it is best to fit a complete new set.

49 With new parts obtained as required, reassembly can begin.

50 Place the side-gear and thrust washer in the differential case.

51 Position the two pinion gears and thrust washer exactly opposite each other in the case so that they are in mesh with the side-gear and also aligned with the pinion shaft holes in the case.

52 Position the pinion shaft in the differential case hole, line the shaft lockpin hole with the pin hole in the case. Tap the shaft into position and secure with the lockpin.

53 Place the side-gear and thrust washer in the differential case cover and refit the cover to the differential case. Line up the previously made marks.

54 Make sure that the crownwheel and its seating is quite clean and then place the crownwheel in position on the differential case. Line up the previously made marks unless new parts are being fitted.

55 Secure the differential case cover and crownwheel with new bolts and washers. If the bolt threads are not pre-coated, apply thread sealant.

56 If the differential case bearings have been removed these should next be refitted. Using a piece of suitable diameter tube, very carefully fit the bearings with the smaller diameter taper outwards. The bearing cage must not in anyway be damaged.

57 Place the shim previously removed behind the pinion gear and using a suitable diameter tube, drive the pinion rear bearing into position. Make sure it is the right way round with the larger diameter against the pinion gear.

58 Slide a new pinion bearing preload spacer on the pinion shaft. The end with the largest diameter (shorter end) should be placed on the pinion shaft first.

59 Refit the front and rear pinion bearing cones (outer tracks) to the axle casing using a suitable diameter drift. Make sure they are the correct way round and fully seated.

60 Well lubricate the pinion bearings with axle oil and insert the front bearing into the casing.

61 Fit a new pinion oil seal in the carrier casting with a suitable diameter drift. Make sure it is fitted squarely as well as the correct way round. Lubricate the oil seal lip.

62 Carefully insert the drive pinion shaft flange into the seal and hold it firmly in position against the front bearing.

63 The pinion assembly may now be inserted into the carrier casing from the rear and engaged with the pinion shaft flange.

64 Fit a new pinion shaft nut. Hold the pinion shaft flange with a self-grip wrench or other suitable means, and tighten the pinion shaft nut slowly. As the nut is tightened the pinion shaft will be pulled onto the front bearing and into the flange. Also the shaft endplay will be reduced. When there is still a little endplay the pinion flange and front bearing will be felt to bottom. This means that contact will have been made with the collapsible spacer.

65 From this point a much greater torque will have to be applied to turn the pinion shaft nut as the collapsible spacer will be progressively compressed.

66 Continue to tighten the pinion shaft nut slowly until the required pinion bearing preload is obtained. **Do not** overtighten otherwise a new collapsible spacer will have to be fitted. Whilst tightening the pinion nut rotate the pinion shaft several times to ensure that the bearings are seating correctly.

67 Lubricate the differential bearings with axle oil and refit the differential case into the axle casing. If the crownwheel and pinion gears are of the non-hunting or partial non-hunting type, fit the differential assembly so that the marked teeth on the pinion indexes between the marked teeth on the ring gear. (White paint is usually used). With the hunting type of crownwheel and pinion gears this indexing is not necessary.

68 Slide the differential assembly along the bearing bores until a slight amount of backlash is felt between the gearteeth. Hold the differential assembly in this position.

69 Refit and set the adjusting nuts in the bores until they just contact the bearings.

70 Carefully position the bearing caps on the carrier casting, ensuring that they are fitted on their original sides as noted and marked during dismantling.

71 Refit the bearing cap bolts and spring washers. As the bolts are tightened turn the adjusting nuts with a suitably shaped hooked tool. (A screwdriver can be used with care).

72 If the adjusting nuts do not turn freely as the cap bolts are tightened, remove the bearing caps and check for damaged threads or incorrectly positioned caps. Tighten the cap bolts to the required torque wrench setting to ensure correct seating.

73 Back off the cap bolts by 5lbf ft (0.7 kgfm) to allow for adjustment of crownwheel/pinion mesh.

74 If possible mount a dial indicator gauge so that the probe is resting on one of the teeth of the crownwheel and determine the backlash between the crownwheel and pinion. The backlash is varied by rotating

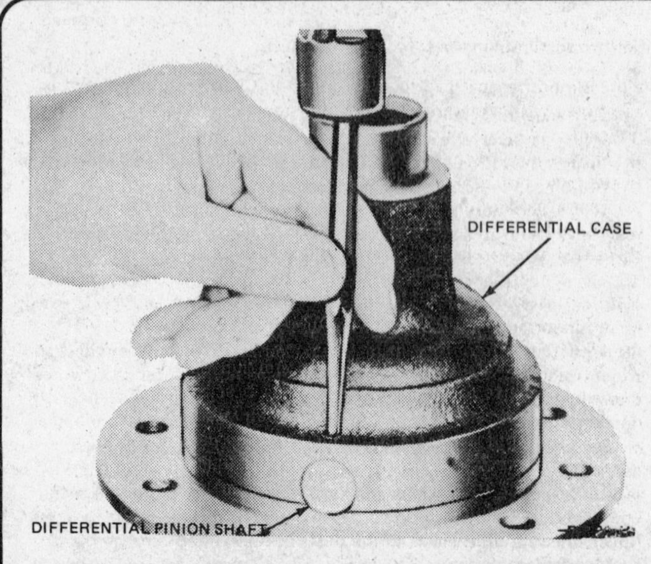

Fig. 13.112 Removing differential pinion shaft lockpin

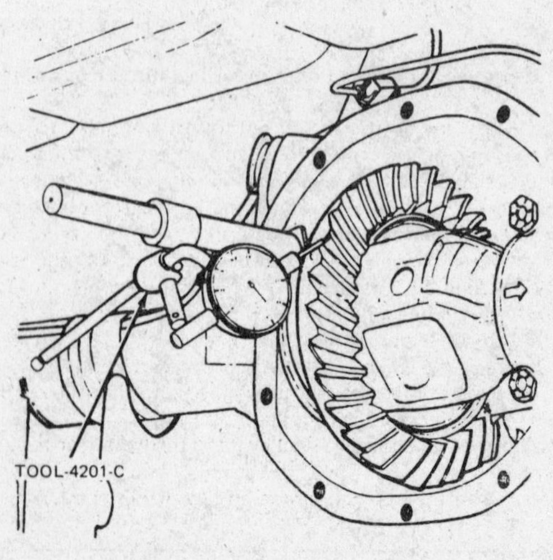

Fig. 13.113 Checking pinion/ring gear backlash

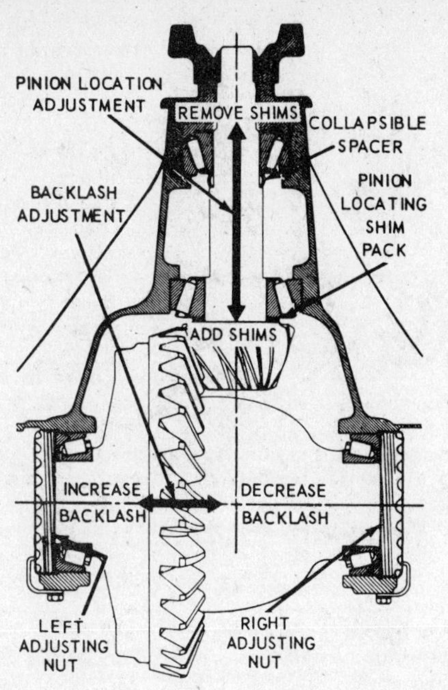

Fig. 13.114 Ring gear and pinion adjustment diagram

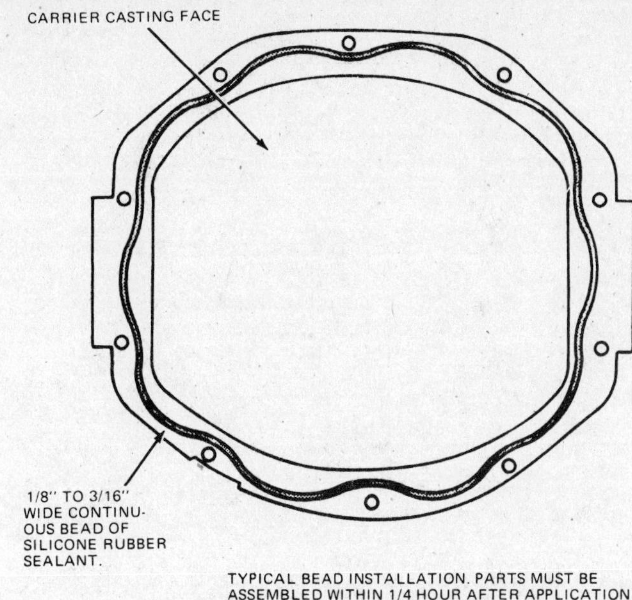

Fig. 13.115 Differential rear cover sealing bead

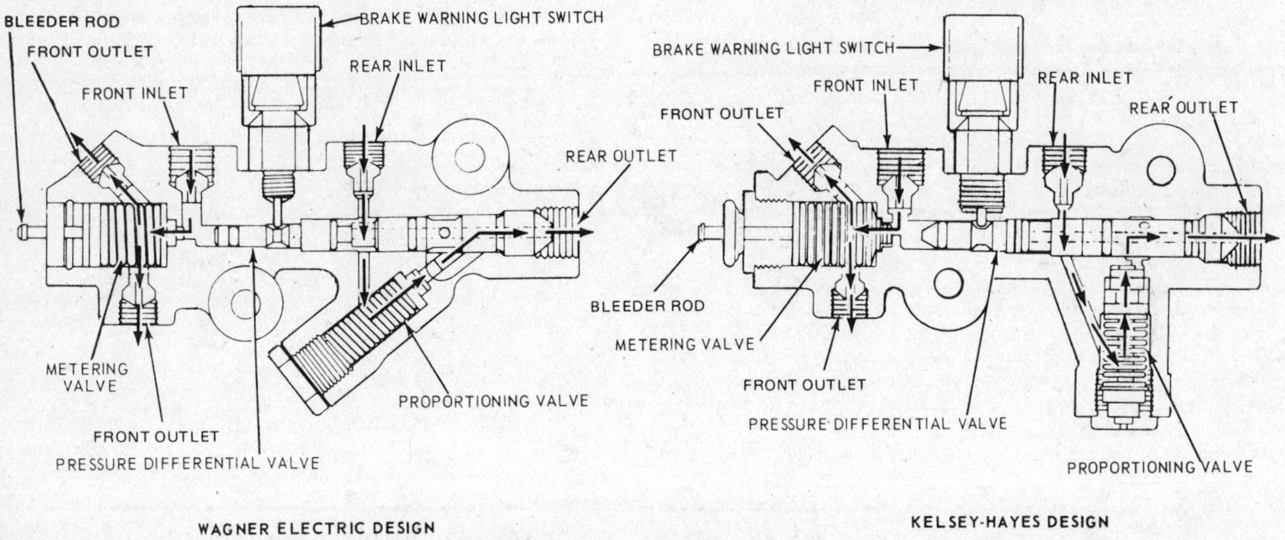

WAGNER ELECTRIC DESIGN

KELSEY-HAYES DESIGN

Fig. 13.116 Pressure differential/proportioning valves

the adjustment nuts so moving the crownwheel into or out of mesh as required.

75 The best check the do-it-yourself enthusiast can make to ascertain the correct meshing of the crownwheel and pinion is to smear a little engineer's (Prussian) blue or lead-oxide onto the crownwheel and then rotate the pinion. The contact mark should appear right in the middle of the crownwheel teeth. Refer to Fig. 8.11 where the correct tooth pattern is shown. Also given are incorrect tooth patterns and the method of obtaining the correct pattern. Obviously this will take time and patience but will be well worth it.

76 With the adjustment nuts tight, lock them to the bearing caps with the locks. Recheck the mesh of the crownwheel and pinion.

77 Before refitting the rear cover make quite sure that the mating faces are free from traces of jointing compound.

78 Apply a bead of silicone type sealant and refit the rear cover. Fit the axleshafts.

79 Fill the axle with the correct grade and quantity of oil.

9 Braking system

Pressure differential/proportioning valve

1 The control valve located in the brake hydraulic line may consist of a pressure differential valve as described in Chapter 9, or it may be combined with a metering valve and proportioning valve in a single housing.

2 The purpose of the metering valve is to regulate hydraulic pressure to the front disc brakes.

3 The proportioning valve reduces hydraulic pressure to the rear brakes during heavy braking to produce balanced braking between front and rear and to prevent rear wheel lock-up.

Vacuum booster pushrod adjustment

4 An incorrectly adjusted pushrod can give rise to brake drag due to incomplete release of the master cylinder piston, and/or 'clunk' heard when brake pedal applied.

5 Adjustment of the servo pushrod will not normally be required unless the master cylinder or servo unit have been renewed.

6 Before fitting the master cylinder to the booster, check the distance between the tip of the vacuum booster pushrod and the face of the booster to which the master cylinder is to be mounted. Take this measurement using a depth gauge or similar while exerting finger pressure on the end of the pushrod to keep it firmly seated.

7 The correct dimension (A in Fig. 13.117) should be between 0.941 in (23.9 mm) and 0.956 in (24.3 mm) while the engine is running with the vacuum pipe connected to the booster.

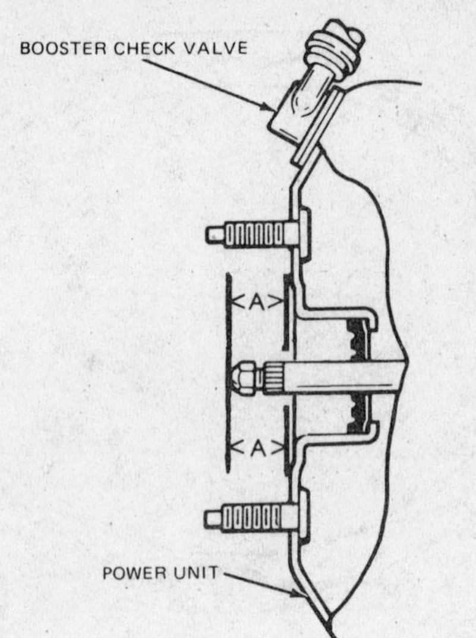

Fig. 13.117 Brake booster pushrod measuring points. For A see text

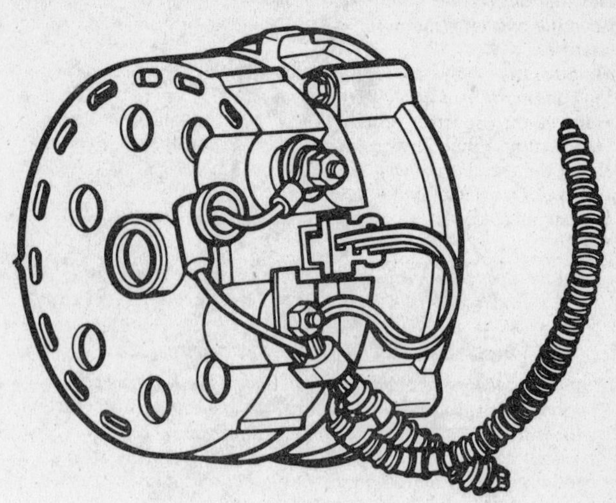

Fig. 13.118 Typical side terminal alternator

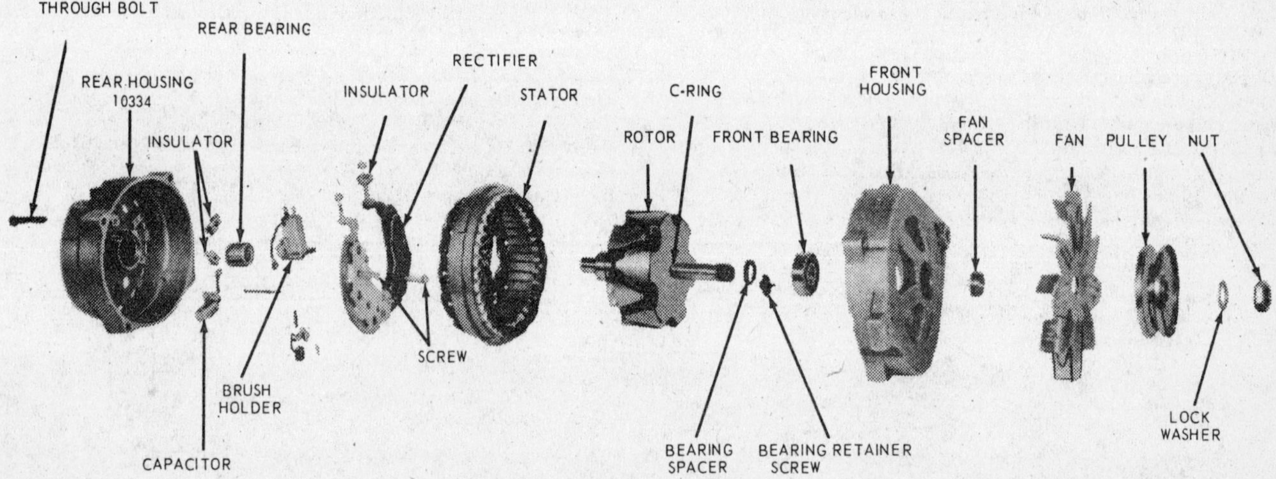

Fig. 13.119 Exploded view of side terminal alternator

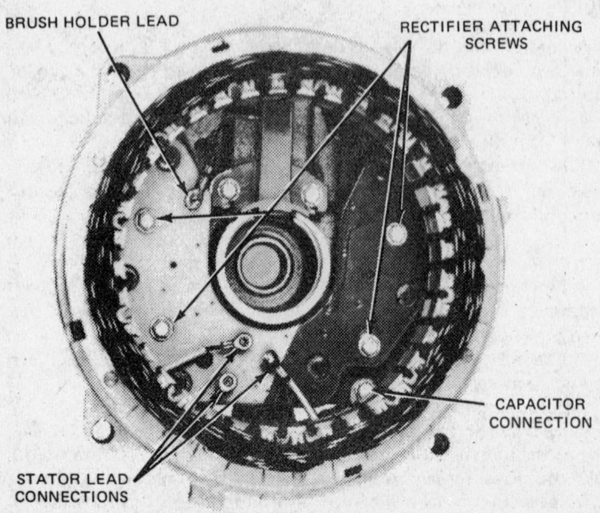

Fig. 13.120 Stator lead connections (side terminal alternator)

8 If necessary, turn the adjuster screw at the end of the pushrod to correct the setting.

10 Electrical system

Alternator (side terminal type) - overhaul

1 Some vehicles are fitted with the side terminal type of alternator. Remove it from the engine for overhaul.

2 Clean away external dirt and scribe a line across the stator and end housing as an aid to reassembly.

3 Remove the four through-bolts and separate the front housing and rotor from the rear housing and stator. Do not attempt to separate the stator and rear housing at this stage.

4 Remove the drive pulley components by unscrewing the retaining nut while the rotor shaft is held still with the appropriate tool inserted into its end. Alternatively, clamp the pulley in a vise with the aid of an old drivebelt.

5 Pull the rotor from the front housing and remove the spacer from the rotor shaft.

6 Renew the bearing in the front housing if it is dry or worn.

7 Unsolder the three stator leads from the rectifier and lift the stator from the rear housing.

8 Unsolder the brush holder lead from the rectifier.

9 Release the capacitor lead from the rectifier (one screw) and then extract the four screws which hold the rectifier to the rear housing. Remove the two terminal nuts from outside the housing and withdraw the rectifier.
10 Remove the brushes and holder (two screws) and clean away any sealing compound from the rear housing or brush holder.
11 Remove the capacitor (one screw).
12 Renew the bearing in the rear housing if it is dry or noisy.
13 Clean the slip rings with glasspaper and wipe other components clean. Do not immerse them in any kind of solvent.
14 Reassembly is a reversal of dismantling, but observe the following points:

(a) *Use a piece of wire to retain the brushes in the raised position while the brush holder is being fitted*
(b) *Make sure that the housing and stator marks made before dismantling are in correct alignment*

Voltage regulator - description, checking and adjustment

15 The independent voltage regulator used in conjunction with the alternator is located within the engine compartment.
16 The regulator may be of mechanical, electro-mechanical or electronic type depending upon the date of production and vehicle model.

Mechanical type

17 This is a sealed unit, no adjustment being possible. If it is suspected of being faulty, due to under- or over-charging of the battery, the following test may be carried out.
18 Connect a voltmeter positive lead to the positive terminal of the battery and the negative lead of the instrument to the negative terminal of the battery. Switch off all electrical loads.
19 Check the reading on the voltmeter.
20 Now connect the red lead of a tachometer to the distributor negative terminal on the ignition coil and the black lead of the instrument to a good ground.
21 Start the engine and increase the speed to between 1800 and 2200 rpm, holding it at this level for two or three minutes.
22 Check the voltmeter reading which should be between 1 and 2 volts higher than the first reading which was taken. Where the difference is less than 1 volt, or greater than 2.5 volts, then the regulator is faulty and must be renewed.
23 If the difference in readings is within the specified range of between 1 and 2 volts, turn on the headlamps and the heater blower: the voltmeter reading should not drop by more than ½ volt. If the drop is greater, again the regulator unit will have to be renewed (assuming the battery and alternator to be in good condition).
24 Always disconnect the battery before removing the voltage regulator.

Electro-mechanical type voltage regulator

25 Voltage regulation on this type of unit is achieved by the use of

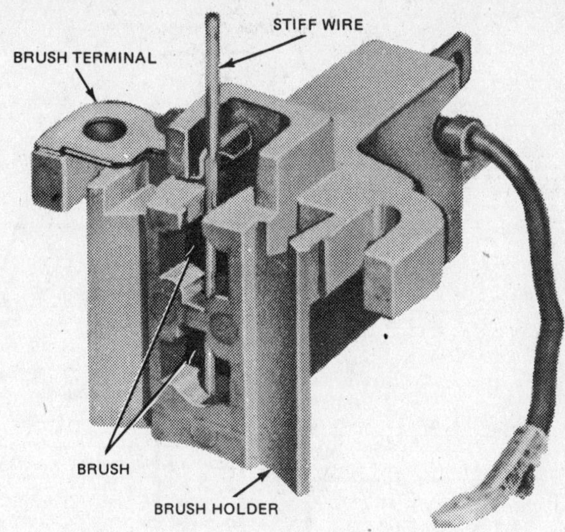

Fig. 13.121 Brush holder (side terminal alternator)

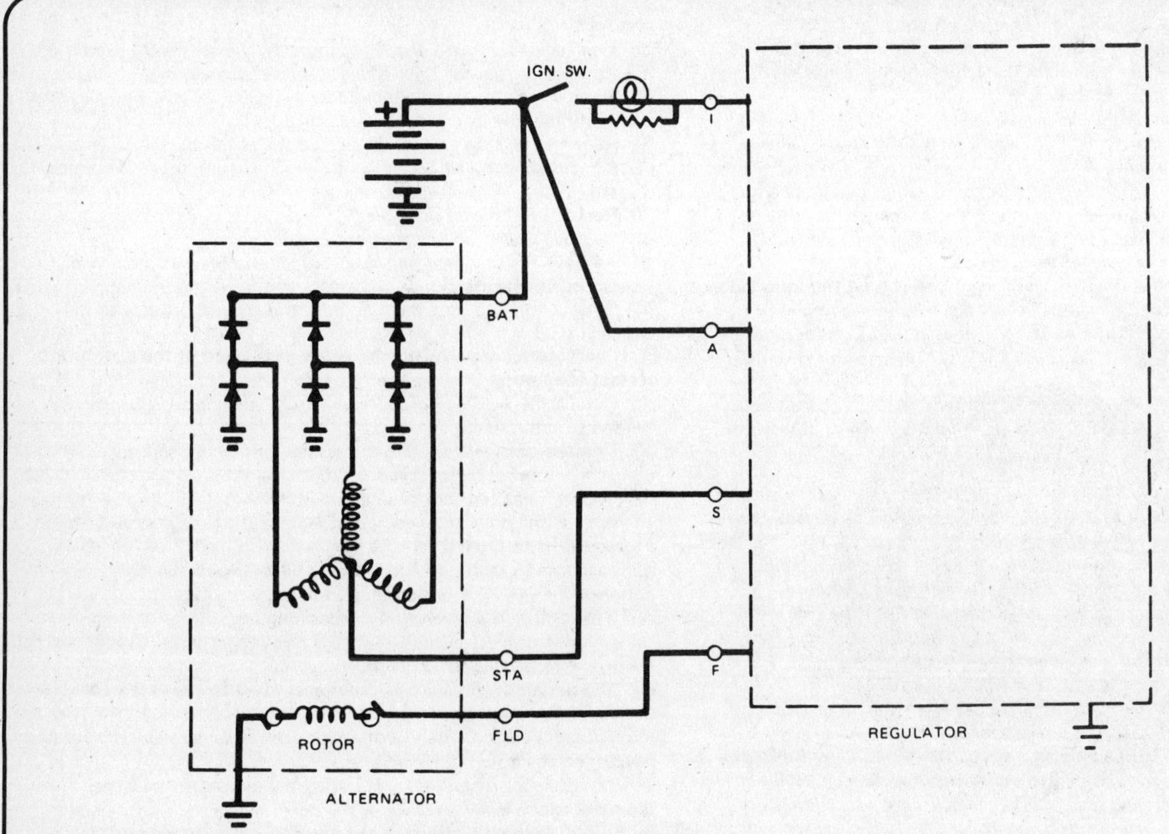

Fig. 13.122 Charging system (electronic regulator and indicator lamp)

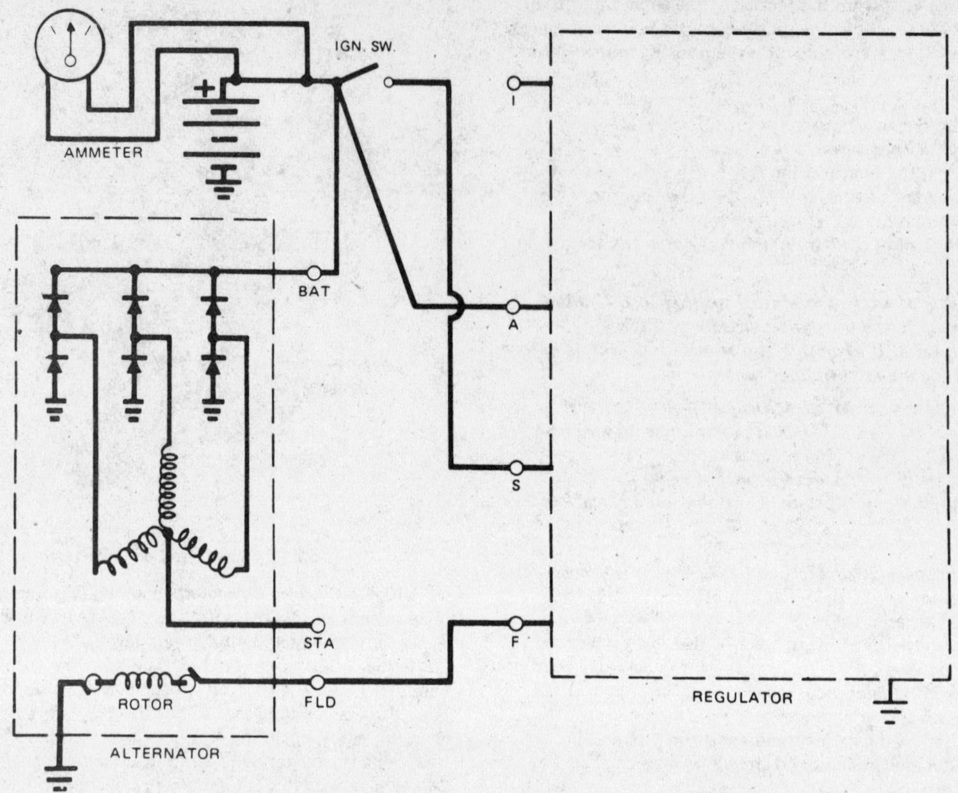

Fig. 13.123 Charging system (electronic regulator and ammeter)

transistors and diodes. Voltage limiter adjustment is possible as described in the following way, otherwise in the event of a fault occurring, the regulator must be renewed complete.
26 Before attempting adjustment, make sure that the regulator is at normal operating temperature with the vehicle having come in from at least a few miles of highway travel.
27 Remove the cover from the regulator.
28 A fiber rod or other type of insulated screwdriver must be used to turn the adjusting screw.
29 Following the test procedure described in earlier paragraphs for the mechanical type regulator, turn the adjuster screw clockwise to increase the voltage setting or counterclockwise to decrease it.

Electronic (solid state) type voltage regulator

30 On later cars, the voltage regulator is of sealed type and must not be dismantled. If a fault develops, renew the regulator complete.
A blue regulator is used for circuits with ammeters, black for circuits with a warning lamp.

All models

31 Never use an old type of regulator unit with a later type alternator.
32 With the later type sealed electronic regulators always observe the following conditions:

(a) Check that the push-on field terminal connector is connected to the field terminal stud on the alternator and not to the ground stud
(b) Always disconnect the wiring plug from the regulator before any testing of the alternator is carried out
(c) Always disconnect the wiring plug from the regulator before releasing the regulator mounting screws. If the wiring plug is disconnected from an ungrounded regulator, the regulator will be destroyed
(d) Never attempt to polarize the alternator or ground its field circuit or the regulator will be ruined
(e) Always disconnect the electric choke heater wire from the stator terminal of the alternator when checking out the charging system. The electric choke should also be checked for ground condition

Starter motor - dismantling and reassembly

33 On later models (1977 on) the starter motor is of slightly modified design.
34 To dismantle this type of motor, extract the cover screw and remove the cover.
35 Unscrew and remove the through-bolts, the starter drive end housing and the starter drive plunger lever return spring.
36 Remove the pivot pin which retains the starter gear plunger lever and withdraw the lever and the armature.
37 Remove the stop ring retainer from the armature shart.
38 Extract the stop ring from its groove in the armature shaft and discard it.
39 Remove the starter drivegear.
40 Remove the brush endplate and insulator.
41 Remove the brushes from their holder and lift out the brush holder, noting its location with respect to the end terminal.
42 Extract the two screws which hold the ground brushes to the frame.
43 Bend up the edges of the sleeve which is inserted into the rectangular aperture in the frame and withdraw the sleeve and retainer.
44 Detach the field coil ground wire from the copper tab which is riveted to the frame.
45 Unless a press is available, this is the limit of dismantling as the coil screws cannot be removed without one. Where a press is available to hold the releasing tool in engagement with the coil screws, remove the screws, the pole shoes and coils and cut the field coil connection at the switch post lead. Cut the positive brush leads from the field coils as close to their coil connecting points as possible. Cut connections will have to be soldered on reassembly.
46 Reassembly is a reversal of dismantling.

Exterior lamps - bulb renewal

47 The design of these lamps varies according to the date of production.
48 The bulb can be renewed on front parking lamps and rear lamps by pulling the bulb holder from the rear of the lamp.
49 To renew a broken lens on later model lamps, pry out the lens and scrape away all trace of the butyl seal. Fit a new seal and lens, holding the lens pressed into position for a few seconds to fix it.

Fuses, circuit breakers and fusible links

50 On later models, the fuse arrangement has been revised and

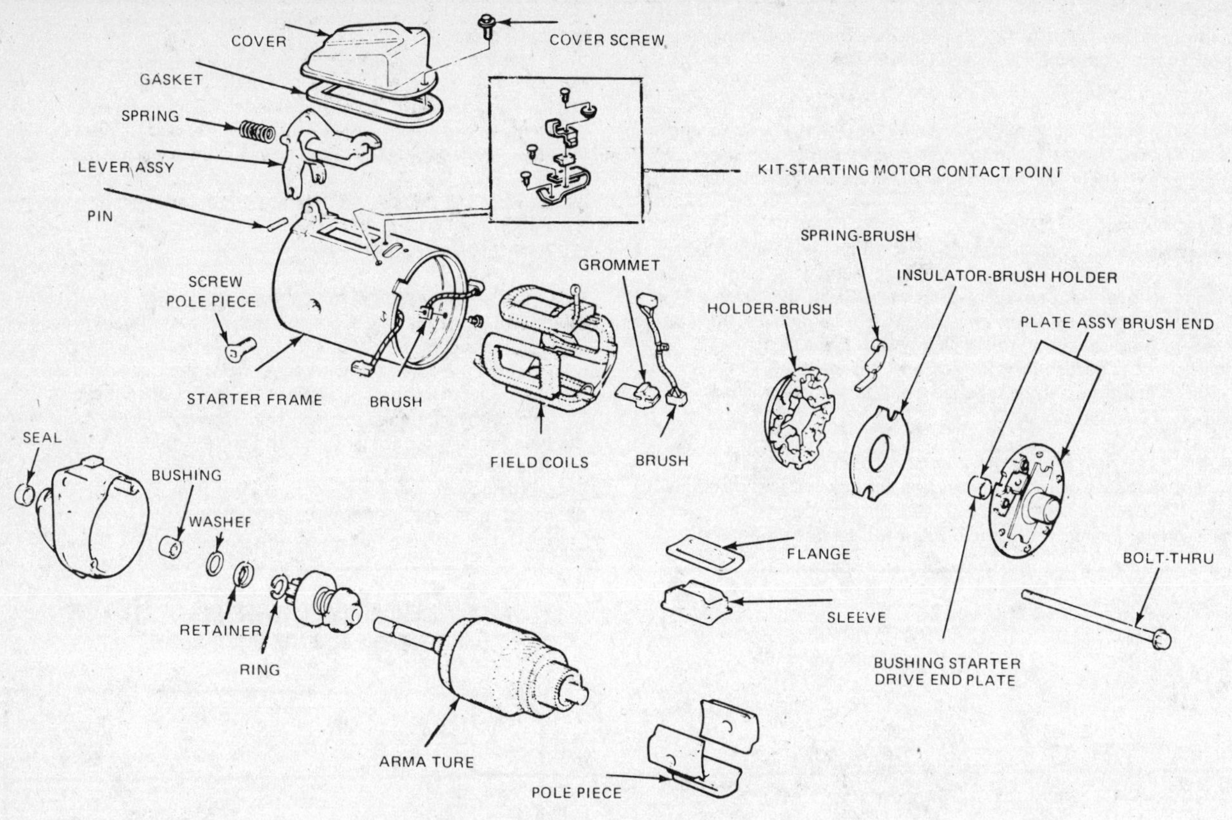

Fig. 13.124 Exploded view of later type starter motor

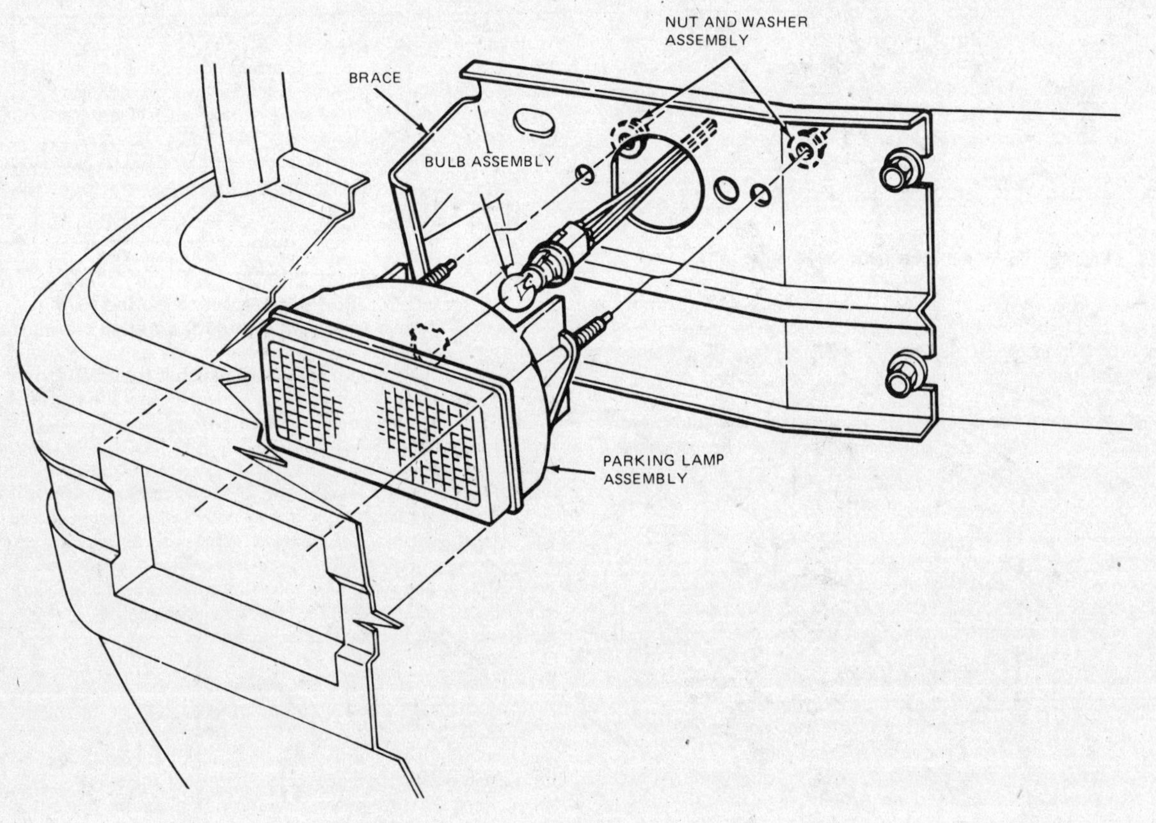

Fig. 13.125 Front parking lamp (typical)

reference should be made to the Specifications at the beginning of this Chapter also to the individual vehicle fuse box.

Dual buzzers

51 The buzzer for the ignition key warning (anti-theft) systems and the buzzer for the seat belt warning system are mounted on the right-hand side of the relay panel above the glove compartment.

Heated rear window (1978)

52 The system incorporates a timer switch which has an inbuilt relay coil which switches off the heated rear window grid after termination.
53 The grid wires should be treated with care. Clean the inside of the rear window with a damp cloth only. Avoid scratching from rings on the fingers or luggage and do not stick labels over the grid wires.
54 If a break does occur in a grid wire, and it is less than 1 in (2.54 mm) in length, it can be repaired using special conductive paint supplied by your dealer.

Radio and tape player - removal and refitting

55 To remove the radio fitted as standard equipment, first disconnect the battery ground cable.
56 Reach up behind the radio and disconnect the power, antenna and speaker leads.
57 From the front of the radio, remove the control knobs and spindle nuts.
58 Remove the ashtray and bracket.
59 Remove the nut from the support at the rear of the radio.
60 Remove the reinforcement from the lower part of the instrument panel.
61 Remove the floor ducts (heater, air conditioner) if necessary.
62 Withdraw the radio from the instrument panel.
63 Refitting is a reversal of removal.

Antenna - removal and refitting

64 Pull the antenna lead from the rear of the radio and release the lead retaining clips.
65 Remove the cowl side trim panel from the right-hand side.
66 Disconnect the antenna cable from the extension cable.
67 Remove the antenna cap and four screws. Pull the cable through the hole in the door hinger pillar and front fender and withdraw the antenna assembly.
68 Refitting is a reversal of removal, but trim the antenna as described in the radio operating instructions.

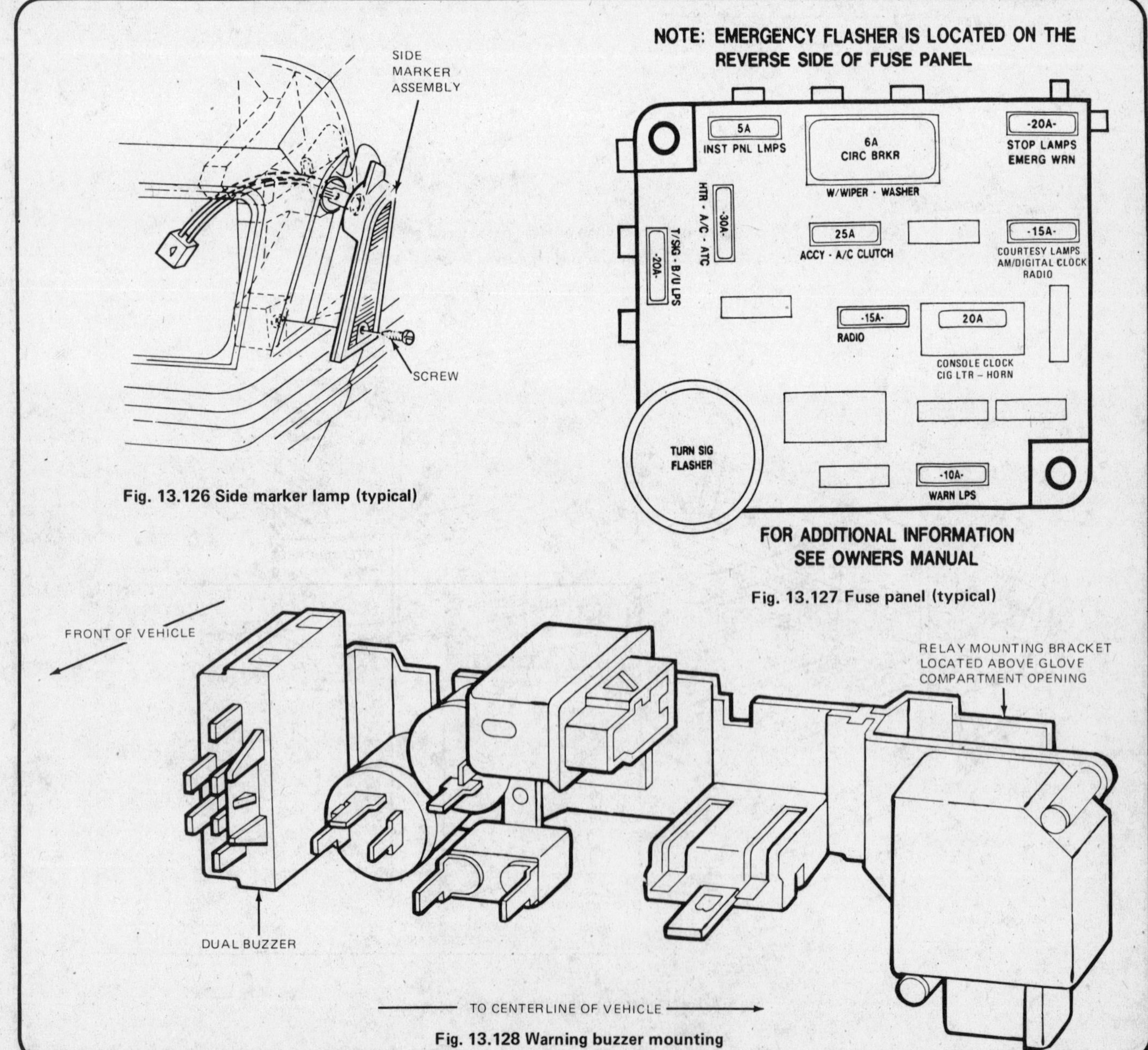

Fig. 13.126 Side marker lamp (typical)

Fig. 13.127 Fuse panel (typical)

Fig. 13.128 Warning buzzer mounting

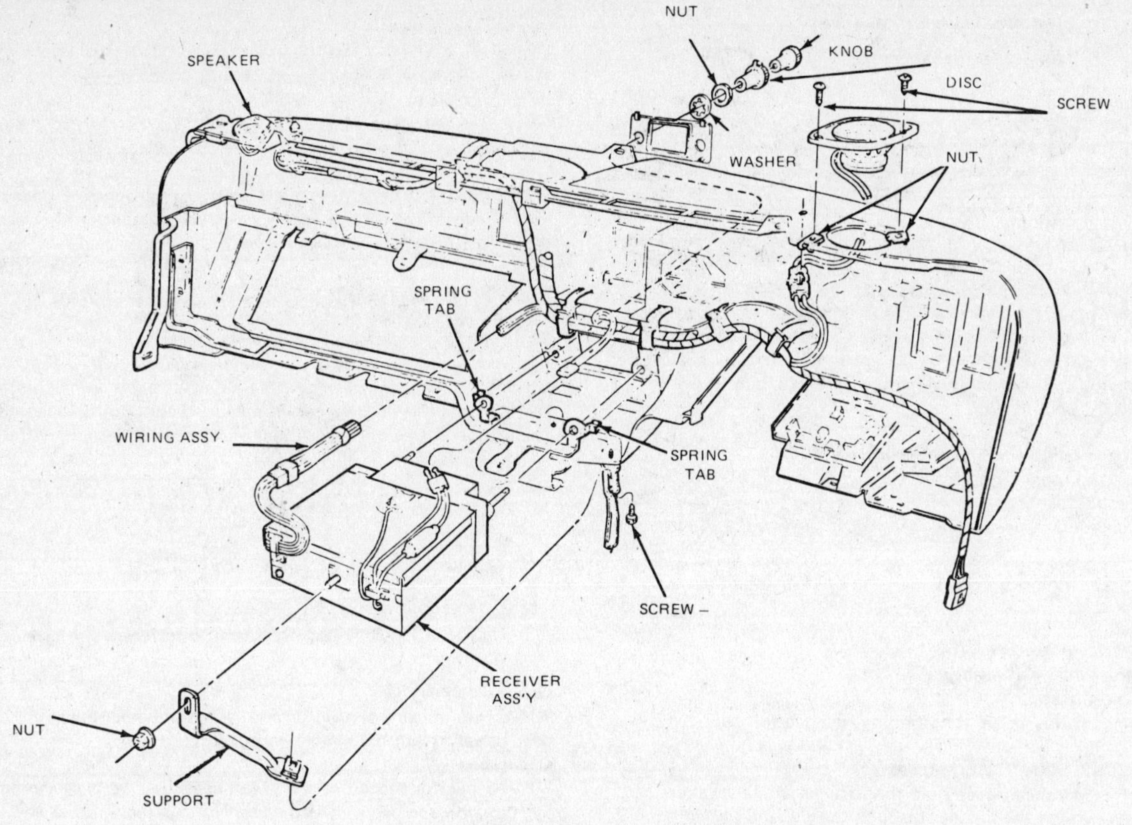

Fig. 13.129 Radio mounting details (typical)

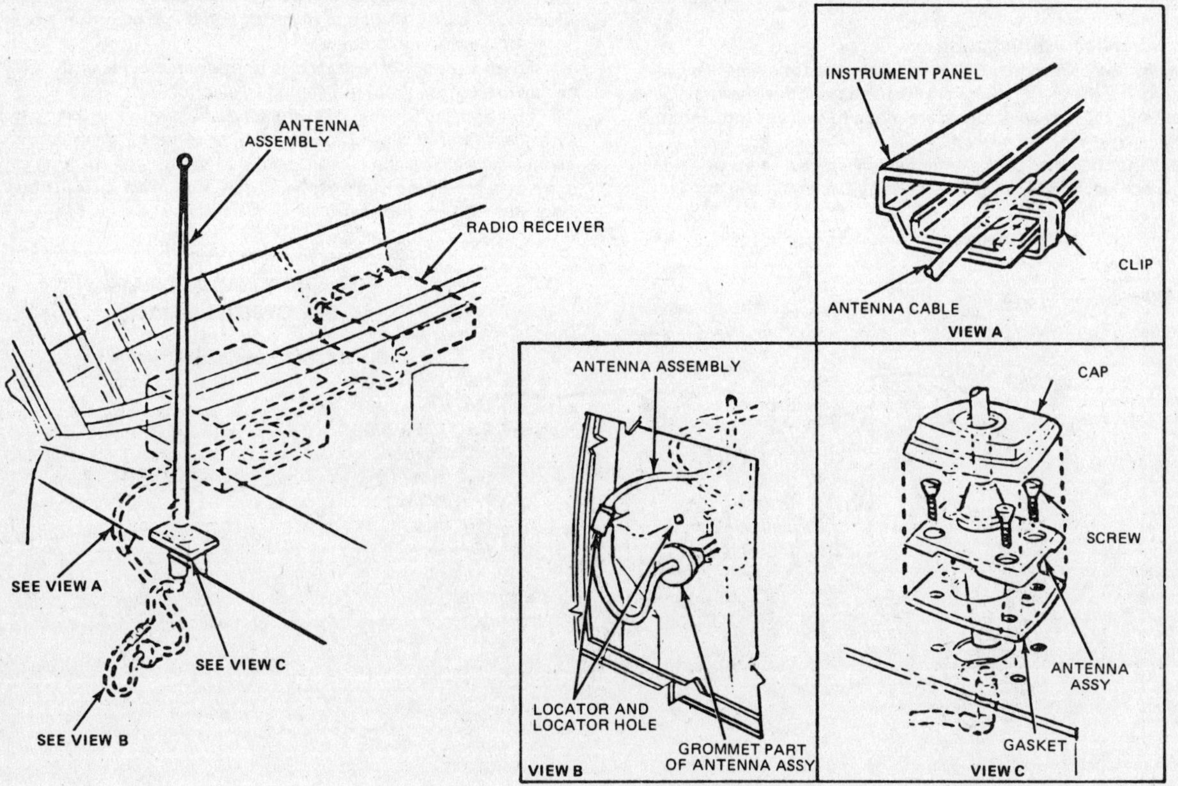

Fig. 13.130 Radio antenna installation (typical)

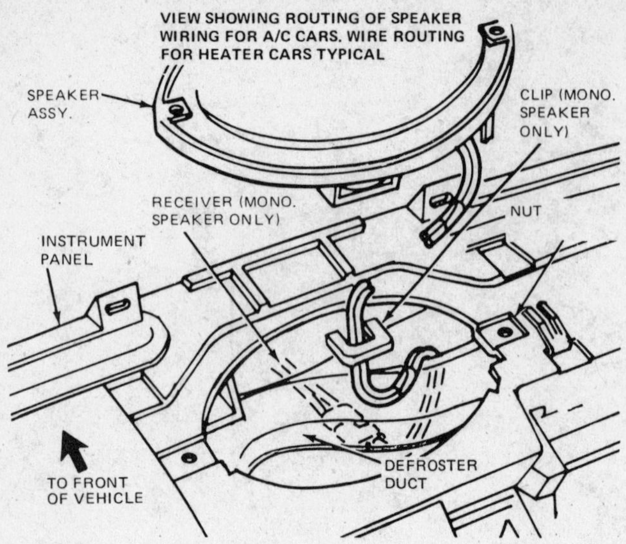

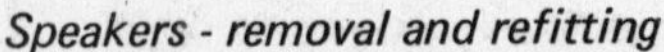
Fig. 13.131 Radio speaker mounting on instrument panel

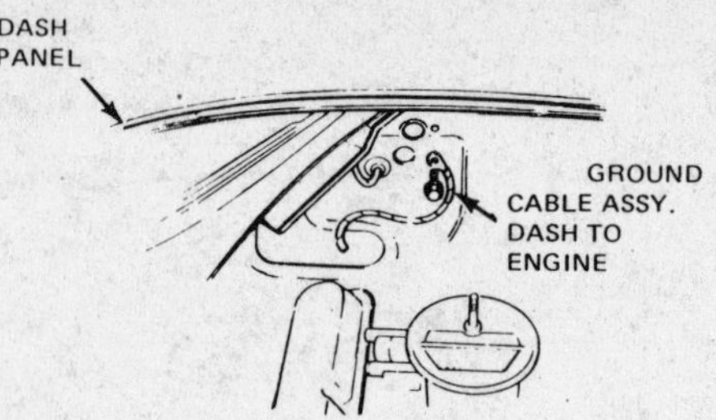

Fig. 13.132 Engine to dash panel grounding

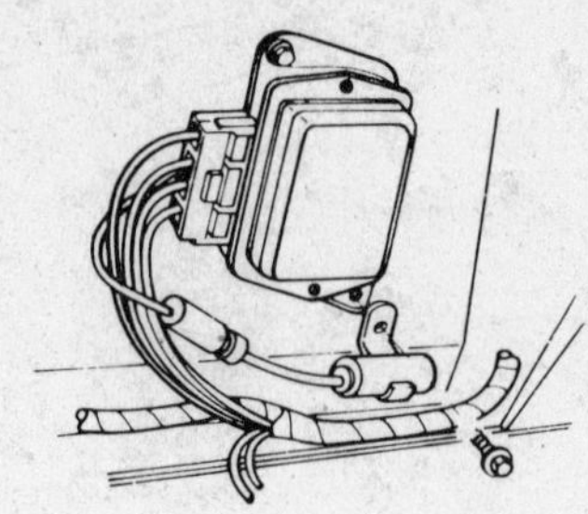

Fig. 13.133 Voltage regulator interference suppressor

Speakers - removal and refitting

69 Remove the ashtray assembly.

70 Remove the glovebox.

71 On cars equipped with air conditioning, remove the right-hand air duct.

72 Disconnect the leads (radio-to-speaker).

73 Unscrew the two nuts which hold the speaker to the speaker mounting plate. Lower the speaker through the glovebox opening.

74 Refitting is a reversal of removal.

75 Where stereo speakers are fitted to the instrument panel, the instrument panel pad must be removed in order to detach the speaker from it.

Radio interference - suppression

76 Factory or dealer installed radios will have the following suppression items installed. If you are fitting a radio for the first time, check that these arrangements are made to prevent interference spoiling the performance of the set.

77 Always tune the radio to the antenna when a new radio or antenna is installed, this is usually done using the small adjuster screw provided in the radio.

Ground cables

78 A ground cable should be connected between the engine and the dash panel within the engine compartment.

Capacitors

79 A capacitor should be fitted between the live (+) terminal on the ignition coil and ground, also at the voltage regulator as shown in Fig. 13.133.

Tape player - cleaning

80 The playback head and capstan in the tape player may require cleaning of oxide residue at intervals if the reproduction becomes weak or wavering in volume.

81 To do this, hold the cartridge door open and clean the playback head with cotton wool moistened in alcohol.

82 To clean the capstan, trip the ON/OFF switch at the cartridge slot with the eraser at the end of a pencil, or something similar, at the same time holding the cotton wool pad against the rotating capstan. Do not overwet the pad or solvent may run down into the bearings and wash out the lubricant.

BK	*Black*	*LG*	*Light green*
BR	*Brown*	*DB*	*Dark blue*
T	*Tan*	*LB*	*Light blue*
R	*Red*	*P*	*Purple*
PK	*Pink*	*G*	*Grey*
O	*Orange*	*W*	*White*
Y	*Yellow*	*(H)*	*Hash*
DG	*Dark green*	*(D)*	*Dot*

Color code for wiring diagrams

Location of vehicle electrical systems – 1977 models

System or circuit	Fig.
Air conditioning and/or heating	*13.138*
Charge, start and run	*13.135*
Exterior lighting	*13.136*
Heated rear window	*13.135*
Horn	*13.138*
Illumination lamps	*13.139*
Immersion heater (engine block)	*13.135*
Power distribution	*13.134*
Protection and convenience	*13.137*
Radio	*13.138*
Windshield wipe/wash	*13.137*

Location of vehicle electrical systems – 1978 models

System or circuit	Fig.
Air conditioning and/or heating	*13.144*
Charge, start and run	*13.141*
Exterior lighting	*13.142*
Heated rear window	*13.143*
Horn	*13.143*
Illumination lamps	*13.144*
Immersion heater (engine block)	*13.141*
Power distribution	*13.140*
Protection and convenience	*13.145*
Radio	*13.143*
Windshield wipe/wash	*13.143*

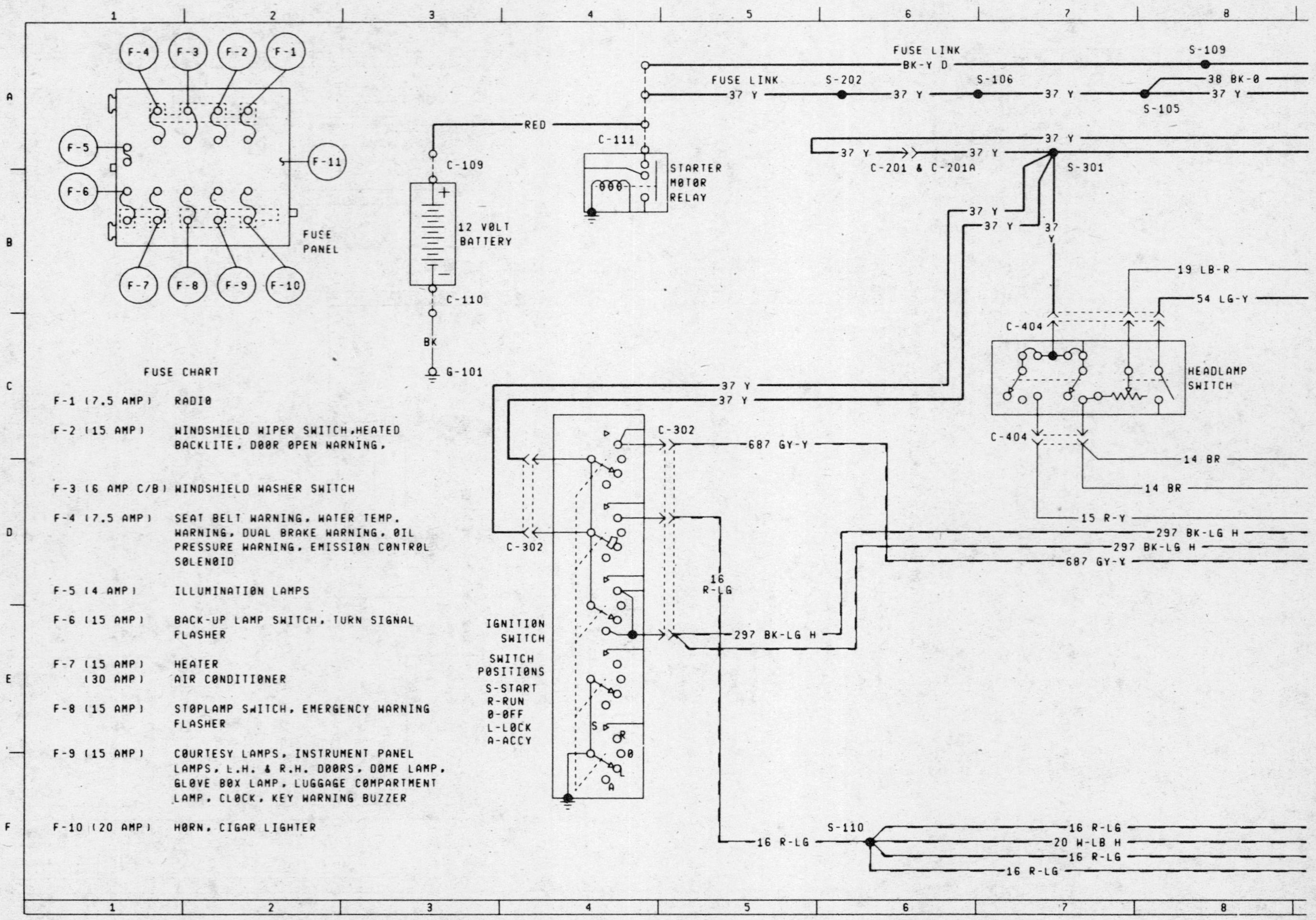
FUSE CHART
F-1 (7.5 AMP) RADIØ
F-2 (15 AMP) WINDSHIELD WIPER SWITCH, HEATED BACKLITE, DØØR ØPEN WARNING.
F-3 (6 AMP C/B) WINDSHIELD WASHER SWITCH
F-4 (7.5 AMP) SEAT BELT WARNING, WATER TEMP. WARNING, DUAL BRAKE WARNING, ØIL PRESSURE WARNING, EMISSIØN CØNTRØL SØLENØID
F-5 (4 AMP) ILLUMINATIØN LAMPS
F-6 (15 AMP) BACK-UP LAMP SWITCH, TURN SIGNAL FLASHER
F-7 (15 AMP) HEATER
(30 AMP) AIR CØNDITIØNER
F-8 (15 AMP) STØPLAMP SWITCH, EMERGENCY WARNING FLASHER
F-9 (15 AMP) CØURTESY LAMPS, INSTRUMENT PANEL LAMPS, L.H. & R.H. DØØRS, DØME LAMP, GLØVE BØX LAMP, LUGGAGE CØMPARTMENT LAMP, CLØCK, KEY WARNING BUZZER
F-10 (20 AMP) HØRN, CIGAR LIGHTER
FUSE PANEL
12 VØLT BATTERY
STARTER MØTØR RELAY
IGNITIØN SWITCH
SWITCH PØSITIØNS
S-START
R-RUN
Ø-ØFF
L-LØCK
A-ACCY
HEADLAMP SWITCH
FUSE LINK
BK-Y D
FUSE LINK
37 Y
38 BK-Ø
RED
BK
G-101
C-109
C-110
C-111
C-201 & C-201A
C-302
C-404
S-109
S-202
S-106
S-105
S-301
S-110
19 LB-R
54 LG-Y
14 BR
15 R-Y
297 BK-LG H
687 GY-Y
16 R-LG
20 W-LB H

Fig. 13.134 Wiring diagram, 1977 models: power distribution circuits. For color code see page 280

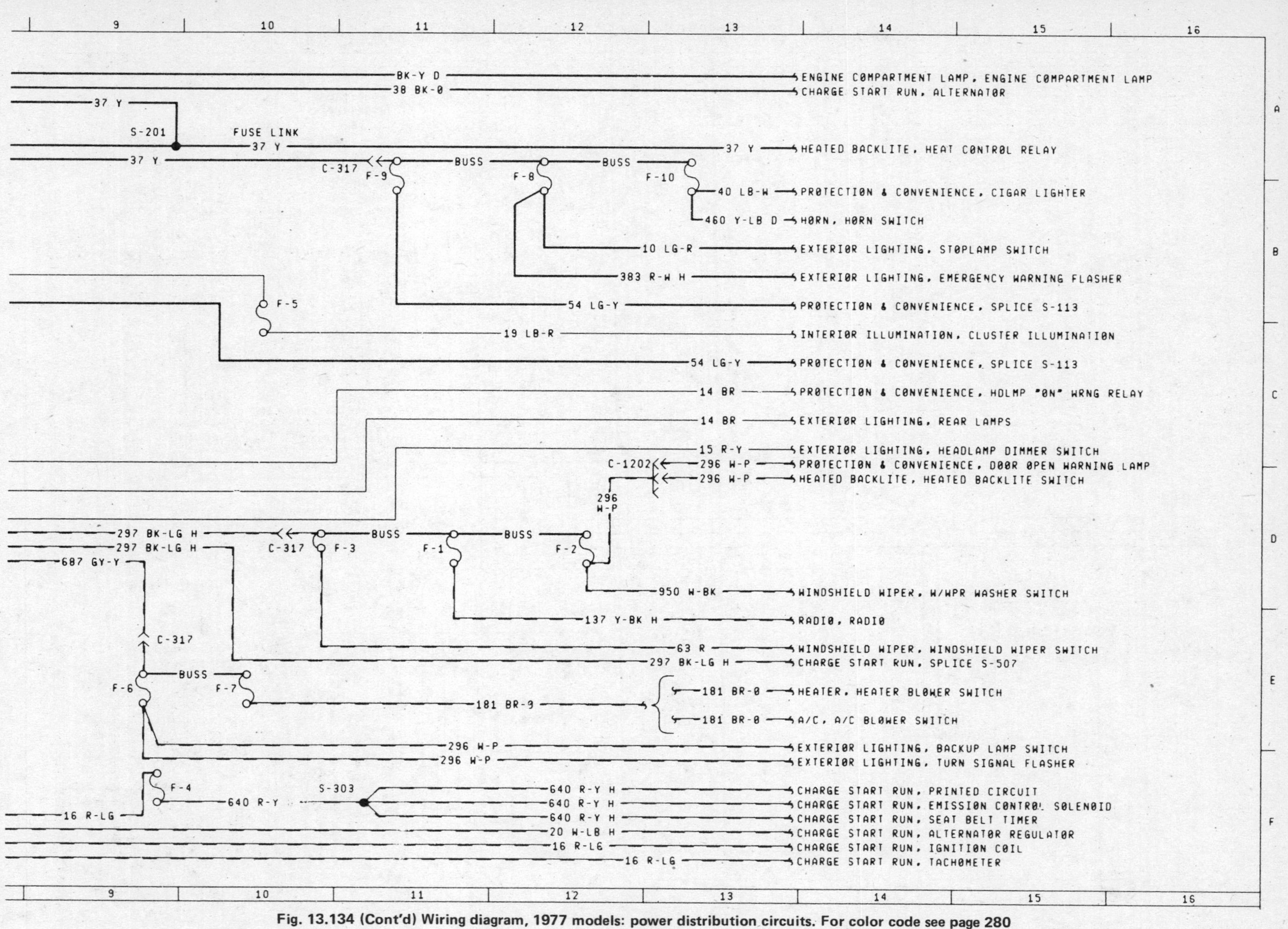

Fig. 13.134 (Cont'd) Wiring diagram, 1977 models: power distribution circuits. For color code see page 280

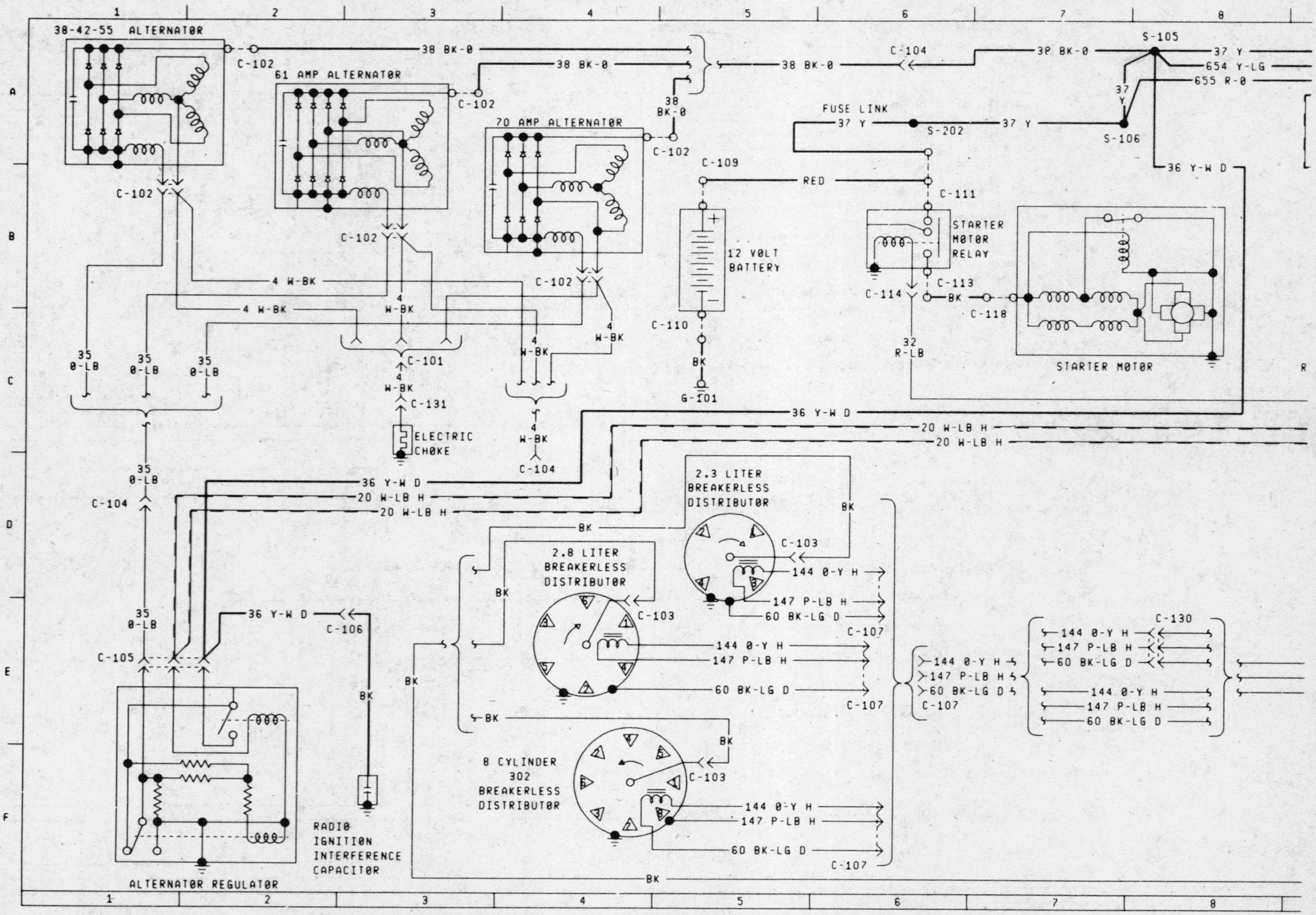

Fig. 13.135 Wiring diagram, 1977 models: charge, start and run circuits. For color code see page 280

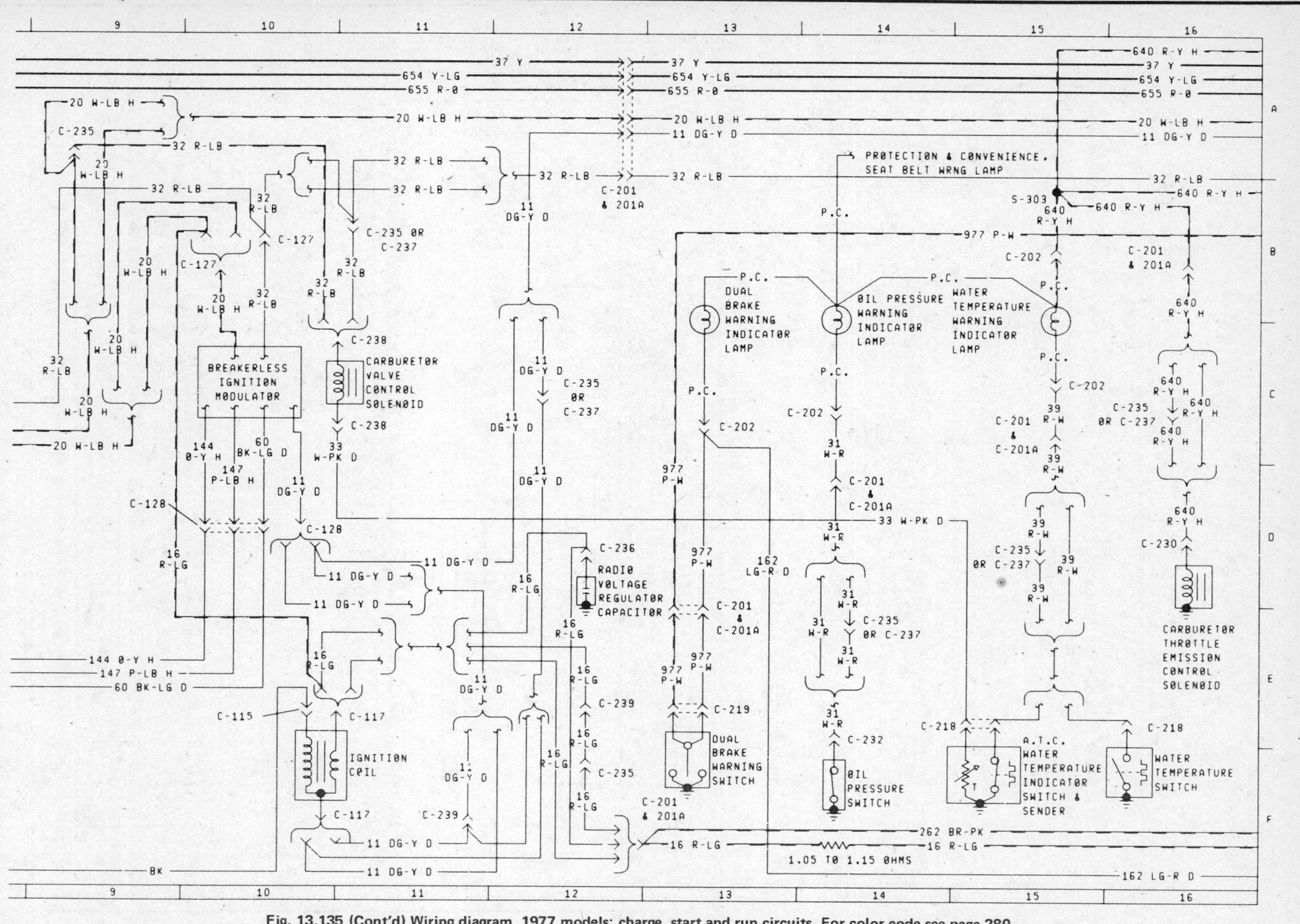

Fig. 13.135 (Cont'd) Wiring diagram, 1977 models: charge, start and run circuits. For color code see page 280

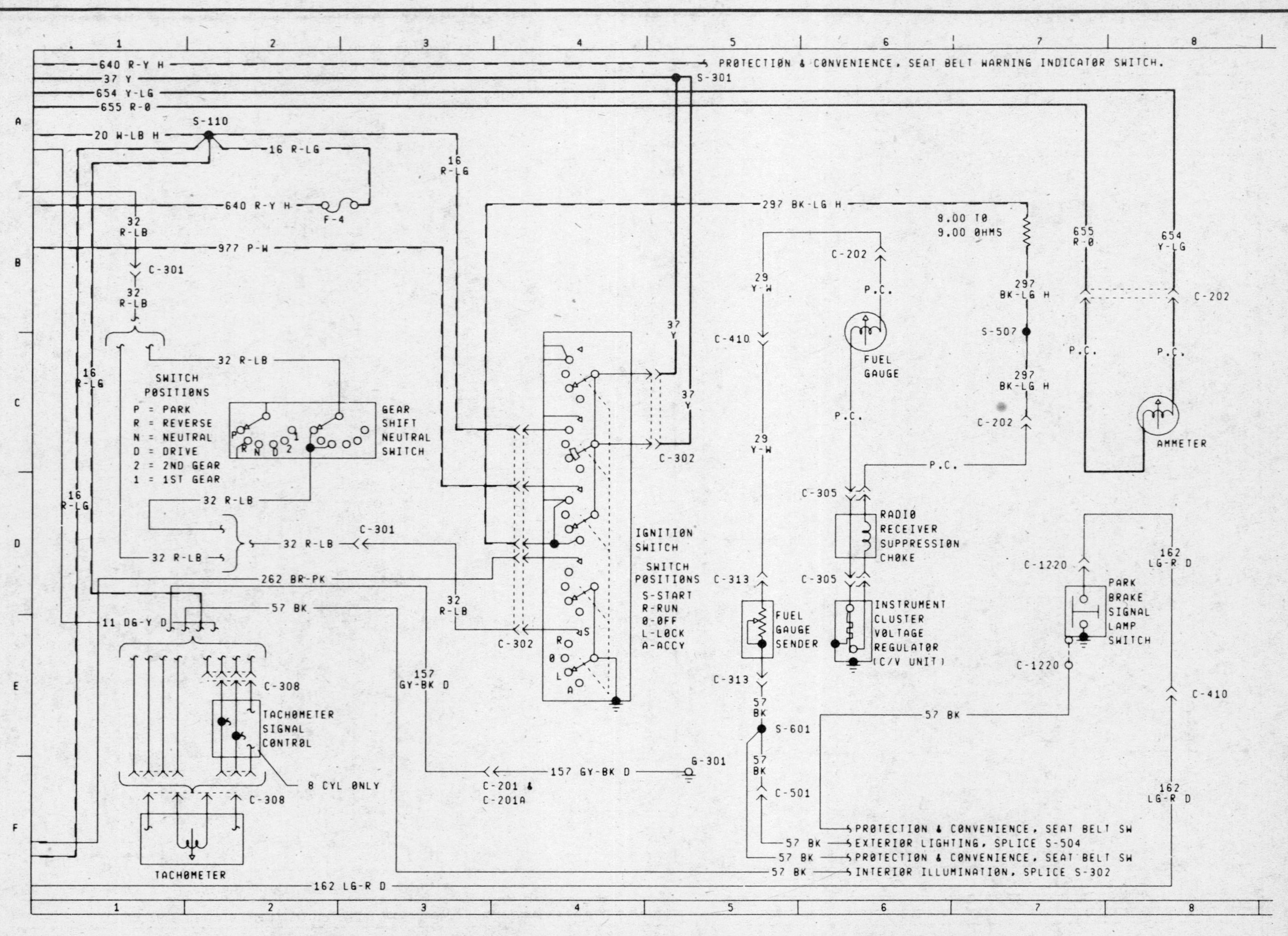

Fig. 13.135 (cont'd) Wiring diagram, 1977 models: charge, start and run circuits. For colour code see page 280

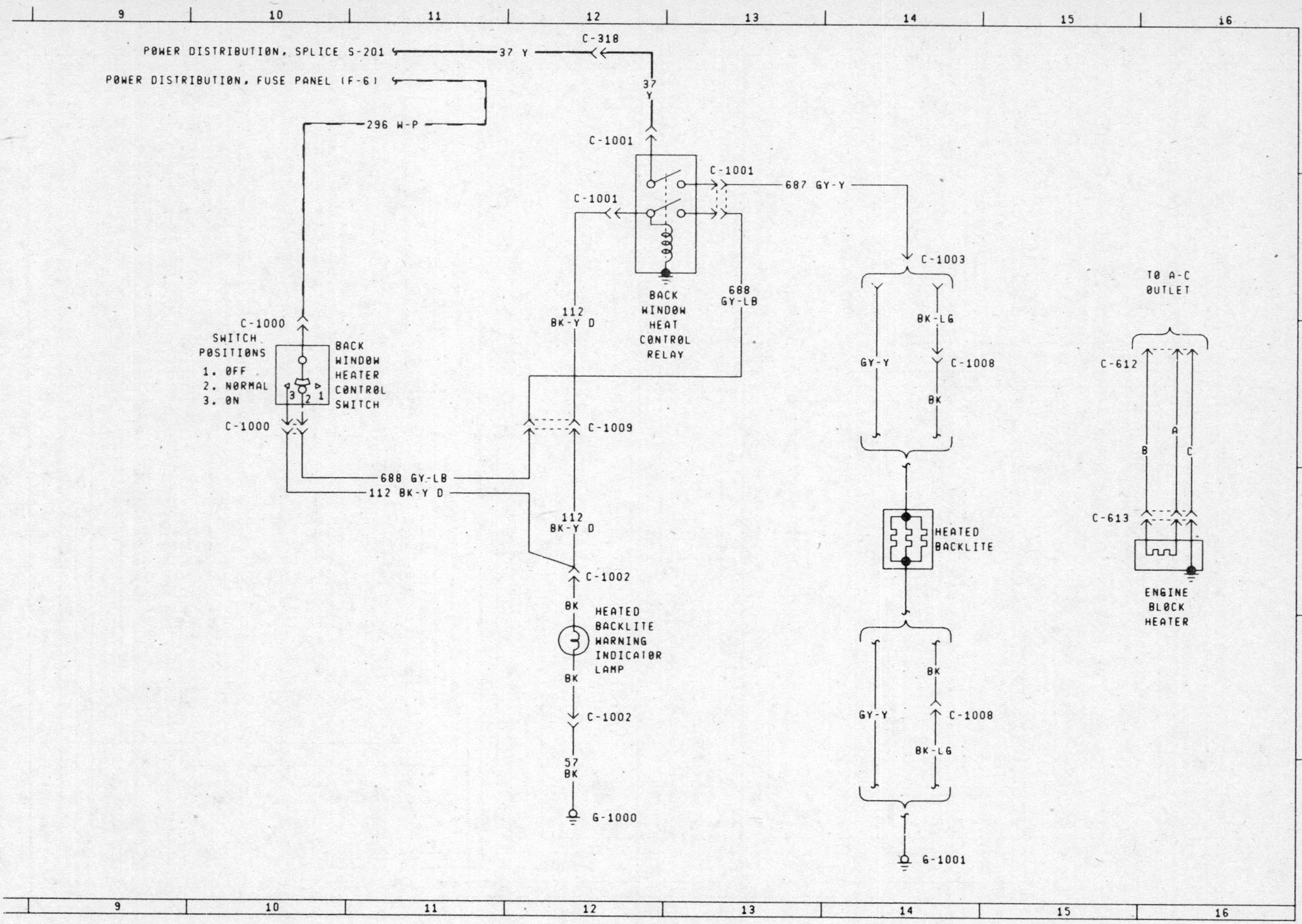

9 10 11 12 13 14 15 16

A B C D E F

POWER DISTRIBUTION, SPLICE S-201
37 Y
C-318
POWER DISTRIBUTION, FUSE PANEL (F-6)
296 W-P
37 Y
C-1001
C-1001
687 GY-Y
C-1001
BACK WINDOW HEAT CONTROL RELAY
688 GY-LB
112 BK-Y D
C-1003
BK-LG
GY-Y
C-1008
BK
TO A-C OUTLET
C-612
B
A
C
C-613
ENGINE BLOCK HEATER
C-1000
SWITCH POSITIONS
1. OFF
2. NORMAL
3. ON
BACK WINDOW HEATER CONTROL SWITCH
3 2 1
C-1000
C-1009
688 GY-LB
112 BK-Y D
112 BK-Y D
HEATED BACKLITE
C-1002
BK
HEATED BACKLITE WARNING INDICATOR LAMP
BK
C-1002
57 BK
G-1000
BK
GY-Y
C-1008
BK-LG
G-1001

Fig. 13.135 (cont'd) Wiring diagram, 1977 models: charge, start and run circuits. For colour code see page 280

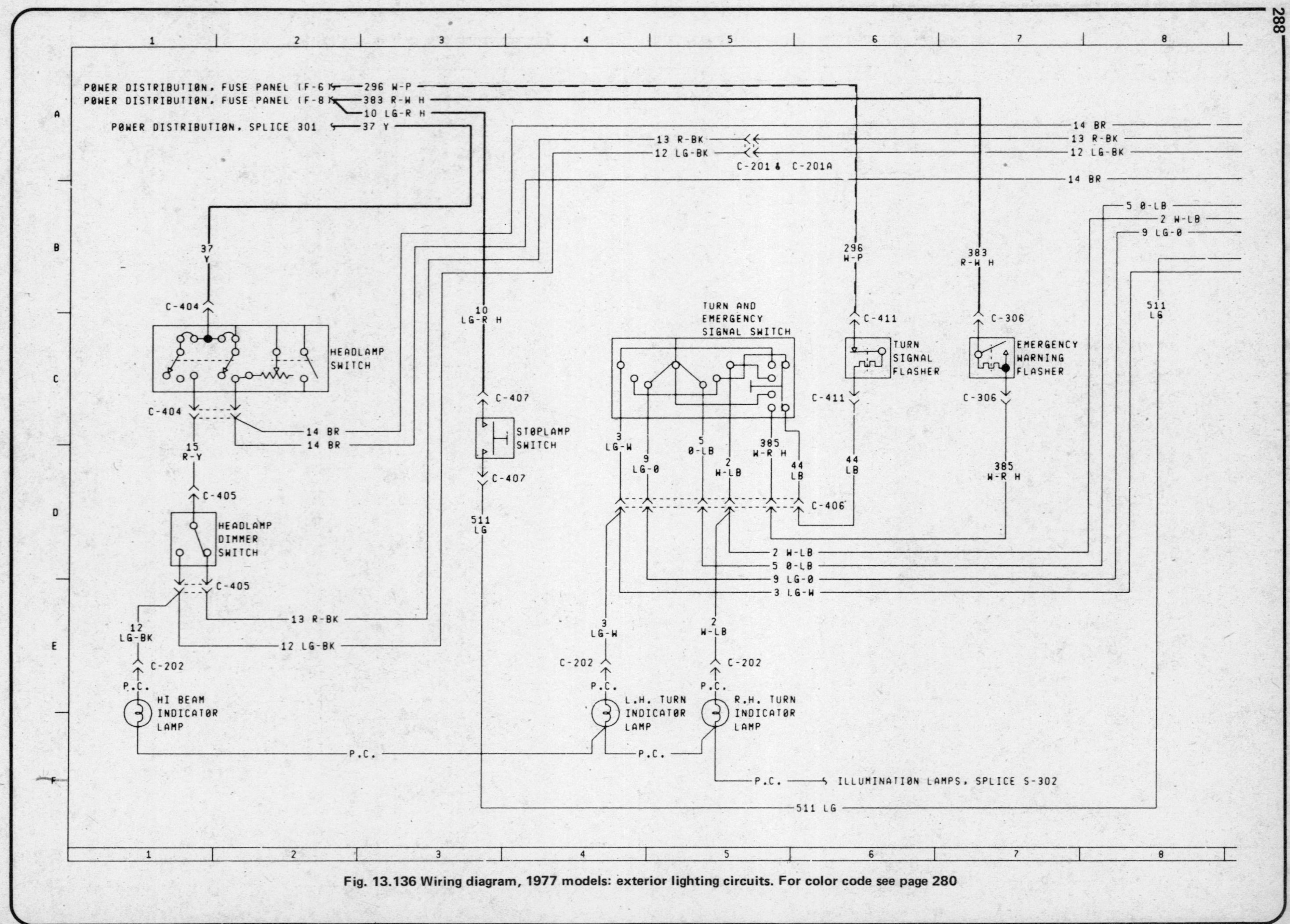

Fig. 13.136 Wiring diagram, 1977 models: exterior lighting circuits. For color code see page 280

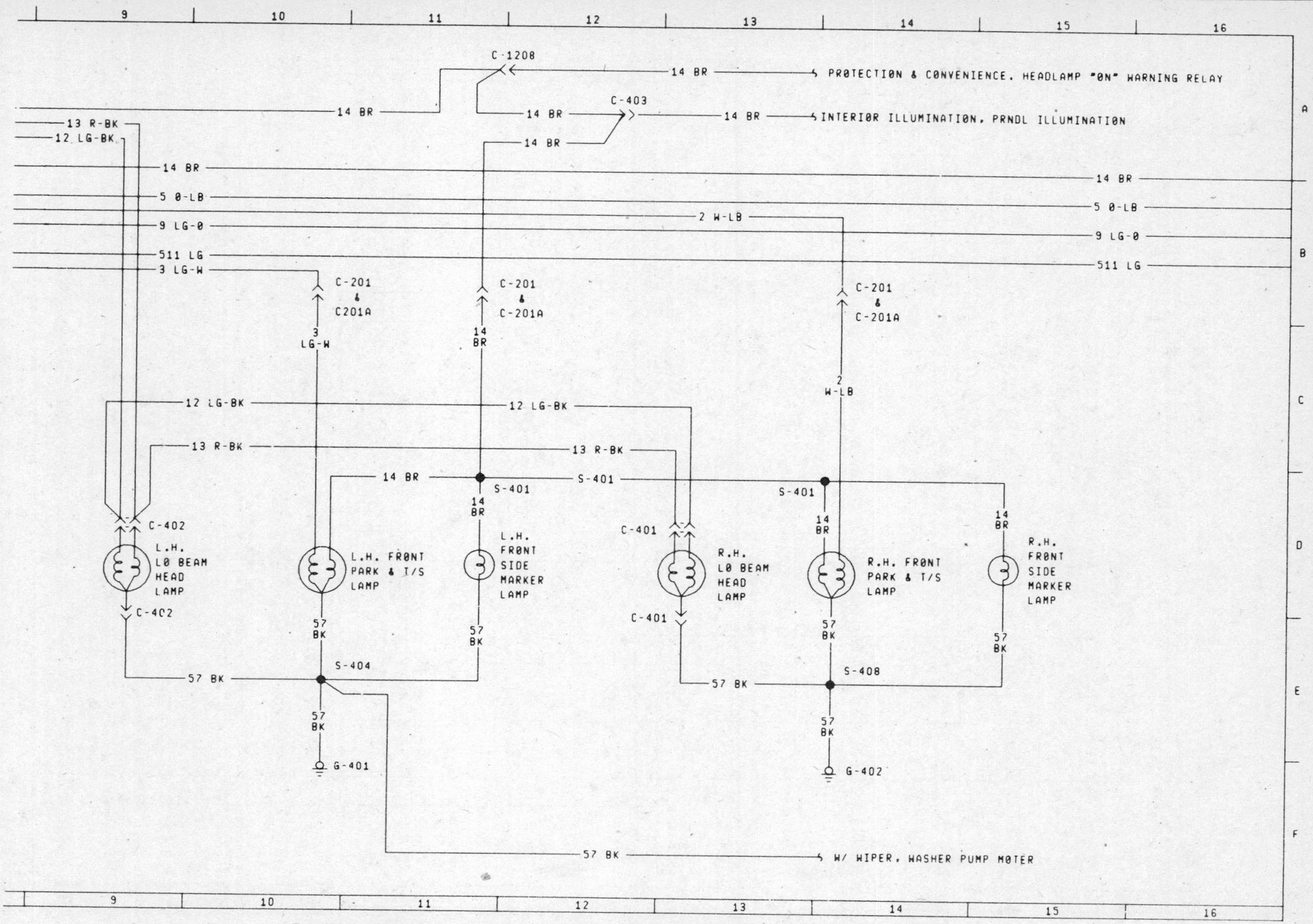

9 10 11 12 13 14 15 16

A B C D E F

C-1208
14 BR
PROTECTION & CONVENIENCE. HEADLAMP "ON" WARNING RELAY
C-403
14 BR
INTERIOR ILLUMINATION, PRNDL ILLUMINATION
13 R-BK
12 LG-BK
14 BR
5 O-LB
2 W-LB
9 LG-O
511 LG
3 LG-W
C-201 & C201A
C-201 & C-201A
C-201 & C-201A
3 LG-W
14 BR
2 W-LB
12 LG-BK
13 R-BK
S-401
C-402
L.H. LO BEAM HEAD LAMP
L.H. FRONT PARK & T/S LAMP
L.H. FRONT SIDE MARKER LAMP
C-401
R.H. LO BEAM HEAD LAMP
R.H. FRONT PARK & T/S LAMP
R.H. FRONT SIDE MARKER LAMP
57 BK
S-404
S-408
G-401
G-402
W/ WIPER, WASHER PUMP MOTER

Fig. 13.136 (Cont'd) Wiring diagram, 1977 models: exterior lighting circuits. For color code see page 280

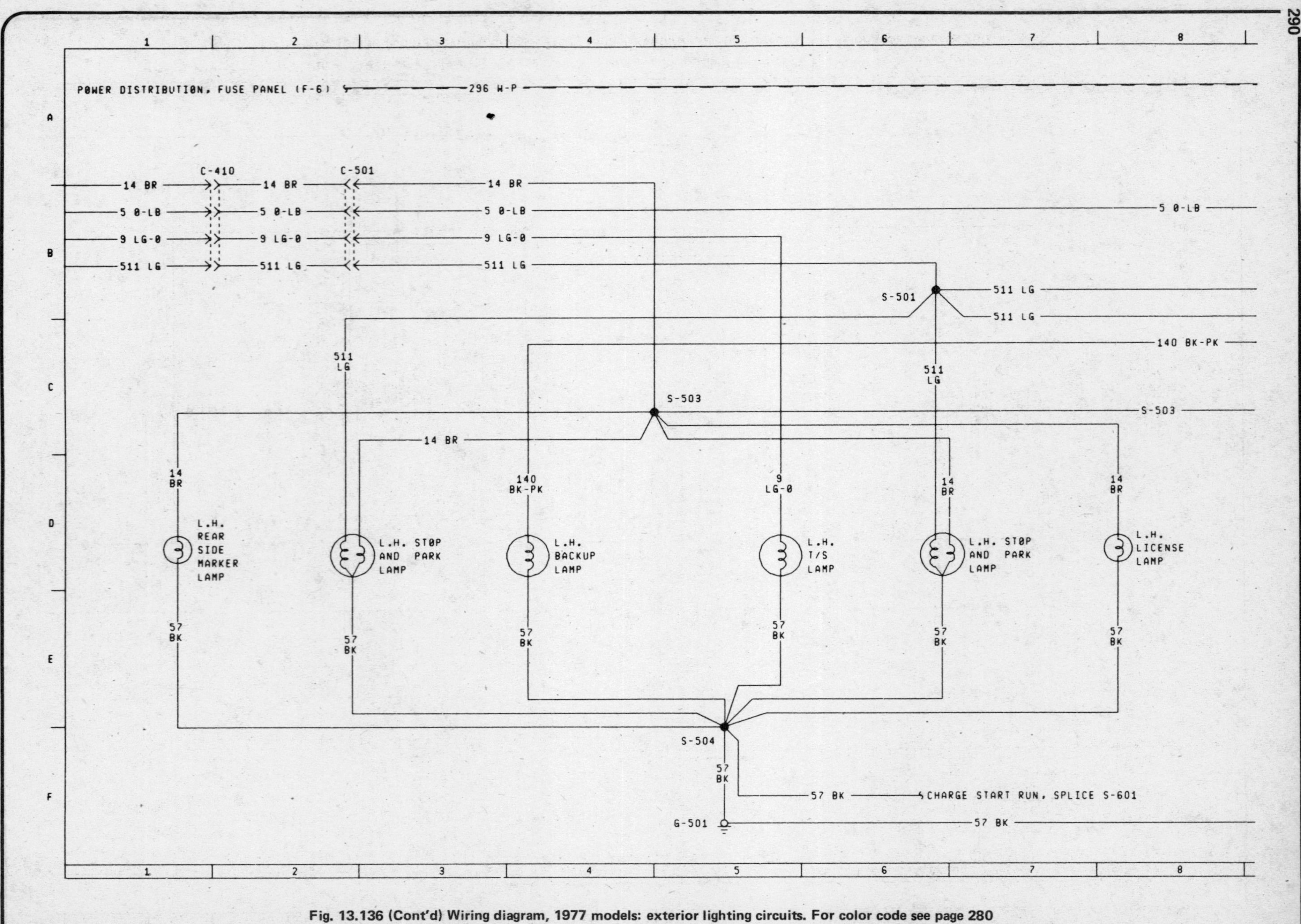

Fig. 13.136 (Cont'd) Wiring diagram, 1977 models: exterior lighting circuits. For color code see page 280

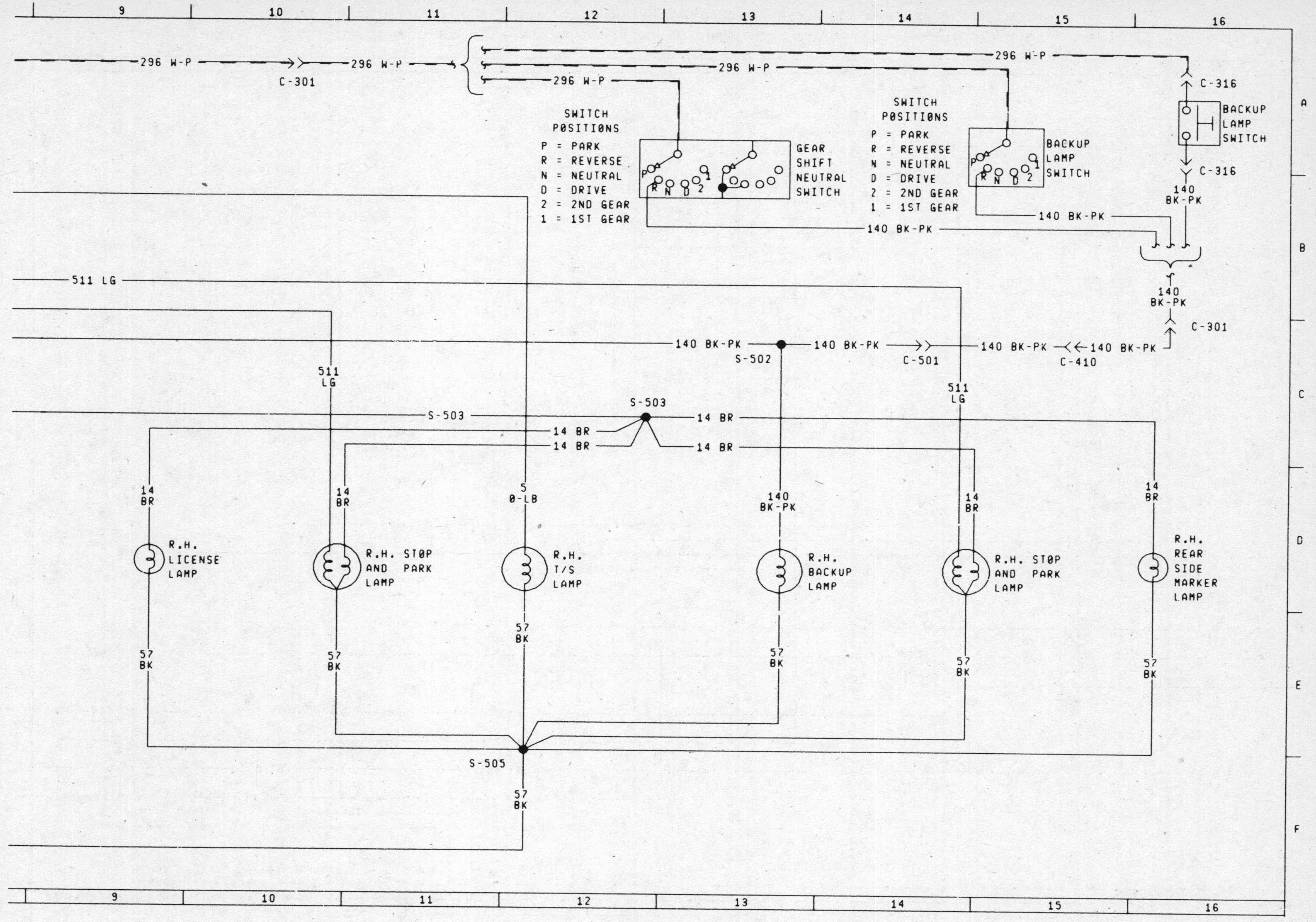

296 W-P
C-301
C-316
BACKUP LAMP SWITCH
SWITCH POSITIONS
P = PARK
R = REVERSE
N = NEUTRAL
D = DRIVE
2 = 2ND GEAR
1 = 1ST GEAR
GEAR SHIFT NEUTRAL SWITCH
140 BK-PK
511 LG
S-502
C-501
C-410
S-503
14 BR
5 O-LB
57 BK
S-505
R.H. LICENSE LAMP
R.H. STOP AND PARK LAMP
R.H. T/S LAMP
R.H. BACKUP LAMP
R.H. REAR SIDE MARKER LAMP

Fig. 13.136 (Cont'd) Wiring diagram, 1977 models: exterior lighting circuits. For color code see page 280

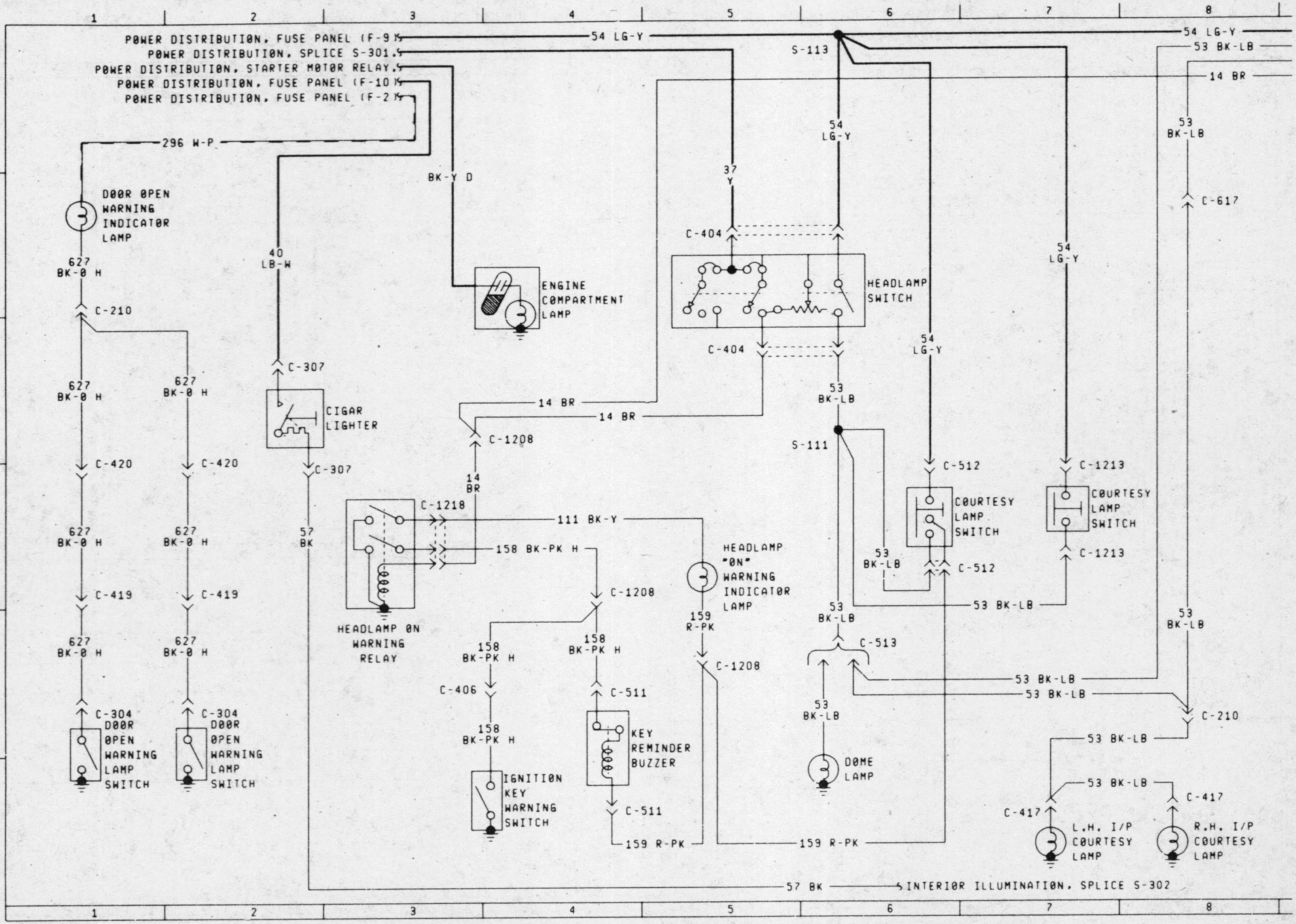

POWER DISTRIBUTION, FUSE PANEL (F-9)
POWER DISTRIBUTION, SPLICE S-301
POWER DISTRIBUTION, STARTER MOTOR RELAY
POWER DISTRIBUTION, FUSE PANEL (F-10)
POWER DISTRIBUTION, FUSE PANEL (F-2)
54 LG-Y
53 BK-LB
14 BR
296 W-P
BK-Y D
S-113
DOOR OPEN WARNING INDICATOR LAMP
627 BK-0 H
C-210
C-420
C-419
C-304
DOOR OPEN WARNING LAMP SWITCH
40 LB-W
C-307
CIGAR LIGHTER
57 BK
ENGINE COMPARTMENT LAMP
C-1208
C-1218
HEADLAMP ON WARNING RELAY
111 BK-Y
158 BK-PK H
C-406
IGNITION KEY WARNING SWITCH
C-511
KEY REMINDER BUZZER
159 R-PK
HEADLAMP "ON" WARNING INDICATOR LAMP
37 Y
C-404
HEADLAMP SWITCH
S-111
C-512
COURTESY LAMP SWITCH
C-1213
C-513
DOME LAMP
C-617
C-417
L.H. I/P COURTESY LAMP
R.H. I/P COURTESY LAMP
INTERIOR ILLUMINATION, SPLICE S-302

Fig. 13.137 Wiring diagram, 1977 models: protection and convenience circuits. For color code see page 280

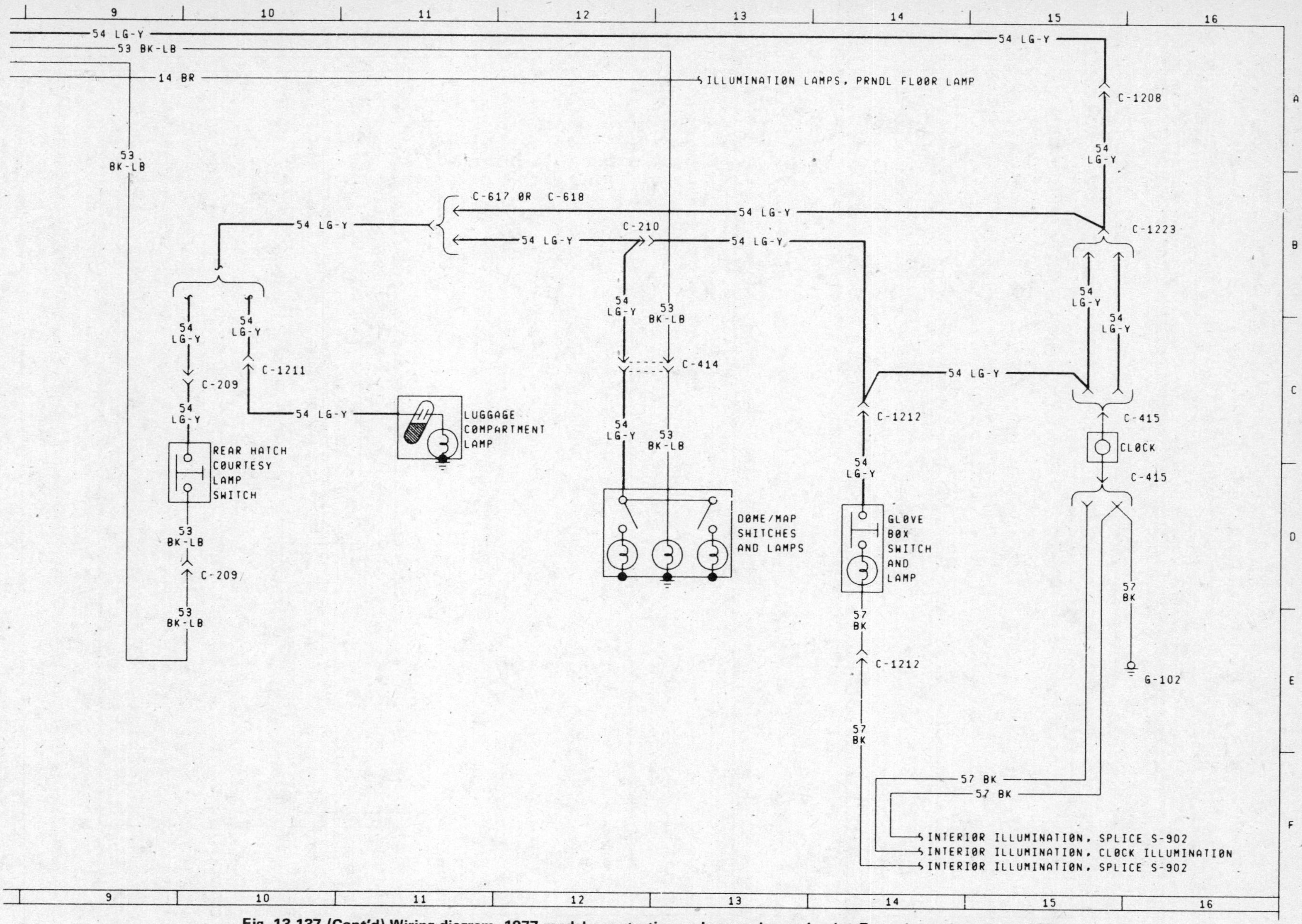

9 10 11 12 13 14 15 16

A B C D E F

54 LG-Y
53 BK-LB
14 BR
ILLUMINATION LAMPS, PRNDL FLOOR LAMP
C-1208
C-617 OR C-618
C-210
C-1223
C-1211
C-209
C-414
C-1212
C-415
CLOCK
REAR HATCH COURTESY LAMP SWITCH
LUGGAGE COMPARTMENT LAMP
DOME/MAP SWITCHES AND LAMPS
GLOVE BOX SWITCH AND LAMP
57 BK
G-102
INTERIOR ILLUMINATION, SPLICE S-902
INTERIOR ILLUMINATION, CLOCK ILLUMINATION
INTERIOR ILLUMINATION, SPLICE S-902

Fig. 13.137 (Cont'd) Wiring diagram, 1977 models: protection and convenience circuits. For color code see page 280

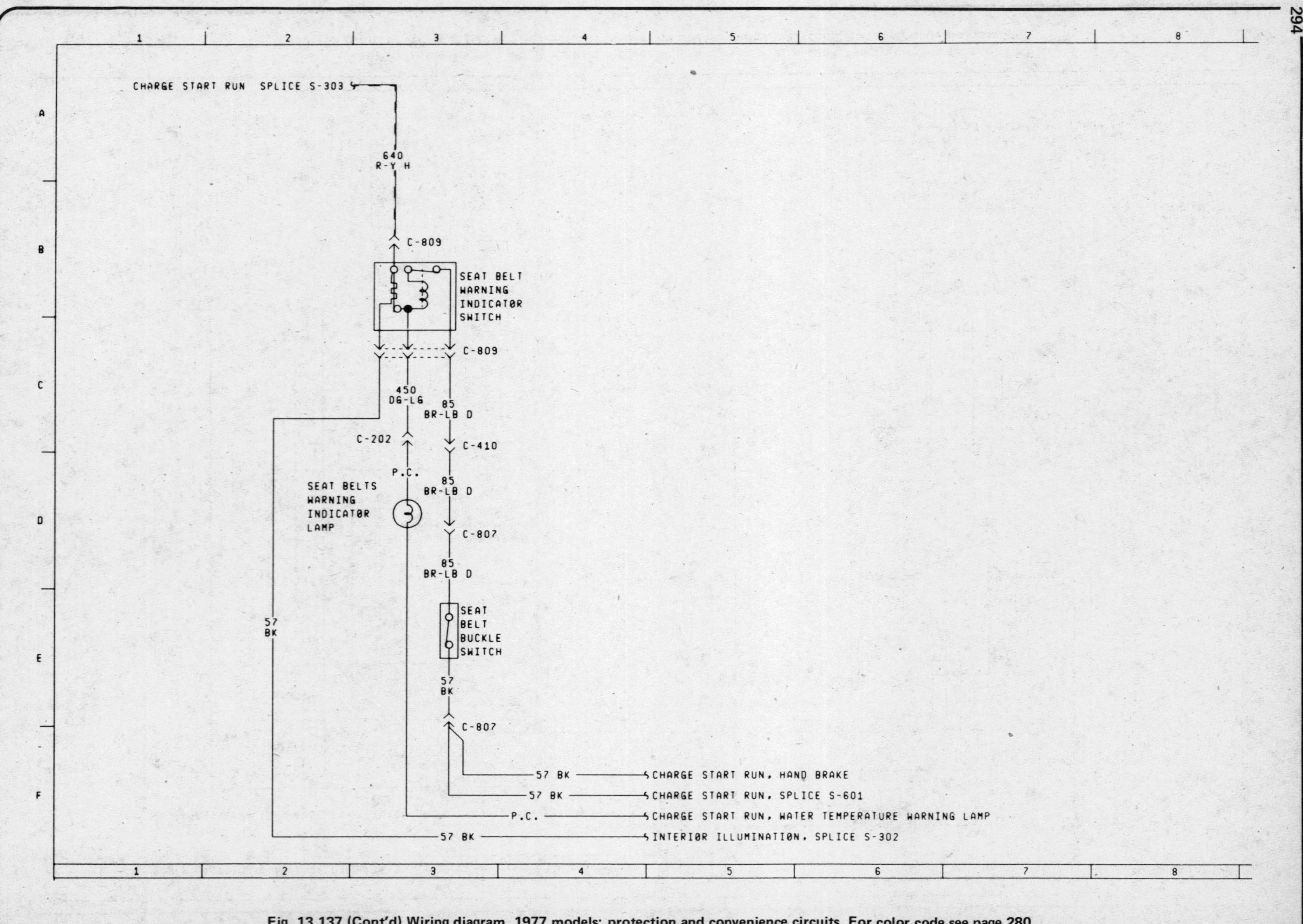

Fig. 13.137 (Cont'd) Wiring diagram, 1977 models: protection and convenience circuits. For color code see page 280

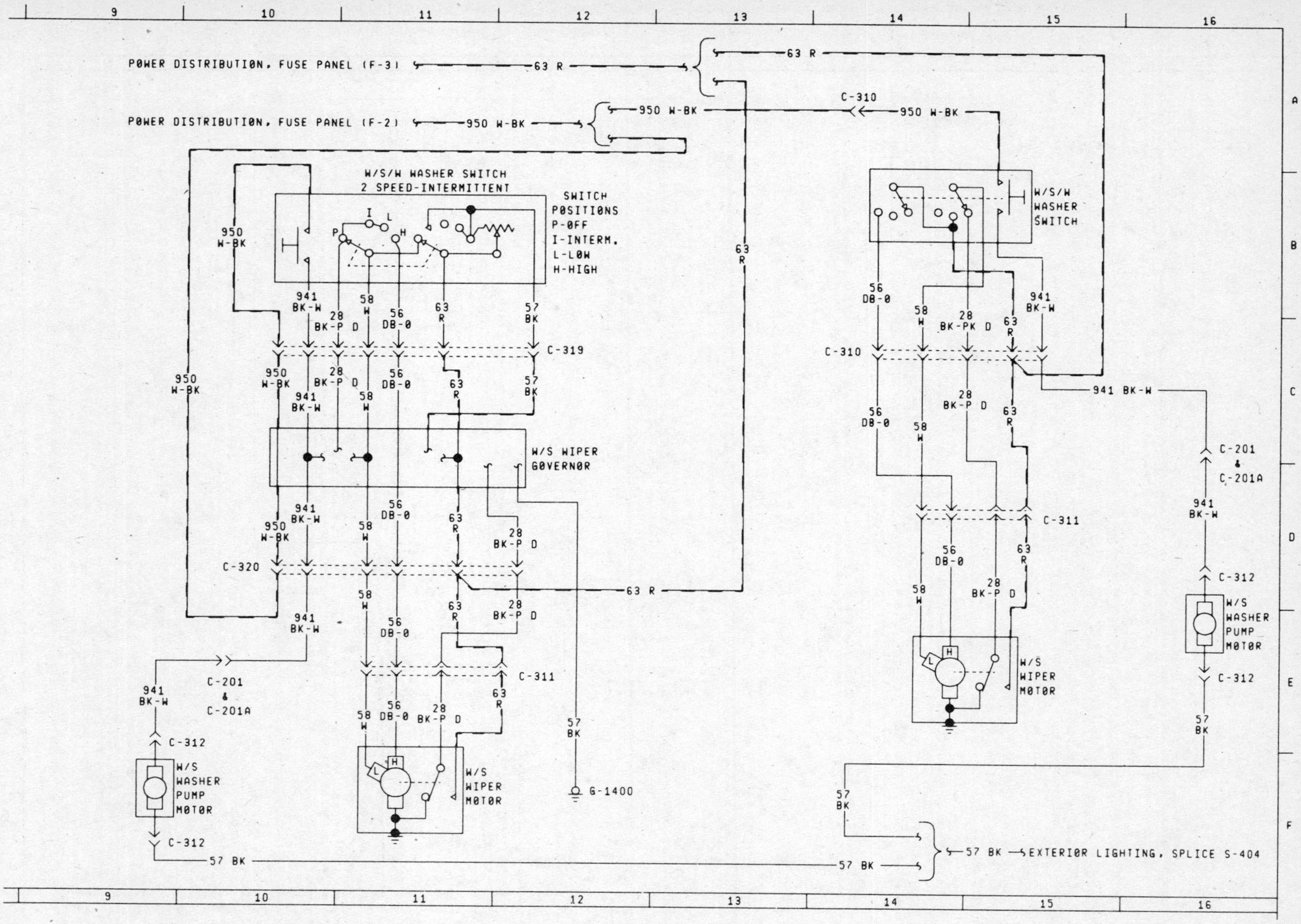

Fig. 13.137 (Cont'd) Wiring diagram, 1977 models: protection and convenience circuits. For color code see page 280

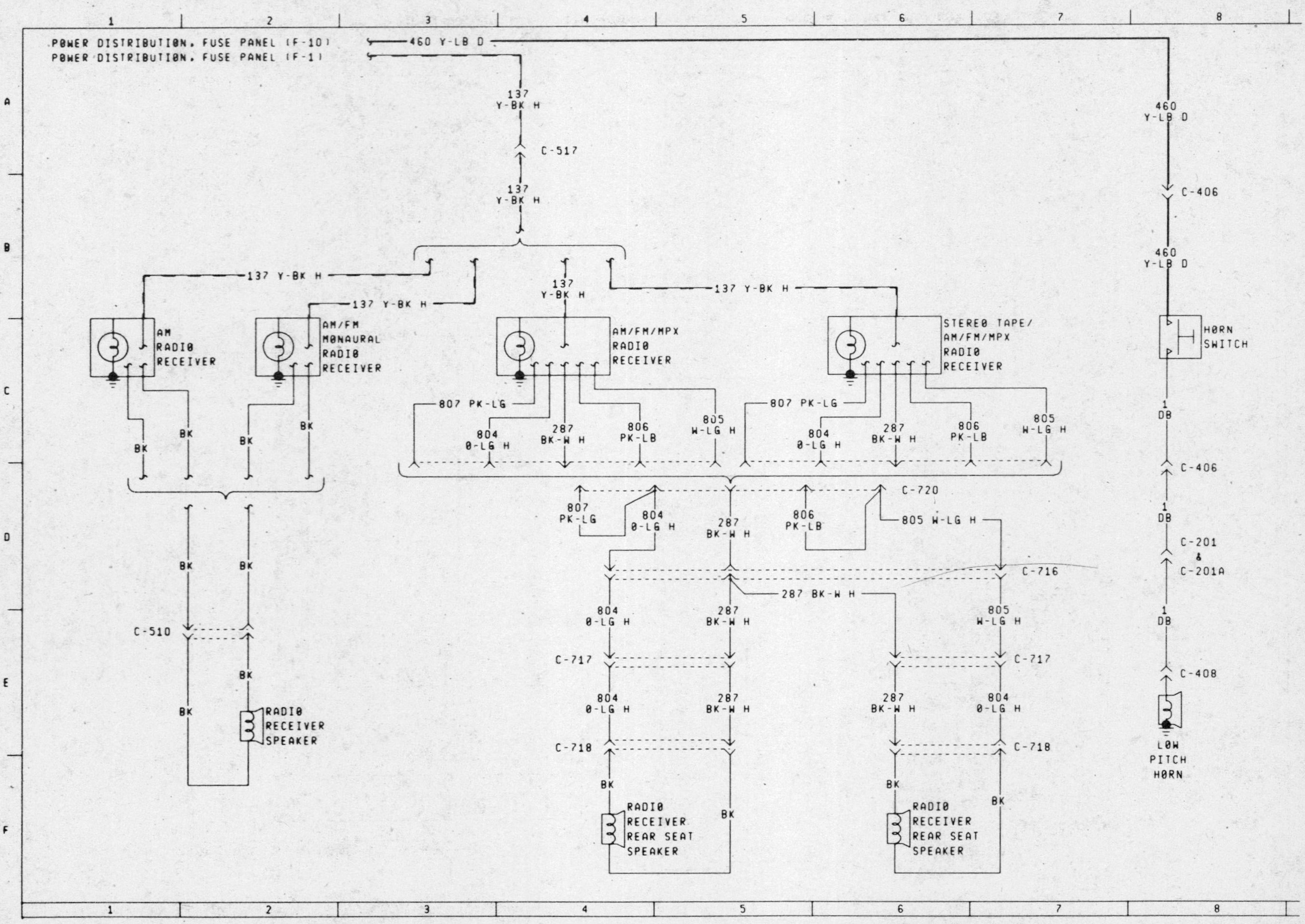

POWER DISTRIBUTION, FUSE PANEL (F-10)
POWER DISTRIBUTION, FUSE PANEL (F-1)
460 Y-LB D
137 Y-BK H
C-517
AM RADIO RECEIVER
AM/FM MONAURAL RADIO RECEIVER
AM/FM/MPX RADIO RECEIVER
STEREO TAPE/ AM/FM/MPX RADIO RECEIVER
HORN SWITCH
807 PK-LG
804 O-LG H
287 BK-W H
806 PK-LB
805 W-LG H
BK
C-720
C-716
C-717
C-718
C-510
C-406
C-201 & C-201A
C-408
1 DB
RADIO RECEIVER SPEAKER
RADIO RECEIVER REAR SEAT SPEAKER
LOW PITCH HORN

Fig. 13.138 Wiring diagram, 1977 models: radio, horn and air conditioning circuits. For color code see page 280

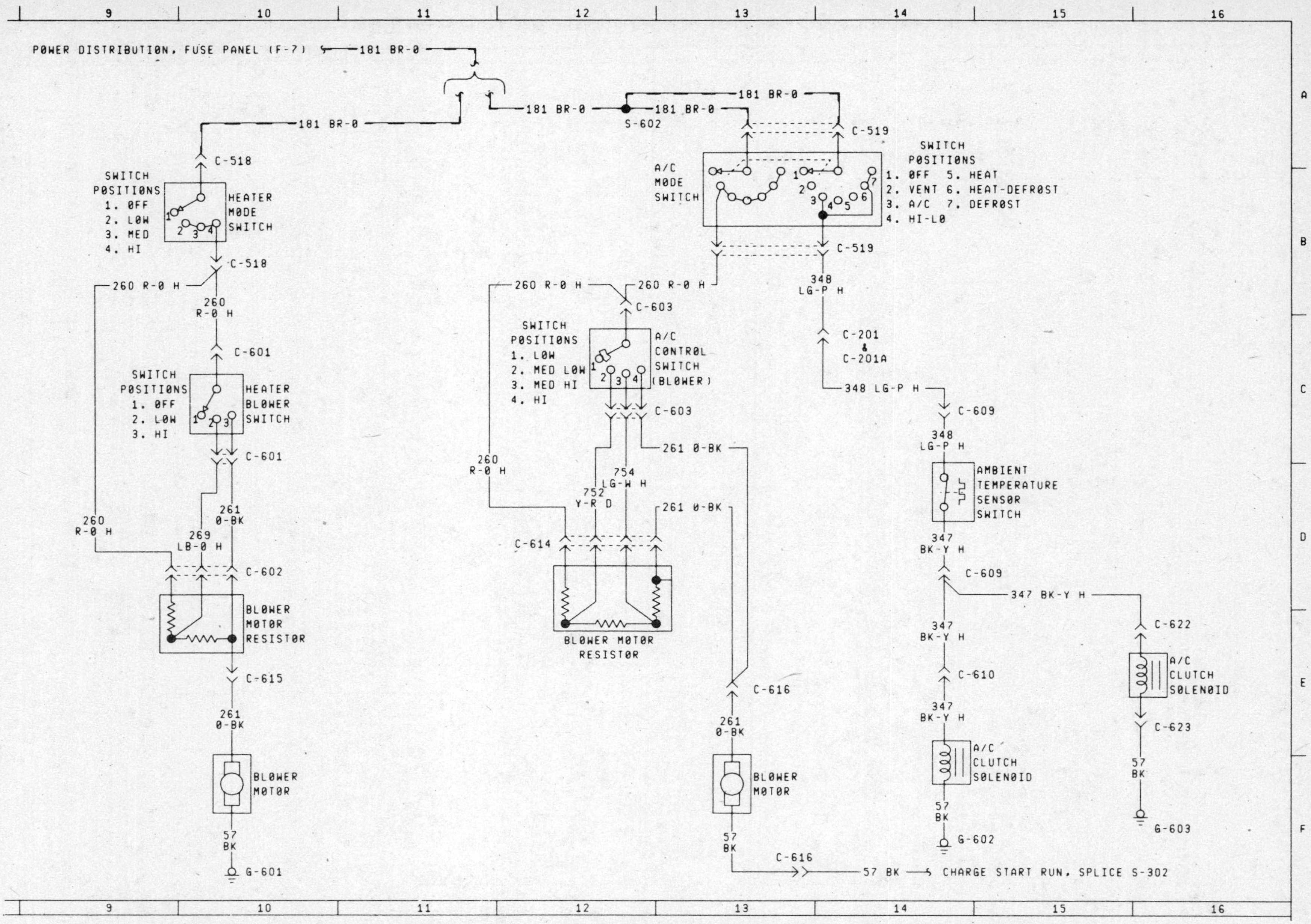

POWER DISTRIBUTION, FUSE PANEL (F-7) — 181 BR-O

181 BR-O
181 BR-O
S-602
181 BR-O
181 BR-O
C-519
A/C MODE SWITCH
SWITCH POSITIONS
1. OFF 5. HEAT
2. VENT 6. HEAT-DEFROST
3. A/C 7. DEFROST
4. HI-LO
C-519
348 LG-P H
C-201 & C-201A
348 LG-P H
C-609
348 LG-P H
AMBIENT TEMPERATURE SENSOR SWITCH
347 BK-Y H
C-609
347 BK-Y H
C-622
A/C CLUTCH SOLENOID
C-623
57 BK
G-603
347 BK-Y H
C-610
347 BK-Y H
A/C CLUTCH SOLENOID
57 BK
G-602

C-518
SWITCH POSITIONS
1. OFF
2. LOW
3. MED
4. HI
HEATER MODE SWITCH
C-518
260 R-O H
260 R-O H
C-601
SWITCH POSITIONS
1. OFF
2. LOW
3. HI
HEATER BLOWER SWITCH
C-601
261 O-BK
269 LB-O H
260 R-O H
C-602
BLOWER MOTOR RESISTOR
C-615
261 O-BK
BLOWER MOTOR
57 BK
G-601

260 R-O H
260 R-O H
C-603
SWITCH POSITIONS
1. LOW
2. MED LOW
3. MED HI
4. HI
A/C CONTROL SWITCH (BLOWER)
C-603
261 O-BK
754 LG-W H
752 Y-R D
260 R-O H
261 O-BK
C-614
BLOWER MOTOR RESISTOR
C-616
261 O-BK
BLOWER MOTOR
57 BK
C-616
57 BK — CHARGE START RUN, SPLICE S-302

9 10 11 12 13 14 15 16
A B C D E F

Fig. 13.138 (Cont'd) Wiring diagram, 1977 models: radio, horn and air conditioning circuits. For color code see page 280

13

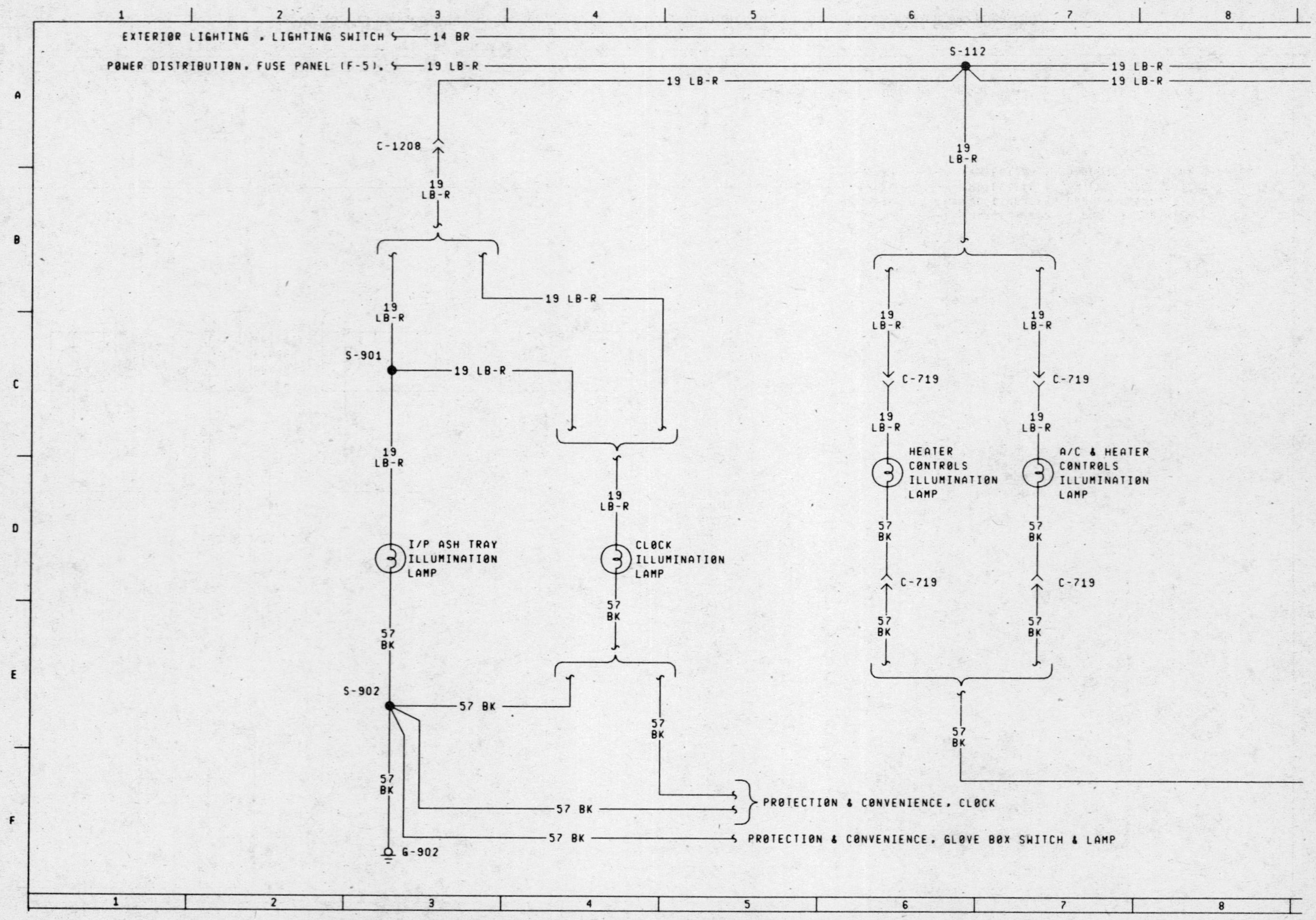

1 2 3 4 5 6 7 8

A B C D E F

EXTERIOR LIGHTING , LIGHTING SWITCH — 14 BR

POWER DISTRIBUTION, FUSE PANEL (F-5), — 19 LB-R

S-112

19 LB-R

19 LB-R

19 LB-R

C-1208

19 LB-R

19 LB-R

S-901

19 LB-R

19 LB-R

19 LB-R

I/P ASH TRAY ILLUMINATION LAMP

CLOCK ILLUMINATION LAMP

57 BK

S-902

57 BK

57 BK

57 BK

57 BK

G-902

PROTECTION & CONVENIENCE, CLOCK

PROTECTION & CONVENIENCE, GLOVE BOX SWITCH & LAMP

C-719

HEATER CONTROLS ILLUMINATION LAMP

A/C & HEATER CONTROLS ILLUMINATION LAMP

57 BK

Fig. 13.139 Wiring diagram, 1977 models: illumination lamp circuits. For color code see page 280

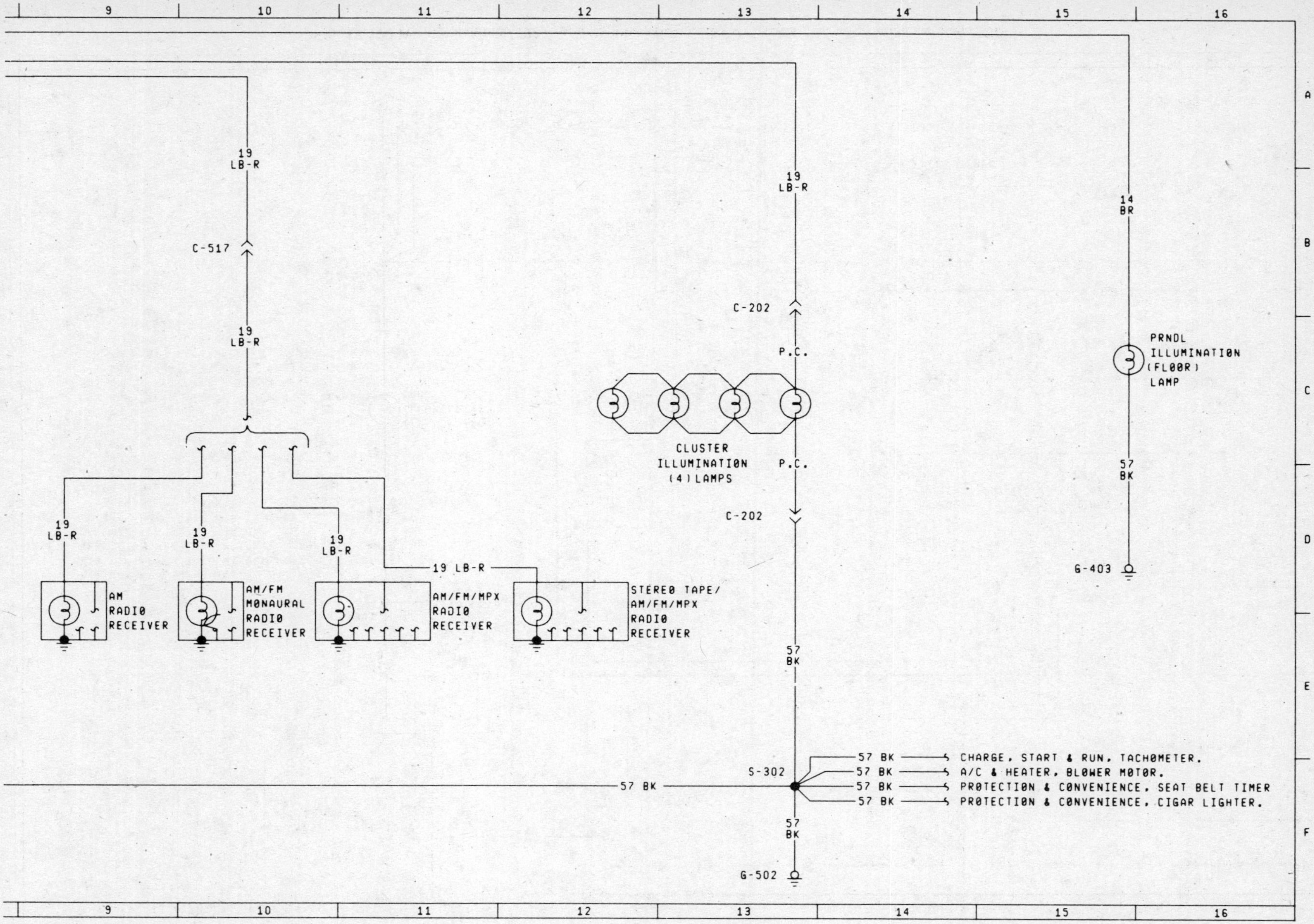

9 10 11 12 13 14 15 16

A B C D E F

19 LB-R

C-517

19 LB-R

19 LB-R

19 LB-R

19 LB-R

19 LB-R

AM RADIØ RECEIVER

AM/FM MØNAURAL RADIØ RECEIVER

AM/FM/MPX RADIØ RECEIVER

STEREØ TAPE/ AM/FM/MPX RADIØ RECEIVER

19 LB-R

C-202

P.C.

CLUSTER ILLUMINATIØN (4) LAMPS

P.C.

C-202

57 BK

S-302

57 BK — CHARGE, START & RUN, TACHØMETER.
57 BK — A/C & HEATER, BLØWER MØTØR.
57 BK — PRØTECTIØN & CØNVENIENCE, SEAT BELT TIMER
57 BK — PRØTECTIØN & CØNVENIENCE, CIGAR LIGHTER.

57 BK

57 BK

G-502

14 BR

PRNDL ILLUMINATIØN (FLØØR) LAMP

57 BK

G-403

Fig. 13.139 (Cont'd) Wiring diagram, 1977 models: illumination lamp circuits. For color code see page 280

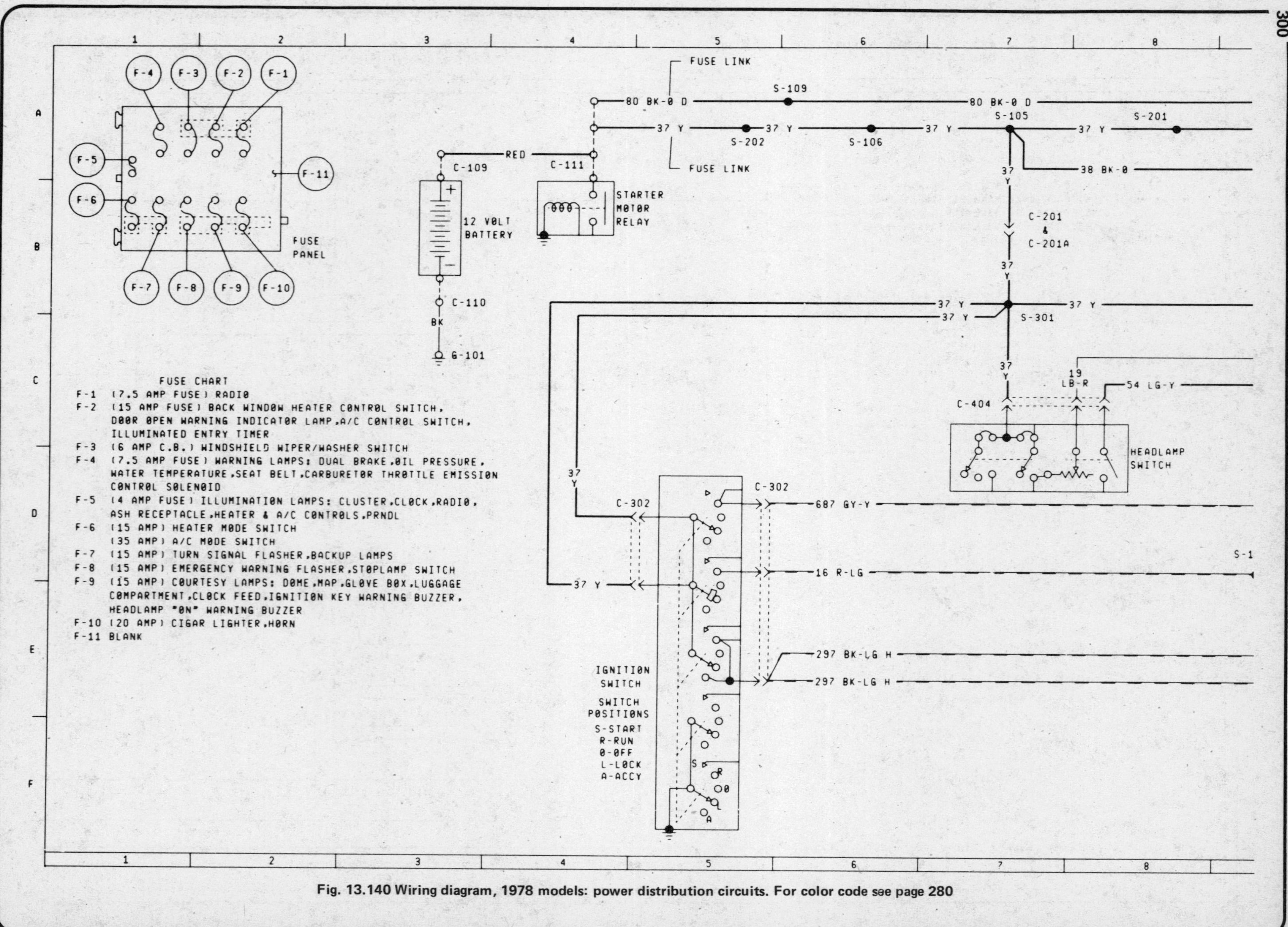

Fig. 13.140 Wiring diagram, 1978 models: power distribution circuits. For color code see page 280

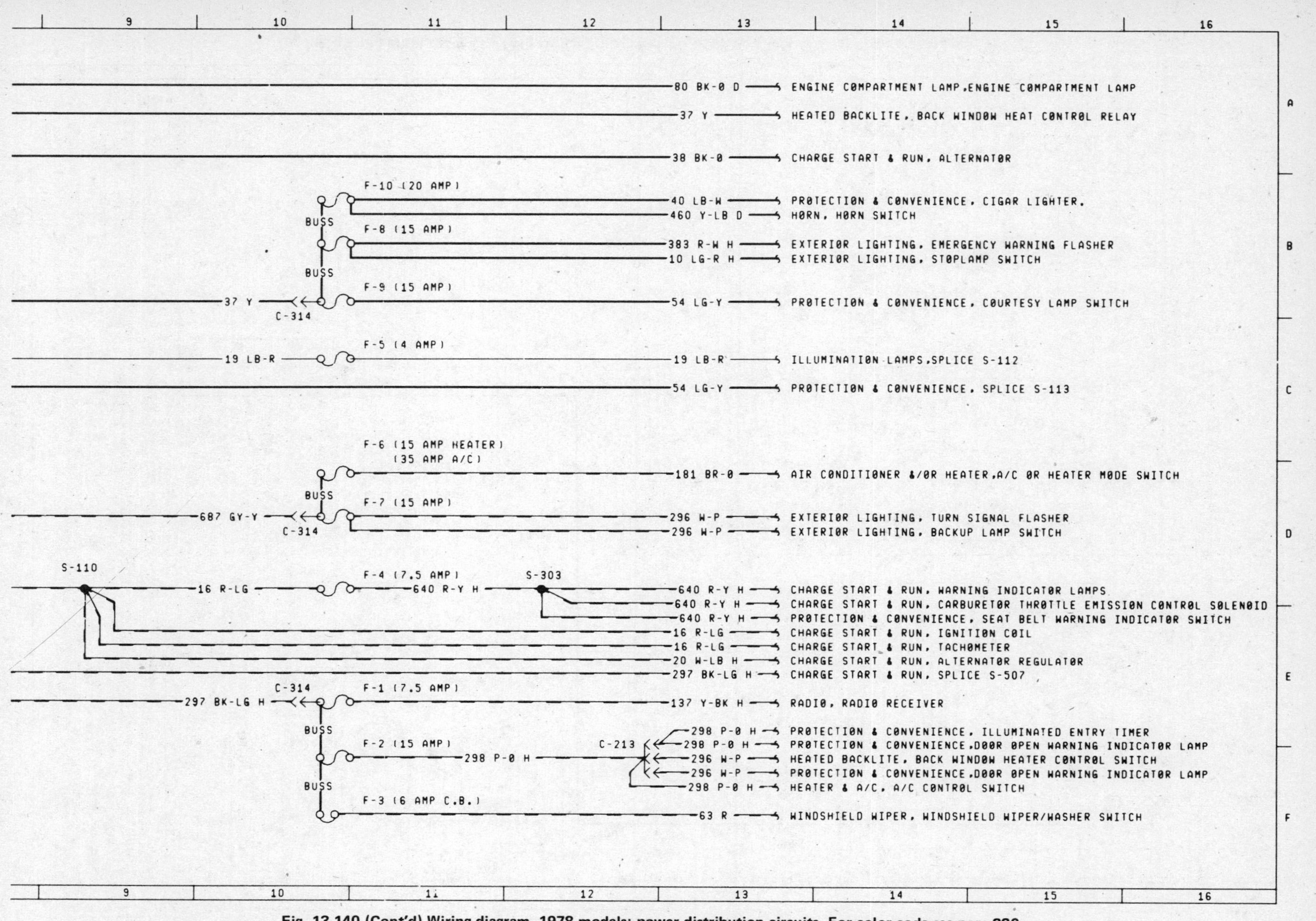

Fig. 13.140 (Cont'd) Wiring diagram, 1978 models: power distribution circuits. For color code see page 280

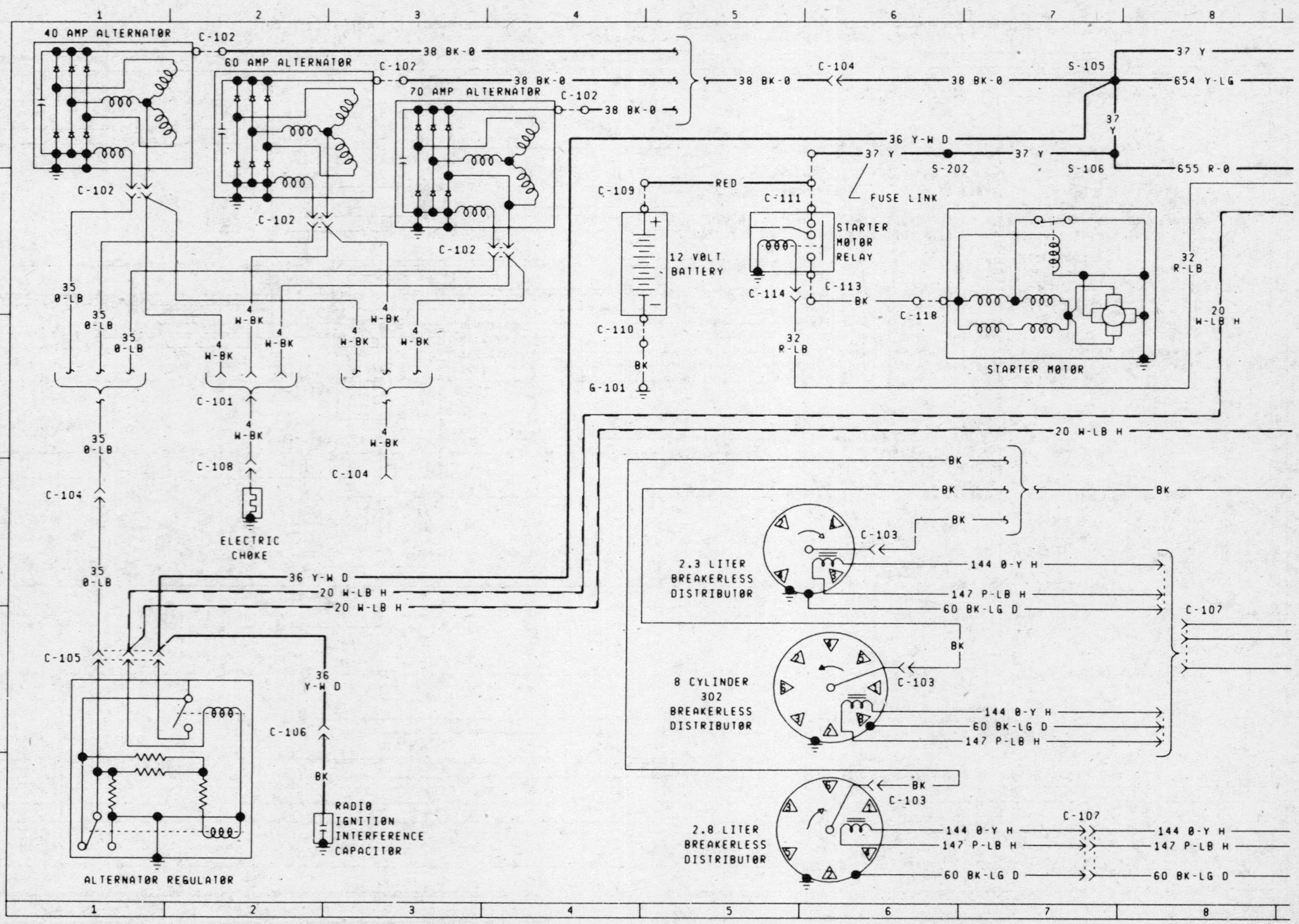

40 AMP ALTERNATØR
60 AMP ALTERNATØR
70 AMP ALTERNATØR
C-102
38 BK-Ø
C-104
S-105
37 Y
654 Y-LG
36 Y-W D
S-202
S-106
655 R-Ø
C-109
RED
C-111
FUSE LINK
12 VØLT BATTERY
STARTER MØTØR RELAY
C-113
C-114
BK
C-118
32 R-LB
STARTER MØTØR
20 W-LB H
C-110
G-101
35 Ø-LB
4 W-BK
C-101
C-108
ELECTRIC CHØKE
C-104
C-105
36 Y-W D
C-106
RADIØ IGNITIØN INTERFERENCE CAPACITØR
ALTERNATØR REGULATØR
2.3 LITER BREAKERLESS DISTRIBUTØR
8 CYLINDER 302 BREAKERLESS DISTRIBUTØR
2.8 LITER BREAKERLESS DISTRIBUTØR
C-103
C-107
144 Ø-Y H
147 P-LB H
60 BK-LG D

Fig. 13.141 Wiring diagram, 1978 models: charge, start and run circuits. For color code see page 280

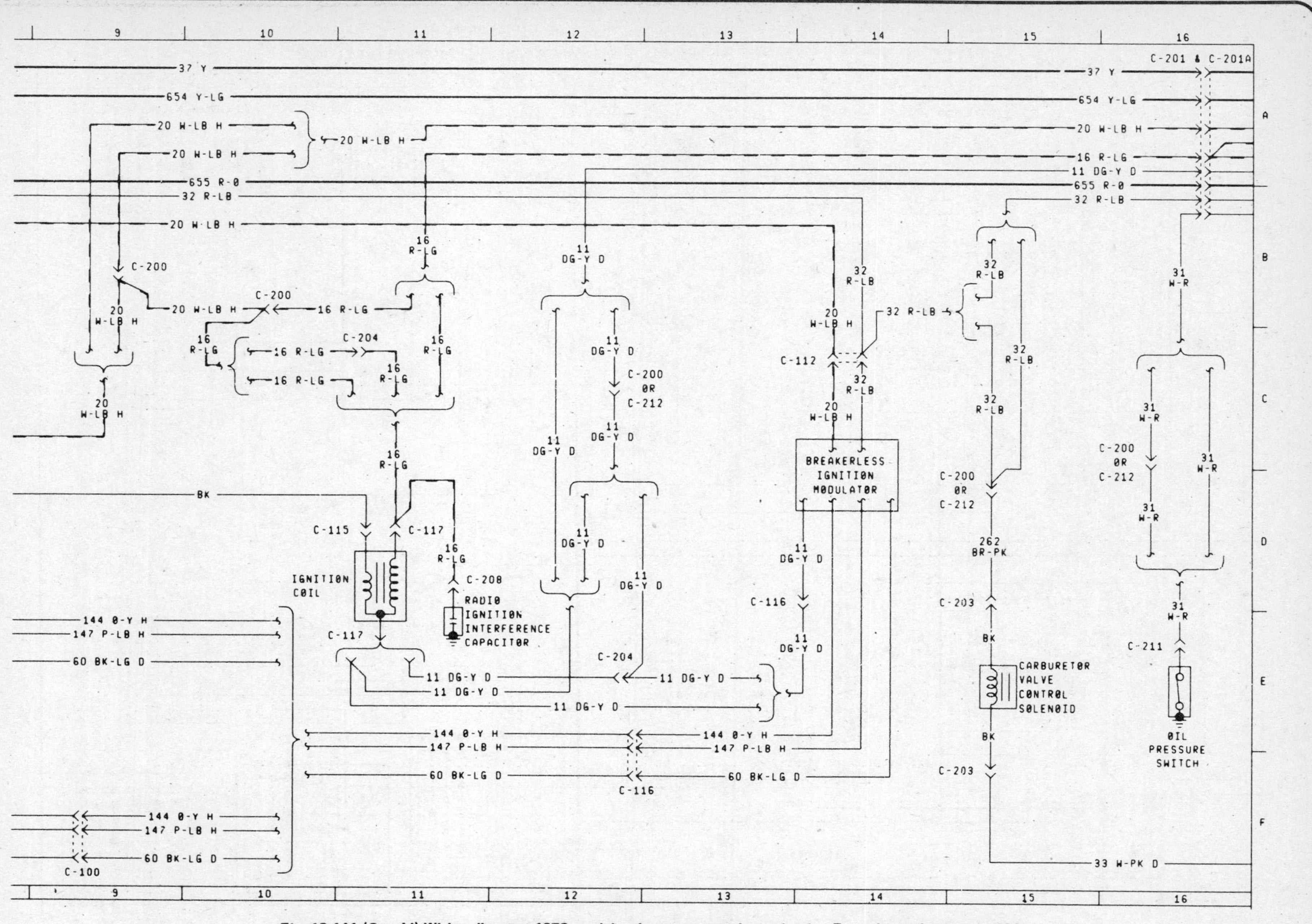

Fig. 13.141 (Cont'd) Wiring diagram, 1978 models: charge, start and run circuits. For color code see page 280

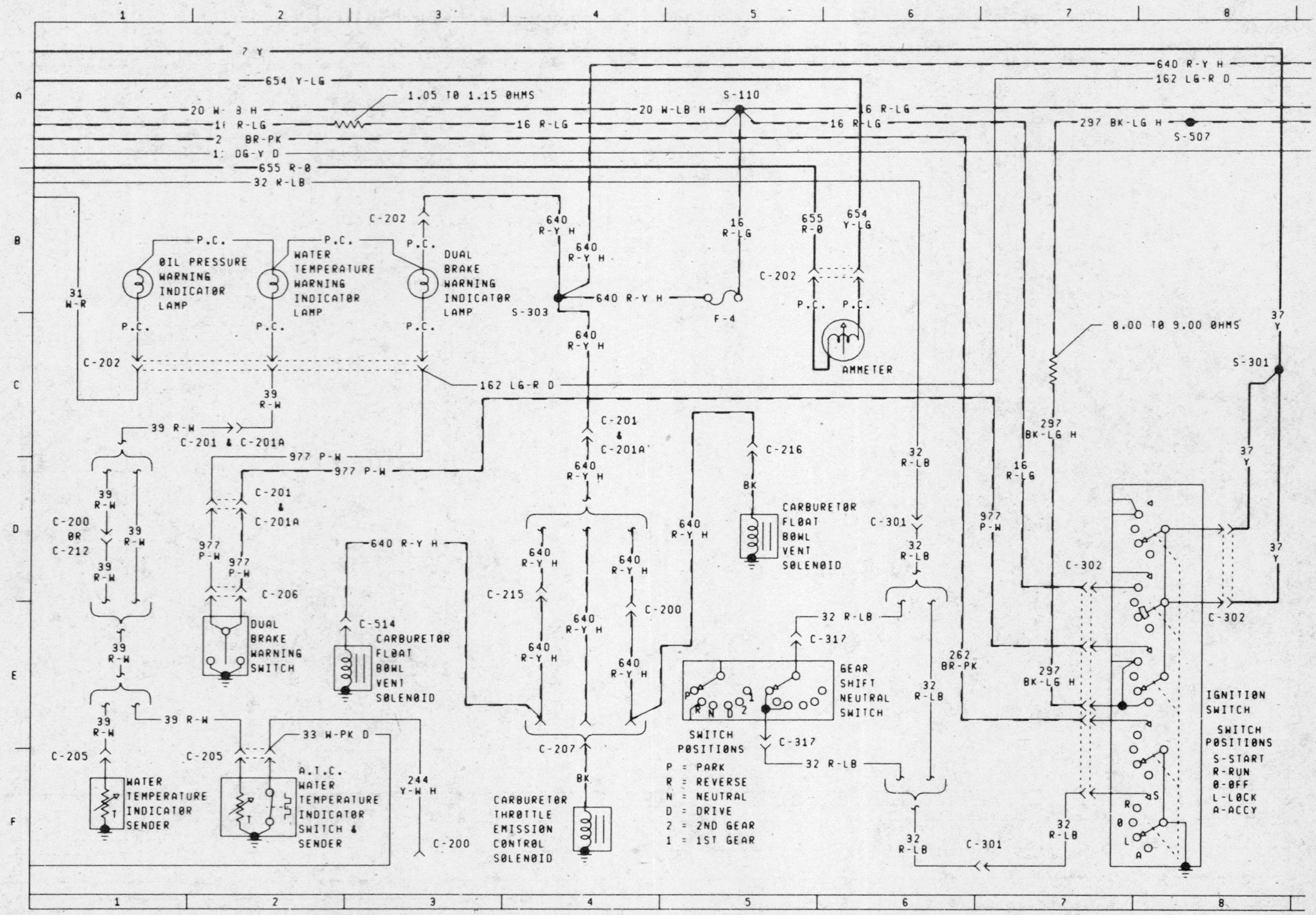
7 Y
654 Y-LG
1.05 TO 1.15 OHMS
20 W-LB H
16 R-LG
BR-PK
DG-Y D
655 R-O
32 R-LB
S-110
640 R-Y H
162 LG-R D
297 BK-LG H
S-507
31 W-R
C-202
P.C.
OIL PRESSURE WARNING INDICATOR LAMP
WATER TEMPERATURE WARNING INDICATOR LAMP
DUAL BRAKE WARNING INDICATOR LAMP
S-303
F-4
AMMETER
8.00 TO 9.00 OHMS
S-301
37 Y
39 R-W
C-201 & C-201A
977 P-W
C-200 OR C-212
C-206
DUAL BRAKE WARNING SWITCH
C-514
CARBURETOR FLOAT BOWL VENT SOLENOID
C-215
C-200
C-216
BK
C-301
C-302
C-317
GEAR SHIFT NEUTRAL SWITCH
262 BR-PK
C-205
WATER TEMPERATURE INDICATOR SENDER
33 W-PK D
A.T.C. WATER TEMPERATURE INDICATOR SWITCH & SENDER
244 Y-W H
C-207
CARBURETOR THROTTLE EMISSION CONTROL SOLENOID
SWITCH POSITIONS
P = PARK
R = REVERSE
N = NEUTRAL
D = DRIVE
2 = 2ND GEAR
1 = 1ST GEAR
IGNITION SWITCH
SWITCH POSITIONS
S-START
R-RUN
O-OFF
L-LOCK
A-ACCY

Fig. 13.141 (Cont'd) Wiring diagram, 1978 models: charge, start and run circuits. For color code see page 280

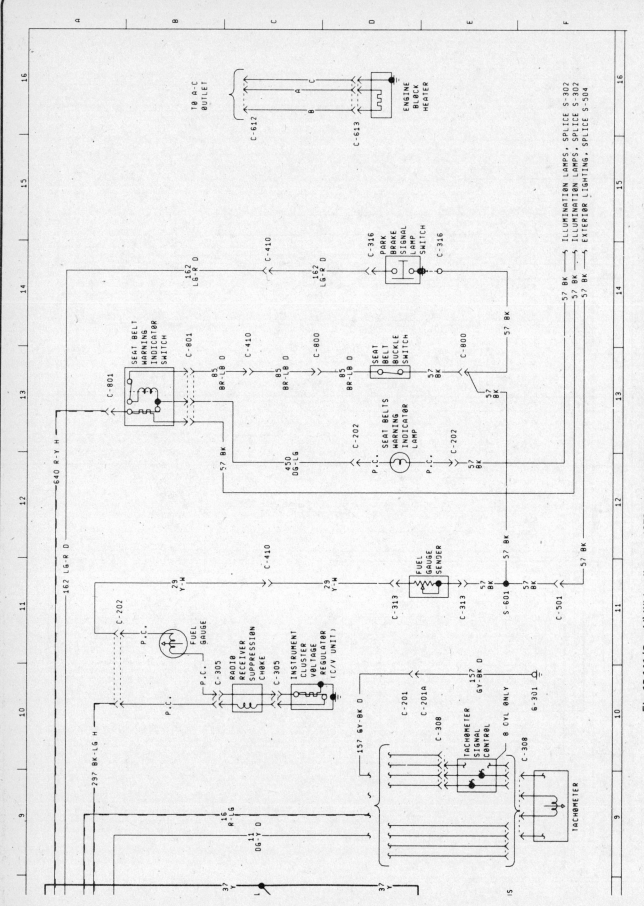

Fig. 13.141 (Cont'd) Wiring diagram, 1978 models: charge, start and run circuits. For color code see page 280

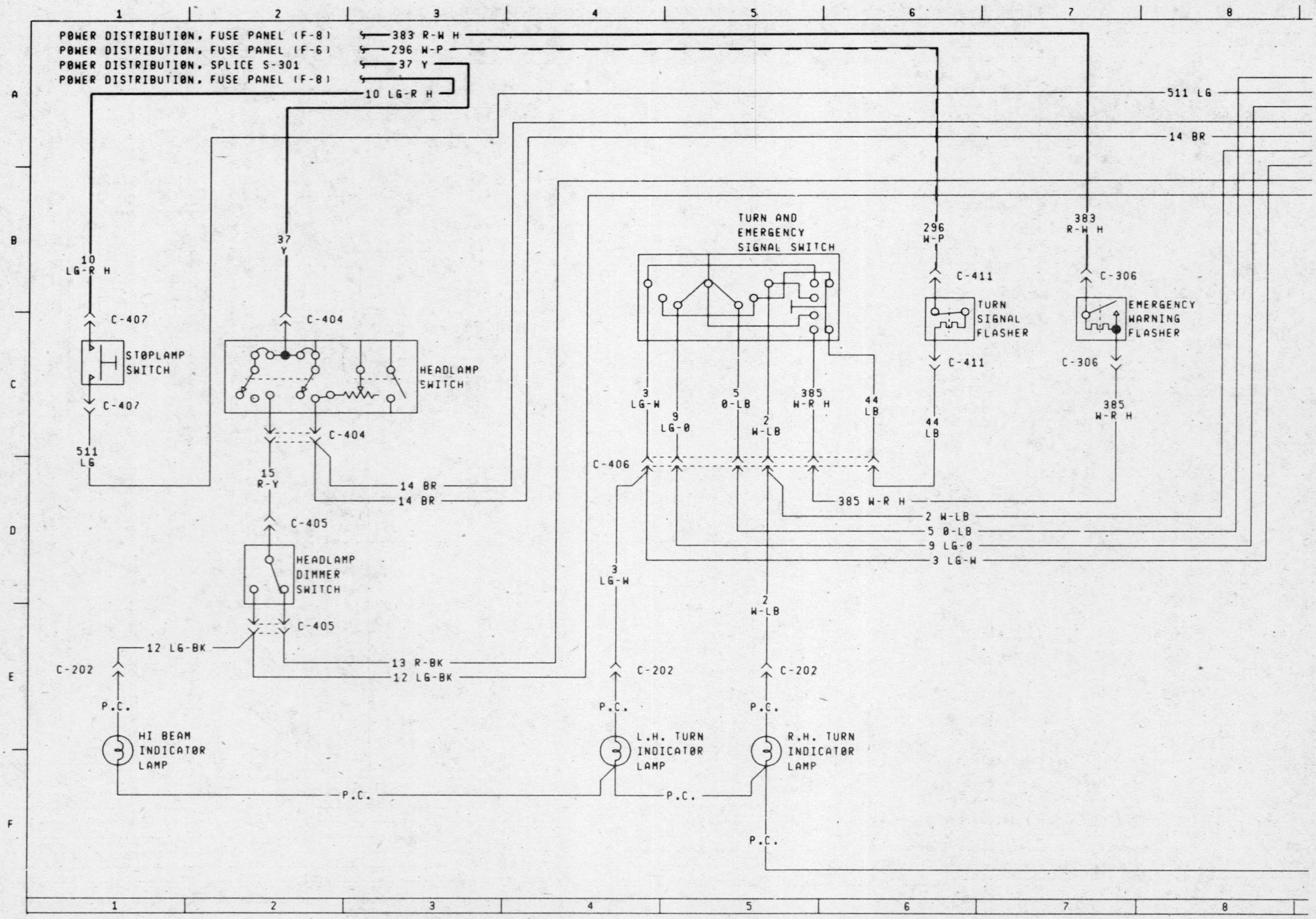

POWER DISTRIBUTION, FUSE PANEL (F-8) 383 R-W H
POWER DISTRIBUTION, FUSE PANEL (F-6) 296 W-P
POWER DISTRIBUTION, SPLICE S-301 37 Y
POWER DISTRIBUTION, FUSE PANEL (F-8) 10 LG-R H

511 LG
14 BR

10 LG-R H
C-407
STOPLAMP SWITCH
C-407
511 LG

37 Y
C-404
HEADLAMP SWITCH
C-404
15 R-Y
14 BR
14 BR
C-405
HEADLAMP DIMMER SWITCH
C-405
12 LG-BK
13 R-BK
12 LG-BK

TURN AND EMERGENCY SIGNAL SWITCH
3 LG-W
9 LG-O
5 O-LB
2 W-LB
385 W-R H
44 LB
C-406

296 W-P
C-411
TURN SIGNAL FLASHER
C-411
44 LB

383 R-W H
C-306
EMERGENCY WARNING FLASHER
C-306
385 W-R H

385 W-R H
2 W-LB
5 O-LB
9 LG-O
3 LG-W

3 LG-W
2 W-LB

C-202
P.C.
HI BEAM INDICATOR LAMP

C-202
P.C.
L.H. TURN INDICATOR LAMP

C-202
P.C.
R.H. TURN INDICATOR LAMP

P.C.
P.C.
P.C.

Fig. 13.142 Wiring diagram, 1978 models: exterior lighting circuits. For color code see page 280

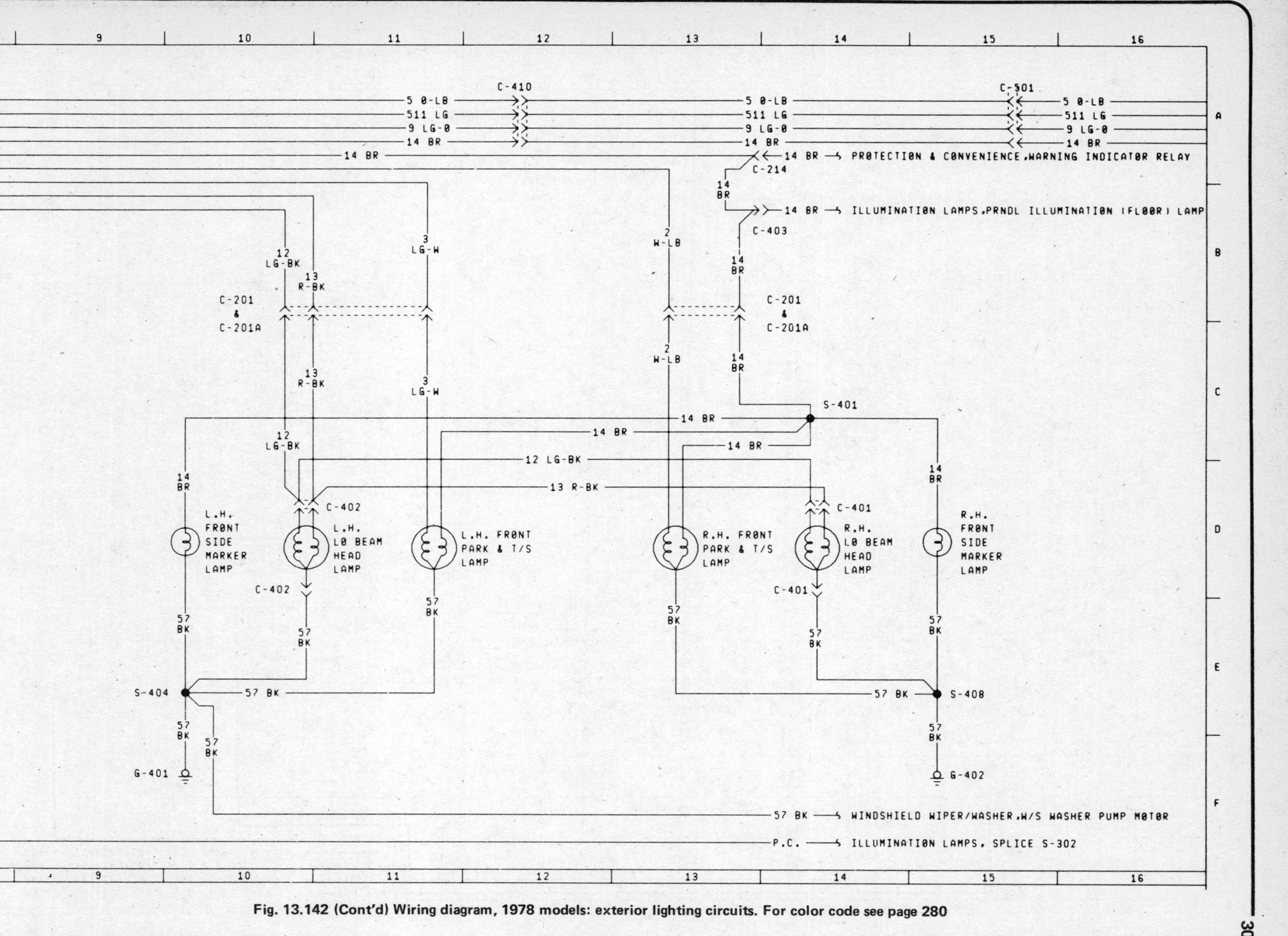

Fig. 13.142 (Cont'd) Wiring diagram, 1978 models: exterior lighting circuits. For color code see page 280

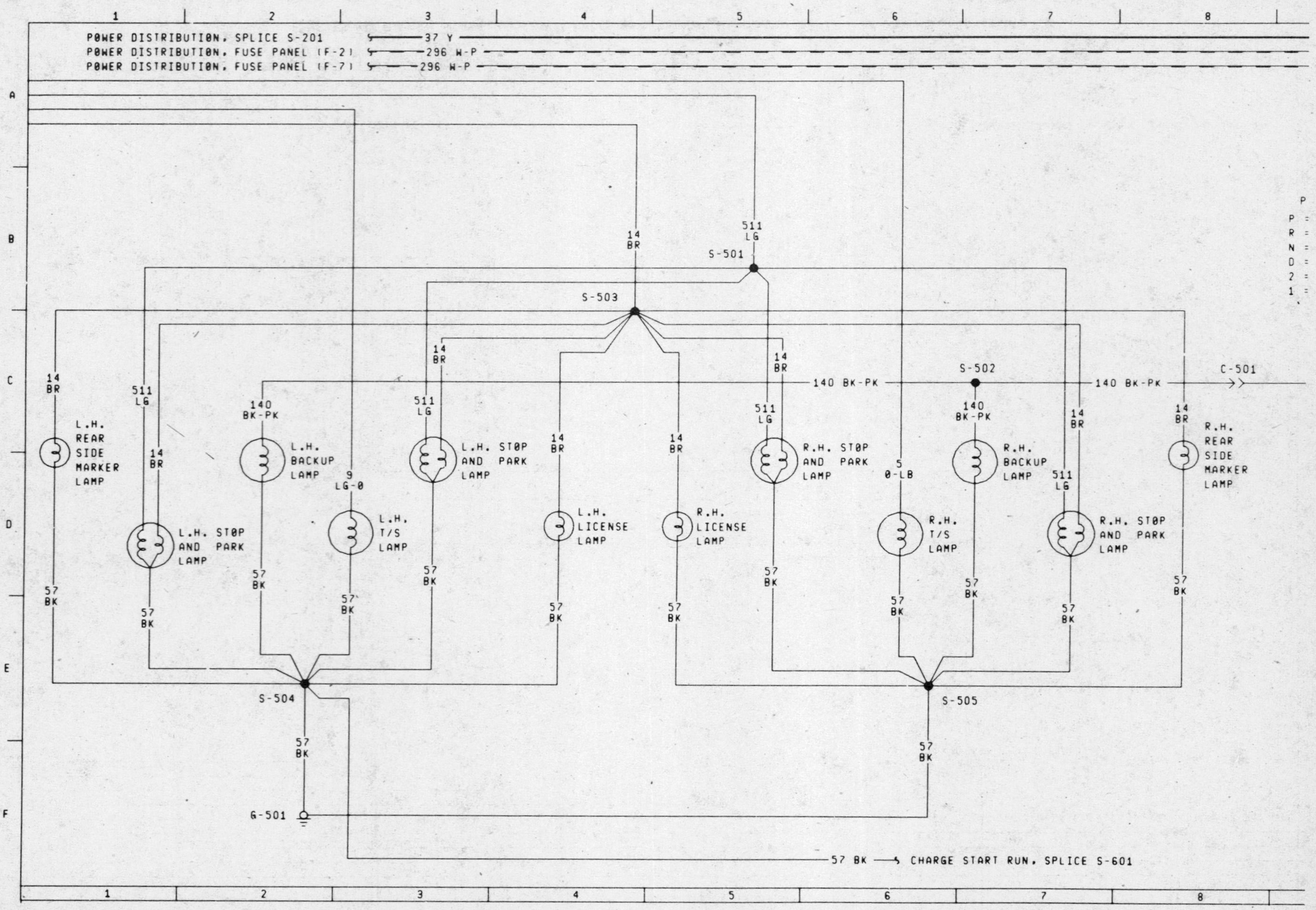

1 2 3 4 5 6 7 8

POWER DISTRIBUTION, SPLICE S-201 — 37 Y
POWER DISTRIBUTION, FUSE PANEL (F-2) — 296 W-P
POWER DISTRIBUTION, FUSE PANEL (F-7) — 296 W-P

A
B
C
D
E
F

P
P =
R =
N =
D =
2 =
1 =

14 BR
511 LG
S-501
S-503
S-502
C-501
140 BK-PK
140 BK-PK

L.H. REAR SIDE MARKER LAMP — 14 BR — 57 BK
L.H. STOP AND PARK LAMP — 511 LG — 14 BR — 57 BK
L.H. BACKUP LAMP — 140 BK-PK — 57 BK
L.H. T/S LAMP — 9 LG-O — 57 BK
L.H. STOP AND PARK LAMP — 511 LG — 14 BR — 57 BK
L.H. LICENSE LAMP — 14 BR — 57 BK
R.H. LICENSE LAMP — 14 BR — 57 BK
R.H. STOP AND PARK LAMP — 511 LG — 14 BR — 57 BK
R.H. T/S LAMP — 5 O-LB — 57 BK
R.H. BACKUP LAMP — 140 BK-PK — 57 BK
R.H. STOP AND PARK LAMP — 511 LG — 14 BR — 57 BK
R.H. REAR SIDE MARKER LAMP — 14 BR — 57 BK

S-504
S-505
57 BK
57 BK
G-501

57 BK — CHARGE START RUN, SPLICE S-601

1 2 3 4 5 6 7 8

Fig. 13.142 (Cont'd) Wiring diagram, 1978 models: exterior lighting circuits. For color code see page 280

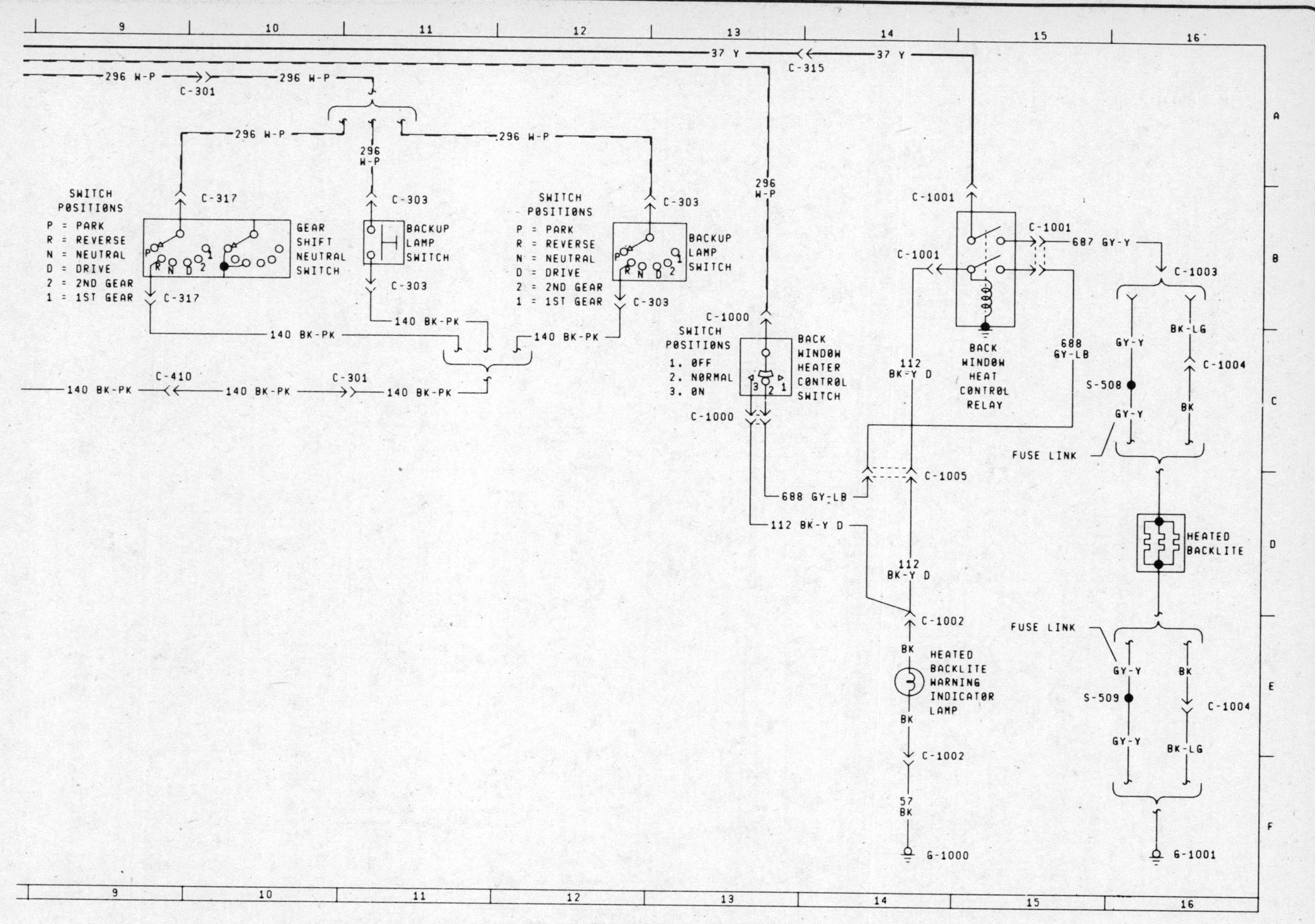

Fig. 13.142 (Cont'd) Wiring diagram, 1978 models: exterior lighting circuits. For color code see page 280

13

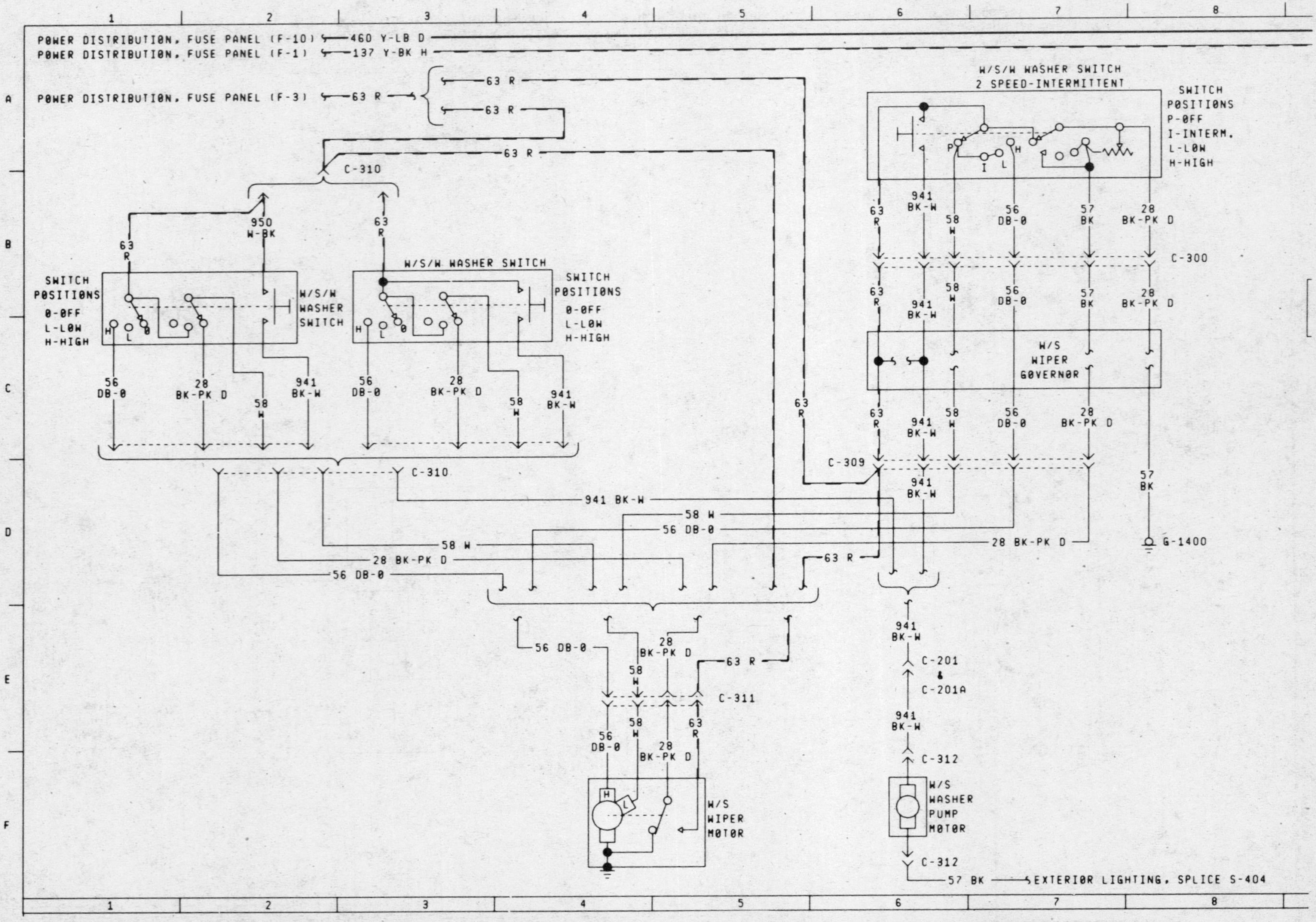

POWER DISTRIBUTION, FUSE PANEL (F-10) — 460 Y-LB D
POWER DISTRIBUTION, FUSE PANEL (F-1) — 137 Y-BK H
POWER DISTRIBUTION, FUSE PANEL (F-3) — 63 R

W/S/W WASHER SWITCH
SWITCH POSITIONS
0-OFF
L-LOW
H-HIGH

W/S/W WASHER SWITCH
SWITCH POSITIONS
0-OFF
L-LOW
H-HIGH

W/S/W WASHER SWITCH
2 SPEED-INTERMITTENT
SWITCH POSITIONS
P-OFF
I-INTERM.
L-LOW
H-HIGH

W/S WIPER GOVERNOR

W/S WIPER MOTOR

W/S WASHER PUMP MOTOR

C-300, C-309, C-310, C-311, C-312, C-201 & C-201A, G-1400

63 R, 950 W-BK, 56 DB-O, 28 BK-PK D, 58 W, 941 BK-W, 57 BK

57 BK — EXTERIOR LIGHTING, SPLICE S-404

Fig. 13.143 Wiring diagram, 1978 models: windshield wash/wipe, radio and horn circuits. For color code see page 280

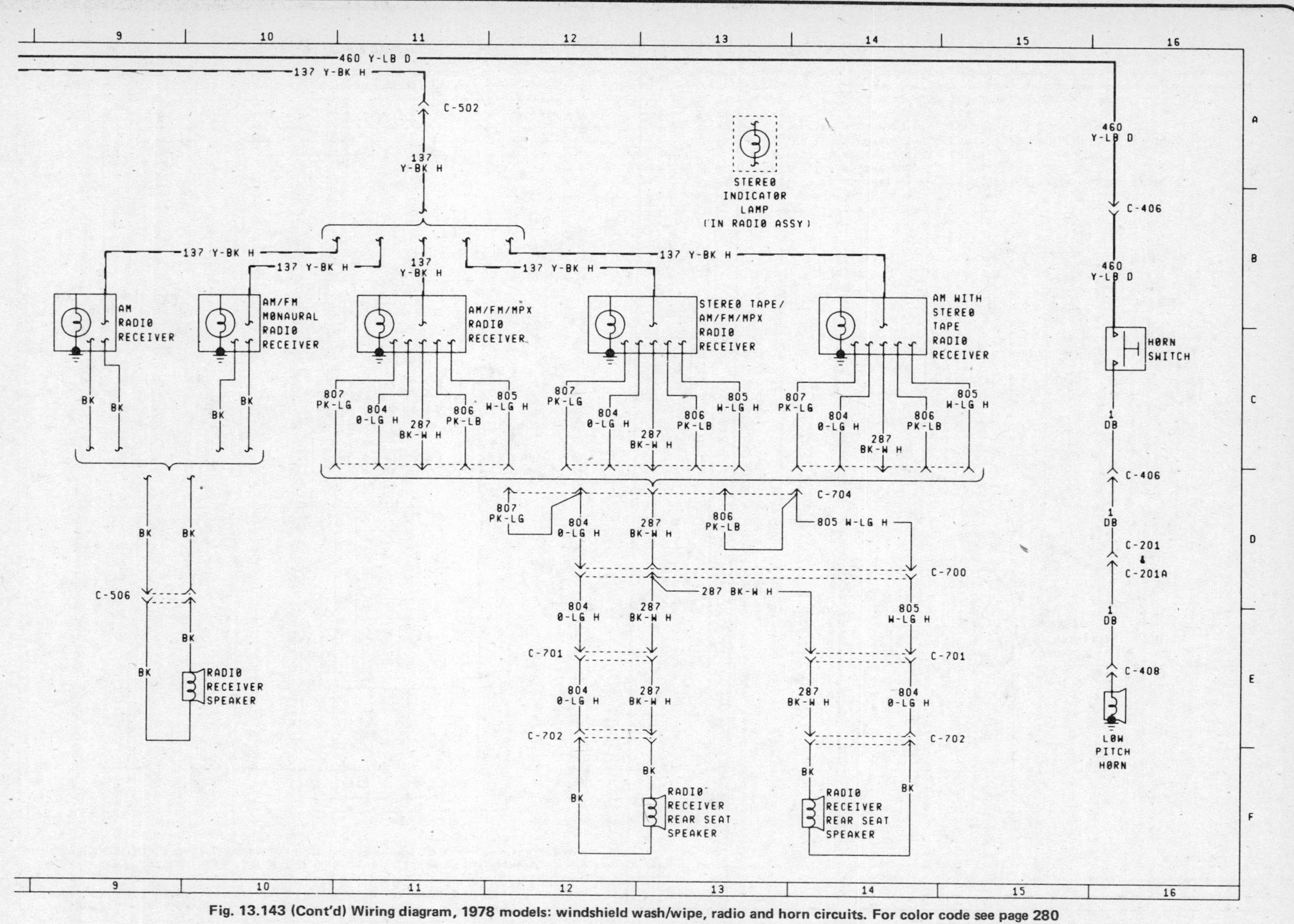

Fig. 13.143 (Cont'd) Wiring diagram, 1978 models: windshield wash/wipe, radio and horn circuits. For color code see page 280

13

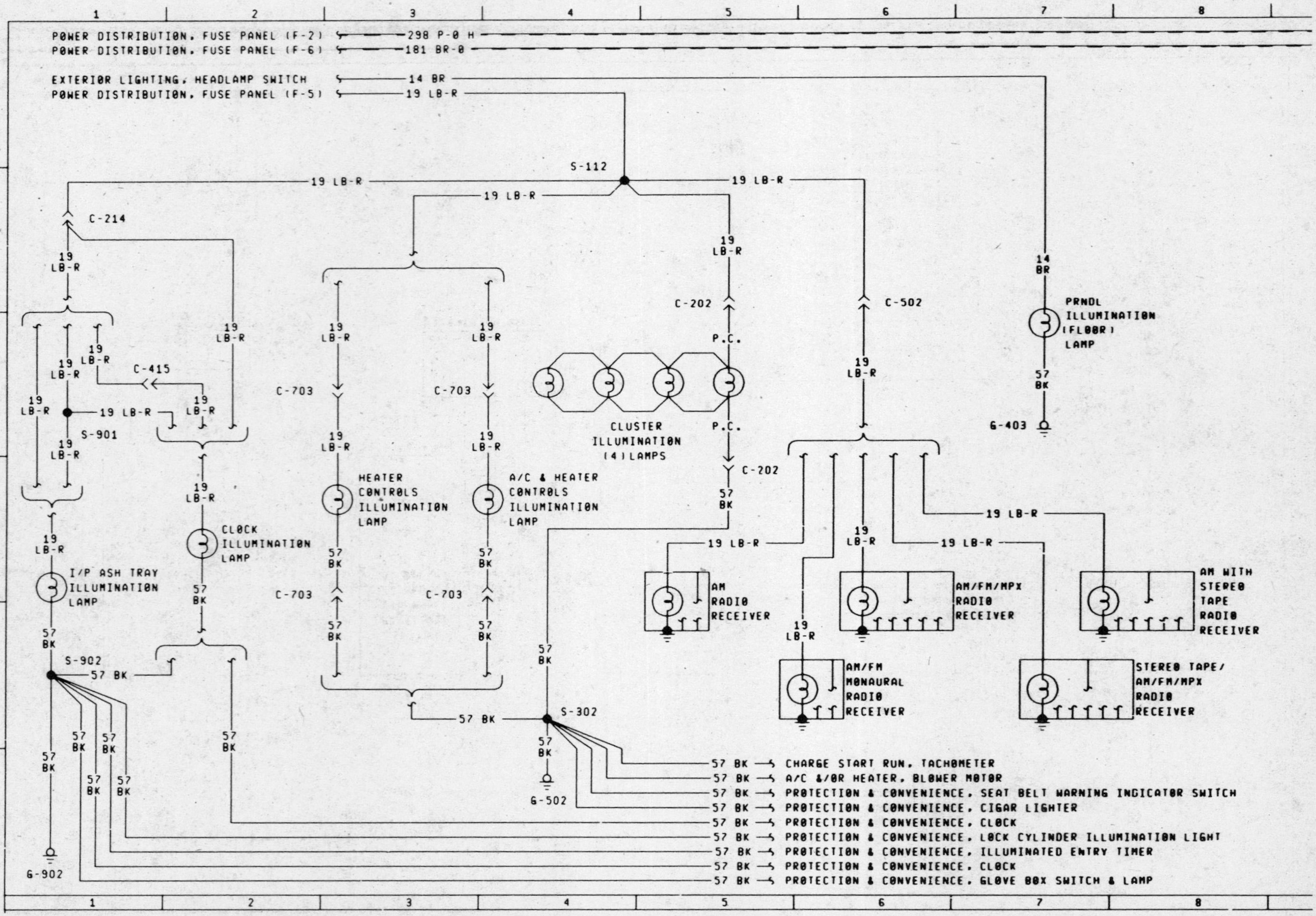

Fig. 13.144 Wiring diagram, 1978 models: illumination lamp, air conditioning or heater circuits. For color code see page 280

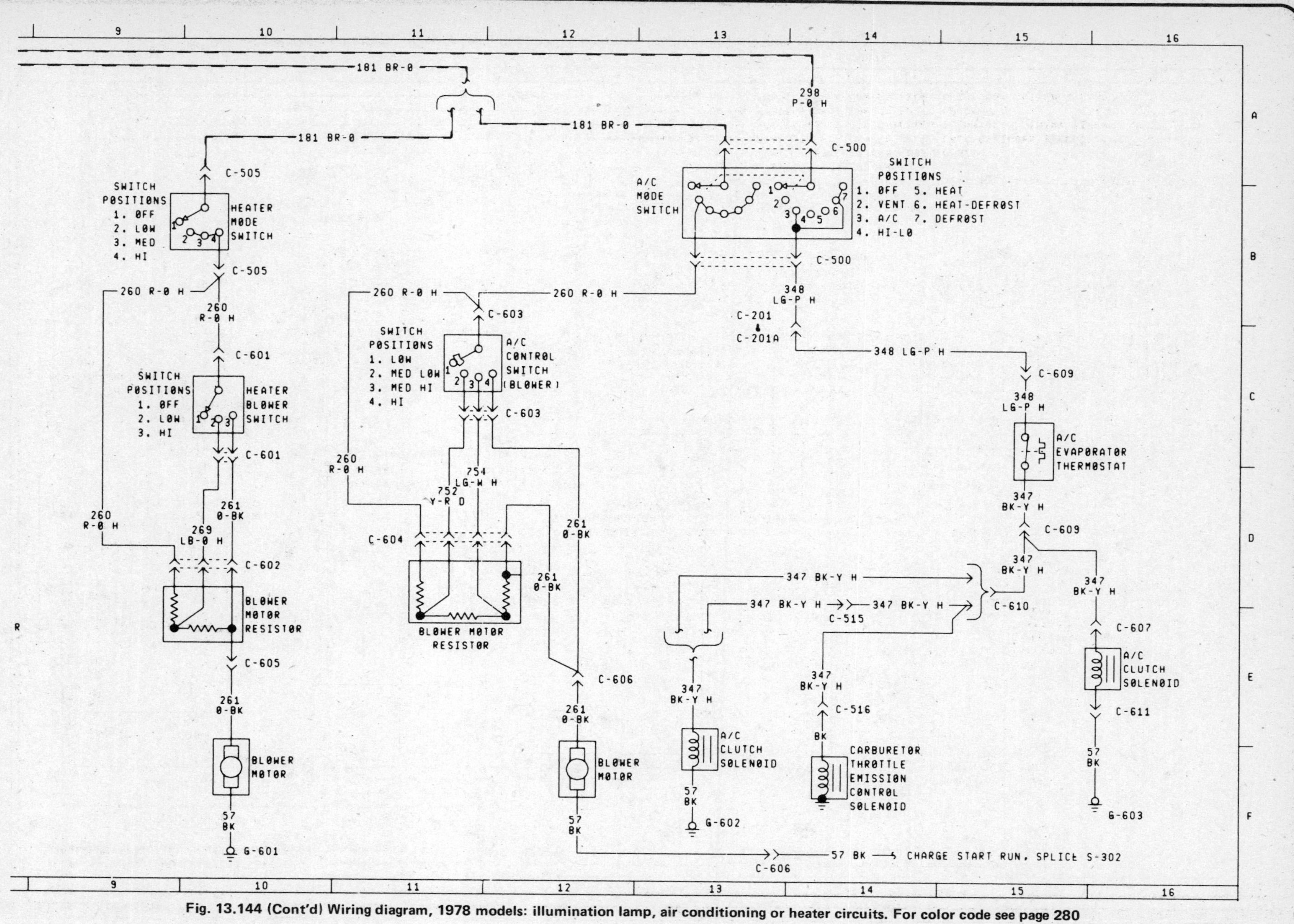

Fig. 13.144 (Cont'd) Wiring diagram, 1978 models: illumination lamp, air conditioning or heater circuits. For color code see page 280

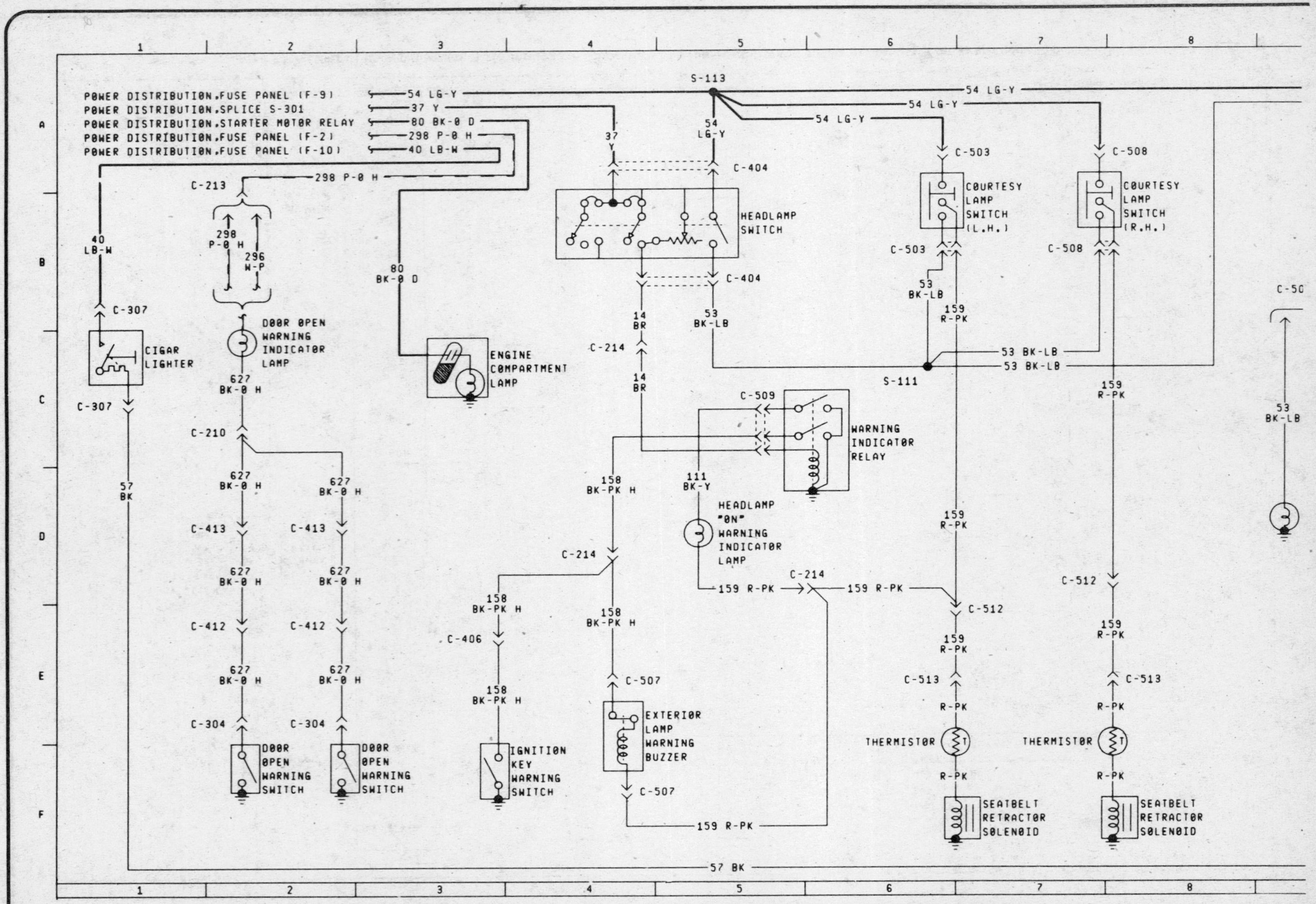

Fig. 13.145 Wiring diagram, 1978 models: protection and convenience circuits. For color code see page 280

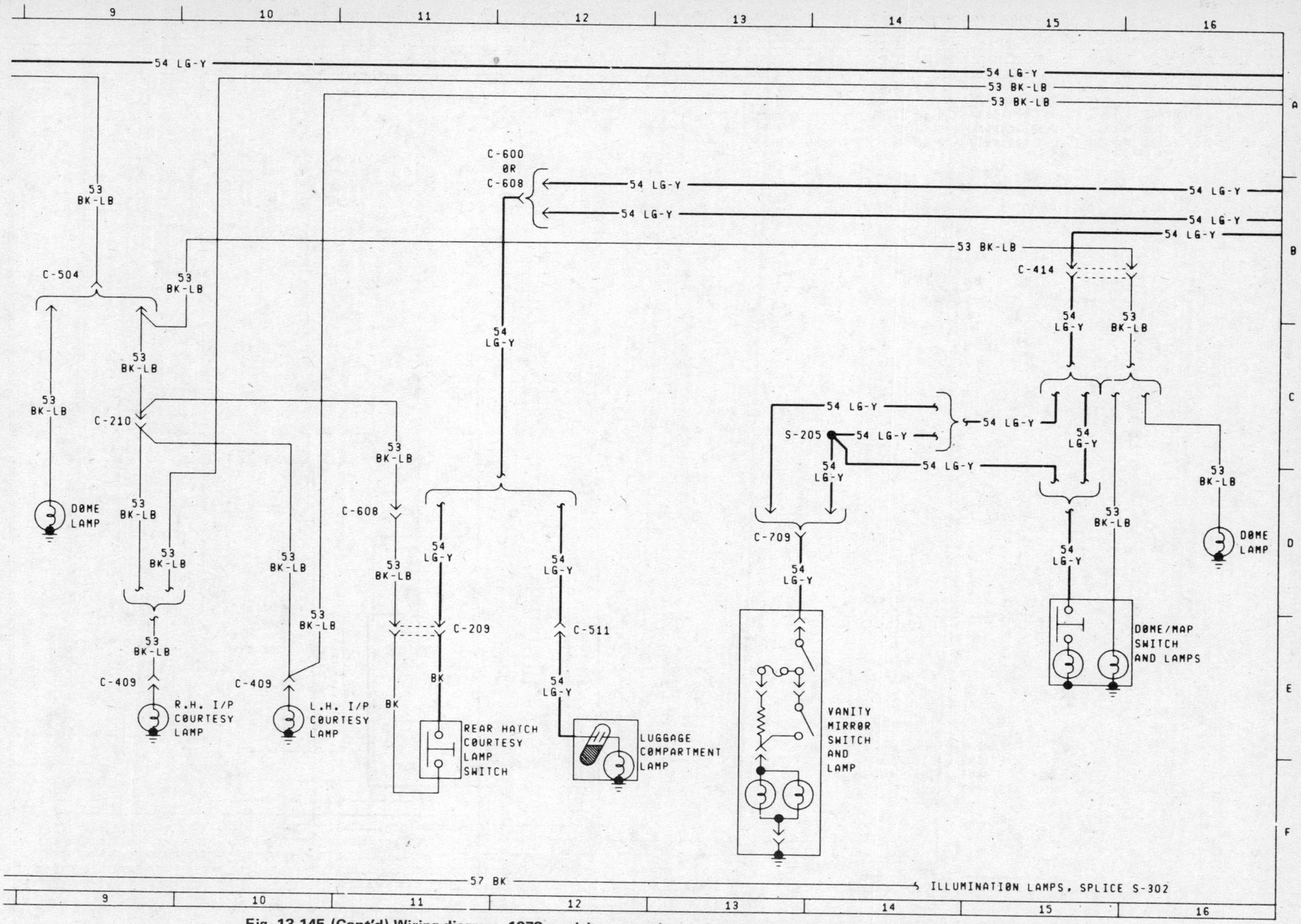

Fig. 13.145 (Cont'd) Wiring diagram, 1978 models: protection and convenience circuits. For color code see page 280

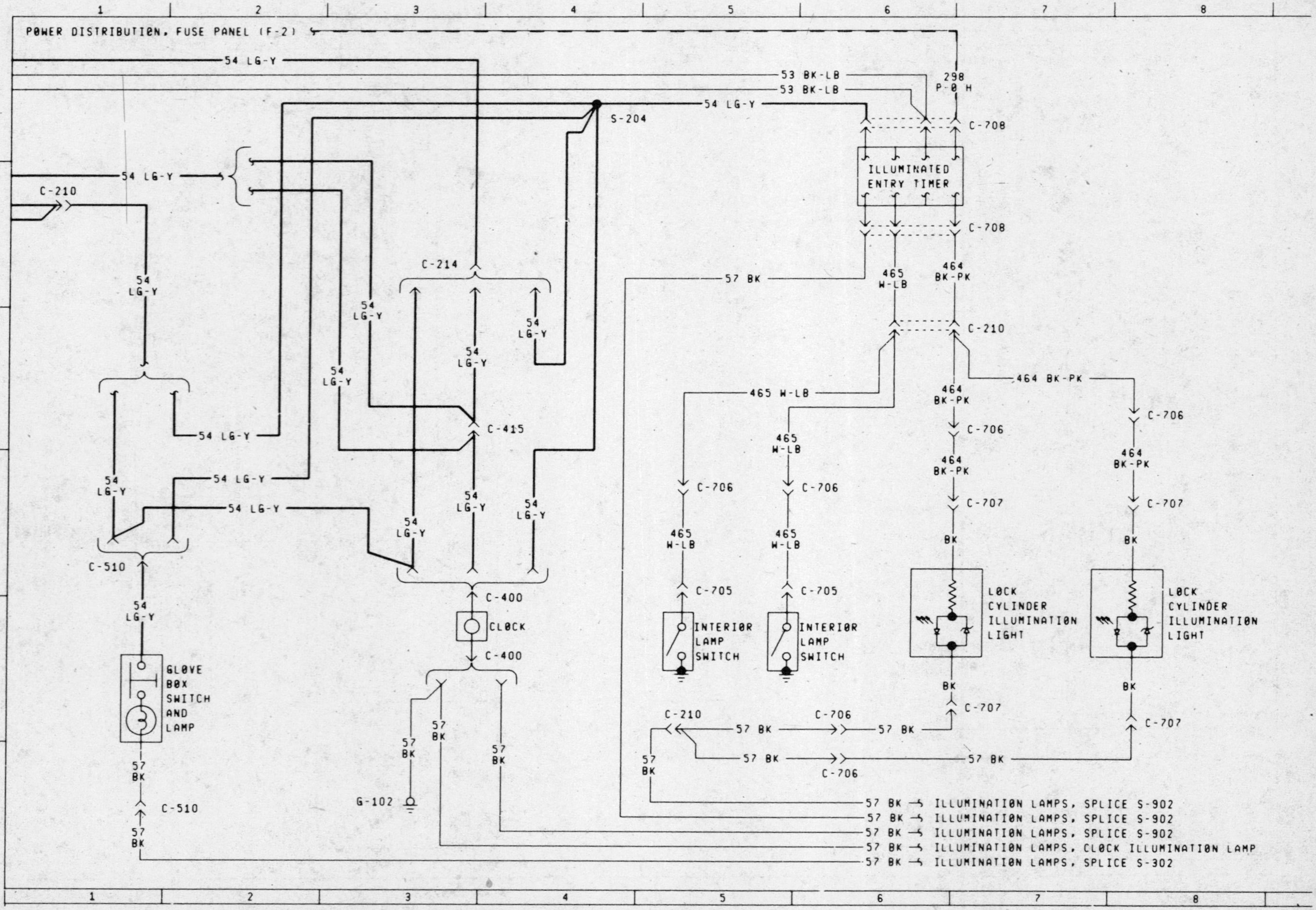
POWER DISTRIBUTION, FUSE PANEL (F-2)
54 LG-Y
53 BK-LB
53 BK-LB
298 P-O H
54 LG-Y
S-204
C-708
ILLUMINATED ENTRY TIMER
C-708
C-210
C-214
C-415
C-400
CLOCK
C-400
C-510
GLOVE BOX SWITCH AND LAMP
57 BK
465 W-LB
464 BK-PK
464 BK-PK
C-706
C-705
C-707
INTERIOR LAMP SWITCH
INTERIOR LAMP SWITCH
LOCK CYLINDER ILLUMINATION LIGHT
LOCK CYLINDER ILLUMINATION LIGHT
G-102
57 BK ILLUMINATION LAMPS, SPLICE S-902
57 BK ILLUMINATION LAMPS, SPLICE S-902
57 BK ILLUMINATION LAMPS, SPLICE S-902
57 BK ILLUMINATION LAMPS, CLOCK ILLUMINATION LAMP
57 BK ILLUMINATION LAMPS, SPLICE S-302

Fig. 13.145 (Cont'd) Wiring diagram, 1978 models: protection and convenience circuits. For color code see page 280

11 Bodywork and fittings

Safety belts

1 The seat belts should be inspected periodically for fraying or damage. Renew as necessary, never attempt to repair or modify.
2 Clean the belts with water and detergent only and if the anchorages are dismantled, ensure that the original sequence of washers and spacers is retained.

Sun roof (removable type)

3 This optional fitment is removable by squeezing the connecting links together to disengage the latching mechanism. A stowage bag for the panel is provided behind the rear seat (2-door models) or rear floor (3-door models).
4 The panel can be adjusted to provide positive closure by moving the latch sleeves up or down and locking them with the setscrews.
5 The panel can be adjusted for alignment if the plastic cover is removed from the two ¼ inch bolts, the bolts loosened and the brackets repositioned.
6 Check regularly that the drain hole at each corner of the roof is clear. Clean with air pressure or a flexible rod if necessary.

Rear view mirrors

Interior type

7 This is of the type which has its mounting pad (base) bonded to the windshield glass.
8 In the event of the mounting pad bacoming loose or a new windshield being fitted, leave the fitting of a new pad to your dealer as special bonding materials are required for this work.

Outside type

9 The mirrors are of remotely controlled cable-operated type.
10 Removal is carried out by unscrewing the bezel nut from the operating lever and removing the trim panel from the door. Unscrew the mirror mounting screws and release the cable retaining clips, then withdraw the mirror with cable attached.

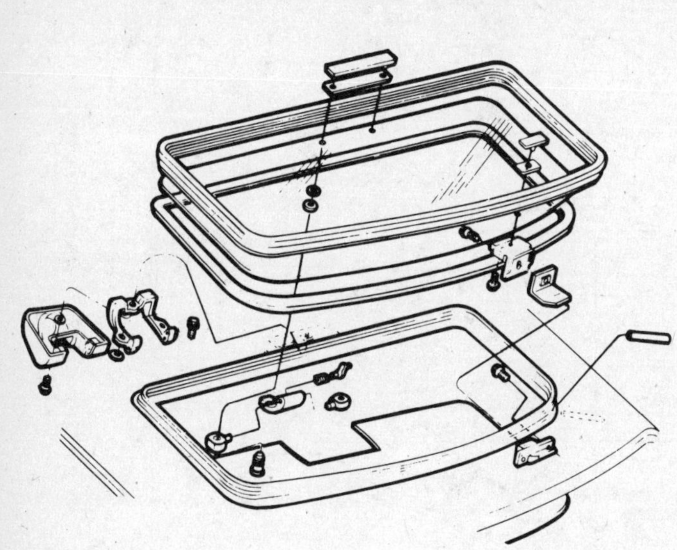

Fig. 13.146 Flip-up type sun roof panel

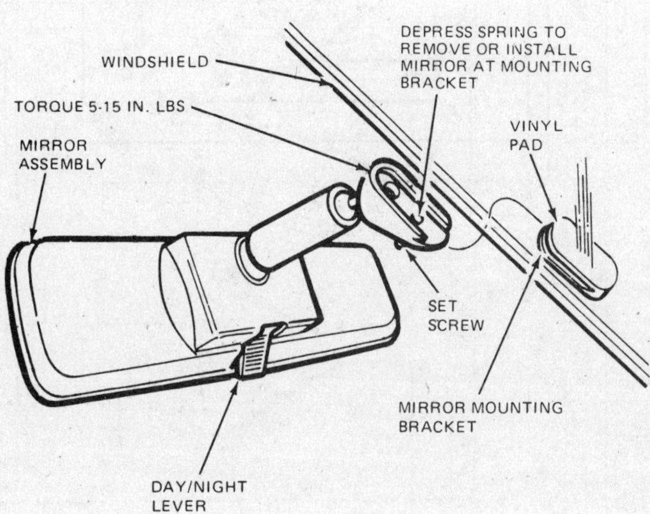

Fig. 13.147 Interior rear view mirror

13

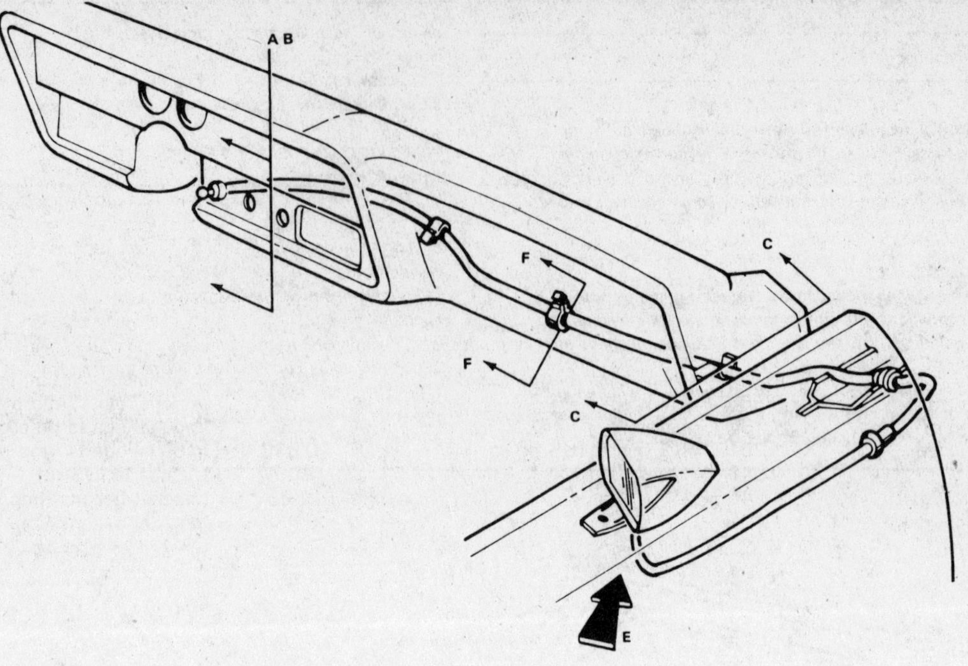

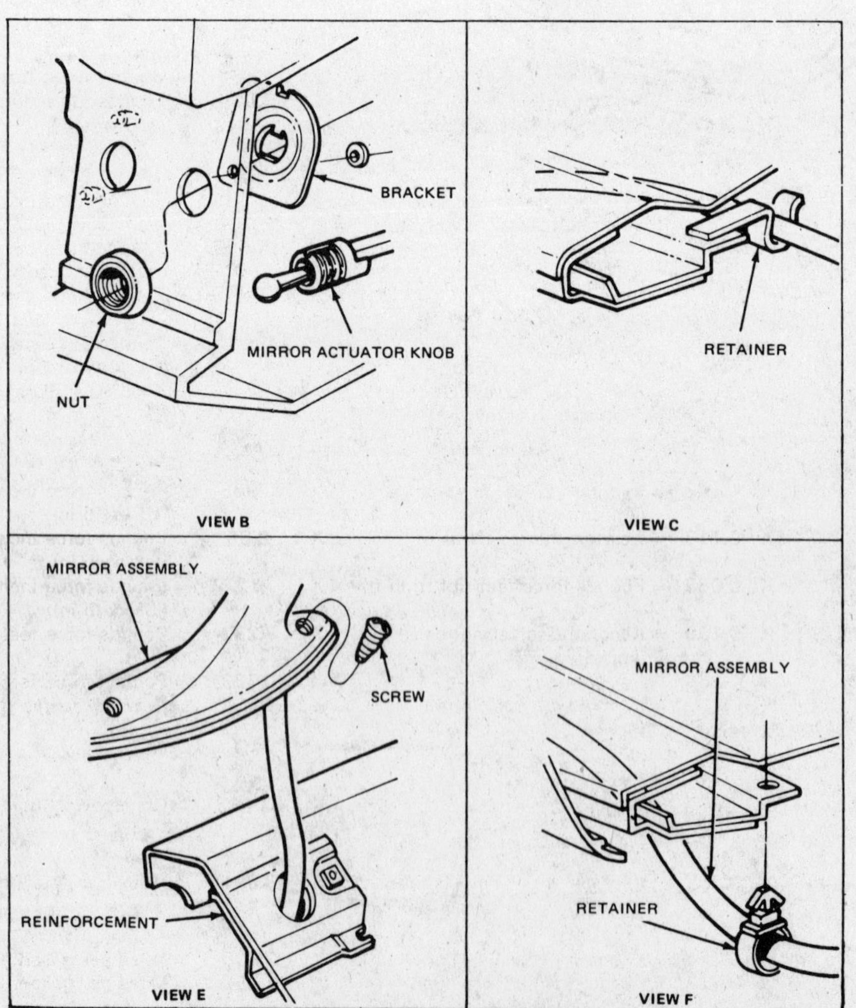

Fig. 13.148 Exterior rear view mirror installation details

Conversion factors

Length (distance)

Inches (in)	X 25.4	= Millimetres (mm)	X 0.0394	= Inches (in)
Feet (ft)	X 0.305	= Metres (m)	X 3.281	= Feet (ft)
Miles	X 1.609	= Kilometres (km)	X 0.621	= Miles

Volume (capacity)

Cubic inches (cu in; in³)	X 16.387	= Cubic centimetres (cc; cm³)	X 0.061	= Cubic inches (cu in; in³)
Imperial pints (Imp pt)	X 0.568	= Litres (l)	X 1.76	= Imperial pints (Imp pt)
Imperial quarts (Imp qt)	X 1.137	= Litres (l)	X 0.88	= Imperial quarts (Imp qt)
Imperial quarts (Imp qt)	X 1.201	= US quarts (US qt)	X 0.833	= Imperial quarts (Imp qt)
US quarts (US qt)	X 0.946	= Litres (l)	X 1.057	= US quarts (US qt)
Imperial gallons (Imp gal)	X 4.546	= Litres (l)	X 0.22	= Imperial gallons (Imp gal)
Imperial gallons (Imp gal)	X 1.201	= US gallons (US gal)	X 0.833	= Imperial gallons (Imp gal)
US gallons (US gal)	X 3.785	= Litres (l)	X 0.264	= US gallons (US gal)

Mass (weight)

Ounces (oz)	X 28.35	= Grams (g)	X 0.035	= Ounces (oz)
Pounds (lb)	X 0.454	= Kilograms (kg)	X 2.205	= Pounds (lb)

Force

Ounces-force (ozf; oz)	X 0.278	= Newtons (N)	X 3.6	= Ounces-force (ozf; oz)
Pounds-force (lbf; lb)	X 4.448	= Newtons (N)	X 0.225	= Pounds-force (lbf; lb)
Newtons (N)	X 0.1	= Kilograms-force (kgf; kg)	X 9.81	= Newtons (N)

Pressure

Pounds-force per square inch (psi; lbf/in²; lb/in²)	X 0.070	= Kilograms-force per square centimetre (kgf/cm²; kg/cm²)	X 14.223	= Pounds-force per square inch (psi; lbf/in²; lb/in²)
Pounds-force per square inch (psi; lbf/in²; lb/in²)	X 0.068	= Atmospheres (atm)	X 14.696	= Pounds-force per square inch (psi; lbf/in²; lb/in²)
Pounds-force per square inch (psi; lbf/in²; lb/in²)	X 0.069	= Bars	X 14.5	= Pounds-force per square inch (psi; lbf/in²; lb/in²)
Pounds-force per square inch (psi; lbf/in²; lb/in²)	X 6.895	= Kilopascals (kPa)	X 0.145	= Pounds-force per square inch (psi; lbf/in²; lb/in²)
Kilopascals (kPa)	X 0.01	= Kilograms-force per square centimetre (kgf/cm²; kg/cm²)	X 98.1	= Kilopascals (kPa)

Torque (moment of force)

Pounds-force inches (lbf in; lb in)	X 1.152	= Kilograms-force centimetre (kgf cm; kg cm)	X 0.868	= Pounds-force inches (lbf in; lb in)
Pounds-force inches (lbf in; lb in)	X 0.113	= Newton metres (Nm)	X 8.85	= Pounds-force inches (lbf in; lb in)
Pounds-force inches (lbf in; lb in)	X 0.083	= Pounds-force feet (lbf ft; lb ft)	X 12	= Pounds-force inches (lbf in; lb in)
Pounds-force feet (lbf ft; lb ft)	X 0.138	= Kilograms-force metres (kgf m; kg m)	X 7.233	= Pounds-force feet (lbf ft; lb ft)
Pounds-force feet (lbf ft; lb ft)	X 1.356	= Newton metres (Nm)	X 0.738	= Pounds-force feet (lbf ft; lb ft)
Newton metres (Nm)	X 0.102	= Kilograms-force metres (kgf m; kg m)	X 9.804	= Newton metres (Nm)

Power

Horsepower (hp)	X 745.7	= Watts (W)	X 0.0013	= Horsepower (hp)

Velocity (speed)

Miles per hour (miles/hr; mph)	X 1.609	= Kilometres per hour (km/hr; kph)	X 0.621	= Miles per hour (miles/hr; mph)

*Fuel consumption**

Miles per gallon, Imperial (mpg)	X 0.354	= Kilometres per litre (km/l)	X 2.825	= Miles per gallon, Imperial (mpg)
Miles per gallon, US (mpg)	X 0.425	= Kilometres per litre (km/l)	X 2.352	= Miles per gallon, US (mpg)

Temperature

Degrees Fahrenheit = (°C x 1.8) + 32

Degrees Celsius (Degrees Centigrade; °C) = (°F - 32) x 0.56

**It is common practice to convert from miles per gallon (mpg) to litres/100 kilometres (l/100km), where mpg (Imperial) x l/100 km = 282 and mpg (US) x l/100 km = 235*

Safety first!

Regardless of how enthusiastic you may be about getting on with the job at hand, take the time to ensure that your safety is not jeopardized. A moment's lack of attention can result in an accident, as can failure to observe certain simple safety precautions. The possibility of an accident will always exist, and the following points should not be considered a comprehensive list of all dangers. Rather, they are intended to make you aware of the risks and to encourage a safety conscious approach to all work you carry out on your vehicle.

Essential DOs and DON'Ts

DON'T rely on a jack when working under the vehicle. Always use approved jackstands to support the weight of the vehicle and place them under the recommended lift or support points.
DON'T attempt to loosen extremely tight fasteners (i.e. wheel lug nuts) while the vehicle is on a jack — it may fall.
DON'T start the engine without first making sure that the transmission is in Neutral (or Park where applicable) and the parking brake is set.
DON'T remove the radiator cap from a hot cooling system — let it cool or cover it with a cloth and release the pressure gradually.
DON'T attempt to drain the engine oil until you are sure it has cooled to the point that it will not burn you.
DON'T touch any part of the engine or exhaust system until it has cooled sufficiently to avoid burns.
DON'T siphon toxic liquids such as gasoline, antifreeze and brake fluid by mouth, or allow them to remain on your skin.
DON'T inhale brake lining dust — it is potentially hazardous (see *Asbestos* below)
DON'T allow spilled oil or grease to remain on the floor — wipe it up before someone slips on it.
DON'T use loose fitting wrenches or other tools which may slip and cause injury.
DON'T push on wrenches when loosening or tightening nuts or bolts. Always try to pull the wrench toward you. If the situation calls for pushing the wrench away, push with an open hand to avoid scraped knuckles if the wrench should slip.
DON'T attempt to lift a heavy component alone — get someone to help you.
DON'T rush or take unsafe shortcuts to finish a job.
DON'T allow children or animals in or around the vehicle while you are working on it.
DO wear eye protection when using power tools such as a drill, sander, bench grinder, etc. and when working under a vehicle.
DO keep loose clothing and long hair well out of the way of moving parts.
DO make sure that any hoist used has a safe working load rating adequate for the job.
DO get someone to check on you periodically when working alone on a vehicle.
DO carry out work in a logical sequence and make sure that everything is correctly assembled and tightened.
DO keep chemicals and fluids tightly capped and out of the reach of children and pets.
DO remember that your vehicle's safety affects that of yourself and others. If in doubt on any point, get professional advice.

Asbestos

Certain friction, insulating, sealing, and other products — such as brake linings, brake bands, clutch linings, torque converters, gaskets, etc. — contain asbestos. *Extreme care must be taken to avoid inhalation of dust from such products since it is hazardous to health.* If in doubt, assume that they *do* contain asbestos.

Fire

Remember at all times that gasoline is highly flammable. Never smoke or have any kind of open flame around when working on a vehicle. But the risk does not end there. A spark caused by an electrical short circuit, by two metal surfaces contacting each other, or even by static electricity built up in your body under certain conditions, can ignite gasoline vapors, which in a confined space are highly explosive. Do not, under any circumstances, use gasoline for cleaning parts. Use an approved safety solvent.

Always disconnect the battery ground (–) cable *at the battery* before working on any part of the fuel system or electrical system. Never risk spilling fuel on a hot engine or exhaust component.

It is strongly recommended that a fire extinguisher suitable for use on fuel and electrical fires be kept handy in the garage or workshop at all times. Never try to extinguish a fuel or electrical fire with water.

Torch (flashlight in the US)

Any reference to a "torch" appearing in this manual should always be taken to mean a hand-held, battery-operated electric light or flashlight. It DOES NOT mean a welding or propane torch or blowtorch.

Fumes

Certain fumes are highly toxic and can quickly cause unconsciousness and even death if inhaled to any extent. Gasoline vapor falls into this category, as do the vapors from some cleaning solvents. Any draining or pouring of such volatile fluids should be done in a well ventilated area.

When using cleaning fluids and solvents, read the instructions on the container carefully. Never use materials from unmarked containers.

Never run the engine in an enclosed space, such as a garage. Exhaust fumes contain carbon monoxide, which is extremely poisonous. If you need to run the engine, always do so in the open air, or at least have the rear of the vehicle outside the work area.

If you are fortunate enough to have the use of an inspection pit, never drain or pour gasoline and never run the engine while the vehicle is over the pit. The fumes, being heavier than air, will concentrate in the pit with possibly lethal results.

The battery

Never create a spark or allow a bare light bulb near a battery. They normally give off a certain amount of hydrogen gas, which is highly explosive.

Always disconnect the battery ground (–) cable *at the battery* before working on the fuel or electrical systems.

If possible, loosen the filler caps or cover when charging the battery from an external source (this does not apply to sealed or maintenance-free batteries). Do not charge at an excessive rate or the battery may burst.

Take care when adding water to a non maintenance-free battery and when carrying a battery. The electrolyte, even when diluted, is very corrosive and should not be allowed to contact clothing or skin.

Always wear eye protection when cleaning the battery to prevent the caustic deposits from entering your eyes.

Mains electricity (household current in the US)

When using an electric power tool, inspection light, etc., which operates on household current, always make sure that the tool is correctly connected to its plug and that, where necessary, it is properly grounded. Do not use such items in damp conditions and, again, do not create a spark or apply excessive heat in the vicinity of fuel or fuel vapor.

Secondary ignition system voltage

A severe electric shock can result from touching certain parts of the ignition system (such as the spark plug wires) when the engine is running or being cranked, particularly if components are damp or the insulation is defective. In the case of an electronic ignition system, the secondary system voltage is much higher and could prove fatal.

Use of English

As this book has been written in England, it uses the appropriate English component names, phrases, and spelling. Some of these differ from those used in America. Normally, these cause no difficulty, but to make sure, a glossary is printed below. In ordering spare parts remember the parts list may use some of these words:

English	American	English	American
Accelerator	Gas pedal	Locks	Latches
Aerial	Antenna	Methylated spirit	Denatured alcohol
Anti-roll bar	Stabiliser or sway bar	Motorway	Freeway, turnpike etc
Big-end bearing	Rod bearing	Number plate	License plate
Bonnet (engine cover)	Hood	Paraffin	Kerosene
Boot (luggage compartment)	Trunk	Petrol	Gasoline (gas)
Bulkhead	Firewall	Petrol tank	Gas tank
Bush	Bushing	'Pinking'	'Pinging'
Cam follower or tappet	Valve lifter or tappet	Prise (force apart)	Pry
Carburettor	Carburetor	Propeller shaft	Driveshaft
Catch	Latch	Quarterlight	Quarter window
Choke/venturi	Barrel	Retread	Recap
Circlip	Snap-ring	Reverse	Back-up
Clearance	Lash	Rocker cover	Valve cover
Crownwheel	Ring gear (of differential)	Saloon	Sedan
Damper	Shock absorber, shock	Seized	Frozen
Disc (brake)	Rotor/disk	Sidelight	Parking light
Distance piece	Spacer	Silencer	Muffler
Drop arm	Pitman arm	Sill panel (beneath doors)	Rocker panel
Drop head coupe	Convertible	Small end, little end	Piston pin or wrist pin
Dynamo	Generator (DC)	Spanner	Wrench
Earth (electrical)	Ground	Split cotter (for valve spring cap)	Lock (for valve spring retainer)
Engineer's blue	Prussian blue	Split pin	Cotter pin
Estate car	Station wagon	Steering arm	Spindle arm
Exhaust manifold	Header	Sump	Oil pan
Fault finding/diagnosis	Troubleshooting	Swarf	Metal chips or debris
Float chamber	Float bowl	Tab washer	Tang or lock
Free-play	Lash	Tappet	Valve lifter
Freewheel	Coast	Thrust bearing	Throw-out bearing
Gearbox	Transmission	Top gear	High
Gearchange	Shift	Torch	Flashlight
Grub screw	Setscrew, Allen screw	Trackrod (of steering)	Tie-rod (or connecting rod)
Gudgeon pin	Piston pin or wrist pin	Trailing shoe (of brake)	Secondary shoe
Halfshaft	Axleshaft	Transmission	Whole drive line
Handbrake	Parking brake	Tyre	Tire
Hood	Soft top	Van	Panel wagon/van
Hot spot	Heat riser	Vice	Vise
Indicator	Turn signal	Wheel nut	Lug nut
Interior light	Dome lamp	Windscreen	Windshield
Layshaft (of gearbox)	Countershaft	Wing/mudguard	Fender
Leading shoe (of brake)	Primary shoe		

Index

C

D

E

Haynes Automotive Manuals

NOTE: New manuals are added to this list on a periodic basis. If you do not see a listing for your vehicle, consult your local Haynes dealer for the latest product information.

ACURA

*12020 **Integra** '86 thru '89 **& Legend** '86 thru '90

AMC

Jeep CJ - *see JEEP (50020)*
14020 **Mid-size models,** Concord, Hornet, Gremlin & Spirit '70 thru '83
14025 **(Renault) Alliance & Encore** '83 thru '87

AUDI

15020 **4000** all models '80 thru '87
15025 **5000** all models '77 thru '83
15026 **5000** all models '84 thru '88

AUSTIN-HEALEY

Sprite - *see MG Midget (66015)*

BMW

*18020 **3/5 Series** not including diesel or all-wheel drive models '82 thru '92
*18021 **3 Series** except 325iX models '92 thru '97
18025 **320i** all 4 cyl models '75 thru '83
18035 **528i** & 530i all models '75 thru '80
18050 **1500 thru 2002** except Turbo '59 thru '77

BUICK

Century (front wheel drive) - *see GM (829)*
*19020 **Buick, Oldsmobile & Pontiac Full-size (Front wheel drive)** all models '85 thru '98 **Buick** Electra, LeSabre and Park Avenue; **Oldsmobile** Delta 88 Royale, Ninety Eight and Regency; **Pontiac** Bonneville
19025 **Buick Oldsmobile & Pontiac Full-size (Rear wheel drive)** **Buick** Estate '70 thru '90, Electra'70 thru '84, LeSabre '70 thru '85, Limited '74 thru '79 **Oldsmobile** Custom Cruiser '70 thru '90, Delta 88 '70 thru '85,Ninety-eight '70 thru '84 **Pontiac** Bonneville '70 thru '81, Catalina '70 thru '81, Grandville '70 thru '75, Parisienne '83 thru '86
19030 **Mid-size Regal & Century** all rear-drive models with V6, V8 and Turbo '74 thru '87
Regal - *see GENERAL MOTORS (38010)*
Riviera - *see GENERAL MOTORS (38030)*
Roadmaster - *see CHEVROLET (24046)*
Skyhawk - *see GENERAL MOTORS (38015)*
Skylark '80 thru '85 - *see GM (38020)*
Skylark '86 on - *see GM (38025)*
Somerset - *see GENERAL MOTORS (38025)*

CADILLAC

*21030 **Cadillac Rear Wheel Drive** all gasoline models '70 thru '93
Cimarron - *see GENERAL MOTORS (38015)*
Eldorado - *see GENERAL MOTORS (38030)*
Seville '80 thru '85 - *see GM (38030)*

CHEVROLET

*24010 **Astro & GMC Safari Mini-vans** '85 thru '93
24015 **Camaro V8** all models '70 thru '81
24016 **Camaro** all models '82 thru '92
Cavalier - *see GENERAL MOTORS (38015)*
Celebrity - *see GENERAL MOTORS (38005)*
24017 **Camaro & Firebird** '93 thru '97
24020 **Chevelle, Malibu & El Camino** '69 thru '87
24024 **Chevette & Pontiac T1000** '76 thru '87
Citation - *see GENERAL MOTORS (38020)*
*24032 **Corsica/Beretta** all models '87 thru '96
24040 **Corvette** all V8 models '68 thru '82
*24041 **Corvette** all models '84 thru '96
10305 **Chevrolet Engine Overhaul Manual**
24045 **Full-size Sedans** Caprice, Impala, Biscayne, Bel Air & Wagons '69 thru '90
24046 **Impala SS & Caprice and Buick Roadmaster** '91 thru '96
Lumina - *see GENERAL MOTORS (38010)*
24048 **Lumina & Monte Carlo** '95 thru '98
Lumina APV - *see GM (38035)*
24050 **Luv Pick-up** all 2WD & 4WD '72 thru '82
*24055 **Monte Carlo** all models '70 thru '88
Monte Carlo '95 thru '98 - *see LUMINA (24048)*
24059 **Nova** all V8 models '69 thru '79
*24060 **Nova and Geo Prizm** '85 thru '92
24064 **Pick-ups '67 thru '87** - Chevrolet & GMC, all V8 & in-line 6 cyl, 2WD & 4WD '67 thru '87; Suburbans, Blazers & Jimmys '67 thru '91
*24065 **Pick-ups '88 thru '98** - Chevrolet & GMC, all full-size pick-ups, '88 thru '98; Blazer & Jimmy '92 thru '94; Suburban '92 thru '98; Tahoe & Yukon '98
24070 **S-10 & S-15 Pick-ups** '82 thru '93, **Blazer & Jimmy** '83 thru '94,
*24071 **S-10 & S-15 Pick-ups** '94 thru '96 **Blazer & Jimmy** '95 thru '96
*24075 **Sprint & Geo Metro** '85 thru '94
*24080 **Vans - Chevrolet & GMC,** V8 & in-line 6 cylinder models '68 thru '96

CHRYSLER

25015 **Chrysler Cirrus, Dodge Stratus, Plymouth Breeze** '95 thru '98
25025 **Chrysler Concorde, New Yorker & LHS, Dodge** Intrepid, **Eagle** Vision, '93 thru '97
10310 **Chrysler Engine Overhaul Manual**
*25020 **Full-size Front-Wheel Drive** '88 thru '93
K-Cars - *see DODGE Aries (30008)*
Laser - *see DODGE Daytona (30030)*
*25030 **Chrysler & Plymouth Mid-size** front wheel drive '82 thru '95
Rear-wheel Drive - *see Dodge (30050)*

DATSUN

28005 **200SX** all models '80 thru '83
28007 **B-210** all models '73 thru '78
28009 **210** all models '79 thru '82
28012 **240Z, 260Z & 280Z** Coupe '70 thru '78
28014 **280ZX** Coupe & 2+2 '79 thru '83
300ZX - *see NISSAN (72010)*
28016 **310** all models '78 thru '82
28018 **510 & PL521 Pick-up** '68 thru '73
28020 **510** all models '78 thru '81
28022 **620 Series Pick-up** all models '73 thru '79
720 Series Pick-up - *see NISSAN (72030)*
28025 **810/Maxima** all gasoline models, '77 thru '84

DODGE

400 & 600 - *see CHRYSLER (25030)*
*30008 **Aries & Plymouth Reliant** '81 thru '89
30010 **Caravan & Plymouth Voyager Mini-Vans** all models '84 thru '95
*30011 **Caravan & Plymouth Voyager Mini-Vans** all models '96 thru '98
30012 **Challenger/Plymouth Saporro** '78 thru '83
30016 **Colt & Plymouth Champ (front wheel drive)** all models '78 thru '87
*30020 **Dakota Pick-ups** all models '87 thru '96
30025 **Dart, Demon, Plymouth Barracuda, Duster & Valiant** 6 cyl models '67 thru '76
*30030 **Daytona & Chrysler Laser** '84 thru '89
Intrepid - *see CHRYSLER (25025)*
*30034 **Neon** all models '95 thru '97
*30035 **Omni & Plymouth Horizon** '78 thru '90
*30040 **Pick-ups** all full-size models '74 thru '93
*30041 **Pick-ups** all full-size models '94 thru '96
*30045 **Ram 50/D50 Pick-ups & Raider and Plymouth Arrow Pick-ups** '79 thru '93
30050 **Dodge/Plymouth/Chrysler** rear wheel drive '71 thru '89
*30055 **Shadow & Plymouth Sundance** '87 thru '94
*30060 **Spirit & Plymouth Acclaim** '89 thru '95
*30065 **Vans - Dodge & Plymouth** '71 thru '96

EAGLE

Talon - *see Mitsubishi Eclipse (68030)*
Vision - *see CHRYSLER (25025)*

FIAT

34010 **124 Sport Coupe & Spider** '68 thru '78
34025 **X1/9** all models '74 thru '80

FORD

10355 **Ford Automatic Transmission Overhaul**
*36004 **Aerostar Mini-vans** all models '86 thru '96
*36006 **Contour & Mercury Mystique** '95 thru '98
36008 **Courier Pick-up** all models '72 thru '82
36012 **Crown Victoria & Mercury Grand Marquis** '88 thru '96
10320 **Ford Engine Overhaul Manual**
36016 **Escort/Mercury Lynx** all models '81 thru '90
*36020 **Escort/Mercury Tracer** '91 thru '96
*36024 **Explorer & Mazda Navajo** '91 thru '95
36028 **Fairmont & Mercury Zephyr** '78 thru '83
36030 **Festiva & Aspire** '88 thru '97
36032 **Fiesta** all models '77 thru '80
36036 **Ford & Mercury Full-size,** Ford LTD & Mercury Marquis ('75 thru '82); Ford Custom 500,Country Squire, Crown Victoria & Mercury Colony Park ('75 thru '87); Ford LTD Crown Victoria & Mercury Gran Marquis ('83 thru '87)
36040 **Granada & Mercury Monarch** '75 thru '80
36044 **Ford & Mercury Mid-size,** Ford Thunderbird & Mercury Cougar ('75 thru '82); Ford LTD & Mercury Marquis ('83 thru '86); Ford Torino,Gran Torino, Elite, Ranchero pick-up, LTD II, Mercury Montego, Comet, XR-7 & Lincoln Versailles ('75 thru '86)
36048 **Mustang V8** all models '64-1/2 thru '73
36049 **Mustang II** 4 cyl, V6 & V8 models '74 thru '78
36050 **Mustang & Mercury Capri** all models Mustang, '79 thru '93; Capri, '79 thru '86
*36051 **Mustang** all models '94 thru '97
36054 **Pick-ups & Bronco** '73 thru '79
36058 **Pick-ups & Bronco** '80 thru '96
36059 **Pick-ups, Expedition & Mercury Navigator** '97 thru '98
36062 **Pinto & Mercury Bobcat** '75 thru '80
36066 **Probe** all models '89 thru '92
36070 **Ranger/Bronco II** gasoline models '83 thru '92
*36071 **Ranger** '93 thru '97 & **Mazda Pick-ups** '94 thru '97
36074 **Taurus & Mercury Sable** '86 thru '95
*36075 **Taurus & Mercury Sable** '96 thru '98
*36078 **Tempo & Mercury Topaz** '84 thru '94
36082 **Thunderbird/Mercury Cougar** '83 thru '88
*36086 **Thunderbird/Mercury Cougar** '89 and '97
36090 **Vans** all V8 Econoline models '69 thru '91
*36094 **Vans** full size '92-'95
*36097 **Windstar Mini-van** '95-'98

GENERAL MOTORS

*10360 **GM Automatic Transmission Overhaul**
*38005 **Buick Century, Chevrolet Celebrity, Oldsmobile Cutlass Ciera & Pontiac 6000** all models '82 thru '96
*38010 **Buick Regal, Chevrolet Lumina, Oldsmobile Cutlass Supreme & Pontiac Grand Prix** front-wheel drive models '88 thru '95
*38015 **Buick Skyhawk, Cadillac Cimarron, Chevrolet Cavalier, Oldsmobile Firenza & Pontiac J-2000 & Sunbird** '82 thru '94
*38016 **Chevrolet Cavalier & Pontiac Sunfire** '95 thru '98
38020 **Buick Skylark, Chevrolet Citation, Olds Omega, Pontiac Phoenix** '80 thru '85
38025 **Buick Skylark & Somerset, Oldsmobile Achieva & Calais and Pontiac Grand Am** all models '85 thru '95
38030 **Cadillac Eldorado** '71 thru '85, **Seville** '80 thru '85, **Oldsmobile Toronado** '71 thru '85 **& Buick Riviera** '79 thru '85
*38035 **Chevrolet Lumina APV, Olds Silhouette & Pontiac Trans Sport** all models '90 thru '95
General Motors Full-size Rear-wheel Drive - *see BUICK (19025)*

(Continued on other side)

** Listings shown with an asterisk (*) indicate model coverage as of this printing. These titles will be periodically updated to include later model years - consult your Haynes dealer for more information.*

Haynes North America, Inc., 861 Lawrence Drive, Newbury Park, CA 91320-1514 • (805) 498-6703

Haynes Automotive Manuals (continued)

NOTE: New manuals are added to this list on a periodic basis. If you do not see a listing for your vehicle, consult your local Haynes dealer for the latest product information.

GEO

Metro - *see CHEVROLET Sprint (24075)*
Prizm - *'85 thru '92 see CHEVY (24060), '93 thru '96 see TOYOTA Corolla (92036)*
*40030 **Storm** all models '90 thru '93
Tracker - *see SUZUKI Samurai (90010)*

GMC

Safari - *see CHEVROLET ASTRO (24010)*
Vans & Pick-ups - *see CHEVROLET*

HONDA

42010 **Accord CVCC** all models '76 thru '83
42011 **Accord** all models '84 thru '89
42012 **Accord** all models '90 thru '93
42013 **Accord** all models '94 thru '95
42020 **Civic 1200** all models '73 thru '79
42021 **Civic 1300 & 1500 CVCC** '80 thru '83
42022 **Civic 1500 CVCC** all models '75 thru '79
42023 **Civic** all models '84 thru '91
*42024 **Civic & del Sol** '92 thru '95
*42040 **Prelude CVCC** all models '79 thru '89

HYUNDAI

*43015 **Excel** all models '86 thru '94

ISUZU

Hombre - *see CHEVROLET S-10 (24071)*
*47017 **Rodeo** '91 thru '97; **Amigo** '89 thru '94; **Honda Passport** '95 thru '97
*47020 **Trooper & Pick-up**, all gasoline models Pick-up, '81 thru '93; Trooper, '84 thru '91

JAGUAR

*49010 **XJ6** all 6 cyl models '68 thru '86
*49011 **XJ6** all models '88 thru '94
*49015 **XJ12 & XJS** all 12 cyl models '72 thru '85

JEEP

*50010 **Cherokee, Comanche & Wagoneer Limited** all models '84 thru '96
50020 **CJ** all models '49 thru '86
*50025 **Grand Cherokee** all models '93 thru '98
50029 **Grand Wagoneer & Pick-up** '72 thru '91 Grand Wagoneer '84 thru '91, Cherokee & Wagoneer '72 thru '83, Pick-up '72 thru '88
*50030 **Wrangler** all models '87 thru '95

LINCOLN

Navigator - *see FORD Pick-up (36059)*
59010 **Rear Wheel Drive** all models '70 thru '96

MAZDA

61010 **GLC Hatchback (rear wheel drive)** '77 thru '83
61011 **GLC (front wheel drive)** '81 thru '85
*61015 **323 & Protogé** '90 thru '97
*61016 **MX-5 Miata** '90 thru '97
*61020 **MPV** all models '89 thru '94
Navajo - *see Ford Explorer (36024)*
61030 **Pick-ups** '72 thru '93
Pick-ups '94 thru '96 - *see Ford Ranger (36071)*
61035 **RX-7** all models '79 thru '85
*61036 **RX-7** all models '86 thru '91
61040 **626** (rear wheel drive) all models '79 thru '82
*61041 **626/MX-6 (front wheel drive)** '83 thru '91

MERCEDES-BENZ

63012 **123 Series Diesel** '76 thru '85
*63015 **190 Series** four-cyl gas models, '84 thru '88
63020 **230/250/280** 6 cyl sohc models '68 thru '72
63025 **280 123 Series** gasoline models '77 thru '81
63030 **350 & 450** all models '71 thru '80

MERCURY

See FORD Listing.

MG

66010 **MGB** Roadster & GT Coupe '62 thru '80
66015 **MG Midget, Austin Healey Sprite** '58 thru '80

MITSUBISHI

*68020 **Cordia, Tredia, Galant, Precis & Mirage** '83 thru '93
*68030 **Eclipse, Eagle Talon & Ply. Laser** '90 thru '94
*68040 **Pick-up** '83 thru '96 **& Montero** '83 thru '93

NISSAN

72010 **300ZX** all models including Turbo '84 thru '89
*72015 **Altima** all models '93 thru '97
*72020 **Maxima** all models '85 thru '91
*72030 **Pick-ups** '80 thru '96 **Pathfinder** '87 thru '95
72040 **Pulsar** all models '83 thru '86
*72050 **Sentra** all models '82 thru '94
*72051 **Sentra & 200SX** all models '95 thru '98
*72060 **Stanza** all models '82 thru '90

OLDSMOBILE

*73015 **Cutlass** V6 & V8 gas models '74 thru '88
For other OLDSMOBILE titles, see BUICK, CHEVROLET or GENERAL MOTORS listing.

PLYMOUTH

For PLYMOUTH titles, see DODGE listing.

PONTIAC

79008 **Fiero** all models '84 thru '88
79018 **Firebird** V8 models except Turbo '70 thru '81
79019 **Firebird** all models '82 thru '92
For other PONTIAC titles, see BUICK, CHEVROLET or GENERAL MOTORS listing.

PORSCHE

*80020 **911** except Turbo & Carrera 4 '65 thru '89
80025 **914** all 4 cyl models '69 thru '76
80030 **924** all models including Turbo '76 thru '82
*80035 **944** all models including Turbo '83 thru '89

RENAULT

Alliance & Encore - *see AMC (14020)*

SAAB

*84010 **900** all models including Turbo '79 thru '88

SATURN

87010 **Saturn** all models '91 thru '96

SUBARU

89002 **1100, 1300, 1400 & 1600** '71 thru '79
*89003 **1600 & 1800** 2WD & 4WD '80 thru '94

SUZUKI

*90010 **Samurai/Sidekick & Geo Tracker** '86 thru '96

TOYOTA

92005 **Camry** all models '83 thru '91
92006 **Camry** all models '92 thru '96
92015 **Celica Rear Wheel Drive** '71 thru '85
*92020 **Celica Front Wheel Drive** '86 thru '93
92025 **Celica Supra** all models '79 thru '92
92030 **Corolla** all models '75 thru '79
92032 **Corolla** all rear wheel drive models '80 thru '87
92035 **Corolla** all front wheel drive models '84 thru '92
*92036 **Corolla & Geo Prizm** '93 thru '97
92040 **Corolla Tercel** all models '80 thru '82
92045 **Corona** all models '74 thru '82
92050 **Cressida** all models '78 thru '82
92055 **Land Cruiser** FJ40, 43, 45, 55 '68 thru '82
92056 **Land Cruiser** FJ60, 62, 80, FZJ80 '80 thru '96
*92065 **MR2** all models '85 thru '87
92070 **Pick-up** all models '69 thru '78
*92075 **Pick-up** all models '79 thru '95
*92076 **Tacoma** '95 thru '98, **4Runner** '96 thru '98, **& T100** '93 thru '98
*92080 **Previa** all models '91 thru '95
92085 **Tercel** all models '87 thru '94

TRIUMPH

94007 **Spitfire** all models '62 thru '81
94010 **TR7** all models '75 thru '81

VW

96008 **Beetle & Karmann Ghia** '54 thru '79
96012 **Dasher** all gasoline models '74 thru '81
*96016 **Rabbit, Jetta, Scirocco, & Pick-up** gas models '74 thru '91 & Convertible '80 thru '92
96017 **Golf & Jetta** all models '93 thru '97
96020 **Rabbit, Jetta & Pick-up** diesel '77 thru '84
96030 **Transporter 1600** all models '68 thru '79
96035 **Transporter 1700, 1800 & 2000** '72 thru '79
96040 **Type 3 1500 & 1600** all models '63 thru '73
96045 **Vanagon** all air-cooled models '80 thru '83

VOLVO

97010 **120, 130 Series & 1800 Sports** '61 thru '73
97015 **140 Series** all models '66 thru '74
*97020 **240 Series** all models '76 thru '93
97025 **260 Series** all models '75 thru '82
*97040 **740 & 760 Series** all models '82 thru '88

TECHBOOK MANUALS

10205 **Automotive Computer Codes**
10210 **Automotive Emissions Control Manual**
10215 **Fuel Injection Manual, 1978 thru 1985**
10220 **Fuel Injection Manual, 1986 thru 1996**
10225 **Holley Carburetor Manual**
10230 **Rochester Carburetor Manual**
10240 **Weber/Zenith/Stromberg/SU Carburetors**
10305 **Chevrolet Engine Overhaul Manual**
10310 **Chrysler Engine Overhaul Manual**
10320 **Ford Engine Overhaul Manual**
10330 **GM and Ford Diesel Engine Repair Manual**
10340 **Small Engine Repair Manual**
10345 **Suspension, Steering & Driveline Manual**
10355 **Ford Automatic Transmission Overhaul**
10360 **GM Automatic Transmission Overhaul**
10405 **Automotive Body Repair & Painting**
10410 **Automotive Brake Manual**
10415 **Automotive Detaiing Manual**
10420 **Automotive Eelectrical Manual**
10425 **Automotive Heating & Air Conditioning**
10430 **Automotive Reference Manual & Dictionary**
10435 **Automotive Tools Manual**
10440 **Used Car Buying Guide**
10445 **Welding Manual**
10450 **ATV Basics**

SPANISH MANUALS

98903 **Reparación de Carrocería & Pintura**
98905 **Códigos Automotrices de la Computadora**
98910 **Frenos Automotriz**
98915 **Inyección de Combustible 1986 al 1994**
99040 **Chevrolet & GMC Camionetas** '67 al '87 Incluye Suburban, Blazer & Jimmy '67 al '91
99041 **Chevrolet & GMC Camionetas** '88 al '95 Incluye Suburban '92 al '95, Blazer & Jimmy '92 al '94, Tahoe y Yukon '95
99042 **Chevrolet & GMC Camionetas Cerradas** '68 al '95
99055 **Dodge Caravan & Plymouth Voyager** '84 al '95
99075 **Ford Camionetas y Bronco** '80 al '94
99077 **Ford Camionetas Cerradas** '69 al '91
99083 **Ford Modelos de Tamaño Grande** '75 al '87
99088 **Ford Modelos de Tamaño Mediano** '75 al '86
99091 **Ford Taurus & Mercury Sable** '86 al '95
99095 **GM Modelos de Tamaño Grande** '70 al '90
99100 **GM Modelos de Tamaño Mediano** '70 al '88
99110 **Nissan Camionetas** '80 al '96, **Pathfinder** '87 al '95
99118 **Nissan Sentra** '82 al '94
99125 **Toyota Camionetas y 4Runner** '79 al '95

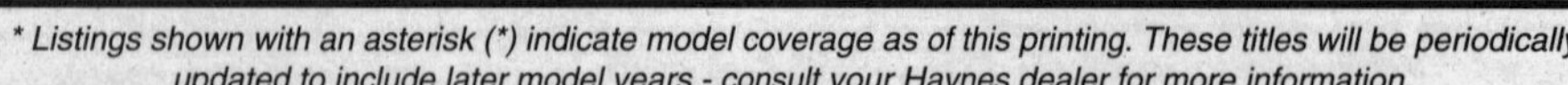

** Listings shown with an asterisk (*) indicate model coverage as of this printing. These titles will be periodically updated to include later model years - consult your Haynes dealer for more information.*

Over 100 Haynes motorcycle manuals also available